Lecture Notes in Computer

Commenced Publication in 1973
Founding and Former Series Editors:
Gerhard Goos, Juris Hartmanis, and Jan van L

Editorial Board

David Hutchison
  Lancaster University, UK
Takeo Kanade
  Carnegie Mellon University, Pittsburgh, PA, USA
Josef Kittler
  University of Surrey, Guildford, UK
Jon M. Kleinberg
  Cornell University, Ithaca, NY, USA
Friedemann Mattern
  ETH Zurich, Switzerland
John C. Mitchell
  Stanford University, CA, USA
Moni Naor
  Weizmann Institute of Science, Rehovot, Israel
Oscar Nierstrasz
  University of Bern, Switzerland
C. Pandu Rangan
  Indian Institute of Technology, Madras, India
Bernhard Steffen
  University of Dortmund, Germany
Madhu Sudan
  Massachusetts Institute of Technology, MA, USA
Demetri Terzopoulos
  University of California, Los Angeles, CA, USA
Doug Tygar
  University of California, Berkeley, CA, USA
Moshe Y. Vardi
  Rice University, Houston, TX, USA
Gerhard Weikum
  Max-Planck Institute of Computer Science, Saarbruecken, Germany

Dave Thomas (Ed.)

ECOOP 2006 – Object-Oriented Programming

20th European Conference
Nantes, France, July 3-7, 2006
Proceedings

 Springer

Volume Editor

Dave Thomas
Bedarra Research Lab.
1 Stafford Road, Suite 421, Ottawa, Ontario, Canada K2H 1B9
E-mail: dave@bedarra.com

Library of Congress Control Number: Applied for

CR Subject Classification (1998): D.1, D.2, D.3, F.3, C.2, K.4, J.1

LNCS Sublibrary: SL 2 – Programming and Software Engineering

ISSN   0302-9743
ISBN-10   3-540-35726-2 Springer Berlin Heidelberg New York
ISBN-13   978-3-540-35726-1 Springer Berlin Heidelberg New York

This work is subject to copyright. All rights are reserved, whether the whole or part of the material is
concerned, specifically the rights of translation, reprinting, re-use of illustrations, recitation, broadcasting,
reproduction on microfilms or in any other way, and storage in data banks. Duplication of this publication
or parts thereof is permitted only under the provisions of the German Copyright Law of September 9, 1965,
in its current version, and permission for use must always be obtained from Springer. Violations are liable
to prosecution under the German Copyright Law.

Springer is a part of Springer Science+Business Media

springer.com

© Springer-Verlag Berlin Heidelberg 2006
Printed in Germany

Typesetting: Camera-ready by author, data conversion by Scientific Publishing Services, Chennai, India
Printed on acid-free paper   SPIN: 11785477   06/3142   5 4 3 2 1 0

Preface

The 20th Anniversary of ECOOP was held in Nantes, France, July 3-7, 2006. For 20 years ECOOP has been a leading conference in Europe. Each year ECOOP brings together researchers, graduate students, and software practitioners to exchange ideas, progress, and challenges. The conference covered the full spectrum of the field with many sessions to accommodate the varied interests of the participants including outstanding invited speakers, refereed technical papers, tutorials, workshops, demonstrations, and a poster session.

This year, the Program Committee received 162 submissions, covering the entire spectrum of object-orientation: aspects, modularity and adaptability; architecture and patterns; components, frameworks and product lines; concurrency, real-time and embedded; mobility and distribution; collaboration and workflow, domain specific, dynamic, multi-paradigm and constraint languages; HCI and user interfaces; language innovations; compilation and virtual machines; methodology, process and practices; model engineering, design languages and transformations; persistence and transactions; theoretical foundations; and tools. The PC committee accepted 20 papers for publication after a careful and thorough reviewing process. Papers were evaluated based on significance, originality, and soundness.

Eric Jul, Chair of the Selection Committee, presented the Dahl-Nygaard Prize to Erich Gamma, Richard Helm, Ralph Johnson, and (posthumously) to John Vlissides, popularly known as the "Gang of Four." Their significant practical work on design patterns changed the vocabulary and best practices in our software development.

Erich Gamma, Serge Abiteboul, and Ralph Johnson presented invited talks which complimented the technical papers. A highlight of this 20th ECOOP was the special anniversary invited panel that provided their perspectives on our field. The invited talks and the special panel papers are published in the proceedings.

ECOOP 2006's success was due to the dedication of many people. First I would like to thank the authors for submitting a high number of quality papers. The selection of a subset of papers to be published from these took a lot of careful reviewing and discussion. Secondly I would like to thank our invited speakers and panelists for their contributions. They provided a rich context for discussions and future directions. I would like to thank the members of the Program Committee for their careful reviews, and for thorough and balanced discussions during the selection process, which was held February 2–3 in Paris. I thank the General Chairs of the conference, Pierre Cointe and Jean Bézivin, for organizing the conference and Antoine Beugnard and Thomas Ledoux, Tutorial Co-chairs, Charles Consel and Mario Südholt, Workshop Co-chairs, Julien Cohen and Hervé Grall, Demonstration and Poster Co-chairs. Special thanks to Jean-François Perrot for organizing the invited 20th anniversary panel.

June 2006   Dave Thomas

Organization

ECOOP 2006 was organized by the Computer Science Department of the Ecole des Mines de Nantes, the University of Nantes, the CNRS LINA laboratory and by INRIA, under the auspices of AITO (Association Internationale pour les Technologies Objets), and in cooperation with ACM SIGPLAN and SIGSOFT.

Executive Committee

Program Chair
    Dave Thomas (Bedarra Research Labs)
Organizing Chairs
    Jean Bézivin (University of Nantes-LINA, INRIA)
    Pierre Cointe (Ecole des Mines de Nantes-INRIA, LINA)

Organizing Committee

Workshops
    Charles Consel (LABRI, INRIA)
    Mario Südholt (INRIA-Ecole des Mines de Nantes, LINA)
Tutorials
    Antoine Beugnard (ENST Bretagne)
    Thomas Ledoux (Ecole des Mines de Nantes-INRIA, LINA)
Webmaster and Registration Chair
    Didier Le Botlan (CNRS-Ecole des Mines de Nantes, LINA)
Local Arrangement Chair
    Christian Attiogbé (University of Nantes, LINA)
Sponsors and Industrial Relations
    Gilles Muller (Ecole des Mines de Nantes-INRIA, LINA)
Treasurer
    Catherine de Charette (Ecole des Mines de Nantes)
Publicity Chairs
    Olivier Roux (Ecole Centrale de Nantes, IRCCYN)
    Nathalie Le Calvez (Ecole des Mines de Nantes)

Posters and Demos Chairs
    Julien Cohen (Polytech' Nantes, LINA)
    Hervé Grall (Ecole des Mines de Nantes-INRIA, LINA)
Student Volunteer Chair
    Yann-Gaël Guéhéneuc (University of Montreal)
20th Anniversary Chair
    Jean-François Perrot (University of Paris VI)
Doctoral Symposium Chair
    Mircea Trofin (Dublin City University)
Workshops Review Committee
    Uwe Aßmann (University of Dresden)
    Shigeru Chiba (Tokyo Institute of Technology)
    Krystof Czarnecki (University of Waterloo)
    Erik Ernst (Aarhus University)
    Luigi Liquori (INRIA)
    Wolfgang De Meuter (Vrije Universiteit Brussel)
    Christian Perez (IRISA)
    Calton Pu (Georgia Tech)
Doctoral Symposium Committee
    Ada Diaconescu (Dublin City University)
    Stephanie Balzer (ETH Zurich)
    Robert Bialek (University of Copenhagen)
    Simon Denier (Ecole des Mines de Nantes/INRIA)

Sponsoring Organizations

Silver Sponsors

Bronze Sponsors

Institution Sponsors

Program Committee

Mehmet Akşit (University of Twente, Netherlands)
Jonathan Aldrich (Carnegie Mellon University, USA)
David F. Bacon (IBM Research, USA)
Don Batory (University of Texas at Austin, USA)
Françoise Baude (University of Nice Sophia-Antipolis, France)
Andrew Black (Portland State University, USA)
Gilad Bracha (SUN Java Software, USA)
Luca Cardelli (Microsoft Research, UK)
Craig Chambers (University of Washington, USA)
Shigeru Chiba (Tokyo Institute of Technology, Japan)
William Cook (University of Texas at Austin, USA)
Wolfgang De Meuter (Vrije Universiteit Brussel, Belgium)
Theo D'Hondt (Vrije Universiteit Brussel, Belgium)
Christophe Dony (University of Montpellier, France)
John Duimovich (IBM, Canada)
Erik Ernst (Aarhus University, Denmark)
Michael D. Ernst (Massachusetts Institute of Technology, USA)
Patrick Eugster (Purdue University, USA)
Bjørn Freeman-Benson (Eclipse Foundation, USA)
Bill Harrison (Trinity College, Dublin, Ireland)
Eric Jul (Microsoft Research/Univ. of Copenhagen, Denmark)
Gerti Kappel (Vienna University of Technology, Austria)
Gregor Kiczales (University of British Columbia, Canada)
Karl Lieberherr (Northeastern University, USA)
Boris Magnusson (University of Lund, Sweden)
Jacques Malenfant (University of Paris VI, France)
Erik Meijer (Microsoft, USA)
Mira Mezini (Darmstadt University, Germany)
Birger Mller-Pedersen (University of Oslo, Norway)
Douglas C. Schmidt (Vanderbilt University, USA)
Clemens Szyperski (Microsoft, USA)
Frank Tip (IBM, USA)
Mads Torgersen (Microsoft, USA)
Vasco T. Vasconcelos (University of Lisbon, Portugal)
Cristina Videira Lopes (University of California, Irvine, USA)
Wolfgang Weck (Independent Software Architect, Switzerland)
Roel Wuyts (Université Libre de Bruxelles, Belgium)
Matthias Zenger (Google Switzerland)

Referees

Marwan Abi-Antoun	Gabriela Arevalo	Stephanie Balzer
João Araújo	Sushil Bajracharya	Klaas van den Berg

Alexandre Bergel
Lodewijk Bergmans
Jean Bézivin
Kevin Bierhoff
Elisa Gonzalez Boix
Philippe Bonnet
Johan Brichau
Luis Caires
Ciera Christopher
Thomas Cleenewerck
William Clinger
Pascal Costanza
Ward Cunningham
Tom Van Cutsem
Michel Dao
Marcus Denker
Brecht Desmet
Stéphane Ducasse
Roland Ducournau
Pascal Durr
Chris Dutchyn
Peter Ebraert
Michael Eichberg
Andrew Eisenberg
Luc Fabresse
Johan Fabry
Jingsong Feng
Stephen Fink
Markus Gälli
Jacques Garrigue
Vaidas Gasiunas
Simon Gay
Tudor Girba
Sofie Goderis
Ryan Golbeck
Mark Grechanik

Orla Greevy
Gurcan Gulesir
Philip Guo
Wilke Havinga
Görel Hedin
Tony Hoare
Christian Hofmann
Terry Hon
Marianne Huchard
Ali Ibrahim
Andy Kellens
Adam Kiezun
David Kitchin
Gerhard Kramler
Ivan Krechetov
Viktor Kuncak
Patrick Lam
Peter Lee
Adrian Lienhard
Chuan-kai Lin
Antonia Lopes
Pablo Gomes Ludermir
Donna Malayeri
Francisco Martins
Stephen McCamant
Elke Michlmayr
Todd Millstein
Stijn Mostinckx
Marion Murzek
István Nagy
Srinivas Nedunuri
Trung Ngo
Isabel Nunes
Manuel Oriol
Klaus Ostermann
Ellen Van Paesschen

Jeffrey Palm
Jeff Perkins
Laura Ponisio
Christoph von Praun
Rosario Pugliese
Antonio Ravara
Derek Rayside
Reza Razavi
Tom Rodriguez
Coen De Roover
Kenneth Russell
Alexandru Salcianu
Nathanael Schärli
Andrea Schauerhuber
Wieland Schwinger
Jan Schwinghammer
João Costa Seco
Martina Seidl
Arjun Singh
Therapon Skotiniotis
Hasan Sozer
Tom Staijen
Veronika Stefanov
Bedir Tekinerdoğan
Matthew Tschantz
Jorge Vallejos
Sebastien Vaucouleur
Sylvain Vauttier
Jonathan Walpole
Ben Wiedermann
Mike Wilson
Manuel Wimmer
Pengcheng Wu
Chen Xiao

Table of Contents

Keynote

Languages

Type Theory

Keynote

Tools

Modularity

Design Patterns – 15 Years Later

Erich Gamma

IBM Rational Zurich Research Lab, Oberdorfstr. 8,
8001 Zurich, Switzerland
erich_gamma@ch.ibm.com

Abstract. Design patterns are now a 15 year old thought experiment. And, today, for many, software design patterns have become part of the standard development lexicon. The reason is simple: rather than constantly redis-covering solutions to recurring design problems developers can refer to a body of literature that captures the best practices of system design. This talks looks back to the origins of design patterns, shows design patterns in action, and provides an overview of where patterns are today.

D. Thomas (Ed.): ECOOP 2006, LNCS 4067, p. 1, 2006.
© Springer-Verlag Berlin Heidelberg 2006

CodeQuest:
Scalable Source Code Queries with Datalog

Elnar Hajiyev, Mathieu Verbaere, and Oege de Moor

Programming Tools Group,
Oxford University Computing Laboratory,
Wolfson Building, Parks Road, Oxford OX1 3QD, UK
{Elnar.Hajiyev, Mathieu.Verbaere, Oege.de.Moor}@comlab.ox.ac.uk,
http://progtools.comlab.ox.ac.uk/projects/codequest/

Abstract. Source code querying tools allow programmers to explore relations between different parts of the code base. This paper describes such a tool, named *CodeQuest*. It combines two previous proposals, namely the use of logic programming and database systems.

As the query language we use *safe Datalog*, which was originally introduced in the theory of databases. That provides just the right level of expressiveness; in particular recursion is indispensable for source code queries. Safe Datalog is like Prolog, but all queries are guaranteed to terminate, and there is no need for extra-logical annotations.

Our implementation of Datalog maps queries to a relational database system. We are thus able to capitalise on the query optimiser provided by such a system. For recursive queries we implement our own optimisations in the translation from Datalog to SQL. Experiments confirm that this strategy yields an efficient, scalable code querying system.

1 Introduction

Understanding source code is vital to many tasks in software engineering. Source code querying tools are designed to help such understanding, by allowing programmers to explore relations that exist between different parts of the code base. Modern development environments therefore provide querying facilities, but these are usually fixed: one cannot define new relationships that are particular to the project in hand.

It can be very useful, however, to define such project-specific queries, for instance to enforce coding style rules (*e.g.* naming conventions), to check correct usage of an API (*e.g.* no call to a GUI method from an enterprise bean), or to ensure framework-specific rules (*e.g.* in a compiler, every non-abstract AST class must override the *visitChildren* method). Apart from such checking tasks, we might want new ways of navigating beyond the fixed set of relations provided in a development environment. When cleaning up a piece of legacy software, it is for example useful to know what methods are never called (directly or indirectly) from the *main* method. A good querying tool allows the programmer to define all these tasks via simple, concise queries. Note that none of these examples is easily

D. Thomas (Ed.): ECOOP 2006, LNCS 4067, pp. 2–27, 2006.
© Springer-Verlag Berlin Heidelberg 2006

implemented with today's dominant code querying tool, namely *grep*. Built-in querying and navigating facilities of Eclipse, widely used by the IDE users, are limited to a fixed number of certain queries.

The research community has long recognised the need for flexible code queries, and many solutions have been proposed. We shall discuss this previous work in detail in Sect. 6. For now it suffices to say that two crucial ideas have emerged from that earlier research: a logical query language like Prolog to formulate queries, and a relational database to store information about the program.

All these earlier attempts, however, fall short on at least one of three counts: the system is not scalable to industrial-size projects, or the query language is not sufficiently expressive, or the queries require complex annotations to guarantee efficiency. Scalability is typically not achieved because no query optimisation is used, and/or all data is held in main memory. Expressiveness requires recursive queries, to inspect the graph structures (the type hierarchy and the call graph, for example) that are typically found in code queries. Yet the use of recursion in SQL and XQuery is cumbersome, and in Prolog recursion over graphs often leads to non-termination. In Prolog that problem may be solved via tabling plus mode annotations, but such annotations require considerable expertise to get right.

1.1   Contributions

This paper solves all these deficiencies, and it presents a code querying tool that is scalable, expressive and purely declarative. We achieve this through a synthesis of the best ideas of the previous work on code querying. To wit, our contributions are these:

- The identification of *safe Datalog* (a query language originating in database theory) as a suitable source code query language, in the sweet spot between expressiveness and efficient implementation.
- The implementation of Datalog via an optimising compiler to SQL, which is in turn implemented on a relational database system. Our compiler performs a specialised version of the well-known 'magic sets' transformation, which we call 'closure fusion'.
- A method of incrementally updating the database relations when a compilation unit is changed.
- A comprehensive set of experiments, with two different commercial database systems (Microsoft SQL Server and IBM DB2) as a backend for our query compiler, to show the scalability of our approach. We also demonstrate that for this application, a special implementation of recursion outperforms the built-in recursion provided by these database systems.
- Detailed comparison with other state-of-the-art code querying tools, in particular JQuery (an Eclipse plugin tailored for code queries) [2, 24, 34] and XSB (a general optimising compiler for tabled Prolog [3,39]), demonstrating that on small projects our approach is competitive, and on large projects superior.

1.2   Paper Organisation

The paper is organised as follows. First we provide a brief introduction to Datalog; we also present its semantics with an emphasis on the concepts that are important to the implementation of *CodeQuest* (Sect. 2). That implementation is presented in Sect. 3. It is also here that we discuss a number of alternative implementations of recursion, via built-in facilities of the underlying database system, and via a procedural implementation of our own. Next, in Sect. 4, we turn to the tricky problem of incrementally updating the database when a change is made to the source program. Clearly this is crucial to the use of *CodeQuest* in the context of refactoring, where queries are interspersed with frequent changes. The heart of the paper is Sect. 5: there we demonstrate, through careful experiments with a wide variety of queries, that our implementation method yields a truly scalable system. The experiments are conducted with two major database systems to factor out any implementation accidents in our measurements. We also assess the efficiency of incrementally rebuilding the database with a series of refactoring queries. In Sect. 6, we provide a comprehensive account of all the previous work on code queries that has inspired the construction of *CodeQuest*. Finally, we conclude in Sect. 7.

2   Datalog

Datalog is a query language originally put forward in the theory of databases [20]. Syntacticly it is a subset of a logic language Prolog, but has a different evaluation strategy. It also poses certain stratification restrictions on the use of negation and recursion. As a result, in contrast to Prolog, Datalog requires no extra-logical annotations in order to guarantee termination of the queries. At the same time it has the right level of expressiveness for the type of applications discussed above.

Datalog's basic premise is that data is arranged according to relations. For example, the relation *hasName* records names of program elements. Variables are used to find unknown elements; in our syntax, variable names start with a capital letter. So one might use the *hasName* relation as follows:

$$hasName(L, \text{`List'})$$

is a query to find all program elements with the name *List*; the variable L will be instantiated to all program elements that have that name.

Unary relations are used to single out elements of a particular type. So for example, one might write

$$method(M), hasName(M, \text{`add'}),$$
$$interface(L), hasName(L, \text{`List'}),$$
$$hasChild(L, M)$$

Here the comma stands for logical 'and'. This query checks that the *List* interface contains a method named *add*. It also illustrates an important issue: a method is a program element, with various attributes, and the name of the method is just one of those attributes. It is incorrect to write *hasChild*('List', 'add'), because names do not uniquely identify program elements. At present *CodeQuest* does not have a type system, so this incorrect predicate would just evaluate to 'false'.

Above, we have used primitive relations that are built into our version of Datalog only. One can define relations of one's own, for instance to define the notion of subtypes (semi-colon (;) stands for logical 'or', and (:−) for reverse implication):

$$hasSubtype(T, S) :- extends(S, T) \; ; \; implements(S, T).$$

This says that T has a (direct) subtype S when S extends T or S implements T. Of course *CodeQuest* provides many such derived predicates by default, including *hasSubtype*. Unlike primitives such as *extends* or *implements*, these derived predicates are not stored relations, instead they are deduced from the primitives. A full list of all primitive and derived predicates provided in *CodeQuest* can be found on the project web page [5].

In summary, basic Datalog is just a logic programming language, quite similar to Prolog, but without data structures such as lists. The arguments of relations are program elements (typically nodes in the abstract syntax tree) and names. Like other logic programming languages, Datalog is very compact compared to query languages in the SQL tradition. Such conciseness is very important in a code querying tool, as verbosity would defeat interactive use.

Recursion. Code queries naturally need to express properties of tree structures, such as the inheritance hierarchy and the abstract syntax tree. They also need to express properties of graphs, such as the call graph, which may be cyclic. For these reasons, it is important that the query language supports recursion. To illustrate, here is a definition of direct or indirect subtypes:

$$hasSubtypePlus(T, S) :- hasSubtype(T, S) \; ;$$
$$hasSubtype(T, MID), hasSubtypePlus(MID, S).$$

Now seasoned logic programmers will recognise that such definitions pose a potential problem: in Prolog we have to be very careful about variable bindings and possible cycles to guarantee termination. For efficiency, we also need to worry about overlapping recursive calls. For example, the above would not be an adequate program in XSB, a state-of-the-art version of Prolog [3, 39]. Instead, we would have to distinguish between whether T is known or S is known at the time of query evaluation. Furthermore, we would have to annotate the predicate to indicate that its evaluation must be *tabled* to avoid inefficiency due to overlapping recursive calls. JQuery [2, 24, 34], the code querying system that is the main inspiration for *CodeQuest*, similarly requires the developer to think about whether T or S is known during query evaluation.

CodeQuest foregoes all such extra-logical annotations: one simple definition of a recursive relation suffices. We believe this is an essential property of a code querying language, as the queries should be really easy to write, and not require any understanding of the evaluation mechanism. Termination is never an issue, as all recursions in *CodeQuest* terminate, due to certain restrictions explained below.

Semantics. Datalog relations that are defined with recursive rules have a least-fixpoint semantics: they denote the smallest relation that satisfies the given implication. To illustrate, the above clause for *hasSubtypePlus* defines it to be the least relation X that satisfies

$$X \supseteq hasSubtype \cup (hasSubtype \circ X)$$

where ($\circ$) stands for sequential relational composition (*i.e.* $(a, c) \in (R \circ S)$ iff $\exists b : (a, b) \in R \wedge (b, c) \in S$). The existence of such a smallest solution X is guaranteed in our version of Datalog because we do not allow the use of negation in a recursive cycle. Formally, that class of Datalog programs is said to be *stratified*; interested readers may wish to consult [9] for a comprehensive survey.

It follows that we can reason about relations in Datalog using the relational calculus and the Knaster-Tarski fixpoint theorem [29, 11, 18]: all our recursions correspond to monotonic mappings between relations (f is monotonic if $X \subseteq Y$ implies $f(X) \subseteq f(Y)$). For ease of reference, we quote that theorem here:

Theorem 1 (Knaster-Tarski). *Let f be a monotonic function on (tuples of) relations. Then there exists a relation R such that $R = f(R)$ and for all relations X we have*

$$f(X) \subseteq X \quad implies \quad R \subseteq X$$

The relation R is said to be the least fixpoint *of f.*

In particular, the theorem implies that we can compute least fixpoints by iterating from the empty relation: to find the R in the theorem, we compute $\emptyset, f(\emptyset), f(f(\emptyset)), \ldots$ until nothing changes. Because our relations range over a finite universe (all program elements), and we insist that all variables in the left-hand side of a clause are used at least once positively (that is not under a negation) on the right-hand side, such convergence is guaranteed to occur in a finite number of steps. Together with the restriction to stratified programs, this means we handle the so-called *safe* Datalog programs. *CodeQuest* does not place any further restrictions on the use of recursion in Datalog.

Closure fusion. Another very simple consequence of Knaster-Tarski, which we have found to be effective as an optimisation in *CodeQuest*, is *closure fusion*. The reflexive transitive closure R^* of a relation R is defined to be the least fixpoint of

$$X \mapsto id \cup (R \circ X)$$

where *id* is the identity relation.

Theorem 2 (closure fusion). *The relation $R^* \circ S$ is the least fixpoint of*

$$X \mapsto S \cup (R \circ X)$$

Furthermore, $S \circ R^*$ is the least fixpoint of

$$X \mapsto S \cup (X \circ R)$$

In words, this says that instead of first computing R^* (via exhaustive iteration) and then composing with S, we can start the iteration with S. As we shall see, this saves a lot of work during query evaluation. Due to the strictly declarative nature of Datalog, we can do the optimisation automatically, while compiling the use of recursive queries.

To illustrate closure fusion, suppose that we wish to find all types in a project that are subtypes of the *List* interface:

$$listImpl(X) :- type(L), hasName(L, \text{`List'}), hasSubtypePlus(L, X).$$

A naïve evaluation of this query by fixpoint iteration would compute the full *hasSubtypePlus* relation. That is not necessary, however. Applying the second form of the above theorem with $R = hasSubtype^*$ and

$$S(L, X) :- type(L), hasName(L, \text{`List'}), hasSubtype(L, X).$$

we obtain the result

$$listImpl(X) \qquad\qquad :- hasSubtypePlus'(L, X).$$
$$hasSubtypePlus'(L, X) :- type(L), hasName(L, \text{`List'}), hasSubtype(L, X).$$
$$hasSubtypePlus'(L, X) :- hasSubtypePlus'(L, MID), hasSubtype(MID, X).$$

Readers who are familiar with the deductive database literature will recognise this as a special case of the so-called *magic sets* transformation [12]. In the very specialised context of *CodeQuest*, it appears closure fusion on its own is sufficient to achieve good performance.

3   *CodeQuest* Implementation

CodeQuest consists of two parts: an implementation of Datalog on top of a relational database management system (RDBMS), and an Eclipse [1] plugin for querying Java code via that Datalog implementation. We describe these two components separately.

3.1   Datalog Implementation

Our implementation of Datalog divides relations into those that are stored in the database on disk, and those that are computed via queries. When we are given a particular query, the relevant rules are compiled into equivalent SQL. The basics of such a translation are well understood [30, 27]; somewhat surprisingly, these works do not include careful performance experiments. Details of the translation that we employ can be found in [23].

The most interesting issue is the implementation of recursion. As noted in the previous section, we restrict ourselves to *safe* Datalog programs, and that implies we can compute solutions to recursive equations by exhaustive iteration.

Modern database systems allow the direct expression of recursive SQL queries via so-called Common Table Expressions (CTEs), as described in the SQL-99 standard. This is one of the implementations available in *CodeQuest*. A major disadvantage, however, is that most database systems impose the additional restriction that only bag (multiset) operations may be used inside the recursion: one cannot employ set union, for example. That implies the semantics of CTEs do not quite coincide with our intended semantics of Datalog. In particular, while in our semantics, all recursions define a finite relation, the corresponding CTE may fail to terminate because there are an infinite number of duplicates in the resulting relation. We shall see a concrete example of that phenomenon later on, when we write queries over the call graph of a program.

It follows that it is desirable to provide an alternative implementation of recursion. Suppose we have a recursive rule of the form:

$$result :- f(result).$$

where $f(R)$ is some combination of R with other relations. We can then find a least fixpoint with the following naive algorithm:

$$result = \emptyset;$$
do {
$$\quad oldresult = result;$$
$$\quad result = f(oldresult);$$
}
while ($result \neq oldresult$)

All modern database systems allow us to express this kind of computation in a procedural scripting variant of SQL. Furthermore such scripts get directly executed on the database server; they are sometimes called *stored procedures*. We shall refer to this implementation as *Proc1* in what follows. We stress once more that because of our restriction to *safe* Datalog, *Proc1* always terminates, in contrast to the CTE implementation. In our experiments, *Proc1* is also sometimes faster than CTEs.

The above method of computing least fixpoints is of course grossly inefficient. If we know that $f(R)$ distributes over arbitrary unions of relations, significant improvements are possible. A sufficient requirement for such distribution is that $f(R)$ uses R only once in each disjunct. Such recursions are called linear, and in our experience most recursions in code queries satisfy that criterion. The following semi-naïve algorithm uses a worklist to improve performance when f distributes over arbitrary unions:

$$result = f(\emptyset);$$
$$todo = result;$$
while ($todo \neq \emptyset$)
{
$$\quad todo = f(todo) - result;$$
$$\quad result = result \cup todo;$$
}

This algorithm, expressed as a stored procedure, will be referred to as *Proc2*. One might expect *Proc2* to outperform *Proc1*, but as we shall see, this depends on the characteristics of the underlying database system. Of course many more interesting fixpoint finding algorithms could be devised, and undoubtedly they would help to improve performance. In this paper, however, our aim is to assess the feasibility of implementing Datalog on top of a database system. We therefore restrict ourselves to the comparison of just these three variants: *CTE*, *Proc1* and *Proc2*.

Because our aim is a proof of concept, we have to ensure that our results do not depend on the peculiarities of one relational database management system. For that reason, we provide two backends for *CodeQuest*, one that targets Microsoft SQL Server 2005, and the other IBM DB2 v8.2. Our use of these systems is somewhat naïve, and no attempt has been made to tune their performance. It is very likely that an expert would be able to significantly improve performance by careful selection of the system parameters.

3.2 Querying Java Code

It is our aim to compare *CodeQuest* to JQuery, the leading code querying system for Java. For that reason, we have striven to make the *CodeQuest* frontend as similar as possible to JQuery, to ensure the experiments yield an accurate comparison. For the same reason, the information we extract from Java source and store in the database is the same with the information that JQuery collects. For elements, it consists exhaustively of packages, compilation units, classes, interfaces, all class members and method parameters. As for relational facts, we store hasChild, calls, fields reads/writes, extends, implements and returns relationships.

All these facts are not computed by *CodeQuest*: they are simply read off the relevant data structures in Eclipse, after Eclipse has processed a Java compilation unit. In what follows, the process of collecting information, and storing it in the database is called *parsing*. It is not to be confused with the translation from strings into syntax trees that happens in the Eclipse Java compiler. Naturally parsing is expensive (we shall determine exactly how expensive in Sect. 5), so in the next section we shall consider how *CodeQuest* achieves its parsing incrementally, making appropriate changes to the database relations when a compilation unit is modified.

We are currently working on the implementation of a robust user interface of our plugin for a neat integration within Eclipse. We also wish to develop a similar add-in for Visual Studio.

4 Incremental Database Update

Source code queries are typically performed for software development tasks within an interactive development environment, where frequent changes of the source code occur. Hence, the database of code facts needs be kept up-to-date with the source code developers are working on. Developers cannot afford, however, a reparsing of their entire project between successive modifications and queries. A querying tool, embedded in a development environment, must provide an incremental update mechanism.

Yet such a feature is inherently similar to the tough problem of incremental compilation. Keeping the database in a consistent state, by specifying strong conditions for which the update of some facts must occur, is a complex task. To illustrate, consider a Java project with two packages a and b. Package a contains a class A and package b a class B declared with the code:

```
package b;
import a.A;
public class B {
    A theField;
}
```

At this stage, the type of *theField* is the class $a.A$. If we introduce a new class A in the package b, although no previously existing file has changed, the type of *theField* is now bound to $b.A$, and the relationship in the database should be updated accordingly.

Conveniently, Eclipse provides an auto-build feature that triggers a background incremental compilation of a project after each resource modification on that project. Eclipse tries to recompile as few compilation units as possible, but keeps the project in a consistent compiled state.

We leverage the auto-build feature of Eclipse to incrementally update the database when the developer modifies a Java resource. On notification by the Eclipse platform, we remove from the database all facts related to compilation units that are being deleted or recompiled. The cleaning is performed by deleting all compilation unit nodes and their children. These are computed using an *ad hoc* stored procedure generated by *CodeQuest* from the following query:

$$hasChildPlus(T, S) :- \ hasChild(T, S) \ ;$$
$$hasChild(T, MID), hasChildPlus(MID, S).$$
$$nodesToDelete(N) \ :- \ compilationUnitsToDelete(N) \ ;$$
$$compilationUnitsToDelete(C), hasChildPlus(C, N).$$

All primitive relations, where one of these deleted children is involved, are also deleted, as well as empty packages. Then, *CodeQuest* simply reparses and stores facts about the compilation units that have been recompiled by Eclipse.

One might argue that compilation units provide too coarse a level of granularity for reparsing. Indeed, in principle one might attempt to do this at the level of class members, say, but keeping track of the relevant dependencies is likely to be complex. Furthermore, object-oriented programs have rather small compilation units. For the projects used in our experiments, the average number of lines of code per compilation unit varies from 81 to 233 lines per unit (see Table 1). That level of granularity, although pretty coarse, has proved to be very workable for our experiments with a series of refactoring queries discussed in the following section.

5 Experiments

In order to determine the performance characteristics – the usability, efficiency and scalability properties of the *CodeQuest* system, we have performed a number of experiments. We compare *CodeQuest* with two alternative approaches, namely JQuery (a mature code querying system by Kris de Volder *et al.* [34, 24]), and XSB which is an optimising implementation of Prolog.

The experiments can be divided into four categories:

- **General queries:** these are generally useful queries, of the kind one might wish to run on any project. They include both recursive and non-recursive queries. We shall use them to compare all three systems.
- **Project specific queries:** some examples of queries that are more specific and specialised for a particular project. It is our contention that such queries, relating to style rules and API conventions, are often desirable and necessitate a flexible code querying system beyond the capabilities of today's IDEs.
- **Program understanding:** program understanding is the most common use of source code querying system. It typically requires a series of queries to be run; here we take a series inspired by previous work on querying systems.
- **Refactoring:** this is the process of restructuring software to improve its design but maintain the same functionality. Typically it involves a series of queries to be executed and the appropriate changes applied to the source. This experiment illustrates that our method of keeping the database up-to-date (described in Sect. 4) is effective.

5.1 Experimental Setup

In our experiments we are going to compare the three versions of *CodeQuest* (*CTE, Proc1* and *Proc2*) on two different database systems (MS SQL and DB2), with the well known source code querying tool JQuery. To rule out the possibility that JQuery's performance problems are due to the fact that it was written in Java, we also compare against XSB, a state of the art optimising compiler for tabled Prolog that is written in C. We have not written an interface between XSB and Eclipse, however. Instead we modified the *CodeQuest* plugin to write its facts to a text file that is then read in by the XSB interpreter. In summary, there are eight different systems to compare: six versions of *CodeQuest* itself, plus JQuery and XSB.

For our experiments, we shall use four open-source Java applications of different size. The chosen projects range from very small one-man software projects to huge industrial multi-team projects with many developers around the world involved. Characteristics of the projects are summarised in the Table 1.

Most experiments were run on a Pentium IV 3.2GHz/HT machine with 1GB of memory running Windows XP. The XSB numbers, however, were obtained under Debian GNU/Linux with a quad Xeon 3.2Ghz CPU and 4GB of memory, as we encountered memory violations with XSB when trying to load a large number of facts on a machine with a lesser specification. The reader should therefore bear in mind that our experimental setup is giving an advantage to XSB; as we shall see, that only strengthens our conclusions about scalability.

5.2   Running Experiments

Initial parsing. Before the queries can be run on a project it is parsed into a database and the time required is shown in Table 2. For all four projects, the time taken to build the relations in MSSQL is 5 to 7 times as much as it takes to compile them in Eclipse. The factor does *not* increase with the size of the project. For DB2, the situation is similar, but the factor is slightly higher (11 to 14). While this is a significant cost, it should be stressed that such complete builds are rare. When changes are applied to the program, the database is updated incrementally and usually there is no need for complete reparsing of the project. We shall measure the cost of such incremental updates when discussing queries for refactoring. We note that the cost of parsing in JQuery is very similar to that for *CodeQuest*, somewhere in between the MSSQL and DB2 versions. However, JQuery is not able to parse Eclipse. We do not provide parsing times for XSB, because as pointed out above, there we load facts indirectly, via a text file produced with a modification of the *CodeQuest* Eclipse plugin.

The high initial parsing cost of code querying systems is only justified if subsequent queries evaluate faster, and that is what we investigate next.

General queries. We start by considering three example queries, that represent typical usage of a code querying tool. They are not specific to a particular project.

The first query is checking a common style rule, namely that there are no declarations of non-final public fields. When such fields occur, we want to return both the field F and the enclosing type T. As a Datalog clause, this query might read as follows:

$$query1(T, F) :- type(T), hasChild(T, F), field(F),$$
$$hasStrModifier(F, 'public'), \mathbf{not}(hasStrModifier(F, 'final')).$$

The above query is non-recursive. A little more interesting is the second example. Here, we wish to determine all methods M that write a field of a particular

Table 1. Summary information on benchmark Java projects

Application	Description	Number of java files	Source LOC	Source Classes
Jakarta Regexp	Java Regular Expression package	14	3265	14
JFreeChart	Java library for generating charts	721	92916	641
abc +Polyglot	extensible AspectJ compiler + framework	1644	133496	1260
Eclipse	Open Source Java IDE	12197	1607982	10338

Table 2. Required parsing time for the Java projects (hh:mm:ss)

Application	Compile	Relation parsing (MSSQL/DB2/JQuery)	Ratio (parse/compile) (MSSQL/DB2/JQuery)
Jakarta Regexp	00:00:01	00:00:07/00:00:12/00:00:06	07/12/06
JFreeChart	00:00:15	00:01:29/00:03:25/00:02:35	06/14/10
abc (+Polyglot)	00:00:28	00:02:41/00:06:12/00:04:45	06/13/10
Eclipse	00:09:23	00:44:45/01:34:46/—:—:—	05/11/—

type, say T. In fact, fields whose type is a subtype of T qualify as well. We therefore specify:

$$query2(M, T) :- method(M), writes(M, F), hasType(F, FT),$$
$$hasSubtypeStar(T, FT).$$

Here the main relation of interest is $hasSubtypeStar(T, FT)$, which relates a type T to its subtype FT. It is defined as:

$$hasSubtypeStar(T, T) :- type(T).$$
$$hasSubtypeStar(T, S) :- hasSubtypePlus(T, S).$$

where $hasSubtype$ and $hasSubtypePlus$ are relations previously discussed in Sect. 2.

The third query is to find all implementations $M2$ of an abstract method $M1$. Naturally Eclipse also provides a way of answering this query, and indeed it is a good example of how those fixed facilities are subsumed by a general code querying system. The query reads:

$$query3(M1, M2) :- hasStrModifier(M1, \text{`abstract'}), overrides(M2, M1),$$
$$\mathbf{not}(hasStrModifier(M2, \text{`abstract'})).$$

The definition of *overrides* does also make use of the recursively defined *hasSubtypePlus*:

$$overrides(M1, M2) :- strongLikeThis(M1, M2),$$
$$hasChild(C1, M1), hasChild(C2, M2),$$
$$inheritableMethod(M2), hasSubtypePlus(C2, C1).$$

In words, we first check that $M1$ has the same signature and visibility as $M2$, since a protected method (say) cannot override a public one. We also check that $M2$ can actually be overridden (so it's not static, for example). When these two conditions are satisfied, we find the containing types of $M1$ and $M2$, and check that one is a subtype of the other.

Let us now consider different systems and their properties. Figure 1 presents the evaluation times of each system for the three queries. For each query, we show eight different ways of evaluating it [systems are listed in the legend of the chart in the same top-down order as the corresponding bars apper in left-right order; in the colour version of this paper, the correspondence is further enhanced

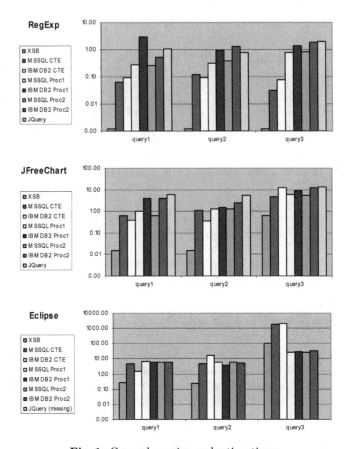

Fig. 1. General queries evaluation times

via colours]. On the vertical axis, we show the time taken in seconds – note that this is log-scale.

CodeQuest vs. JQuery. Most of the *CodeQuest* implementations proved to be more efficient than JQuery, for each of the three queries. The bars for JQuery are missing for the last graph because it was impossible to parse Eclipse with JQuery. It appears, therefore, that while JQuery is very effective for medium size projects, it does not scale to large projects. That is in line with the design goals of JQuery, namely to provide a light-weight, pure Java Eclipse plugin.

CodeQuest vs. XSB. It is natural to wonder whether a more efficient implementation of tabled Prolog such as XSB would yield a system similar to JQuery but with better efficiency characteristics. Our experiments confirm that this is indeed the case, and that Prolog outperforms *CodeQuest*. Notice, however, the exponential growth of time (with respect to the size of the project) required by XSB. Furthermore we have observed that XSB strongly depends on main memory, and for large projects that memory consumption becomes prohibitive (as we shall see in a query involving the call graph below). It therefore lacks scalability, whereas *CodeQuest* shows much slower growth of time against project size, for each of the queries. It is also important to mention that programs and queries for the XSB system were optimised by hand (distinguishing modes, appropriate use of cut, and tabling), so that their evaluation occurs in the best possible order and excludes all unnecessary computations. Less carefully optimised programs for XSB require considerably more time to execute as will be shown in the following subsection.

CTEs vs. Procs. We now turn to the comparison of the two implementations of recursion that we described in Sect. 3: via a built-in feature of the DBMS, namely Common Table Expressions, or via stored procedures. There is a remarkable difference in evaluation times between these two approaches. *CodeQuest Proc1* and *Proc2* have slightly worse performance than *CodeQuest* CTEs for all non-recursive queries as well as for recursive queries over small code bases. The situation changes significantly, however, with the recursive queries over large amounts of source code. It seems that it is the creation of intermediate tables in the stored procedures approach that causes a certain overhead. But the least fixpoint computation algorithm, implemented using stored procedures, proves to be more efficient, as we see in computationally expensive queries.

Proc1 vs. Proc2. *Proc2* has an optimised algorithm for computing the fixpoint of recursively defined relations. It is therefore equivalent to *Proc1* for non-recursive queries, and it should be more efficient for recursive ones. The downside of the *Proc2* algorithm is that it extensively creates and drops temporary tables. Thus, there is no efficiency gain for recursive queries over small size projects. Somewhat to our surprise, *Proc2* also does worse than *Proc1* on top of DB2, contrary to the situation for MSSQL. In more complex queries, for instance those that involve the call graph (discussed below), *Proc2* pays off even on DB2.

MSSQL vs. IBMDB2. It is clear from the graphs that usually the *CodeQuest* implementation on top of IBM DB2 is less efficient than on top of MS SQL Server. We have found that this may be somewhat sensitive to the exact form of the SQL that is produced by our compiler from Datalog. For instance, in DB2 it is better to avoid generating *not exists* clauses in the code. Furthermore, we note that: 1) we did not resort to the help of a professional database administrator and it is very likely that the database systems we were using could be tuned to increase performance significantly; 2) creation and deletion operations in IBM DB2 are generally more expensive than in MS SQL Server and since they are extensively used in the *Proc2* algorithm, the performance gain through a lesser number of joins was overwhelmed by the performance loss of a bigger number of creation/deletion of temporary tables. Nevertheless, both implementations prove that the concept of building a query system with a RDBMS at its backend is both efficient and scalable.

Project specific queries. While one can spend a lot of time trying to come up with the best possible optimisations for a general query, it is not quite possible when queries are written frequently and are specific to different projects. In this subsection we want to run exactly such experiments.

Most of the coding style constraints in an object oriented software system are implicit and cannot be enforced by means of the programming language. Therefore it is desirable to run queries to ensure that such constraints are satisfied. *abc* is an AspectJ compiler based on an extensible compiler framework called Polyglot [10,35]. One of the coding style constraints in Polyglot is the following: every concrete AST class (an AST class is one that implements the *Node* interface), that has a child (a field which is also subtype of *Node*) must implement a *visitChildren* method. In order to check whether that constraint holds, we write the following query:

$$existsVChMethod(C) :- class(C), hasChild(C, M), method(M),$$
$$hasName(M, \text{`visitChildren'}).$$
$$nodeInterface(N) \quad :- interface(N), hasName(N, \text{`Node'}).$$
$$concreteClass(C) \quad :- class(C), \mathbf{not}(hasStrModifier(C, \text{`abstract'})).$$
$$query1(C) :- nodeInterface(N), concreteClass(C),$$
$$hasSubtypePlus(N, C), hasChild(C, F), hasType(F, T),$$
$$hasSubtypeStar(N, T), \mathbf{not}(existsVChMethod(C)).$$

The *existsVChMethod(C)* looks up all the classes that have methods called *visitChildren*. The *nodeInterface(N)* respectively finds the interface with the name *Node* and *concreteClass(C)* all the classes that are not abstract. The final part of the query is read as follows: find all concrete classes that are subtypes of type *Node* and have a child (field) of the same type, but there exists no method called *visitChildren* in that class.

The evaluation times of this query are given in Fig. 2(query1). In contrast to the general queries, we did not perform any complex hand-tuning of the Prolog queries. An obvious equivalent of the *CodeQuest* query has been taken.

The next query also applies to *abc* and the Polyglot framework. We would like to find all the methods that are not called (transitively) from *abc*'s *main* method. We expect to receive a list of methods that are defined to be called externally, or perhaps via reflection. Potentially we may encounter dead code here if a function neither reachable from the *main* nor from any of the extending modules.

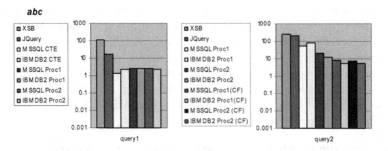

Fig. 2. Project specific queries evaluation times

$$polyCall(M1, M2) \quad :- \; calls(M1, M2).$$
$$polyCall(M1, M2) \quad :- \; calls(M1, M3), overrides(M2, M3).$$

$$polyCallPlus(X, Y) \; :- \; polyCall(X, Y).$$
$$polyCallPlus(X, Z) \; :- \; polyCallPlus(X, Y), polyCall(Y, Z).$$

$$mainCalls(Dummy) :- \; method(Main), hasName(Main, \text{'main'}),$$
$$polyCallPlus(Main, Dummy).$$

$$query2(Dummy) \quad :- \; method(Dummy), \mathbf{not}(mainCalls(Dummy)).$$

We were unable to make this query evaluate successfully on systems other than *CodeQuest* with closure fusion (on the DB2 version, it takes 13 seconds). As the main purpose of this paper is to evaluate *CodeQuest* relative to other systems, we decided to run the query on *abc* sources only, excluding Polyglot. Naturally that means we do not catch call chains that occur via Polyglot, so the results of the query will be highly inaccurate.

In the results (Fig. 2(query2)) we have explicitly included query evaluation time for *CodeQuest* with and without the closure fusion optimisation. It is evident that this optimisation is highly effective for this example. Another important detail to mention here is that recursive relations such as *polyCallPlus* may have loops. For example, if method $m1$ (transitively) calls method $m2$ and method $m2$ again (transitively) calls method $m1$. Computation of recursive relations of this kind is almost impossible using Common Table Expressions in SQL. There are various work-arounds to this problem, but none of them is efficient and general. This is the reason why the numbers for the CTEs based implementation of *CodeQuest* are missing for this query. Finally, we note that for the XSB query, we did have to apply some obvious optimisations by hand to make it terminate at all, even when the code base was reduced by excluding Polyglot.

Program understanding. The most typical usage of a source code querying tool is undoubtedly program understanding. In this subsection we give an example of a program exploration scenario that involves a series of queries to be run consecutively as a programmer browses through the source. This scenario was loosely inspired by an earlier paper on JQuery [24].

JFreeChart is a free Java library for generating charts. Suppose a user would like to find out when the graph plots are redrawn. They might start by listing the packages and the classes defined in each one:

$$query1(P, T) :- \; package(P), hasChild(P, CU), hasChild(CU, T), type(T).$$

The user immediately spots the *plot* package where all kinds of plots are defined. Drawing is a standard operation and will be most likely defined in the supertype of all plots. Thus, he can pick any of the plot-types and search for its supertype:

$$query2(SuperT) :- \; type(PickedType), hasSubtypePlus(SuperT, PickedType).$$

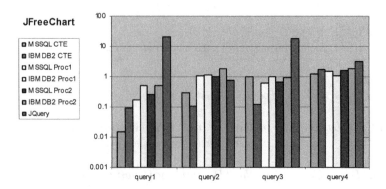

Fig. 3. Program understanding queries evaluation times

where *PickedType* is the type, chosen by the programmer. The result of this query will find an abstract *Plot* class. To list all its methods, the user defines the following query:

$$query3(M) :- hasChild(AbstractPlotType, M), method(M).$$

In the list the user finds an abstract method *draw* and he can finally define a query to spot all calls to this method or any overriding method in an extending class:

$$query4(M2) :- hasChild(C2, M2), polyCalls(M2, DrawM).$$
$$query4(M2) :- hasChild(C2, M2), polyCalls(M2, TargetM),$$
$$overrides(TargetM, DrawM).$$

Both JQuery and RDBMSs support some form of caching. As the cache warms up it requires typically less time to evaluate subsequent queries. This is especially crucial factor for JQuery since it is known to have strong caching strategies and run much faster on a warm cache. Figure 3 presents the comparison graph for the above scenario for JQuery and *CodeQuest*.

The *CodeQuest* system again shows better results. In retrospect, this is not that surprising, since RDBMSs also traditionally possess caching mechanisms to limit the number of disk I/Os. In addition to that, as described in Sect. 7 further optimisations can be included in the *CodeQuest* system itself.

Refactoring. The following refactoring scenario is inspired by a feature request for JFreeChart [40]. The task is to create an interface for combined plot classes and make it declare methods common to these classes, notably *getSubplots()*. We compare JQuery with the *Proc2* version of *CodeQuest* . We start by writing a query to locate the combined plot classes:

$$classesToRefactor(C) :- class(C), hasName(C, Name),$$
$$re\_match('\%Combined\%', Name),$$
$$declaresMethod(C, M), hasName(M, 'getSubplots').$$

In words, this query looks for a class whose name contains the substring *Combined*, which furthermore declares a method named *getSubplots*. Evaluation of this query yields four elements: *CombinedDomainCategoryPlot*, *CombinedDomainXYPlot*, *CombinedRangeCategoryPlot* and *CombinedRangeXYPlot*.

We perform the first refactoring, by making the four classes implement a new interface *CombinedPlot* that declares a single method *getSubplots()*. This refactoring involves a sequence of operations in Eclipse, in particular the application of built-in refactorings such as *'Extract Interface'* and *'Use Supertype Where Possible'* as well as some minor hand coding.

The next step is to look for other methods than *getSubplots()*, common to the four refactored classes, whose declarations could be pulled up in the new interface. A query for this task reads as follows:

$overridingMethod(M) :- overrides(M, N).$
$declares(C, S) \qquad :- class(C), declaresMethod(C, M),$
$\qquad\qquad\qquad hasSignature(M, S), \mathbf{not}(overridingMethod(M)).$

$declarations(S) :- class(C1), hasName(C1, \text{`CombinedDomainCategoryPlot'}),$
$\qquad\qquad class(C2), hasName(C2, \text{`CombinedDomainXYPlot'}),$
$\qquad\qquad class(C3), hasName(C3, \text{`CombinedRangeCategoryPlot'}),$
$\qquad\qquad class(C4), hasName(C4, \text{`CombinedRangeXYPlot'}),$
$\qquad\qquad declares(C1, S), declares(C2, S),$
$\qquad\qquad declares(C3, S), declares(C4, S).$

In words, we look for signatures of methods that are defined in all four classes of interest, which furthermore do not override some method in a supertype. Of course one might wish to write a more generic query, but as this is a one-off example, there is no need. The query yields two method signatures, **double** *getGap()* and **void** *setGap(**double**)*, which are related to the logic of the new interface. Hence, we perform a second refactoring to include these declarations in *CombinedPlot*.

This scenario provides a tiny experiment for measuring the efficiency of our incremental update mechanism and compare it to the one implemented in JQuery. An important difference between these two update mechanisms is the following. In *CodeQuest*, the update runs as a background task just after any incremental compilation is performed by Eclipse. In JQuery, the update occurs only when

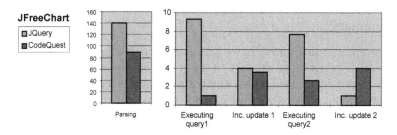

Fig. 4. Query evaluation and incremental update times for the Refactoring example

user explicitly executes the update action. The results are shown in Fig. 4. The sequence of measurements consists of the initial parsing time (which neither system needs to repeat after the first loading of the project), followed by two queries and updates.

In the given scenario the update times of the two systems are comparable. However, this refactoring example requires an update of very few facts. JQuery's performance considerably deteriorates when performing a larger change since it involves the deletion and recreation of many tiny files on the hard drive. For instance, if we apply the *Rename* rafactoring to the *org.jfree.data.general* package, update of 185 files will be required. It takes JQuery longer to update its factbase (over 5 mins) than to reparse the entire project again, whereas *CodeQuest* completes the update within 30 secs.

5.3 Effect of RDBMS Optimiser

Relational database systems not only enable code querying tools to be scalable for projects of virtually any size; another advantage lies in the powerful query optimisers, based on over forty years of intensive research. In order to illustrate the effect of the RDBMS optimiser we ran the project specific queries again, but this time with the optimiser switched off. *query1* (coding style constraints) was evaluated using CTEs based implementation of *CodeQuest* and *query2* (methods not transitively called from *main*) using *Proc2*. The evaluation time of *query1* with and without the internal IBM DB2 SQL optimiser is 2.7 and 5 seconds respectively. The difference becomes even more tangible for *query2*: 3.8 and 404 seconds respectively. Clearly it does not make sense for a code querying tool to try to re-implement all the work on optimisation already done for databases.

5.4 Memory Usage

We conclude this experimental section with a few brief remarks about memory usage. Both JQuery and XSB are memory hungry, and simply crash when there is not sufficient main memory available. Simple experiments confirm this behaviour: indeed, JQuery is unable to parse the source of Eclipse, and in XSB we could load it only under Debian Sid on a machine with 4GB of RAM. This sharply contrasts with the memory behaviour of database systems: these will use main memory where available, but performance is scalable. Because these results are entirely as expected, we do not present detailed numbers.

5.5 Summary

In this section we ran a variety of tests to measure performance of *CodeQuest* and to compare it against other similar systems. *CodeQuest* proved to be at least as efficient as JQuery in all case studies. Furthermore, simple techniques for storing intermediate results in temporary tables instead of recomputing them in every subsequent query could be added to already existent caching mechanisms of RDBMSs which would further leverage their performance. Of course that increased efficiency comes at the price of using a relational database system — there is much merit in JQuery's lightweight approach, which does not require any additional software components.

By today's standards, considering both parameters of the hardware systems at hand and the size of software projects that require querying, *CodeQuest* is definitely competitive with XSB. The memory based computations of an optimised Prolog program are fast but not scalable. Non-optimised Prolog queries are clearly less efficient than the same queries evaluated with *CodeQuest*.

Today's industrial databases are able to evaluate recursive queries as described in the SQL99 standard. However, it appears that built-in recursion is often less efficient than custom algorithms using stored procedures. Furthermore, in some cases the built-in facilities do not work at all, in particular when an infinite number of duplicate entries might be generated in intermediate results. So, the choice between different implementations of *CodeQuest* with the tested RDBMS comes down to *Proc1* and *Proc2*. Formally *Proc2* is an optimised variant of *Proc1* and should therefore be more preferable. But in practice it requires creating and dropping temporary tables during each iteration step. If a database system has the cost of creation and dropping tables higher than a certain limit, then the optimisation becomes too expensive. In our experiments, *Proc2* is more efficient than *Proc1* in most of the queries when used in MS SQL Server and vice-versa when used in IBM DB2. More generally, code generation strategy (*CTE*, *Proc1* or *Proc2*) is tightly coupled with an internal RDBMS SQL optimiser. As a consequence of that, the choice of the appropriate *CodeQuest* implementation depends not only on the exact type of queries that a user may want to run, but also on the RDBMS and in particular on the SQL optimiser being used to run produced SQL code.

6   Related Work

There is a vast body of work on code queries, and it is not possible to cover all of it in a conference paper. We therefore concentrate on those systems that have provided an immediate inspiration for the design and implementation of *CodeQuest*. First we focus on work from the program maintenance community, then we discuss related research in the program analysis community, and we conclude with some recent developments that are quite different to *CodeQuest*, and could be seen as alternative approaches to address the same problems.

Storing the program in a database. In the software maintenance community, there is a long tradition of systems that store the program in a database. One of the earliest proposals of this kind was Linton's Omega system [32]. He stores 58 relations that represent very detailed information about the program in the INGRES database system. Queries are formulated in the INGRES query language QUEL, which is quite similar to SQL. There is no way to express recursive queries. Linton reports some performance numbers that indicate a poor response time for even simple queries. He notes, however, that future query optimisers ought to do a lot better; our experiments confirm that prediction.

The next milestone in this line of work is the C Information Abstraction system, with the catchy acronym CIA [14]. CIA deviates from Omega in at least two important ways. First, based on the poor performance results of Omega, CIA only stores certain relations in the database, to reduce its size. Second, it aims for an incremental construction of the database — although the precise mechanism for achieving that is not detailed in [14], and there are no performance experiments to evaluate such incremental database construction. In *CodeQuest* we also store only part of the program, but it is our belief that modern database systems can cope with much larger amounts of data. Like CIA, we provide incremental updating of the database, and the way to achieve that efficiently was described in Sect. 4. CIA does not measure the effects of the optimiser provided by a particular database system, and in fact it is claimed the system is independent of that choice.

Despite their disadvantages, Omega and CIA have had quite an impact on industrial practice, as numerous companies now use a database system as a code repository, *e.g.* [13, 42].

Logic query languages. Both Omega and CIA inherited their query language from the underlying database system. As we have argued in Sect. 2, recursive queries, as provided in a logic programming language, are indispensable. Indeed, the XL C++ Browser [26] was one of the first to realise Prolog provides a nice notation to express typical queries over source code. The implementation is based directly on top of a Prolog system, implying that all the facts are held in main memory. As our experiments show, even with today's vastly increased memory sizes, using a state-of-the-art optimising compiler like XSB, this approach does not scale.

A particularly interesting attempt at overcoming the problem of expressiveness was put forward by Consens *et al.* [15]. Taking the search of graphs as its primary focus, GraphLog presents a query language with just enough power to express properties of paths in graphs, equivalent to a subset of Datalog, with a graphical syntax. In [15] a convincing case is made that the GraphLog queries are easier to write than the Prolog equivalent, and the authors state: "One of our goals is to have such implementations produced automatically by an optimizing GraphLog to Prolog translator." Our experiments show that to attain scalability, a better approach is to map a language like GraphLog to a relational database system.

Also motivated by the apparent inadequacy of relational query languages as found in the database community, Paul and Prakash revisited the notion of relational algebra [36]. Their new relational algebra crucially includes a closure operator, thus allowing one to express the traversals of the type hierarchy, call graph and so on that code queries require. The implementation of this algebra is done on top of the *Refine* system, again with an in-memory representation of the relevant relations [8]. Paul and Prakash report that hand-written queries in the *Refine* language typically evaluate a factor 2 to 10 faster than their declarative formulations. *CodeQuest* takes some of its inspiration from [36], especially in our use of relational algebra to justify optimisations such as closure fusion. Of course the connection between Datalog (our concrete syntax) and relational algebra with a (generalised) closure operator has been very thoroughly explored in the theoretical database community [7].

Also spurred on by the desire to have a convenient, representation-independent query language, Jarzabek proposed PQL, a Program Query Language [25]. PQL contains quite detailed information on the program, to the point where it is possible to formulate queries about the control flow graph. The query syntax is akin to that of SQL, but includes some operators for graph traversal. While SQL syntax undoubtedly has the benefit of being familiar to many developers, we feel that advantage is offset by its verbosity. Jarzabek points out that PQL admits many different implementations, and he describes one in Prolog. If so desired, it should be possible to use *CodeQuest* as a platform for implementing a substantial subset of PQL.

Another logic programming language especially for the purpose of source code queries is ASTLog, proposed by Crew [16]. Unlike PQL, it is entirely focussed on traversing the syntax tree, and there is no provision for graph manipulation. That has the advantage of a very fast implementation, and indeed ASTLog was used within Microsoft on some quite substantial projects.

The immediate source of inspiration for our work was JQuery, a source-code querying plugin for Eclipse [24, 34]. JQuery represents a careful synthesis of all these previous developments. It uses a logic programming language named TyRuBa [4]. This is similar to Prolog, but crucially, it employs tabled resolution for evaluating queries, which avoids many of the pitfalls that lead to non-termination. Furthermore, JQuery has a very nice user interface, where the results of queries can be organised in hierarchical views. Finally, it allows incremental building of the fact base, and storing them on disk during separate runs of the query interpreter. The main differences with *CodeQuest* are that TyRuBa requires mode annotations on predicates, and the completely different evaluation mechanism in *CodeQuest*. As our experiments show, that different evaluation mechanism is more scalable. The increased efficiency comes however at the price of less expressive power, as TyRuBa allows the use of data structures such as lists in queries, whereas *CodeQuest* does not. In JQuery, such data structures are used to good effect in building up the graphical views of query results. We feel this loss of expressiveness is a price worth paying for scalability.

Datalog for program analysis. The idea of using a tabled implementation of Prolog for the purpose of program analysis is a recurring theme in the logic programming community. An early example making the connection is a paper by Reps [38]. It observes that the use of the 'magic sets' transformation [12] (a generalised form of our closure fusion) helps in deriving demand-driven program analyses from specifications in Datalog.

A more recent paper in this tradition is by Dawson *et al.* [17], which gives many examples, and evaluates their use with the XSB system. We note that many of the examples cited there can be expressed in Datalog, without queries that build up data structures. As it is the most mature piece of work in applying logic programming to the realm of program analysis, we decided to use XSB for the experiments reported in Sect. 5. Our focus is not on typical dataflow analyses, but instead on source code queries during the development process.

Very recently Martin *et al.* proposed another PQL (not to be confused with Jarzabek's language discussed above), to find bugs in compiled programs [33,31]. Interestingly, the underlying machinery is that of Datalog, but with a completely different implementation, using BDDs to represent solution sets [43]. Based on their results, we believe that a combination of the implementation technology of *CodeQuest* (a relational database system) and that of PQL (BDDs) could be very powerful: source code queries could be implemented via the database, while queries that require deep semantic analysis might be mapped to the BDD implementation.

Other code query languages. Aspect-oriented programming represents a separate line of work in code queries: here one writes patterns to find all places in a program that belong to a cross-cutting concern. The most popular aspect-oriented programming language, AspectJ, has a sophisticated language of such patterns [28]. In IBM's Concern Manipulation Environment, that pattern language is deployed for interactive code queries, and augmented with further primitives to express more complex relationships [41]. We subscribe to the view that these pattern languages are very convenient for simple queries, but they lack the flexibility needed for sophisticated queries of the kind presented in this paper.

It comes as no surprise that the work on identifying cross-cutting concerns and code querying is converging. For example, several authors are now proposing that a new generation of AspectJ might use a full-blown logic query language instead [22,21]. The results of the present paper seem to suggest Datalog strikes the right balance between expressiveness and efficiency for this application also.

To conclude, we would like to highlight one effort in the convergence of aspects and code queries, namely Magellan. Magellan employs an XML representation of the code, and XML queries based on XQuery [19,37]. This is natural and attractive, given the hierarchical nature of code; we believe it is particularly suitable for queries over the syntax tree. XQuery is however rather hard to optimise, so it would be difficult to directly employ our strategy of relying on a query optimiser. As the most recent version of Magellan is not yet publicly available, we were unable to include it in our experimental setup. An interesting venue for further research might be to exploit the fact that semi-structured queries can be translated into Datalog, as described by Abiteboul *et al.* [6] (Chapter 6).

7   Conclusion

In this paper, we have demonstrated that Datalog, implemented on top of a modern relational database system, provides just the right balance between expressive power and scalability required for a source code querying system. In particular, recursion allows an elegant expression of queries that traverse the type hierarchy or the call graph. The use of a database system as the backend yields the desired efficiency, even on a very large code base.

Our experiments also indicate that even better performance is within reach. A fairly simple, direct implementation of recursion via stored procedures often outperforms the built-in facilities for recursion provided in today's database systems. More careful implementation of recursion, especially in conjunction with the query optimiser, is therefore a promising venue for further work.

At present the queries that can be expressed with *CodeQuest* are constrained by the relations that are stored in the database; we have closely followed JQuery in that respect, in order to make the experimental comparison meaningful. It is, in particular, impossible to phrase queries over the control flow of the program. There is however nothing inherently difficult about storing the relevant information. In fact, we plan to make the choice of relations configurable in *CodeQuest*, so the database can be adapted to the kind of query that is desired for a particular project.

We are particularly keen to see *CodeQuest* itself used as an engine for other tools, ranging from different query languages through refactoring, to pointcut languages for aspect-orientation. At present we are in the process of providing *CodeQuest* with a robust user interface; once that is complete, it will be released on the project website [5].

Acknowledgements

Elnar Hajiyev would like to thank Shell corporation for the generous support that facilitated his MSc at Oxford during 2004-5, when this research was started. We would also like to thank Microsoft Research (in particular Dr. Fabien Petitcolas) for its support, including a PhD studentship for Mathieu Verbaere. Finally, this research was partially funded through EPSRC grant EP/C546873/1. Members of the Programming Tools Group at Oxford provided helpful feedback at all stages of this research. We are grateful to Kris de Volder for many interesting discussions related to the topic of this paper.

References

1. *Eclipse.* http://www.eclipse.org.
2. *JQuery.* http://www.cs.ubc.ca/labs/spl/projects/jquery/.
3. *XSB.* http://xsb.sourceforge.net/.
4. *The TyRuBa metaprogramming system.* http://tyruba.sourceforge.net/.
5. *CodeQuest.* http://progtools.comlab.ox.ac.uk/projects/codequest/.
6. Serge Abiteboul, Peter Buneman, and Dan Suciu. *Data on the Web: From Relations to Semistructured Data and XML.* Morgan Kaufmann Publishers, 2000.
7. Serge Abiteboul, Richard Hull, and Victor Vianu. *Foundations of Databases.* Addison-Wesley, 1995.
8. Leonor Abraido-Fandino. An overview of Refine 2.0. In *Procs. of the Second International Symposium on Knowledge Engineering and Software Engineering*, 1987.
9. Krzysztof R. Apt and Roland N. Bol. Logic programming and negation: A survey. *Journal of Logic Programming*, 19/20:9–71, 1994.
10. Pavel Avgustinov, Aske Simon Christensen, Laurie Hendren, Sascha Kuzins, Jennifer Lhoták, Ondřej Lhoták, Oege de Moor, Damien Sereni, Ganesh Sittampalam, and Julian Tibble. *abc*: An extensible AspectJ compiler. In *Aspect-Oriented Software Development (AOSD)*, pages 87–98. ACM Press, 2005.

11. Roland Backhouse and Paul Hoogendijk. Elements of a relational theory of datatypes. In Bernhard Möller, Helmut Partsch, and Stephen Schuman, editors, *Formal Program Development*, volume 755 of *Lecture Notes in Computer Science*, pages 7–42. Springer Verlag, 1993.

12. François Bancilhon, David Maier, Yehoshua Sagiv, and Jeffrey D. Ullman. Magic sets and other strange ways to implement logic programs. In *Proceedings of the Fifth ACM SIGACT-SIGMOD Symposium on Principles of Database Systems, March 24-26, 1986, Cambridge, Massachusetts*, pages 1–16. ACM, 1986.

13. Cast. Company website at: http://www.castsoftware.com.

14. Yih Chen, Michael Nishimoto, and C. V. Ramamoorthy. The C information abstraction system. *IEEE Transactions on Software Engineering*, 16(3):325–334, 1990.

15. Mariano Consens, Alberto Mendelzon, and Arthur Ryman. Visualizing and querying software structures. In *ICSE '92: Proceedings of the 14th international conference on Software engineering*, pages 138–156, New York, NY, USA, 1992. ACM Press.

16. Roger F. Crew. ASTLOG: A language for examining abstract syntax trees. In *USENIX Conference on Domain-Specific Languages*, pages 229–242, 1997.

17. Stephen Dawson, C. R. Ramakrishnan, and David Scott Warren. Practical program analysis using general purpose logic programming systems. In *ACM Symposium on Programming Language Design and Implementation*, pages 117–126. ACM Press, 1996.

18. Henk Doornbos, Roland Carl Backhouse, and Jaap van der Woude. A calculational approach to mathematical induction. *Theoretical Computer Science*, 179(1–2):103–135, 1997.

19. Michael Eichberg, Michael Haupt, Mira Mezini, and Thorsten Schäfer. Comprehensive software understanding with sextant. In *ICSM '05: Proceedings of the 21st IEEE International Conference on Software Maintenance (ICSM'05)*, pages 315–324, Washington, DC, USA, September 2005. IEEE Computer Society.

20. Hervé Gallaire and Jack Minker. *Logic and Databases*. Plenum Press, New York, 1978.

21. Stefan Hanenberg Günter Kniesel, Tobias Rho. Evolvable pattern implementations need generic aspects. In *Proc. of ECOOP 2004 Workshop on Reflection, AOP and Meta-Data for Software Evolution*, pages 116–126. June 2004.

22. Kris Gybels and Johan Brichau. Arranging language features for more robust pattern-based crosscuts. In *2nd International Conference on Aspect-oriented Software Development*, pages 60–69. ACM Press, 2003.

23. Elnar Hajiyev. CodeQuest: Source Code Querying with Datalog. MSc Thesis, Oxford University Computing Laboratory, September 2005. Available at http://progtools.comlab.ox.ac.uk/projects/codequest/.

24. Doug Janzen and Kris de Volder. Navigating and querying code without getting lost. In *2nd International Conference on Aspect-Oriented Software Development*, pages 178–187, 2003.

25. Stan Jarzabek. Design of flexible static program analyzers with PQL. *IEEE Transactions on Software Engineering*, 24(3):197–215, 1998.

26. Shahram Javey, Kin'ichi Mitsui, Hiroaki Nakamura, Tsuyoshi Ohira, Kazu Yasuda, Kazushi Kuse, Tsutomu Kamimura, and Richard Helm. Architecture of the XL C++ browser. In *CASCON '92: Proceedings of the 1992 conference of the Centre for Advanced Studies on Collaborative research*, pages 369–379. IBM Press, 1992.

27. Karel Ježek and Vladimír Toncar. Experimental deductive database. In *Workshop on Information Systems Modelling*, pages 83–90, 1998.

28. Gregor Kiczales, Erik Hilsdale, Jim Hugunin, Mik Kersten, Jeffrey Palm, and William G. Griswold. An overview of AspectJ. In J. Lindskov Knudsen, editor, *European Conference on Object-oriented Programming*, volume 2072 of *Lecture Notes in Computer Science*, pages 327–353. Springer, 2001.

29. Bronislaw Knaster. Un théorème sur les fonctions d'ensembles. *Annales de la Societé Polonaise de Mathematique*, 6:133–134, 1928.

30. Kemal Koymen. A datalog interface for SQL (abstract). In *CSC '90: Proceedings of the 1990 ACM annual conference on Cooperation*, page 422, New York, NY, USA, 1990. ACM Press.

31. Monica S. Lam, John Whaley, V. Benjamin Livshits, Michael C. Martin, Dzintars Avots, Michael Carbin, and Christopher Unkel. Context-sensitive program analysis as database queries. In *PODS '05: Proceedings of the twenty-fourth ACM SIGMOD-SIGACT-SIGART symposium on Principles of database systems*, pages 1–12, New York, NY, USA, 2005. ACM Press.

32. Mark A. Linton. Implementing relational views of programs. In Peter B. Henderson, editor, *Software Development Environments (SDE)*, pages 132–140, 1984.

33. Michael Martin, Benjamin Livshits, and Monica S. Lam. Finding application errors using PQL: a program query language. In *Proceedings of the 20th annual ACM SIGPLAN OOPSLA Conference*, pages 365–383, 2005.

34. Edward McCormick and Kris De Volder. JQuery: finding your way through tangled code. In *OOPSLA '04: Companion to the 19th annual ACM SIGPLAN OOPSLA conference*, pages 9–10, New York, NY, USA, 2004. ACM Press.

35. Nathaniel Nystrom, Michael R. Clarkson, and Andrew C. Myers. Polyglot: An extensible compiler framework for Java. In *12th International Conference on Compiler Construction*, volume 2622 of *Lecture Notes in Computer Science*, pages 138–152, 2003.

36. Santanu Paul and Atul Prakash. Querying source code using an algebraic query language. *IEEE Transactions on Software Engineering*, 22(3):202–217, 1996.

37. Magellan Project. Web page at: http://www.st.informatik.tu-darmstadt.de/ static/pages/projects/Magellan/XIRC.html. 2005.

38. Thomas W. Reps. Demand interprocedural program analysis using logic databases. In *Workshop on Programming with Logic Databases, ILPS*, pages 163–196, 1993.

39. Konstantinos Sagonas, Terrance Swift, and David S. Warren. XSB as an efficient deductive database engine. In *SIGMOD '94: Proceedings of the 1994 ACM SIGMOD international conference on Management of data*, pages 442–453, New York, NY, USA, 1994. ACM Press.

40. Eric Sword. Create a root *combinedplot* interface. JFreeChart feature request: http://sourceforge.net/tracker/index.php?func=detail&aid=1234995& group_id=15494&atid=365494, 2005.

41. Peri Tarr, William Harrison, and Harold Ossher. Pervasive query support in the concern manipulation environment. Technical Report RC23343, IBM Research Division, Thomas J. Watson Research Center, 2004.

42. Michael Thompson. Bluephoenix: Application modernization technology audit. Available at: http://www.bitpipe.com/detail/RES/1080665824_99.html., 2004.

43. John Whaley, Dzintars Avots, Michael Carbin, and Monica S. Lam. Using datalog and binary decision diagrams for program analysis. In Kwangkeun Yi, editor, *Proceedings of the 3rd Asian Symposium on Programming Languages and Systems*, volume 3780, pages 97–118. Springer-Verlag, November 2005.

Efficient Object Querying for Java

Darren Willis, David J. Pearce, and James Noble

Computer Science, Victoria University of Wellington, NZ
{darren, djp, kjx}@mcs.vuw.ac.nz

Abstract. Modern programming languages have little or no support for querying objects and collections. Programmers are forced to hand code such queries using nested loops, which is both cumbersome and inefficient. We demonstrate that first-class queries over objects and collections improve program readability, provide good performance and are applicable to a large number of common programming problems. We have developed a prototype extension to Java which tracks all objects in a program using AspectJ and allows first-class queries over them in the program. Our experimental findings indicate that such queries can be significantly faster than common programming idioms and within reach of hand optimised queries.

1 Introduction

No object stands alone. The value and meaning of objects arise from their relationships with other objects. These relationships can be made explicit in programs through the use of pointers, collection objects, algebraic data types or other relationship constructs (e.g. [5,27,28,29]). This variety suggests that programming languages provide good support for relationships. We believe this is not entirely true — many relationships are *implicit* and, as such, are not amenable to standard relationship constructs. This problem arises from the great variety of ways in which relationships can manifest themselves. Consider a collection of student objects. Students can be related by name, or student ID — that is, distinct objects in our collection can have the same name or ID; or, they might be related by age bracket or street address. In short, the abundance of such implicit relationships is endless.

Most programming languages provide little support for such arbitrary and often dynamic relationships. Consider the problem of *querying* our collection to find all students with a given name. The simplest solution is to traverse the collection on demand to find matches. If the query is executed frequently, we can improve upon this by employing a hash map from names to students to get fast lookup. This is really a *view* of the original collection optimised for our query. Now, when students are added or removed from the main collection or have their names changed, the hash map must be updated accordingly.

The two design choices outlined above (traversal versus hash map) present a conundrum for the programmer: which should he/she choose? The answer, of course, depends upon the ratio of queries to updates — something the programmer is unlikely to know beforehand (indeed, even if it is known, it is likely to

D. Thomas (Ed.): ECOOP 2006, LNCS 4067, pp. 28–49, 2006.
© Springer-Verlag Berlin Heidelberg 2006

change). Modern OO languages compound this problem further by making it difficult to move from one design to the other. For example, consider moving from using the traversal approach to using a hash map view. The easiest way to ensure both the collection and the hash map are always consistent is to encapsulate them together, so that changes to the collection can be intercepted. This also means providing a method which returns the set of all students with a given name by exploiting the hash map's fast lookup. The problem is that we must now replace the manual traversal code — which may be scattered throughout the program — with calls to this new method and this is a non-trivial task.

In this paper, we present an extension to Java that supports efficient querying of program objects. We allow queries to range over collection objects and also the set of all instantiated objects. In this way, manual code for querying implicit relationships can be replaced by simple query statements. This allows our query evaluator to optimise their execution, leading to greater efficiency. In doing this, we build upon a wealth of existing knowledge on query optimisation from the database community. Our focus differs somewhat, however, as we are interested in the value of querying as a programming construct in its own right. As such, we are not concerned with issues of persistence, atomic transactions, roll-back and I/O efficient algorithms upon which the database community expends much effort. Rather, our "database" is an object-oriented program that fits entirely within RAM.

This paper makes the following contributions:

- We develop an elegant extension to the Java language which permits object querying over the set of all program objects.
- We present experimental data looking at the performance of our query evaluator, compared with good and bad hand-coded implementations. The results demonstrate that our system is competitive with an optimised hand-coded implementation.
- We present a technique which uses AspectJ to efficiently track object extent sets.
- We present experimental data looking at the performance of our object tracking system on the SPECjvm98 benchmark suite. The results demonstrate that our approach is practical.

2   Object Querying

Figure 1 shows the almost generic diagram of students attending courses. Versions of this diagram are found in many publications on relationships [5,6,11,31]. Many students attend many courses; Courses have a course code, a title string and a teacher; students have IDs and (reluctantly, at least at our university's registry) names. A difficulty with this decomposition is representing students who are also teachers. One solution is to have separate **Student** and **Teacher** objects, which are related by name. The following code can then be used to identify students who are teachers:

```
List<Tuple2<Faculty,Student>> matches = new ArrayList<..>();
for(Faculty f : allFaculty) {
  for(Student s : allStudents) {
    if(s.name.equals(f.name)) {
      matches.add(new Tuple2<Faculty,Student>(f,s));
}}}
```

In database terms, this code is performing a *join* on the name field for the `allFaculty` and `allStudent` collections. The code is cumbersome and can be replaced with the following *object query*, which is more succinct and, potentially, more efficient:

```
List<Tuple2<Faculty,Student>> matches;
matches = selectAll(Faculty f=allFaculty, Student s=allStudents
                    : f.name.equals(s.name));
```

This gives exactly the same set of results as the loop code. The `selectAll` primitive returns a list of tuples containing all possible instantiations of the *domain variables* (i.e. those declared before the colon) where the *query expression* holds (i.e. that after the colon). The domain variables determine the set of objects which the query ranges over: they can be initialised from a collection (as above); or, left uninitialised to range over the entire *extent set* (i.e. the set of all instantiated objects) of their type. Queries can define as many domain variables as necessary and can make use of the usual array of expression constructs found in Java. One difference from normal Java expressions is that boolean operators, such as `&&` and `||`, do not imply an order of execution for their operands. This allows flexibility in the order they are evaluated, potentially leading to greater efficiency.

As well as its simplicity, there are other advantages to using this query in place of the loop code. The query evaluator can apply well-known optimisations which the programmer might have missed. By leaving the decision of which optimisation to apply until runtime, it can make a more informed decision based upon dynamic properties of the data itself (such as the relative size of input sets) — something that is, at best, difficult for a programmer to do. A good example, which applies in this case, is the so-called *hash-join* (see e.g. [26]). The idea is to avoid enumerating all of `allFaculty` × `allStudents` when there are few matches. A hash-map is constructed from the largest of the two collections which maps the value being joined upon (in this case `name`) back to its objects. This still requires $O(sf)$ time in the worst-case, where $s = |{\tt allStudents}|$ and $f = |{\tt allFaculty}|$, but in practice is likely to be linear in the number of matches (contrasting with a nested loop which *always* takes $O(sf)$ time).

Figure 2 illustrates a hash-join implementation of the original loop. We believe it is highly unlikely a programmer would regularly apply this optimisation in practice. This is because it is noticeably more complicated than the nested-loop implementation and requires considerable insight, on behalf of the programmer, to understand the benefits. Even if he/she had appreciated the value of using a hash join, the optimal ordering (i.e. whether to map from names to Faculty

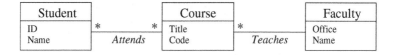

```
class Student { String name; int ID; ... }
class Faculty { String name; String office; ... }

class Course {
 String code, title;
 Faculty teacher;
 HashSet<Student> roster;
 void enrol(Student s) { roster.add(s); }
 void withdraw(Student s) { roster.remove(s); }
}
```

Fig. 1. A simple UML diagram, describing students that attend courses and teachers that teach them and a typical implementation. Protection specifiers on fields and accessor methods are omitted for simplicity.

```
// selectAll(Faculty f=allFaculty, Student s=allStudents
//              : f.name.equals(s.name));

HashMap<String,List<Faculty>> tmp = new HashMap<...>();
for(Faculty f : allFaculty) {
  List<Faculty> fs = tmp.get(f.name);
  if(fs == null) {
   fs = new ArrayList<Faculty>();
   tmp.put(f.name,fs);
  }
  fs.add(f);
}

List<Tuple2<Faculty,Student>> matches = new ArrayList<..>();
for(Student s : allStudents) {
  List<Faculty> fs = tmp.get(s.name);
  if(fs != null) {
    for(Faculty f : fs) {
     matches.add(new Tuple2<Faculty,Student>(f,s));
    }
  }
}
```

Fig. 2. Illustrating a hash-join implementation of the simple query (shown at the top) from Section 2. The code first creates a map from `Faculty` names to `Faculty` objects. Then, it iterates over the `allStudents` collection and looks up those `Faculty` members with the same name.

or from names to Students) depends upon the relative number of students and faculty (mapping to the smaller is generally the best choice [26]). Of course, a clever programmer could still obtain optimal performance by manually enumerating all possible orderings and including a runtime check to select the best one. But, is this really likely to happen in practice? Certainly, for larger queries, it becomes ridiculously impractical as the number of valid orderings grows exponentially. Using a query in place of a manual implementation allows the query evaluator to perform such optimisations. And, as we will see in Section 4, there is a significant difference between a good hand-coded implementation and a poor one — even for small queries.

2.1   Querying Object Extents

While object querying could be limited to collections alone, there is additional benefit in allowing queries to range over the set of all instantiated objects. An interesting example lies in expressing and enforcing *class invariants*. Class invariants are often captured using universal/existential quantifiers over object extents (e.g. [3,30,34,35]). Queries provide a natural approach to checking these invariants.

In a conventional OO language, such as Java, it is possible to express and enforce some class invariants using simple assertions. For example:

```
class BinTree {
  private BinTree left;
  private BinTree right;
  private Object value;

  public BinTree(BinTree l, BinTree r) {
    left = l; right = r;
    assert left != right;
  }
  void setLeftTree(BinTree l) {
    left = l;
    assert left != right;
  }
  ...
}
```

Here, the class invariant `left!=right` is enforced by asserting it after every member function. This allows programmers to identify the exact point during a program's execution that an incorrect state is reached — thus preventing a *cause-effect gap* [12].

A limitation of this approach is that it cannot easily express more wide-ranging class invariants. The above tries (unsuccessfully) to enforce the invariant that there is no aliasing between trees. In other words, that no `BinTree` object has more than one parent and/or the same subtrees. The simple approach using assert can only *partially* express this because it is limited to a particular instance of BinTree — there is no way to quantify over all instances. The programmer could rectify this by maintaining a collection of the class's instances in a static class variable. This requires a separate implementation for each class and, once in place, is difficult to disable (e.g. for software release). Another option is to maintain a back-pointer in each BinTree object, which points to its parent. Then, before assigning a tree to be a subtree of another, we check whether it already has a parent. Again, this approach suffers from being difficult to disable and requiring non-trivial implementation. Indeed, properly maintaining this parent-child relationship is a tricky task that could easily be implemented incorrectly — potentially leading to a false impression that the class invariant holds.

Using an object query offers a cleaner, more succinct and more manageable solution:

```
assert null == selectA(BinTree a, BinTree b :
                       (a.left == b.left && a != b) ||
                       (a.right == b.right && a != b) ||
                       (a.left == b.right));
```

This uses the selectA primitive which returns a matching tuple (if there is one), or null (otherwise). Using selectA (when applicable) is more efficient that selectAll because the query evaluator can stop as soon as the first match is made. Notice that, in the query, a and b can refer to the same BinTree object, hence the need to guard against this in the first two cases.

Other examples of interesting class invariants which can be enforced using object queries include the singleton pattern [13]:

```
assert 1 == selectAll(Singleton x).size();
```

and, similarly, the fly-weight pattern [13]:

```
assert null == selectA(Value x, Value y : x.equals(y) && x != y);
```

The above ensures that flyweight objects (in this case Value objects) are not duplicated, which is the essence of this pattern.

2.2 Dynamic Querying

So far, we have assumed that queries are statically compiled. This means they can be checked for well-formedness at compile time. However, our query evaluator maintains at runtime an Abstract Syntax Tree (AST) representation of the query for the purposes of query optimisation. An AST can be constructed at runtime by the program and passed directly to the query evaluator. This form of *dynamic query* has the advantage of being more flexible, albeit at the cost of runtime type checking. The syntax of a dynamic query is:

```
List<Object[]> selectAll(Query stmt);
```

Since static typing information is not available for dynamic queries, we simply implement the returned tuples as `Object` arrays. The `Query` object encapsulates the domain variables and query expression (a simple AST) making up the query. The following illustrates a simple dynamic query:

```
List<Object[]> findEquivInstances(Class C, Object y) {
  // build selectAll(C x : x.equals(y));
  Query query = new Query();
  DomainVar x = query.newDomainVar(C);
  query.addConjunct(new Equals(x,new ConstRef(y)));
  // run query
  return query.selectAll();
}
```

This returns all instances, x, of class c where `x.equals(y)` holds. This query cannot be expressed statically, since the class c is unknown at compile time. Dynamic queries are more flexible: in particular, we can construct queries in direct response to user input.

3   Implementation

We have prototyped a system, called the *Java Query Language (JQL)*, which permits queries over object extents and collections in Java. The implementation consists of three main components: a compiler, a query evaluator and a runtime system for tracking all active objects in the program. The latter enables the query evaluator to range over the extent sets of all classes. Our purpose in doing this is twofold: firstly, to assess the performance impact of such a system; secondly, to provide a platform for experimenting with the idea of using queries as first-class language constructs.

3.1   JQL Query Evaluator

The core component of the JQL system is the query evaluator. This is responsible for applying whatever optimisations it can to evaluate queries efficiently. The evaluator is called at runtime with a tree representation of the query (called the *query tree*). The tree itself is either constructed by the JQL Compiler (for static queries) or by the user (for dynamic queries).

Evaluation Pipeline. The JQL evaluator evaluates a query by pushing tuples through a staged pipeline. Each stage, known as a *join* in the language of databases, corresponds to a condition in the query. Only tuples matching a join's condition are allowed to pass through to the next. Those tuples which make it through to the end are added to the result set. Each join accepts two lists of tuples, L(eft) and R(ight), and combines them together producing a single list. We enforce the restriction that, for each intermediate join, either both inputs come from the previous stage or one comes directly from an input collection and

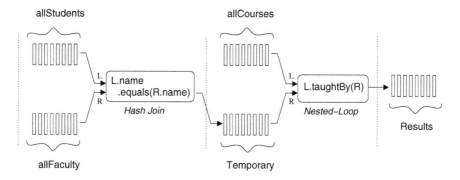

Fig. 3. Illustrating a query pipeline

the other comes from the previous stage. This is known as a *linear processing tree* [19] and it simplifies the query evaluator, although it can lead to inefficiency in some cases.

The way in which a join combines tuples depends upon its type and the operation (e.g. ==, < etc) it represents. JQL currently supports two join types: *nested-loop join* and *hash join*. A nested-loop join is a two-level nested loop which iterates each of L × R and checks for a match. A hash join builds a temporary hash table which it uses to check for matches. This provides the best performance, but can be used only when the join operator is == or equals(). Future implementations may take advantage of B-Trees, for scanning sorted ranges of a collection.

Consider the following simple query for finding all students who teach a course (presumably employed as an RA):

```
r = selectAll(Student s=allStudents, Faculty f=allFaculty,
    Course c=allCourses : s.name.equals(f.name) && c.taughtBy(f));
```

Figure 3 illustrates the corresponding query pipeline. Since the first join represents an equals() operation, it is implemented as a hash-join. The second join, however, represents an arbitrary method call and must be implemented as a nested-loop. The tuples which are produced from the first join have the form ⟨*Student, Faculty*⟩ and are stored in a temporary location before being passed into the second join.

Join Ordering. The ordering of joins in the pipeline can dramatically effect the time needed to process the query. The cost of a single join is determined by its input size, (i.e. $|L| \times |R|$) while its *selectivity* affects the input size (hence, cost) of subsequent joins. Selectivity is the ratio of the number of tuples which do not match to the input size[1]. Thus, highly selective joins produce relatively few matches compared with the amount of input. To find a minimal cost ordering, we must search

---

[1] We follow Lencevicius [20] with our meaning of selectivity here. While this contrasts with the database literature (where it means the opposite), we feel this is more intuitive.

every $n!$ possible configurations and, in fact, this is known to be an NP-complete problem [18]. A further difficulty is that we cannot know the true selectivity of a given join without first running it. One approach is to use a fixed selectivity heuristic for each operation (e.g. == is highly selective, while != is not). Alternatively, we can *sample* the join's selectivity by testing a small number of tuples and seeing how many are matched before evaluating the whole query [15,20].

The JQL evaluator supports both approaches for estimating selectivity. For the fixed heuristic approach, the following selectivity values are used: 0.95 for == and `equals()`; 0.5 for <, <=, >, >= and `compare()`; 0.2 for !=; finally, 0.1 for arbitrary methods. The sampling approach passes 10 randomly selected tuples from the input through each join and uses the number of matches as an estimator of selectivity. We find that, even with a sample size of just 10 tuples, surprisingly accurate results can be obtained.

We have implemented several join ordering strategies in an effort to assess their suitability. We now briefly discuss each of these in turn:

- EXHAUSTIVE: This strategy enumerates each possible configuration, selecting that with the lowest cost. To determine the overall cost of a pipeline, we use essentially the same procedure as outlined above.
- MAX_SELECTIVITY: This strategy orders joins based solely on their selectivity, with the most selective coming first. This simple approach has the advantage of avoiding an exponential search and, although it will not always find the best ordering, we find it generally does well in practice. This is essentially the same strategy as that used in the PTQL system [14].

Many other heuristics have been proposed in the literature (see e.g. [18,19,37,36]) and, in the future, we hope to implement more strategies to help determine which is most suited to this domain.

3.2   JQL Compiler

The JQL compiler is a prototype source-to-source translator that replaces all `selectAll` / `selectA` statements with equivalent Java code. When a query statement is encountered the compiler converts the query expression into a sequence of Java statements that construct a query tree and pass this to the query evaluator. The value of using a compiler, compared with simply writing dynamic queries (as in Section 2.2), is twofold: firstly, the syntax is neater and more compact; secondly, the compiler can check the query is well-formed, the value of which has been noted elsewhere [4,9,10].

The query tree itself is a fairly straightforward Abstract Syntax Tree. For ease of implementation, our prototype requires that queries be expressed in CNF. This way the query can be represented as an array of expressions, where each is ANDed together.

3.3   JQL Runtime System

To track the extent sets of all objects, we use AspectJ to intercept and record all calls to `new`. The following example illustrates a simple aspect which does this:

```
aspect MyAspect {
  pointcut newObject() : call(* *.new(..)) && !within(MyAspect);
  after() : newObject() { System.out.println("new called"); }
}
```

This creates a pointcut, newObject(), which captures the act of calling new on any class except MyAspect. This is then associated with advice which executes whenever a join point captured by newObject() is triggered (i.e. whenever new is called). Here, after() indicates the advice executes immediately after the join point triggers. Notice that we must use !within(MyAspect) to protect against an infinite loop which could arise if MyAspect allocates storage inside the advice, resulting in the advice triggering itself.

Implementation. To track all program objects in the program we use an Aspect (similar to above) which advises all calls to new() with code to record a reference to the new object. This aspect is shown in Figure 4. One exception

```
public aspect TrackingAspect {
  Hashtable<Class,ExtentSet> extentSets = new Hashtable<...>();

  pointcut newObject() : call(*.new(..)) && !within(TrackingAspect.*);

  after() returning(Object o) : newObject() {
     Class C = o.getClass();
     getExtentSet(C).add(o);
  }

  ExtentSet getExtentSet(Class C) {
    // Find extent set for C.  If there is none, create one.
    ExtentSet set;
    synchronized(extentSets) {
      set = extentSets.get(C);
      if(set == null) {
        set = new ExtentSet();
        extentSets.put(C, set);
        Class S = C.getSuperClass();
        if(S != null) {
          getExtentSet(S).link(set);        // Link superclass set
        }
        for(Class I : C.getInterfaces()) {
          getExtentSet(I).link(set);        // Link interface set
        }
      }
    }
  }
}
```

Fig. 4. An aspect for tracking all objects in the program

is the use of "`returning(...)`" which gives access to the object reference returned by the **new** call. We use this aspect to provide a facility similar to the 'allInstances' message in Smalltalk, without having to produce a custom JVM.

The TrackingAspect maintains a map from classes to their ExtentSets. An ExtentSet (code not shown) holds every object of its class using a weak reference. Weak references do not prevent the garbage collector from reclaiming the object they refer to and, hence, an ExtentSet does not prevent its objects from being reclaimed. In addition, an ExtentSet has a redirect list which holds the ExtentSets of all its class's subclasses. In the case of an interface, the redirect list refers to the ExtentSet of all implementing classes and subinterfaces. The reason for using redirect lists is to avoid storing multiple references for objects whose class either implements some interface(s) or extends another class. Note that only ExtentSets which correspond to concrete classes will actually contain object references, as interfaces and abstract classes cannot be instantiated.

An important consideration is the effect of synchronisation. We must synchronise on the Hashtable and, hence, we are essentially placing a lock around object creation. In fact, the multi-level nature of the extent set map can help somewhat. This is because new ExtentSets will only be added to the outer Hashtable infrequently. A more advanced data structure should be able to exploit this and restrict the majority of synchronisation to within individual ExtentSets. This way, synchronisation only occurs between object creations of the same class. We have experimented with using ConcurrentHashmap for this purpose, although we saw no performance improvements. We hope to investigate this further in the future and expect it likely the two tier structure of the extent sets will obviate most of the synchronisation penalty.

4   Performance

We consider that the performance of the JQL system is important in determining whether it could gain widespread use. Ideally, the system should be capable of evaluating queries as fast as the optimal hand-coded loop. This is difficult to achieve in practice due to the additional overheads introduced by the pipeline design, and in the necessary search for good join orders. However, we argue that merely being competitive with the best hand-coded loops is a sufficient indicator of success, since it is highly unlikely a programmer will often write optimal hand-coded loops in large-scale programs.

Therefore, in this section we investigate the performance of the JQL system in a number of ways. Firstly, we compare its performance against hand-coded loops across three simple benchmarks to determine its competitiveness. Secondly, we evaluate the overhead of the object tracking mechanism using the SPECjvm98 benchmarks [1].

In all experiments which follow, the experimental machine was an Intel Pentium IV 2.5GHz, with 1GB RAM running NetBSD v3.99.11. In each case, Sun's Java 1.5.0 (J2SE 5.0) Runtime Environment and Aspect/J version 1.5M3 were used. Timing was performed using the standard System.currentTimeMillis()

method, which provides millisecond resolution (on NetBSD). The source code for the JQL system and the three query benchmarks used below can be obtained from http://www.mcs.vuw.ac.nz/~djp/JQL/.

4.1 Study 1 — Query Evaluation

The purpose of this study was to investigate the query evaluator's performance, compared with equivalent hand-coded implementations. We used three queries of different sizes as benchmarks for comparison. Two hand-coded implementations were written for each: HANDOPT and HANDPOOR. The former represents the best implementation we could write. This always used hash-joins when possible and employed the optimal join ordering. The HANDPOOR implementation was the exact opposite, using only nested-loop joins and the worst join ordering possible — a pessimistic but nonetheless possible outcome for novice or distracted programmers. Our purpose with these implementations was to determine the range of performance that could be expected for hand-coded queries. This is interesting for several reasons: firstly, the programmer is unlikely to apply all the optimisations (e.g. hash-joins) that are possible; secondly; the programmer is unlikely to select an optimal join order (indeed, the optimal may vary dynamically as the program executes). The question, then, was how close the JQL evaluator performance was, compared with the HANDOPT implementation.

Table 1. Details of the three benchmark queries

Name	Details
OneStage	`selectAll(Integer a=L1, Integer b=L2 : a == b);` This benchmark requires a single pipeline stage. Hence, there is only one possible join ordering. The query can be optimised by using a hash-join rather than a nested loop implementation.

TwoStage	`selectAll(Integer a=L1, Integer b=L2, Integer c=L3`
	`        : a == b && b != c);`
	
	This benchmark requires two pipeline stages. The best join ordering has the joins ordered as above (i.e. == being first). The query can be further optimised by using a hash-join rather than a nested loop implementation for the == join.

ThreeStage	`selectAll(Integer a=L1, Integer b=L2, Integer c=L3,`
	`          Integer d=L4 : a == b && b != c && c < d);`
	
	This benchmark requires three pipeline stages. The best join ordering has the joins ordered as above (i.e. == being first). The query is interesting as it makes sense to evaluate b != c before c < d, even though the former has lower selectivity. This query can be optimised using a hash-join as before.

Experimental setup. The three query benchmarks are detailed in Table 1. The queries range over the lists of Integers L1, ..., L4 which, for simplicity, were always kept the same size. Let n be the size of each list. Then, each was generated by initialising with each integer from $\{1, \ldots, n\}$ and randomly shuffling. Note, the worst case time needed to evaluate StageOne, StageTwo and StageThree queries is $O(n^2)$, $O(n^3)$ and $O(n^4)$, respectively.

For each query benchmark, four implementations were tested: the two hand-coded implementations (HANDOPT, HANDPOOR); and, the JQL query evaluator using the MAX_SELECTIVITY and EXHAUSTIVE join ordering strategies. For all JQL tests, join selectivity was estimated using the fixed heuristic outlined in Section 3.1, but not the sampling approach. The reason for this is simply that, for these queries, the two approaches to estimating selectivity produced very similar results.

Each experiment consisted of measuring the average time taken for an implementation to evaluate one of the query benchmarks for a given list size. The average time was measured over 10 runs, with 5 ramp-up runs being performed beforehand. These parameters were sufficient to generate data with a variation coefficient (i.e. standard deviation over mean) of ≤ 0.15 — indicating low variance between runs. Experiments were performed for each query and implementation at different list sizes (i.e. n) to gain insight into how performance varied with n.

Discussion. The results of the experiments are shown in Figure 5. The main observation is that there is a significant difference between the HANDOPT and HANDPOOR implementations, even for the small OneStage query. Furthermore, while the performance of JQL is always marginally slower (regardless of join ordering strategy) than HANDOPT, it is always much better than HAND-POOR. We argue then, that the guaranteed performance offered by JQL is very attractive, compared with the range of performance offered by hand-coded implementations — especially as it's unlikely a programmer will achieve anything close to HANDOPT in practice.

The ThreeStage benchmark is the most complex of those studied and highlights a difference in performance between the MAX_SELECTIVITY and EX-HAUSTIVE join ordering strategies used by JQL. This difference arises because the MAX_SELECTIVITY heuristic does not obtain an optimal join ordering for this benchmark, while the EXHAUSTIVE strategy does. In general, it seems that the EXHAUSTIVE strategy is the more attractive. Indeed, for queries that have relatively few joins, it is. It is also important to remember that it uses an exponential search algorithm and, hence, for large queries this will certainly require a prohibitive amount of time. In general, we believe that further work investigating other possible join ordering heuristics from the database community would be valuable.

4.2   Study 2 — Object Extents Tracking

The purpose of this study was to investigate the performance impact of the JQL object tracking system. This is necessary to permit querying over the object

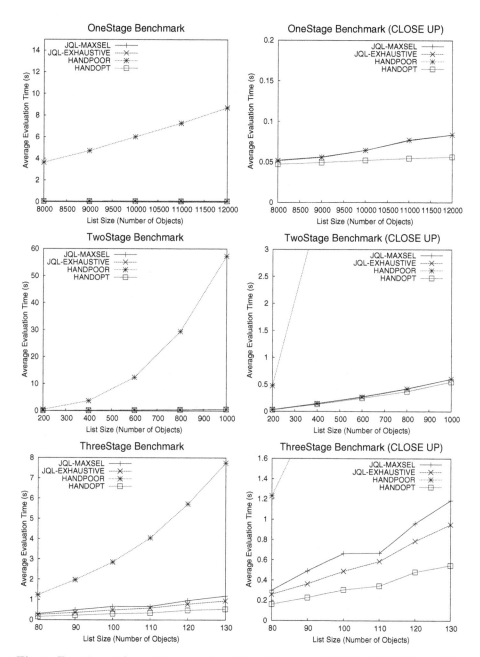

Fig. 5. Experimental results comparing the performance of JQL with different join ordering strategies against the hand-coded implementations. Data for the OneStage, TwoStage and ThreeStage benchmarks are shown at the Top, Middle and Bottom respectively. The charts on the right give a close ups of the three fastest implementations for each benchmark. Different object sizes are plotted to show the general trends.

Table 2. The benchmark suite. Size indicates the amount of bytecode making up the benchmark, excluding harness code and standard libraries. Time and Heap give the execution time and maximum heap usage for one run of the benchmark. # Objects Created gives the total number of objects created by the benchmark during one run.

Benchmark	Size (KB)	# Objects Created	Time (s)	Heap (MB)	Multi- Threaded
_201_compress	17.4	601	6.4	55	N
_202_jess	387.2	5.3×10^6	1.6	61	N
_205_raytrace	55.0	5.0×10^6	1.6	60	N
_209_db	9.9	1.6×10^5	11.5	63	N
_213_javac	548.3	11152	3.9	78	N
_222_mpegaudio	117.4	1084	6.0	26	N
_227_mtrt	56.0	5.2×10^6	2.6	64	Y
_228_jack	127.8	6.9×10^5	2.3	59	N

extent sets. However, each object creation causes, at least, both a hashtable lookup and an insertion. Keeping an extra reference of every live object also causes memory overhead. We have used the SPECjvm98 benchmark suite to test the memory and execution overhead incurred.

Experimental setup. The benchmarks used for these experiments are described in Table 2. To measure execution time, we averaged time taken by each benchmark with and without the tracker enabled. These timings were taken over 10 runs with a 5-run rampup period. This was sufficient to generate data with a variation coefficient of ≤ 0.1, again indicating very low variance between runs. For memory overhead measurements, we monitored the resource usage of the JVM process using top while running the benchmark and recorded the peak measurement. For these experiments the JVM was run with a 512MB heap.

Discussion. The relative slowdowns for each benchmark's execution time are shown in Figure 6. The memory overhead incurred for each benchmark is shown in Figure 7.

Both memory overhead and execution overhead are directly influenced by the number of objects created. Execution overhead is linked to how much time is spent creating objects, rather than operating on them. mpegaudio and compress, for example, create relatively few objects and spend most of their runtime working with those objects. Hence, they show relatively minor slowdown. jess and raytrace, on the other hand, create millions of objects in the space of a few seconds. This leads to a fairly significant slowdown.

Memory overhead is also influenced by relative size of objects created. A benchmark like raytrace creates hundreds of thousands of small Point objects, likely smaller than the WeakReference objects necessary to track them. This means the relative overhead of the tracker for each object is very large. db, on the other hand, creates a hundred thousand-odd String instances, which outweigh the WeakReferences. Compared to these bulky Strings, the tracker's overhead is minor.

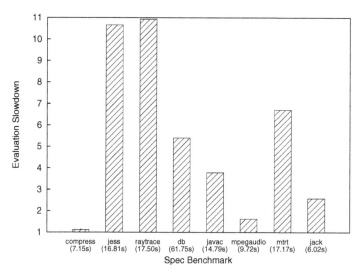

Fig. 6. Slowdown factors for SPECjvm98 benchmark programs executed with object tracking enabled. The execution time with tracking enabled is shown below each benchmark; the untracked execution times are given in Table 2. Slowdown factors are computed as the division of the tracked time over the untracked time.

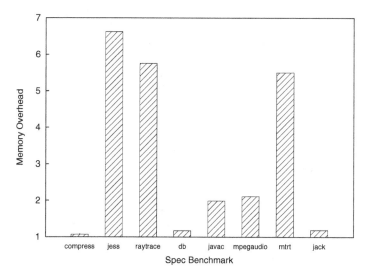

Fig. 7. Memory overhead factors for SPECjvm98 benchmark programs executed with object tracking enabled. Memory overhead is computed as the division of the tracked memory usage over the untracked usage.

We consider these benchmarks show the object tracker is likely to be practical for many Java programs. Certainly, using the system in development would offer significant benefits, for example, if class invariants we used properly. We feel performance data for using the object tracker with various 'real-world' Java applications would be valuable, and plan to investigate this in the future.

5   Discussion

In this section, we discuss various issues with the JQL system and explore interesting future directions.

5.1   Side Effecting Queries

One of the issues we have not addressed is that of side-effecting queries. That is, queries using a method which mutates the objects it is called upon. While this is possible in principle, we believe it would be difficult to use in a sensible way. This is because the query evaluator is free to optimise queries as it sees fit — there is no evaluation order which can be relied upon. Indeed, there is no guarantee upon what combinations of the domain variable's objects such a method will be called. For example:

```
r = selectAll(Object x, Object y : x.equals(y) && x.fn(y));
```

Even for this simple query, it is difficult to predict upon which objects `fn()` will be called. The most likely scenario is that `x.equals(y)` will be the first join in the pipeline — in which case `x.fn(y)` is only called on those x and y which are `equals()`. However, if the JQL's sampling strategy for estimating selectivity is used, then `fn()` could be placed before `equals()` in the pipeline. In this case, `x.fn(y)` is called for all possible x and y combinations.

We make the simplifying assumption that all methods used as part of a query (such as `fn()` above) have no side effects. This applies to the use of `equals()` and `compare()` as well as all other method calls. Since JQL cannot enforce this requirement (at least, not without complex static analysis), it falls upon the programmer to ensure all methods used are in fact side-effect free.

5.2   Incrementalisation

An interesting observation is that, to improve performance, the results of a query can be cached and reused later. This approach, often called incrementalisation [7,24], requires that the cached results are updated in line with changes to the objects and collections they derive from.

Determining whether some change to an object/collection affects a cached query result it is not without difficulty. We could imagine intercepting all field reads/writes (perhaps using AspectJ's field read/write pointcuts) and checking whether it affects any cached query results. While this might be expensive if there are a large number of cached queries, it could be lucrative if the cache is restricted to a small number of frequently called queries. Alternatively, cached queries could be restricted to those involving only `final` field values. This way, we are guaranteed objects involved in a query cannot change, thereby simplifying the problem.

While incrementalisation can improve performance, its real power lies in an ability to improve program structure by eliminating many uses of collections. Consider the problem of recording which Students are enrolled in which Courses. In Figure 1, this is achieved by storing a collection of Students in each Course object. With incrementalisation we can imagine taking another route. Instead of adding a Student to a Course's collection, we construct a new Enroll object which has fields referencing the Student and Course in question. To access Students enrolled in a particular Course, we simply query for all Enroll objects with a matching Course field. Incrementalisation ensures that, if the query is executed frequently, the cached query result — which is equivalent to the collection in Course that was replaced — is maintained. This provides more flexibility than the original design as, for example, it allows us to efficiently traverse the relationship in either direction with ease. With the original design, we are limited to a single direction of traversal, unless we add a collection to Student that holds enrolled Courses. In fact, this has many similarities with the approach taken to implementing relationships in Rel/J [5].

Incrementalisation is not currently implemented in JQL, although we hope to explore this direction in the future.

6   Related Work

An important work in this area is that of Lencevicius *et al.*, who developed a series of *Query-Based Debuggers* [20,21,22,23] to address the *cause-effect gap* [12]. The effect of a bug (erroneous output, crash, etc) often occur some time after the statement causing it was executed, making it hard to identify the real culprit. Lencevicius *et al.* observed that typical debuggers provide only limited support for this in the form of breakpoints that trigger when simple invariants are broken. They extended this by allowing queries on the object graph to trigger breakpoints — thereby providing a mechanism for identifying when complex invariants are broken. Their query-based debuggers re-evaluate the query whenever a program event occurs that could change the query's result. Thus, a breakpoint triggers whenever one or more objects match the query. To reduce the performance impact of this, they employed a number of query optimisations (such as operator selectivity and join ordering).

Several other systems have used querying to aid debugging. The Fox [32,33] operates on heap dumps of the program generated using Sun's Heap Analysis Tool (HAT), allowing queries to range over the set of objects involved in a given snapshot. The main focus of this was on checking that certain ownership constraints were being properly maintained by a given program. The Program Trace Query Language (PTQL) permits relational queries over program traces with a specific focus on the relationship between program events [14]. PTQL allows the user to query over relations representing various aspects of program execution, such as the set of all method invocations or object creations. The query evaluator in PTQL supports nested-loop joins (but not hash-joins as we do) and performs join ordering using something very similar to our MAX_SELECTIVITY heuristic. The Program Query Language (PQL) is a similar system which allows the programmer to express queries capturing erroneous behaviour over the program trace [25]. A key difference from other systems is that static analysis was used in an effort to answer some queries without needing to run the program. As a fallback, queries which could not be resolved statically are compiled into the program's bytecode and checked at runtime.

Hobatr and Malloy [16,17] present a query-based debugger for C++ that uses the OpenC++ Meta-Object Protocol [8] and the Object Constraint Language (OCL) [38]. This system consists of a frontend for compiling OCL queries to C++, and a backend that uses OpenC++ to generate the instrumentation code necessary for evaluating the queries. In some sense this is similar to our approach, except that we use JQL to specify queries and AspectJ to add the necessary instrumentation for resolving them. Like the others, their focus is primarily on catching violations of class invariants and pre/post conditions, rather than as a general purpose language extension. Unfortunately, no details are given regarding what (if any) query optimisations are employed and/or how program performance is affected by the added instrumentation code.

More recently, the Language INtegrated Query (LINQ) project has added querying capabilities to the $C^\sharp$ language. In many ways, this is similar to JQL and, while LINQ does not support querying over object extent sets, its queries can be used to directly access databases. At this stage, little is known about the query evaluator employed in LINQ and the query optimisations it performs. We hope that our work will motivate studies of this and it will be interesting to see how the LINQ query evaluator performs in practice. The $C\omega$ language [4] preceded LINQ and they have much in common as regards queries.

One feature of LINQ is the introduction of lambda expressions to $C^\sharp$. Lambda expressions can be used in place of iterators for manipulating / filtering collections [2]. In this way, they offer a form of querying where the lambda expression represents the query expression. However, this is more simplistic than the approach we have taken as, by permitting queries over multiple collections, we can exploit a number of important optimisations. Lambda expressions offer no help in this regard as, to apply such optimisations, we must be able to break apart and manipulate the query expression to find operators that support efficient joins and to determine good join orderings.

Another related work is that of Liu et al. [24], who regard all programs as a series of queries and updates. They use static program analysis to determine which queries can be incrementalised to permit efficient evaluation. To do this, they employ a cost model to determine which queries are expensive to compute and, hence, which should be incrementalised. This incrementalisation can be thought of as creating a view which represents the query results and automatically updating when the underlying data is changed. This optimisation could be implemented in JQL (albeit in a dynamic, rather than static setting) and we wish to explore this in the future.

Cook and Rai [10] describe how building queries out of objects (rather than using e.g. SQL strings) can ensure typesafety and prevent spoofing attacks. While these safe query objects have generally been used to generate database queries, they could also act as a front-end to our query system. Similarly, the object extents and query optimisations we describe in this paper could be applied in the context of a safe query object system.

Finally, there are a number of APIs available for Java (e.g. SQLJ, JSQL, etc.) which provide access to SQL databases. These are quite different from the approach we have presented in this work, as they do not support querying over collections and/or object extents. Furthermore, they do not perform any query optimisations, instead relying on the database back end to do this.

7 Conclusion

In this paper, we have presented a language extension for Java (called JQL) which permits queries over object collections and extent sets. We have motivated this as a way of improving both program readability and flexibility and also in providing a stronger guarantee of performance. The latter arises from the query evaluator's ability to perform complex optimisations — many of which the programmer is unlike to do in practice. Through an experimental study we have demonstrated there is a large difference in performance between a poor hand-coded query and a good one. Furthermore, our prototype implementation performs very well compared with optimised hand-coded implementations of several queries. We have also demonstrated that the cost of tracking all objects in the program is practical. We would expect that, with direct support for querying from the JVM, the performance overhead of this would improve significantly.

The complete source for our prototype implementation is available for download from http://www.mcs.vuw.ac.nz/~djp/JQL/ and we hope that it will motivate further study of object querying as a first-class language construct.

Acknowledgements

The authors would like to thank Stuart Marshall for some insightful comments on an earlier draft of this paper. This work is supported by the University Research Fund of Victoria University of Wellington, and the Royal Society of New Zealand Marsden Fund.

References

1. The Standard Performance Corporation. SPEC JVM98 benchmarks, http://www.spec.org/osg/jvm98, 1998.
2. H. G. Baker. Iterators: Signs of weakness in object-oriented languages. *ACM OOPS Messenger*, 4(3), July 1993.
3. M. Barnett, R. DeLine, M. Fahndrich, K. Rustan, M. Leino, and W. Schulte. Verification of object-oriented programs with invariants. *Journal of Object Technology*, 3(6):27–56, 2004.

4. G. Bierman, E. Meijer, and W. Schulte. The essence of data access in $c\omega$. In *Proceedings of the European Conference on Object-Oriented Programming (ECOOP)*, volume 3586 of *Lecture Notes in Computer Science*, pages 287–311. Springer-Verlag, 2005.

5. G. Bierman and A. Wren. First-class relationships in an object-oriented language. In *Proceedings of the European Conference on Object-Oriented Programming (ECOOP)*, volume 3586 of *Lecture Notes in Computer Science*, pages 262–282. Springer-Verlag, 2005.

6. G. Booch, I. Jacobson, and J. Rumbaugh. *The Unified Modeling Language User Guide*. Addison-Wesley, 1998.

7. S. Ceri and J. Widom. Deriving production rules for incremental view maintenance. In *Proceedings of the International Conference on Very Large Data Bases (VLDB)*, pages 577–589. Morgan Kaufmann Publishers Inc., 1991.

8. S. Chiba. A metaobject protocol for C++. In *Proceedings of the ACM conference on Object-Oriented Programming, Systems, Languages and Applications (OOPSLA)*, pages 285–299. ACM Press, 1995.

9. W. R. Cook and A. H. Ibrahim. Programming languages & databases: What's the problem? Technical report, Department of Computer Sciences, The University of Texas at Austin, 2005.

10. W. R. Cook and S. Rai. Safe query objects: Statically typed objects as remotely executable queries. In *Proceedings of the International Conference on Software Engineering (ICSE)*, pages 97–106. IEEE Computer Society Press, 2005.

11. D. F. D'Souza and A. C. Wills. *Objects, Components, and Frameworks with UML: The Catalysis Approach*. Addison-Wesley, 1998.

12. M. Eisenstadt. My hairiest bug war stories. *Communications of the ACM*, 40(4):30–37, 1997.

13. E. Gamma, R. Helm, R. E. Johnson, and J. Vlissides. *Design Patterns: Elements of Reusable Object-Oriented Software*. Addison-Wesley, 1994.

14. S. Goldsmith, R. O'Callahan, and A. Aiken. Relational queries over program traces. In *Proceedings of the ACM Conference on Object-Oriented Programming, Systems, Languages and Applications (OOPSLA)*, pages 385–402. ACM Press, 2005.

15. P. J. Haas, J. F. Naughton, and A. N. Swami. On the relative cost of sampling for join selectivity estimation. In *Proceedings of the thirteenth ACM symposium on Principles of Database Systems (PODS)*, pages 14–24. ACM Press, 1994.

16. C. Hobatr and B. A. Malloy. The design of an OCL query-based debugger for C++. In *Proceedings of the ACM Symposium on Applied Computing (SAC)*, pages 658–662. ACM Press, 2001.

17. C. Hobatr and B. A. Malloy. Using OCL-queries for debugging C++. In *Proceedings of the IEEE International Conference on Software Engineering (ICSE)*, pages 839–840. IEEE Computer Society Press, 2001.

18. T. Ibaraki and T. Kameda. On the optimal nesting order for computing n-relational joins. *ACM Transactions on Database Systems.*, 9(3):482–502, 1984.

19. R. Krishnamurthy, H. Boral, and C. Zaniolo. Optimization of nonrecursive queries. In *Proceedings of the ACM Conference on Very Large Data Bases (VLDB)*, pages 128–137. Morgan Kaufmann Publishers Inc., 1986.

20. R. Lencevicius. *Query-Based Debugging*. PhD thesis, University of California, Santa Barbara, 1999. TR-1999-27.

21. R. Lencevicius. On-the-fly query-based debugging with examples. In *Proceedings of the Workshop on Automated and Algorithmic Debugging (AADEBUG)*, 2000.

22. R. Lencevicius, U. Hölzle, and A. K. Singh. Query-based debugging of object-oriented programs. In *Proceedings of the ACM conference on Object-Oriented Programming, Systems, Languages and Applications (OOPSLA)*, pages 304–317. ACM Press, 1997.

23. R. Lencevicius, U. Hölzle, and A. K. Singh. Dynamic query-based debugging. In *Proceedings of the European Conference on Object-Oriented Programming (ECOOP)*, volume 1628 of *Lecture Notes in Computer Science*, pages 135–160. Springer-Verlag, 1999.

24. Y. A. Liu, S. D. Stoller, M. Gorbovitski, T. Rothamel, and Y. E. Liu. Incrementalization across object abstraction. In *Proceedings of the ACM conference on Object-Oriented Programming, Systems, Languages and Applications (OOPSLA)*, pages 473–486. ACM Press, 2005.

25. M. Martin, B. Livshits, and M. S. Lam. Finding application errors and security flaws using PQL: a program query language. In *Proceedings of the ACM conference on Object-Oriented Programming, Systems, Languages and Applications (OOPSLA)*, pages 365–383. ACM Press, 2005.

26. P. Mishra and M. H. Eich. Join processing in relational databases. *ACM Computing Surveys*, 24(1):63–113, 1992.

27. J. Noble. Basic relationship patterns. In N. Harrison, B. Foote, and H. Rohnert, editors, *Pattern Languages of Program Design 4*, chapter 6, pages 73–94. Addison-Wesley, 2000.

28. J. Noble and J. Grundy. Explicit relationships in object-oriented development. In *Proceedings of the conference on Technology of Object-Oriented Languages and Systems (TOOLS)*. Prentice-Hall, 1995.

29. D. J. Pearce and J. Noble. Relationship aspects. In *Proceedings of the ACM conference on Aspect-Oriented Software Development (AOSD)*, pages 75–86. ACM Press, 2005.

30. C. Pierik, D. Clarke, and F. de Boer. Creational invariants. In *Proceedings of the Workshop on Formal Techniques for Java-like Programs (FTfJP)*, pages 78–85, 2004.

31. R. Pooley and P. Stevens. *Using UML: Software Engineering with Objects and Components*. Addison-Wesley, 1999.

32. A. Potanin, J. Noble, and R. Biddle. Checking ownership and confinement. *Concurrency and Computation: Practice and Experience*, 16(7):671–687, 2004.

33. A. Potanin, J. Noble, and R. Biddle. Snapshot query-based debugging. In *Proceedings of the IEEE Australian Software Engineering Conference (ASWEC)*, pages 251–261. IEEE Computer Society Press, 2004.

34. K. Rustan, M. Leino, and P. Müller. Object invariants in dynamic contexts. In *Proceedings of the European Conference on Object-Oriented Programming (ECOOP)*, volume 3086 of *Lecture Notes in Computer Science*, pages 491–516. Springer-Verlag, 2004.

35. K. Rustan, M. Leino, and P. Müller. Modular verification of static class invariants. In *Proceedings of the Formal Methods Conference (FM)*, volume 3582 of *Lecture Notes in Computer Science*, pages 26–42, 2005.

36. M. Steinbrunn, G. Moerkotte, and A. Kemper. Heuristic and randomized optimization for the join ordering problem. *The VLDB Journal*, 6(3):191–208, 1997.

37. A. N. Swami and B. R. Iyer. A polynomial time algorithm for optimizing join queries. In *Proceedings of the International Conference on Data Engineering*, pages 345–354, Washington, DC, USA, 1993. IEEE Computer Society.

38. J. Warmer and A. Kleppe. *The Object Constraint Language: precise modeling with UML*. Addison-Wesley Longman Publishing Co., Inc., Boston, MA, USA, 1999.

Automatic Prefetching by Traversal Profiling in Object Persistence Architectures*

Ali Ibrahim and William R. Cook

Department of Computer Sciences, University of Texas at Austin
{aibrahim, wcook}@cs.utexas.edu

Abstract. Object persistence architectures support transparent access to persistent objects. For efficiency, many of these architectures support queries that can *prefetch* associated objects as part of the query result. While specifying prefetch manually in a query can significantly improve performance, correct prefetch specifications are difficult to determine and maintain, especially in modular programs. Incorrect prefetching is difficult to detect, because prefetch is only an optimization hint. This paper presents AUTOFETCH, a technique for automatically generating prefetch specifications using traversal profiling in object persistence architectures. AUTOFETCH generates prefetch specifications based on previous executions of similar queries. In contrast to previous work, AUTOFETCH can fetch arbitrary traversal patterns and can execute the optimal number of queries. AUTOFETCH has been implemented as an extension of Hibernate. We demonstrate that AUTOFETCH improves performance of traversals in the OO7 benchmark and can automatically predict prefetches that are equivalent to hand-coded queries, while supporting more modular program designs.

1 Introduction

Object persistence architectures allow programs to create, access, and modify *persistent objects*, whose lifetime extends beyond the execution of a single program. Examples of object persistence architectures include object-relational mapping tools [10, 6, 28, 24], object-oriented databases [8, 21], and orthogonally persistent programming languages [25, 2, 19, 22].

For example, the Java program in Figure 1 uses Hibernate [6] to print the names of employees, their managers, and the projects they work on. This code is typical of industrial object-persistence models: a string representing a query is passed to the database for execution, and a set of objects is returned. This query returns a collection of employee objects whose first name is "John". The fetch keyword indicates that related objects should be loaded along with the main result objects. In this query, both the manager and multiple projects are prefetched for each employee.

---

* This work was supported by the National Science Foundation under Grant No. 0448128.

D. Thomas (Ed.): ECOOP 2006, LNCS 4067, pp. 50–73, 2006.
© Springer-Verlag Berlin Heidelberg 2006

```
1  String query = "from Employee e
2    left join fetch e.manager left join fetch e.projects
3    where e.firstName = 'John' order by e.lastName";
4  Query q = sess.createQuery(query);
5  for (Employee emp : q.list()) {
6    print(emp.getName() + ": " + emp.getManager().getName());
7    for (Project proj : emp.getProjects()) {
8      printProject(prog);
9    }
10 }
```

Fig. 1. Java code using `fetch` in a Hibernate query

While specifying prefetch manually in a query can significantly improve performance, correct prefetch specifications are difficult to write and maintain manually. The prefetch definitions (line 2) in the query must correspond exactly to the code that uses the results of the query (lines 6 through 8).

It can be difficult to determine exactly what related objects should be prefetched. Doing so requires knowing all the operations that will be performed on the results of a query. Modularity can interfere with this analysis. For example, the code in Figure 1 calls a `printProject` method which can cause additional navigations from the project object. It may not be possible to statically determine which related objects are needed. This can happen if class factories are used to create operation objects with unknown behavior, or if classes are loaded dynamically.

As a program evolves, the code that uses the results of a query may be changed to include additional navigations, or remove navigations. As a result, the query must be modified to prefetch the objects required by the modified program. This significantly complicates evolution and maintenance of the system. If a common query is reused in multiple contexts, it may need to be copied in order to specify different prefetch behaviors in each case.

Since the prefetch annotations only affect performance, it is difficult to test or validate that they are correct – the program will compute the same results either way, although performance may differ significantly.

In this paper we present and evaluate AUTOFETCH, which uses traversal profiling to automate prefetch in object persistence architectures. AUTOFETCH records which associations are traversed when operating on the results of a query. This information is aggregated to create a statistical profile of application behavior. The statistics are used to automatically prefetch objects in future queries.

In contrast, previous work focused on profiling application behavior in the context of a single query. While this allowed systems such as PrefetchGuide [13] to prefetch objects on the initial execution of query, AUTOFETCH has several advantages. AUTOFETCH can prefetch arbitrary traversal patterns in addition to recursive and iterative patterns. AUTOFETCH can also execute fewer queries once patterns across queries are detected. AUTOFETCH's disadvantage of not optimizing initial query executions can be eliminated by combining AUTOFETCH with previous work.

When applied to an unoptimized version of the Torpedo benchmark, AUT-OFETCH performs as well as a hand-tuned version. For the OO7 benchmark, AUTOFETCH eliminates up to 99.8% of queries and improves performance by up to 99.7%. We also examined the software engineering benefits of AUTOFETCH, by showing that a modular version of a web-based resume application using AUTOFETCH performs as well as a less-modular, hand-optimized version.

2   Background

The object persistence architectures examined in this paper combine elements of *orthogonal persistence* [1] with the pragmatic approach of relational data access libraries, also known as *call level interfaces* [30].

Orthogonal persistence states that persistence behavior is independent of (orthogonal to) all other aspects of a system. In particular, any object can be persistent, whether an object is persistent does not affect its other behaviors, and an object is persistent if it is reachable from a persistent root. Orthogonal persistence has been implemented, to a degree, in a variety of programming languages [25, 2, 19, 22].

A key characteristic of orthogonal persistence is that objects are loaded when needed. Using a reference in an object is called *traversing* the reference, or *navigating* between objects – such that the target object is loaded if necessary. We use the term *navigational query* to refer to queries that are generated implicitly as a result of navigation.

Relational data access libraries are a pragmatic approach to persistence: they allow execution of arbitrary SQL queries, and the queries can return any combination of data that can be selected, projected, or joined via SQL. Examples include ODBC [15] and JDBC [12]. The client application determines how the results of a query are used – each row of the query result may be used as is, or it may be mapped to objects. Since data is never loaded automatically, the programmer must specify in a query all data required for an operation – the concept of prefetching data that might be loaded automatically does not apply.

The object persistence architectures considered in this paper are hybrids of orthogonal persistence and data access libraries. Examples include EJB [24], JDO [28], Hibernate [6], and Toplink [10]. They support automatic loading of objects as needed. But they also include query languages and the ability to manually prefetch related objects. While query languages can significantly increase performance, they reduce orthogonality because they are special operations that only apply to persistent data.

For example, in EJB 2.1, a query can return objects or a value:

select object(p) **from** Person p **where** p.firstName="John"

The set of objects loaded by a query are called *root* objects. Use of the root objects may result in navigation to related objects, each of which will require an additional query to load.

In client-server architectures, the cost of executing a query, which involves a round-trip to a database, typically dominates other performance measures. This is because the latency cost of communicating with the database is significantly greater than the cost of processing the query or producing results [4]. Other factors, like number of joins or subqueries, or the number of columns returned form a query, are insignificant compared to latency. The relative impact of latency on system performance is likely to increase, given that improvements in latency lag improvements in bandwidth and processing power [27]. As a result, number of queries will increasingly dominate all other concerns. In effect, overall response time is directly related to the number of queries executed in a task.

Object persistence architectures have developed a variety of mechanisms for avoiding navigational queries, by allowing programmers to manually specify prefetch of related objects. Prefetch of related objects is especially important in addressing the $n + 1$ select problem in which a related object is accessed for each result of a query. Without prefetch, if there are n results for a query, then there will be $n + 1$ loads. Most JDO vendors extended the standard to allow prefetch to be specified at the class level. Hibernate, and now EJB 3.0, allow prefetch to be specified within each query using the fetch keyword. Using fetch, a query can specify which related objects to load along with the root objects. These related objects can be either single objects or collections of related objects, depending on whether the association is single- or multi-valued. For example, this EJB 3.0 query returns a collection of persons where the children have been fetched as well:

select distinct p **from** Person p **left join fetch** p. children
where p.firstName=John

Previous versions of Hibernate only allowed one collection prefetch, however, Hibernate 3.1 allows multiple collections prefetches. Hibernate executes a query with a prefetch by augmenting the query with an appropriate join. This strategy causes the data for the container object to be replicated when a collection association is fetched. For a nested collection, the root container is replicated once for each combination of subcollection and sub-subcollection items. Thus replication is multiplied with each level of subcollection. Independent fetch collections are especially expensive because they cause the result set to include the cross-product of independent collection hierarchy elements. If Hibernate used a different query strategy that allowed for multiple SQL queries to be executed, while correlating the results in the client, then this problem could be eliminated.

Safe Query Objects are a type-safe alternative to string-based query interfaces [7]. Safe queries use methods in standard object-oriented languages to specify query criteria and sorting, so that a query is simply a class. Unlike string-based query languages, there is no natural place to specify prefetch in a Safe Query. Thus Safe Queries would benefit significantly from automatic prefetching.

3 Automating Prefetch

In this section we present AUTOFETCH, a solution to the problem of manual prefetch in object persistence architectures. Instead of the programmer manually specifying prefetches, AUTOFETCH adds prefetch specifications automatically. By profiling traversals on query results, AUTOFETCH determines the prefetches that can help reduce the number of navigational queries, i.e. queries executed as a program traverses an association.

To formalize this approach, we define type and object graphs as an abstract representation of persistent data. A type graph represents the class model, or structure of the database. Object graphs represent data. A complete database is represented as an object graph. Queries are functions whose range is a set of subgraphs of the database object graph.

Traversals represent the graph of objects and associations that are actually used in processing each result of a query. These traversals are aggregated into *traversal profiles*, which maintain statistics on the likelihood of traversing specific associations. Queries are classified into *query classes* based on a heuristic that groups queries that are likely to have similar traversals.

For each query executed, AUTOFETCH computes a prefetch specification based on the traversal profile for the query class. The prefetch specification is incorporated into the query and executed by the underlying database.

3.1 Profiling Traversals

In this section we develop a model for profiling the traversals performed by an object-oriented application. The concept of *profiling* is well known [3, 11]; it involves collecting statistics about the behavior of a program. Profiling is typically used to track control flow in an application – to find hot spots or compute code coverage. In this paper, profiling is used to track data access patterns – to identify what subset of a database is needed to perform a given operation.

We develop a formal model for types, objects, queries, and traversals. The type and object models are derived from work on adaptive programming [18].

Type Graph: Let T be the finite set of type names and F be the finite set of field names. A type graph is a directed graph $G_T = (T, A)$.

- T is a set of types.
- A is a partial function $T \times F \xrightarrow{?} T \times \{single, collection\}$ representing a set of associations between types. Given types t and t' and field f, if $A(t, f) = (t', m)$ then there is an association from t to t' with name f and cardinality m, where m indicates whether the association is a single- or multi-valued association.

Inheritance is not modeled in our type graph because it is orthogonal to prefetch. Bi-directional associations are supported through two uni-directional associations. Figure 2 shows a sample type graph. There are three types: Employee, Department, and Company. Each company has a set of departments and a CEO, each department has a set of employees, and each employee may have a supervisor. The formal representation is:

T = {Department, Employee, Company}
F = {employees, departments, CEO, supervisor}
A(Department, employees) ↦ (Employee, collection)
A(Company, departments) ↦ (Department, collection)
A(Company, CEO) ↦ (Employee, single)
A(Employee, supervisor) ↦ (Employee, single)

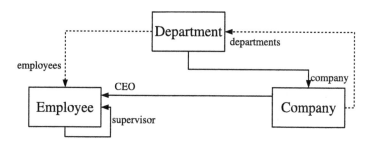

Fig. 2. Simple Type Graph with three types: Employee, Department, and Company. Solid lines represent single associations, while dashed lines represent collection associations.

Object Graph: Let O be the finite set of object names. An object graph is a directed graph $G_O = (O, E, G_T = (T, A), Type)$. G_T is a type graph and $Type$ is a unary function that maps objects to types. The following constraints must be satisfied in the object graph G_O:

- O represents a set of objects.
- $Type : O \rightarrow T$. The type of each object in the object graph must exist in the type graph.
- $E : O \times F \xrightarrow{?} powerset(O)$, the edges in the graph are a partial function from an object and field to a set of target objects.
- $\forall o, f: E(o, f) = S$
  - $A(Type(o), f) = (T', m)$
  - $\forall o' \in S, Type(o') = T'$.
  - if $m = single$, then $|S| = 1$.
  Each edge in the object graph corresponds to an edge in the type graph, single associations have exactly one target object.

An example object graph is shown in Figure 3 which is based on the type graph in Figure 2. Edges that contain a dark oval represent collection associations. Null-valued single associations are not represented by edges in the object graph, however, empty collection associations are represented as edges whose target is an empty set. We chose this representation because most object persistence architectures represent associations as a reference to a single target object or collection. A null-valued association is usually represented as a special reference in the source object. This means that the persistence architecture can tell if a single-valued association is null without querying the database. On the

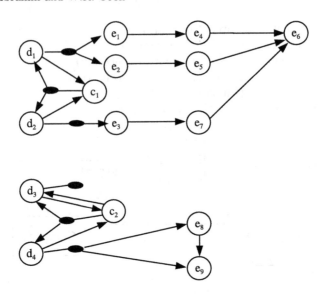

Fig. 3. An example of an object graph based on the type graph in Figure 2. Collection associations contain an oval in the middle of the edge.

other hand, the persistence architecture will query the database if a collection association reference is empty, because the collection reference does not have any information on the cardinality of the collection. The ability to represent traversals to empty collections is important when we discuss traversals in Section 3.1, because it allows AUTOFETCH to represent navigational queries that load empty collections.

Queries. A query is a function that returns a subgraph of the database object graph. The subgraph consists of a set of connected object graphs each of which has a distinguished *root* object. The definition of every query includes an *extent type* and *criteria*. The extent type is the type of all the root objects. The criteria are the conditions that an object satisfies to be returned as a root object.

Our approach to prefetching is independent of a particular query language, however, the query language must support an object-oriented view of persistent data, and the underlying persistence data store must allow prefetching associations of the extent type.

Queries are executed by the program to return their results. However, queries are first-class values, because they can be dynamically constructed or passed or returned from procedures. A single program point could execute different queries, depending on the program flow.

Traversals. A traversal captures how the program navigates the object graphs that the query returns. A program may traverse all the objects and associations in the result of the query, or it may traverse more or less. Only program navigations that would result in a database load for the query without prefetch are included in the traversal.

A traversal is represented as a forest where each tree's root is a root object in the result of a query and each tree is a subgraph of the entire object graph. Let R denote a single tree from the traversal on the object graph $G_O = (O, E)$.

$$R = O \times (F \rightarrow \{R\}) \text{ where } (o, (f, r)) \in R \text{ implies } |E(o, f)| = |r|$$

If the program navigates to the same object multiple times in a traversal, only the shortest path from the root of the traversal is included in R. Figure 4 shows a sample traversal on the object graph in Figure 3 for a query which returned 3 departments: d_1, d_2, d_3. Edges with dark ovals represent collection associations.

If a program navigates an association, it may not be included in the traversal if it would not result in database load. An association navigation does not result in a database load in three cases:

- The association is a null-valued single association.
- The association is a single valued association whose target had already been navigated to from the root object with a shorter path.
- The association's target was cached by the program.

If a program navigates an empty collection association, there will be a database query and the navigation will be included in the traversal. The last item illustrates an interesting link between caching and query execution; AUTOFETCH is able to adapt to the caching mechanism of the application by adjusting query prefetch to ignore associations that are likely to be cached.

An important point is that a single query may be used in different contexts that generate different traversals. This will commonly happen if a library function runs a query to load a set of objects, but this library function is called from multiple transactions. Each transaction will have a different purpose and therefore may traverse different associations.

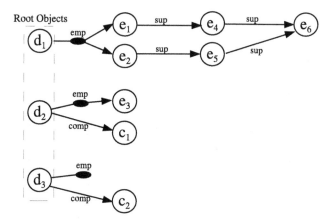

Fig. 4. An example of a traversal on the object graph in Figure 3. Collection associations contain an oval in the middle of the edge.

Traversal Profiles. A traversal profile represents the aggregation of the traversals for a set of queries. Each traversal profile is a tree representation of all the previous traversals mapped to the type graph. Let P represent a traversal profile for a type graph $G_T = (T, A)$:

$$P = T \times N \times N \times (F \rightarrow P)$$

such that for all $(t, used, potential, (f, p)) \in P$

1. $A(t, f)$ is defined
2. $used \leq potential$.

Each node in the tree contains statistics on the traversals to this node: the number of times this node needed to be loaded from the database ($used$), and the number of opportunities the program had to load this node from the database ($potential$), i.e. the number of times the program had a direct reference to an object representing this node.

Algorithm 1. $combine((o, AO), (used, potential, t, AP))$

---

   for all $(f, (used, potential, t, A)) \in AO$ **do**
     $w(f) = (used, potential + 1, t, A)$
   end for
   for all $f, P \in AP$ **do**
     for all $r \in AO(f)$ **do**
       $w(f) = combine(r, w(f));$
     end for
   end for
   return $(used + 1, potential, t, w)$

The traversal, a forest of object trees R, is combined with a traversal profile by combining each object tree R in the traversal with the profile using a function $combine \ (R \times P \rightarrow P)$. The combination algorithm is straightforward. Given a traversal and traversal profile, $combine$ increments the $used$ statistic for the root of the traversal profile and the potential statistic for all the children of the root. The combine method is then recursively called for each child traversal profile and its matching (same association) children of the root node in R. The statistics for the root node of the traversal profile are ignored since they represent the statistics for the root objects returned by a query and AUTOFETCH assumes those objects should always be fetched. Figure 5 shows a traversal profile updated from an empty traversal profile and the traversal in Figure 4. The traversal profile statistics are given above each type as (used/potential).

3.2 Query Classification

Query classification determines a set of queries that share a traversal profile. The aim of query classification is to group queries which are likely to have similar

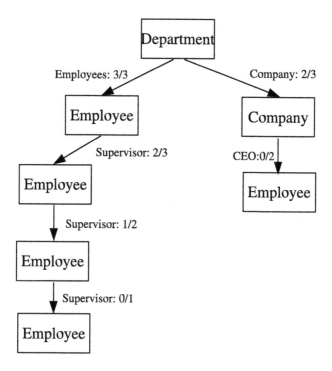

Fig. 5. Traversal profile for query class after traversal in Figure 4. Statistics are represented as (used/potential).

traversals. A simple classification of queries is to group all queries that have the same query string. There are several reasons why this is not effective.

First, a given query may be used to load data for several different operations. Since the operations are different, the traversals for these operations may be different as well. This situation typically arises when query execution is centralized in library functions that are called from many parts of a program. Classifying based only on the criteria will not distinguish between these different uses of a query, so that very different traversals may be classified as belonging to the same class. This may lead to poor prediction of prefetch. The classification in this case is too coarse.

A second problem is that query criteria are often constructed dynamically. If each set of criteria is classified as a separate query, then commonality between operations may not be identified. At the limit, every query may be different, leading to a failure to gather sufficient data to predict prefetch.

Queries may also be classified by the program state when the query is executed. This is motivated by the observation that traversals are determined by the control flow of the program after query execution. Program state includes the current code line, variable values, library bindings, etc. Classifying queries based on the entire program state is infeasible as the program state may be very large and will likely be different for every query. However, a set of salient features of the program state can be reasonable both in memory and computation. Computation refers to cost of computing the program state features when a query is invoked.

The line number where a query is executed is a simple feature of the program state to calculate and has a small constant memory size, however, it does not capture enough of the program state to accurately determine the traversal of the query results. Specifically the problem is that line number where the query is executed does not provide enough information on how the results of the query will be used outside of the invoking method.

The natural extension to the using the line number where the query is executed is using the entire call stack when the query is executed. Our hypothesis is that the call stack gives more information about the future control flow, because it is highly likely that the control flow will return through the methods in the call stack. The call stack as the salient program state feature is easy to compute and bounded in size. In the programs we have considered, we have found that the call stack classifies queries at an appropriate granularity for prefetch.

Unfortunately, a call stack with line numbers will classify 2 queries with different extent types together if the 2 queries occur on the same line. To address this, AUTOFETCH uses the pair of the query string and the call stack when the query is executed to classify queries. This limits AUTOFETCH's ability to prefetch for dynamic queries. Optimally, the call stack would contain information on the exact program statement being executed at each frame.

3.3   Predicting Traversals

Given that an operation typically traverses a similar collection of objects, it is possible to predict future traversals based on the profiling of past traversals. The predicted traversal provides a basis to compute the prefetch specification. The goal of the prefetch specification is to minimize the time it will take to perform the traversal. A program will be most efficient if each traversal is equal to the query result object graph, because in this case only one round-trip to the database will be required and the program will not load any more information from the database than is needed. The heuristic used in AUTOFETCH is to prefetch any node in the traversal profile for which the probability of traversal is above a certain threshold.

Before each query execution, AUTOFETCH finds the traversal profile associated with the query class. If no traversal profile is found, a new traversal profile is created and no prefetches are added to the query. Otherwise, the existing traversal profile is used to compute the prefetch specification.

First, the traversal profile is trimmed such that the remaining tree only contains the associations that will be loaded with high probability (above a set threshold) given that the root node of the traversal profile has been loaded. For each node n and its parent node $p(n)$ in the traversal profile, the probability that the association between n and $p(n)$ will be traversed given that p(n) has been loaded can be estimated as $used(n)/potential(n)$. Using the rules of conditional probability, the probability that the association is navigated given that the root node is loaded is:

$$f(n) = (used(n)/potential(n)) * f(p(n))$$

The base case is that the $f(root)$ in the traversal profile is 1. A depth first traversal can calculate this probability for each node without recomputing any values. This calculation ensures that traversal profile nodes are prefetched only if their parent node is prefetched, because $f(n) \leq f(p(n))$.

Second, if there is more than one collection path in the remaining tree, an arbitrary collection path is chosen and other collection paths are removed. Collection paths are paths from the root node to a leaf node in the tree that contain at least 1 collection association. This is to avoid creating a query which joins multiple many-valued associations.

The prefetch specification is a set of prefetch directives. Each prefetch directive corresponds to a unique path in the remaining tree. For example, given the traversal profile in Figure 5 and the prefetch threshold of 0.5, the prefetch specification would be: (employees, employees.supervisor, company). The query is augmented with the calculated prefetch specification. Regardless of the prefetch specification, profiling the query results remains the same.

4 Implementation

The implementation of AUTOFETCH is divided into a traversal profile module and an extension to Hibernate 3.1, an open source Java ORM tool.

4.1 Traversal Profile Module

The traversal profile module maintains a 1-1 mapping from query class to traversal profile. When the hibernate extension asks for the prefetch specification for a query, the module computes the query class which is used to lookup the traversal profile which is used to compute the prefetch specification. The module computes the query class as the pair of the query string and the current program stack trace and uses this as the key to lookup the traversal profile. To decrease the memory requirements for maintaining the set of query classes, each stack trace contains a maximum number of frames. If a stack trace is larger than this limit, AUTOFETCH removes top-level frames until the stack trace is under the limit. Each frame is a string containing the name of a method and a line number. If a traversal profile does not exist for a query class, the module adds a mapping from that query class to an empty traversal profile. Finally, the module computes a prefetch specification for the query using the traversal prediction algorithm in Section 3.3 applied to the traversal profile.

4.2 Hibernate

Hibernate was modified to incorporate prefetch specifications and to profile traversals of its query results. The initial AUTOFETCH implementation used Hibernate 3.0 which did not support multiple collection prefetches. Fortunately, Hibernate 3.1 contains support for multiple collection prefetches and AUTOFETCH was migrated to this version. Support for multiple collection prefetches turns out to be critical for improving performance in some of the evaluation benchmarks.

Original query

HQL:

> from Department d where d.name = 'foo'

SQL:

> select * from Department as d where d.name = 'foo'

Query with a single prefetch

HQL:

> from Department d
> left outer join fetch d.employees where x.name = 'foo'

SQL:

> select * from Department as d
> left outer join Employee as e on e.deptId = d.id
> where d.name = 'foo'

Fig. 6. Augmenting queries with prefetch specifications

Hibernate obtains the prefetch specification for a query from the traversal profile module. The code in Figure 6 illustrates how a HQL query is modified to include prefetches and the SQL generated by Hibernate. Queries which already contain a prefetch specification are not modified or profiled allowing the programmer to manually specify prefetch. The hibernate extensions profile traversals by instrumenting each persistent object with a dynamically generated proxy. The proxy intercepts all method calls to the object and if any object state is accessed that will require a database load, the proxy increments the appropriate node in the traversal profile for the query class. Hibernate represents single association references with a key. Therefore, accessing the key is not considered as an object access because it never requires a database query. Collections are instrumented by modifying the existing Hibernate collection classes. Although there is a performance penalty for this type of instrumentation, we found that this penalty was not noticeable in executing queries in our benchmarks. This performance penalty may be ameliorated through sampling, i.e. only instrumenting a certain percentage of queries. The AUTOFETCH prototype does not support all of Hibernate's features. For example, AUTOFETCH does not support prefetching or profiling for data models which contain weak entities or composite identifiers. Support for these features was omitted for simplicity.

5   Evaluation

We evaluated AUTOFETCH using the Torpedo and OO7 benchmarks. The Torpedo benchmark measures on the number of queries that an ORM tool executes in a simple auction application, while the OO7 benchmark examines the performance

of object-oriented persistence mechanisms for an idealized CAD (computer assisted design) application. We also examined the software engineering benefits of
avoiding manual specification of prefetches in a resume application.

Both benchmarks were executed on an Intel®Pentium®4 2.8 GHz machine
with 1 Gb of RAM. The OO7 benchmark connects to a database on a separate
machine, an Intel®Pentium®4 2.4 Ghz machine with 885 Mb of RAM on the
same University of Texas Computer Science department local area network. The
AUTOFETCH parameters maximum extent level and stack frame limit were set
to 12 and 20 respectively unless otherwise noted. The benchmarks did not use
any caching across transactions.

5.1 Torpedo Benchmark

The Torpedo benchmark [23] measures the number of SQL statements executed
by an ORM tool over a set of test cases. The benchmark consists of a Java client
and a J2EE auction server. The client issues requests to the auction server,
such as placing a bid or retrieving information for a particular auction. There
are seven client test cases which were designed to test various aspects of the
mapping tool such as caching or prefetching. The number of SQL statements
executed is used as the measure of the performance of the mapping tool. The
benchmark can be configured to use different object-relational mapping tools
(EJB, JDO, Hibernate) as the persistence backend.

We created two versions of the Hibernate persistence backend, the original
tuned backend included with the benchmark and that same backend minus the
prefetch directives. The latter backend can be configured to have AUTOFETCH
enabled or disabled. We ran the Torpedo benchmark for each version and possible

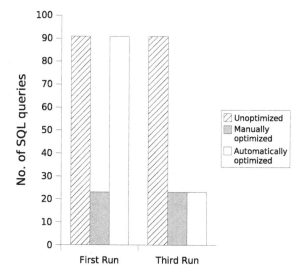

Fig. 7. Torpedo benchmark results. The y-axis represents the number of queries executed. Maximum extent level is 12.

options three times in succession. The results of the first and third iterations are shown in Figure 7. The second run was omitted in the graph since the first and second iterations produce the same results. A single set of iterations is sufficient, because the benchmark is deterministic with respect to the number of queries.

As Figure 7 shows, the prefetch directives reduce the number of queries executed. Without either the prefetch directives nor AUTOFETCH enabled the benchmark executed three times as many queries. Without prefetch directives but with AUTOFETCH enabled, the benchmark executes many queries on the first and second iterations; however, from the third iteration (and onward) it executes as many queries as the version with programmer-specified prefetches.

A simple query classification method using the code line where the query was executed as the query class would not have been sufficient to match the performance of manually specified prefetches for this benchmark. For example, the findAuction method is used to load both detailed and summary information about an auction. The detailed auction information includes traversing several associations for an auction such as the auction bids. The summary auction information only includes fields of the auction object such as the auction id or date. These different access patterns require different prefetches even though they use the same backend function to load the auction.

5.2   OO7 Benchmark

The OO7 benchmark [5] was designed to measure the performance of OODB management systems. It consists of a series of traversals, queries, and structural modifications performed on databases of varying sizes and statistical properties. We implemented a Java version of the OO7 benchmark based on code publicly available from the benchmark's authors. Following the lead in Han [13], we omitted all structural modification tests as well as any traversals that included updates, because updates have no effect on AUTOFETCH behavior and otherwise these traversals were not qualitatively different from the included traversals. Q4 was omitted because it requires using the medium or large OO7 databases. Traversal CU was omitted because caching and AUTOFETCH are orthogonal, and the traversal's performance is very sensitive to the exact caching policy.

Only a few of the OO7 operations involve object navigation, which can be optimized by AUTOFETCH. Traversal T1 is a complete traversal of the OO7 object graph, both the assembly and part hierarchies. Traversal T6 traverses the entire assembly hierarchy, but only accesses the composite and root atomic parts in the part hierarchy. Traversal T1 has a depth of about 29 while Traversal T6 has a depth of about 10. Neither the queries nor traversals T8 or T9 perform navigation; however, they are included to detect any performance penalties for traversal profiling.

We added a reverse traversal, RT, which chooses atomic parts and finds their root assembly, associated module, and associated manual. Such traversals were omitted from the OO7 benchmark because they were considered not to add anything to the results. They are significant in the context of prefetch, since single-valued associations can be prefetched more easily than multi-valued associations.

Table 1. Comparison with prefetch disabled and with AUTOFETCH. Maximum extent
level is 12. Small OO7 benchmark. Metrics for each query/traversal are average number
SQL queries and average time in milliseconds. Percentages are for percent improvement
of AUTOFETCH over baseline.

Query	Iteration	No Prefetch		AUTOFETCH			
		queries	ms	queries	%	ms	%
Q1	1	11	45	11	–	43	(4%)
	2	11	44	11	–	43	(2%)
	3	11	43	11	–	43	–
Q2	1	2	10	2	–	9	(10%)
	2	2	10	2	–	10	–
	3	2	11	2	–	10	(9%)
Q3	1	2	59	2	–	58	(2%)
	2	2	89	2	–	59	(34%)
	3	2	58	2	–	60	-(3%)
Q6	1	2	70	2	–	69	(1%)
	2	2	66	2	–	65	(2%)
	3	2	67	2	–	81	-(21%)
Q7	1	2	532	2	–	504	(5%)
	2	2	472	2	–	508	-(8%)
	3	2	498	2	–	471	(5%)
Q8	1	2	43	2	–	48	-(12%)
	2	2	46	2	–	46	–
	3	2	48	2	–	44	(8%)
T1	1	3096	21750	2909	(6%)	20875	(4%)
	2	3096	22160	2907	(6%)	20694	(7%)
	3	3096	21009	38	(98.8%)	248	(98.8%)
T6	1	1146	8080	1099	(4%)	8266	-(2%)
	2	1146	7900	1096	(4%)	8115	-(3%)
	3	1146	7831	2	(99.8%)	21	(99.7%)
T8	1	2	36	2	–	38	-(6%)
	2	2	46	2	–	36	(22%)
	3	2	36	2	–	40	-(11%)
T9	1	2	40	2	–	35	(13%)
	2	2	44	2	–	38	(14%)
	3	2	40	2	–	36	(10%)
RT	1	10	63	4	(60%)	43	(32%)
	2	10	63	3	(70%)	39	(38%)
	3	10	61	3	(70%)	39	(36%)

Table 1 summarizes the results of the OO7 benchmark. Neither the queries
nor traversals T8 or T9 show any improvement with prefetch enabled. This is to
be expected since they do not perform any navigational queries. These queries

Table 2. The number of queries executed by AUTOFETCH with Hibernate 3.0 and AUTOFETCH with Hibernate 3.0 for traversals T1, T6, and RT. Only 3rd iteration shown. Maximum extent level is 12. Small OO7 benchmark.

AUTOFETCH Version	T1	T6	RT
AUTOFETCH with Hibernate 3.0	2171	415	3
AUTOFETCH with Hibernate 3.1	38	2	3

are included for completeness, and to show that AUTOFETCH does not have high overhead when not needed.

Both traversals T1 and T6 show a large improvement in the number of queries and time to execute the traversal. T6 shows a larger improvement than T1 even though T1 is a deeper traversal, because some of the time executing traversal T1 is spent traversing the object graph in memory; repeatedly traversing the part hierarchies. The number of queries and the time to execute a traversal are tightly correlated as expected. Both T1 and T6 are top-down hierarchical traversals which require multiple collection prefetches to execute few queries. Table 2 shows a comparison of the number of queries executed by AUTOFETCH with Hibernate 3.1 and AUTOFETCH with Hibernate 3.0 which was unable to prefetch multiple collection associations. The ability to fetch multiple collection associations had a greater effect on deep traversals such as T1 and T6 than on shallow traversals such as RT.

Figure 8 shows that the maximum depth of the traversal profile is important to the performance of prefetch system in the presence for deep traversals. The tradeoff for increasing the maximum depth of the traversal profile is an increase in the memory requirements to store traversal profiles. It should be noted that deep

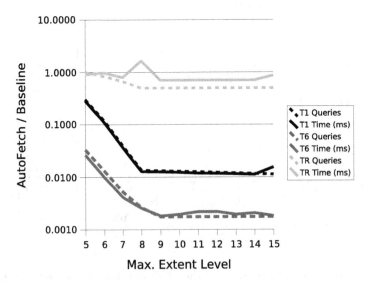

Fig. 8. Varying maximum extent level from 5 to 15. Only 3rd iteration shown. Small OO7 database.

traversals such as T1 and T6 in OO7 are relatively rare in enterprise business applications.

5.3   Resume Application

In addition to the synthetic benchmarks, we applied AUTOFETCH to a resume application that uses the AppFuse framework [29]. AppFuse is a template for a model-view-controller (MVC) architecture that integrates many popular Java libraries and tools. AppFuse includes a flexible data layer which can be configured to use one of several persistence providers. Users of the framework define interfaces for data access objects (DAO) that are implemented using the persistence provider.

Hibernate is used as the persistence provider in the sample resume application. The resume application data model is centered around a Resume class. A Resume contains basic resume data fields and associations to related objects, including education listings, work experiences, and references. The ResumeDAO class includes methods to load and store resumes. A simple implementation of the ResumeDAO and Resume classes is shown in Fig 9. The ResumeDAO.getResume(Long) method loads a resume without prefetching any of its associated objects. To load the work experience in a resume, a programmer first uses ResumeDAO to load the resume, and then getExperiences() to load the work experience.

```
interface ResumeDAO {
  Resume getResume(Long resumeId);
  ...
}

class Resume {
  List getEducations() { ... }
  List getExperiences() { ... }
  List getReferences() { ... }
  ...
}
```

Fig. 9. Struts resume code without any optimizations

Although this implementation is very natural, it is inefficient because the resume application has several pages that display exactly one kind of associated object; a page for work experience, a page for references, etc. For these pages, the application would execute 2 queries: one to load the resume and another to load the associated objects. There are several alternative implementations:

1. Modify the ResumeDAO.getResume(Long) method to prefetch all associations.
2. Add ResumeDAO methods which load a resume with different prefetch directives.

3. Add ResumeDAO methods which directly load associated objects without loading the resume first.

The actual implementation uses the third approach. The first alternative always loads too much data and would be infeasible if the data model contained cycles. The other two alternatives are fragile and redundant. For example, if a new user interface page was added to the application that displayed two resume associations, then a new method would have to be added to the ResumeDAO class. The code is also redundant because we have to copy either the ResumeDAO.getResume(Long) method in the second alternative or the Resume getter methods in the third alternative. By incorporating AUTOFETCH, the simple code in Figure 9 should perform as well as the optimized code after some initial iterations.

We tested the code in Figure 9 version with AUTOFETCH and found that indeed it was able to execute a single query for all the controller layer methods after the initial learning period. Our modified code has the advantage of being smaller, because we eliminated redundant methods in ResumeDAO class. With AUTOFETCH, DAO methods are more general because the same method may be used with different traversal patterns. AUTOFETCH also increases the independence of the user interface or view layer from the business logic or controller layer, because changes in the traversal pattern of the user interface on domain objects do not require corresponding changes in the controller interface.

5.4   General Comments

In all of the evaluation benchmarks, the persistent data traversals were the same given the query class. Consequently, AUTOFETCH never prefetched more data than was needed, i.e. AUTOFETCH had perfect precision. While our intuition is that persistent data traversals are usually independent of the program branching behavior, it is an open question whether our benchmarks are truly representative in this respect. Similarly, it is difficult to draw general conclusions about the parameters of the AUTOFETCH such as the maximum extent level or stack frame limit without observing a larger class of persistent programs. The maximum extent level was set to 12, because this produced reasonable memory consumption on our benchmarks. The stack frame limit was set to 20 to preserve enough information from the stack frame about control flow in the presence of the various architectural layers in the Torpedo benchmark and the recursive traversals in the OO7 benchmark.

6   Related Work

Han et al. [13] classify prefetching algorithms into five categories: page-based prefetching, object-level/page-level access pattern prefetching, manually specified prefetches, context-based prefetches, and traversal/path-based prefetches.

Page-based prefetching has been explored in object-oriented databases such as ObjectStore [17]. Page-based prefetching is effective when the access patterns of an application correspond to the clustering of the objects on disk. Since the clustering is usually static, it cannot efficiently support multiple data access patterns. Good clustering of objects is difficult to achieve and can be expensive to maintain when objects are updated frequently. However, when it works it provides very low-cost prefetching. Finally, if the amount of object data that should be prefetched is larger than a page, than this prefetching algorithm will be unable to prefetch all the objects needed.

Object-level or page-level access pattern prefetching relies on monitoring the sequence of object or page requests to the database. Curewitz et al. [9] implemented an access pattern prefetching algorithm using compression algorithms. Palmer and Zdonik [26] implemented a prefetch system, Fido, that stores access patterns and uses a nearest neighbor algorithm to detect similar patterns and issue prefetch requests. Knafla [16] models object relationship accesses as discrete time Markov chains and uses this model in addition to a sophisticated cost model to issue prefetch requests. The main drawback to these approaches is that they detect object-level patterns, i.e. they perform poorly if the same objects are not repeatedly accessed. Repeated access to the same objects is not typical of many enterprise applications with large databases.

Bernstein et al. [4] proposed a context-controlled prefetch system, which was implemented as an extension of Microsoft Repository. Each persistent object in memory is associated with a context. This context represents a set of related objects, either objects that were loaded in the same query or objects that are a member of the same collection association. For each attribute access of an object O, the system prefetches the requested attribute for all objects in O's context. When iterating through the results of a query or collection association, this prefetch strategy will avoid executing $n + 1$ queries where n is the number of query results. A comparison of this strategy and AUTOFETCH is given below. While AUTOFETCH only profiles associations, Bernstein et al. use "MA prefetch" to prefetch scalar attributes for classes in which the attributes reside in separate tables. MA prefetch improves the performance of the OO7 benchmark queries, which were not improved by AUTOFETCH, because OO7 attributes and associations are separated into multiple tables. The implemented system only supported single-level prefetches, although prefetching multiple levels (path prefetch) is mentioned as an extension in the paper. The system also makes extensive use of temporary tables, which are not needed by AUTOFETCH.

Han et al. [14, 13] extended the ideas of Bernstein et al. to maintain not only the preceding traversal which led to an object, but the entire type-level *path* to reach an object. Each query is associated with an attribute access log set which contains all the type level paths used to access objects from the navigational root set. The prefetch system then monitors the attribute access log and prefetches objects if either an iterative or recursive pattern is detected. The prefetch system, called PrefetchGuide, can prefetch multiple levels of objects in the object graph if it observes multi-level iteration or recursive patterns. However, unlike the Bernstein prefetch implementation, there are no results on prefetching for arbitrary queries, instead only purely navigational queries are supported. PrefetchGuide is implemented in a prototype ORDBMS.

While the systems created by Bernstein and Han prefetch data within the context of a top-level query, AUTOFETCH uses previous query executions to predict prefetch for future queries. Context-based prefetch always executes at least one query for each distinct association path. AUTOFETCH, in contrast, can modify the top-level query itself, so that only one query is needed. AUTOFETCH can also detect traversal patterns across queries, e.g. if certain unrelated associations are always accessed from a given query result, AUTOFETCH prefetches those objects even though it would not constitute a recursive or iterative pattern within that single query. One disadvantage of AUTOFETCH is that the initial queries are executed without any prefetch at all. The consequence of this disadvantage, is that the performance on the initial program iteration is equivalent to a program with unoptimized queries. However, it would be possible to combine AUTOFETCH with a system such as PrefetchGuide. In such a combined system, PrefetchGuide could handle prefetch in the first query, and also catch cases where the statistical properties of past query executions do not allow AUTOFETCH to predict correct prefetches. We believe that such a combination would provide the best of both worlds for prefetch performance.

Automatic prefetch in object persistence architectures is similar to prefetching memory blocks as a compiler optimization. Luk and Mowry[20] have looked at optimizing recursive data structure access by predicting which parts of the structure will be accessed in the future. One of their approaches, history pointers, is similar in philosophy to our traversal profiles.

7   Future Work

We presented a simple query classification algorithm which only relies on the call stack at the moment the query is executed. Although we found this to work quite well in practice, a more complex classification algorithm could include other features of program state: the exact control path where the query was executed, or the value of program variables. This richer program state representation might classify queries too finely. Unsupervised learning techniques could be applied to richer program state representations to learn a classification that clusters the queries according to the similarity of their traversals. Consider the following program fragment, where findAllFoos executes a query:

```
List  results  = findAllFoos();
if (x > 5)
   doTraversal1( results );
else
   doTraversal2( results );
```

A learning algorithm could learn a better classification strategy than the one described in this paper. In this case, the value of the variable x should be used to distinguish two query classes.

A cost model for database query execution is necessary for accurate optimization of prefetching. AUTOFETCH currently uses the simple heuristic that it is always better to execute one query rather than two (or more) queries if the data loaded by the second query is likely to be needed in the future. This heuristic relies on the fact that database round-trips are expensive. However, there are other factors that determine cost of prefetching a set objects: the cost of the modified query, the expected size of the set of prefetched objects, the connection latency, etc. A cost model that takes such factors into account will have better performance and may even outperform manual prefetches since the system would be able to take into account dynamic information about database and program execution.

8   Conclusion

Object prefetching is an important technique for improving performance of applications based on object persistence architectures. Current architectures rely on the programmer to manually specify which objects to prefetch when executing a query. Correct prefetch specifications are difficult to write and maintain as a program evolves, especially in modular programs. In this paper we presented AUTOFETCH, a novel technique for automatically computing prefetch specifications. AUTOFETCH predicts which objects should be prefetched for a given query based on previous query executions. AUTOFETCH classifies queries executions based on the client state when the query is executed, and creates a traversal profile to summarize which associations are traversed on the results of the query. This information is used to predict prefetch for future queries. Before a new query is executed, a prefetch specification is generated based on the classification of the query and its traversal profile. AUTOFETCH improves on previous approaches by collecting profile information across multiple queries, and using client program state to help classify queries. We evaluated AUTOFETCH using both sample applications and benchmarks and showed that we were able to improve performance and/or simplify code.

References

1. M. P. Atkinson and O. P. Buneman. Types and persistence in database programming languages. *ACM Comput. Surv.*, 19(2):105–170, 1987.
2. M. P. Atkinson, L. Daynes, M. J. Jordan, T. Printezis, and S. Spence. An orthogonally persistent Java. *SIGMOD Record*, 25(4):68–75, 1996.
3. T. Ball and J. R. Larus. Efficient path profiling. In *International Symposium on Microarchitecture*, pages 46–57, 1996.
4. P. A. Bernstein, S. Pal, and D. Shutt. Context-based prefetch for implementing objects on relations. In *Proceedings of the 25th VLDB Conference*, 1999.
5. M. J. Carey, D. J. DeWitt, and J. F. Naughton. The 007 benchmark. *SIGMOD Rec.*, 22(2):12–21, 1993.
6. D. Cengija. Hibernate your data. *onJava.com*, 2004.
7. W. R. Cook and S. Rai. Safe query objects: statically typed objects as remotely executable queries. In *ICSE '05: Proceedings of the 27th international conference on Software engineering*, pages 97–106. ACM Press, 2005.

8. G. Copeland and D. Maier. Making Smalltalk a database system. In *Proceedings of the 1984 ACM SIGMOD international conference on Management of data*, pages 316–325. ACM Press, 1984.

9. K. M. Curewitz, P. Krishnan, and J. S. Vitter. Practical prefetching via data compression. In *Proceedings of the 1993 ACM SIGMOD International Conference on Management of Data (SIGMOD '93)*, 1993.

10. J.-A. Dub, R. Sapir, and P. Purich. Oracle Application Server TopLink application developers guide, 10g (9.0.4). Oracle Corporation, 2003.

11. J. A. Fisher and S. M. Freudenberger. Predicting conditional branch directions from previous runs of a program. In *ASPLOS-V: Proceedings of the fifth international conference on Architectural support for programming languages and operating systems*, pages 85–95. ACM Press, 1992.

12. G. Hamilton and R. Cattell. JDBC^{TM}: A Java SQL API. Sun Microsystems, 1997.

13. W.-S. Han, Y.-S. Moon, and K.-Y. Whang. PrefetchGuide: capturing navigational access patterns for prefetching in client/server object-oriented/object-relational DBMSs. *Information Sciences*, 152(1):47–61, 2003.

14. W.-S. Han, Y.-S. Moon, K.-Y. Whang, and I.-Y. Song. Prefetching based on type-level access pattern in object-relational DBMSs. In *Proceedings of the 17th International Conference on Data Engineering*, pages 651–660. IEEE Computer Society, 2001.

15. ISO/IEC. Information technology - database languages - SQL - part 3: Call-level interface (SQL/CLI). Technical Report 9075-3:2003, ISO/IEC, 2003.

16. N. Knafla. Analysing object relationships to predict page access for prefetching. In *Eighth International Workshop on Persistent Object Systems: Design, Implementation and Use, POS-8*, 1998.

17. C. Lamb, G. Landis, J. A. Orenstein, and D. Weinreb. The ObjectStore database system. *Commun. ACM*, 34(10):50–63, 1991.

18. K. J. Lieberherr, B. Patt-Shamir, and D. Orleans. Traversals of object structures: Specification and efficient implementation. *ACM Trans. Program. Lang. Syst.*, 26(2):370–412, 2004.

19. B. Liskov, A. Adya, M. Castro, S. Ghemawat, R. Gruber, U. Maheshwari, A. C. Myers, M. Day, and L. Shrira. Safe and efficient sharing of persistent objects in Thor. In *Proceedings of the 1996 ACM SIGMOD international conference on Management of data*, pages 318–329. ACM Press, 1996.

20. C.-K. Luk and T. C. Mowry. Compiler-based prefetching for recursive data structures. In *Architectural Support for Programming Languages and Operating Systems*, pages 222–233, 1996.

21. D. Maier, J. Stein, A. Otis, and A. Purdy. Developments of an object-oriented DBMS. In *Proc. of ACM Conf. on Object-Oriented Programming, Systems, Languages and Applications*, pages 472–482, 1986.

22. A. Marquez, S. Blackburn, G. Mercer, and J. N. Zigman. Implementing orthogonally persistent Java. In *Proceedings of the Workshop on Persistent Object Systems (POS)*, 2000.

23. B. E. Martin. Uncovering database access optimizations in the middle tier with TORPEDO. In *Proceedings of the 21st International Conference on Data Engineering*, pages 916–926. IEEE Computer Society, 2005.

24. V. Matena and M. Hapner. Enterprise Java Beans Specification 1.0. Sun Microsystems, 1998.

25. R. Morrison, R. Connor, G. Kirby, D. Munro, M. Atkinson, Q. Cutts, A. Brown, and A. Dearle. The Napier88 persistent programming language and environment. In *Fully Integrated Data Environments*, pages 98–154. Springer, 1999.

26. M. Palmer and S. B. Zdonik. Fido: A cache that learns to fetch. In *Proceedings of the 17th International Conference on Very Large Data Bases*, 1991.
27. D. A. Patterson. Latency lags bandwith. *Commun. ACM*, 47(10):71–75, 2004.
28. C. Russell. Java Data Objects (JDO) Specification JSR-12. Sun Microsystems, 2003.
29. Raible's wiki: StrutsResume. `http://raibledesigns.com/wiki/Wiki.jsp?page=StrutsResume`, March 2006.
30. M. Venkatrao and M. Pizzo. SQL/CLI – a new binding style for SQL. *SIGMOD Record*, 24(4):72–77, 1995.

The Runtime Structure of Object Ownership

Nick Mitchell

IBM TJ Watson Research Center
19 Skyline Drive, Hawthorne NY 10532
nickm@us.ibm.com

Abstract. Object-oriented programs often require large heaps to run properly or meet performance goals. They use high-overhead collections, bulky data models, and large caches. Discovering this is quite challenging. Manual browsing and flat summaries do not scale to complex graphs with 20 million objects. Context is crucial to understanding responsibility and inefficient object connectivity.

We summarize memory footprint with help from the dominator relation. Each dominator tree captures unique ownership. Edges between trees capture responsibility. We introduce a set of *ownership structures*, and quantify their abundance. We aggregate these structures, and use thresholds to identify important aggregates. We introduce the *ownership graph* to summarize responsibility, and *backbone equivalence* to aggregate patterns within trees. Our implementation quickly generates concise summaries. In two minutes, it generates a 14-node ownership graph from 29 million objects. Backbone equivalence identifies a handful of patterns that account for 80% of a tree's footprint.

1 Introduction

In this paper, we consider the problem excessive memory footprint in object-oriented programs: for certain intervals of time, the live objects exceed available or desired memory bounds. Excessive memory footprint has many root causes. Some data structures impose a high per-element overhead, such as hash sets with explicit chaining, or tree maps. Data models often include duplicate or unnecessary fields, or extend modeling frameworks with a high base-class memory cost. There may be objects that, while no longer needed, remain live [34, 39], such as when the memory for an Eclipse [17] plugin persists beyond its last use. Often, to mask unresolved performance problems, applications aggressively cache data (using inefficient data structures and bulky data models).

To isolate the root causes for large object graph size requires understanding both responsibility and internal content: the program may hold on to objects longer than expected, or may use data structures built up in inefficient ways. We analyze this combination of *ownership structures* by summarizing the state of the heap — at any moment in time within the interval of excessive footprint. In contrast, techniques such as heap [34, 35, 40, 43], space [36], shape [32], lexical [6], or cost-center [37] profiling collect aggregate summaries of allocation sites. Profiling dramatically slows down the program, gives no information about responsibility

D. Thomas (Ed.): ECOOP 2006, LNCS 4067, pp. 74–98, 2006.
© Springer-Verlag Berlin Heidelberg 2006

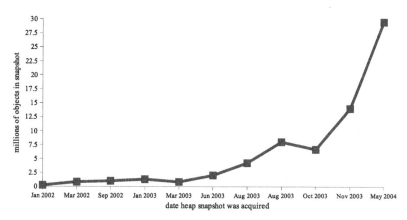

Fig. 1. Growth in the size of Java heaps in recent years

Table 1. A commonly used, but not especially useful, graph summary: aggregate objects by data type, and then apply a threshold to show only the top few

type	objects	bytes
primitive arrays	3,657,979	223,858,288
java/lang/String	2,500,389	80,012,448
java/util/HashMap$Entry	2,307,577	73,842,464
java/util/HashMap$Entry[]	220,683	57,726,696
customer data type	338,601	48,758,544
java/lang/Object[]	506,735	24,721,536

or internal content, and conflates the problem of excessive temporary creation with the problem of excessive memory footprint.

The task of summarizing the state of the heap [12, 20, 9, 29, 19, 32] at any moment in time [3, 31, 18, 25] is one of graph summarization. In this case, the graph's nodes are objects, and the edges are references between them. Summarizing the responsibility and internal content of these graphs is, from our experience with dozens of large-scale object-oriented programs, quite challenging. In part, this is because these object graphs are very large. In Figure 1, we show typical object graph sizes from a variety of large-scale applications. Over the years, this figure shows that the problem has grown worse. Contemporary server applications commonly have tens of millions of live objects at any moment in time.

Furthermore, the way objects are linked together defeats easy summarization. A good summary would identify a small number of features that account for much of the graph's size. Achieving this 80/20 point, especially for large, complex graphs, is challenging. Many commercial memory analysis tools [3, 31, 18] *aggregate* by data type, and then chooses a *threshold* to show those biggest types. This technique produces a table such as Table 1. Typically, generic data types float to the top. Even for the customer-specific types, the table gives us no sense of who is responsible, or how the instances are structured; e.g. are the instance of these types part of a single large collection, or several smaller ones? These same tools also provide *filters* to ignore third-party providers such as J2SE, AWT, and database code. But, as the table shows, those third parties often form the bulk of the graph's size. In addition, they often provide the collections that (perhaps inefficiently) glue together the graph's objects.

Filters, aggregations, and thresholds are essential elements of summarization, but must be applied carefully. Thresholds help to focus on the biggest contributors, but the biggest contributors are not single data types, or even single locations in the graph. As we will show in Section 4, those 3.6 million primitive arrays in Table 1 are placed in many distinct locations. Thus, at first sight, they appear to be scattered throughout the (18-million node) graph. However, we will show that only two distinct *patterns* of locations that account for 80% of the largest data structure's size. This careful combination of aggregation and thresholding can produce concise summaries of internal content.

The same care is necessary when summarizing responsibility. If the object graph is *tree-like* (i.e. a diamond-free flow graph), the problem of summarizing ownership structure reduces to that of summarizing content; responsibility is clear when each object has a single owner. As we will quantify later, object graphs are not at all tree-like. For example, in many cases two unrelated program mechanisms share responsibility for the objects in a data structure; in turn, those two mechanisms themselves are shared by higher-level mechanisms. The result is a vast web of responsibility. We can not arbitrarily filter out edges that result in sharing, even if it does have the desirable property of reducing the responsibility structure to a tree [23].

This paper has four main contributions.

Analysis Methodology. We decompose the analysis of ownership structures into two subproblems, by leveraging the dominator forest [22, 14, 33] of the graph. We use the dominator relation for two reasons. First, it identifies the maximum *unique* ownership within the graph. This aligns well with our distinction between responsibility and content. The edges between trees in this forest capture responsibility, and the elements of a dominator tree capture content. Second, a graph has a single, well-defined dominator forest; a depth-first traversal, in contrast, also produces a spanning tree, but one that depends on an arbitrary ordering of graph roots.

Catalog of Ownership Structures. We develop a catalog of ownership structures, for both responsibility and for internal content. For example, for content we introduce six categories of *backbones*, those structures that allow collections to grow or shrink. We justify their importance by quantifying their prevalence in large-scale applications; being common, they will serve as powerful units of aggregation and filtering. In addition, we demonstrate that categorizing content by backbone structure provides a powerful, if flat, summary of content.

Algorithm for Summarizing Responsibility in Graphs. Beyond flat summaries, we provide summarization algorithms that use this catalog of structures. The summary of responsibility is an *ownership graph*, itself a graph, where each node is an aggregation of ownership structures. We show how the dominator relation alone is a powerful tool for summarizing responsibility; e.g. in one server application, it reduces 29 million nodes to 191 thousand dominator trees (a 99% reduction). We also show how six other structures of responsibility allow us to reduce that summary to a 14-node ownership graph. Our implementation generates that summary automatically in around two minutes.

Algorithm for Summarizing Content in Trees. We summarize the content of a tree by aggregating according to *backbone equivalence*. We introduce two equivalence relations that group together the nodes that may be in widely divergent tree locations, but should be considered as part of a single unit. For example, in a hash set that contains hash sets of strings, there may be millions of strings. All of the strings are backbone-equivalent. In Section 4.3, we demonstrate that this enables a form of analysis that identifies the largest patterns in the largest trees. For example, we show how to locate the set of distinct patterns within a tree in which a dominant data type (such as those shown in Table 1) occur. We demonstrate that a handful of patterns account for most of a hot type's footprint, despite it being in millions of distinct locations in the tree.

Section 3 covers the catalog and algorithms for responsibility, and Section 4 covers the issues of content. We begin with a short discussion of the input to our analysis: seven snapshots from large-scale applications, and seven benchmarks.

2   Object Reference Graphs

To diagnose a memory footprint problem, we analyze a snapshot of its live objects and the references between them.[1] We treat a snapshot as a directed graph, commonly termed an *object reference graph*. The nodes of this graph represent objects and the edges represent a field of one object referring to another. In addition to objects and references, we assume only that the snapshot associates a data type and an instance size with each object. Typically, object reference graphs are neither connected, nor flow graphs (in the sense of [22], where the graph is rooted); we will see more detail and quantifications in Section 3.

Table 2 introduces the applications and SPEC JVM98 benchmarks [41] we study in this paper. Real applications frequently have ten or even twenty million live objects; for this paper, we decided to present a spectrum of graph sizes from real applications. Notice that even A2' is large; it represents a web application server just after server startup has completed. For all fourteen snapshots, the numbers reflect only live objects. We use the JVM's built-in support for generating snapshots, which halts all threads, forces a garbage collection, then writes the snapshot to disk. In the case of the benchmarks, we use the maximally-sized run, and take several dozen snapshots over the course of each benchmark's run. We document the largest of those snapshots.

---

[1] To manually trigger a heap snapshot with the IBM JVM, send a SIGQUIT signal to the JVM process. In the rare case of a short spike in memory footprint, set the heap size so as to cause an out of memory exception upon the spike. At this point, the JVM automatically triggers a heap snapshot.

Table 2. The heap snapshots we analyze in this paper. They include both real applications and benchmarks, divided into the top and bottom half of this table.

application	objects	bytes	description
A1	29,181,452	1,433,937,576	telecom transaction server
A2	20,952,120	1,041,348,768	multi-user collaboration server
A3	17,871,063	818,425,984	e-commerce transaction server
A2'	4,391,183	241,631,368	A2, just after server startup
A4	4,289,704	232,742,536	catalog management server
A5	4,099,743	269,782,704	rich client
A6	3,757,828	99,909,500	an Eclipse-based rich client
mtrt	509,170	13,590,874	
db	342,725	10,569,334	
javac	316,857	10,593,467	
jess	83,815	9,827,946	SPECjvm98 benchmarks
jack	37,949	4,193,140	
mpegaudio	9,997	947,196	
compress	7,696	808,741	

3   Summarizing Responsibility Within Graphs

This section introduces a way to summarize the responsibility for the memory footprint of an object reference graph. We first introduce important structural and semantic *graph* properties, and quantify the extent to which these properties occur in both real applications and benchmarks. We then present an algorithm to compute an *ownership graph*, a new graph that succinctly summarizes the ownership structures within a given graph.

3.1   Four Common Graph Structures

We identify four common graph properties of subgraphs within an object reference graph. They do not depend on features of the language, runtime environment, or application. Figure 2 illustrates these four purely structural graph properties: halos, unique ownership, shared ownership, and butterflies.

Halos. Many object reference graphs include structures such as illustrated in Figure 2(a). This graph has two roots, one of which is a proper graph root (a node with no parents). The three objects that form a cycle combine to make up the second root. We term this cycle at the top of the graph a "halo". A halo is a strongly-connected component in which no constituent has a parent outside of the component's subgraph.[2]

---

[2] Sometimes, the objects in a halo are garbage; e.g. HPROF [43] does not collect garbage prior to writing a heap snapshot to disk. More often, non-Java mechanisms reference members of a halo, but the snapshot does not report them; e.g. if the garbage collector is not type accurate, this information may not be available.

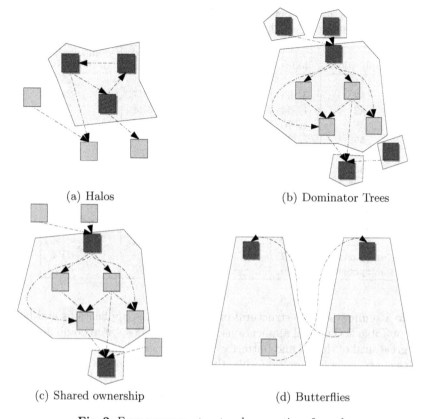

(a) Halos

(b) Dominator Trees

(c) Shared ownership

(d) Butterflies

Fig. 2. Four common structural properties of graphs

Dominator Trees. The dominator relation [22] applied to graphs of memory describes the unique ownership of objects [7]. A relatively small set of nodes often dominate large subsets of the graph. The immediate dominator relation imposes a spanning forest over the graph. Figure 2(b) illustrates a graph whose dominator forest consists of five trees: four single-node trees and one five-node tree. We highlight the root of each dominator tree with a darker shade.

Shared Ownership. For those nodes that are roots of the dominator forest, but not roots of the graph, the ownership responsibility is shared. Figure 2(c) highlights the two dominator trees of Figure 2(b) with shared ownership. Table 3 shows how, among a number of real applications, more than 75% of the dominator trees have shared ownership; we discuss this table in more detail below.

Butterflies. Mutually shared ownership arises when one node of a dominator tree points to the root of another dominator tree, while a node of that other dominator tree points back to the root of the first tree. Figure 2(d) illustrates a case where two dominator trees mutually own each other; we refer to these structures as "butterflies". These structures are common in real applications, where 7–54% of dominator trees are involved in butterflies.

Table 3. The structural properties of graphs; the fifth and sixth columns show the fraction of the dominator trees that are shared and involved in butterflies

application	halos	avg. objects per domtree	shared domtrees	domtrees in a butterfly
A1	152	153	81%	25%
A2	3,496	41	91%	24%
A3	1,064	310	87%	54%
A2'	1,776	39	76%	9%
A4	3,828	27	78%	42%
A5	3,492	43	67%	7%
A6	826	103	72%	13%
mtrt	25	3	2%	<1%
db	7	5	32%	<1%
javac	27	8	49%	16%
jess	8	3	6%	<1%
jack	27	3	24%	<1%
mpegaudio	117	8	40%	<1%
compress	26	6	45%	<1%

Table 3 summarizes the structural properties for the applications and benchmarks of Table 2. The real applications have many halos, large dominator trees, and a great deal of shared and butterfly ownership. Only one benchmark, javac, exhibits characteristics somewhat like the real applications.

3.2   Three Structures Derived from the Language and Data Types

We supplement structural information with three pieces of semantic information: contingent ownership, the class loader frontier, and context-identical dominator trees, as illustrated in Figure 3. The first two draw upon language features, and the third takes object data types into account.

Contingent Ownership. Some language mechanisms reference objects, but do not impact their lifetime. We choose to filter out these references, for the purposes of summarizing the responsibility for graph nodes. Java applications commonly use two such mechanisms: weak references, and the finalizer queue. The constructor of a WeakReference creates a new object that references a provided object; the garbage collector ignores this reference when determining liveness. For example, in the situation illustrated by Figure 3(a), one of the two referents to the bottom dominator tree is from a weak reference. From structural perspective, the bottom tree has shared ownership; but it is more natural to consider the weak ownership to be *contingent* upon the persistence of the strong reference. Similarly, instances of a class with a finalize method will be referenced by the finalizer queue; but, again, these references do not impact liveness. In addition, we choose to filter references due to Java soft references. These references informs the garbage collector that, in the absence of other strong references, to free the object when memory becomes tight.

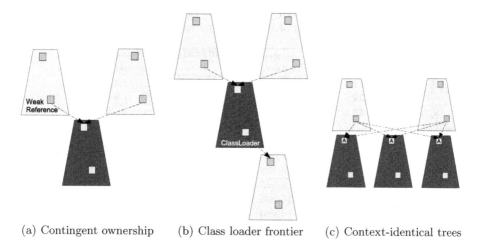

(a) Contingent ownership   (b) Class loader frontier   (c) Context-identical trees

Fig. 3. Three common semantic properties of graphs

Definition 1 (Contingent Ownership). *We say that an edge (n', n) offers contingent ownership to n if n' is weak, soft, or part of the finalizer queue, and there exists at least one other edge (n'', n) such that n'' is not weak, soft, or part of the finalizer queue. We say that a reference (n, n') offers strong contingent ownership if there is exactly one such n''.*

Table 4 shows the fraction of shared dominator trees that have this property. The real applications all have thousands of dominator trees with contingent ownership, and on average 52% of the contingent ownership is strong. The benchmarks have a higher proportion of strong contingent ownership: 78%.

Class Loader Frontier. Real applications have a large boundary between dominator trees headed by class loader mechanisms and trees of non-class loading mechanisms. Figure 3(b) illustrates a case with four dominator trees located on either side of this boundary. This boundary is large because real applications make heavy use of class loaders, and they commonly have shared ownership. Table 5 shows that real applications have as many as 38 thousand dominator trees headed by class loader data types; on average, 29% of the class loader dominator trees from these seven snapshots were shared. Further complicating matters, these shared class loader dominator trees tend to reach nearly all objects. This is because, in real applications, the class objects very often reach a substantial portion of the graph. Next, the class loader dominator trees are usually reachable from a wide assortment of application, framework, and JVM mechanisms. For example, to isolate plugins, the Eclipse IDE uses a separate class loader for each plugin; its plugin system reaches the class loader mechanism, which in turn reaches many of the objects. The result is a highly tangled web of edges that connect the class loader and other trees.

We say that dominator trees that are headed by an instance of a class loader data type, and that are on either side of the boundary between class loader

Table 4. The number of dominator trees that are contingently owned, and strongly so, compared to the total number of shared dominator trees

application	shared domtrees	contingently owned	strongly contingent
A1	155,069	2,630	1,235
A2	472,177	5,324	1,943
A3	502,534	3,964	2,331
A2'	85,100	3,851	1,624
A4	121,623	33,208	29,984
A5	121,623	3,502	785
A6	26,430	733	294
mtrt	2,545	45	34
db	20,795	26	22
javac	19,830	1,514	1,503
jess	1,796	24	20
jack	3,103	113	100
mpegaudio	506	79	19
compress	542	116	105

mechanisms and all others are said to be on the *class loader frontier*. The fourth column of Table 5 shows the number of dominator trees that lie on this frontier. All of the benchmarks have a small, and roughly equal number of shared class loader dominator trees that are on this frontier; this, despite a widely varying range of shared dominator trees across the benchmarks (as shown in the second column of Table 4). The real applications have a varied, and much larger, class loader frontier. This reflects a richer usage of the class loader mechanism, compared to the benchmarks.

Table 5. The number of dominator trees headed by class loader mechanisms, the number of those that have shared ownership, and the number of dominator trees that are on the class loader frontier

application	class loader total	class loader shared	class loader frontier
A1	8,297	1,032	4,550
A2	26,676	1,008	3,030
A3	38,395	133	3,768
A2'	19,080	959	2,449
A4	5,475	396	1,127
A5	5,410	363	1,259
A6	1,017	120	522
mtrt	51	8	29
db	46	8	21
javac	48	8	22
jess	135	8	23
jack	48	8	29
mpegaudio	47	8	23
compress	47	8	22

Context Equality. Often, a large number of non-contingently owned dominator trees are headed by nodes of the same type and have identical ownership.
Figure 3(c) illustrates a case of three context-identical dominator trees: all three
are headed by nodes of type A, and the set of dominator trees to which their
predecessors belong is the same. For example, in a server application, this kind
of structure occurs with the per-user session data. The session data structures
are often simultaneously stored in two collections, under two different roots.
Hence, each is shared, but in the same way. In another common situation, an
application allocates and manages Java data structures outside of Java. All that
is visible from a Java heap snapshot are many of those data structures with no
visible Java roots: the same type of data structures, all in the same (in this case,
empty) context. We can leverage this kind of similarity.

Definition 2 (Context-identical). *Let n be a node in a graph, $R(n)$ be the
root node of the dominator tree in which that node belongs, $P(n)$ be the set of
predecessor nodes of n that do not have contingent ownership over n, and $T(n)$
be the type of a node n. Let $I(n) = \{T(R(p)) : p \in P(R(n))\}$, i.e. the types of
the root nodes of the predecessors of n's dominator tree root. We say two nodes
n_1 and n_2 are part of* context identical *dominator trees if $T(R(n_1)) = T(R(n_2))$
and $I(n_1) = I(n_2)$.*

Under this definition of equality, we can group dominator trees into equivalence
classes. Table 6 shows the number and average size of context-identical equivalence classes for our suite of applications and benchmarks. In real applications,
there are typically many thousands of such classes, with a dozen or so dominator
trees per class.

Table 6. The number and average size of the context-identical equivalence classes from
a variety of applications and benchmarks

application	context-identical equiv. classes	avg. domtrees per equiv. class
A1	4,420	13
A2	32,087	6
A3	36,464	9
A2'	3,190	10
A4	1,837	31
A5	2,078	15
A6	2,011	5
mtrt	140	11
db	9	1,706
javac	438	16
jess	72	7
jack	71	14
mpegaudio	8	3
compress	5	21

3.3   The Ownership Graph

We demonstrate an algorithm that, given an object reference graph, produces a new *ownership graph* that concisely summarizes responsibility within the input graph. To compute the ownership graph, the algorithm performs a chain of *graph edits*, each of which filters, aggregates, or applies thresholds to the nodes in an object reference graph.

Definition 3 (Graph Edit). *Given a graph G, a graph edit E_G is (C, D_n, D_e); C is the collapsing relation, an $N : 1$ relation among the nodes of G; D_n and D_e are, respectively, the node and edge delete sets, and are subsets of the nodes and edges of G, respectively. We term the range of the collapsing relation as the set of canonical nodes of the edit. The deleted graph is the subgraph of G consisting of edges either in D_e or whose target is in D_n; its nodes are the nodes of G.*

Applying a graph edit yields a new, reduced, graph that preserves the reachability of the input graph. When applying a chain of graph edits, each edit takes as input the reduced graph generated by the previous graph edit.

Definition 4 (Reduced Graph). *Given a graph edit E_G, define the reduced graph of E_G to be the graph R whose nodes are the canonical nodes of E_G and whose edges are the union of edges from G renamed according to the collapsing relation, and edges from the transitive closure of the deleted graph of E_G.*

Each node in a reduced graph represents an aggregation of nodes from previous graphs. Since each collapsing relation is a tree relation (i.e. it is $N : 1$ from nodes to nodes of the input graph), the correspondence between a node of a reduced graph to the nodes of any previous reduced graph is just the transitive closure of the inverse of the collapsing relations.

Definition 5 (Contained Nodes). *Let R be a reduced graph derived, via a chain of graph edits, from a graph G. Define the contained node set of $r \in R$ relative to G to be the set of $g \in G$ encountered on a traversal, from r, of the composition of the inverse of the collapsing relations of the chain of graph edits that led to R.*

Using a combination of five kinds graph edits, some applied multiple times, we construct concise ownership graphs. We now define those five kinds of edits, and subsequently describe an ownership graph construction algorithm.

Dominator Edit. Compute a representative for each halo of the input graph; we find the set of representatives that, on any depth-first traversal of the input, have only back edges incoming. The union of this set of halo representatives with those nodes that have no incoming edges form the *root set* of the graph. Given this root set, compute the dominator forest of the input graph.[3] From

---

[3] The dominator algorithm we use [22] assumes that the input is a flow graph. In our case, we use an implicit start vertex: one that points to the computed root set.

this forest, we define a graph edit (C, D_e, D_n). The collapsing relation C maps a node to its dominator forest root; the deleted edge set D_e consists of edges that cross the class loader frontier or that have only contingent ownership; the deleted node set D_n is empty. This edit collapses the dominator trees into single nodes. It will also remove the shared ownership from dominator trees that are strongly contingently owned.

Context-identical Edit. For each node n of the input graph, compute a representative type T_n. In the case where each node is a dominator tree, we choose this representative type to be the node type of the head of the dominator tree; this will not necessarily be the case when this graph edit is applied subsequent to graph edits other than the `dominator` edit. In the case where each node is a collection of dominator trees whose heads are of uniform type, we choose the representative type to be that type. Otherwise, we say the representative type is undefined. Let the parent set of a node n, P_n, be the set of predecessor nodes of n. Group the nodes of the input graph according to equality, for each graph node n, of the pair (P_n, T_n). For the remaining equivalence classes, choose an arbitrary representative node. The context-identical collapsing relation maps each node to that representative. The deleted edge set and deleted node set are empty.

Butterfly Edit. Compute the strongly connected components of the input graph. Choose a representative node from each component. The collapsing relation maps each node to the representative of the component to which it belongs. The deleted edge set and deleted node set are empty.

Reachable Edit. Given a reduced graph R, for each node $r \in R$ determine the contained node set of R relative to the original input graph G. Recall from Section 2 that we assume a heap snapshot associates an instance size attribute with each node. Compute the *uniquely-owned* size for each $r \in R$, which is the sum over each node $g \in G$ in the contained set of r of the instance size of g. Next, compute the *shared-owned* size for each node $r \in R$, which is the sum over all nodes r' reachable from r of uniquely-owned size of r'. Choose a threshold of this shared-owned property, a size below which would not be worth the effort of further study. We have found that a reasonable threshold is the maximum of one megabyte and one standard deviation above the mean size of all shared-owned sizes of the graph's nodes. The collapsing relation of this graph edit is the identity. The deleted edge set is empty. The deleted node set is those nodes whose shared-owned size falls below the threshold.

Miscellaneous Edit. Given a reduced graph R, determine the subset of the contained set of R relative to the original graph G that have been deleted; that is, those union of the contained set, relative to G, of nodes in a D_n of some reduced graph on the chain between G and R. We term this the "miscellaneous" set. Compute the sum M of the instance sizes of the members of the miscellaneous set. Compute the shared-owned size, S_r of each nodes $r \in R$. Choose a fraction ϵ of M so that the deleted node set of this graph edit is the set of nodes of $r \in R$ with $S_r - M < \epsilon$; this isolates any node that is responsible for only a

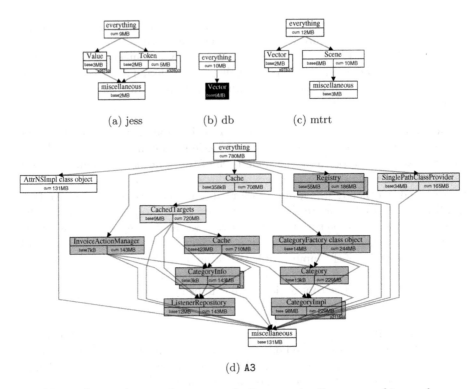

(a) jess   (b) db   (c) mtrt

(d) A3

Fig. 4. Our implementation automatically generates these ownership graphs

small amount of space, i.e. ϵM, on top of the miscellaneous size. The collapsing relation is the identity, and the deleted edge set is empty.

The Ownership Graph Algorithm. The ownership graph is the reduced graph resulting from the final edit in a chain of graph edits. We will need to apply certain edits more than once, because one edit may reintroduce a structure that another edit aggregates. Consider a variant of the graph of Figure 2(d), where one node in each of the two dominator tree references a third dominator tree. A dominator edit produces a graph of three nodes. A butterfly edit of that graph aggregates the two butterfly-connected nodes into one. The resulting two-node graph has a single edge between the former butterfly and that node representing the third dominator tree. Reapplying the dominator edit produces a single-node graph. The chain of graph edits we use to produce an ownership graph is: dominator, context-identical, butterfly, dominator, reachable-threshold, miscellaneous-threshold, context-identical, and finally dominator.

We have implemented this algorithm, and it consistently and quickly produces small ownership graphs. Recall that the two threshold edits may populate a pseudo-aggregate (`miscellaneous`) that represents the memory that falls below the chosen threshold. When rendering an ownership graph, we introduce a second pseudo-node (`everything`), to represent the entire snapshot; it refers to every

Table 7. The size and time to compute ownership graphs

application	nodes in full graph	nodes in ownership graph	seconds to construct
A1	29,181,452	14	148
A2	20,952,120	15	98
A3	17,871,063	11	82
A4	4,391,183	3	26
A2'	4,289,704	19	24
A5	4,099,743	13	27
A6	3,757,828	3	18
mtrt	509,170	2	8
db	342,725	1	7
javac	316,857	8	8
jess	83,815	2	7
jack	37,949	1	7
mpegaudio	9,997	1	5
compress	7,696	1	6

root in the graph. Table 7 shows the size and time to compute[4] ownership graphs. We do not count the two pseudo-nodes towards an ownership graph's node count. The computation time figures include the code to compute the graph halos, a DFS spanning tree, the dominator tree, all of the graph edits, and the time to render the graph to SVG (scalable vector graphics). For application A3, the full graph has nearly 18 million nodes; the ownership graph, computed in 82 seconds, consists of 11 nodes.

Figure 4 shows the output, generated automatically, from three of the benchmarks and application A3. Our rendering code draws a stack of nodes whenever an ownership graph node represents a context-identical aggregate. Each node shows the uniquely-owned bytes ("base") represented by that aggregate. Each non-leaf node also show shared-owned bytes ("cum"). Finally, we color the nodes based on the source package that primarily contributes to that aggregate's base size: dark gray for customer code, light gray for framework code (such as the application server, servlet processing, XML parsing code), black for standard Java library code, and white for everything else.

4 Summarizing Content Within Trees

This section shows how to summarize the nodes within a tree [12, 9, 20, 21, 25], using the concept of backbones. A backbone in a tree is a mechanism whereby collections of objects grow or shrink. The backbone of a linked list is the chain of "element" objects that store the inter-element linkage; in this case, the backbone structure is recursive. Section 4.1 introduces a categorization of the contents of a data structures based on how the objects contribute to backbones. This categorization alone provides powerful, but *flat* summaries of a tree's content.

---

[4] On a 1.8GHz Opteron, using Sun's Linux 1.5.0_06 64-bit JVM and the -server flag.

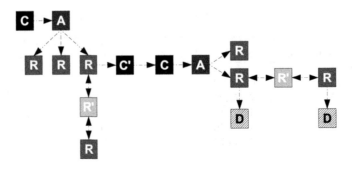

Fig. 5. A categorization of the nodes in a tree according to backbone structure

To summarize the *locations* of excessive memory footprint, Section 4.2 shows how to use a backbone categorization to aggregate backbones into equivalence classes, based on two notions of equality. We show that the equivalence relations successfully aggregate large number of backbones. Finally Section 4.3 shows how applying thresholds after having aggregated by backbone equivalence provides succinct summaries of tree content.

Note that, in some cases, a node in the ownership graph will be a dominator tree, and the approach described in this section applies directly. In other cases, it will be a collection of trees. To analyze a forest of trees, we take the union of the summaries of each tree.

4.1   The Elements of a Backbone

We identify six elements of a backbone within a tree, as shown in Figure 5. Array backbone types, those nodes labeled A, are responsible for horizontal growth or shrinkage in a graph. Recursive backbone types, nodes labeled R, can change the depth of a graph. We refer to the union of A and R types as *backbone types*. In some cases, a recursive backbone includes nodes of a non-backbone type (R') that are sandwiched between the recursive backbone nodes. Above any backbone is a node that represents the container (C) to which they belong. There are often non-backbone nodes placed between one container and another, or between a backbone and a nested container; these *container sandwich* nodes are labeled C'. Underneath the backbone nodes, whether array or recursive, are the nodes that dominate the true data of the container (D). These six groups of types cover much of the structure within trees. We bundle any other structures not covered by the main six groups into the D group.

For example, an XML document can grow by adding elements or by adding attributes to an existing element. The elements grow recursively, but sometimes a `TextImpl` node is sandwiched between two `ElementImpl` nodes. The attributes grow along an array backbone, with data of type `AttributeImpl` under a container of type `Vector`. Between an element's recursive backbone and the `Vector` container is a container sandwich of type `AttributeMap`.

We categorize node types into one of these six groups. From this categorization of types, it is straightforward to categorize the nodes themselves. Array types

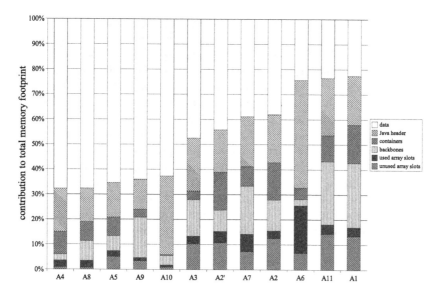

Fig. 6. The contribution of backbone overheads to total memory footprint

have instances that point to a number of nodes of the same type; the format of heap snapshots usually distinguishes array types for us. We currently identify only one-hop recursion, where nodes of a type point to nodes of the same type. This simple rule is very effective. Even in the XML document example of the previous paragraph, where there are recursive sandwich types, the recursive-typed nodes still point to nodes of the same type. A container type is a non-backbone type that has node instances that point to backbone types. Given a subpath in the tree that begins and ends with a node from R, all nodes between those endpoints are from R'. Given a subpath that begins with A, C, or R and that ends with C, all nodes between the endpoints are from C'. Finally, there will be a set of nodes that are pointed to by nodes of backbone type; the union of the types of nodes dominated by them form D.

Categorizing objects in this way yields powerful summaries of content, such as the ones shown in Figure 6. This figure includes five additional snapshots from real server applications, A7-A11, that we do not otherwise study in this paper. Each of the six categories in the figure represents the sum of the instance size of each node. We split the array backbone overhead into two subcategories: the memory devoted to unused slots in the array, and slots used for actual references. We assume that a `null` reference value in an array is not meaningful data; in our experience, this is nearly always the case. We also include the contribution of the Java object header, assuming eight bytes per header. We include header overhead, as its contribution varies for similar reasons as backbone overheads in general: many small collections leads to a higher C overhead, but also a higher object header overhead. We deduct this header cost from the costs associated with the other backbone overheads.

The amount of storage in the D group varies from as much as 68% to as little as 23%. On average, the data consumes 47% of the heap. This fraction is not well correlated with snapshot size; e.g. the snapshot A4 has over 20 million nodes, and yet has the highest fraction of data, while application A2', with a quarter the number of nodes, has a much lower fraction of data. Furthermore, the distribution to the various overheads is not constant: there is no hard and fast rule about how to impose a high backbone cost. It is certainly a property of the application; e.g. A2 and A2', which represent the same application in steady state, and just after server startup, have similar profiles. One application might have a few large data structures, versus many small ones; another might use an open-chained hashing implementation, rather than one with explicit chaining (the former would avoid a high R cost). Appendix A describes the data models we use in the implementations for this paper. Our layout nearly eliminates backbone and object header overheads, which is one of the ways we achieve high scalability.

4.2   Aggregates of Backbone Equivalence

Most real applications have a tremendous number of backbone nodes. As the second column of Table 8 shows, our real applications have anywhere from 67 thousand to 10 million distinct locations in their dominator trees that serve as either array or recursive backbones. This is far too many for a human to comprehend. Fortunately, there is much commonality in those backbone locations. We group the backbone nodes into equivalence classes, based on two equivalence properties: one based on type equality of paths and the second based on a notion of backbone-folding equality. While the second subsumes the first, to achieve a well-performing implementation, it is important to apply them one after the other, as computing context equality can be expensive.

Table 8. The number of backbone nodes and the number of root-type-path and backbone-folding equivalence classes (summed over all dominator trees)

application	backbone nodes	root-type-path equiv. classes	backbone-folding equiv. classes
A1	10,864,774	21,820	7,689
A2	4,704,630	23,561	10,381
A3	3,690,480	345,863	21,482
A2'	772,299	13,855	6,550
A4	342,570	9,630	5,046
A5	630,784	14,847	7,793
A6	107,802	3,907	1,840
mtrt	78,153	3,092	448
db	17,173	91	50
javac	116,274	18,818	9,025
jess	15,069	148	101
jack	2,690	289	154
mpegaudio	2,017	117	77
compress	1,985	175	48

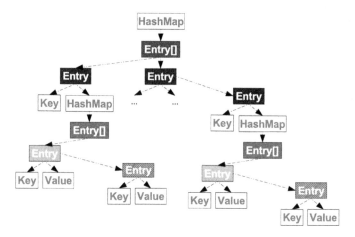

Fig. 7. A hash map of inner hash maps. There are two backbone types (`Entry[]` and `Entry`), ten nodes of those two types, nine backbone equivalence classes under root type path equality, and four backbone-folding equivalence classes.

Root-type-path Equality. Let the *root path* of a tree node be the list of nodes from the tree root to that node, inclusive; the *root type path* is similarly the list of those node types. We compute the A and R node types, and the instances of those types in the tree under analysis. We then form equivalence classes of these instances, using root type path equality.

It is often the case that a large number of backbone nodes in a tree have equal root type paths. Forming equivalence classes based on this notion of equality can therefore produce a more succinct summary of a tree's content than an enumeration of the backbone nodes. The third column in Table 8 shows the number of root type path equivalence classes in a number of applications and benchmarks.

Consider the common case of root type path equality shown in Figure 7: a hash map of inner hash maps, where all of maps use explicit chaining. There are two backbone types (`Entry[]` and `Entry`) and ten backbone nodes. Of those ten, there are nine distinct classes of backbone nodes under root type path equality. The only non-singleton class has the two top-left `Entry` nodes. Every other backbone node has a unique root type path. For example, the third `Entry` in the upper hash map is located under an `Entry` object, a property that the other two `Entry` nodes do not have. This difference skews every other node instance under that chained `Entry`, rendering little root type equivalence. We chose this example for illustrative purposes only. In practice, we see that from Table 8 that there are quite a large number of backbone nodes with type-identical root type paths. The figures in this table represent the sum over all dominator trees in each heap snapshot.

Backbone-folding Equality. Root type path equality identifies nine backbone equivalence classes in the tree of Figure 7. We feel there should only be four distinct classes. The upper `Entry[]` array is rightly in a singleton class, but the three upper `Entry` instances, the two lower `Entry[]` instances, and the four lower `Entry` instances should form a total of three classes, respectively. Imagine that the lower hash maps contain values of type string: a hash map of hash maps that map to string values. We feel that each of those strings should be the same, despite being located in potentially thousands of separate (lower) hash maps, and despite each lower hash map being under a wide variety of depths of (upper) Entry recursion.

To capture this finer notion of equivalence, we observe that it is recursive structures, through combinations of R and R′ nodes, that lead to the kind of skew that foils root type path equality. We compute the set of A, R, and R′ nodes and, to each backbone node, associate a regular expression. The canonical set of regular expressions form the equivalence classes (c.f. the RDS types and instances of [32] and the DSGraphs of [20, 21]). The regular expression of a node is its root type path, except that any R′ node is optional and any R node can occur one or more times in any position. For example, the two D nodes from Figure 5 are backbone-folding equivalent, because they share the regular expression $CAR^{+}(R'?)CARL^{+}(R'?)$, where + and ? have the standard meanings of "one or more" and "optional".

The fourth column in Table 8 shows the number of equivalence classes of backbone nodes under backbone-folding equality. Even for graphs with tens of millions of nodes, aggregation alone (i.e. without filters or thresholds) collapses all dominator trees down to at most 21 thousand backbone equivalence classes.

4.3   Using Thresholds to Identify Large Patterns in Large Trees

Applying thresholds after having aggregated backbones can yield succinct summaries of content. As a first threshold, we usually care to study only the largest trees, or at least to study the largest trees first. Within a large tree, we consider two useful thresholds of backbone aggregates: a biggest contributing pattern analysis, and a suspect locator analysis.

A *biggest contributing pattern* analysis looks for the equivalence classes that contribute most to a given tree. Table 9 shows the result of a biggest-contributor analysis to the largest dominator tree in each application and benchmark. There are often hundreds of equivalence classes within the largest tree. However, only a few patterns summarize a substantial fraction of the footprint of the tree. The third column in the table shows how many of those equivalence classes account for 80% of the size of the tree (tabulating the largest equivalence classes first). With just two exceptions, a small handful of classes account for most of the footprint of the largest tree. Even for the two exceptions, A1 and javac, 80% of the largest tree's size is accounted for by 35 and 53 patterns.

Sometimes, it is helpful to know where certain suspicious data types are placed in an expensive tree. A *suspect locator* analysis identifies the distinct classes of locations in which a chosen data type occurs. There may be millions of instances of this type, but they will not be in a million different equivalence classes. Furthermore, as Table 10 shows, for all of our applications and benchmarks, a only a handful of equivalence classes account for most of the contribution of that type in any one tree. This is despite the fact that, in some cases, there are hundreds of distinct patterns in which the largest data type is located. More generally,

Table 9. A biggest contributing pattern analysis shows that a few hot patterns account for 80% of the largest dominator tree's memory footprint

application	equiv. classes in largest tree	80% contributors in largest tree
A1	761	35
A2	20	10
A3	1	1
A2'	11	2
A4	2	1
A5	1172	3
A6	77	3
mtrt	43	10
db	1	1
javac	566	53
jess	1	1
jack	22	1
mpegaudio	2	1
compress	2	1

this suspect locator analysis can apply to other notions of suspects, such as the major contributors to backbone overhead: if my C overhead is so high, then tell me the patterns that contribute most. We will explore this more general form of analysis in future work.

5   Related Work

Techniques that *summarize* the internal structure of heap snapshots are relatively uncommon. Recent work [27, 29] introduces a system for counting, via general queries, both aggregate and reachability properties of an object reference graph. They have also done insightful characterization studies [28, 30]. Another recent work [25], akin to [12], summarizes reachability properties for each root in the graph. To our knowledge, these works do not aggregate the internal structural of the graphs according to context. Other related domains include:

Shape Analysis. Static shape analysis builds conservative models of the heap at every line of code [12, 9, 19, 20, 21]. They often use abstract interpretation to form type graphs (such as the RSRSG [9] or the DSGraph [20]); these summaries capture recursive structures, somewhat analogous to the regular expressions we form in Section 4.2. The work we discussed above [25] can be thought of as a kind of dynamic shape analysis.

Heap Profiling. This phrase usually applies to techniques that track the object allocations of an application for a period of time [6, 36, 34, 35, 37, 40, 32]. Mostly, the allocation site profiles are used to populate aggregate call graphs, and interpreted as one would a profile of execution time. Sometimes, the data is used to help design garbage collectors [15]. Some works combine static shape analysis with dynamic profile collection [32].

Table 10. A suspect locator analysis shows that a few hot patterns contain 80% of the bytes due to instances of the dominant data type

application	equiv. classes in largest tree	80% contributors classes in largest tree
A1	427	14
A2	7	1
A3	33	2
A2'	2	2
A4	1	1
A5	248	5
A6	6	3
mtrt	13	7
db	1	1
javac	1	1
jess	1	1
jack	1	1
mpegaudio	1	1
compress	1	1

Ownership Types. There is a large body of recent work on representing the ownership of objects in the static type system [8, 26, 4, 2, 7, 5, 1, 11, 24]. Some recent refinements have addressed issues such as sharing [26] and dominance [7]. The primary goal of this work is to enable better static analysis, such as less conservative alias analysis, or catching deadlocks at compile time [4].

Leak Analysis. An application that leaks memory will eventually be found to have an excessive memory footprint. Much of the prior work on memory leak detection either focuses on identifying allocation sites [13, 43, 42, 38, 3, 18], or on mostly-manual heap snapshot differencing [10, 31]. Our previous work [23] analyzes a pair of heap snapshots, and automates the detection of the heads of possibly leaking data structures. It neither address shared ownership, nor how to summarize the content underneath the leaking structures.

Visualization. The work of [14] introduces the idea of using the dominator tree to visualize object ownership. They also provide an clever composition of trees that mirrors the stack of activation records. In a similar vein, [33] presents an alternative visualization strategy that takes into account object references, domination, and characteristics of object usage. Similar to our previous work [23], they use heuristics to impose an ownership tree on a graph. None of these summarize nodes; by using the dominator spanning tree, they do filter out edges. Other tools require a human to browse what are essentially raw object reference graphs [10, 31, 3]. In some cases, these tools aggregate, but only locally; e.g. [10] aggregates outgoing edges by the referred-to type. Many tools also provide flat summaries that aggregate graph nodes by type, size, etc. The work of [25] includes a visualization component that describes reachability-from-root and age properties of objects in a heap snapshot, but concedes that it does not scale to graphs much larger than several thousand nodes.

6   Future Work

We see three exciting areas of future work. First, Section 4.3 demonstrated how to locate the patterns that explain the hottest elements of a flat summary by type. This is a powerful style of analysis, and we can extend it to be driven by a more general notion of suspects. For example, we can use it to locate the few patterns that explain most of the Java object header overhead. We can also introduce new kinds of suspects, such as large base class overhead.

Second, the ownership graph provides a visual representation of responsibility. We feel that there is a need for schematic visual representations of content. The backbone equivalence classes provide a good model for this summary. There is much work to be done in finding the powerful, yet concise, visual metaphors that will capture these patterns.

Third, we feel that the methodology employed in this paper, and the ownership structures we have identified can be useful in understanding the structure graphs from other domains. For example, many of the difficult aspects of graph size (scale, scattering of suspects in disparate locations in a graph, sharing of responsibility) have analogs in the performance realm. In performance, flat summaries usually only point out leaf methods, and yet the structure of a call graph is highly complex. We will explore this synergy.

7   Conclusion

It is common these days for large-scale object-oriented applications to be developed by integrating a number of existing frameworks. As beneficial as this may be to the development process, it has negative implications on understanding what happens at run time. These applications have very complicated policies governing responsibility and object lifetime. From a snapshot of the heap, we are left to reverse engineer those policies. On top of that, even uniquely-, non-contingently-owned objects have complex structure. Data structures that are essentially trees, like XML documents, are large, and represented with a multitude of non-tree edges. The common data types within them may be scattered in a million places; e.g. the attributes of an XML document's elements occur across the width and throughout the depth of the tree.

We have presented a methodology and algorithms for analyzing this web of complex ownership structures. In addition to their usefulness for summarizing memory footprint, we hope they are helpful as an exposition of the kinds of structures that occur in large-scale applications. Work that tackles object ownership from viewpoints other than runtime analysis may benefit from this study.

Acknowledgments

The author thanks Glenn Ammons, Herb Derby, Palani Kumanan, Derek Rayside, Edith Schonberg, and Gary Sevitsky for their assistance with this work.

References

1. Aldrich, J., Chambers, C.: Ownership domains: Separating aliasing policy from mechanism. In: The European Conference on Object-Oriented Programming. Volume 3086 of Lecture Notes in Computer Science., Oslo, Norway, Springer-Verlag (2004)
2. Aldrich, J., Kostadinov, V., Chambers, C.: Alias annotations for program understanding. In: Object-oriented Programming, Systems, Languages, and Applications. (2002)
3. Borland Software Corporation: OptimizeIt^{TM} Enterprise Suite. http://www.borland.com/us/products/optimizeit (2005)
4. Boyapati, C., Lee, R., Rinard, M.: Ownership types for safe programming: preventing data races and deadlocks. In: Object-oriented Programming, Systems, Languages, and Applications. (2002)
5. Boyapati, C., Liskov, B., Shrira, L.: Ownership types for object encapsulation. In: Symposium on Principles of Programming Languages. (2003)
6. Clack, C., Clayman, S., Parrott, D.: Lexical profiling: Theory and practice. Journal of Functional Programming 5(2) (1995) 225–277
7. Clarke, D., Wrigstad, T.: External uniqueness is unique enough. In: The European Conference on Object-Oriented Programming. Volume 2743 of Lecture Notes in Computer Science., Springer-Verlag (2003) 176–200
8. Clarke, D.G., Noble, J., Potter, J.M.: Simple ownership types for object containment. In: The European Conference on Object-Oriented Programming. Volume 2072 of Lecture Notes in Computer Science., Budapest, Hungary, Springer-Verlag (2001) 53–76
9. Corbera, F., Asenjo, R., Zapata, E.L.: A framework to capture dynamic data structures in pointer-based codes. IEEE Transactions on Parallel and Distributed Systems 15(2) (2004) 151–166
10. De Pauw, W., Sevitsky, G.: Visualizing reference patterns for solving memory leaks in Java. Concurrency: Practice and Experience 12 (2000) 1431–1454
11. Dietl, W., Müller, P.: Universes: Lightweight ownership for JML. Special Issue: ECOOP 2004 Workshop FTfJP, Journal of Object Technology 4(8) (2005) 5–32
12. Ghiya, R., Hendren, L.J.: Is it a tree, a DAG, or a cyclic graph? a shape analysis for heap-directed pointers in c. In: Symposium on Principles of Programming Languages. (1996)
13. Hastings, R., Joynce, B.: Purify — fast detection of memory leaks and access errors. In: USENIX Proceedings. (1992) 125–136
14. Hill, T., Noble, J., Potter, J.: Scalable visualizations of object-oriented systems with ownership trees. Journal of Visual Languages and Computing 13 (2002) 319–339
15. Hirzel, M., Hinkel, J., Diwan, A., Hind, M.: Understanding the connectivity of heap objects. In: International Symposium on Memory Management. (2002)
16. Hitchens, R.: Java NIO. First edn. O'Reilly Media, Inc. (2002)
17. Holzner, S.: Eclipse. First edn. O'Reilly Media, Inc. (2004)
18. IBM Corporation: Rational PurifyPlus (2005)
19. Jeannet, B., Loginov, A., Reps, T., Sagiv, M.: A relational approach to interprocedural shape analysis. In: International Static Analysis Symposium. Lecture Notes in Computer Science, New York, NY, Springer-Verlag (2004)
20. Lattner, C., Adve, V.: Data structure analysis: A fast and scalable context-sensitive heap analysis. Technical Report UIUCDCS-R-2003-2340, Computer Science Deptartment, University of Illinois (2003)

21. Lattner, C., Adve, V.: Automatic pool allocation: Improving performance by controlling data structure layout in the heap. In: Programming Language Design and Implementation, Chicago, IL (2005) 129–142
22. Lengauer, T., Tarjan, R.E.: A fast algorithm for finding dominators in a flow graph. ACM Transactions on Programming Languages and Systems **1**(1) (1979) 121–141
23. Mitchell, N., Sevitsky, G.: Leakbot: An automated and lightweight tool for diagnosing memory leaks in large Java applications. In: The European Conference on Object-Oriented Programming. Volume 2743 of Lecture Notes in Computer Science., Springer-Verlag (2003) 351–377
24. Parkinson, M., Bierman, G.: Separation logic and abstraction. In: Symposium on Principles of Programming Languages. (2005)
25. Pheng, S., Verbrugge, C.: Dynamic shape and data structure analysis in java. Technical Report 2005-3, School of Computer Science, McGill University (2005)
26. Pollet, I., Charlier, B.L., Cortesi, A.: Distinctness and sharing domains for static analysis of Java programs. In: The European Conference on Object-Oriented Programming. Volume 2072 of Lecture Notes in Computer Science., Springer-Verlag (2001) 77–98
27. Potanin, A.: The Fox — a tool for object graph analysis. Undergraduate Honors Thesis (2002)
28. Potanin, A., Noble, J., Biddle, R.: Checking ownership and confinement. Concurrency and Computation: Practice and Experience **16**(7) (2004) 671–687
29. Potanin, A., Noble, J., Biddle, R.: Snapshot query-based debugging. In: Australian Software Engineering Conference, Melbourne, Australia (2004)
30. Potanin, A., Noble, J., Frean, M., Biddle, R.: Scale-free geometry in object-oriented programs. In: Communications of the ACM. (2005)
31. Quest Software: JProbe® Memory Debugger. http://www.quest.com/jprobe (2005)
32. Raman, E., August, D.I.: Recursive data structure profiling. In: ACM SIGPLAN Workshop on Memory Systems Performance. (2005)
33. Rayside, D., Mendel, L., Jackson, D.: A dynamic analysis for revealing object ownership and sharing. In: Workshop on Dynamic Analysis. (2006)
34. Rojemo, N., Runciman, C.: Lag, drag, void and use — heap profiling and space-efficient compilation revisited. In: International Conference on Functional Programming. (1996) 34–41
35. Runciman, C., Rojemo, N.: New dimensions in heap profiling. Journal of Functional Programming **6**(4) (1996) 587–620
36. Sansom, P.M., Peyton Jones, S.L.: Time and space profiling for non-strict higher-order functional languages. In: Symposium on Principles of Programming Languages, San Francisco, CA (1995) 355–366
37. Sansom, P.M., Peyton Jones, S.L.: Formally based profiling for higher-order functional languages. ACM Transactions on Programming Languages and Systems **19**(2) (1997) 334–385
38. Shaham, R., Kolodner, E.K., Sagiv, M.: Automatic removal of array memory leaks in java. In: Computational Complexity. (2000) 50–66
39. Shaham, R., Kolodner, E.K., Sagiv, M.: Estimating the impact of heap liveness information on space consumption in Java. In: International Symposium on Memory Management. (2002)
40. Shaham, R., Kolodner, E.K., Sagiv, S.: Heap profiling for space-efficient java. In: Programming Language Design and Implementation. (2001) 104–113
41. SPEC Corporation: The SPEC JVM Client98 benchmark suite. http://www.spec.org/osg/jvm98 (1998)

42. Sun Microsystems: Heap Analysis Tool. https://hat.dev.java.net/ (2002)
43. Sun Microsystems: HPROF JVM profiler.
    http://java.sun.com/developer/technicalArticles/Programming/HPROF.html
    (2005)

A   Modeling Gigantic Graphs

To program graph analysis algorithms in Java, we must be careful to avoid our own memory footprint problems. We could easily find ourselves modeling the Java heap of a large server inside the Java heap on a development machine. To write scalable graph analysis algorithms in Java, we made two implementation decisions. We do not store graphs in an object-oriented style. Instead, we represent node attributes and edges as columns of data, and store each column as a separate file on disk. There is no `Node` data type. Rather, code refers to nodes as 32-bit integer identifiers, ranging densely from 0 to the number of nodes; the same is true for the edges (limiting us to two billion nodes). This storage layout avoids an object header for each node, and avoids any container cost to represent the outgoing and incoming edges for each node.

In addition to lowering footprint requirements, this style of storage aids performance. It permits direct use of the `java.nio` package [16] to memory map attributes on demand. This gives us constant time reloading of graphs, transparent persistence of graphs and attributes, the operating system takes care of caching for us (even across process boundaries), and we can run any analysis with the default Java heap size, independent of the size of the graph under analysis.[5]

---

[5] `java.nio` is not without its faults; e.g. it currently lacks an explicit unmap facility.

On Ownership and Accessibility

Yi Lu and John Potter

Programming Languages and Compilers Group
School of Computer Science and Engineering
University of New South Wales, Sydney
{ylu, potter}@cse.unsw.edu.au

Abstract. Ownership types support information hiding by providing statically enforceable object encapsulation based on an ownership tree. However ownership type systems impose fixed ownership and an inflexible access policy. This paper proposes a novel type system which generalizes ownership types by separating object accessibility and reference capability. With the ability to hide owners, it provides a more flexible and useful model of object ownership.

1   Introduction

The object-oriented community is paying increasing attention to techniques for object level encapsulation and alias protection. Formal techniques for modular verification of programs at the level of objects are being developed hand in hand with type systems and static analysis techniques for restricting the structure of runtime object graphs. Ownership type systems have provided a sound basis for such structural restrictions by being able to statically represent an extensible object ownership hierarchy. The trick to ownership systems is to hide knowledge of the identity of an object outside its owner. This form of information hiding is useful for modular reasoning, data abstraction and confidentiality.

Ownership types support instance-level information hiding by providing a statically enforceable object encapsulation model based on an ownership tree. Traditional class-level private fields are not enough to hide object instances. For example, an object in a private field can be easily returned through a method call. However, the encapsulation mechanism used by ownership types is still not flexible enough to express some common design patterns such as iterators and callback objects. Moreover, ownership types, to date, lack ownership variance. This means, for instance, that all elements stored in a list must be owned by the same owner due to the recursive structure of the list.

This paper proposes a novel type system which generalizes ownership types with an access control system in which *object accessibility* and *reference capability* are treated orthogonally. The rationale behind this mechanism is that one only needs to hold access permission for an object in order to use it; the capability of the object can be adapted to the current access context. This allows more flexible and expressive programming with ownership types.

Our system allows programmers to trade off flexibility/accessibility with useability/capability. We allow object accessibility to be variant; intuitively it is

D. Thomas (Ed.): ECOOP 2006, LNCS 4067, pp. 99–123, 2006.
© Springer-Verlag Berlin Heidelberg 2006

safe to allow accessibility to be reduced as computation proceeds. On the other hand, we allow reference capability associated with an object to be abstracted in contexts where it is used. Our resulting type system is flexible enough to encode iterator and callback-like design patterns. It also allows objects, such as recursive data structures, to hold references to elements owned by different objects.

This paper is organized as follows: Section 2 gives an introduction to object encapsulation and the mechanisms used in ownership types; it also discusses the limitations of ownership types. Section 3 proposes the variant ownership object model and its key mechanisms with some program examples. Section 4 presents a small object-oriented programming language to allow us to formalize the static semantics, dynamic semantics and some important properties. Section 5 follows with discussion and related work. Section 6 briefly concludes the paper.

2   Ownership Types

Earlier object encapsulation systems, such as *Islands* [13] and *Balloons* [2], use full encapsulation techniques to forbid both incoming and outgoing references to an object's representation. However, full encapsulation techniques are overly strong, because outgoing references from the representation are harmless and are often needed to express typical object-oriented idioms. Ownership types [11, 10, 7] provide a more flexible mechanism than previous systems; they weaken the restriction of full encapsulation by allowing outgoing references while still preventing representation exposure from outside of the encapsulation. The work on ownership types emanated from some general principles for *Flexible Alias Protection* [20] and the use of dominator trees in structuring object graphs [22].

Ownership type systems establish a fixed per object ownership tree, and enforce a reference containment invariant, so that objects cannot be referenced from outside of their owner — an object owns its representation and any other external object wanting to access the representation must do so via the owner. Ownership types are parameterized by names of runtime objects, called *contexts* in the type system [10]. Contexts include all objects and a pre-defined context called world which is used to name the root of the ownership tree. The world context is in scope throughout the program. All root objects are created in the world context and all live objects are reachable from the root objects.

In defining ownership the first context parameter of a class is the owner of the object. An object's owner is fixed for its lifetime, thus naturally establishing an *ownership tree* in the heap. The rest of the context parameters are optional; they are used to type and reference the objects outside the current encapsulation, which is how ownership types free objects from being fully encapsulated, as in early approaches to alias protection.

Types are formed by binding the formal context parameters of a class. In order to declare a type for a reference, one must be able to name the owner that encapsulates the object. An encapsulation is protected from incoming references because the owners of objects inside the encapsulation cannot be named from the outside. The key mechanism is the use of variable this to name the current object (or context), which is different from object to object — it is impossible to name this in an object from outside of the object. Only objects inside the current object can name the this context, because the name of this can only be propagated as context arguments for objects owned by this object.

Since an object can only name its dominators (either direct or indirect owners) using formal context parameters, the pre-defined context world or the local context this, it can never declare a correct type for any object not owned by these contexts. In the following simple example, the private Data object is in the this context. Since it is impossible to name the this variable in a Personnel object from outside, it is impossible to give a correct type for the private Data object and reference it.

```
class Personnel<o> {
  Data<this> privateData;
  Data<this> getData() { return privateData; } }
```

We now highlight two problems with the standard ownership example of a linked list in which the linked nodes are protected within their list owner.

```
class List<o, d> {
  Node<this, o> head;
  Iterator<this, d> getIter() { return new Iterator<this, d>(head); } }

class Node<o, d> {
  Node<o, d> next;
  Data<d> data;
  Node(Node<o, d> next, Data<d> data) {
    this.next = next; this.data = data; } }

class Iterator<o, d> {
  Node<o, d> current;
  Iterator(Node<o, d> node) { current = node; }
  Data<d> element() { return current.data; }
  void next() { current = current.next; }
  void add(Data<d> data) {
    current.next = new Node<o, d>(current.next, data); } }

class Data<o> { void useMe(){ ... } }
```

A list object is implemented by a sequence of linked node objects. The node objects form the representation of the list object, in other words, they are owned by the list object. The owner of the node objects is the this context in the List class which refers to the current list object. The List class provides iterator objects to be used by the client to read the elements stored by the list or add new elements.

The first problem for iterators with ownership is well known. Iterator objects need to be able to reference the internal data representation of the list in order to traverse it efficiently. In ownership types, this requires that iterators are owned by the list, living within the list's internal representation. The problem is obvious — iterators cannot be referenced from outside of the list due to the encapsulation property. In the client code given below, `list` owns the iterator object returned by `list.getIter()`, but `iter` cannot be declared as `Iterator<list,o>`, because `list` is not a constant.

```
class Client<o> {
  void m() {
    List<this, o> list = new List<this, o>(); // OK
    Iterator<this, o> iter = list.getIter();  // ERROR, owner mismatch
    iter.add(new Data<o>());                  // OK
    iter.add(new Data<world>());     // ERROR, owner of Data mismatch
    iter.add(new Data<this>());      // ERROR, owner of Data mismatch
    iter.element().useMe(); } }               // OK
```

The second problem is a less well-known expressiveness problem due to the recursive nature of the `Node` class. All `Data` objects stored in the list must have the same type; in particular they must be owned by the same context. In the above example, the client can only add objects with type `Data<o>` into the list.

For the first problem with iterators, a number of solutions have been proposed (to be discussed in Section 5). Compared to these, our proposal is more flexible and somewhat less ad hoc. To solve the second problem, we employ a powerful mechanism which allows ownership contexts to be abstract or variant (that is, appearing as an abstraction with bounds) while still maintaining enough control on object access. The resulting type system is statically type checkable and more expressive than previous ownership type systems.

3   Variant Ownership Types

In this section, we give an informal overview of *variant ownership types* which are more flexible and expressive than ownership types. The two new concepts involved are the *accessibility context* and *context variance*.

3.1   The Accessibility Context

We separate the access permissions for an object from the definition of its class, by adding another context to ownership types (in addition to the normal context arguments) as an access modifier, which alone determines its accessibility. In comparison to conventional class-level field access modifiers, such as *public/protected/private* as used in Java and C++, our system provides instance-level object access modifiers that are dynamic contexts. This extra context is specified by the creator of the object in its creation type, and controls the accessibility of the object. Only objects which can name the access modifier have access permission. In the owners-as-dominators model, owners control access, but in our model, accessors do not need to have the owner in scope. For a given ownership hierarchy, our new approach has more flexibility, and strictly subsumes the owners-as-dominators model. In ownership types, if object l can reference object l' then l must be inside $owner(l')$. In our type system, we use a separate context $acc(l)$ to determine the accessibility of an object; if object l can reference object l' then l must be inside $acc(l')$. This is the *accessibility invariant* for our system.

A typical type consists of three parts: [access] Class⟨capabilities⟩ comprising a class name with a list of contexts. In a type, the capability list binds the formal parameters of the type's class definition to actual contexts; the access modifier context (the prefix in square brackets) restricts accessibility to objects inside the given context.

Class definitions are parameterized by formal contexts. These formal parameters, together with this and world, define the contexts that are available for types within the class. Note that a class definition does not have a formal parameter for denoting the accessibility of its instances; there is no need.

Access modifiers are independent from the definition of their objects, that is, the access modifier is an annotation on a type rather than a context parameter in the class definition. Note that, in our type system, the ownership tree is still built from the owner context (the first context argument of a type). The modifier does not affect the ownership tree, instead, it generalizes the strong containment invariant of ownership, allowing more general reference structures.

We could use access modifiers to provide various levels of protection on objects. When an object's access modifier is the world context, it can be considered as a public object which is accessible by any other object. When an object's access modifier is the owner of the defining object (i.e., the owner parameter of the current class), it is partially protected — it can be only used by those within the owner context. When an object's access modifier is the defining object (i.e., the this context), it is private to the defining object and cannot be accessed from outside the defining object.

In the following example, variable a has world accessibility and owner this. We interpret this dynamically. Variable a is a field of the current B object that may hold references to A objects; any such A object must be inside (owned by) the current B object this because the owner is given as this. Having world accessibility implies that the referenced object can be used by any other object via B's a field. The new expression creates a new A object owned by the current B object with world accessibility. Such an object may safely be assigned to the a field of the current object, but not to other B objects.

```
class A<o> { ... }

class B<o> {
  [world] A<this> a;
  m() { a = new [world]A<this>; } }
```

Access modifiers allow indirect exposure of internal states in a controlled manner. Objects in variable a can act as interface objects or proxy objects between the internal objects of the current B object and accessing objects on the outside. However, the type system ensures these interface objects cannot directly expose the internal objects to the accessing objects on the outside. This breaks the strong owners-as-dominators containment invariant enforced in ownership types while still retaining enough control on object access.

The access modifier of an object is decided by its creator and does not change over the object's lifetime. However, to allow a more flexible programming style, our type system allows the access modifier to be varied inwards. In the following example, the assignment a1 = a2 being OK implies that objects accessed via a2 can also be accessed via a1. This variance is safe because the set of objects that can access o is a subset of the objects that can access world. In other words, an object in variable a2 can become less accessible when it is assigned to variable a1; the converse does not apply. This is typical of access control mechanisms in security applications where it is safe to increase the security level by restricting the number of subjects that may access an object. We use this variance in our type system, and its usage is *implicit* (via binding) and very similar to the way type subsumption works in any typed language. As with subtyping, this variance of accessibility applies to language-level expressions; at runtime, an object's accessibility is fixed, and is determined by its creation type.

```
class C<o> {
  [o] A<o> a1;
  [world] A<o> a2;
  [this] A<o> a3;
  m() {
    a1 = a2;        // OK, o inside world
    a1 = a3;        // ERROR, o outside this
    a2 = a1;        // ERROR, world outside o
    a2 = a3;        // ERROR, world outside this
    a3 = a1;        // OK, this inside o
    a3 = a2; } }    // OK, this inside world
```

When the owner context and access modifier are the same, the variant ownership type [o] A<o> is the same as the A<o> in ownership types. Hence our model with modifiers subsumes the owners-as-dominators model. The following example illustrates how separating access from the owner allows us to achieve different kinds of access protection.

```
class D<o> {
  [o] A<o> a1;         // partly protected
  [this] A<this> a2;// encapsulated
  [this] A<o> a3;      // encapsulated, but field is writable from outside
  [o] A<this> a4; } // not encapsulated, field is read-only from outside

class E<o> {
  [o] D<o> d;
  m() {
    [o]A<o> x = d.a1;   // OK to read the reference
    d.a1 = x;           // OK to update the field

    ... = d.a2;         // ERROR to read, cannot name context inside
                        // d.a2's access modifier ('this' in d)
```

```
d.a2 = ...  // ERROR to write, cannot name d.a2's owner ('this' in d)

... = d.a3; // ERROR to read, cannot name context inside 'this' in d
d.a3 = new [o]A<o>; // OK to write, 'this' in d inside o

[o]A<*> y = d.a4;   // OK to read, the owner of d.a4 is abstracted
d.a4 = ... } }      // ERROR to write, cannot name d.a4's owner
```

When an object is encapsulated by its defining object this, it is not accessible from outside. The reference in field a3 is protected from being accessed from outside of the object. However a client can assign the field itself with an expression of type [p]A<o> where this is known to be inside p (= o in the example). This reference does not break the accessibility invariant because the modifier is variant inwards (from p to this). Such accessibility restrictions are useful but cannot be expressed by any of the existing ownership type systems which use an invariant owner to control access.

In contrast to a3, the field a4 can be read from outside (via context abstraction, which will be discussed in the next subsection) but is not updatable from outside of the object. The field a4 can be considered as an object-level (instead of traditional class-level) read-only field — it is not updatable by a client from outside, but can be updated from objects within the current context. Again, this kind of object-level read-only restriction is not supported by previous ownership type systems.

3.2 Context Variance

Type variance is a recently developed approach for increasing code genericity in typed programming languages. Use-site variance on parametric types [15] has been implemented in the new version of Java 1.5 with wildcards [25]. Our type system adds variance to context arguments rather than type arguments. By allowing context variance, not only do we achieve code genericity, but we also allow a much more flexible reference structure than the original ownership types by removing the naming restriction of object contexts. Technically, use-site variance is a form of existential types, in our case, existential contexts. The technical detail and formalization are discussed in Section 4. Here we introduce the context variances informally with examples.

Programmers may *explicitly* declare the variance of context arguments wherever they form types. For a concrete context K, we write K+ for inward variance which means any context inside K, K− for outward variance which means any context outside K and ∗ for full abstraction which means any context. Recall that concrete contexts are those of formal context parameters, the current context this and the world context. Figure 1 shows these variances for a given context K.

The following subtype relations show the variant ownership types with two contexts K and K′ where K dominates K′ (domination is the reflexive and transitive relation of ownership). For simplicity, access modifiers are all defaulted (to the world context) because they are orthogonal to the context argument variance.

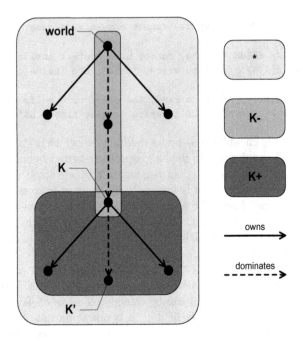

Fig. 1. Context Variances

$$C\langle K'\rangle <: C\langle K'+\rangle <: C\langle K+\rangle <: C\langle *\rangle$$
$$C\langle K\rangle <: C\langle K-\rangle <: C\langle K'-\rangle <: C\langle *\rangle$$

Variance on context arguments is not to be confused with variance on the access modifier which is variant implicitly. Moreover, access modifiers can never be abstracted while argument variances are a form of context abstraction. For convenience, when all context arguments are fully abstract, we will elide all the * contexts. For instance, in the following example, [o] A is short for [o] A<*>. Also because we use the world context as default access modifier, A is short for [world] A<*>.

```
class F<o> { [o] A a; }
```

```
class G<o> {
  F<this> f1;              // invariant on context argument
  F<*> f2;                 // fully abstract on context argument
  F<this+> f3;             // inward variance on context argument
  F<this-> f4;             // outward variance on context argument
  A<this> a;
  m() {
    [this] A x = f1.a;     // OK to read
    f1.a = x;              // OK to write

    ... = f2.a;// ERROR, cannot name context inside f2.a's
               // access modifier (which is abstracted)
```

```
f2.a = ... // ERROR (in most cases),
           // cannot name context outside f2.a's access modifier
f2.a = a;  // OK! the only exception, world outside any context!

...= f3.a;// ERROR, cannot name context inside f3.a's access modifier
f3.a = new [o]A<o>();   // OK, f3.a's access modifier inside o

x = f4.a;  // OK, 'this' inside f4.a's access modifier
f4.a = ... // ERROR (in most cases),
           // cannot name context outside f4.a's access modifier
f4.a = a; } } // OK! the only exception, world outside any context!
```

The choice of variance is made when types are used. Programmers can use any combination of invariance, inward/outward variance or full abstraction to express context arguments in a type. Invariant contexts are most usable but least flexible because one must be able to name the concrete context. `f1` is most usable, because `f1.a` is both readable and writable; but `f1` is less flexible because it can only be accessed from within the current context. Fully abstract contexts are most flexible but least usable because all information about the context is hidden; `f2` is least usable because `f2.a` is neither readable nor writable (except for the special case with the world context as shown in the example). The type of `f2.a` is `[?]A` where the `?` denotes an unknown context; the only thing we know about `?` is that it is inside world. Unknown contexts are not for programmer use, but are used in our semantics. They are simply shorthand for an anonymous context with given variance which is existentially quantified. However, the combinations of fully abstract and invariant context arguments are useful as we are about to see in revisiting the list example. Inward/outward variant contexts give a choice between invariance and full abstraction where some information of the context is available to give programmers just enough information they need to use the context, as we see with `f3.a` and `f4.a`. Within class `G` their types are `[this+?]A` (respectively `[this-?]A`) where the unknown contexts are bounded inside (respectively outside) this.

We extend the above example with some more complicated cases of variance which involve nested variances and mixed inward/outward variances. The type system is able to derive the ordering information in the presence of nested variances. Some of the types involved are:

   h1.f1 : F<o+?+>   and   h1.f1.a : [o+?+?]A<*>

we can derive that o+?+? is inside o. Also we find:

   h1.f2 : F<o+?->   and   h2.f1 : F<o-?+>

The variance o+?- contains contexts o and world but not this. Similarly o-?+ contains o and this but not world.

```
class H<o> {
  F<o+> f1;
  F<o-> f2; }
```

```
class I<o> {
  H<o+> h1;
  H<o-> h2;
  [o] A a;
  m() {
    h1.f1.a = a;              // OK, h1.f1.a's access modifier inside o
    a = h2.f2.a;              // OK, o inside h2.f2.a's access modifier

    h1.f2 = new F<o>;         // OK
    h1.f2 = new F<world>;     // OK
    h1.f2 = new F<this>;      // ERROR
    h2.f1 = new F<o>;         // OK
    h2.f1 = new F<this>;      // OK
    h2.f1 = new F<world>; } } // ERROR
```

Now we are in a good position to revisit the list example we discussed in the previous section.

3.3   The List Example: Revisited

We revisit the list example with a solution to the two problems considered previously: iterator accessibility and fixed ownership of data.

```
class List<o, d> {
  [this] Node<this, d> head;
  [o]Iterator<this, d> getIter(){return new [o]Iterator<this, d>(head);}}

class Node<o, d> {
  [o] Node<o, d> next;
  [d] Data data;
  Node([o]Node<o, d> next, [d]Data data) {
    this.next = next;
    this.data = data; } }

class Iterator<o, d> {
  [o] Node<o, d> current;
  Iterator([o]Node<o, d> Node) { current = Node; }
  [d]Data element() { return current.data; }
  void next() { current = current.next; }
  void add([d]Data data) {
    current.next = new Node<o, d>(current.next, data); } }

class Data<o> { void useMe(){ ... } }
```

The implementation of the List and Iterator classes is almost the same as for ownership types except the type of iterators created by the list has the access modifier the same to the owner of the list, which essentially means anyone who can name the owner of the list is allowed to access its iterators. By creating iterators with accessibility as o, the list object authorizes the iterators to act as its interface objects and to be used by the client to manipulate on itself.

However, the list's representation (that is, the `Node` objects) is always protected from the client and never exposed to the outside directly. To access the nodes, the client must use either the list itself or the iterators created by the list.

In the `Node` class, the type of `data` field is `[d] Data`. As we have mentioned, this is shorthand for `[d] Data<*>` where the owner of these `Data` objects is abstract. The `Node` class is a recursive structure so all the node objects must have the same type. However, with our owner abstraction, each node may contain data objects owned by different contexts as shown in the client program.

```
class Client<o> {
  void m() {
    List<this, o> list = new List<this, o>();   // OK
    [this]Iterator<*, o> iter = list.getIter(); // OK
    iter.add(new [o]Data<o>());       // OK, o inside o, o matches *
    iter.add(new Data<world>());      // OK, o inside world, world matches *
    iter.add(new [this]Data<this>());            // ERROR, o outside this!
    iter.add(new [o]Data<this>()); // OK, o is inside o, this matches *
    iter.element().useMe();                      // OK
    iter.current = ... } }        // ERROR, access modifier abstracted
```

The client creates the list object as usual, but in order to obtain a reference to iterator objects returned by the list, it must declare a type which abstracts the owner of iterators (which is the list object, see the `List` class). However, in the type of iterators, the second context argument remains concrete, which is necessary in order to reference data objects returned by iterators. Moreover, with context variance, now the client can add data objects owned by various contexts into the list. Objects with type `[this] Data<this>` cannot be added into the list because the access modifier is variant outwards (from `this` to `o`) which is not sound hence not permitted by the type system. Note that the type system guarantees iterators cannot expose the node objects to the client.

4   The Formal Language

In this section, we formalize variant ownership types in a core language based on *Featherweight Java* [14] extended with field assignment. We incorporate contexts and formalize the main properties.

4.1   Syntax

The abstract syntax for the source languages is given in Table 1. The metavariable T ranges over types; N ranges over nameable contexts (or concrete contexts); K ranges over contexts; V ranges over context variances; L ranges over class definitions; M ranges over method definitions; e ranges over expressions; C, D range over class names; f and m range over field names and method names respectively; X, Y range over formal context parameters; and x ranges over variable names with this as a special variable name to reference the target object for the current call. The overbar is used for a sequence of constructs; for example,

Table 1. Abstract Syntax for Source Language

T	::= [N] C⟨$\overline{V}$⟩	types
N	::= X | this | world	nameable contexts
K	::= N	contexts
V	::= K | K+ | K− | ∗	context variances
L	::= class C⟨$\overline{X}$⟩ ⊲ D⟨$\overline{Y}$⟩ {$\overline{T}$ $\overline{f}$; $\overline{M}$}	classes
M	::= T m($\overline{T}$ $\overline{x}$) {e}	methods
e	::=	terms
	x	variable
	| new T($\overline{e}$)	new
	| e.f	select
	| e.m($\overline{e}$)	call
	| e.f = e	assignment

Table 2. Extended Syntax for Type System

K	::= ... | K+? | K−? | ?	contexts
P	::= $\overline{L}$ e	programs
Γ	::= • | Γ, X ⪯ Y | Γ, x : T	environments

$\overline{e}$ is used for a possibly empty sequence $e_1..e_n$, $\overline{T}$ $\overline{x}$ stands for a possibly empty sequence of pairs $T_1 x_1..T_n x_n$, etc. In the class production, inheritance ⊲ D⟨$\overline{Y}$⟩ is optional because our type system does not need a top type.

The syntax distinguishes between concrete (nameable) contexts N and those contexts K allowing the abstract contexts. Table 2 shows the extended syntax used by the type system, which is not accessible by programmers. Abstract contexts K+?, K−? and ? correspond to context variances K+, K− and ∗. The difference between K+ and K+? is that K+ means all contexts inside K while K+? is one context in the set of K+. Actually, K+? is a bounded existential context whose name is anonymous; but we do know it is inside K. The unbound existential context ? is an arbitrary context; we know nothing about it (except it is inside the upper bound context world in the context hierarchy). Figure 2 shows the concept of existential contexts. A program P is a pair consisting of a fixed sequence of class definitions and an expression e which is the body of the main method. The environment Γ may contain the types of variables and domination relations between formal context parameters.

4.2   Static Semantics

The same syntactical abbreviation for sequences is used in the typing rules. A sequence of judgements can be simplified with an overbar on the argument, such as Γ; N ⊢ $\overline{T}$. Substitution $[\overline{V}/\overline{X}]$T is used to substitute $\overline{V}$ for $\overline{X}$ in T; this substitution also requires $|\overline{V}| = |\overline{X}|$. Sometimes we use implications, denoted by ⟹ , to avoid repeating rules with similar structure. Other symbols used in the type system are: • means empty set; _ and ... match any single or multiple things; 1..n means an enumeration from 1 to n.

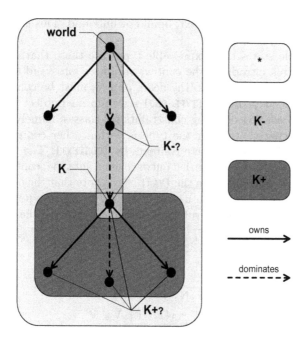

Fig. 2. Existential Contexts

In ownership type systems the contexts used to form types are actual runtime objects. In order to prove the desired dynamic properties, we need to incorporate the bindings of context parameters into the type system. Typically, the expression judgement $\Gamma; N \vdash e : T$ holds for the current context N. The context N is bound to the current object (the target object of current call); in the static semantics N is always bound to the variable this or world for the top-level program expression, while in the dynamic semantics N is bound to the location of the actual object in heap or world. Note that the bindings for all context parameters in the current environment can be determined from the type of N at runtime. To simplify the dynamic semantics we will annotate locations with their object type.

[VAR-ANY] $\dfrac{}{\Gamma \vdash V \subseteq *}$ [VAR-IN'] $\dfrac{\Gamma \vdash K \preceq K'}{\Gamma \vdash K+ \subseteq K'+}$

[VAR-CRT] $\dfrac{}{\Gamma \vdash N \subseteq N}$ [VAR-OUT'] $\dfrac{\Gamma \vdash K' \preceq K}{\Gamma \vdash K- \subseteq K'-}$

[VAR-IN] $\dfrac{}{\Gamma \vdash K+_? \subseteq K+}$ [VAR-TRA] $\dfrac{\Gamma \vdash V \subseteq V'' \quad \Gamma \vdash V'' \subseteq V'}{\Gamma \vdash V \subseteq V'}$

[VAR-OUT] $\dfrac{}{\Gamma \vdash K-_? \subseteq K-}$

The [VAR] rules define the valid context variances. Since context variances represent sets of contexts, the [VAR] rules really just define the subset relations between them. Contexts can be considered as singleton sets containing only one element. The only rule that can be applied to the unbound existential context ? is the [VAR-ANY] rule. By inspection it is also clear that we cannot have anything as a subset of any existential context, bound or unbound. This is a key property of the system.

The [TYPE] rule states that expressible types are those that are supertypes of object types; this introduces the context variances into valid types. In order to maintain an ownership tree on the heap, objects must be constructed using new with concrete contexts. By [TYPE-OBJ] a well-formed object type must satisfy the standard context ordering constraints for classes, namely that the first argument, the owner context for the type is within other context arguments; all contexts must be valid concrete contexts by [CONTEXT]. The [SUB-VAR] rule allows the access modifier to be varied outwards in a subtype; context arguments can also be narrowed according to the [VAR] rules. Note that the class definitions are global so that we simply use class $C[\overline{X}] \lhd D[\overline{Y}]$ ... to hypothesize a valid class definition in the [SUB-EXT] rule and some other rules in the type system.

$$[\text{TYPE}] \quad \frac{\Gamma; N \vdash_o T_o \quad \Gamma \vdash T_o <: T}{\Gamma; N \vdash T}$$

$$[\text{TYP-OBJ}] \quad \frac{|\overline{N}| = \text{arity}(C) \quad \Gamma; N \vdash N', \overline{N} \quad \Gamma \vdash N_1 \preceq \overline{N}}{\Gamma; N \vdash_o [N'] \, C\langle \overline{N} \rangle}$$

$$[\text{SUB-VAR}] \quad \frac{\Gamma \vdash N' \preceq N \quad \Gamma \vdash \overline{V} \subseteq \overline{V'}}{\Gamma \vdash [N] \, C\langle \overline{V} \rangle <: [N'] \, C\langle \overline{V'} \rangle}$$

$$[\text{SUB-EXT}] \quad \frac{\text{class } C\langle \overline{X} \rangle \lhd D\langle \overline{Y} \rangle \ ... \quad T = [N] \, D\langle [\overline{V}/\overline{X}]\overline{Y} \rangle \quad \Gamma \vdash T <: T}{\Gamma \vdash [N] \, C\langle \overline{V} \rangle <: T}$$

Our subtyping rules need to handle context abstraction correctly, and avoid breaking accessibility constraints through assignments to fields, or method parameters, with some of their types' contexts hidden. The main idea of our system is to substitute existential contexts for any variant contexts in the type of an object (via an opening process as we see later) when we determine the types of its fields/methods, and to prohibit binding to fields or method parameters which include existential contexts in their types. Let us use the phrase *existential type* to describe a type containing an existential context. By guaranteeing that existential types cannot be supertypes, we achieve the desired prohibition (note the subtyping premise in all [EXP] rules involve binding). We now explain how the [SUB] rules achieve this. We cannot use [SUB-VAR] to find an existential supertype because its premise would require there to be some subset of an existential context, which the [VAR] rules preclude. It follows that no existential type can be a subtype of itself, because the alternative [SUB-EXT] is not applicable for the reflexive case. Finally any type T judged to be a supertype by [SUB-EXT] must be a supertype of itself according to the last premise of the rule. It follows that no type judged to be a supertype by these rules can contain an existential context.

Legal concrete contexts include formal context parameters, the current context this and the world context. Recall that the current context N, in the static semantics, is always bound to this or world. Context ordering rules define the domination relation between contexts. Domination is the reflexive and transitive closure of ownership. Direct ownership is captured in the [ORD-OWN] rule by looking up the owner from the type of the context via [LKP-OWN] (appearing at the end of this subsection). The only direct ownership relation available in the static semantics is for the this context; it is owned by the first context parameter of its type (see [LKP-OWN] and [LKP-OWN']). The this context is the only context that is given a static type; this is both a context parameter and a variable naming the current object. At runtime, this is bound to the location of the target object. The ordering on existential contexts is not surprising; $? \preceq$ world by the [ORD-WLD] rule, but no other ordering is derivable for $?$.

$$[\text{CTX-LCL}] \quad \frac{\Gamma; N \vdash N : [N''] \, C\langle \overline{N} \rangle \qquad N' \in \overline{N} \cup \{N\}}{\Gamma; N \vdash N'}$$

$$[\text{CTX-WLD}] \quad \frac{}{\Gamma; N \vdash \text{world}}$$

$$[\text{ORD-OWN}] \quad \frac{}{\Gamma \vdash N \preceq \text{owner}_\Gamma(N)}$$

$$[\text{ORD-TRA}] \quad \frac{\Gamma \vdash K \preceq K'' \qquad \Gamma \vdash K'' \preceq K'}{\Gamma \vdash K \preceq K'}$$

$$[\text{ORD-RFL}] \quad \frac{}{\Gamma \vdash N \preceq N}$$

$$[\text{ORD-ENV}] \quad \frac{X \preceq X' \in \Gamma}{\Gamma \vdash X \preceq X'}$$

$$[\text{ORD-WLD}] \quad \frac{}{\Gamma \vdash K \preceq \text{world}}$$

$$[\text{ORD-IN}] \quad \frac{}{\Gamma \vdash K+_? \preceq K}$$

$$[\text{ORD-OUT}] \quad \frac{}{\Gamma \vdash K \preceq K-_?}$$

The [PROGRAM] rule simply checks the expression in the main method; world is the only concrete context available at this level.

$$[\text{PROGRAM}] \quad \frac{\vdash \overline{L} \qquad \bullet; \text{world} \vdash e : T}{\vdash \overline{L} \, e}$$

Class well-formedness is checked in the [CLASS] rule. Each class defines its own environment formed from its formal contexts and the type of this object. In the original ownership type system, the owner parameter X_1 had to be dominated by all other context parameters, we follow the same convention here. Note that the only direct ownership relation known to the class, that is this $\preceq X_1$, is not included in the class environment; instead we capture it in the [ORD-OWN] rule to make it generally derivable, in particular for its use in the dynamic semantics. Furthermore, field types and methods need to be checked for well-formedness.

If a class is extended from another then the supertype needs to be valid in the environment formed from the class, and the owner of the supertype must be the same as the owner of the current context. Not surprisingly, new field names need to be distinguished from the field names used in the supertype. Moreover, the supertype is bound to a super variable in the environment that is used only by the [METHOD] rule to check the correctness of overridden methods. We implicitly assume the access modifier for the types of both this and super variables is the default access modifier world.

$$[\text{CLASS}] \quad \frac{\Gamma = X_1 \preceq \overline{X}, \text{this} : C\langle \overline{X} \rangle, \text{super} : D\langle \overline{Y} \rangle \qquad X_1 = Y_1 \qquad \Gamma; \text{this} \vdash D\langle \overline{Y} \rangle, \overline{T} \quad \Gamma \vdash \overline{M} \qquad \overline{f} \cap \text{dom}(\text{fields}(D\langle \overline{Y} \rangle, \text{this})) = \bullet}{\vdash \text{class } C\langle \overline{X} \rangle \lhd D\langle \overline{Y} \rangle \, \{\overline{T} \, \overline{f}; \, \overline{M}\}}$$

In the [METHOD] rule, all types are checked for well-formedness and a new environment is constructed by extending the class environment with method parameters and their types. The method body is checked in the new environment and the current context this. Methods can be overridden in the traditional way — covariant on the return type and contravariant on the types of method parameters.

$$\text{[METHOD]} \quad \frac{\begin{array}{c}\Gamma; \text{this} \vdash \mathsf{T}, \overline{\mathsf{T}} \quad \Gamma, \overline{\mathsf{x}} : \overline{\mathsf{T}}; \text{this} \vdash e : \mathsf{T}'' \quad \Gamma \vdash \mathsf{T}'' <: \mathsf{T} \\ \text{method}(\Gamma(\text{super}), \text{this}, m) = \mathsf{T}' \; m(\overline{\mathsf{T}'} \; \_)... \implies \\ \Gamma \vdash \mathsf{T} <: \mathsf{T}' \quad \Gamma \vdash \overline{\mathsf{T}'} <: \overline{\mathsf{T}} \end{array}}{\Gamma \vdash \mathsf{T} \; m(\overline{\mathsf{T}} \; \overline{\mathsf{x}}) \; \{e\}}$$

In the [EXP-NEW] rule, new objects are created using concrete contexts (according to [TYP-OBJ]) in order to establish an ownership tree in heap. For simplicity, we force all the fields of the object to be initialized at creation time. The internal context of the newly created object is an anonymous context inside its owner. The [EXP-SEL] and [EXP-CAL] rules lookup the types of fields or methods for the target expression e. They need to decide if they are able to name the internal context of e by using the auxiliary function $\text{rep}_\mathsf{T}()$ which simply checks if e is the current context (i.e. this). If e is the current context then it is used as the internal context of e in the lookup functions fields() and method(); otherwise, an anonymous context is used instead thus hiding the internal context (see [LKP-REP]).

All rules for expressions that involve some form of binding, such as [EXP-ASS], [EXP-CAL] and [EXP-NEW], use a subtype constraint to ensure that the type of the target of the binding does not involve any existential contexts (recall the [SUB] rules). A more conventional formulation of these rules would shift the subtype check onto a subsumption rule, but that cannot be done here — we need to use distinct types for the source and target of the binding in the rules.

$$\text{[EXP-VAR]} \quad \frac{\Gamma(x) = \mathsf{T}}{\Gamma; \mathsf{N} \vdash x : \mathsf{T}}$$

$$\text{[EXP-NEW]} \quad \frac{\Gamma; \mathsf{N} \vdash_o \mathsf{T} \quad \Gamma; \mathsf{N} \vdash \overline{e} : \overline{\mathsf{T}'} \quad \text{fields}(\mathsf{T}, \text{owner}(\mathsf{T})+_?) = \overline{f} \; \overline{\mathsf{T}} \quad \Gamma \vdash \overline{\mathsf{T}'} <: \overline{\mathsf{T}}}{\Gamma; \mathsf{N} \vdash \text{new} \; \mathsf{T}(\overline{e}) : \mathsf{T}}$$

$$\text{[EXP-SEL]} \quad \frac{\Gamma; \mathsf{N} \vdash e : \mathsf{T} \quad \text{fields}(\mathsf{T}, \text{rep}_\mathsf{T}(\mathsf{N}, e))(f) = \mathsf{T}'}{\Gamma; \mathsf{N} \vdash e.f : \mathsf{T}'}$$

$$\text{[EXP-ASS]} \quad \frac{\Gamma; \mathsf{N} \vdash e' : \mathsf{T}' \quad \Gamma; \mathsf{N} \vdash e.f : \mathsf{T} \quad \Gamma \vdash \mathsf{T}' <: \mathsf{T}}{\Gamma; \mathsf{N} \vdash e.f = e' : \mathsf{T}'}$$

$$\text{[EXP-CAL]} \quad \frac{\begin{array}{c}\Gamma; \mathsf{N} \vdash e : \mathsf{T} \quad \Gamma; \mathsf{N} \vdash \overline{e} : \overline{\mathsf{T}} \quad \Gamma \vdash \overline{\mathsf{T}} <: \overline{\mathsf{T}'} \\ \text{method}(\mathsf{T}, \text{rep}_\mathsf{T}(\mathsf{N}, e), m) = \mathsf{T}' \; m(\overline{\mathsf{T}'} \; \_)... \end{array}}{\Gamma; \mathsf{N} \vdash e.m(\overline{e}) : \mathsf{T}'}$$

When accessing the fields or methods via an expression e, we determine their types, given the type of e. These in turn use [LKP-DEF] to find a correct substitution for parameters of T's class. The opening process requires the replacement of context variances with corresponding existential contexts. This process is similar to the usual unpack/open for conventional existential types. The major difference is that our open process does not introduce fresh context variables into the current environment. Instead, we keep the existential context anonymous by annotating context variances with a special symbol ?. This technique not only eliminates the need for the pack/close operation (since anonymous contexts do not have to be bound to an environment, they naturally become global), but also makes the proofs simpler. Moreover, this technique is capable of handling complicated variances which would need nested open/close operations.

$$[\text{LKP-DEF}] \quad \frac{L = \text{class } C\langle \overline{X}\rangle \ \ldots \qquad \text{open}(T) = C\langle \overline{K}\rangle}{\text{defin}(T, K) = [\overline{K}/\overline{X}, K/\textbf{this}]L}$$

$$[\text{LKP-FLD}] \quad \frac{\text{defin}(T, K) = \text{class } \ldots \lhd T' \ \{\overline{T} \ \overline{f}; \ \ldots \}}{\text{fields}(T, K) = \overline{f} \ \overline{T}, \text{fields}(T', K)}$$

$$[\text{LKP-MTH}] \quad \frac{\text{defin}(T, K) = \text{class } \ldots \ T' \ m(\overline{T} \ \overline{x})\{e\} \ \ldots}{\text{method}(T, K, m) = T' \ m(\overline{T} \ \overline{x})\{e\}}$$

$$[\text{LKP-MTH}'] \quad \frac{\text{defin}(T, K) = \text{class } \ldots \lhd T' \ \{ \ \ldots \ ; \overline{M}\} \qquad m \notin \overline{M}}{\text{method}(T, K, m) = \text{method}(T', K, m)}$$

$$[\text{LKP-ARI}] \quad \frac{\text{class } C\langle \overline{X}\rangle \ \ldots}{\text{arity}(C) = |\overline{X}|}$$

$$[\text{OPEN}] \quad \frac{}{\text{open}(C\langle \overline{K}\rangle) = C\langle \overline{K}\rangle}$$

$$[\text{OPN-ANY}] \quad \frac{}{\text{open}(C\langle \overline{K}, *, \overline{V}\rangle) = \text{open}(C\langle \overline{K}, ?, \overline{V}\rangle)}$$

$$[\text{OPN-IN}] \quad \frac{}{\text{open}(C\langle \overline{K}, K+, \overline{V}\rangle) = \text{open}(C\langle \overline{K}, K+_?, \overline{V}\rangle)}$$

$$[\text{OPN-OUT}] \quad \frac{}{\text{open}(C\langle \overline{K}, K-, \overline{V}\rangle) = \text{open}(C\langle \overline{K}, K-_?, \overline{V}\rangle)}$$

$$[\text{LKP-OWN}] \quad \frac{\Gamma; \bullet \vdash e : T}{\text{owner}_\Gamma(e) = \text{owner}(T)}$$

$$[\text{LKP-OWN}'] \quad \frac{}{\text{owner}([N] \ C\langle \overline{V}\rangle) = V_1}$$

$$[\text{LKP-REP}] \quad \frac{e \neq N}{\text{rep}_T(N, e) = \text{owner}(T)+_?}$$

$$[\text{LKP-REP}'] \quad \frac{}{\text{rep}_T(N, N) = N}$$

4.3 Dynamic Semantics and Properties

The extended syntax and features used by the dynamic semantics are given in Table 3. The ownership information is usually only used in static type checking. However, in order to obtain a formal proof for some of the key properties of the type system, we need to establish a connection between the static and dynamic semantics by including ownership relations in the dynamic semantics. Terms and contexts are extended with locations, which are annotated with the type of object they refer to. A heap is a mapping from locations to objects; an object maps fields to locations. Object creation extends the heap, introducing a new location which is then forever associated with its object; field assignment updates an object but does not directly affect the heap.

Table 3. Extended Syntax with Dynamic Features

l, l_T		typed locations
e	$::= ... \mid l$	terms
N	$::= ... \mid l$	nameable contexts
o	$::= \overline{f} \mapsto \overline{l}$	objects
H	$::= \overline{l} \mapsto \overline{o}$	heaps

There are also a few auxiliary definitions to help formalize the properties. Locations are annotated with their type. From this we can lookup the accessibility context for an object stored at that location. The objects in the heap form an ownership tree just as in other ownership type systems. However, the reference containment invariant is different. An object needs to be inside another object's modifier in order to access it.

[EXP-LOC]
$$\Gamma; N \vdash l_T : T$$

[LKP-ACC]
$$\frac{\bullet; \bullet \vdash l : [N]\ C\langle \overline{V} \rangle}{acc(l) = N}$$

[HEAP]
$$\frac{\forall l \in dom(H) \cdot \bullet; \bullet \vdash l : T \qquad H(l) = \overline{f} \mapsto \overline{l} \qquad fields(T, l) = \overline{f}\ \overline{T} \qquad \bullet; \bullet \vdash \overline{l} : \overline{T'} \qquad \Gamma \vdash \overline{T'} <: \overline{T} \qquad \bullet \vdash l \preceq acc(\overline{l})}{\vdash H}$$

The reduction rules are defined in a big step fashion. The context N in $\Downarrow_N$ refers to the target object of the current call, or the world context in case of the main method. At the time of method invocation in [RED-CAL], the target object of the body of the invoked method is l. Notice that the variable this is not substituted in $[\overline{l}/\overline{x}]e'$. Instead, this is replaced by l in the substitution provided by the lookup function $method(T, l, m)$.

[EXECUTION]
$$\frac{\bullet; e \Downarrow_{world} H; l}{\overline{L}\ e \Downarrow l}$$

[RED-CAL]
$$\frac{H; e \Downarrow_N H'; l \qquad H'; \overline{e} \Downarrow_N H''; \overline{l} \qquad \bullet; N \vdash l : T \qquad method(T, l, m) = ...(\_\ \overline{x})\{e'\} \qquad H''; [\overline{l}/\overline{x}]e' \Downarrow_l H'''; l'}{H; e.m(\overline{e}) \Downarrow_N H'''; l'}$$

[RED-NEW]
$$\frac{H; \overline{e} \Downarrow_N H'; \overline{l} \qquad l_T \notin dom(H') \qquad \overline{f} = dom(fields(T, l_T)) \qquad H'' = H', l_T \mapsto \{\overline{f} \mapsto \overline{l}\}}{H; new\ T(\overline{e}) \Downarrow_N H''; l_T}$$

[RED-ASS]
$$\frac{H; e \Downarrow_N H'; l \qquad H'; e' \Downarrow_N H''; l'}{H; e.f = e' \Downarrow_N H''[l \mapsto H''(l)[f \mapsto l']]; l'}$$

[RED-SEL]
$$\frac{H; e \Downarrow_N H'; l}{H; e.f \Downarrow_N H'; H'(l)(f)}$$

Finally we formalize some of the key properties of the type system. We present a standard subject reduction result in Theorem 1, together with a statement that goodness of a heap is invariant through expression reductions. This implies that the heap invariants are maintained through program execution.

Theorem 1 (Subject Reduction). *Given* $\vdash P$ *and* $\vdash H$, *if* $\bullet; N \vdash e : T$ *and* $H; e \Downarrow_N H'; l$ *then* $\bullet; N \vdash l : T'$ *for some* T' *such that* $\bullet \vdash T' <: T$ *and* $\vdash H'$.

Proof. The proof proceeds by induction on the form of $H; e \Downarrow_N H'; l$. Notice the heap needs to be well-formed over reduction to maintain the accessibility invariant.

Theorem 2 is the accessibility invariant enforced by the type system, which is proved as part of Theorem 1.

Theorem 2 (Accessibility Invariant). *Given* $\vdash P$ *and* $\vdash H$, *if* $(f \mapsto l') \in H(l)$ *then* $\bullet \vdash l \preceq acc(l')$.

Proof. This property is enforced by the [HEAP] rule and proved in Theorem 1.

5 Discussion and Related Work

Object encapsulation enforces a separation between the internal state of an object, and external dependencies. Ownership types achieve object encapsulation by establishing an object ownership tree, and in the owners-as-dominators model, prevent object references from breaching the encapsulated state. Ownership types use the ability to name objects as owners, to permit access to the objects they own. Ownership types can be considered as an access control system where other objects are permitted to access an object if they can name all of its context arguments, including its owner. The reference capability of an object is determined by its actual context arguments; these are used by the object as permissions for accessing other objects. In ownership types an object's accessibility and capability are essentially the same thing — as determined by the actual context arguments of the object's ownership type.

In this paper, we have separated accessibility and capability by introducing the concept of access modifier. The capability of an object remains the same as in ownership types, although now the context arguments can be abstract or variant from the site of use. However accessibility to the object now requires the ability of other objects to name its access modifier. Moreover, to completely free accessibility from capability, the access modifier is not declared in the object's class definition, that is, it is not part of its formal capability. Accessibility to an object is therefore independent of the reference capability of the object. The access context is the only context that must be named in order to access the object; this yields a much more flexible access control policy. Note that the access modifier cannot be abstracted — it must be named to gain access. The capability (context arguments) can be abstract or variant to express less rigid reference structures as we have seen from the examples. Moreover, an object's accessibility also implies its lifetime. The separation of accessibility from capability naturally means an object's lifetime is independent from its capability, but solely dependent on its accessibility.

The soundness of our approach lies in the fact that an object can only be accessible to those objects created (directly or indirectly) by the owner of the object. This is because the owner's internal context can only be named from within the owner. This highlights the role of the creator — only the creator can authorize the created objects to access its own representation by defining their accessibility and capability appropriately.

Obviously, our type system subsumes ownership types; ownership types are special cases of our type system where the access modifier is the same as the owner context and no context argument is abstracted. Moreover, the techniques used in our type system may be applicable in other similar type systems for more flexibility and expressiveness, such as Effective Ownership [17], Acyclic Types [16] and Ownership Domains [1].

Aldrich and Chambers noted that ownership types cannot express the event callback design pattern [1]. Typically, a callback object is created by a listener object to observe some event. In the event, the callback object is invoked and will notify the listener object. Callback objects share some of the problems of iterators. The problem occurs when the callback object needs to directly mutate the listener's internal representation rather than use the listener's interface. The callback problem does not have such a serious performance issue as iterators do. The issue here is really about adding some flexibility to the callback classes. For example, instead of adding more methods (to be called by callback objects in different events) into the listener class, each callback class may implement its own code to mutate its listener. In our system, callback objects can be expressed in exactly the same way as iterators — we may simply promote the access modifier (permitted by the listener object) of callback objects high enough in the ownership hierarchy so that they can be named by the user of the callback objects.

Syntactic overhead for our types is that of ownership types plus an extra access modifier for each type. As we have seen, with carefully selected defaults type annotations can be reduced significantly. For instance, access modifiers can be omitted for globally accessible objects; abstract contexts can be omitted completely. Moreover, the ideas of *Generic Ownership* [21] can also be employed here to reduce the amount of type annotations in the presence of class type parameters.

As for ownership types, our type system allows separate compilation. It is statically checkable and does not require any runtime support. Our dynamic semantics can easily handle typecasting with runtime checks because it incorporates full owner information. However, in practice, the overhead for having owner information available at runtime may be significant for systems with a large number of small objects because each object will have two extra fields to identify its owner and access contexts. In security sensitive applications, this cost may well be worthwhile.

5.1   Related Work

Ownership Type Systems Without Owners-As-Dominators. There have been a number of proposals made to improve the expressiveness of ownership types. Some of them tend to break the strong owners-as-dominators encapsulation of ownership types. Some of them tend to retain the owners-as-dominators encapsulation by using harmless cross-encapsulation references. We will discuss each of them individually.

Most proposals to break strong encapsulation of owners-as-dominators are essentially methods to increase nameability of internal contexts. Our proposal is also an owners-as-dominators encapsulation breaking technique. The difference is that we do not expose internal names, but use abstraction to hide the names of internal contexts. Compared to previous attempts, our type system appears to be more flexible and less ad hoc.

JOE [9] allows internal contexts to be named through read-only local variables (variables that cannot be assigned after initialization) so that internal representation can be accessed from outside; the justification for this approach is that encapsulation breeches are localized on the stack. The following code shows a simple example of JOE, where a method parameter is used to name the owner context of the Node object.

```
void joe(List<o, d> list) { Node<list, d> node = list.head; }
```

Ownership Domains [1] use a similar method where read-only fields (final fields in Java) are used to name internal domains (partitions of contexts) instead of read-only variables. The effect of moving variables to fields allows ownership domains types to have a more flexible reference structure than ownership types and JOE. To provide some safety with this approach, only domains declared as public can be named via final fields. Access policy between domains is explicitly declared and public domains are typically linked to private domains (which are unnameable from outside). For soundness, object creation is restricted to the owner domain of the current object or its locally defined subdomains. The following code shows a simple example of ownership domains. Iterator objects are created in a public domain of the list object and used as interface objects by the client. Note that a subclass of **Iterator** is needed to propagate the name of the private domain **owned** (as an extra domain parameter) to the iterator objects. We consider this to be a limited version of our context abstraction: essentially the Iterator interface hides the Node owner that is a required capability for the ListIterator object.

```
class List<o, d> assumes o->d {
  domain owned; link owned->d;
  public domain iters; link iters->owned, iters->d;
  Node<owned, d> head;
  Iterator<iters, d> getIter() {
    return new ListIterator<iters, d, owned>(head); } }

// in client class
final Link<some, world> list = ...
Iterator<list.iters, world> iter = list.getIter();
```

In practice, some problems may arise with read-only variables/fields. For example, in order to access an object in a context/public domain, it must firstly obtain a reference to the owner object of the context and then must place the owner in a read-only variable. Only in this way can the context be named through the name of the read-only variable and a valid type be constructed for the object to be accessed. When accessing an object buried deep in the ownership tree, the programmer may need to declare many read-only variables and obtain references to each object along an ownership branch.

Moreover, the restriction on where objects can be created may limit some common programming practices, the factory design pattern for instance, where objects need to be created in various contexts/domains given by clients. The explicitly defined domains add finer-grained structures to the system at the cost of more domain and link annotations. Domains can be used to express some architectural constraints more precisely than ownership types do, because these constraints can be expressed directly as links which defines access policy between each pair of domains.

The *inner class* solution was suggested for ownership types by Clarke in his PhD thesis [7] and adopted by Boyapati et al. [4]. The idea of inner classes is very simple; inner classes can name the outer object directly. The following example shows the `Iterator` class is written as an inner class of the `List` class, who can name the list object's internal context directly via `List.this`.

```
class List<o, d> {
  Node<this, d> head;
  class Iterator<o, d> { Node<List.this, d> current; ... } }
```

Inner classes are lexically scoped and can only be used in limited places where the usage of the objects are specific and can be foreseen by the programmer. In general they are not as flexible as our type system.

The closest work to our type system may be the model of *Simple Ownership Types* [10]. In this model, there is a separation of *owner* and *rep* contexts. The owner context of the object determines which other objects may access it (like our accessibility context), while the rep context determines those contexts it may access (like `this`). The containment invariant states that if l references l' then $rep(l) \preceq owner(l')$. There are a number of major differences between the two models. The owner context in simple ownership types is a formal parameter of the class definition; it controls access to the object rather than defining the containment structure of objects/contexts — we prefer to reserve the notion of owner for the latter role. To preserve soundness this prevents the owner context from being variant. Moreover, as for all context parameters, the owner context must be a dominator of the rep context (which can be thought of as the object itself). Although simple ownership types use an explicit form of existential types to hide the internal contexts, it does not support variance of context arguments, as our system does.

Ownership Type Systems With Owners-As-Dominators. The proposals to retain the owners-as-dominators encapsulation allow some references to cross encapsulation boundary but ensure these reference cannot update the internal states directly (called *observational representation exposure* in [3]), that is, any update still has to be initialized by the owner object.

The *Universes* System [18, 19] uses read-only references to cross the boundary of encapsulation. Its read-only references are restricted and can only return read-only references. For example, they are able to express iterators by using a read-only reference to access the internal implementation of the list object. However, these iterators can only return data elements in read-only mode, that is, the elements in the list cannot be updated in this way (unless using dynamic casting with its associated runtime overheads [19]).

Effective Ownership [17] employs an encapsulation-aware effect system which allows arbitrary reference structure but still retain an owners-as-dominators encapsulation on object representation. It guarantees that any update to an object's internal state must occur (directly or indirectly) via a call on a method of its owner. In contrast to Universes, effective ownership's cross-encapsulation references can be used to mutate data elements via references held by a list object, while still protecting the list's representation from being modification. One limitation of effective ownership is that the iterator objects cannot be used to update the list's internal implementation, such as adding or removing elements from the list, because of the strong owners-as-dominators effect encapsulation.

Other Type Systems for Alias Protection. Many type systems have been proposed for alias protection. Confined types [26] manage aliases based on a package level encapsulation which provides a lightweight but weaker constraint than instance-level object encapsulation. Uniqueness techniques [27, 13] allow local reasoning and can prevent representation exposure by forbidding sharing; a reference is unique if it is the only reference to an object. External uniqueness combines the benefit of ownership types with uniqueness [8]. Boyland et al designed a system to unify uniqueness and read-only capability [5] where a reference is combined with a capability. Adoption [12, 6] can be used to provide information hiding similar to object encapsulation, but it is not clear how common object-oriented patterns such as iterators can be expressed in this approach. Alias types [23, 28] allow fine control on aliases at the cost of more complex annotations.

Variance on Parametric Types. The idea of use-site variance on type arguments of parametric class was first introduced informally by Thorup and Torgersen but only for covariance [24]. Igarashi and Viroli added contravariance and bivariance (complete abstraction) in their *Variant Parametric Types* and formalized type variances as bounded existential types. Our type system uses a similar technique, where, instead of types with subtyping, we rely on the containment ordering of ownership. Usually type systems with existential types would need some form of pack/unpack or close/open pairing to distinguish between typing contexts where the existential type is visible or not. Igarashi and Viroli used this idea directly in their type system, without exposing the existential types in the language syntax. Our use of the *, K+ and K− context variances in the language syntax and ?, K+? and K−? in the type system is somewhat akin to the use of pack/unpack mechanisms for existential types, but simpler. In particular, we avoid introducing new names for contexts into environments by keeping them anonymous (for example, K+? denotes an anonymous context which is inside K). Moreover since anonymous existential contexts are not bound to an environment they naturally become global, in other words, there is no need to pack/close them.

6   Conclusion

This paper has presented *variant ownership types* that generalize ownership types by separating accessibility of a type from its capability. Combined with context variance, the resulting type system significantly improves the expressiveness and utility of ownership types. The authors wish to acknowledge the support of the Australian Research Council Grant DP0665581.

References

1. J. Aldrich and C. Chambers. Ownership domains: Separating aliasing policy from mechanism. In *In European Conference on Object-Oriented Programming (ECOOP)*, July 2004.
2. P. S. Almeida. Balloon types: Controlling sharing of state in data types. *Lecture Notes in Computer Science*, 1241:32–59, 1997.
3. A. Birka and M. D. Ernst. A practical type system and language for reference immutability. In *OOPSLA '04: Proceedings of the 19th annual ACM SIGPLAN Conference on Object-Oriented Programming, Systems, Languages, and Applications*, pages 35–49. ACM Press, 2004.
4. C. Boyapati, B. Liskov, and L. Shrira. Ownership types for object encapsulation. In *Proceedings of the 30th ACM SIGPLAN-SIGACT Symposium on Principles of Programming Languages*, pages 213–223. ACM Press, 2003.
5. J. Boyland, J. Noble, and W. Retert. Capabilities for sharing: A generalisation of uniqueness and read-only. In *In European Conference on Object-Oriented Programming (ECOOP)*, pages 2–27, 2001.
6. J. T. Boyland and W. Retert. Connecting effects and uniqueness with adoption. In *POPL '05: Proceedings of the 32nd ACM SIGPLAN-SIGACT Symposium on Principles of Programming Languages*, pages 283–295, New York, NY, USA, 2005. ACM Press.
7. D. Clarke. *Object Ownership and Containment*. PhD thesis, School of Computer Science and Engineering, The University of New South Wales, Sydney, Australia, 2001.
8. D. Clarke and T. Wrigstad. External uniqueness is unique enough. In *In European Conference on Object-Oriented Programming (ECOOP)*, July 2003.
9. D. G. Clarke and S. Drossopoulou. Ownership, encapsulation and disjointness of type and effect. In *17th Annual Conference on Object-Oriented Programming, Systems, Languages, and Applications (OOPSLA)*, November 2002.
10. D. G. Clarke, J. Noble, and J. M. Potter. Simple ownership types for object containment. In *European Conference on Object-Oriented Programming (ECOOP)*, 2001.
11. D. G. Clarke, J. M. Potter, and J. Noble. Ownership types for flexible alias protection. In *Proceedings of the 13th ACM SIGPLAN Conference on Object-Oriented Programming, Systems, Languages, and Applications*, pages 48–64. ACM Press, 1998.

12. M. Fahndrich and R. DeLine. Adoption and focus: practical linear types for imperative programming. In *PLDI '02: Proceedings of the ACM SIGPLAN 2002 Conference on Programming Language Design and Implementation*, pages 13–24, New York, NY, USA, 2002. ACM Press.

13. J. Hogg. Islands: aliasing protection in object-oriented languages. In *OOPSLA '91: Proceedings of Conference on Object-Oriented Programming Systems, Languages, and Applications*, pages 271–285, New York, NY, USA, 1991. ACM Press.

14. A. Igarashi, B. Pierce, and P. Wadler. Featherweight Java: A minimal core calculus for Java and GJ. In L. Meissner, editor, *Proceedings of the 1999 ACM SIGPLAN Conference on Object-Oriented Programming, Systems, Languages, and Applications (OOPSLA'99)*, volume 34(10), pages 132–146, N. Y., 1999.

15. A. Igarashi and M. Viroli. On variance-based subtyping for parametric types. In *Proceedings of the 16th European Conference on Object-Oriented Programming*, pages 441–469. Springer-Verlag, 2002.

16. Y. Lu and J. Potter. A type system for reachability and acyclicity. In *Proceedings of the 19th European Conference on Object-Oriented Programming*, pages 479–503. Springer-Verlag, 2005.

17. Y. Lu and J. Potter. Protecting representation with effect encapsulation. In *Proceedings of the 33th ACM SIGPLAN-SIGACT Symposium on Principles of Programming Languages*. ACM Press, 2006.

18. P. Müller and A. Poetzsch-Heffter. Universes: A type system for controlling representation exposure. *Programming Languages and Fundamentals of Programming*, 1999.

19. P. Müller and A. Poetzsch-Heffter. Universes: A type system for alias and dependency control. Technical Report 279, Fernuniversität Hagen, 2001.

20. J. Noble, J. Vitek, and J. Potter. Flexible alias protection. In *European Conference on Object-Oriented Programming (ECOOP)*, 1998.

21. A. Potanin, J. Noble, and R. Biddle. Generic ownership: practical ownership control in programming languages. In *OOPSLA Companion*, pages 50–51, 2004.

22. J. Potter, J. Noble, and D. Clarke. The ins and outs of objects. In *Australian Software Engineering Conference*. IEEE Press, 1998.

23. F. Smith, D. Walker, and G. Morrisett. Alias types. *Lecture Notes in Computer Science*, 1782:366–381, 2000.

24. K. K. Thorup and M. Torgersen. Unifying genericity - combining the benefits of virtual types and parameterized classes. In *ECOOP*, pages 186–204, 1999.

25. M. Torgersen, C. P. Hansen, E. Ernst, P. von der Ahé, G. Bracha, and N. M. Gafter. Adding wildcards to the java programming language. In *SAC*, pages 1289–1296, 2004.

26. J. Vitek and B. Bokowski. Confined types. In *Proceedings of the 14th Annual Conference on Object-Oriented Programming, Systems, Languages, and Applications*, pages 82–96. ACM Press, 1999.

27. P. Wadler. Linear types can change the world! In M. Broy and C. Jones, editors, *IFIP TC 2 Working Conference on Programming Concepts and Methods, Sea of Galilee, Israel*, pages 347–359. North Holland, 1990.

28. D. Walker and G. Morrisett. Alias types for recursive data structures. *Lecture Notes in Computer Science*, 2071:177–206, 2001.

Scoped Types and Aspects for Real-Time Java

Chris Andreae[3], Yvonne Coady[1], Celina Gibbs[1],
James Noble[3], Jan Vitek[4], and Tian Zhao[2]

[1] University of Victoria, CA
[2] University of Wisconsin–Milwaukee, USA
[3] Victoria University of Wellington, NZ
[4] Purdue University, USA

Abstract. Real-time systems are notoriously difficult to design and implement, and, as many real-time problems are safety-critical, their solutions must be reliable as well as efficient and correct. While higher-level programming models (such as the Real-Time Specification for Java) permit real-time programmers to use language features that most programmers take for granted (objects, type checking, dynamic dispatch, and memory safety) the compromises required for real-time execution, especially concerning memory allocation, can create as many problems as they solve. This paper presents Scoped Types and Aspects for Real-Time Systems (STARS) a novel programming model for real-time systems. Scoped Types give programmers a clear model of their programs' memory use, and, being statically checkable, prevent the run-time memory errors that bedevil models such as RTSJ. Our Aspects build on Scoped Types guarantees so that Real-Time concerns can be completely separated from applications' base code. Adopting the integrated Scoped Types and Aspects approach can significantly improve both the quality and performance of a real-time Java systems, resulting in simpler systems that are reliable, efficient, and correct.

1   Introduction

The Real-Time Specification for Java (RTSJ) introduces abstractions for managing resources, such as non-garbage collected regions of memory [4]. For instance, in the RTSJ, a series of *scoped memory* classes let programmers manage memory explicitly: creating nested memory regions, allocating objects into those regions, and destroying regions when they are no longer needed. In a hard real-time system, programmers must use these classes, so that their programs can bypass Java's garbage collector and its associated predictability and performance penalties. But these abstractions are far from abstract. The RTSJ forces programmers to face more low-level details about the behaviour of their system than ever before — such as how scoped memory objects correspond to allocated regions, which objects are allocated in those regions, how those the regions are ordered — and then rewards any mistakes by throwing dynamic errors at runtime. The difficulty of managing the inherent complexity associated with real-time concerns ultimately compromises the development, maintenance and evolution of safety critical code bases and increases the likelihood of fatal errors at runtime.

This paper introduces Scoped Types and Aspects for Real-Time Systems (STARS), a novel approach for programming real-time systems that shields developers from many

D. Thomas (Ed.): ECOOP 2006, LNCS 4067, pp. 124–147, 2006.
© Springer-Verlag Berlin Heidelberg 2006

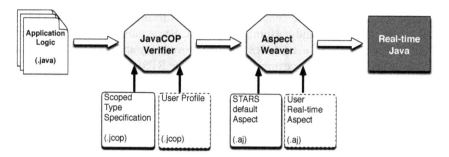

Fig. 1. Overview of STARS. Application logic is written according to the Scoped Types discipline. The JAVACOP verifier uses scoped types rules (and possibly some user-defined application-specific constraints) to validate the program. Then, an aspect weaver combines the application logic with the real-time behaviour. The result is a real-time Java program that can be executed on any STARS-compliant virtual machine.

accidental complexities that have proven to be problematic in practice. Scoped Types use a program's package hierarchy to represent the structure of its memory use, making clear where objects are allocated and thus where they are accessible. Real-Time Aspects then weave in allocation policies and implementation-dependent code — separating real-time concerns further from the base program. Finally, Scoped Types' correctness guarantees, combined with the Aspect-oriented implementation, removes the need for memory checks or garbage collection at runtime, increasing the resulting system's performance and reliability. Overall, STARS is a methodology that guides real-time development and provides much needed tool support for the verification and the modularization of real-time programs.

Fig. 1 illustrates the STARS methodology. Programmers start by writing application logic in Java with no calls to the RTSJ APIs. The code is then verified against a set of consistency rules — STARS provides a set of rules dealing with memory management; users may extend these rules with application-specific restrictions. If the program type checks, the aspects implementing the intended real-time semantics of the program can be woven into the code. The end result is a Real-time Java program which can be run in any real-time JVM which supports the STARS API.

The paper thus makes the following contributions:

1. **Scoped Types.** We use a lightweight pluggable type system to model hierarchical memory regions. Scoped Types is based on familiar Java concepts like packages, classes, and objects, can be explained with a few informal rules, and requires no changes to Java syntax.
2. **Static Verification** via the JAVACOP pluggable types checker [1]. We have encoded Scoped Types into a set of JAVACOP rules used to validate source code. We also show how to extend the built-in rules with application-specific constraints.
3. **Aspect-based real-time development.** We show how an aspect-oriented approach can decouple real-time concerns from the main application logic.
4. **Implementation in a real-time JVM.** We demonstrate viability of STARS with an implementation in the Ovm framework [2]. Only minor changes (18 lines of code in all) were needed to support STARS.

5. **Empirical evaluation.** We conducted a case study to show the impact STARS has on both code quality and performance in a 20 KLoc hard real-time application. Refactoring RTSJ code to a STARS program proved easy and the resulting program enjoyed a 28% performance improvement over the RTSJ equivalent.

Compared with our previous work, STARS presents two major advances. First, Scoped Types enforce a per-owner relation [10, 18] via techniques based on Confined Types [9, 22]. The type system described here refines the system described in [21] which includes a proof of correctness, but no implementation. In fact, the refactoring discussed in that paper does not type check under the current type system. Secondly, the idea of using aspects to localize real-time behaviour is also new.

The paper proceeds as follows. After a survey of background and previous work, Section 2 presents an overview of the STARS programming model while Section 3 overviews the current STARS prototype implementations. Section 4 follows with a case study using STARS in the implementation of a real-time collision detection system. Finally we conclude with discussion and future work.

1.1 Background: The Challenges of Real-Time Memory Management

The Real-time Specification for Java (RTSJ) provides real-time extensions to Java that have shown to be effective in the construction of large-scale systems [2, 17, 20]. Two key benefits of the RTSJ are first, that it allows programmers to write real-time programs in a type-safe language, thus reducing opportunities for catastrophic failures; and second, that it allows hard-, soft- and non-real-time tasks to interoperate in the same execution environment. To achieve this second benefit, the RTSJ adopts a mixed-mode memory model in which garbage collection is used for non-real time activities, while manually allocated regions are used for real-time tasks. Though convenient, the interaction of these two memory management disciplines causes significant complexity, and consequently is often the culprit behind many runtime memory errors.

The problem, in the case of real-time tasks, is that storage for an allocation request (i.e. new) must be serviced differently from standard Java allocation. In order to handle real-time requests, the RTSJ extends the Java memory management model to include dynamically checked regions known as *scoped memory areas* (or also memory scopes), represented by subclasses of ScopedMemory. A scoped memory area is an allocation context which provides a pool of memory for threads executing in it. Individual objects allocated in a scoped memory area cannot be deallocated, instead, an entire scoped memory area is torn down as soon as all threads exit that scope. The RTSJ defines two distinguished scopes for *immortal* and *heap* memory, respectively for objects with unbounded lifetimes and objects that must be garbage collected. Two new kinds of threads are also introduced: *real-time* threads which may access scoped memory areas; and *no heap real-time* threads, which in addition are protected from garbage collection pauses, but which suffer dynamic errors if they attempt to access heap allocated objects.

Scoped memory areas provide methods enter(Runnable) and executeIn-Area(Runnable) that permit application code to execute within a scope, allocating and accessing objects within that scope. Using nested calls, a thread may enter or execute runnables in multiple scopes, dynamically building up the scope hierarchy. The differences between these two methods are quite subtle [4]: basically, enter must

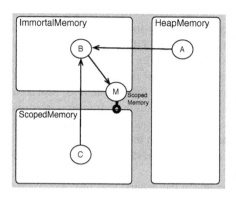

1. HeapMemory is garbage collected memory with no timeliness guarantees.
2. ImmortalMemory is not subject to reclamation.
3. ScopedMemory can be reclaimed in a single step if no thread is active in the area.
4. Immortal data can be referenced from any region. Scoped data can only be referenced from same scope or a nested scope. Violations lead to dynamic `Illegal-AssignmentErrors`.
5. `NoHeapRealtimeThread` cannot load heap references.

Fig. 2. Memory Management in the Real-time Specification for Java

be used to associate a scope with a thread, whereas `executeInArea` (temporarily) changes a thread's active scope to a scope it has previously `entered`. Misuse of these methods is punished by dynamic errors, e.g. a `ScopedCycleException` is thrown when a user tries to `enter` a `ScopedMemory` that is already accessible. Reference counting on `enters` ensures that all the objects allocated in a scope are finalized and reclaimed when the last thread leaves that scope.

Real-time developers must take these memory scopes and threading models into account during the design of a real-time system. Scoped memory areas can be nested to form a dynamic, tree-shaped hierarchy, where child memory areas have strictly shorter lifetimes than their parents. Because the hierarchy is established dynamically, memory areas can move around within the hierarchy as the program runs. Dynamically enforced safety rules check that a memory scope with a longer lifetime does not hold a reference to an object allocated in a memory scope with a shorter lifetime. This means that heap memory and immortal memory cannot hold references to objects allocated in scoped memory, nor can a scoped memory area hold a reference to an object allocated in an inner (more deeply nested) scope. Once again, errors are only detected at runtime and are rewarded with dynamic errors or exceptions.

Given that safety and reliability are two goals of most real-time systems, the fact that these safety rules are checked *dynamically* seems, in retrospect, to be an odd choice. The only guarantee that RTSJ gives to a programmer is that their programs will fail in a controlled manner: if a dynamic assignment into a dynamically changing scope hierarchy trips a dynamic check, the program will crash with an `IllegalAssignmentError`.

1.2   Related Work: Programming with Scoped Memory

Beebee and Rinard provided one of the early implementations of the RTSJ memory management extensions [3]. They found it "close to impossible" to develop error-free real-time Java programs without some help from debugging tools or static analysis. The difficulty of programming with RTSJ motivated Kwon, Wellings and King to propose Ravenscar-Java [16], which mandates a simplified computational model. Their goal was to decrease the likelihood of catastrophic errors in mission critical systems. Further work along these lines transparently associates scoped memory areas with methods, avoiding the need for explicit manipulation of memory areas [15]. Limitations of this approach include the fact that memory areas cannot be multi-threaded.

In contrast, systems like Islands [13], Ownership Types [10], and their successors restrict the scope of references to enable modular reasoning. The idea of using ownership types for the safety of region-based memory was first proposed by Boyapati et al. [5], and required changes to the Java syntax and explicit type annotations. Research in type-safe memory memory management, message-based communication, process scheduling and the file system interface management for Cyclone, a dialect of C, has shown that it is possible to prevent dangling pointers even in low-level codes [11]. The RTSJ is more challenging than Cyclone as scopes can be accessed concurrently and are first-class values.

Scoped types are one of the latest developments in the general area of type systems for controlled sharing of references [21]. This paper builds on Scoped Types and proposes a practical programming model targeting the separation of policy and mechanism within real-time applications. The key insight of Scoped Types is the necessity to make the nested scope structure of the program explicit: basically, every time the programmer writes an allocation expression of the form new Object(), the object's type shows where the object fits into the scope structure of the program. It is not essential to know which particular scope it will be allocated in, but rather the object's hierarchical relationship to other objects. This ensures that when an assignment expression, e.g. obj.f=new F(), is encountered, Scoped Types can statically (albeit conservatively) ensure that the assignment will not breach the program's scope structure.

2   The STARS Programming Model

STARS guides the design and implementation of real-time systems with a simple, explicit programming model. As the STARS name suggests, this is made up of two parts, Scoped Types, and Aspects. First, Scoped Types ensure that the relative memory location of any object is obvious in the program text. We use nested packages to define a *static* scope hierarchy in the program's code; a pluggable type checker ensures programs respect this hierarchy; at runtime, the dynamic scope structure simply instantiates this static hiearchy. Second, we use Aspect-Oriented Programming to decouple the real-time parts of STARS programs from their application logic. Aspects are used as declarative specifications of the real-time policies of the applications (the size of scoped memory areas or scheduling parameters of real time threads), but also to link Scoped Types to their implementations within a real-time VM.

The main points of the STARS programming model are illustrated in Fig. 3. The main abstraction is the *scoped package*. A scoped package is the static manifestation of an RTSJ scoped memory area. Classes defined within a scoped package are either *gates* or *scoped classes*. Every instance of a gate class has its own unique scoped memory area, and every instance of a scoped class will be allocated in the memory area belonging to a gate object in the same package. Because gate classes can have multiple instances, each scoped package can correspond to multiple scoped memory areas at runtime (one for each gate instance), just as a Java class can correspond to multiple instances. Then, the dynamic structure of the nested memory areas is modelled by the static structure of the

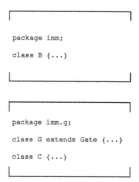

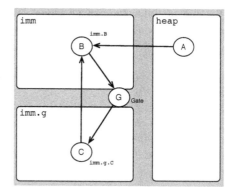

Fig. 3. The STARS Programming Model. Each runtime scope has a corresponding Java package. Objects defined in a package are always allocated in a corresponding scope. A scope's Gate is allocated in its parent scope.

nested scoped packages, in just the same way that the dynamic structure of a program's objects is modelled by the static structure of the program's class diagram.

Scoped types are allowed to refer to types defined in an ancestor package, just as in RTSJ, objects allocated in a scope are allowed to refer to an ancestor scope: the converse is forbidden. The root of the hierarchy is the package imm, corresponding to RTSJ's immortal memory. There will be as many scoped memory areas nested inside the immortal memory area as there are instances of the gate classes defined in imm's immediate subpackages.

STARS does impact the structure of Real-time Java programs. By giving an additional meaning to the package construct, we *de facto* extend the language. This form of overloading of language constructs has the same rationale as the definition of the RTSJ itself — namely to extend a language without changing its syntax, compiler, or intermediate format. In practice, STARS changes the way packages are used: rather than grouping classes on the basis of some logical criteria, we group them by lifetime and function. In our experience, this decomposition is natural as RTSJ programmers must think in terms of scopes and locations in their design. Thus it is not surprising to see that classes that end up allocated in the same scope are closely coupled, and so grouping them in the same package is not unrealistic. We argue that this package structure is a small price to pay for STARS' static guarantees, and for the clarity it brings to programs' real-time, memory dependent code.

2.1 Scoped Types: Static Constraints

The following Scoped Types rules ensure static correctness of STARS programs. In this rules, we assume that a scoped package contains exactly one *gate class* and zero or more scoped classes or interfaces (the *scoped types*). By convention, the gate is named with the package's name with the first letter capitalized. The descendant relation on packages is a partial order on packages defined by package nesting. The distinguished package imm is the root of the scope hierarchy. In the following we use S and G to denote respectively scoped and gate types, we use C to refer to any class. We use p to refer to the fully qualified name of a package. We refer to types not defined in a scoped package as *heap types*.

Rule 1 (Scoped Types).

1. *The package* imm *is a scoped package. Any package nested within a scoped package is scoped.*
2. *Any type not defined in a scoped package is a heap type.*
3. *The type of a gate class* p . G *defined within a scoped package* p *is a gate type.*
4. *The type of any non-gate interface or class* p . S *defined within a scoped package* p *is a scoped type. The type of an array with elements of scoped type is a scoped type.*

Rule 2 (Visibility).

1. *An expression of scoped type* p . S *is visible in any type defined in* p *or any of its subpackages.*
2. *An expression of gate type* p . G *is visible in any type defined in the immediate super-package of* p. *An exception to this rule is the local variable* this *which can be used within a gate class.*
3. *The type of the top-level gate* imm . G *is visible in heap types.*
4. *An expression of heap type is only visible in other heap types.*

The visibility rule encodes the essence of the RTSJ access rules. An object can be referenced from its defining memory area (denoted statically by a package), or from a memory area with shorter lifetime (a nested package). Gate classes are treated differently, as they are handles used from a parent scope to access a memory area. They must only be accessible to the code defined in the parent scope. The reason other types in the same scope package cannot refer to a gate is that we must avoid confusion between gates of the same type; a parent can instantiate many gates of the same type and the contents of these gates must be kept separate. Even though a gate's type is not visible in its own class, a single exception is made so that a gate object can refer to itself through the this pointer (because we know which gate "this" is).

Rule 3 (Widening). *An expression of a scoped type* p . S *can be widened only to another scoped type in* p. *An expression of a gate type* p . G *cannot be widened to any other types.*

Rule 3 is traditional in confined type systems where types are used to enforce structural properties on the object graph. Preventing types from being be cast to arbitrary supertypes (in particular Object) makes it possible to verify Rule 2 statically.

Rule 4 (Method Inheritance). *An invocation of some method* m *on an expression of scoped type* p . S *where* p *is a scoped package is valid if* m *is defined in a class* p . S' *in the same package. An invocation of a method* m *on an expression of gate type* p . G *is valid only if* m *is defined in* p . G.

Rule 4 prevents a more subtle form of reference leak: within an inherited method, the receiver (i.e. this) is implicitly cast to the method's defining class — this could lead to a leak if one were to invoke a method inherited from a heap class.

Rule 5 (Constructor Invocation). *The constructor of a scoped class* p.S *can only be invoked by methods defined in* p.

Rule 5 prevents a subpackage from invoking new on a class that is allocated in a different area than the currently executing object. This rule is not strictly necessary, as an implementation could potentially reflect upon the static type of the object to dynamically obtain the proper scope. In our prototype, we use factory methods to create objects.

Rule 6 (Static Reference Fields). *A type* p.S *defined in a scoped package* p *is not allow to declare static reference fields.*

A static variable would be accessible by different instances of the same class allocated in different scopes.

2.2 Correctness

The fact that a package can only have one parent package trivially ensures that the RTSJ single parent rule will hold. Moreover, a scope-allocated object o may only reference objects allocated in the scope of o, or scopes with a longer lifetime, preventing any RTSJ IllegalAssignmentError. For example, suppose that the assignment o.f=o' is in the scope s, where o and o' have types p.C and p'.C' respectively. If p.C is a scoped type, then the rules above ensure that o and o' can only be allocated in s or its outer scopes. By Rules 2 and 3, the type of the field f is defined in p', which is visible to p.C. Thus, the package p' is the same as or a super-package of p and consequently o' must be allocated in the scope of o or its outer scope. The same is true if p.C is a gate type, in which case o either represents s or a direct descendant of s. A formal soundness argument can be found in the extended version of this paper.

3   The STARS Prototype Implementation

The STARS prototype has two software components — a checker, which takes plain Java code that is supposed to conform to the Scoped Types discipline, and verifies that it does in fact follow the discipline, and an series of AspectJ aspects that weaves in the necessary low-level API calls to run on a real-time virtual machine.

3.1   Checking the Scoped Types Discipline

We must ensure that only programs that follow the scoped types discipline are accepted by the system: this is why we begin by passing our programs through a checker that enforces the discipline. Rather than implement a checker from scratch, we have employed the JAVACOP "pluggable types" checker [1]. Pluggable types [6] are a relatively recent idea, developed as extensions of soft type systems [8] or as a generalization of the ideas behind the Strongtalk type system [7]. The key idea is that pluggable types layer a new static type system over an existing (statically or dynamically typed) language, allowing programmers to have greater guarantees about their programs' behaviour, but without the expense of implementing entirely new type systems or programming languages. JAVACOP is a pluggable type checker for Java programs — using JAVACOP, pluggable type systems are designed by a series of syntax-directed rules that are layered on top of the standard Java syntax and type system and then checked when the program is compiled. STARS is a pluggable type system, and so it is relatively straightforward to check with JAVACOP. The design and implementation of JAVACOP is described in [1].

The JAVACOP specification of the Scoped Type discipline is approximately 300 lines of code. Essentially, we provide two kinds of facts to JAVACOP to describe Scoped Types. First we define which classes must be considered scoped or gate types; and then we to restrict the code of those classes according to the Scoped Type rules.

Defining Scoped Types is relatively easy. Any class declared within the imm package or any subpackage is either a scoped type or a gate. Declaring a scoped type in the JAVACOP rule language is straightforward: a class or interface is scoped if it is in a scoped package and is not a gate. A gate is a class declared within a scoped package and with a name that case-insensitively matches that of the package. Array types are handled separately: an array is scoped if its element types are scoped.

```
1  declare gateNamed(ClassSymbol s){
2      require(s.packge.name.equalsIgnoreCase(s.name));
3  }
4  declare scoped(Type t){
5      require(!t.isArray);
6      require(!gateNamed(t.getSymbol));
7      require(scopedPackage(t.getSymbol.packge));
8  }
9  declare scoped(Type t){
10     require(t.isArray && scoped(t.elemtype));
11 }
12 declare gate(Type t){
13     require(!t.isArray);
14     require(gateNamed(t.getSymbol));
15     require(scopedPackage(t.getSymbol.packge));
16 }
```

The rule that enforces visibility constraints is only slightly more complex. The following rule matches on a class definition (line 1) and ensure that all types of all syntax tree nodes found within that definition (line 2) meet the constraints of Scoped Types. A number of types and syntactic contexts, such as Strings and inheritance declarations, are deemed "safe" (safeNodes on line 3, definition omitted) and can be used in any context. Lines 4-5 ensure that top level gates are only visible in the heap. Lines 7-8 ensure that a gate is only visible in its parent package. Lines 10-11 ensure that the visibility of a scoped type is limited to its defining package and subpackages. Lines 13-16 apply if c is defined within a scoped package and ensure that types used within a scoped package are visible.

```
1  rule scopedTypesVisibilityDefn1(ClassDef c){
2   forall(Tree t : c){
3    where(t.type != null && !safeNode(t)){
4    where(topLevelGate(t.type)){
5     require(!scopedPackage(c.sym.packge)):
6      warning(t,"Top level gate visible only in heap"); }
7    where(innerGate(t.type)){
8     require(t.type.getSymbol.packge.owner == c.sym.packge):
9      warning(t,"gate visible only in immediate superpackage"); }
10   where(scoped(t.type)){
11    require(t.type.getSymbol.packge.isTransOwner(c.sym.packge)):
12     warning(t,"type visible only in same or subpackage"); }
13   where(scoped(c.sym.type)){
14    require(scopedPackage(t.type.getSymbol.packge) ||
15        specialPackage(t.type.getSymbol.packge)    ||
16        visibleInScopedOverride(t)):
17     warning(t,"Type not visible in scoped package."); }
18   }
19  }
20 }
```

We restrict widening of scoped types with the following rule. It states that if we are trying to widen a scoped type, then the target must be declared in the same scoped package, and if the type is a gate widening disallowed altogether. The safeWidening-Location predicate is an escape hatch that allows annotations that override the default rules.

```
1  rule scopedTypesCastingDef2(a <: b @ pos){
2   where(!safeWideningLocation(pos)){
3    where(scoped(a)){
4     require(a.getSymbol.packge == b.getSymbol.packge) :
5      warning(pos,"Illegal scoped type widening."); }
6    where(gate(a)){
7     require(b.isSameType(a)) :
8      warning(pos,"May not widen gate."); }
9   }
10 }
```

JAVACOP allows users to extend the Scoped Types specification with additional restrictions. It is thus possible to use JAVACOP to restrict the set of allowed programs further. The prototype implementation has one restriction, though, it does not support AspectJ syntax. JAVACOP is thus not able to validate the implementation of aspects. As long as aspects remain simple and declarative, this will not be an issue. But in the longer term we would like to see integration of a pluggable type checker with an Aspect language.

3.2   Aspects for Memory Management and Real-Time

Though the design of memory management in a real-time system may be clear, typically, its implementation will be unclear, because it is inherently tangled throughout the code. For this reason we chose an aspect-oriented approach for modularizing scope management. This part of STARS is implemented using a (subset of) the Aspect-Oriented Programming features provided by AspectJ [14]. For performance, predictability and safety reasons we stay away from dynamic or esoteric features such as *cflow* and features that require instance-based aspect instantiation such as *perthis* and *pertarget*.

After the program has been statically verified, aspects are composed with the plain Java base-level application. The aspects weave necessary elements of the RTSJ API into the system. This translation (and the aspects) depend critically upon the program following the Scoped Type discipline: if the rules are broken, the resulting program will no longer obey the RTSJ scoped memory discipline, and then either fail at runtime with just the kind of an exception we aim to prevent; or worse, if running on a virtual machine that omits runtime checks, fail in some unchecked manner.

STARS programs are written against a simple API, shown in Fig. 4. The use of the API is intentionally simple. Gate classes must extend `scope.Gate`, which gives access to only two methods: `waitForNextPeriod()`, which is used to block a thread until its next release event, and `runInThread()`, which is used to start a new real-

```
1  package scope;
2
3  public class STARS {
4    static public boolean waitForNextPeriod() { ... }
5    public @WidenScoped void runInThread(Runnable r) {}
6  }
7
8  public class Gate extends STARS {
9    private MemoryArea mem;
10 }
11
12 privileged abstract aspect ScopedAspect {
13   abstract pointcut InScope();
14   pointcut NewGate(Gate g) : execution(Gate+.new(..))
15                              && target(g)
16                              && InScope();
17   pointcut GateCall(Gate g) :
18                              execution(public void Gate+.*(..))
19                              && this(g);
20   pointcut RunInThread(Runnable r, STARS g) :
21                              execution(void STARS+.runInThread(..))
22                              && target(g)
23                              && args(r);
24   ...
25 }
```

Fig. 4. STARS Interface. The `scope` package contains two classes, STARS and Gate, and an abstract aspect ScopedAspect. Every gate class inherits from Gate and has access to two methods `waitForNextPeriod()` and `runInThread()`. Every STARS aspect extends ScopedAspect, must define pointcut InScope and has access to a number of predefined pointcuts.

time thread. The single argument of `runInThread` is an instance of class that implements the `Runnable` interface. The semantics of the method is that the argument's `run` method will be executed in a new thread. The characteristics of the thread are left unbound in the Java code.

STARS aspects must deal with two concerns: the specifics of the memory area associated with each gate and the binding between invocations of `runInThread()` and real-time threads. Specifying memory area parameters is done by declaring a `before` advice to the initialization of a newly allocated gate. The privileged nature of the aspect allows the assignment to the `Gate.mem` private field. The `ScopedMemory` class is abstract, the advice must specify one of its subclasses `LTMemory` and `VTMemory` which provide linear time and variable time allocation of objects in scoped memory areas respectively. It must also declare a size for the area.

```
1  before(Gate g): NewGate(g) && execution(MyGate.new(..)){
2    g.mem = new VTMemory( sz );
3  }
```

The above example shows an advice for class `MyGate`. The memory area associated has size `sz` and is of type `VTMemory`. The code can get more involved when `Size-Estimators` are used to determine the proper size of the area.

It is noteworthy that the `mem` field is not accessible from the application logic as it is declared private. This means that memory areas are only visible from aspects. (As an aside, strict application of the scoped type discipline would preclude use of those classes in any case.)

3.3 Instrumentation and Virtual Machine Support

The implementation of STARS relies on a small number of changes to a real-time Java virtual machine. In our case, we needed only add 18 lines to the Ovm framework [2] and 105 of lines of AspectJ to provide the needed functionality.

The added functionality consists of the addition of three new methods to the abstract class `MemoryArea`. These methods expose different parts of the implementation of the `MemoryArea.enter()`. The `STARSenter()` method increments the reference count associated to the area, changes allocation context and returns an opaque reference to the VM's representation of the allocation context before the change. `STARSexit()` leaves a memory area, possible reclaiming its contents and restores the previous allocation context passed in as argument. `STARSrethrow()` is used to leave a memory area with an exception. Three methods of the class `LibraryImports` which mediates between the user domain and the VM's executive were made public. They are: `setCurrentArea()` to change the allocation context, `getCurrentArea()` to obtain the allocation context for the current thread, and `areaOf()` to obtain the area in which an object was allocated. All of these methods operate on opaque references.

```
1 Opaque MemoryArea.STARSenter();
2 void    MemoryArea.STARSrethrow(Opaque,Throwable);
3 void    MemoryAreaSTARSexit(Opaque area);
4
5 static Opaque LibraryImports.setCurrentArea(Opaque area);
6 static Opaque LibraryImports.getCurrentArea();
7 static Opaque LibraryImports.areaOf(Object ref);
```

We show two key advices from the ScopedAspect introduced in Figure 4. The first advice executes before the instance initializer of any scoped class or array (lines 1-4). This advice obtains the area of o – which is the object performing the allocation – and sets the allocation context to that area. The reasoning is that if we are executing a new then the target class must be visible. We thus ensure that it is co-located.

```
1 before(Object o): AllocInScope(o) {
2   return LibraryImports
3           .setCurrentArea(LibraryImports.areaOf(o));
4 }
```

We use the second advice to modify the behaviour of any call to a gate (recall that these can only originate from the immediate parent package). This around advice uses the memory region field of the gate to change allocation context. When the method returns we restore the previous area.

```
1 void around(Gate g) : GateCall(g) {
2   Opaque x = g.mem.STARSenter();
3   try {
4     try {
5       proceed(g);
6     } catch(Throwable e) { g.mem.STARSrethrow(x, e); }
7   } finally { g.mem.STARSexit(x); }
8 }
```

3.4 Extensions and Restrictions

We have found that, for practical reasons, a small numbers of adjustments needed to be made to the core of the scoped type system.

Intrinsics. Some important features of the standard Java libraries are presented as static methods on JDK classes. Invoking static methods from a scoped package, and especially ones that are not defined in the current package, is illegal. This is too restrictive and we relaxed the JAVACOP specification to allow calls to static methods in the following classes System, Double, Float, Integer, Long, Math, and Number. Moreover, we have chosen to permit the use of java.lang.String in scoped packages. Whether this is wise is debatable – for debugging purposes it is certainly useful to be able to construct messages, but it opens up an opportunity for runtime memory errors. It is conceivable that the JAVACOP rules will be tightened in the future to better track the use of scope allocated strings.

Exceptions. All subclasses of `Throwable` are allowed in a scoped package. This is safe within the confines of standard use of exceptions. If an exception is allocated and thrown within a scoped package, it is either caught by a handler within that package or escape out of the memory area. In which case it will be caught by the around advice at the gate boundary and `STARSrethrow` will allocate a RTSJ `ThrowBoundary-Error` object in the parent scope and rethrow the newly allocated error. One drawback of this rule is that a memory error could occur if a programmer managed to return/assign a scope-allocated error object to a parent area. Luckily there is a simple solution that catches most reasonable use-cases. We define a JAVACOP rule that allows exceptions to be created only if they are within a `throw` statement.

```
1  declare treeVisInScoped(Tree t){
2    require(NewClass n, Throw th;
3           n <- env.tree && th<-env.next.tree){
4      require(th.expr == n);
5      require(t == n.clazz);
6    }
7  }
```

Annotations. We found that in rare cases it may be necessary to let users override the scoped type system — typically where (library) code is clearly correct, but where it fails the conservative Scoped Types checker. For this we provide two Java 5 annotations that are recognised by the JAVACOP rules. `@WidenScoped` permits to declare that an expression which performs an otherwise illegal widening is deemed safe. `@MakeVisible` takes a type and makes it visible within a class or method.

Reflection. In the current implementation we assume that reflection is not used to manipulate scoped types. But a better solution would be to have reflection enforce the STARS semantics. This can be achieved by making the implementation of reflection scope-aware. Of course, whether reflection should be used in a hard real-time system, considering its impact on compiler analysis and optimization is open for discussion.

Native methods. Native methods are an issue for safety. This is nothing new, even normal Java virtual machines depend on the correctness of the implementation of native methods for type safety. We take the approach that native methods are disallowed unless explicitly permitted in a JAVACOP specification.

Finalizers. While the STARS prototype allows finalizers, we advocate that they should not be used in scoped packages. This because there is a well-known pathological case where a `NoHeapRealtimeThread` can end up blocking for the garbage collector due to the interplay of finalization and access to scope by `RealtimeThreads`. This constraint is not part of the basic set of JAVACOP rules. Instead we add it as a user-defined extension to the rule set. This is done by the following rule:

```
1  rule nofinalizers(MethodDef m){
2   where(m.name.equals("finalize") && m.params.length == 0){
3     require(ClassSymbol c; c <- m.sym.owner) {
4       require(!scopedPackage(c.packge)):
5     warning(m,"Scoped class may not define a finalizer");
6     }
7   }
8  }
```

4   Case Study: A Real-Time Collision Detector

We conducted a case study to demonstrate the relative benefits of STARS. The software system used in this experiment is modeling a real-time *collision detector* (or CD). The collision detector algorithm is about 25K Loc and was originally written with the Real-time Specification for Java. As a proof-of-concept for our proposal, we refactored the CD to abide by the scoped type discipline and to use aspects.

The architecture of the STARS version of the CD is given in Fig. 5. The application has three threads, a plain Java thread running in the heap to generate simulated work-loads, a 5Hz thread whose job is to communicate results of the algorithm to an output device and finally a 10Hz `NoHeapRealtimeThread` which periodically acquires a data frame with positions of aircrafts from simulated sensors. The system must de-

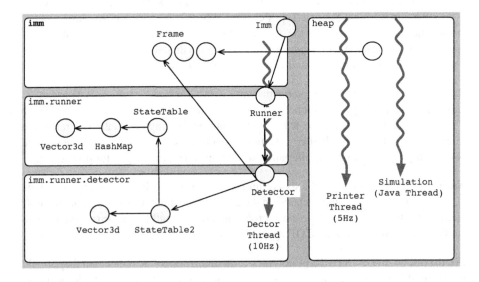

Fig. 5. Collision Detector. The CD uses two scoped memory areas. Two threads run in the heap: the first simulates a workload, the second communicate with an output device. The memory hierarchy consists of `imm` (immortal memory) for the simulated workload, `imm.runner` for persistent data, and `imm.runner.detector` for frame specific data.

tect collision before they happen. The numbers of planes, airports, and nature of flight restrictions are variables to the system.

The refactoring was done in three stages. First, we designed a scope structure for the program based on the `ScopedMemory` areas used in the CD. Second, we moved classes amongst packages so that the STARS-CD package structure matched the scope structure. Third, we removed or replaced explicit RTSJ memory management idioms with equivalent constructs of our model.

Fig. 6 compares the package structure of the two versions. In the original CD the packages `atc` and `command` were responsible of computing trajectories based on a user-defined specification. They were not affected by the refactoring. Package `detector` contained all of the RTSJ code as well the program's `main()`. Finally `util` contained a number of general purpose utility classes. We split the code in the `detector` package in four groups. The package `heap` contains code that runs in the heap–this is the main and the data reporting thread. The package `imm` contains classes that will be allocated in immortal memory and thus never reclaimed. Below immortal memory there is one scope that contains the persistent state of the application, we defined a package `imm.runner` for this. The main computation is done in the last package, `imm.runner.detector`. This is the largest real-time package which contains classes that are allocated and reclaimed for each period.

The entire code of the real-time aspect for the CD is given in Fig. 7. This aspect simply declares the memory area types for the `imm.runner` and `imm.runner.-detector` gates. Then it gives an around advice that specifies that the thread used by the CD algorithm is a `NoHeapRealtimeThread` and gives appropriate scheduling and priority parameters.

The overall size of the Scoped CD has increased because we had to duplicate some of the utility collection classes. This duplication is due to our static constraints. A number of collection classes were used in the `imm.runner` package to represent persistent state, and in the `imm.runner.detector` package to compute collisions. While we could have avoided the duplication by fairly simple changes to the algorithm and the use of problem specific collections, our goal was to look at the 'worst-case' scenario, so we tried to make as few changes to the original CD as possible. The methodology

CD packages	classes per package	Scoped CD packages	classes per package
atc	989	atc	989
command	21198	command	21198
util	927	util	927
detector	1041		
		heap	105
		imm	120
		imm.runner	162
		imm.runner.detector	1587
		collections	8322

Fig. 6. Package structure of the CD (left) and the STARS CD (right)

```
1  privileged aspect CDAspect extends ScopedAspect{
2
3    before(Gate g): NewGate(g) && execution(Runner.new(..)){
4      g.mem = new LTMemory(Constants.SIZE*2,Constants.SIZE*2);
5    }
6
7    before(Gate g): NewGate(g) && execution(Detector.new(..)){
8      g.mem = new LTMemory(Constants.SIZE);
9    }
10
11   void around(STARS g, Runnable r): RunInThread(r, g){
12     Thread t = new NoHeapRealtimeThread(
13         new PriorityParameters(Constants.PRIORITY),
14         new PeriodicParameters(null,
15             new RelativeTime(Constants.PERIOD, 0),
16             null, null, null),
17         null, ((Gate) g).mem, null, r);
18     t.start();
19   }
20 }
```

Fig. 7. Real-time Aspect for the CD. The aspect specifies the characteristics of memory areas as well as that of the real-time thread used by the application. The CD logic does not refer to any of the RTSJ APIs.

used to duplicate collection classes is straightforward: we define a scoped replacement for the `Object` class and replace all occurrences of `Object` in the libraries with the scoped variant. There were some other minor changes, but these were also fairly straightforward.

4.1   Patterns and Idioms

RTSJ programmers have adopted or developed a number of programming idioms to manipulate scopes. After changing the structure of the original CD, we need to convert these idioms into corresponding idioms that abide by our rules. In almost every case, the resulting code was simpler and more general, because it could directly manipulate standard Java objects rather than having to create and manage special RTSJ scope meta-objects explicitly.

Scoped Run Loop. At the core of the CD is an instance of the ScopedRunLoop pattern identified in [19]. The `Runner` class creates a `Detector` and periodically executes the detector's `run()` method within a scope. Fig. 8 shows both the RTSJ version and the STARS version. In the RTSJ version, the runner is a `NoHeapRealtimeThread` which has in its `run()` method code to create a new scoped memory (lines 11-12) and a run loop which repeatedly enters the scope passing a detector as argument (lines 17-18).

In the STARS version, `Runner` and `Detector` are gates to nested packages. Thus the call to `run()` on line 16 will enter the memory area associated with the detector. Objects allocated while executing the method are allocated in this area. When the method returns these objects will be reclaimed. Fig. 9 illustrates how a `Runner` is started. In the RTSJ version a scoped memory area is explicitly created (lines 2-3) and the real-time arguments are provided (lines 6-11). In the STARS version most of this is implicit due to the fact that a runner is a gate and the use of the `runInThread()` method which is advised to create a new thread. What should be noted here is that STARS clearly separates the real-time support from the non-real-time code. In fact we can define an alternative aspect which allows the program to run in a standard JVM.

```
1  public class Runner extends          1  public class Runner
2          NoHeapRealtimeThread {        2          extends Gate {
3                                        3
4  public Runner(                        4
5          PriorityParameters r,         5
6          PeriodicParameters p,         6
7          MemoryArea m) {               7
8    super(r, p, m);                     8
9  }                                     9
10 public void run() {                   10 public void run() {
11   final LTMemory cdmem =              11   StateTable st =
12   new LTMemory(CDSIZE,CDIZE);         12     new StateTable();
13   StateTable st =                     13   Detector cd =
14   new StateTable();                   14     new Detector(st, SIZE);
15   Detector cd =                       15   while (waitForNextPeriod())
16   new Detector(st, SIZE);             16     cd.run();
17   while (waitForNextPeriod())         17 }
18     cdmem.enter(cd);                  18 }
19 }                                     19
20 }                                     20
```

Fig. 8. Scoped Run Loop Example. The Runner class: RTSJ version (on the left) and Scoped version (on the right).

```
1  public void run() {                  1  public void run(){
2    LTMemory memory =                   2    Runner rt =
3    new LTMemory(MSZ, MSZ);             3      new Runner();
4    NoHeapRealtimeThread rt =           4    runInThread(rt);
5    new Runner(new PriorityParameters(P), 5  }
6    new  PeriodicParameters(null,       6
7    new RelativeTime(PER,0),            7
8    new RelativeTime(5,0),              8
9    new RelativeTime(50,0),             9
10   null,null),                        10
11   memory);                           11
12   rt.start();                        12
13 }                                    13
```

Fig. 9. Starting up. The `imm.Imm.run()` method: RTSJ version (left-hand side) and Scoped version (right-hand side).

Multiscoped Object. A multiscoped object is an object which is used in several allocation contexts as defined in [19]. In the RTSJ CD the `StateTable` class keeps persistent state and is allocated in the area that is not reclaimed on each period. This table has one entry per plane holding the plane's call sign and its last known position. There is also a method `createMotions()` invoked from the transient scope. The class appears in Fig. 10.

This code is particularly tricky because the state table object is allocated in the persistent area and the method `createMotions()` is executed in the transient area (when called by the `Detector`). The object referred to by `pos` (line 8) is transient and one must be careful not to store it in the parent scope. When a new plane is detected, `old` is null (line 11) and a new position vector must be added to the state table. The complication is that at that point the allocation context is that of the transient area, but the `HashMap` was allocated in the persistent scope (line 2). So we must temporarily change allocation context. This is done by defining an inner class whose sole purpose is to create a new vector and add it to the hash map (lines 23-39). The context switch

```
 1  class StateTable {
 2    HashMap prev = new HashMap();
 3    Putter putter = new Putter();
 4
 5    List createMotions(Frame f) {
 6      List ret = new LinkedList();
 7      for (...) {
 8        Vector3d pos = new Vector3d();
 9        Aircraft craft = iter.next(newpos);
10        ...
11        Vector3d old = (Vector3d) prev.get(craft);
12        if (old == null) {
13          putter.c = craft;
14          putter.v = pos;
15          MemoryArea current =
16            MemoryArea.getMemoryArea(this);
17          mem.executeInArea(putter);
18        }
19      }
20      return ret;
21    }
22
23    class Putter implements Runnable {
24      Aircraft c;
25      Vector3d v;
26      public void run() {
27        prev.put(c, new Vector3d(v));
28      }
29    }
30  }
```

Fig. 10. RTSJ StateTable. This is an example of a RTSJ multiscoped object – an instance of class allocated in one scope but with some of its methods executing in a child scope. Inspection of the code does not reveal in which scope `createMotions()` will be run. It is thus incumbent on the programmer to make sure that the method will behave correctly in any context.

is performed in lines 15-17 by first obtaining the area in which the StateTable was allocated, and finally executing the Putter in that area (line 17). This code is a good example of the intricacy (insanity?) of RTSJ programming.

The scoped solution given in Fig. 11 makes things more explicit. The StateTable class is split in two. One class, imm.runner.StateTable, for persistent state and a second class, imm.runner.detector.StateTable2 that has the update method. This split makes the allocation context explicit. A StateTable2 has a reference to the persistent state table. The createMotions() method is split in two parts, one that runs in the transient area (lines 23-30) and the other that performs the update to the persistent data (lines 8-14).

Since our type system does not permit references to subpackages the arguments to StateTable.put() are primitive. The most displeasing aspect of the refactoring is that we had to duplicate the Vector3d class - there are now two identical versions - in each imm.runner and imm.runner.detector. We are considering extensions to the type system to remedy this situation.

```
1  package imm.runner;
2  public class Vector3d { ... }
3
4  public class StateTable {
5    HashMap prev = new HashMap();
6
7    void put(Aircraft craft, float x, float y, float z) {
8      Vector3d old = prev.get(craft);
9      if (old==null)
10       prev.put(craft, new Vector3d(x, y, z));
11     else
12       old.set(x, y, z);
13   }
14 }
15
16 package imm.runner.detector;
17 class Vector3d { ... }
18
19 class StateTable2 {
20   StateTable table;
21
22   List createMotions(Frame f) {
23     List ret = new LinkedList();
24     for (...) {
25       Vector3d pos = new Vector3d();
26       ...
27       table.put(craft, pos.x, pos.y, pos.z);
28     }
29     return ret;
30   }
31 }
```

Fig. 11. STARS StateTable. With scoped types the table is split in two. This makes the allocation context for data and methods explicit.

4.2   Performance Evaluation

We now compare the performance of three versions of the CD: with the RTSJ, with STARS, and with a real-time garbage collector. The latter was obtained by ignoring the STARS annotations, with all objects allocated in the heap. The benchmarks were run on an AMD Athlon(TM) XP1900+ running at 1.6GHz, with 1GB of memory. The operating system is Real-time Linux with a kernel release number of 2.4.7- timesys-3.1.214. We rely on AspectJ 1.5 as our weaver. We use the Ovm virtual machine framework [2] with ahead-of-time compilation ("engine=j2c, build=run"). The GCC 4.0.1 compiler is used for native code generation. The STARS VM was built with dynamic read and write barriers turned off. The application consists of three threads, 10Hz, 5Hz, and plain Java. Priority preemptive scheduling is performed by the RTSJVM.

Fig. 12 shows the difference in running time between the three versions of the CD. Some of the variation is due to the workloads – collisions require more computational resources.

The results suggest that STARS outperforms both RTSJ and Real-time GC. On average, STARS is about 28% faster per frame than RTSJ and RTGC. This means that the overhead of before advice attached to every allocation is negligible. This is only a single data point, we feel that more aggressive barrier elimination could reduce the overhead of RTSJ programs and that the performance of our RTGC is likely not yet optimal. Nevertheless, the data presented here suggested that there is a potentially significant performance benefit in adopting STARS.

5   Discussion and Future Work

The combination of Scoped Types with Aspects is a promising means of structuring policy with its corresponding mechanism. When a real-time program is in this form, we can get the benefit of high level abstractions along with increased flexibility of their key mechanisms as aspects. The approach further allows for flexible combinations of lightweight static verification. The prototype implementation of STARS shows that the benefits of our approach can be obtained using mostly off-the-shelf technologies, in particular, existing aspect-oriented languages and static verifiers, with minimal changes to a real-time Java virtual machine. There is also potential for significant performance improvements. In our benchmark we have seen that a STARS program may run 28% faster than the corresponding RTSJ program.

This work has illustrated how aspects can extract and localize real-time concerns. In our case study the entire real-time specific portion of the application could be extracted as a simple declarative aspect. But the STARS interface is intentionally spartan and covers only part of the Real-time Specification for Java API. We hope that our approach can be extended to address a much larger set of real-time applications.

One of the advantages of STARS is its truly lightweight type system. So lightweight, in fact, that one only needs make a judicious choice of package names to denote nesting of memory regions. The attraction is that no changes are needed in the language and tool chain, and that the rules are simple to explain. We do not attempt to sweep the costs of adopting STARS under the rug. As we have seen in the case study, there are cases where we had to change interfaces from objects to primitive types, thus forfeiting some

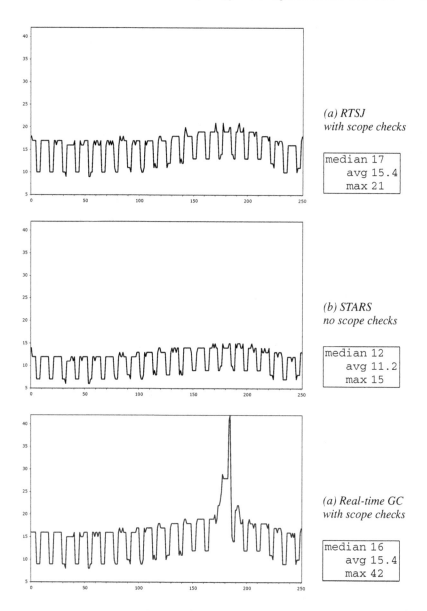

Fig. 12. Performance Evaluation. Comparing the performance of the collision detection implemented with (a) RTSJ, (b) STARS and (c) Java with a real-time garbage collector. We measure the time needed to process one frame of input by a 10Hz high-priority thread. The x-axis shows input frames and the y-axis processing time in milliseconds. The RTGC spikes at 43ms when the GC kicks in. No deadlines are missed. The average per frame processing time of STARS is 28% less than that of RTSJ and RTGC. Variations in processing time are due to the nature of the algorithm.

of the software engineering benefits of Java. We were forced to duplicate the code of some common libraries in order to abide by the rules of scoped types. While there are clear software engineering drawbacks to code duplication, the actual refactoring effort in importing those classes was small. With adequate tool support the entire refactoring effort took less than a day. The hard part involved discovering and disentangling the scope structure of the programs that we were trying to refactor.

The benefits in terms of correctness can not be overemphasized. Every single practitioner we have met has remarked on the difficulty of programming with RTSJ-style scoped memory. In our own work we have encountered numerous faults due to incorrect scope usage. As a reaction against this complexity many RTSJ users are asking for real-time garbage collection. But RTGC is not suited for all applications. In the context of safety critical systems a number of institutions are investigating restricted real-time 'profiles' in which the flexibility of scoped memory is drastically curtailed [12]. But even in those proposals, there are no static correctness guarantees. Considering the cost of failure, the effort of adopting a static discipline such as the one proposed here is well justified.

We see several areas for future work. One direction is to increase the expressiveness of the STARS API to support different kinds of real-time systems and experiment with more applications to further validate the approach. Another issue to be addressed is to extend JAVACOP to support AspectJ syntax. In the current system, we are not checking aspects for memory errors. This is acceptable as long as aspects remain simple and declarative, but real-time aspects may become more complex as we extend STARS, and their static verification will become a more pressing concern. Finally we want to investigate extensions to the type system to reduce, or eliminate, the need for code duplication.

Acknowledgments. This work is supported in part by the National Science Foundation under Grant No. 0509156, and in part by the Royal Society of New Zealand Marsden Fund. Filip Pizlo and Jason Fox implemented the Collision Detector application, Ben Titzer wrote supporting libraries. We are grateful to David Holmes and Filip Pizlo for their comments, and to the entire Ovm team at Purdue.

References

1. Chris Andreae, James Noble, Shane Markstrum, and Todd Millstein. A framework for implementing pluggable type systems. Submitted, March 2006.
2. Jason Baker, Antonio Cunei, Chapman Flack, Filip Pizlo, Marek Prochazka, Jan Vitek, Austin Armbuster, Edward Pla, and David Holmes. A real-time Java virtual machine for avionics. In *Proceedings of the 12th IEEE Real-Time and Embedded Technology and Applications Symposium (RTAS 2006)*. IEEE Computer Society, 2006.
3. William S. Beebee, Jr. and Martin Rinard. An implementation of scoped memory for real-time Java. In *Proceedings of the First International Workshop on Embedded Software (EM-SOFT)*, 2001.
4. Greg Bollella, James Gosling, Benjamin Brosgol, Peter Dibble, Steve Furr, and Mark Turnbull. *The Real-Time Specification for Java*. Addison-Wesley, June 2000.
5. Chandrasekhar Boyapati, Alexandru Salcianu, William Beebee, and Martin Rinard. Ownership types for safe region-based memory management in real-time Java. In *ACM Conference on Programming Language Design and Implementation*, June 2003.

6. Gilad Bracha. Pluggable type systems. In *OOPSLA 2004 Workshop on Revival of Dynamic Languages*, 2004.
7. Gilad Bracha and David Griswold. Strongtalk: Typechecking smalltalk in a production environment. In *In Proc. of the ACM Conf. on Object-Oriented Programming, Systems, Languages and Applications (OOPSLA)*, September 1993.
8. Robert Cartwright and Mike Fagan. Soft typing. In *Proceedings of the ACM SIGPLAN 1991 conference on Programming language design and implementation*, pages 278–292. ACM Press, 1991.
9. Dave Clarke, Michael Richmond, and James Noble. Saving the world from bad Beans: Deployment-time confinement checking. In *Proceedings of the ACM Conference on Object-Oriented Programming, Systems, Languages, and Appplications (OOPSLA)*, Anaheim, CA, November 2003.
10. David G. Clarke, John M. Potter, and James Noble. Ownership types for flexible alias protection. In *OOPSLA '98 Conference Proceedings*, volume 33(10) of *ACM SIGPLAN Notices*, pages 48–64. ACM, October 1998.
11. Dan Grossman, Greg Morrisett, Trevor Jim, Michael Hicks, Yanling Wang, and James Cheney. Region-based memory management in Cyclone. In *Proceedings of Conference on Programming Languages Design and Implementation*, pages 282–293, June 2002.
12. HIJA. European High Integrity Java Project. www.hija.info., 2006.
13. John Hogg. Islands: Aliasing Protection in Object-Oriented Languages. In *Proceedings of the OOPSLA '91 Conference on Object-Oriented Programming Systems, Languages and Applications*, 1991.
14. Gregor Kiczales, Erik Hilsdale, Jim Hugunin, Mik Kersten, Jeffrey Palm, and William G. Griswold. An overview of AspectJ. *Lecture Notes in Computer Science*, 2072:327–355, 2001.
15. Jagun Kwon and Andy Wellings. Memory management based on method invocation in RTSJ. In *OTM Workshops 2004, LNCS 3292, pp. 33–345*, 2004.
16. Jagun Kwon, Andy Wellings, and Steve King. Ravenscar-Java: A high integrity profile for real-time Java. In *Joint ACM Java Grande/ISCOPE Conference*, November 2002.
17. NASA/JPL and Sun. Golden gate. research.sun.com/projects/goldengate, 2003.
18. James Noble, John Potter, and Jan Vitek. Flexible alias protection. In *Proceedings of the 12th Eurpean Conference on Object-Oriented Programming (ECOOP)*, Brussels, Belgium, July 1998.
19. Filip Pizlo, Jason Fox, David Holmes, and Jan Vitek. Real-time java scoped memory: design patterns and semantics. In *Proceedings of the IEEE International Symposium on Object-Oriented Real-Time Distributed Computing*, May 2004.
20. David Sharp. Real-time distributed object computing: Ready for mission-critical embedded system applications. In *Proceeding of the Third International Symposium on Distribtued-Objects and Applications*, 2001.
21. Tian Zhao, James Noble, and Jan Vitek. Scoped Types for Realtime Java. In *International Real-Time Systems Symposium (RTSS 2004)*, Lisbon, Portugal, December 2004. IEEE.
22. Tian Zhao, Jens Palsberg, and Jan Vitek. Type-based confinement. *Journal of Functional Programming*, 16(1), January 2006.

Transparently Reconciling Transactions with Locking for Java Synchronization

Adam Welc, Antony L. Hosking, and Suresh Jagannathan

Department of Computer Science
Purdue University
West Lafayette, IN 47907, USA
{welc, hosking, suresh}@cs.purdue.edu

Abstract. Concurrent data accesses in high-level languages like Java and C# are typically mediated using mutual-exclusion locks. Threads use locks to *guard* the operations performed while the lock is held, so that the lock's guarded operations can never be interleaved with operations of other threads that are guarded by the same lock. This way both *atomicity* and *isolation* properties of a thread's guarded operations are enforced. Recent proposals recognize that these properties can also be enforced by concurrency control protocols that avoid well-known problems associated with locking, by transplanting notions of *transactions* found in database systems to a programming language context. While higher-level than locks, software transactions incur significant implementation overhead. This overhead cannot be easily masked when there is little contention on the operations being guarded.

We show how mutual-exclusion locks and transactions can be reconciled transparently within Java's monitor abstraction. We have implemented monitors for Java that execute using locks when contention is low and switch over to transactions when concurrent attempts to enter the monitor are detected. We formally argue the correctness of our solution with respect to Java's execution semantics and provide a detailed performance evaluation for different workloads and varying levels of contention. We demonstrate that our implementation has low overheads in the uncontended case (7% on average) and that significant performance improvements (up to $3\times$) can be achieved from running contended monitors transactionally.

1 Introduction

There has been much recent interest in new concurrency abstractions for high-level languages like Java and C#. These efforts are motivated by the fact that concurrent programming in such languages currently requires programmers to make careful use of mutual-exclusion locks to mediate access to shared data. Threads use locks to *guard* the operations performed while the lock is held, so that the lock's guarded operations can never be interleaved with operations of other threads that are guarded by the same lock. Rather, threads attempting to execute a given guarded sequence of operations will execute the entire sequence serially, without interruption, one thread at a time. In this way, locks, when used properly, can enforce both *atomicity* of their guarded operations (they execute as a single unit, without interruption by operations of other threads that

D. Thomas (Ed.): ECOOP 2006, LNCS 4067, pp. 148–173, 2006.
© Springer-Verlag Berlin Heidelberg 2006

are guarded by the same lock), and *isolation* from the side-effects of all operations by other threads guarded by the same lock.

Unfortunately, synchronizing threads using locks is notoriously difficult and error-prone. Undersynchronizing leads to safety violations such as race conditions. Even when there are no race conditions, it is still easy to mistakenly violate atomicity guarantees [14]. Oversynchronizing impedes concurrency, which can degrade performance even to the point of deadlock. To improve concurrency, some languages provide lower-level synchronization primitives such as *shared* (i.e., read-only) locks in addition to the traditional mutual-exclusion (i.e., read-write) locks. Correctly using these lower-level locking primitives requires even great care by programmers to understand thread interactions on shared data.

Recent proposals recognize that properties such as *atomicity* and *isolation* can be enforced by concurrency control protocols that avoid the problems of locking, by transplanting notions of *transactions* found in database systems to the programming language context [17, 20, 36]. Concurrency control protocols ensure *atomicity* and *isolation* of operations performed within a transaction while permitting concurrency by allowing the operations of different transactions to be interleaved only if the resulting schedule is *serializable*: the transactions (and their constituent operations) *appear* to execute in some serial order. Any transaction that might violate serializability is aborted in mid-execution, its effects are revoked, and it is retried. Atomicity is a powerful abstraction, permitting programmers more easily to reason about the effects of concurrent programs independently of arbitrary interleavings, while avoiding problems such as deadlock and priority inversion. Moreover, transactions relieve programmers of the need for careful (and error-prone) placement of locks such that concurrency is not unnecessarily impeded while correctness is maintained. Thus, transactions promote programmability by reducing the burden on programmers to resolve the tension between fine-grained locking for performance and coarse-grained locking for correctness.

Meanwhile, there is comprehensive empirical evidence that programmers almost always use mutual-exclusion locks to enforce properties of atomicity and isolation [14]. Thus, making transaction-like concurrency abstractions available to programmers is generating intense interest. Nevertheless, lock-based programs are unlikely to disappear any time soon. Certainly, there is much legacy code (including widespread use of standard libraries) that utilizes mutual-exclusion locks. Moreover, locks are extremely efficient when contention for them is low – in many cases, acquiring/releasing an uncontended lock is as cheap as setting/clearing a bit using atomic memory operations such as compare-and-swap. In contrast, transactional concurrency control protocols require much more complicated tracking of operations performed within the transaction as well as validation of those operations before the transaction can finish. Given that transaction-based schemes impose such overheads, many programmers will continue to program using exclusion locks, especially when the likelihood of contention is low. The advantages of transactional execution (i.e., improved concurrency, deadlock-freedom) accrue only when contention would otherwise impede concurrency and serializability violations are low.

These tradeoffs argue for consideration of a hybrid approach, where existing concurrency abstractions (such as Java's monitors) used for atomicity and isolation can be mediated both by locks and transactions. In fact, whether threads entering a monitor acquire a lock or execute transactionally, so long as the language-defined properties of the monitor are enforced, all is well from the programmer's perspective. Dynamically choosing which style of execution to use based on observed contention for the monitor permits the best of both worlds: low-cost locking when contention is low, and improved concurrency using transactions when multiple threads attempt to execute concurrently within the monitor.

Complicating this situation is the issue of nesting, which poses both semantic and implementation difficulties. When a nested transaction completes, isolation semantics for transactions mandate that its effects are not usually globally visible until the outermost transaction in which it runs successfully commits. Such nesting is referred to as *closed*, and represents the purest expression of nested transactions as preserving atomicity and isolation of their effects. In contrast, Java monitors expressed as synchronized methods/blocks reveal all prior effects upon exit, even if the synchronized execution is nested inside another monitor. Obtaining a meaningful reconciliation of locks with transactions requires addressing this issue.

Our Contribution

In this paper, we describe how locks and transactions can be *transparently* reconciled within Java's monitor abstraction. We have implemented monitors for Java that execute using locks when contention is low and switch over to transactions when concurrent attempts to enter the monitor are detected. Our implementation is for the Jikes Research Virtual Machine (RVM). To our knowledge, ours is the first attempt to consider hybrid execution of Java monitors using both mutual-exclusion and transactions within the same program.

Our treatment is transparent to applications: programs continue to use the standard Java synchronization primitives to express the usual constraints on concurrent executions. A synchronized method/block may execute transactionally even if it was previously executed using lock-based mutual exclusion, and vice versa. Transactional execution dynamically toggles back to mutual-exclusion whenever aborting a given transaction becomes infeasible, such as at native method calls. In both cases, hybrid execution does not violate Java semantics, and serves only to improve performance.

We make the following contributions:

1. The design and implementation of a Java run-time system that supports implementation of Java monitors (i.e., synchronized methods/blocks) using both mutual-exclusion and software transactions based on optimistic concurrency. A given monitor will execute using either concurrency control mechanism depending on its contention profile.
2. An efficient implementation of monitors as closed nested transactions. We introduce a new mechanism called *delegation* that significantly reduces the overhead of nested transactions when contention is low. Support for delegation is provided through extensions to the virtual machine and run-time system.
3. A formal semantics that defines safety criteria under which mutual exclusion and transactions can co-exist. We show that for programs that conform to prevalent atomicity idioms, Java monitors can be realized using either transactions or mutual-

exclusion with no change in observable behavior. In this way, we resolve the apparent mismatch in the visibility of the effects of Java monitors versus closed nested transactions.

4. A detailed implementation study that quantifies the overheads of our approach. We show that over a range of single-threaded benchmarks the overheads necessary to support hybrid execution (i.e., read barriers, meta-data information on object headers, etc.) is small, averaging less than 10%. We also present performance results on a comprehensive synthetic benchmark that show how transactions that co-exist with mutual-exclusion locks lead to clear run-time improvements over mutual-exclusion only and transaction-only non-hybrid implementations.

2   A Core Language

To examine notions of safety with respect to transactions and mutual exclusion, we define a two-tiered semantics for a simple dynamically-typed call-by value language similar to Classic Java [16] extended with threads and synchronization. The first tier describes how programs written in this calculus are evaluated to yield a *schedule* that defines a sequence of possible thread interleavings, and a memory model that reflects how and when updates to shared data performed by one thread are reflected in another. The second tier defines constraints used to determine whether a schedule is safe based on a specific interpretation of what it means to protect access to shared data; this tier thus captures the behavior of specific concurrency control mechanisms.

Before describing the semantics, we first introduce the language informally (see Figure 1). In the following, we take metavariables L to range over class declarations, C to range over class names, t to denote thread identifiers, M to range over methods, m to range over method names, f and x to range over fields and parameters, respectively, ℓ to range over locations, and v to range over values. We use P for process terms, and e for expressions.

SYNTAX:

$$
\begin{aligned}
P &::= (P \mid P) \mid \text{t}[e] \\
L &::= \text{class } C \, \{\overline{f} \, \overline{M}\} \\
M &::= \text{m}(\overline{x}) \, \{\, e \,\} \\
e &::= x \mid \ell \mid \text{this} \mid \text{e.f} \mid \text{e.f} := e \mid \text{new } C() \\
&\quad \mid \text{e.m}(\overline{e}) \mid \text{let } x = e \text{ in } e \text{ end} \mid \text{guard} \{e\} \, e \\
&\quad \mid \text{spawn } (e)
\end{aligned}
$$

Fig. 1. A simple call-by-value object-based concurrent language

A program defines a collection of class definitions, and a collection of processes. Classes are all uniquely named, and define a collection of instance fields and instance methods which operate over these fields. Every method consists of an expression whose value is returned as the result of a call to that method. Every class has a unique (nullary) constructor to initialize object fields. Expressions can read the contents of a field, store a new value into an instance field, create a new object, perform a method call, define local bindings to enforce sequencing of actions, or guard the evaluation of a subexpression.

To evaluate an expression of the form, guard{e_1} e, e_1 is first evaluated to yield a reference ℓ; we refer to ℓ as a *monitor*. A monitor acts as a locus of contention, and mediates the execution of the guard body. When contention is restricted to a single thread, the monitor behaves like a mutual exclusion lock. When contention generalizes to several threads, the monitor helps to mediate the execution of these threads within the guard body by enforcing serializability on their actions.

Mutual exclusion results when monitor contention is restricted to a single thread. In contrast, transactions can be used to allow multiple threads to execute concurrently within the same region. In this sense, a transaction defines the set of object and field accesses made by a thread within a guarded region. When a thread exits a region, it consults the monitor to determine if its transaction is serializable with the transactions of other threads that have executed within the same region. If so, the transaction is allowed to commit, and its accesses are available for the monitor to mediate the execution of future transactions in this region; if not, the transaction aborts, and the thread must start a new transaction for this region.

Since we are interested in transparently using either of these protocols, two obvious questions arise: (1) when is it *correct* to have a program use mixed-mode execution for its guarded regions; (2) when is it *profitable* to do so? We address the first question in the following section, and the second in Section 5.

3   Semantics

The semantics of the language are given in Figure 2. A value is either the distinguished symbol null, a location, or an object $C(\overline{\ell})$, that denotes an instance of class C, in which field f_i has value ℓ_i.

In the following, we use over-bar to represent a finite ordered sequence, for instance, $\overline{f}$ represents $f_1 f_2 \dots f_n$. The term $\overline{\alpha}\alpha$ denotes the extension of the sequence $\overline{\alpha}$ with a single element α, and $\overline{\alpha}\,\overline{\alpha}'$ denotes sequence concatenation, $S.\text{OP}_t$ denotes the extension of schedule S with operation OP_t. Given schedules S and S', we write $S \preceq S'$ if S is a subsequence of S'.

Program evaluation and schedule construction is specified by a reduction relation, $P, \Delta, \Gamma, S \Longrightarrow P', \Delta', \Gamma', S'$ that maps program states to new program states. A state consists of a collection of evaluating processes (P), a thread store (Δ) that maps threads to a local cache, a global store (Γ) that maps locations to values, and a schedule (S) that defines a collection of interleaved actions. This relation is defined up to congruence of processes ($P|P' = P'|P$, etc.). An auxiliary relation $\leadsto_t$ is used to describe reduction steps performed by a specific thread t. Actions that are recorded by a schedule are those that read and write locations, and those that acquire and release locks, the latter generated as part of guard evaluation. Informally, threads evaluate expressions using their local cache, loading and flushing their cache at synchronization points defined by guard expressions. These semantics roughly correspond to a release consistency memory model similar to the Java memory model [22].

The term $t[\mathcal{E}[e]]$ evaluated in a reduction rule is identified by the thread t in which it occurs; thus $\mathcal{E}_P^t[e]$ denotes a collection of processes containing a process with thread

PROGRAM STATES

$$t \in Tid$$
$$P \in Process$$
$$x \in Var$$
$$\ell \in Loc$$
$$v \in Val \quad = \texttt{null} \mid \texttt{C}(\overline{\ell}) \mid \ell$$
$$\sigma \in Store \quad = Loc \rightarrow Val$$
$$\Gamma \in SMap \quad = Loc \rightarrow Store$$
$$\Delta \in TStore \quad = Tid \rightarrow Store$$
$$\text{OP}_t^\Gamma\,\ell, \text{OP}_t\,\ell \in Ops \quad = \{\mathbf{rd}, \mathbf{wr}\} \times Tid \times Loc+$$
$$\{\mathbf{acq}, \mathbf{rel}\} \times Tid \times Loc \times SMap$$
$$S \in Schedule = Ops^*$$
$$\Lambda \in State \quad = Process \times Store \times Schedule$$

EVALUATION CONTEXTS

$$\mathcal{E} ::= \bullet \mid \mathcal{E}.\mathtt{f} := \mathtt{e} \mid \ell.\mathtt{f} := \mathcal{E}$$
$$\mid \mathcal{E}.\mathtt{m}(\overline{\mathtt{e}}) \mid \ell.\mathtt{m}(\overline{\ell}\; \mathcal{E}\; \overline{\mathtt{e}})$$
$$\mid \texttt{let } \mathtt{x} = \mathcal{E} \texttt{ in e end}$$
$$\mid \texttt{guard}\,\{\mathcal{E}\}\,\mathtt{e}$$

$$\mathcal{E}_P^t[\mathtt{e}] ::= P \mid \mathtt{t}[\mathcal{E}[\mathtt{e}]]$$

SEQUENTIAL EVALUATION RULES

$$\texttt{let } \mathtt{x} = \mathtt{v} \texttt{ in e end}, \sigma, S \rightsquigarrow_t \mathtt{e}[\mathtt{v}/\mathtt{x}], \sigma, S$$

$$\frac{mbody(\mathtt{m}, \mathtt{C}) = (\overline{\mathtt{x}}, \mathtt{e}) \quad \sigma(\ell) = \mathtt{C}(\overline{\ell})}{\ell.\mathtt{m}(\overline{\mathtt{v}}), \sigma, S \rightsquigarrow_t [\overline{\mathtt{v}}/\overline{\mathtt{x}}, \ell/\texttt{this}]\mathtt{e}, \sigma, S}$$

$$\frac{field(\mathtt{C}) = \overline{\mathtt{f}} \quad \sigma(\ell) = \mathtt{C}(\overline{\ell}) \quad S' = S.\mathbf{rd}_t\,\ell}{\ell.\mathtt{f}_i, \sigma, S \rightsquigarrow_t \ell_i, \sigma, S'}$$

$$\frac{\begin{array}{c}\sigma(\ell) = \mathtt{C}(\overline{\ell''}) \quad \sigma(\ell') = \mathtt{v} \\ \sigma' = \sigma[\ell''_i \mapsto \mathtt{v}] \\ S' = S.\mathbf{rd}_t\,\ell'.\mathbf{wr}_t\,\ell''_i\end{array}}{\ell.\mathtt{f}_i := \ell', \sigma, S \rightsquigarrow_t \ell', \sigma', S'}$$

$$\frac{\begin{array}{c}\ell', \overline{\ell} \text{ fresh} \\ \sigma' = \sigma[\ell' \mapsto \mathtt{C}(\overline{\ell}), \overline{\ell} \mapsto \texttt{null}] \\ S' = S.\mathbf{wr}_t\,\ell_1 . \ldots \mathbf{wr}_t\,\ell_n.\mathbf{wr}_t\,\ell' \\ \ell_1, \ldots, \ell_n \in \overline{\ell}\end{array}}{\texttt{new } \mathtt{C}(), \sigma, S \rightsquigarrow_t \ell', \sigma', S'}$$

GLOBAL EVALUATION RULES

$$\frac{\Delta(\mathtt{t}) = \sigma \qquad e, \sigma, S \rightsquigarrow_{t,\Gamma} e', \sigma', S'}{\mathcal{E}_P^t[\mathtt{e}], \Delta, \Gamma, S \implies \mathcal{E}_P^t[\mathtt{e}'], \Delta[\mathtt{t} \mapsto \sigma'], \Gamma, S'}$$

$$\frac{\begin{array}{c}\sigma = \Delta(\mathtt{t}) \quad \sigma' = \sigma \circ \Gamma(\ell) \\ \Delta' = \Delta[\mathtt{t} \mapsto \sigma'] \\ \ell \notin lockset(S, \mathtt{t}) \\ \mathcal{E}_P^t[\mathtt{e}], \Delta', \Gamma, \phi \implies^* P' \mid \mathtt{t}[\mathtt{v}], \Delta'', \Gamma', S' \\ \Gamma'' = \Gamma'[\ell \mapsto \Gamma'(\ell) \circ \Delta''(\mathtt{t})]\end{array}}{\begin{array}{c}\mathcal{E}_P^t[\texttt{guard}\,\{\ell\}\,\mathtt{e}], \Delta, \Gamma, S \\ \implies \mathcal{E}_{P'}^t[\mathtt{v}], \Delta'', \Gamma'', S.\mathbf{acq}_t^\Gamma\,\ell.S'.\mathbf{rel}_t^{\Gamma'}\,\ell\end{array}}$$

$$\frac{\mathtt{t}' \text{ fresh} \quad \Delta' = \Delta[\mathtt{t}' \mapsto \Delta(\mathtt{t})] \quad P' = P \mid \mathtt{t}'[\mathtt{e}]}{\mathcal{E}_P^t[\texttt{spawn}\,(\mathtt{e})], \Delta, \Gamma, S \implies \mathcal{E}_{P'}^t[\texttt{null}], \Delta', \Gamma, S}$$

Fig. 2. Semantics

identifier t executing expression e with context $\mathcal{E}$. The expression "picked" for evaluation is determined by the structure of evaluation contexts.

Most of the rules are standard: holes in contexts can be replaced by the value of the expression substituted for the hole, `let` expressions substitute the value of the bound variable in their body. Method invocation binds the variable `this` to the current receiver object, in addition to binding actuals to parameters, and evaluates the method body in this augmented environment. Read and write operations augment the schedule in the obvious way. Constructor application returns a reference to a new object whose fields are initialized to null.

To evaluate expression e within a separate thread, we first associate the new thread with a fresh thread identifier, set the thread's local store to be the current local store of its parent, and begin evaluation of e using an empty context.

Let ℓ be the monitor for a guard expression. Before evaluating the body, the local store for the thread evaluating the guard is updated to load the current contents of the global store at location ℓ. In other words, global memory is indexed by the set of locations that act as monitors: whenever a thread attempts to synchronize against one of these monitors (say, ℓ), the thread augments its local cache with the store associated with ℓ in the global store. The body of the guard expression is then evaluated with respect to this updated cache. When the expression completes, the converse operation is performed: the contents of the local cache are flushed to the global store indexed by ℓ. Thus, threads that synchronize on different references will not have their updates made visible to one another. Observe that the semantics do not support a single global store; to propagate effects performed in one thread to all other threads would require encoding a protocol that uses a global monitor for synchronization. To simplify the presentation, we prohibit nested guard expressions from synchronizing on the same reference ($\ell \notin lockset(S, t)$).

3.1 Schedules

When the body of the guard is entered, the schedule is augmented to record the fact that there was monitored access to e via monitor ℓ by thread t ($\mathbf{acq}_t^\Gamma \ell$). When evaluation of the guard completes, the schedule is updated to reflect that reference ℓ is no longer used as a monitor by t ($\mathbf{rel}_t^{\Gamma'} \ell$). The global store recorded in the schedule at synchronization acquire and release points will be used to define safety conditions for mutual-exclusion and transactional execution as we describe below.

These semantics make no attempt to enforce a particular concurrency model on thread execution. Instead, we specify safety properties that dictate the legality of an interleaving by defining predicates on schedules. To do so, it is convenient to reason in terms of *regions*, subschedules produced as a result of guard evaluation:

$$region(S) = \{S_i \preceq S | S_i = \mathbf{acq}_t^\Gamma \ell.S_i'.\mathbf{rel}_t^{\Gamma'} \ell\}$$

For any region $R = \mathbf{acq}_t^\Gamma \ell.S_i'.\mathbf{rel}_t^{\Gamma'} \ell$, $T(R) = t$, and $\mathcal{L}(R) = \ell$.

The predicate $msafe(S)$ defines the structure of schedules that correspond to an interpretation of guards in terms of mutual exclusion:

Definition 1. *Msafe*

$$\frac{\forall R \in region(S) \ T(R) = t, \mathcal{L}(R) = \ell}{t \neq t' \rightarrow \mathbf{acq}_{t'}^{\Gamma'} \ell \notin R}{msafe(S)}$$

For a schedule to be safe with respect to concurrency control based on mutual exclusion, multiple threads cannot concurrently execute within the body of a guarded region protected by the same monitor. Thus if thread t is executing within a guard protecting expression e using monitor ℓ, no other thread can attempt to acquire ℓ until t relinquishes it.

We can also interpret thread execution within guarded expressions in terms of transactions. Under this interpretation, multiple threads can execute transactionally within the same guarded expression concurrently. To ensure the legality of such concurrent executions, we impose constraints that capture notions of transactional *isolation* and *atomicity* on schedules:

Definition 2. *Isolated*

$$\forall R \in region(S) = \mathbf{acq}_t^\Gamma \ell.S'.\mathbf{rel}_t^{\Gamma'} \ell$$
$$\forall \mathbf{rd}_t \ell' \in S'$$
$$\frac{\Gamma(\ell) = \sigma \wedge \Gamma'(\ell) = \sigma' \rightarrow \sigma(\ell') = \sigma'(\ell')}{isolated(S)}$$

Isolation ensures that locations read by a guarded region are not changed during the region's evaluation. The property is enforced by requiring that the global store associated with a region's monitors is not modified during the execution of the region. Note that the global store Γ' at the point control exits a guarded expression does reflect global updates performed by other threads, but does not reflect *local* updates performed by the current thread that have yet to be propagated. Thus, the isolation rule captures visibility constraints on schedules corresponding to execution within a guard expression; namely, any location read within the schedule cannot be modified by other concurrently executing threads.

Definition 3. *Atomic*

$$\forall N, R \in region(S), \quad \ell = \mathcal{L}(N) \quad R = S_b.N.S_a$$
$$\frac{\mathcal{T}(N) = \mathcal{T}(R) = t \wedge t \neq t' \rightarrow \mathbf{acq}_{t'}^\Gamma \ell \notin S_a}{atomic(S)}$$

Atomicity ensures that the effects of a guarded region are not propagated to other threads until the region completes. Observe that our semantics propagate updates to the global store when a guarded region exits; these updates become visible to any thread that subsequently executes a guard expression using the same monitor. Thus, a nested region may have its effects made visible to any thread whose execution is mediated by the same monitor. This would violate our intuitive notion of atomicity for the enclosing guarded region since its partial effects (i.e., the effects performed by the inner region) would be visible before it completes. Our atomicity rule thus captures the essence of a closed nested transaction model: the effects of a nested transaction are visible to the parent, via the local store, but are propagated to other threads only when the outermost transaction completes.

Our safety rules are distinguished from other attempts at defining atomicity properties [14, 15] for concurrent programs because they do not rely on mutual-exclusion semantics for lock acquisition and release. For example, consider a schedule in which two threads interleave execution of two guarded regions protected by the same monitor. Such an execution is meaningless for semantics in which synchronization is defined in terms of mutual-exclusion, but quite sensible if guarded regions are executed transactionally. Isolation is satisfied if the actions performed by the two threads are non-overlapping. Atomicity is satisfied even if these guarded regions execute in a nested context because the actions performed within a region by one thread are not witnessed by the other due to the language's release consistency memory model.

Definition 4. *Tsafe.* We also define $tsafe(S)$ (read "transaction-safe") to hold if both $atomic(S)$ and $isolated(S)$ hold.

3.2 Safety

In order to allow implementations to choose adaptively either a transactional or mutual-exclusion based protocol for guarded regions, dictated by performance considerations, it must be the case that there is no observable difference in the structure of the global store as a consequence of the decisions taken. We show that programs that satisfy *atomicity* and *isolation* exhibit this property.

Suppose program P induces schedule S_P and $tsafe(S_P)$ holds. Now, if $msafe(S_P)$ also holds, then any region in S_P can be implemented either transactionally or using mutual-exclusion. Suppose, however, that $msafe(S_P)$ does not hold. This is clearly possible: consider an interleaving in which distinct threads concurrently evaluate guard expressions protected by the same monitor, but whose bodies access disjoint locations.

Our soundness theorem shows that every such schedule can be permuted to one that satisfies both *msafe* and *tsafe*. In other words, for every transaction-safe schedule, there is an equivalent schedule that also satisfies constraints defining mutual-exclusion. Thus, as long as regions in a program obey atomicity and isolation, they can be implemented by either one of the mutual-exclusion or closed nested transaction mechanisms without violating program semantics.

Theorem 1. *Soundness.* Let

$$\mathsf{t}[e], \Delta_0, \Gamma_0, \phi \Longrightarrow^* \mathsf{t}[v], \Delta, \Gamma, S$$

and suppose $tsafe(S)$ holds but $msafe(S)$ does not. Then, there exists a schedule S_f such that

$$\mathsf{t}[e], \Delta_0, \Gamma_0, \phi \Longrightarrow^* \mathsf{t}[v], \Delta', \Gamma', S_f$$

where $tsafe(S_f)$ and $msafe(S_f)$ hold, and in which $\Gamma = \Gamma'$.

Proof Sketch. Let S be $tsafe$, $R \preceq S$, and suppose $msafe(R)$ does not hold, and thus $msafe(S)$ does not hold. Suppose $R = \mathbf{acq}_\mathsf{t}^\Gamma \ell.S'.\mathbf{rel}_\mathsf{t}^{\Gamma'} \ell$. Since $msafe(R)$ does not hold, there must be some $R' \preceq S$ such that $R' = \mathbf{acq}_{\mathsf{t}'}^{\Gamma''} \ell.S''.\mathbf{rel}_{\mathsf{t}'}^{\Gamma'''} \ell$ where $\mathbf{acq}_{\mathsf{t}'}^{\Gamma''} \ell \in S'$. Since $isolated(S)$ holds, $isolated(R)$ must also hold, and thus none of the actions performed by t' within S' are visible to actions performed by t in S'. Similarly, since atomicity holds, actions performed by t in S' are not visible to operations executed by t' in S'. Suppose that $\mathbf{rel}_{\mathsf{t}'}^{\Gamma''''} \ell$ follows R in S. Then, effects of S' may become visible to operations in S'' (e.g., through nested synchronization actions). But, then $isolated(R')$ would not hold. However, because $tsafe(S)$ holds, we can construct a permuted schedule S_P of S' in which actions performed by R' are not interleaved with actions performed by R, thus ensuring that $msafe(S_P)$, $isolated(S_P)$, and $atomic(S_P)$ all hold.

4   Design Overview

Our design is motived by three overarching goals:

1. The specific protocol used to implement guarded regions must be completely transparent to the application. Thus, Java `synchronized` blocks and methods serve as guarded regions, and may be executed either transactionally or exclusively depending upon heuristics applied at run-time.
2. The modifications necessary to support such transparency should not lead to performance degradation in the common case – single-threaded uncontended execution within a guarded region – and should lead to notable performance gain in the case when there is contention for entry to the region.
3. Transparency should not come at the expense of correctness. Thus, transactional execution should not lead to behavior inconsistent with Java concurrency semantics.

Issue 3 is satisfied for any Java program that is transaction-safe as defined in the previous section. Fortunately, recent studies have shown that the overwhelming majority of concurrent Java programs exhibit monitor usage that satisfy the correctness goal by using monitors solely as a mechanism to enforce atomicity and isolation for sequences of operations manipulating shared data [14]. We thus focus our attention in the remainder of this section on the first two goals.

Note that lock-based synchronization techniques for languages such as Java are already heavily optimized for the case where monitors are uncontended [2, 5]. Indeed, the Jikes RVM platform that serves in our experiments already supports very efficient lock acquisition and release in this common case: atomically (using "test-and-set" or equivalent instructions) set a bit in the header of the monitor object on entry and clear it on exit. Only if another thread tries to acquire the monitor does *lock inflation* occur to obtain a "fat" lock and initiate full-blown synchronization with wait queues, etc. Thus, the second of our goals has already been met by the current-state-of-the-art.

Supporting transactional execution of guarded regions in place of such highly-optimized locking techniques is thus a significant engineering challenge, if they are to have any advantage at all. As discussed below, our implementation uses *optimistic* concurrency control techniques to minimize the overhead of accesses to shared data [21].

We also make the obvious but important assumption that a guarded region cannot be executed concurrently by different threads using different protocols (i.e., locking or transactional). Any thread wishing to use a different protocol (e.g., locking) than the one currently installed (e.g., transactional) for a given monitor must wait until all other threads have exited the monitor.

4.1   Nesting and Delegation

Since Java monitors support nesting, our transparency requirement means that transactional monitors must also support nesting. There is no conceptual difficulty in dealing with nesting; recall that the definition of atomicity and isolation captures the essence of the closed nested transaction model [24], and that the prevalent usage of monitors is to enforce atomicity and isolation [14].

Unfortunately, nesting poses a performance challenge since each monitor defines a locus of contention, for which we must maintain enough information to validate the serializability invariants that guarantee atomicity and isolation. Nesting exacerbates this overhead since nested monitors must record separate access sets used to validate serializability.

However, there is no *a priori* reason why accesses must be mediated by the immediately enclosing monitor that guards them. For example, a single global monitor could conceivably be used to mediate all accesses within all monitors. Under transactional execution, a single global monitor effectively serves to implement the atomic construct of Harris and Fraser [17]. Under lock-based execution, a single global monitor defines a global exclusive lock. The primary reason why applications choose *not* to mediate access to shared regions using a single monitor is because of increased contention and corresponding reduced concurrency. In the case of mutual exclusion, a global lock reduces opportunities for concurrent execution; in the case of transactional execution, a global monitor would have to mediate accesses from logically disjoint transactions, and is likely to be inefficient and non-scalable.

Nonetheless, we can leverage this observation to optimize an important specific case for transactional execution of monitors. Consider a thread T acquiring monitor outer, and prior to releasing outer, also acquiring monitor inner. If no other thread attempts concurrent acquisition of inner (i.e., the monitor is uncontended) then the acquisition of inner can be *delegated* to outer. In other words, instead of synchronizing on monitor inner we can establish outer as inner's delegate and synchronize on outer instead. Since monitor inner is uncontended, there is nothing for inner to mediate, and no loss of efficiency accrues because of nesting (provided that the act of setting a delegate is inexpensive). Of course, when monitor inner *is* contended, we must ensure that atomicity and isolation are appropriately enforced. Note that if inner was an exclusive monitor, there would be no benefit in using delegation since acquisition of an uncontended mutual-exclusion monitor is already expected to have low overhead.

Protocol Description. Figure 3 illustrates how the delegation protocol works for a specific schedule; for simplicity, we show only Java-level monitor acquire/release operations. The schedule consists of steps 1 through 6 enumerated in the first column of the schedule table. The right-hand side of Figure 3 describes the state of the transactional monitors, used throughout the schedule, with respect to delegation. A monitor whose delegate has been set is shaded grey; an arrow represents the reference to its delegate. To begin, we assume that the delegates of both monitor outer and monitor inner have not been set. Thread T starts by (transactionally) "acquiring" monitor outer, creating a new transaction whose accesses are mediated by outer and setting outer's delegate to itself (step 1 in Figure 3(a)). Then T proceeds to (transactionally) "acquire" monitor inner. Because there is no delegate for inner, and T is already executing within a transaction mediated by outer, T sets inner's delegate to refer to outer (step 2 in Figure 3(b)).

	T	T'
1	**acq**(outer)	
2	**acq**(inner)	
3		**acq**(inner)
4	**rel**(inner)	
5	**rel**(outer)	
6		**rel**(inner)

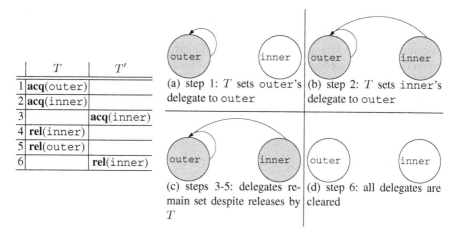

(a) step 1: T sets outer's delegate to outer

(b) step 2: T sets inner's delegate to outer

(c) steps 3-5: delegates remain set despite releases by T

(d) step 6: all delegates are cleared

Fig. 3. Delegation example

This protocol implements a closed nested transaction model: the effects of T's execution within monitor inner are not made globally visible until the outer transaction commits, since only outer is responsible for mediating T's accesses and validating serializability.

The delegates stay set throughout steps 3, 4 and 5 (Figure 3(b)), even after thread T, the setter of both delegates, commits its top-level transaction and "releases" outer. In the meantime, thread T' attempts to "acquire" inner. The delegate of inner is at this point already set to outer so thread T' starts its own transaction whose accesses are mediated by outer. The delegates are cleared only after T''s transaction, mediated by outer, commits or aborts. At this point there is no further use for the delegates.

Note that some precision is lost in this example: the transactional meta-data maintained by outer is presumably greater than what would be necessary to simply implement consistency checks for actions guarded by inner. However, despite nesting, only one monitor (outer) has been used to mediate concurrent data accesses and only one set of transactional meta-data was created for outer. However, observe that if the actions of steps 2 and 3 are reversed so that T' acquires inner before T then inner's delegate would not be set, and T' would begin its new transaction mediated in this case by inner, so transactional meta-data for both outer and inner would be needed.

4.2   Reverting to Mutual Exclusion

Optimistic concurrency control assumes the existence of a revocation mechanism so that the effects of a transaction can be reversed on abort. In real world Java applications some operations (e.g., I/O) are irrevocable, so their effects cannot be reversed. To handle such situations, we force any thread executing transactionally guarded by some monitor, but which attempts an irrevocable operation, to revert immediately to mutual exclusion. To support this, each thread executing transactionally must record the monitors it has "acquired" in order of acquisition. Our implementation reverts to mutual exclusion calls to native methods, and at explicit thread synchronization using wait/notify. At the point where such operations arise, we attempt acquisition of all the monitors that the thread acquired transactionally, in order of acquisition. Successful acquisition of all the monitors implies that all other threads executing transactions against those monitors have completed, exited the monitors, and cleared their respective delegates. From that point on the locking thread can proceed in mutual-exclusion mode, releasing the locks as it exits the monitor scopes. If the transition is unsuccessful (because some other thread acquired the monitors in lock-mode) then the thread executing the irrevocable operation is revoked (i.e., its innermost transaction is aborted) and re-executed from its transaction starting point.

5   Implementation

Our transactional delegation protocol reduces overheads for uncontended nested monitors executed transactionally by deploying nested transaction support only when absolutely necessary. Thus, transactions are employed only for top-level monitors or for contended nested monitors, as described earlier.

Transactions are implemented using an optimistic protocol [21], divided into three phases: *read*, *validate* and *write-back*. Each transaction updates private copies of the objects it manipulates: a copy is created when the transaction (thread) first writes to an object. The validation phase verifies transaction-safety, aborting the transaction and discarding the copies if safety is violated. Otherwise, the write-back phase lazily propagates updated copies to the shared heap, installing each of them atomically.

In the remainder of this section we discuss our strategy for detecting violation of serializability via dependency tracking, our solutions for revocation and re-execution on abort, and details of the implementation platform.

5.1   Platform

Our prototype implementation is based on the Jikes Research Virtual Machine (RVM) [4]. The Jikes RVM is a reserch Java virtual machine with performance comparable to many production virtual machines. Jikes RVM itself is written almost entirely in Java and is self-hosted (i.e., it does not require another virtual machine to run). Java bytecodes in the Jikes RVM are compiled directly to machine code. The Jikes RVM's distribution includes both a *baseline* and an *optimizing* compiler. The baseline compiler performs a straightforward expansion of each bytecode instruction into its corresponding sequence of assembly instructions. Our prototype targets the Intel x86 architecture.

5.2   Read and Write Barriers

Our technique to control and modify accesses to shared data uses compiler-inserted read and write *barriers*. These barriers are code snippets emitted by the compiler to augment each heap read and write operation. They trigger creation of versions (copy-on-write) and redirection of reads to the appropriate version, as well as tracking data dependencies.

5.3   Detecting Validity

Threads executing concurrently in the scope of a given monitor will run as separate transactions. Each transaction hashes its shared data accesses into two private hash maps: a read-map and a write-map, mapping each shared object to a single bit. Once a transaction commits and propagates its updates into the shared heap it also propagates information about its own updates to a global write-map associated with the monitor mediating the transaction. Other transactions whose operations are mediated by the same monitor will then, during their validation phase, intersect their local read-maps with the global write-map to determine if the shared data accesses caused a violation of serializability. When nesting results in an inner monitor running a distinct nested transaction (as opposed to piggy-backing on its delegate-parent) there will be a separate global write-map for each transaction level, so validation must check all global write-maps at all nesting levels. The remaining details of our implementation are the same as in our earlier work [36].

Since for most Java programs reads significantly outnumber writes, reducing the number of read barriers is critical to achieving reasonable performance. Our implementation therefore trades-off accuracy for run-time efficiency in detecting violation of transaction safety. Instead of placing barriers on all reads to shared heap variables (e.g., reading an integer from an object), we assume that the first time a reference is loaded from the heap, it will eventually be used to read from its target object. Thus, read barriers are placed only on loads of *references* from the heap. In other words, we "pre-read" (tagging the local-read map appropriately) all objects whose references are loaded to the stack of a transactional thread. As a result, even objects that are never read, but only written, are conservatively pre-read. This greatly simplifies version management and enables early detection of serializability violations, as described below. This read barrier optimization is applied only for objects and arrays. All other accesses, including all reads from static variables and all writes to shared items incur an appropriate barrier.

5.4 Revocation

Our revocation procedure is identical to our prior work [36], allowing for transaction abort at arbitrary points during its execution. The abort is signaled by throwing a Revoke exception. Undo and re-execution procedures are implemented using a combination of bytecode re-writing and virtual machine modifications. Even though Java monitors are lexically scoped, it is necessary to support transaction aborts at arbitrary points to correctly handle native method calls as well as wait and notify operations, as described in Section 4.2.

In the case of optimistic protocols, the decision about whether a transaction should be committed or aborted is made during the validation phase. Since transactions are lexically scoped, it is relatively easy to encapsulate the computation state at the beginning of the transaction so that it can be reinstated if the transaction aborts, by copying the closure of thread-local state at that point. We use bytecode rewriting in conjunction with a modified exception handling mechanism to restore this saved state on abort.

5.5 Versioning

We use shared data versioning to prevent the effects of incomplete transactions from being made visible to other threads until they commit. We maintain versions of both objects and arrays, as well as static (global) variables. Object and array versioning are handled exactly the same. Statics use a slightly modified approach, requiring boxing and unboxing of the static values.

Because our array versioning procedure is identical to that used for versioning objects, we refer only to objects in the following description. Versions are accessible through a forwarding pointer from the original object. We use a "copy-on-write" strategy for creating new versions. A transaction creates a new (uncommitted) copy right before performing first update to an object, and redirects all subsequent read and write operations to access that version. It is important to note that for transaction safety all programs executed in our system must be race-free (a prerequisite for atomicity): all accesses by all threads to a given shared data item must be guarded by the same monitor [14]. As a result, writes to the same location performed by different threads will be detected as unsafe by our validity check described above. This also means that only the first transaction writing to a given object need create a version for it. Other transactions accessing that object are aborted when the writing transaction commits and discovers the overlap.

Upon successful commit of a transaction, the current version becomes the *committed version* and remains accessible via a *forwarding pointer* installed in the original object. Subsequent accesses are re-directed (in the read and write barriers) via the forwarding pointer to the committed version. When a transaction aborts all its versions are discarded. Note that at most two versions of an object exist at any given time: a committed version and an uncommitted version.

As noted above, the read barriers are only executed on reference loads. In general, multiple on-stack references may end up pointing to *different* versions of *the same* object. This is possible, even though read barriers are responsible for retrieving the most up-to-date version of the object, writes may occur after the reference has been loaded to multiple locations on the stack. The run-time system must thus ensure that the version of an object accessible through an on-stack reference is the "correct" one. The visibility rules for the Java Memory Model [22] mean that at certain synchronization points (e.g., monitor entry, access to volatile variables, etc.) threads are obliged to have the same view of the shared heap. As a result, it is legal to defer fixing on-stack references until specific synchronization points (e.g., monitor enter/exit, wait/notify). At these points all on-stack references must be forwarded to the most up-to-date version. Reference forwarding is implemented using a modified version of thread stack inspection as used by the garbage collector.

In addition to performing reference forwarding at synchronization points, when a version is first created by a transaction, the thread creating the version must forward all references on its stack to point to the new version. This ensures that all subsequent accesses (by the same thread) observe the results of the update.

5.6 Example

We now present an example of how these different implementation features interact. Figure 4 describes actions concerning shared data versioning and serializability violation detection, performed by threads T, T' and T'' executing the schedule shown in Table 1. Figure 4(a) represents the initial state, before any threads have started executing. Wavy lines represent threads, and circles represent objects o1 and o2. The objects

Table 1. A non-serializable schedule

Step	T	T'	T''
1	**acq**(outer)		
2	**wt**(o2)		
3			**acq**(inner)
4			**wt**(o1)
5		**acq**(outer)	
6		**acq**(inner)	
7		**rd**(o1)	
8			**rel**(inner)
9	**rel**(outer)		
10		**rd**(o1)	
11		**rel**(inner)	
12		**rel**(outer)	

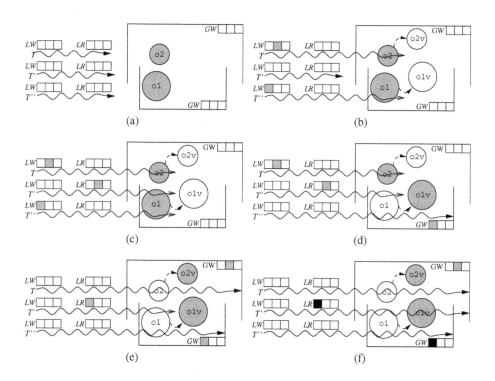

Fig. 4. A non-serializable execution

have not yet been versioned – they are shaded grey because at the moment they contain the most up-to-date values. The larger box (open at the bottom) represents the scope of transactional monitor outer, the smaller box (open at the top) represents the scope of transactional monitor inner. Both the global write map (GW) associated with the monitor and the local maps (write map LW and read map LR) associated with each thread have three slots. Maps that belong to a given thread are located above the wavy line representing this thread. We assume that accesses to object o1 hash to the first slot of every map and accesses to object o2 hash to the second slot of every map

Execution begins with threads T and T'' starting to run transactions whose operations are mediated by monitors outer and inner (respectively) and performing updates to objects o2 and o1 (respectively), as presented in Figure 4(b). The updates trigger creation of copies o2v and o1v for objects o2 and o1, respectively, and tagging of the local write maps. Thread T tags the second slot of its local write map since it modifies object o2, whereas thread T'' tags the first slot of its local write map since it modifies object o1. In Figure 4(c) thread T' starts executing, running the outermost transaction mediated by monitor outer and its inner transaction mediated by monitor inner, and then reads object o1, which tags the local read map. In Figure 4(d) T'' attempts to commit its transaction. Since no writes by other transactions mediated by monitor inner have been performed, the commit is successful: o1v becomes the committed version, the contents of T''''s local write map are transferred to inner's global write map and the local write map is cleared. Similarly, in Figure 4(e), T's transaction commits successfully: o2v becomes the committed version and the local write map is cleared after its contents has been transfered to the global write map associated with monitor outer. In Figure 4(f) thread T' proceeds to again read object o1 and then to commit its transactions (both inner and outer). However, because a new committed version of object o1 has been created, o1v is read by T' instead of the original object. When attempting to commit both its inner and outer transactions, thread T' must intersect its local read map with the global maps associated with both monitor outer and monitor inner. The first intersection is empty (no writes performed in the scope of monitor outer could compromise reads performed by T'), the second however is not – both transactions executed by T' must be aborted and re-executed.

5.7 Header Compression

For performance we need efficient access to several items of meta-data associated with each object (e.g., versions and their identities, delegates, identity hash-codes, access maps, etc.). At the same time, we must keep overheads to a minimum when transactions are not used. The simplest solution is to extend object headers to associate the necessary meta-data. Our transactional meta-data requires up to four 32-bit words. Unfortunately, Jikes RVM does not easily support variable header sizes and extending the header of each object by four words has serious overheads of space and performance, even in the case of non-transactional execution. On the other hand keeping meta-data "on the side" (e.g., in a hash table), also results in a significant performance hit.

We therefore implement a compromise. The header of every object is extended by a single *descriptor word* that is lazily populated when meta-data needs to be associated with the object. If an object is never accessed in a transactional context, its descriptor word remains empty. Because writes are much less common than reads, we treat the information needed for reads as the common case. The first transactional read will place the object's identity hash-code in the descriptor (we generate hash codes independently of native Jikes RVM object hashcodes to ensure good data distribution in the access maps). If additional meta-data needs to be associated with the object (e.g., a new version on write) then the descriptor word is overwritten with a reference to a new *descriptor object* containing all the necessary meta-data (including the hash-code originally stored in the descriptor word). We discriminate these two cases using the low-order bit of the descriptor word.

5.8 Code Duplication

Transactional support (e.g., read and write barriers) is required only when a thread decides to execute a given monitor transactionally. However, it is difficult to determine if a particular method is going to be used only in a non-transactional context. To avoid unnecessary overheads during non-transactional execution, we use bytecode rewriting to duplicate the code of all (user-level) methods actually being executed by the program. Every method can then be compiled in two versions: one that embeds transactional support (transactional methods) and one that does not (non-transactional methods). This allows the run-time system to dynamically build a call chain consisting entirely of non-transactional methods for non-transactional execution. Unfortunately, because of our choice to access most up-to-date versions of objects through forwarding pointers, we cannot fully eliminate read barriers even in non-transactional methods. We can however eliminate all write barriers and make the non-transactional read barriers very fast in the common case – they must simply differentiate objects that have never been accessed transactionally from those that have. In addition to the usual reference load, such barriers consist only of a null check, one condition, and one load. These instructions verify that the descriptor word is empty, indicating that the object has never been accessed transactionally, so no alternate version has ever been created.

5.9 Triggering Transactional Execution

Our implementation must be able to determine whether to execute a given monitor transactionally or exclusively. We use a very light-weight heuristic to detect monitor contention and trigger transactional execution only for contended monitors . The first thread to enter a monitor always executes the monitor exclusively. It is only after a thin mutual-exclusion lock is "inflated" by being turned into a fat lock (on contended acquisition of the lock) that the monitor in question is asserted to be contended. All threads queued waiting for the monitor will then execute transactionally once the currently executing (locking) thread exits the monitor. We recognize that there are more advanced and potentially more conservative heuristics that a production system may wish to use. For example, programmer annotations could be provided to mark the concurrency control mechanism that is to be used for different monitors. Adaptive solutions based on dynamic profiling or solutions utilizing off-line profiles may also provide more refined information on when it is best to execute monitors transactionally.

6   Experiments

The performance evaluation of our prototype implementation is divided into two parts. We use a number of single-threaded benchmarks (from the SPECjvm98 [31] and Java Grande [30] suites) to measure the overheads of supporting hybrid-mode execution (e.g., compiler-inserted barriers, code-duplication, object layout modifications, etc.)

when monitors are uncontended. We also use an extended version of the OO7 object database benchmark [10], to expose the range of performance when executing under different levels of monitor contention. We measure the behavior when all monitors are executed transactionally and when using the hybrid scheme that executes monitors transactionally only when sufficient monitor contention is detected. Our measurements were taken on an eight-way 700MHz Intel Pentium III symmetric multi-processor (SMP) with 2GB of RAM running Linux kernel version 2.4.20-31.9smp (RedHat 9.0). Our implementation uses version 2.3.4+CVS (with 2005/12/08 15:01:10 UTC timestamp) of Jikes RVM for all the configurations used to take the measurements (mutual-exclusion-only, transactions-only and hybrid). We ran each benchmark configuration in its own invocation of the virtual machine, repeating the benchmark six times in each invocation, and discarding the results of the first iteration, in which the benchmark classes are loaded and compiled, to eliminate the overheads of compilation.

6.1 Uncontended Execution

A summary of our performance evaluation results when monitors are uncontended is presented in Figure 5. Our current prototype implementation is restricted to running bytecodes compiled with debugging information for local variables; this information is needed by the bytecode rewriter for generating code to store and restore local state in case of abort. Therefore, we can only obtain results for those SPECjvm98 benchmarks for which source code is available.

In Figure 5(a) we report total summary overheads for a configuration that supports hybrid-mode execution. The overheads are reported as a percentage with respect to a "clean" build of the "vanilla" unmodified Jikes RVM. The average overhead is on the order of 7%, with a large portion of the performance degradation attributed to execution of the compiler-inserted barriers, as described below. Figure 5(b) reveals how different mechanisms for transactional execution affect performance in the uncontended case. The bottom of every bar represents the effect of extending the header of every object by one word (as needed to support transaction-related meta-data). The middle of every bar represents the cost of all other system modifications, excluding compiler-inserted

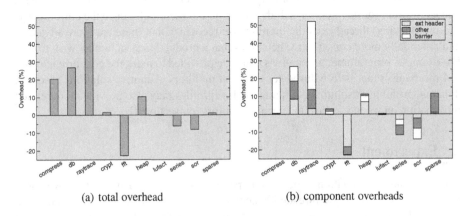

(a) total overhead   (b) component overheads

Fig. 5. Uncontended execution

barriers.[1] The top bar captures overhead from execution of the barriers themselves (mostly read barriers but also barriers on static variable accesses).

Observe that changing the object layout can by itself have a significant impact on performance. In most cases, the version of the system with larger object headers indeed induces overheads over the clean build of Jikes RVM, but in some situations (e.g., FFT or Series), its performance actually improves over the clean build by a significant amount; variations in cache footprint is the most likely cause. The performance impact of the compiler-inserted barriers is also clearly noticeable, especially in the case of benchmarks from the SPECjvm98 suite. When discounting overheads related to the execution of the barriers, the average overhead with respect to the clean build of Jikes RVM drops to a little over 1% on average. This result is consistent with that reported by Blackburn and Hosking [7] for garbage collection read barriers that can incur overheads up to 20%. It would be beneficial for our system to use a garbage collector that might help to amortize the cost of the read barrier. Fortunately, there exist modern garbage collectors (e.g., [6]) that fulfill this requirement.

6.2 Contended Execution

The OO7 benchmark suite [10] provides a great deal of flexibility of benchmark parameters (e.g., database structure, fractions of reads/writes to shared/private data). The multi-user OO7 benchmark [9] allows control over the degree of contention for access to shared data. In choosing OO7 as a benchmark our goal was to accurately gauge the various trade-offs inherent with our implementation over a wide range of different workloads, rather than emulating specific workloads of potential applications. We believe the benchmark captures essential features of scalable concurrent programs that can be used to quantify the impact of the design decisions underlying our implementation.

The OO7 benchmark operates on a synthetic design database, consisting of a set of *composite parts*. Each composite part comprises a graph of *atomic parts*, and a document object containing a small amount of text. Each atomic part has a set of attributes (i.e., fields), and is connected via a bi-directional association to several other atomic parts. The connections are implemented by interposing a separate connection object between each pair of connected atomic parts. Composite parts are arranged in an *assembly* hierarchy; each assembly is either made up of composite parts (a *base* assembly) or other assemblies (a *complex* assembly). Each assembly hierarchy is called a *module*, and has an associated *manual* object consisting of a large amount of text. Our results are all obtained with an OO7 database configured as in Table 2.

Our implementation of OO7 conforms to the standard OO7 database specification. Our traversals are a modified version of the multi-user OO7 traversals. A traversal chooses a single path through the assembly hierarchy and at the composite part level randomly chooses a fixed number of composite parts to visit (the number of composite parts to be visited during a single traversal is a configurable parameter). When the traversal reaches the composite part, it has two choices:

1. Do a *read-only* depth-first traversal of the atomic part subgraph associated with that composite part; or

---

[1] The measurements were taken after artificially removing compiler-inserted barriers from the "full" version of the system. Naturally our system cannot function without barriers.

Table 2. Component organization of the OO7 benchmark

Component	Number
Modules	1
Assembly levels	7
Subassemblies per complex assembly	3
Composite parts per assembly	3
Composite parts per module	500
Atomic parts per composite part	20
Connections per atomic part	3
Document size (bytes)	2000
Manual size (bytes)	100000

2. Do a *read-write* depth-first traversal of the associated atomic part subgraph, swap-ping the x and y coordinates of each atomic part as it is visited.

Each traversal can be done beginning with either a *private* module or a *shared* mod-ule. The parameter's of the workload control the mix of these four basic operations: read/write and private/shared. To foster some degree of interesting interleaving and contention in the case of concurrent execution, our traversals also take a parameter that allows extra overhead to be added to read operations to increase the time spent performing traversals.

Our experiments here use traversals that always operate on the *shared* module, since we are interested in the effects of contention on performance of our system. Our imple-mentation of OO7 conforms to the standard OO7 database specification. Our traversals differ from the original OO7 traversals in adding a parameter that controls entry to mon-itors at varying levels of the database hierarchy. We run 64 threads on 8 physical CPUs. Every thread performs 1000 traversals (enters 1000 monitors) and visits 4M atomic parts during each iteration. When running the benchmarks we varied the following pa-rameters:

- ratio of shared reads to shared writes: from 10% shared reads and 90% shared writes (mostly read-only workload) to 90% shared reads and 10% shared writes (mostly write-only workload).
- level of the assembly hierarchy at which monitors are entered: level one (module level), level three (second layer of complex assemblies) and level six (fifth layer of complex assemblies). Varying the level at which monitors are entered models different granularities of user-level synchronization from coarse-grained through to fine-grained and diversifies the degree of monitor contention.

Figure 6 plots execution times for the OO7 benchmark when all threads execute all monitors transactionally (Figure 6(a)) and when threads execute in hybrid mode, where the mode is chosen based on monitor contention (Figure 6(b)). The execution times are normalized with respect to the performance of the "clean" build of Jikes RVM (90% confidence intervals are also reported). Figure 7 plots the total number of aborts for both transactions-only (Figure 7(a)) and hybrid (Figure 7(b)) executions. Different lines on the graphs represent different levels of user-level synchronization granularity – one being the most coarse-grained and six being the most fine-grained.

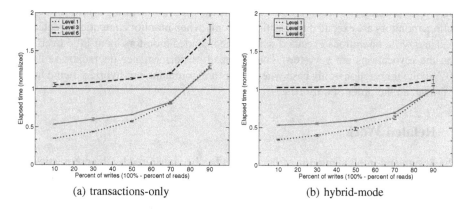

(a) transactions-only   (b) hybrid-mode

Fig. 6. Normalized execution times for the OO7 benchmark

When there is a suitable level of monitor contention, and when the number of writes is moderate, transactional execution significantly outperforms mutual exclusion by up to three times. The performance of the transactions-only scheme degrades as the number of writes increases (and so does the number of generated hash-codes) since the number of bitmap collisions increases, leading to a large number of aborts even at low contention (Figure 7(b)). Extending the size of the maps used to detect serializability violations would certainly remedy the problem, at least in part. However, we cannot use maps of an arbitrary size. This could unfavorably affect memory overheads (especially compared to mutual-exclusion locks) but more importantly we have determined that the time to process potentially multiple maps at the end of the outermost transaction must be bounded. Otherwise, the time spent to process them becomes a source of significant delay (currently each map contains over 16,000 slots). The increased number of aborts certainly has a very significant impact on the difference in performance between the transactions-only and hybrid schemes. The overheads of the transactions-only scheme cannot however be attributed only to the increased abort rate – observe that the shape of

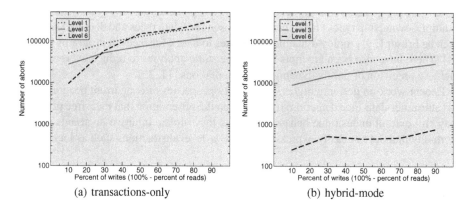

(a) transactions-only   (b) hybrid-mode

Fig. 7. Total number of aborts for the OO7 benchmark

the graphs plotting execution times and aborts are different. During hybrid-mode execution, monitors are executed transactionally only when monitor contention is detected, read and write operations executed within uncontended monitors incur little overhead, and the revocations are very few. Thus, instead of performance degradation of over 70% in the transactions-only case when writes are dominant, our hybrid scheme incurs overhead on the order of only 10%.

7 Related Work

The design and implementation of our system has been inspired by the optimistic concurrency protocols first introduced in the 1980's [21] to improve database performance. Given a collection of transactions, the goal in an optimistic concurrency implementation is to ensure that only a serializable schedule results [1, 19, 32]. Devising fast and efficient techniques to confirm that a schedule is correct remains an important topic of study.

There have been several attempts to reduce overheads related to mutual-exclusion locking in Java. Agesen et al. [2] and Bacon et al. [5] describe locking implementations for Java that attempt to optimize lock acquisition overhead when there is no contention on a shared object. Other recent efforts explore alternatives to lock-based concurrent programming [17, 36, 20, 18]. In these systems, threads are allowed to execute within a guarded region (e.g., protected by monitors) concurrently, but are monitored to ensure that safety invariants (e.g., serializability) are not violated. If a violation of these invariants by some thread is detected, the computation performed by this thread is revoked, any updates performed so far discarded and the thread is re-executed. Our approach differs from these in that it seamlessly integrates different techniques to manage concurrency within the same system. When using our approach, the most appropriate scheme is dynamically chosen to handle concurrency control in different parts of *the same* application.

There is also a large body of work on removing synchronization primitives when it can be shown that there is never contention for the region being guarded [3, 28, 33]. The results derived from these efforts would equally benefit applications running in the system supporting hybrid-mode execution.

There has been much recent interest in devising techniques to detect data races in concurrent programs. Some of these efforts [13, 8] present new type systems using, for example, ownership types [12] to verify the absence of data races and deadlocks. Others such as Eraser [29] employ dynamic techniques to check for races in programs [25, 23, 34]. There have also been attempts to leverage static analyses to reduce overheads and increase precision of purely dynamic implementations [11, 35].

Recent work on deriving higher-level safety properties of concurrent programs [15, 14] subsumes data-race detection. It is based on the observation that race-free programs may still exhibit undesirable behavior because they violate intuitive invariants such as atomicity that are not easily expressed using low-level abstractions such as locks.

8 Conclusions

Existing approaches to providing concurrency abstractions for programming languages offer disjoint solutions for mediating concurrent accesses to shared data throughout the lifetime of the entire application. Typically these mechanisms are either based on mutual exclusion or on some form of transactional support. Unfortunately, none of these techniques is ideally suited for all possible workloads. Mutual exclusion performs best when there is no contention on guarded region execution, while transactions have the potential to extract additional concurrency when contention exists.

We have designed and implemented a system that seamlessly integrates mutual exclusion and optimistic transactions to implement Java monitors. We formally argue correctness (with respect to language semantics) of such a system and provide a detailed performance evaluation of our hybrid scheme for different workloads and varying levels of contention. Our implementation and experiments demonstrate that the hybrid approach has low overheads (on the order of 7%) in the uncontended (base) case and that significant performance improvements (speedups up to $3\times$)can be expected from running contended monitors transactionally.

Acknowledgements

We thank the anonymous referees for their suggestions and improvements to this paper. This work is supported by the National Science Foundation under grants Nos. CCR-0085792, CNS-0509377, CCF-0540866, and CNS-0551658, and by gifts from IBM and Microsoft. Any opinions, findings and conclusions expressed herein are the authors and do not necessarily reflect those of the sponsors.

References

[1] Adya, A., Gruber, R., Liskov, B., and Maheshwari, U. Efficient optimistic concurrency control using loosely synchronized clocks. *ACM SIGMOD Record 24*, 2 (June 1995), 23–34.

[2] Agesen, O., Detlefs, D., Garthwaite, A., Knippel, R., Ramakrishna, Y. S., and White, D. An efficient meta-lock for implementing ubiquitous synchronization. In OOPSLA'99 [26], pp. 207–222.

[3] Aldrich, J., Sirer, E. G., Chambers, C., and Eggers, S. J. Comprehensive synchronization elimination for Java. *Science of Computer Programming 47*, 2-3 (2003), 91–120.

[4] Alpern, B., Attanasio, C. R., Barton, J. J., Cocchi, A., Hummel, S. F., Lieber, D., Ngo, T., Mergen, M., Shepherd, J. C., and Smith, S. Implementing Jalapeño in Java. In OOPSLA'99 [26], pp. 314–324.

[5] Bacon, D., Konuru, R., Murthy, C., and Serrano, M. Thin locks: Featherweight synchronization for Java. In *Proceedings of the ACM Conference on Programming Language Design and Implementation* (Montréal, Canada, June). *ACM SIGPLAN Notices 33*, 5 (May 1998), pp. 258–268.

[6] Bacon, D. F., Cheng, P., and Rajan, V. T. A real-time garbage collector with low overhead and consistent utilization. In *Conference Record of the ACM Symposium on Principles of Programming Languages* (New Orleans, Lousiana, Jan.). *ACM SIGPLAN Notices 38*, 1 (Jan. 2003), pp. 285–298.

[7] Blackburn, S. M., and Hosking, A. L. Barriers: Friend or foe? In *Proceedings of the ACM International Symposium on Memory Management* (Vancouver, Canada, Oct., 2004), D. F. Bacon and A. Diwan, Eds. ACM, 2004, pp. 143–151.

[8] Boyapati, C., Lee, R., and Rinard, M. C. Ownership types for safe programming: preventing data races and deadlocks. In *Proceedings of the ACM Conference on Object-Oriented Programming Systems, Languages, and Applications* (Seattle, Washington, Nov.). *ACM SIGPLAN Notices 37*, 11 (Nov. 2002), pp. 211–230.

[9] Carey, M. J., DeWitt, D. J., Kant, C., and Naughton, J. F. A status report on the OO7 OODBMS benchmarking effort. In *Proceedings of the ACM Conference on Object-Oriented Programming Systems, Languages, and Applications* (Portland, Oregon, Oct.). *ACM SIGPLAN Notices 29*, 10 (Oct. 1994), pp. 414–426.

[10] Carey, M. J., DeWitt, D. J., and Naughton, J. F. The OO7 benchmark. In *Proceedings of the ACM International Conference on Management of Data* (Washington, DC, May). *ACM SIGMOD Record 22*, 2 (June 1993), pp. 12–21.

[11] Choi, J.-D., Lee, K., Loginov, A., O'Callahan, R., Sarkar, V., and Sridharan, M. Efficient and precise datarace detection for multithreaded object-oriented programs. In *Proceedings of the ACM Conference on Programming Language Design and Implementation* (Berlin, Germany, June). *ACM SIGPLAN Notices 37*, 5 (May 2002), pp. 258–269.

[12] Clarke, D. G., Potter, J. M., and Noble, J. Ownership types for flexible alias protection. In *Proceedings of the ACM Conference on Object-Oriented Programming Systems, Languages, and Applications* (Vancouver, Canada, Oct.). *ACM SIGPLAN Notices 33*, 10 (Oct. 1998), pp. 48–64.

[13] Flanagan, C., and Freund, S. N. Type-based race detection for Java. In PLDI'00 [27], pp. 219–232.

[14] Flanagan, C., and Freund, S. N. Atomizer: a dynamic atomicity checker for multithreaded programs. In *Conference Record of the ACM Symposium on Principles of Programming Languages* (Venice, Italy, Jan.). 2004, pp. 256–267.

[15] Flanagan, C., and Qadeer, S. Types for atomicity. In *Proceedings of the 2003 ACM SIG-PLAN International Workshop on Types in Language Design and Implementation* (New Orleans, Louisiana, Jan.). 2003, pp. 1–12.

[16] Flatt, M., Krishnamurthi, S., and Felleisen, M. Classes and mixins. In *Conference Record of the ACM Symposium on Principles of Programming Languages* (San Diego, California, Jan.). 1998, pp. 171–183.

[17] Harris, T., and Fraser, K. Language support for lightweight transactions. In *Proceedings of the ACM Conference on Object-Oriented Programming Systems, Languages, and Applications* (Anaheim, California, Nov.). *ACM SIGPLAN Notices 38*, 11 (Nov. 2003), pp. 388–402.

[18] Harris, T., Marlow, S., Peyton-Jones, S., and Herlihy, M. Composable memory transactions. In *Proceedings of the ACM SIGPLAN Symposium on Principles and Practice of Parallel Programming* (Chicago, Illinois, June). 2005, pp. 48–60.

[19] Herlihy, M. Apologizing versus asking permission: Optimistic concurrency control for abstract data types. *ACM Trans. Database Syst. 15*, 1 (1990), 96–124.

[20] Herlihy, M., Luchangco, V., Moir, M., and Scherer, III, W. N. Software transactional memory for dynamic-sized data structures. In *Proceedings of the Annual ACM Symposium on Principles of Distributed Computing* (Boston, Massachusetts, July). 2003, pp. 92–101.

[21] Kung, H. T., and Robinson, J. T. On optimistic methods for concurrency control. *ACM Trans. Database Syst. 9*, 4 (June 1981), 213–226.

[22] Manson, J., Pugh, W., and Adve, S. The Java memory model. In *Conference Record of the ACM Symposium on Principles of Programming Languages* (Long Beach, California, Jan.). 2005, pp. 378–391.

[23] Mellor-Crummey, J. On-the-fly detection of data races for programs with nested fork-join parallelism. In *Proceedings of the ACM/IEEE Conference on Supercomputing* (Albuquerque, New Mexico, Nov.). 1991, pp. 24–33.

[24] Moss, J. E. B. *Nested Transactions: An Approach to Reliable Distributed Computing.* MIT Press, Cambridge, Massachusetts, 1985.

[25] O'Callahan, R., and Choi, J.-D. Hybrid dynamic data race detection. In *Proceedings of the ACM SIGPLAN Symposium on Principles and Practice of Parallel Programming* (San Diego, California, June). 2003, pp. 167–178.

[26] *Proceedings of the ACM Conference on Object-Oriented Programming Systems, Languages, and Applications* (Denver, Colorado, Nov.). *ACM SIGPLAN Notices 34,* 10 (Oct. 1999).

[27] *Proceedings of the ACM Conference on Programming Language Design and Implementation* (Vancouver, Canada, June). *ACM SIGPLAN Notices 35,* 6 (June 2000).

[28] Ruf, E. Effective synchronization removal for Java. In PLDI'00 [27], pp. 208–218.

[29] Savage, S., Burrows, M., Nelson, G., Sobalvarro, P., and Anderson, T. Eraser: a dynamic data race detector for multithreaded programs. *ACM Trans. Comput. Syst. 15,* 4 (Nov. 1997), 391–411.

[30] Smith, L. A., Bull, J. M., and Obdržálek, J. A parallel Java Grande benchmark suite. In *Proceedings of the ACM/IEEE Conference on Supercomputing* (Denver, Colorado, Nov.). 2001, p. 8.

[31] SPEC. SPECjvm98 benchmarks, 1998. http://www.spec.org/osg/jvm98.

[32] Stonebraker, M., and Hellerstein, J., Eds. *Readings in Database Systems,* third ed. Morgan Kaufmann, 1998.

[33] Ungureanu, C., and Jagannathan, S. Concurrency analysis for Java. In *Proceedings of the International Static Analysis Symposium* (Santa Barbara, California, Jun./Jul.), J. Palsberg, Ed. vol. 1824 of *Lecture Notes in Computer Science.* 2000, pp. 413–432.

[34] von Praun, C., and Gross, T. R. Object race detection. In *Proceedings of the ACM Conference on Object-Oriented Programming Systems, Languages, and Applications* (Tampa, Florida, Oct.). *ACM SIGPLAN Notices 36,* 11 (Nov. 2001), pp. 70–82.

[35] von Praun, C., and Gross, T. R. Static conflict analysis for multi-threaded object-oriented programs. In *Proceedings of the ACM Conference on Programming Language Design and Implementation* (San Diego, California, June). 2003, pp. 115–128.

[36] Welc, A., Jagannathan, S., and Hosking, A. L. Transactional monitors for concurrent objects. In *Proceedings of the European Conference on Object-Oriented Programming* (Oslo, Norway, June), M. Odersky, Ed. vol. 3086 of *Lecture Notes in Computer Science.* Springer-Verlag, 2004, pp. 519–542.

Object Technology – A Grand Narrative?

Steve Cook

Microsoft UK Ltd, Cambridge
steve.cook@microsoft.com

Abstract. This brief article sets out some personal observations about the development of object technology from its emergence until today, and suggests how it will develop in the future.

1 The Beginning

Like many people, my first encounter with object oriented programming was in 1981 when I read the August 1981 special issue of Byte magazine [1] that was entirely devoted to Smalltalk (I still have it). At the time, I was developing graphical user interfaces using the programming languages C and Pascal, and I encountered difficulties in trying to make the procedural structure of my programs correspond cleanly to the problems I was trying to solve. It seemed that something was missing from these languages; and when I saw Smalltalk, I realized what that thing was – objects. In fact I discovered that I was late to the party; objects had been in the Simula language since 1967.

I threw myself for the next ten years into studying and teaching object-oriented programming. My team implemented Smalltalk and used it to build experimental distributed systems. I witnessed the development and competition of Objective-C and C++. Eiffel inspired me by its visionary design. I tried to understand the relationship between functional and OO programming. I participated in the first several OOPSLA and ECOOP conferences.

In those days, objects were controversial. Some academic colleagues of mine were deeply offended by the polymorphism: they saw it as fundamentally undermining the programmer's ability to reason logically about program consequences. Others were unwilling to admin that anything new was going on: objects were variously "just subroutines" or "just data abstractions" or "just entities".

Of course, objects won the day. Although COBOL remains popular for commercial data processing, most widespread programming languages today are object-oriented. All of the basic mechanisms of object-oriented programming are generally taken for granted: inheritance, virtual functions, instances and classes, interfaces, real-time garbage collection. In Microsoft I work daily with the .NET framework, an extensive object-oriented library for building distributed interactive applications, using the languages supported by Microsoft's Common Language Runtime, primarily C# and Visual Basic.

However we should recognize that the path that we've collectively trod over the past 20 years has involved some significant blind alleys, each of which has had a substantial effect on the industry. I've been personally involved in all of them.

D. Thomas (Ed.): ECOOP 2006, LNCS 4067, pp. 174–179, 2006.
© Springer-Verlag Berlin Heidelberg 2006

2 Some Detours

People became very excited about objects. In some quarters, objects became regarded as a solution for all known problems. Let's look critically at some of the proposals that resulted.

2.1 Objects Solve the Reuse Problem

We've all been enticed by promises of reuse. Objects, we were told, are just like hardware components. We were led to believe that once an object has been designed to solve a problem, it can be reused over and over again in different projects, thus reducing the cost and increasing the productivity of software development.

Although there is a grain of truth in this proposition, it has often been treated much too naively. I have seen several large companies kick off major initiatives based on a simplistic interpretation of this suggestion, and spend many millions of dollars investing in structures and organizations for reuse that ultimately did not work. Objects are typically not reusable because of architectural mismatches. You can almost never take an object designed for use in a single application and use it successfully in another. Except for a few very small and self-contained items, almost all objects are constructed with a large number of both functional and non-functional assumptions about the environment in which they live. Such assumptions are encapsulated by object-oriented frameworks and class libraries, without which it would be almost impossible to build modern distributed interactive applications. The design of these frameworks and libraries is a very complicated business, and organizing them to be powerful and easy to use requires enormous skill and investment.

2.2 Objects Solve the Distribution Problem

Objects seemed like a great answer to the problem of how to build a distributed computing system. If we could conceal the difference between invoking an operation on an object locally and remotely, it was said, then distribution became simple. Indeed, there were early experimental implementations of distributed Smalltalk in which the menus would pop up on the wrong screens because of programming errors. The highest-profile manifestation of this principle was CORBA – the Common Object Request Broker Architecture, from the Object Management Group.

The facts about distribution are these:

- invoking a remote operation is orders of magnitude slower than invoking a local one;
- the programmer of a remote operation probably did it in a programming language different from yours;
- the invoker and the invokee will want to change their implementations at different times;
- neither end can trust the other nor the connection to be well-behaved in any way.

The consequence of these facts is that using objects and their interfaces as a basis for implementing distributed systems does not work well. Abstraction is a wonderful thing, but not when the properties that you are abstracting away are in fact the essence of the problem. In a distributed system, it's important to deal explicitly with autonomous systems, with explicit boundaries, in a language-independent format, over limited bandwidth connections, with explicit statements of how interoperation will be managed, and explicit mechanisms to handle failures.

2.3 Objects Solve the Database Problem

During the mid 1990s, object databases were developed [2]. Many investments were made on the assumption that object databases would just blow relational databases away. Object databases were thought to be so conspicuously good that relational databases just wouldn't survive, in the same way that relational databases supplanted their hierarchical predecessors.

It didn't happen. Relational databases remain the mainstay of commercial data processing. Relational databases continue to provide the performance, scalability, autonomy and language independence for which they were designed, while object databases did not provide these qualities. Object databases exist mainly in niche applications, and object-oriented ideas continue to slowly permeate into the relational world. But the "impedance mismatch" between object-oriented programs and the relational containers where they store their data remains a major unsolved bugbear for programmers.

2.4 Objects Solve the Modelling Problem

The early 1990s saw the publication of several books that proposed using object-oriented concepts to model systems. The general idea was to assert that since the "real world" self-evidently consists of objects, then the appropriate approach for developing software is to describe the objects that exist in the real world, decorate these descriptions with suitable properties and methods, and your software system would simply pop out. Some authors went so far as to claim that this provides a suitable method for modelling business processes and organizations, and these models could be directly translated into the software systems that would implement these businesses. Nobody successfully made this work, though, and such a view is rarely proposed today.

Alongside this philosophy went the development of various diagrammatic approaches for designing object-oriented systems, under the moniker of "object-oriented analysis and design". The Unified Modeling Language (UML) [3] was developed in order to unify three different diagrammatic conventions for object-oriented analysis and design. Unfortunately, UML also claimed to unify semantics, even though such semantic unification is in practice impossible. Different object-oriented programming technologies have subtly different meanings for terms like class, instance, interface, inheritance etc, and these cannot be unified. Either UML is another, different programming language, or it is a set of diagrammatical conventions which can be loosely coupled to existing programming languages. This confusion remains unsettled to this date. Furthermore, some proponents of UML propose that it can also be used for modelling tasks outside its original scope, such as modelling of businesses, workflows, databases, and service-oriented systems. Trying to satisfy all of these conflicting needs has led to UML becoming bloated and unwieldy. I doubt that we'll see any future revisions of it.

3 The Present

This section sets out some views about the current state of the art, reflecting on some lessons learnt from the proposals in the previous section.

3.1 Languages

A great deal of research has been done into programming language design since the emergence of object-oriented programming. Nevertheless, there are still many controversies in object-oriented language design, such as: should multiple inheritance be allowed? When is it appropriate to use interfaces vs classes? Should classes be "minimal" or "humane"[1]? Why doesn't my language allow covariant redefinition of result types? Should classes themselves be objects? Should types be declared or inferred? How to deal effectively with concurrency? Why must operations be attached to a single class? Experience with designing object-oriented programs and class libraries has led to many insights, and many of today's object-oriented languages are nicer than those of 20 years ago; but there are no right answers to any of these questions.

3.2 Class Libraries

Object-oriented design has always been difficult to learn. The basic aim of object-orientation has been to create the most efficient representation of your program, the essence of which is to avoid repetition. If you want to create a piece of program, you must always go and see whether it already exists in your class library. This means that the library must be designed to offer such pieces effectively: and here the fun starts. Designing a good class library is a very complex undertaking. In the work I am currently doing, we've found Steven Clarke's "Cognitive Dimensions of Usability" [4] particularly useful in designing a class library for managing modelling metadata. We also refer frequently to Cwalina and Abrams [5] for guidance. The naïve idea that "objects are just there for the picking" seems truly absurd in 2006.

3.3 Service Orientation

We've realized that the individual components of distributed systems need to be dealt with explicitly as autonomous entities, with explicit boundaries, interacting through message exchanges, sharing data schemas and behavioural contracts. This set of tenets has come to be known as "service-orientation". The roots of service orientation lie in the internet. Since the internet provides ubiquitous access to almost all of the computers in the world, it brings the requirements for distributed computing to the surface in a relentless and vivid fashion.

Service-orientation is supported by standards that are subscribed to by all major software vendors, and is widely agreed to provide the path towards global interoperability of distributed systems. Service orientation does not depend on object-oriented technology: it separates description of data and behaviour, and is not bound to any particular programming language or object-oriented semantics. XML is a widespread

---

[1] http://www.martinfowler.com/bliki/HumaneInterface.html

standard for representing structured data, and most implementations of service-orientation use XML documents to transmit data.

3.4 Talking to Data

An interesting development that attempts to bridge the gap between objects and data-bases is Microsoft's LINQ (Language Integrated Query) project [6]. LINQ integrates queries, sets and transform operations directly into the programming language, thereby providing a strongly-typed means of interacting with data from within an object oriented program. LINQ comes in two flavours: Xlinq talks to XML data and Dlinq talks to SQL-based databases.

LINQ is particularly useful, I believe, because it explicitly recognizes the pervasive existence of distinct "technology spaces". In [7] a technology space is defined as "a working context with a set of associated concepts, body of knowledge, tools, required skills, and possibilities". Examples of technology spaces include OO programming, XML, relational databases, and metamodelling. Many of the blind alleys identified in the previous section were based on a hope that objects provide a unifying technology that can be successfully applied to any problem. We've recognized that this is not so, and that different spaces will continue to exist and evolve as new technology challenges are encountered. Therefore we'll have to find efficient and effective ways of bridging between these spaces: and LINQ offers a promising approach to bridging between the object-oriented programming, the XML and the SQL spaces.

3.5 Modelling

We've learnt from our mistakes that objects do not provide a unifying technology. So let's not make the same mistakes with models: they don't provide a unifying technology either. By models, I mean (influenced by UML) diagrammatic depictions of structures and behaviours that can easily be consumed by humans and interpreted by machines. The notion that all of software development will somehow be replaced by modelling is at least as mistaken as "objects are just there for the picking". Models are useful for specific purposes, such as flowcharting, describing entities and relation-ships, conceptual class diagrams, message sequence charting, state diagramming, and especially describing the structures and relationships of architectural components. Specific kinds of models are useful in specific tasks; the modelling language used for a specific task must be designed to be fit for that task. Today's increasing interest in Domain Specific Languages, rather than general-purpose modelling languages, clearly recognizes this.

4 The Future

I've tried to describe some lessons learnt from experience with objects over the last 25 years. Summarizing, objects remain only one of a variety of different ways to solve problems, whilst our frequent mistake was to hope that objects were the "grand narrative" that might lead us to understand and unify everything.

Which leaves us with the question of whether there is anything – any language, representation, set of concepts, ontology, etc - that might solve everything? Could we invent a technology to apply to all possible software development problems? More parochially, is there a perfect OO programming language? I think not, and I guess this means I've evolved into a post-modern programmer [8]. We'll continue to invent new representations that solve the problems at hand, and then we'll have to find ways to find them and fit them together effectively. This means that discovery, bridging and transformation technologies will inevitably become increasingly important.

References

1. BYTE magazine, Volume 6 No 8, August 1981.
2. Atkinson, M., Bancilhon F., DeWitt D., Dittrich K., Maier D., Zdonik, S: The Object-Oriented Database System Manifesto. Deductive and Object-Oriented Databases. Elsevier, Amsterdam (1989).
3. Rumbaugh, J., Jacobson, I., Booch, G: The Unified Modeling Language Reference Manual. Addison-Wesley (1999).
4. Clarke, S. Cognitive Dimensions of Usability http://blogs.msdn.com/stevencl/linklist.aspx
5. Cwalina, K. and Abrams, B: Framework Design Guidelines : Conventions, Idioms, and Patterns for Reusable .NET Libraries. Addison-Wesley (2006).
6. The LINQ project, at http://msdn.microsoft.com/netframework/future/linq/
7. Kurtev, I., Bézivin, J., Aksit, M. Technical spaces: An initial appraisal. CoopIS, DOA 2002 Federated Conferences, Industrial track, Irvine (2002). Available online at http://www.sciences.univ-nantes.fr/lina/atl/www/papers/PositionPaperKurtev.pdf
8. Noble, J and Biddle, R: Notes on Postmodern Programming, at http://www.mcs.vuw.ac.nz/comp/Publications/CS-TR-02-9.abs.html

Peak Objects

William R. Cook

Department of Computer Sciences
University of Texas at Austin
wcook@cs.utexas.edu

I was aware of a need for object-oriented programming long before I learned that it existed. I felt the need because I was using C and Lisp to build medium-sized systems, including a widely-used text editor, CASE and VLSI tools. Stated simply, I wanted flexible connections between providers and consumers of behavior in my systems. For example, in the text editor anything could produce text (files, in-memory buffers, selections, output of formatters, etc) and be connected to any consumer of text. Object-oriented programming solved this problem, and many others; it also provided a clearer way to *think about* the problems. For me, this thinking was very pragmatic: object solved practical programming problems cleanly.

The philosophical viewpoint that "objects model the real world" has never appealed to me. There are many computational models, including functions, objects, algebras, processes, constraints, rules, automata – and each has a particular ability to model interesting phenomena. While some objects model some aspects of the real world, I do not believe they are inherently better suited to this task than other approaches. Considered another way, what percentage of classes in the implementation of a program have any analog in the real world?

In the mid-'80s, when I was learning about objects, it was frequently said that objects could not be explained, they must be experienced. Sufficient experience would lead to an "Ah ha!" insight after which you could smile knowingly and say "it can't be explained... it must be experienced." This is, unfortunately, still true to a degree. Many students (and programmers) do not feel comfortable with dynamic dispatch, the higher-order nature of objects and factories, or complex subtype/inheritance hierarchies. Advanced programmers also struggle to design effective architectures using advanced techniques – where the best approach is not obvious.

In what follows I describe some long-standing myths about object-oriented programming and then suggest future directions.

Classes Are Abstract Data Types

The assumption that classes are *abstract data types* (ADTs) is one of the more persistent myths. It is not clear exactly how it started, but the early lack of a solid theoretical foundation of objects may have contributed.

ADTs consist of a *type* and *operations* on the type – where the type is *abstract*, meaning it name/identity is visible but is concrete representation is hidden. Hiding the representation type generally requires a *static type system*.

Objects, on the other hand, are *collections of operations*. The types of the operations (the object's interface) are completely public (no hidden types), whereas

D. Thomas (Ed.): ECOOP 2006, LNCS 4067, pp. 180–185, 2006.
© Springer-Verlag Berlin Heidelberg 2006

the internal representation is completely invisible from the outside. The idea of *type abstraction*, or partially hiding a type, is not essential to objects, although it does show up when classes are used as types (see below). Since they don't require type abstraction, object work equally well in dynamically and statically typed languages (e.g. Smalltalk and C++).

The relationship between ADTs and objects is well-known [7, 17], yet even experts often treat "data abstraction" and "abstract data type" as synonyms, for example, in the history of CLU [11], and many textbooks. I suspect that the identification of "data abstraction" and "abstract data type" arose because ADTs seem natural and fundamental: they have the familiar structure of abstract algebra, support effective reasoning and verification [9], and have an elegant explanation in type theory [14]. In the late '70s ADTs appeared in practical programming languages, including Ada, Modula-2, and ML. However, ADTs in their pure form have never become as popular as object-oriented programming. It is interesting to consider what would have happened if Stroustrup had added ML-style ADTs, modules, and functors to "C" instead of adding objects [12].

Most modern languages combine both ADTs and objects: Smalltalk has built-in ADTs for integers, which are used to implement the object-oriented numbers. But Smalltalk does not support user-defined ADTs. OCAML allows user-defined ADTs and also objects. Java, C# and C++ have built-in ADTs for primitive types. They also support pure objects via interfaces and a form of user-defined ADTs: when a class is used as a type it acts as a bounded existential, in that it specifies a particular implementation/representation, not just public interface.

Integrating the complementary strengths of ADTs and objects is an active research topic, which now focuses on extensibility, often using syntactic expressions as a canonical example [10, 15, 19, 21]. However, the complete integration of these approaches has not yet been achieved.

Objects Encapsulate Mutable State

Encapsulation is a useful tool for hiding implementation details. Although encapsulation is often cited as one of the strong points of object-oriented programming, complex objects with imperative update can easily break encapsulation.

For imperative classes with simple interfaces, like stacks or queues, the natural object implementation is effective at encapsulation. But if objects that belong to the private representation of an updatable object leak outside the object, then encapsulation is lost. For example, an object representing a graph may use other objects to represent nodes and edges – but public access to these objects can break encapsulation. This problem is the subject of ongoing research; several approaches have been developed to enforce encapsulation with extended type systems [6, 4, 22, 2]. Another approach uses multiple interfaces to prevent updates to objects that pass outside an encapsulation boundary [18].

With Orthogonal Persistence, We Don't Need Databases

Orthogonal persistence is a natural extension of the traditional concept of variable *lifetime* to allow objects or values to persist beyond a single program execution [1]. Orthogonal persistence is a very clean model of persistent data – in effect it provides garbage collection with persistent roots. Unfortunately, orthogonal persistence by itself does not eliminate the need for databases.

There are three main problems with orthogonal persistence: performance, concurrency, and absolutism – yet they are, I believe, all solvable [8]. The first problem is that orthogonal persistence does not easily support the powerful optimizations available in relational databases [13]. Until orthogonal persistence supports similar optimizations – without introducing non-uniform query languages – I believe it will not be successful outside small research systems. The second problem is the need for control of concurrent access to persistent data. Databases again have well-developed solutions to this problem, but they must be adapted to work with orthogonal persistence [3]. The final problem with orthogonal persistence is its absolutism: taken to the limit, anything can be persistent, including threads, user interface objects, and operating system objects. It also requires that object behavior (class definitions and methods) be stored along with an object's data. While this may be appropriate for some applications, a more pragmatic approach will likely be more successful in a wider range of applications, which just need to store ordinary data effectively.

We must also address the cultural problem: object-oriented programmers rarely have a deep understanding of database performance or transaction models. Database researchers don't seem very interested in how databases are actually incorporated into large systems.

Objects Are the Best Model for Distributed Programming

One of the grand projects at the end of the last millennium was the development of distributed object models. There were many contributors and results to this effort, but some of the most visible were CORBA, DCOM, and Java RMI [20]. I believe that this project met its goals, but was a mostly a failure because the goals were not the right goals. The problem is that *distance does matter* [16] and communication partners don't want to share stubs. I suspect the world wide web would have failed if the HTTP protocol had been designed and implemented using CORBA. Web services are a step in the right direction, but the document-oriented communication style must be better integrated with the application programming model.

Classes Are Types

Object-oriented programming emphasizes the use of interfaces to separate clients and services, yet when classes are used as types they specify the implementation, not just the interface, of objects. It is even possible to inspect the runtime implementation of objects, thus breaking encapsulation, by indiscriminate use of `instanceof`. Programs that include many tests of the form `if (x instanceof C) ...` are quite common but undermine many of the benefits of using objects.

It is possible to define a language in which classes *are not* types. Such a language would be a more pure object-oriented language. Classes would only be used to construct objects. Only interfaces could be used as types – for arguments, return values, and declarations of variables. Following tradition, part of the work could be titled "`instanceof` Considered Harmful".

Simula Was the first Object-Oriented Language

Although Simula was the first imperative object-oriented language, I believe that Church's untyped lambda-calculus was the first object-oriented language [5]. It is also the only language in which everything is an object – since it has no primitive data types. As a starting point, compare the Church booleans to the True and False classes in Smalltalk (note that ^e means return e):

Class	Smalltalk method	Church Boolean
True	iffalse: a ifTrue: b ^a value	$\lambda a.\lambda b.a$
False	iffalse: a ifTrue: b ^b value	$\lambda a.\lambda b.b$

Future

What does the future hold? In the late '90s I started working on enterprise software and found that object-oriented programming in its pure form didn't provide answers to the kinds of problems I was encountering.

It is still too difficult to build ordinary applications – ones with a user interface, a few algorithms or other kinds of program logic, various kinds of data (transactional, cached, session state, configuration), some concurrency, workflow, a security model, running on a desktop, mobile device, and/or server.

I find myself yearning for a new paradigm, just as I yearned for objects in the '80s. New paradigms do not appear suddenly, but emerge from long threads of development that often take decades to mature. Both pure functional programming (exemplified by Haskell) and object-oriented programming (Smalltalk & Java) are examples.

Thus it should be possible to see traces of future paradigms in ideas that exist today. There are many promising ideas, including generative programming, reflection, partial evaluation, process algebra, constraint/logic programming, model-driven development, query optimization, XML, and web services. It is unlikely that focused research in any of these areas will lead to a breakthrough that triggers a paradigm shift. What is needed instead is a wholistic approach to the problem of building better software more easily, while harnessing specific technologies together to create a coherent paradigm.

I want a more declarative description of systems. I find myself using domain-specific languages: for semantic data models, security rules, user interfaces, grammars, patterns, queries, consistency constraints, upgrade transformations, workflow processes. Little bits of procedural code may be embedded in the declarative framework, acting as procedural plugins.

Current forms of abstraction were designed to express isolated data abstractions, rather than families of interrelated abstractions. Today object models, e.g. a business application or the HTML document object model, have hundreds or thousands of interrelated abstractions. A the same time, it is very desirable to place each *feature* of a program into a separate module, even though the implementation of the features may be fairly interconnected.

Designs typically include aspects like security or persistence that are conceptually global, yet must be configured and specialized to each individual part of the system. The concept of an *aspect* is a powerful one – yet current aspect-oriented programming languages are only an initial step toward fulfilling the promise of this concept.

The underlying infrastructure for these higher levels will most likely be built using object-oriented programming. But at the higher levels of application programming, the system may not follow any recognizable object-oriented style.

For years there have been suggestions that object-oriented programming has reached its peak, that nothing new is to be discovered. I believe that objects will continue to drive innovation and will ultimately play a key role in the future of software development. However, it is still to be seen whether objects can maintain their position as a fundamental unifying concept for software designs, or if a new paradigm will emerge.

References

1. M. P. Atkinson and O. P. Buneman. Types and persistence in database programming languages. *ACM Comput. Surv.*, 19(2):105–170, 1987.
2. A. Banerjee and D. A. Naumann. Ownership confinement ensures representation independence for object-oriented programs. *J. ACM*, 52(6):894–960, 2005.
3. S. Blackburn and J. N. Zigman. Concurrency — the fly in the ointment? In *POS/PJW*, pages 250–258, 1998.
4. C. Boyapati, B. Liskov, and L. Shrira. Ownership types for object encapsulation. In *POPL '03: Proceedings of the 30th ACM SIGPLAN-SIGACT symposium on Principles of programming languages*, pages 213–223. ACM Press, 2003.
5. A. Church. *The Calculi of Lambda Conversion*. Princeton University Press, 1951.
6. D. G. Clarke, J. Noble, and J. Potter. Simple ownership types for object containment. In *ECOOP '01: Proceedings of the 15th European Conference on Object-Oriented Programming*, pages 53–76. Springer-Verlag, 2001.
7. W. Cook. Object-oriented programming versus abstract data types. In *Proc. of the REX Workshop/School on the Foundations of Object-Oriented Languages*, volume 173 of *Lecture Notes in Computer Science*. Springer-Verlag, 1990.
8. W. R. Cook and A. Ibrahim. Integrating programming languages & databases: What's the problem? Available from
   `http://www.cs.utexas.edu/users/wcook/projects/dbpl/`, 2005.
9. C. A. R. Hoare. Proof of correctness of data representations. *Acta Inf.*, 1:271–281, 1972.
10. S. Krishnamurthi, M. Felleisen, and D. P. Friedman. Synthesizing object-oriented and functional design to promote re-use. In *ECCOP '98: Proceedings of the 12th European Conference on Object-Oriented Programming*, pages 91–113. Springer-Verlag, 1998.
11. B. Liskov. A history of clu. In *HOPL-II: The second ACM SIGPLAN conference on History of programming languages*, pages 133–147, New York, NY, USA, 1993. ACM Press.
12. D. B. MacQueen. Modules for standard ml. In *Proc. of the ACM Conf. on Lisp and Functional Programming*, 1984.

13. D. Maier. Representing database programs as objects. In F. Bancilhon and P. Buneman, editors, *Advances in Database Programming Languages, Papers from DBPL-1*, pages 377–386. ACM Press / Addison-Wesley, 1987.

14. J. C. Mitchell and G. D. Plotkin. Abstract types have existential type. In *Proc. of the ACM Symp. on Principles of Programming Languages*, pages 37–51. ACM, 1985.

15. M. Odersky and M. Zenger. Independently extensible solutions to the expression problem. In *Proc. FOOL 12*, Jan. 2005.

16. D. A. Patterson. Latency lags bandwith. *Commun. ACM*, 47(10):71–75, 2004.

17. B. C. Pierce. *Types and Programming Languages*. MIT Press, 2002.

18. N. Scharli, A. P. Black, and S. Ducasse. Object-oriented encapsulation for dynamically typed languages. In *OOPSLA '04: Proceedings of the 19th annual ACM SIGPLAN conference on Object-oriented programming, systems, languages, and applications*, pages 130–149. ACM Press, 2004.

19. M. Torgersen. The expression problem revisited - four new solutions using generics. In *Proceedings of ECOOP*, volume 3086 of *Lecture Notes in Computer Science*, pages 123–146. Springer, 2004.

20. M. Völter, M. Kircher, and U. Zdun. *Remoting Patterns: Foundations of Enterprise, Internet and Realtime Distributed Object Middleware*. Wiley, 2005.

21. P. Wadler. The Expression Problem. `http://www.cse.ohio-state.edu/~gb/cis888.07g/java-genericity/20`, November 1998.

22. T. Zhao, J. Palsber, and J. Vite. Lightweight confinement for featherweight java. In *OOPSLA '03: Proceedings of the 18th annual ACM SIGPLAN conference on Object-oriented programing, systems, languages, and applications*, pages 135–148. ACM Press, 2003.

From ECOOP'87 to ECOOP 2006 and Beyond

Ole Lehrmann Madsen

Department of Computer Science, University of Aarhus
Åbogade 34, DK-8200 Århus N, Denmark
ole.l.madsen@daimi.au.dk

Abstract. ECOOP'87 marks the point in time where object-oriented programming started to become mainstream in research as well as in industry. In this paper we will reflect upon the contributions of object-orientation since then and discuss what we consider important challenges for the future.

1 Introduction

This paper is a personal viewpoint to be presented in a panel at ECOOP 2006 on *"Summing up the Past and trying to outline the Future"*. It is not a scientific paper and there has been no attempt to include all relevant references.

ECOOP'87 in Paris was an important milestone in the history of object-oriented programming. ECOOP'87 and the first OOPSLA'86 in Portland mark the point in time where object-oriented programming started to become mainstream in research as well as in industry. For this author the SIMULA languages [4], Smalltalk [9] and C++ [21] were important programming language milestones towards the success of object-oriented programming. In addition, the development of object-oriented methodologies [6] was also important for the increasing adaptation of object-orientation.

The history of object-orientation started more than 20 years before ECOOP'87. The SIMULA languages were developed in the early sixties by Ole-Johan Dahl and Kristen Nygaard. SIMULA 67 contained most of the central concepts now available in mainstream object-oriented languages. And SIMULA was one of the languages described in the first History of Programming Languages conferences in 1978 [24]. In the seventies and eighties, Smalltalk was developed by Alan Kay, Adele Goldberg and co-workers. The highly dynamic Smalltalk system was clearly a major reason for the huge interest in object-orientation. And finally C++ as developed by Bjarne Stroustrup in the early eighties demonstrated that object-oriented concepts could be used for development of efficient software systems.

There is no doubt that ECOOP for more than 20 years has served as the main scientific conference for object-oriented software systems. In this paper we will reflect upon what we consider the main contributions of object-oriented programming since ECOOP'87 and discuss challenges for the future.

2 The Past: Since ECOOP'87

In the mid-eighties there was a lot of excitement about object-oriented programming, but at the same time also a discussion about what it was really all about [19]. A common

D. Thomas (Ed.): ECOOP 2006, LNCS 4067, pp. 186–191, 2006.
© Springer-Verlag Berlin Heidelberg 2006

view was to understand object-orientation from a technical point-of-view. Typically object-oriented programming was identified with the Smalltalk programming model of objects and messages and/or programming using inheritance [22]. For people with a SIMULA/BETA background the attempt was to explain object-oriented programming without recourse to specific language constructs [17, 13]. The Smalltalk model was seen as limited, but useful for exploratory programming – and of course impressive by its simplicity, powerful user interface classes, and programming environment.

In the Scandinavian School of object-orientation, modeling was in focus. That is objects and classes were seen as representations (models) of phenomena and concepts from the application domain. Inheritance – or *subclassing* as we preferred calling it – was considered a mechanism for representing classification hierarchies. Objects and classes are well-suited for representing physical material and associated concepts. When creating models of real world systems, the ability to represent concurrent activities was a must. This was reflected in the ECOOP'87 paper on *"Classification of Actions"* [10]. Since the start of ECOOP the subject of concurrent object-oriented programming [5] has fortunately been central.

In the mid-eighties there seemed to be too much focus on object-orientation as a means for code reuse and extensibility at the expense of modeling. The arrival of methodologies based on object-oriented concepts as an alternative to functional decomposition was a major step forward with respect to obtaining a more balanced view on modeling and the technical aspects of programming. For some period, the importance of methodologies, modeling and graphical modeling languages like UML, however, seemed to be overestimated. One of the strengths of object-orientation is that it is possible to obtain a proper balance between modeling and programming.

ECOOP has played an important role in presenting research that contributed to the understanding of the principles and theories of object-orientation and of course in presenting new ideas. Below we comment on what we believe are some of the more interesting developments within object-oriented software systems during the last twenty years.

Inheritance has of course been a major subject and various forms of inheritance have been proposed including numerous discussions on the pros and cons of multiple inheritance. For multiple inheritance some of the proposals have been quite complex. Fortunately, we have seen a movement towards simpler mechanisms. A central theme has been whether or not inheritance is a mechanism for code reuse (incremental modification) or a mechanism for representing classification hierarchies. It is also a common viewpoint that inheritance and subtyping are different but related concepts. If one strive at simple languages and support for modeling, inheritance should represent classification hierarchies and be used for subtyping.

Genericity. Since the paper by Bertrand Meyer [16], genericity has been an important research issue and besides Eiffel genericity is supported by most mainstream languages. There are many forms of genericity including simple templates, parameterized classes, virtual classes and wildcards as in Java.

Concurrent object-oriented programming is an important issue and many interesting research papers have been published at ECOOP. Sometimes one has had the impression that some of the ideas have been reinvented from the long line of research in concurrent programming in the seventies and early eighties. The research in concurrent object-oriented programming does not seem to have had a major influence on mainstream object-oriented programming languages where the monitor style is dominant. Even the SIMULA style of active objects – which we find superior to most other alternatives – has not caught on.

Prototype-based languages are one of the most interesting developments within object-orientation. The SELF language [23] is an excellent example of a language supporting prototype-based programming.

Software components [20] have been proposed as a new technology which differs from objects. The technology has definitely something to offer, but instead of insisting that it is beyond object-oriented programming, it would be more productive to unify the concepts of component and object. And we see no reason why a component may not be perceived as an object.

Design patterns [8] are a major achievement. Naming and capturing well-known abstractions is essential to the practice of software development.

Aspect-oriented programming [12], and **composition filters** [1] and the idea of language support for separation of concerns is a promising new approach to modularization of programs.

Agile methods [2,7] and other work on light-weight methodologies have proved their usefulness in practice and many hardcore programmers have started to realize that methodologies is not just something that management insist on.

The above list is by no means complete. There are many more areas where useful contributions have been made including reflection, constraint-based programming, exception handling, implementation, application frameworks, object persistence and data bases, type theory and theory in general.

3 The Present: ECOOP 2006

Object-technology has matured with respect to research and practice. In our opinion, we think that the main reasons for the success of object-orientation are:

1. **Good support for modeling.** Programs reflect reality in a *natural* way. Objects, object attributes, classes, etc. are good means for building *physical models* [13] of concepts and phenomena from the application domain. There is a rich *conceptual framework* [11] for organizing knowledge about the problem domain including conceptual means such as classification, generalization, specialization, composition, and whole/part. We do think that most books on object-technology pay too little attention to the conceptual aspects of modeling. The technical aspects of object-technology seem to be totally dominating.

2. **Good support for reusability and extensibility.** At the programming level, object-oriented language mechanisms like class, subclass and virtual procedure provided new possibilities for reuse and extensibility of existing code. In addition, object-orientation has resulted in new architectural principles in the form of application frameworks, design patterns, components and distributed object systems.

3. **Unifying perspective on most phases of the software life cycle.** The perhaps most significant advantage of object-orientation is that it has provided a unifying perspective on most phases of the software life cycle including

analysis, design, and implementation. In addition, object-orientated concepts apply to other areas such as databases, and distributed systems. This is the case for the conceptual framework as well as language constructs.

As of today, we see the following interesting research challenges:

A design pattern identifies an abstraction over an architectural element. Abstraction mechanisms in programming languages also define abstractions. We believe that programming language abstractions should be developed to subsume design patterns.

Aspects-oriented programming still needs to demonstrate its usefulness in practice. We also think that too much work on aspects is characterized by being very technical and thereby difficult to understand at a conceptual level. Object-orientation was originally founded on a conceptual framework and perhaps a similar conceptual framework for aspects is needed.

Concurrent programming is still difficult in practice and the large amount of research within this area does not seem to have influenced mainstream object-oriented languages.

Class-based versus prototype-based languages are both useful from a conceptual as well as a technical point of view. We believe that a conceptual and technical unification would be desirable [15].

Object-orientation has matured as the main technology for development of software. On the darker side, we are facing CASE tools, software development environments, a multitude of programming languages, class libraries, component technologies, database systems, distributed object systems, web services, etc. Compared to the situation with SIMULA and Smalltalk more than 20 years ago, the complexity of object-technology is huge. Of course the concepts and technology have evolved and the requirements have increased, but there is room for a considerable reduction in complexity. Finally, one may regret that the exciting style of dynamic programming with Smalltalk has failed to have a significant impact on practice.

4   The Future: Beyond ECOOP 2006

In year 20 after the first ECOOP conference, object-oriented programming has matured as the main software technology in use. It is, however, about time for new and exciting ideas to appear on the scene. Software systems still have a large complexity and this does not seem to decrease in the future. We should identify new research challenges and focus on these instead of continuing with minor improvements of current ideas and theories.

The complexity of software systems in general is huge and calls for new advances in principles and technology. *Pervasive computing* is the next generation of computing environments with information and communication technology (ICT) everywhere, for everyone, at all times. The use of mobile devices is increasing and ICT will more and more become an integrated part of our environments. Users expect their applications and data to be accessible everywhere, at any time and from whatever terminal at hand. This implies that large enterprise systems and production systems must function in a pervasive computing context. Pervasive computing has gone beyond the proof-of-concept stage where, primarily, it has been systems in small-scale in more or less closed environments. The next step involves solutions to problems that can ensure a successful enrolment of pervasive computing in large-scale organizations and in society in general.

Examples include life/mission critical areas such as healthcare, and aero-space technology, but also home-control systems for energy control, and security and integrated home systems for audio, video, pictures and other personal materials. Society is already highly dependent on ICT, but the pervasive computing systems of the future will have an even more significant impact on people's lives. In order for these systems to be accepted by the users, they put very high demands on software quality, usability, and social and commercial readiness. A major challenge for the future will therefore be to carry out research and innovation in the area of such *critical pervasive computing systems* [3].

One set of requirements is with respect to usability. A user will have to deal with a large variety of different interfaces, as well as with multiple forms of interaction with the same service. This could be from a mobile phone, a PC or a large screen. In some instances, the user or the service may need to choose the best possible interaction device for the job, given the devices available, or the user may desire to move the interaction from one interface to another. With the increasing number of new devices, the user will expect to be able to combine the functionality of different devices not necessarily foreseen by the manufacturer of the devices. This will give rise to contingency situations where meaningful feedback should be given to the user in order to be able to understand the cause of a given problem.

Another set of requirements relate to software quality – in order for new pervasive computing systems to be accepted by the user, the quality must be significantly better than what we know from personal computers, mobile phones and other ICT-based devices. In a similar way, it is essential that people thrust the systems, which puts high demands on security, privacy and safety. In general, critical pervasive computing implies a large number of interesting challenges within software architecture, programming models, programming languages, contingency and dependability.

In the PalCom project [18], some of these issues are being considered including an open architecture for pervasive computing. In addition, the notion of *palpable system* is being developed. A palpable system is capable of being noticed and mentally apprehended, and it supports people in understanding what is going on at the level of their choice. The overall philosophy is that instead of promoting the disappearing computer, people should be aware of the computing systems in their environments and the systems should support that the user is in control.

To handle these challenges we need new breakthroughs in usability and software systems. The object-oriented community should be leading with respect to identifying new research challenges and providing solutions, perhaps as new languages. Being aware that great ideas do not appear every day (or year) ECOOP should continue to be the main conference for presenting research that contributes to our understanding of object-orientation. It is, however, about time that some new and exciting ideas enter the area of object-orientation if ECOOP (and OOPSLA) shall continue to be the most interesting software conferences of the future.

References

1. M. Aksit, L. Bergmans, S. Vural: An Object-Oriented Language-Database Integration Model: The Composition-Filters Approach, ECOOP'92, LNCS 615, Springer-Verlag, 1992.
2. K. Beck: Extreme Programming Explained: Embrace Change. Addison-Wesley, 2000.
3. Critical Pervasive Computing: Research proposal. Department of Computer Science, Aarhus University, 2005.
4. G. Birtwistle, O.-J. Dahl, B. Myrhaug, K. Nygaard: SIMULA BEGIN. Studentlitteratur, Lund, Sweden, 1979.
5. J.-P. Briot, A. Yonezawa: Inheritance and Synchronization in Concurrent OOP. ECOOP'87, LNCS 276, Springer-Verlag, 1987.
6. P. Coad, E. Yourdon: Object-Oriented Analysis. Yourdon Press Computing Series, 1990.
7. A. Cockburn: Crystal Clear: A Human-Powered Methodology for Small Teams. Addison-Wesley, 2004.
8. E. Gamma, R. Helm, R.E. Johnson, J. Vlissides: Design Patterns: Elements of Object-Oriented Software Architecture. Addison-Wesley, 1994.
9. A. Goldberg, D. Robson: Smalltalk-80, the Language and its Implementation, Addison-Wesley, 1983.
10. B.B. Kristensen, O.L. Madsen, B. Møller-Pedersen, K. Nygaard: Classification of Actions or Inheritance also for Methods. ECOOP'87, LNCS 276, Springer-Verlag, 1987.
11. B.B. Kristensen, O.L. Madsen, B. Møller-Pedersen, K. Nygaard: Object-Oriented Programming in the BETA Programming Language, ACM Press/Addison-Wesley, 1993.
12. G. Kiczales, J. Lamping, A. Mendhekar, C. Maeda, C.V. Lopes, J.-M. Loingtier, J. Irwin: Aspect-Oriented Programming, ECOOP'97, LNCS 1247, Springer-Verlag, 1997.
13. O.L. Madsen, B. Møller-Pedersen: What Object-Oriented Programming may be and what it does not have to be. ECOOP'88, LNCS 322, Springer Verlag, 1988.
14. O.L. Madsen: Open Issues in Object-Oriented Programming – A Scandinavian Perspective. Software Practice and Experience, Vol. 25, No. S4, Dec. 1995.
15. O.L. Madsen: Towards a Unified Programming Language. ECOOP 2000, LNCS 1850, Springer Verlag, 2000.
16. B. Meyer: Genericity versus Inheritance. OOPSLA'86, SIGPLAN Notices, 21(11), 1986.
17. K. Nygaard: Basic Concepts in Object-Oriented Programming. SIGPLAN Notices, 21(10), 1986.
18. PalCom: Palpable Computing – a new perspective on ambient computing. www.ist-palcom.org
19. T. Rentsch: Object Oriented Programming. SIGPLAN Notices, 17(9), 1982.
20. C. Szyperski: Component Software – Beyond Object-Oriented Programming. Addison-Wesley, 1997.
21. B. Stroustrup: The C++ Programming Language. Addison-Wesley, 1986.
22. B. Stroustrup: What is "Object-Oriented Programming"? ECOOP'87, LNCS 276, Springer-Verlag, 1987.
23. D. Ungar, R.B Smith: SELF: The Power of Simplicity. OOPSLA'87, SIGPLAN Notices, 22(12), 1987.
24. R.L. Wexelblat: History of Programming Languages, ACM/Academic Press, 1981.

The Continuing Quest for Abstraction

Henry Lieberman

Media Laboratory, Massachusetts Institute of Technology, Cambridge, MA, USA

Abstract. The history of Object-Oriented Programming can be interpreted as a continuing quest to capture the notion of *abstraction* – to create computational artifacts that represent the essential nature of a situation, and to ignore irrelevant details. Objects are defined by their essential behavior, not by their physical representation as data. The basic Object-Oriented paradigm of organizing programs as active objects and message passing has now been accepted by the mainstream, for which ECOOP can be justifiably proud. Future developments in the field will focus on capturing computational *ideas* that can't be expressed well simply by functional abstraction. Programming will evolve from textual programming languages to using natural language, graphics, demonstrated actions, and other techniques.

1 The Revolution Is Dead. Long Live the Revolution!

ECOOP has plenty to be proud of in its 20-year history of promoting Object-Oriented Programming. Object-Oriented Programming is a revolution, that, largely, we've won. At the start of ECOOP, and its sister conference, OOPSLA, in the eighties, OOP was a fringe movement exemplified only by a few research programming languages, and which saw little use outside the research community. Now, OOP is mainstream, and popular programming languages such as Java, C++, C#, Python, etc. have at least some form of the object-oriented concept. We all can be proud of that success.

Of course, like all revolutions, widespread acceptance of the concept didn't quite happen in exactly the way the original revolutionaries (including myself) envisioned. And the ideas didn't get accepted in their pure form, as they originally appeared in Actors and Smalltalk; along the way they were only incompletely understood by the mainstream, diluted, and got mixed with more conventional approaches. You can't win them all. But they did take hold.

Overall, the result was positive. While battles still remain to be won on many fronts, the basic idea of organizing programs as objects, methods, and message passing is accepted widely both in academia and industry. The success of object-oriented programming was achieved because of its ability to facilitate modularity, separation of concerns, reuse, extensibility, transparency, and parallelism in programming. Object-oriented programming, in its original form, is a done deal. Where do we go from here?

D. Thomas (Ed.): ECOOP 2006, LNCS 4067, pp. 192 – 197, 2006.
© Springer-Verlag Berlin Heidelberg 2006

2   The Search for Abstraction

I think that the history, and the success, of object-oriented programming is attributable, in large part, to the ability of objects to facilitate *abstraction*. By abstraction, I mean the ability to disregard inessential aspects of a situation, and to focus on the essential aspects. The key idea of object-oriented programming, in my view, is that objects are defined by their *behavior* (responses to messages) and not by their physical representation, i.e., particular patterns of bits inside a computer. Behavior is essential, bit patterns are not.

Object-oriented programming succeeded by taking an ontological position on the basic "stuff" of which computer programs and their data are made. In the early history of computing, computers were seen as manipulators of bit patterns. Programs are bits. Data are bits. This was fine when programming was done in assembly language. No pretension was made that a programmer was doing anything except manipulating bits. Problem is, people don't think very well about patterns of bits.

High-level programming languages were introduced as an ontological shift in what computers were about. Different languages took different stances on what that shift should be. FORTRAN said that computers were about manipulating numbers and the mathematical formulae that describe relationships between numbers. COBOL said that computers were about manipulating English-like descriptions of databases (actually, maybe not such a bad idea, as we'll see later on in this paper). Simula said that computers were about manipulating simulations. LISP said that computers were about manipulating symbols and lists.

Those last two are significant. Because it isn't very far, once you think about computers as manipulating simulations, or manipulating symbols, to arrive at the point where you realize that computers are really about manipulating *ideas*. Humans think in ideas. Why not computers? That's why Simula and LISP were able to give birth to object-oriented programming in a way that descendents of FORTRAN, COBOL, ALGOL and other languages were not.

It is encouraging to me that, while I have been away from working directly in the field in recent years, much work in the field of Object-Oriented Programming still seems focused on the goal of abstraction and capturing ideas in programming. While I think there was a slowdown in innovation in the field in the nineties, as people's energies were focused on facilitating OOP's entrance to the mainstream, now I think that research in the area is going in some healthy directions. Particularly, work in two areas seems like it has a well-motivated concern with how to capture kinds of abstraction that aren't well served by the original conception of object-oriented programming, that relies purely on functional abstraction to capture ideas.

First, there is the Patterns movement. Patterns are an attempt to capture some high-level design rationale in systems that go beyond simply abstracting them into a function. Because the only way a function (or conventional object) can abstract something is to create a variable for it, systems of objects and patterns of message passing between objects, such as protocols, were not well captured by previous abstraction mechanisms. These ideas can be easily expressed by people in natural language (a signal that programming languages *should* be able to handle them), but are hard for conventional programming languages to capture. Thus pattern languages represent a true advance. However, work continues in making them more capable and precise, and developing tools to help programmers work with them.

Second, there is the Aspects movement. Aspects were motivated, again, by the limits of functional abstraction. Again, researchers noted that there were significant ideas about how programs should be organized that crossed functional boundaries. Again, also, these ideas were easily expressed by programmers in natural language, but difficult to capture in programming languages. While Patterns try to capture notions that are bigger, in some sense, than a single object, Aspects try to model notions that cut across small pieces of multiple objects, and would otherwise necessitate multiple unsynchronized edits and traces.

Finally, I think a future direction that will be important is to understand the *dynamic* nature of abstraction. By and large, current ideas of abstraction in programming languages are about *static* abstraction; at the time of programming, the programmer decides what abstractions need to be made and how they are expressed. But increasingly, abstraction will have to be done on-the-fly, by applications as they are running and interacting with users. The reason for this is the increasing prevalence of *context-sensitive* applications, sparked by interest in mobile, distributed and personalized applications.

In some sense, abstraction and context-sensitivity are in opposition. Abstraction gains its power from *ignoring* details of a particular situation, which is the last thing you want to do if you want to make an application context-sensitive! But the key to resolving this dilemma is to introduce abstraction dynamically. If the program can decide, on the fly, what aspects to ignore or to take into account according to the particular situation, it can be both general and adaptable at the same time. This will bring object-oriented programming much closer to machine learning.

3   Computers Are About Manipulating Ideas

Computers are about manipulating *ideas*. Not numbers, strings, arrays, lists, or even code per se. Ideas. They are about taking ideas that people have in their heads, and, when they are expressible computationally, translating them into a form where computers can manipulate them. The future of Object-Oriented Programming, then, will be in understanding new computational ideas and how they can be expressed. Maybe the word "object" is really just another word for "idea".

I think we should consider radically new ways of representing ideas that are not just limited to conventional textual programming languages, though they may play a part in the process. People have a wide range of representing and communicating ideas in a variety of media, and our programming systems ought to as well. We should work towards ways of letting people express ideas directly, minimizing the amount of specialized knowledge and arcane procedures necessary to express ideas in computational form. That will benefit the usability of our programming systems, and extend the possibility of their use to new audiences.

Perhaps it is obvious, but people naturally express ideas with words. So one direction that we ought to be going in, is to allow people to express programming concepts in words. Not in keywords, reserved words, or identifiers. Simply in words.

The next section will present some work I have done with my colleague Hugo Liu in exploring the perhaps crazy, idea that people could program computers directly in natural language. Other interesting approaches to expressing computational ideas in natural language are also being explored, such as Lotfi Zadeh's Computing with Words [9].

There are, of course, other ways to express ideas than talking about them with words. Ideas can also be expressed visually, and the idea of visual programming has been explored, notably in research reported in IEEE Human-Centric Computing (formerly Visual Languages). I think the field of Object-Oriented Programming should take the idea of visual programming more seriously. Some of the objections often raised against visual programming, such as visual programs "taking up more screen space" are obsolete and/or easily overcome. Visual programming could empower a whole new generation of people to do programming, who are "visual thinkers" by nature, who are currently disenfranchised by the overly verbal and symbolic nature of today's programming languages. Approaches which use graphical manipulation to introduce new ways of working with programs, such as the remarkable SubText of Jonathan Edwards [1], represent innovations that deserve more attention.

Finally, ideas are expressed not only in words or pictures, but in actions. There is the possibility that the computer could use a sequence of actions performed by, or observed from, the user as a representation. I am a big proponent of this approach, under the name of Programming by Example. I won't go further into it here, but refer the reader to my 2001 book [2] and 2006 collection on End-User Programming [3].

4 Object-Oriented Programming in Natural Language

In this section, I want to present, from my current work, an example of what I think will be an important, but perhaps controversial, direction for Object-Oriented Programming. I don't mean to say that all programming should be done this way, but I think it is an example of new kinds of approaches that ought to be considered.

In the Metafor project [4, 5, 6, 7, 8] we are exploring the idea of using descriptions in a natural language like English as a representation for programs. While we cannot yet convert arbitrary English descriptions to fully specified code, we can use a reasonably expressive subset of English as a conceptualization, visualization, editing and debugging tool. Simple descriptions of program objects and their behavior are converted to scaffolding (underspecified) code fragments, that can be used as feedback for the designer, and which can later be elaborated.

Roughly speaking, noun phrases can be interpreted as program objects; verbs can be functions, adjectives can be properties. It is our contention that today's natural language technology has improved to the point that reasonable, simple, descriptions of simple procedural and object oriented programming ideas can be understood (providing, of course, the user is trying to cooperate with the system, not fool it). There's no need to impose a rigid, unforgiving syntax on a user. Interactive dialogues can provide disambiguation when necessary, or if the system is completely stuck, it falls back on the user.

The principal objection to natural language programming rests in the supposed *ambiguity* of natural language. But ambiguity can be your friend. A surprising amount of information about program structure can be inferred by our parser from relations implicit in the linguistic structure. We refer to this phenomenon as *programmatic semantics*.

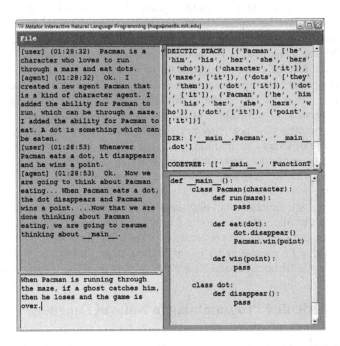

Fig. 1. The Metafor natural language programming system. At the lower left is the user's natural language input. At the lower right the automatically generated code. The two top windows trace the parser's actions and are not intended for the end user.

Metafor has some interesting capabilities for *refactoring* programs. Different ways of describing objects in natural language can give rise to different representation and implementation decisions as embodied in the details of the code. Conventional programming requires making up-front commitments to overspecified details, and saddles the user with having to perform distributed, error-prone edits in order to change design decisions. Metafor uses the inherent "ambiguity" of natural language as an advantage, automatically performing refactoring as the system learns more about the user's intent. For example,

a) *There is a bar. (Single object. But what kind of "bar"?)*
b) *The bar contains two customers. (unimorphic list. Now, a place serving alcohol)*
c) *It also contains a waiter. (unimorphic wrt. persons)*
d) *It also contains some stools. (polymorphic list)*
e) *The bar opens and closes. (class / agent)*
f) *The bar is a kind of store. (inheritance class)*
g) *Some bars close at 6pm. (subclass or instantiatable)*

More details about Metafor and natural language programming appear in the references. Many details and problems still need to be worked out. But we present this as an example that radical new approaches to the programming problem need to be considered if Object-Oriented Programming is to advance in the future.

I look forward to the next 20 years of ECOOP!

References

1. Jonathan Edwards. Subtext: Uncovering the Simplicity of Programming. 20th annual ACM SIGPLAN Conference on Object-Oriented Programming Systems, Languages, and Applications (OOPSLA). October 2005, San Diego, California.
2. Henry Lieberman, ed., *Your Wish is My Command: Programming by Example*, Morgan Kaufmann, San Francisco, 2001.
3. Henry Lieberman, Fabio Paterno and Volker Wulf, eds., *End-User Development*, Springer, 2006.
4. Hugo Liu and Henry Lieberman (2004) Toward a Programmatic Semantics of Natural Language. Proceedings of VL/HCC'04: the 20th IEEE Symposium on Visual Languages and Human-Centric Computing. pp. 281-282. September 26-29, 2004, Rome. IEEE Computer Society Press.
5. Hugo Liu and Henry Lieberman (2005) Programmatic Semantics for Natural Language Interfaces. Proceedings of the ACM Conference on Human Factors in Computing Systems, CHI 2005, April 5-7, 2005, Portland, OR, USA. ACM Press.
6. Hugo Liu and Henry Lieberman (2005) Metafor: Visualizing Stories as Code. Proceedings of the ACM International Conference on Intelligent User Interfaces, IUI 2005, January 9-12, 2005, San Diego, CA, USA, to appear. ACM 2005.
7. Henry Lieberman and Hugo Liu. Feasibility Studies for Programming in Natural Language. H. Lieberman, F. Paterno, and V. Wulf (Eds.) Perspectives in End-User Development, to appear. Springer, 2006.
8. Rada Milhacea, Henry Lieberman and Hugo Liu. NLP for NLP: Natural Language Processing for Natural Language Programming, International Conference on Computational Linguistics and Intelligent Text Processing, Mexico City, Springer Lecture Notes in Computer Science, February 2006.
9. Lotfi Zadeh, Precisiated natural language (PNL), *AI Magazine*, Volume 25, Issue 3 Pages: 74 – 91, Fall 2004.

Early Concurrent/Mobile Objects
– Modeling a Simple Post Office –

Akinori Yonezawa

Dept of Computer Science, University of Tokyo
yonezawa@is.s.u-tokyo.ac.jp
http://www.yl.is.s.u-tokyo.ac.jp

Abstract. This essay just sketches my early investigations on the concept of objects which models concurrent activities of mobile entities that interact with each other in space.

1 A Bit of History and Motivations

In early 70's, research motivations were conceived at the Actor group led by Carl Hewitt and supported by AI Lab., and Laboratory for Computer Science, MIT. They were eager to

- find a universal *concurrent* computational model[1],
- whose level is similar to that of the lambda-calculus,
- which allows us to model and simulate activities of almost all entities
- that interact with each other and move around in space.

The entire research group was convinced that basic entities in the model should be process- or procedure-like things that mutually interact with *message passing*. The message passing is required to be *asynchronous* in the sense that an entity can send a message to an entity at anytime even when the destination entity is not ready or able to receive a message. This assumption was taken because maximum concurrency needs to be expressible at the modeling level[8]. Almost all members, who were only concerned with computation/execution but not with modeling, were uninterested in *mobility* of entities. I myself, however, were rather more interested in modeling, describing the world, and simulating it with some huge powerful machinery. To me, it was natural to capture mobile aspects of entities in the world.

Even in early days of computer science, the term "object" was used in many CS sub-domains. In particular, the group leaded by Barbara Liskov, designing a structured programming language called CLU, was using the term "objects" to refer to instances of abstract data types being defined by the novel program module feature in CLU. CLU was not the first system to use the term. To mention a few, early Lisp systems, early Smalltalk systems, and the Hydra Operating System used the term "objects" frequently. But these notions of objects did not deal with *message transmissions* which take place among objects. Of course, the interactions among objects were called *message passing*, but they were merely meant to be dynamically dispatched method calls (or procedure calls).

---

[1] A more restricted formal calculus was proposed by Robin Milner[5].

D. Thomas (Ed.): ECOOP 2006, LNCS 4067, pp. 198–202, 2006.
© Springer-Verlag Berlin Heidelberg 2006

2 Concurrent Objects

After some trials of developing frameworks, I came up with my own notion of objects which abstract away or model entities that interact with each other in the domain (or world). To me, it was very suitable for modeling things in the world. In explaining my notion of *concurrent objects*, I often used an anthropomorphic analogy. Things are modeled as autonomous information processing agents called *concurrent objects*, and their mutual message transmissions abstract away various forms of communications found in human or social organizations in such a way that they can be realized by the current computer technology without great difficulties.

In our approach, the domain to be modeled/designed/implemented is represented as a collection of *concurrent objects* and the interaction of the domain components is represented as *concurrent* message passing among such objects. Domains where our approach is powerful include distributed problem solving, modeling of human cognitive process, modeling and implementation of real-time systems and operating systems, design and implementation of distributed event simulation etc.

Although it is not so difficult to give a thorough mathematical account of the notion of concurrent objects, for the sake of convenience, let me give an intuitive characterization of concurrent objects (COs) below. Each CO

- has a globally unique identity/name,
- may have a protected, yet updatable local memory,
- has a set of procedures that manipulate the memory,
- receives a message that activates one of the procedures,
- has a single FIFO queue for arrived messages, and
- has autonomous thread(s) of control.

In each CO, memory-updating procedures are activated one at a time with the corresponding message arrival order. The contents of the memory of a CO, which is the local state of the CO, can be defined at the time of message arrival, owing to its single FIFO message queue. Each CO can send messages to the set of COs whose ids the CO knows about at the time of sending. This means that communication is point-to-point and any CO can send messages as long as it remembers the names of destination COs. As the memory of a CO can be updatable, a CO can forget names of other COs. So the set of objects to which a CO can send messages varies from time o time. So communication topology is dynamic. Also any CO can dynamically create COs.

3 What Can Be Contained in Messages

In our framework, message passing is the sole means for information exchange among COs. So what can be contained in messages needs to be explained. Here is what I designed: Messages are allowed to contain not only *names* or *ids* of COs, but also COs *themselves*. In implementation terms, this means that messages can contain not only pointers to COs, but also the code of COs. This mechanism corresponds to what has been called *code migration* or *code mobility*.

Messages are sent by COs, not by other components in our framework. When a message contains a CO (not its id), the CO is actually (forced to be) moved by COs. This mechanism is rather too strong in modeling interactions among domain components. Thus, I restricted message passing in such a way that a message ontaining a CO should be transmitted *only* when CO sends the very CO itself, not when other COs do. This restriction allows a CO to move with its own will, but never be forced by other COs. It should be noted that while a CO is moving, it can send and receive messages.

4 Modeling Customers Coming to a Post Office

To see suitability of my concurrent object framework, I modeled concurrent activities in a simple post office, following an example given in the Simula book[1]. Activities in the post office include customers entering/exiting, interactions of post office clerks and customers (buying/selling stamps), and customers mailing in the mailbox. Figure 1 illustrates the post office. Post office clerks are collectively represented by the counter-section. First, we model customers as concurrent objects. Also we need to model the post office building. Customers go into the post office through its entrance door. So it is natural to model the building as a concurrent object D representing the entrance door. Now two kinds

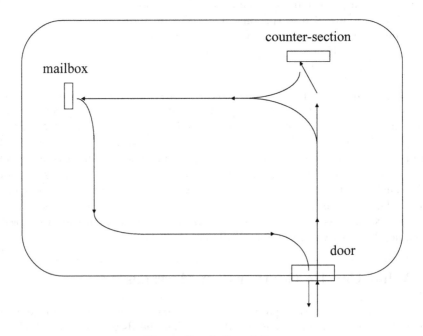

Fig. 1. Simple Post Office

of objects, customer objects and the door object, are in our domain. The next thing to do is how to model the interactions of the two kinds of objects. In the message passing paradigm, arrivals or transmissions of messages are the sole event of interaction among COs. An event of a customer C going through the door is naturally represented as an arrival of a message M at the door object D where M *contains* the customer object C itself (not the id of C). Then, the door object D sends to the customer object C a message M' requesting C to move to the counter-section object CS. As the customer object C does not know where the counter-section object CS is, the door object D should supply the information of the location/name of the counter-section object. This information is, of course, given in the message M' reqeusting the customer to change its location.

5   Needs for Autonomous Mobility and Ambients

In explaining the modeling of the post office above, it was rather vague *how* a message M containing a customer object C arrives at the door object. There are two possibilities: (1) Another concurrent object sends M containing C, or (2) C itself sends M. As I noted earlier, I restricted the movement of objects in such a way that objects can only be moved by themselves. So the second possiblity is the right interpretation. This means that concurrent objects move by themselves, not moved by other COs. In turn, we need to provide a *Go*-instruction which is executed by any concurrent object C. When this instruction is executed, it is transformed into a transmission of a message containing C to some specified destination object.

Here is another point of note. Customers of a post office are not necessary local people who are familiar with the layout of the post office. So when a customer enters the post office, he needs to know where the counter-section or the mailbox is. This information corresponds to what is known as *ambients*. In our modeling, the locations (or names) of the counter-section or the mailbox are given to the customer object by the door object after the customer object arrives at the door object. This ambient information is given in a message sent by the door object to the customer object. As information contained in incoming messages can be stored, updated, and retrieved in the local memory of a CO, it is fair to say that my framework has addressed issues associated with "ambients" of mobile objects[6].

6   ABCL, a Language for Concurrent Objects

We presented the first sketch of our concurrent object-oriented language ABCL [9] at the third French workshop on Object-Oriented Languages, held in Paris in 1985. This workshop was organized by Pierre Cointe and Jean Bezivin. They graciously invited me and indeed I joined the European community of object-oriented programming for the first time. This was a great opportunity for me to come back to the international scenes after some fruitless domestic years in Tokyo. Henry Liebermann also presented his work at the workshop. This workshop was truly the predecessor of the first ECOOP (1987) and the first OOPSLA (1986). I owe very much to this workshop for my own OO research career.

The design of our full language ABCL/1[10], its prototype implementation, and some applications were presented at the first OOPSLA in 1986. My presentation was enthusiastically received by Kristen Nygaard who was the Scandinavian/European leader of object-oriented computing. I was very happy with his strong encouragement. I distributed the ABCL language manuals at the conference site. Later on, a thorough treatment of our concurrent object model was published as a book[11] in 1990. The semantic framework of our ABCL languages was given by N. Kobayashi and myself in 1994[3], and the novel language implementations for high performance computing machines were developed with S. Matsuoka, K. Taura. and M. Yasugi[12]. The problems of inheritance mechanisms with concurrent object-oriented languages, coined *inheritance anomaly*, were found by J.-P. Briot, S. Matsuoka and myself[2][4]. Furthermore, our work on a very efficient implementation of our mobile object language called *Java-GO*[7] was published in 1999.

References

1. Birtwistle, G., Dahl, O.-J., Myhrhang, B., Nygaard, K.: *SIMULA Begin* Auerbach, Philadelphia, 1973.
2. Briot, J.-P., Yonezawa, A.: *Inheritance and Synchronization in Concurrent OOP*, Proc. ECOOP'87, Springer LNCS No. 276, 1987.
3. Kobayashi, N., Yonezawa, A.: Asynchronous Communication Model Based on Linear Logic, *Formal Aspects of Computing*, Springer-Verlag, 1994.
4. Matsuoka, S., Yonezawa, A.: *Analysis of Inheritance Anomaly in Object-Oriented Concurrent Programming Languages, Research Directions in Concurrent Object-Oriented Programming* (Eds. G. Agha, P. Wegner and A. Yonezawa), The MIT Press, 1993, pp.107 - 150.
5. Milner, R.: *The polyadic pi-calculus: a tutorial*, Technical Report ECD-LFCS-91-180, Laboratory for Foundations of Computer Science, Edingburgh University, October 1991.
6. Cardelli, L: *Abstractions for Mobile Computation*, Secure Internet Programming: Security Issues for Mobile and Distributed Objects, Springer LNCS No. 1603, 1999.
7. Sekiguchi, T., Masuhara, H., Yonezawa, A.: *A Simple Extension of Java Language for Controllable Transparent Migration and its Portable Implementation* Proc. Coordination Languages and Models, Springer LNCS No. 1594, 1999.
8. Yonezawa, A., Hewitt, C.: *Modelling Distributed Systems*, Machine Intelligence No.9,(1978) 41–50.
9. Yonezawa, A., Matsuda, H., Shibayama, E.: *An Approach to Object-oriented Concurrent Programming – A Language ABCL –*, Proc. 3rd Workshop on Object-Oriented Languages, Paris, 1985.
10. Yonezawa, A., Briot, J.-P., Shibayama, E.: *Object-oriented Concurrent Programming in ABCL/1*, Proc. ACM OOPSLA'86, Portland Oregon, USA, (1986) 258–268.
11. Yonezawa, A. (Ed.): *ABCL: an Object-Oriented Concurrent System*, MIT Press 1990, 329 pages.
12. Yonezawa, A., Matsuoka, S., Yasugi, M., Taura, K.: *Implementing Concurrent Object-Oriented Languages on Multi-computers* IEEE Parallel & Distributed Technology, 1(2):49-61, May 1993.

Turning the Network into a Database
with Active XML*

Serge Abiteboul

INRIA-Futurs & LRI-Univ. Paris 11
`firstname.lastname@inria.fr`

Abstract. Because of information ubiquity, one observes an important trend towards transferring information management tasks from database systems to networks. We introduce the notion of data ring that can be seen as a network version of a database or a content warehouse. A main goal is to achieve better performance for content management without requiring the acquisition of explicit control over information resources. In this paper, we discuss the main traits of data rings and argue that Active XML provides an appropriate basis for such systems.

A brief introduction to Active XML. We follow the web standards as promoted by the W3C [11]: the URL/URI, name space paradigm, the XML (XMLSchema, RDF, etc.) and web service (WSDL, BPEL, etc.) families. In short, an XML document is an unbounded, labeled, ordered tree and web services are protocols for distributed computing. An Active XML (AXML for short) document consists of XML data with embedded calls to web services. AXML documents may be viewed as objects that can be exchanged between peers. Persistency is supported in the spirit of object databases [6]. Furthermore, an AXML document is at the same time a client for web services and possibly a service provider. The service calls embedded in the document provide both intensional (in the sense of deductive databases [3]) and active (in the sense of active databases [10]) data. A survey of the AXML project may be found in [5]. Papers on AXML as well as the open-source code of an AXML peer may be found from [1].

Data ring. The goal is to develop a middleware information system (called a data ring) to support, in a P2P manner, the integrated management and access to a wide range of information with performance, reliability, robustness and more generally, quality of service, tailored to applications. We expect data rings to be self-tuning, and in particular adapt to application needs without human intervention. An example of data ring is a personal data management system combining resources from PDAs, smart home/car appliances, home/work PCs, etc.

By information, we mean first data, traditional as in relational databases, and less so as in content management systems (mails, letters, reports, etc.). By information, we also mean metadata about the data as well as knowledge (e.g.. ontologies) that are used to interpret data and metadata. Last but not least, we

---

* This work has been partially supported by the EU project Edos [7] on the development and distribution of open source software.

D. Thomas (Ed.): ECOOP 2006, LNCS 4067, pp. 203–205, 2006.
© Springer-Verlag Berlin Heidelberg 2006

mean web forms or more generally web services providing access to data sources. This information is published on the web, and accessed via (subscription) queries, web sites and reports. For the model, we insist on two aspects:

- Seamless transition between data and metadata. The use of metadata is essential for linking data resources and in particular classifying them.
- Seamless transition between explicit and intentional data. One should not have to distinguish between data provided by web pages and data provided by web services.

We are concerned with P2P organizations with the following characteristics: The information is heterogeneous, distributed, replicated, dynamic. Furthermore, information sources are autonomous, willing to collaborate and possibly mobile. Clearly, the peers in such systems vary greatly in terms of storage, bandwidth, computing power (e.g., a sensor vs. a very large database).

Some of the functionalities supplied by a data ring are typical DBMS functionalities, e.g.: persistence, query/update, concurrency control, fault tolerance, recovery, access control. Others are more specific, e.g.,: information discovery and enrichment. A comparison between relational databases and data rings is proposed in Figure 1. Most importantly, in a ring, the information is distributed and so are possibly all these functionalities, although it is not expected from a ring participant to support them all. Some peers may provide persistence, others monitoring, indexing, etc.

Our two theses. The first thesis is that "intentional" and "active" data ala AXML should form the basis for the logical model of the data ring. The intensional component enables the sharing of information and knowledge in a distributed context. The active component provides support for aspects such as pub/sub, monitoring, synchronization/reconciliation, network connectivity, awareness.

The second thesis is that AXML is a proper basis for the physical model as well. Consider for instance distributed query optimization, a key issue. We need to be able to describe and exchange distributed query execution plans. A recent work [4] shows how this can be achieved using AXML expressions describing standard algebraic XML operations and send/receive operators over XML streams.

Related work and conclusion. Many ideas found here are influenced by previous works on P2P content warehouse, see [2]. Similar ideas have been promoted in [8]. The author of the present paper has been strongly influenced by on-going works with Ioana Manolescu, Tova Milo and Neoklis Polyzotis.

Some of the underlying technology has already been developed in related software systems, e.g.: structured p2p network such as Chord or Pastry, XML repositories such as Xyleme or DBMonet, file sharing systems such as BitTorrent or Kazaa, distributed storage systems such as OceanStore or Google File System. content delivery network such as Coral or Akamai, multicast systems such as Bullet or Avalanche, Pub/Sub system such as Scribe or Hyper, application

	Relational DBMS	Data Ring
Data & type	Relations, schema, constraints	AXML, schema, ontologies
Query-update	SQL	Xquery, Xupdate
Storage & access	B-tree, hash, fulltext, pages	also DHT & catalogues
Access control	ACL	also crypto, trust
Change control	DB & versions & triggers	also provenance, monitoring
Distribution	Limited	Yes
Incompleteness, fuzziness	Limited	Yes
Discovery of data/services	×	Yes
Messaging, multi-casting	×	Yes

Fig. 1. Some aspects of the comparison of relational DBMS and Data Rings

platform suites as proposed by Sun or Oracle for integrating software components, data integration as provided in warehouse or mediator systems. Of course, all the work in distributed database systems [9] is relevant.

The development of data rings leads to a number of research issues, notably the distribution of certain functionalities such as query optimization (with self tuning), or access control. An important milestone towards the realization of this vision is the completion of "the glue" between the components and in particular:

- The data/knowledge model that is used.
- The API for the various functionalities.
- The format for publishing logical resources as well as physical ones (AXML is just a starting point).

References

1. Active XML web site, activexml.net
2. S. Abiteboul: Managing an XML Warehouse in a P2P Context. CAiSE, 4-13, 2003
3. S. Abiteboul, R. Hull and V. Vianu: Foundations of Databases, Addison-Wesley, Reading-Massachusetts, 1995
4. S. Abiteboul, I. Manolescu, E. Taropa: A Framework for Distributed XML Data Management. EDBT, 1049-1058, 2006
5. S. Abiteboul, T. Milo, O. Benjelloun: The Active XML Project: an overview, INRIA Internal Report,
   ftp://ftp.inria.fr/INRIA/Projects/gemo/gemo/GemoReport-331.pdf
6. Edited by R. Cattell: The Object Database Standard: ODMG-93, Morgan Kaufmann, San Mateo, California, 1994
7. The Edos Project, http://www.edos-project.org/
8. A. Halevy, M. Franklin, D. Maier: Dataspaces: A New Abstraction for Information Management. DASFAA, 1-2, 2006
9. T. Özsu, P. Valduriez: Principles of Distributed Database Systems. 2nd Edition, Prentice Hall, Englewood Cliffs, New Jersey, 666 pages, 1999
10. N. Paton, O. Diaz, Active database systems, ACM Computing Surveys, Vol. 31, No. 1, March 1999
11. W3C - The World Wide Web Consortium, http://www.w3.org/

SuperGlue: Component Programming with Object-Oriented Signals

Sean McDirmid[1] and Wilson C. Hsieh[2]

[1] École Polytechnique Fédérale de Lausanne (EPFL), 1015 Lausanne, Switzerland
sean.mcdirmid@epfl.ch
[2] University of Utah, 84112 Salt Lake City, UT, USA
wilson@cs.utah.edu

Abstract. The assembly of components that can handle continuously changing data results in programs that are more interactive. Unfortunately, the code that glues together such components is often difficult to write because it is exposed to many complicated event-handling details. This paper introduces the SuperGlue language where components are assembled by connecting their **signals**, which declaratively represent state as time-varying values. To support the construction of interactive programs that require an unbounded number of signal connections, signals in SuperGlue are scaled with object-oriented abstractions. With Super-Glue's combination of signals and objects, programmers can build large interactive programs with substantially less glue code when compared to conventional approaches. For example, the SuperGlue implementation of an email client is around half the size of an equivalent Java implementation.

1 Introduction

Programs that are interactive are more usable than their batch program counterparts. For example, an interactive compiler like the one in Eclipse [15] can continuously detect syntax and semantic errors while programmers are typing, while a batch compiler can only detect errors when it is invoked. Interactive programs are often built out of components that can recompute their output state as their input state changes over time. For example, a compiler parser component could incrementally recompute its output parse tree according to changes made in its input token list. Other examples of these kinds of components include many kinds of user-interface widgets such as sliders and tables.

The assembly of components together in interactive programs often involves expressing state-viewing relationships. In object-oriented languages, such relationships are often expressed according to a model-view controller [13] (MVC) architecture. An MVC architecture involves model and view components, and *glue code* that transforms model state into view state. This glue code is often difficult to develop because most languages lack good constructs for transforming state. Instead, changes in state are often communicated as discrete events that must be manually translated by glue code into discrete changes of the transformed state.

This paper introduces SuperGlue, which simplifies component assembly by hiding event handling details from glue code. Components in SuperGlue are assembled by connecting together their *signals* [10], which represent state declaratively as time-varying

D. Thomas (Ed.): ECOOP 2006, LNCS 4067, pp. 206–229, 2006.
© Springer-Verlag Berlin Heidelberg 2006

```
var folder : Mailbox.Folder;
if (folderView.selected.size = 1 &&
    folderView.selected[0] = folder)
  messageView.rows = folder.messages;
```

Fig. 1. SuperGlue code that implements email client behavior

values. Operations on signals are also signals whose values automatically change when the values of their operand signals change. For example, if x and y are signals, then x + y is a signal whose current value is always the sum of the current values for x and y. By operating on signals to produce new signals, SuperGlue code can transform state between components without expressing custom event handlers.

Although signals are abstractions in functional-reactive programming languages [8, 10, 14], SuperGlue is novel in that it is the first language to combine signals with object-oriented abstractions. A program is expressed in SuperGlue as a set of signal connections between components. Because realistic programs often require an unbounded number of connections, each connection cannot be expressed individually. Instead, rules in SuperGlue can express new connections through type-based pattern matching over existing connections. To organize these rules, the types that are used in connection pattern matching are supported with three object-oriented mechanisms:

– **Nesting**, which is used to describe complicated components whose interfaces contain an unbounded number of signals. For example, inner node objects can describe the signals for an unbounded number of nodes in a user-interface tree component.
– **Traits**, which are used to integrate otherwise incompatible objects. For example, a trait can be used to describe how any kind of object is labeled in a user interface.
– **Extension**, which is used to implicitly prioritize connections to the same signal. For example, the connection of true to a bird object's canFly signal is of a lower priority than the connection of false to a penguin object's canFly signal.

These mechanisms form a novel object system that is specifically designed to support connection-based component programming.

As a concrete example of how SuperGlue can reduce the amount of code needed to assemble components together, consider the SuperGlue code in Figure 1, which implements the following master-detail behavior in an email client: "the messages of a folder that is uniquely selected in a folder view tree are displayed as rows in a message view table." This code glues together the **folderView** and **messageView** components, which are respectively a user-interface tree and table. The second line of Figure 1 is a condition that detects when only one node is selected in the folder view. The third line of Figure 1 is a *connection query* that detects if the first (and only) node selected in the folder view is connected to an email folder. If the connection query is true, the connected-to email folder is bound to the folder variable that is declared on the first line of Figure 1. If both of these conditions are true, the fourth line of Figure 1 connects the rows signal of the message view to the messages signal of the selected email folder.

Because the code in Figure 1 is evaluated continuously, how the rows of the message view table are connected can change during program execution. The user could select more than one node in the folder view tree, which causes the first condition to become false, and then deselect nodes until only one node is selected, which causes the first condition to become true. The user can select a node in a folder view tree that is not an email folder, which causes the second condition to become false. When a new email message is added to the folder whose messages are connected to the message view table's rows, a new row is added to the message view table. All of this behavior occurs with only four lines of SuperGlue code. In contrast, implementing this behavior in Java requires more than thirty lines of code because the code is exposed to event-handling details.

SuperGlue components are implemented with either SuperGlue code or Java code. When implemented with Java code, signals are represented with special Java interfaces that enable the wrapping of existing Java libraries. For example, we have implemented SuperGlue components around Java's Swing [24] and JavaMail [23] class libraries. The advantage of this dual language approach is that an expressive language (Java) can be used to implement components, while modularity is significantly enhanced by having components interact through SuperGlue's declarative signals.

This paper describes SuperGlue and how it reduces the amount of glue code needed to build interactive programs out of components. Section 2 details why components are difficult to assemble together in interactive programs. Section 3 introduces SuperGlue and provides examples of how it is used. Section 4 evaluates SuperGlue through a case study that compares an email client implementation in both SuperGlue and Java. Section 5 describes SuperGlue's syntax, semantics, and implementation. Section 6 presents related work and Section 7 summarizes our conclusions.

2 Motivation

We use the implementation of an email client program to show how components in interactive programs are difficult to assemble together. Consider the Java code in Figure 2, which assembles user-interface and email components to implement the following master-detail behavior: "the messages of an email folder that is uniquely selected in the folder view tree are the rows of a message view table." Two observers, which are object-oriented event handlers, are implemented and installed in Figure 2 to implement this behavior. The observer stored in the `messageObserver` variable translates folder message addition and removal events into table view row addition and removal events. The `messageObserver` is installed on an email folder object by the observer stored in `selectionObserver` variable, which in turn is installed on the folder view tree (`folderView`). The `selectionObserver` is implemented to determine when the following condition is true or false: "only one node is selected and this node is an email folder." When this condition becomes true or false, the `messageObserver` is installed or uninstalled on the right email folder.

The Java code in Figure 2 is complicated because of its direct involvement in how state-change events are communicated between components. This involvement is necessary for two reasons. First, the way components transmit and receive events is often incompatible. In Figure 2, the email message addition and removal events transmitted from an email folder cannot be directly received by a user interface table. Second, events often affect state transformations in ways that must be translated manually. In Figure 2,

```
messageObserver = new MessageCountListener() {
  void messageAdded(Message message)
  { messageViewModel.notifyRowInserted(message); }
  void messageRemoved(Message message)
  { messageViewModel.notifyRowDeleted (message); }
};
selectionObserver = new TreeSelectionListener() {
  Folder selected;
  void selectionAdded  (Object node) {
    int  selCount = folderView.getSelectedCount();
    Object selAdd = folderView.getSelected(0);
    if (selCount == 2 && selected != null) {
      selected.removeMessageCountListener(messageObserver);
      messageViewModel.notifyRowsChanged();
      selected = null;
    } else if (selCount == 1 && selAdd instanceof Folder) {
      selected = (Folder) selAdd;
      selected.addMessageCountListener(messageObserver);
      messageViewModel.notifyRowsChanged();
    }
  }
  void selectionRemoved(Object node) { ... }
};
folderView.addSelectionListener(selectionObserver);
```

Fig. 2. Java glue code that implements and installs the observerobjects of a message view component

tree node selection events are transformed into a condition that determines what email folder's messages are displayed. Detecting the discrete boundaries where this condition changes requires substantial logic in the `selectionObserver` implementation. For example, when a new node is selected in the tree view, code is needed to check if one folder was already selected, in which case the condition becomes false, or if one folder has become selected, in which case the condition becomes true.

Two approaches can currently be used to improve how the glue code of an interactive program is written. First, programming languages can reduce event handler verbosity with better syntax; e.g., through closure constructs and dynamic typing. Programming languages that follow this approach include Python [25], Ruby [19], and Scala [21]. However, although glue code in these languages can be less verbose than in Java, it is often not less complicated because programmers must still deal with the same amount of event handling details. In the second approach, standardized interface can be used in component interfaces to hide event handling details from glue code. For example, The `ListModel` Swing interface listed in Figure 3 can be used standardize how element addition and removal events are transmitted and received by different components. Using list model interfaces in our email client example, displaying email messages as rows in a table view can be reduced to the following line of code:

```
tableView.setRows(folder.getMessages());
```

```
interface ListModel {
  int getSize();
  Object getElementAt(int index);
  void    addDataListener(ListDataListener listener);
  void removeDataListener(ListDataListener listener);
}
```

Fig. 3. Swing's **ListModel** Java interface, which describes a list with observable changes in membership

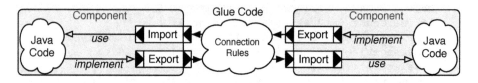

Fig. 4. An illustration of a SuperGlue program's run-time architecture; "use" means the Java code is using imported signals through a special Java interface; "implement" means Java code is providing exported signals by implementing special Java interface

Unfortunately, standardized interfaces cannot easily improve glue code that performs state transformations. For example, the glue code in Figure 2 selects what folder's messages are displayed using a condition. Expressing this condition with standardized interfaces requires redefining how ==, &&, and, most significantly, **if** operations work. Although the resulting code could be syntactically expressed in Java, such code would be very verbose and not behave like normal Java code.

3   SuperGlue

The problems that are described in Section 2 occur when glue code is exposed to events that communicates state changes between components. When event handling can be hidden from glue code with standardized interfaces, these problems disappear and glue code is much easier to write. However, the use of standardized interfaces to express state transformations in glue code requires layering a non-standard semantics on top of the original language. Instead, these standardized interfaces should be supported with their own syntax. In SuperGlue, standardized interfaces are replaced with **signal** language abstractions that represent mutable state declaratively as time-varying values.

The architecture of a SuperGlue program is illustrated in Figure 4. A SuperGlue program is assembled out of components that interact by viewing each others' state through signals. A component views state through its imported signals, and provides state for viewing through its exported signals. SuperGlue code defines program behavior by operating on and connecting the signals of the program's components together. Components in SuperGlue can be implemented either in SuperGlue or Java code, while components are always assembled together with SuperGlue code. Components are implemented in Java code according to special Java interfaces that are described in Section 5. For the rest of this section, we focus on the SuperGlue code that assembles components together.

```
atom Thermometer {
  export temperature : Int;
}
atom Label {
  import text  : String;
  import color : Color;
}
```

Fig. 5. Declarations of the **Thermometer** and **Label** atoms

A component in SuperGlue is an instance of either an *atom*, which is implemented with Java code, or a *compound*, which is implemented with SuperGlue code. Two example atoms are declared in Figure 5. Signals are declared in a component to be either exported or imported and are associated with a type. The **Thermometer** atom declares an exported temperature signal that is the value that a thermometer component measures. The **Label** atom declares an imported text signal that is the value that is displayed by a label component. The **Label** atom also declares an imported color signal that is the foreground color of a label component.

Components in a program are instantiated atoms or compounds. For example, the following code instantiates the **Thermometer** atom to create the **model** component:

```
let model = new Thermometer;
```

Interactions between components are established by connecting their signals together. Signal connection syntax in SuperGlue resembles assignments in a C-like language: the left-hand side of a signal connection is an imported signal that is connected to the right-hand side of a signal connection, which is an expression. As an example of a connection, consider the following glue code:

```
let view = new Label;
view.text = "" + model.temperature + " C";
```

This code connects the text signal that is imported into the **view** component to an expression that refers to the temperature signal that is exported from the **model** component. Because of this connection and the Java implementations of the **Label** and **Thermometer** atoms, whenever the temperature measured by the **model** component changes, the text displayed in the **view** component is updated automatically to reflect this change.

Connections are expressed in rules with conditions that guard when the connections are able to connect signals. When all the conditions of a rule evaluate to true, the rule is *active*, meaning that the source expression of its signal connection can be evaluated and used as the sink signal's value. Connection rules in SuperGlue are expressed as C-like **if** statements. As an example of a rule, consider the following code:

```
if (model.temperature > 30) view.color = red;
```

This code connects the foreground color of the **view** component to the color red when the current temperature measured by the **model** component is greater than 30. When

```
if        (model.temperature > 30) view.color = red;
else if (model.temperature < 0 ) view.color = blue;
else                              view.color = black;
```

Fig. 6. Glue code that causes the color of the **view** label component to change according to the current temperature measured through the **model** thermometer component

the current temperature is not greater than 30, the condition in this code prevents red from being used as the for the foreground color of the **view** component.

Although rules in SuperGlue resemble **if** statements in an imperative language, they have semantics that are declarative. Conditions are evaluated continuously to determine if the connections they guard are active. In our example, the current temperature can dynamically go from below 30 to above 30, which causes the **view** component's foreground color to become red. In SuperGlue's runtime, this continuous evaluation is transparently implemented with event handling that activates the port connection when the current temperature rises above 30.

Multiple rules that connect the same signal form a *circuit* that controls how the signal is connected during program execution. At any given time, any number of rules in a circuit can be active. If all rules in a signal's circuit are inactive, then the signal is unconnected. If exactly one rule in a circuit is active, then the circuit's signal is connected according to that rule. It is also possible that multiple rules in a circuit are active at the same time, while only one of these rules can connect the circuit's imported signal. If these rules cannot be prioritized, then the signal is connected ambiguously.

To explicitly prioritize rules in a circuit, rules can be expressed in the body of an **else** clause so that they are never active when rules that are expressed in the body of the corresponding **if** clause are active. As an example of a circuit, consider the glue code in Figure 6, which continuously connects a different color to the **view** label's foreground color depending on the current temperature. As the current temperature falls below 30, the foreground color of the **view** label changes from red to black. Likewise, as the current temperature falls below 0, the foreground color of the **view** label changes from black to blue. The color connection code in Figure 6 forms a circuit that is illustrated in Figure 7. Conditions, which are ovals, control whether a connection is active based on their test inputs. Multiple connections are organized into a switch that passes through the highest priority connection, which is closest to hi, that is currently active.

With the basic connection model that has been described in this section, each signal connection in a program is encoded separately. This model has two limitations:

- Programs that deal with stateful graph-like structures such as lists and trees cannot be expressed very effectively. Graph-like structures are unbounded in their sizes and therefore cannot be expressed as a fixed number of direct connections between components.
- Many connections conform to patterns that are repeated many times within the same program or across different programs. If each connection must be encoded separately, then these patterns cannot be modularized and connection code can become very repetitive.

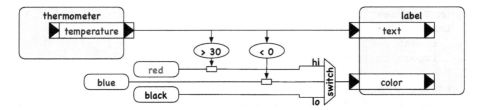

Fig. 7. An illustration of a circuit that connects to the `color` signal of the **view** label component; rounded rectangles are components; boxes that end with triangles are signals; ovals are conditions with outgoing results; and small boxes activate connections according to their incoming condition results; the multiplexor "switch" only passes through the highest (closest to `hi`) active connection

If unaddressed, these two limitations prevent the effective construction of real programs in SuperGlue. Consider the email client that is used as an example in Section 2. This email client consists of a user-interface tree that displays a hierarchy of mailboxes and email folders. Because the size of this tree is not known until run-time, it cannot be expressed with a fixed number of connections. Additionally, the connections in this tree are largely homogeneous; e.g., the connections used to relate one tree node to one email folder are repeated to relate another tree node to another email folder. As a result, specifying each connection individually would result in very repetitive code.

3.1   Connection Nesting and Reification

Connections are not as expressive procedures, and so by themselves cannot scale to express non-trivial programs. In a way that is similar to how procedures are enhanced by being organized into objects, we enhance connections in SuperGlue with object-oriented abstractions to improve their expressiveness. In SuperGlue, connections can be identified at run-time by the types of the signals they connect. A rule can then create a new connection relative to any existing connection that matches a specified type pattern. SuperGlue supports such type-based pattern matching with object-oriented abstractions. Objects in SuperGlue serve two roles: first, they are containers of imported and exported signals; and second, they serve as nodes in a program's connection graphs. Each signal connection in SuperGlue involves objects that reify the import being connected and the expression that the import is being connected to. The types of these objects are then used to identify the connection when rules are evaluated. To better support the use of objects as types in connections, object are supported with nesting, which is described next, traits, which is described in Section 3.2, and extension, which is described in Section 3.3.

Object nesting is similar to pattern nesting in BETA [17] and is used to describe components that contain a large or unbounded number of signals. As an example, the **TreeView** atom is declared in Figure 8 with the `Node` inner object type, which is used to represent user-interface tree nodes. A **TreeView** component imports a root `Node` object, and each of its `Node` object imports its own list of child `Node` objects. In this way, inner `Node` objects can be used to concisely describe the unbounded hierarchical structure of a user-interface tree. The `List` trait used in Figure 8 describes lists of objects of a type specified in brackets. A signal of type `List[T : Node]` contains an integer

```
atom TreeView {
  inner Node {
    import text : String;
    import children : List[T : Node];
  }
  import root      : Node;
  export selected : List[T : Node];
}
```

Fig. 8. The **TreeView** atom and the Node inner object type that is nested in the **TreeView** atom

```
atom Mailbox {
  inner Message {...}
  inner Folder {
    export sub_folders : List[T : Folder];
    export messages      : List[T : Message];
  }
  export root_folder    : Folder;
}
```

Fig. 9. The **Mailbox** atom and the Message and Folder inner object types that are nested in the **Mailbox** atom

size signal and a signal of type Node for each of its elements; e.g., the children signal contains [0] and [1] signals, which are both of type Node. We describe the List trait in Section 3.3.

At run-time, an object in SuperGlue is a vertex in the program's connection graph that is connected to other objects. The declared type of a signal describes the object that is attached to the signal. For example, an imported root signal of declared type Node is attached to a Node object. The type of a signal does not restrict how the signal can be used in a connection. In fact, the types involved in the same connection do not have to be related in any way. Instead, types describe how objects are connected as a result of connections. For example, consider the following SuperGlue code, which uses the **Mailbox** atom that is declared in Figure 9:

```
let folderView = new TreeView;
let mailbox = new Mailbox;
folderView.root = mailbox.root_folder;
```

This rule connects an exported root_folder signal of type Folder to an imported root signal of type Node. The Folder and Node types of the connection's objects are entirely unrelated. Despite the unrelated types, this connection is allowed because other rules can resolve the incompatibilities that occur between these two objects.

Unlike components, inner objects are not instantiated in glue code. Instead, the creation and identity of an inner object is managed inside its containing component. As a result, inner object types can describe a component's interface without revealing details about how the component is implemented. For example, the folder and message objects nested of a mailbox components can be implemented to only have allocated objects while they are being used.

SuperGlue code can abstract over objects based on their types using SuperGlue's variable construct. As an example, consider the following code:

```
var node : folderView.Node;
```

This code declares a `node` variable, which abstracts over all `Node` objects in the **folderView** component. Variables must be bound to values when they are used in rules. A variable is bound to a value when it is used as a connection *target*, which means its signal is being connected in the connection rule. As an example of how a variable is bound when it is a connection target, consider the following code:

```
var node    : folderView.Node;
node.children = folder.sub_folders;
```

Because the `node` variable in this code is the target of a connection, it is always bound to some tree node object when the rule is evaluated. The way that variables are bound when they are used as connection targets resembles how procedure arguments are bound in a procedural language, where evaluating a connection binds the connection's target to a value is analogous to how calling a procedure binds the procedure's arguments to values.

In conjunction with variables, rules can abstract over connections in a program by identifying how objects are connected with *connection queries*. A connection query is a condition of the form `sink = source`, where `sink` and `source` are expressions. A connection query succeeds only if `sink` is connected to a value that is equivalent to `source`, where unbound variables referred to in `source` can become bound to facilitate this equivalence. Whether a variable can be bound to a value depends on the value's type being compatible with the variable's type. As an example, consider the following code:

```
var node    : folderView.Node;
var folder : Mailbox.Folder;
if (node = folder) node.children = folder.sub_folders;
```

This code is evaluated as follows:

1. The `node` variable, which is the target of the rule defined in this code, is bound to a `Node` object whose `children` signal is being accessed.
2. The connection query `node = folder` checks if the targeted `Node` object is connected to a `Folder` object of a **Mailbox** component. If it is, then the `folder` variable is bound to the connecting `Folder` object.
3. If the connection query is true, the imported `children` signal of the `Node` object is connected to the exported `sub_folders` signal of the `Folder` object.

Variables and connection queries allow rules in SuperGlue to be reused in multiple connection contexts. For example, because of the following rule, the root node object of the folder view tree is connected to the root folder object of a mailbox:

```
folderView.root = mailbox.root_folder;
```

```
atom TableView {
  inner Row { ... }
  import rows : List[T : Row];
}
let messageView = new TableView;
var folder : Mailbox.Folder;
if (folderView.selected.size = 1 &&
    folderView.selected[0] = folder)
  messageView.rows = folder.messages;
```

Fig. 10. The **TableView** atom and code that describes how the rows of a message view table are connected in an email client

When the folder view tree's implementation accesses the `children` signal of its root node object, the `node` variable target of the following rule, which was just described, is bound to the root node object:

```
if (node = folder) node.children = folder.sub_folders;
```

Because of the connection query in this rule, the `folder` variable is bound to the root folder object of the mailbox object. As a result, the `children` signal of the root node object is connected to the root folder object's `sub_folders` signal. In turn, the same rule connects the **folderView**.`root.children[0].children` signal to the **mailbox**.`root_folder.sub_folders[0].sub_folders` signal, and so on. Despite the recursion, this rule will terminate because it is only evaluated when a tree node is expanded by a user.

Our use of variables and connection queries to build trees resembles how hierarchical structures are often built in user interfaces using conventional object-oriented languages. For example, in Java's Swing [24] library, **TreeModel** objects often examine the run-time types of objects, which are used as nodes, to compute their child nodes. Compared to this approach, expressing a tree in SuperGlue requires less code because of SuperGlue's direct support for expressing connection graphs.

SuperGlue's signal and object-oriented abstractions are designed to work seamlessly together. Circuits that change how signals are connected at run-time consequently change how objects are connected. Additionally, because signal expressions can be used as the source of a connection query, if and how a connection query is true can change at run-time. As an example, consider the SuperGlue code in Figure 10, some of which was presented in Section 1. The second condition of the rule defined in this code is a connection query that tests if the first and only selected node of a folder view tree is connected to a folder object. As node selection in the folder view changes, the condition can become false if the newly selected node is not a folder object. Alternatively, a different folder object can become bound to the `folder` variable if the newly selected node is another folder. The latter situation would cause the rows of the message view table to be connected to a different list of email messages, which in turn causes the message view table to be refreshed.

3.2 Traits

SuperGlue traits are similar to Java interfaces in that they lack implementations. Traits serve two purposes: they enable the reuse of signal declarations in different component prototypes; and they enable *coercions* that adapt incompatible objects by augmenting them with new behavior.

Unlike the signals that are declared in atoms and compounds, signals are declared in traits with the `port` keyword, meaning whether they are imported or exported is not fixed. As an example, the following SuperGlue code declares the `Labeled` trait with one `label` signal:

```
trait Labeled { port label : String; }
```

An atom or compound can extend a trait by specifying if the trait's signals are imported or exported. As an example, the following code declares that the `Node` inner object type imports the signals of the `Labeled` trait:

```
atom TreeView { inner Node imports Labeled { ... } }
```

Whenever an object that imports a trait is connected to another object that exports the same trait, the trait's declared signals in both objects are connected by default. As an example, first consider having the `Folder` inner object type of a **Mailbox** atom export the `Labeled` trait:

```
atom Mailbox { inner Folder exports Labeled { ... } }
```

When `Node` objects are connected to `Folder` objects, the rule `node.label = folder.label` is implied and does not need to be specified in glue code.

The example in the previous paragraph is not very modular: the `Folder` inner object type, which is an email concern, should not implement the `Labeled` trait, which is a user-interface concern. In general, components should only declare signals that are necessary to express their state and capabilities. Traits for other concerns can be externally implemented as coercions by using variables and connection queries (Section 3.1) to specify how the components' signals are translated between the traits' signals. As an example of a coercion, consider the SuperGlue code in Figure 11, where the `Folder` object does not implement the `Labeled` trait. Instead, the rule in Figure 11 specifies how the `label` signal of an object that imports the `Labeled` trait is connected when the object is connected to a `Folder` object. This rule then applies to each tree **Node** object that is connected to an email `Folder` object.

```
atom Mailbox {
  inner Folder { export name : String; }
  ...
}
var labeled : Labeled;
var folder  : Mailbox.Folder;
if (labeled = folder) labeled.label = "Folder " + folder.name;
```

Fig. 11. An example of how a *Labeled* trait coercion is defined for `Folder` objects that are nested in **Mailbox** components

3.3   Extension

SuperGlue's support for type extension enables the refinement of inner object types and traits. Extension in SuperGlue differs from extension in conventional object-oriented languages in the way that it is used to prioritize rules in circuits. Such prioritization is the only way in SuperGlue to prioritize rules that are specified independently.

Given two SuperGlue variables, one variable is more specific than the other variable if the type of the former variable extends the type of the latter variable. Connections are then prioritized based on the specificity of their involved variables. As an example, consider the following code:

```
trait Bird { port canFly : Boolean; }
trait Penguin extends Bird;
var aBird : Bird;
var aPenguin : Penguin;
aBird.canFly = true;
aPenguin.canFly = false;
```

The *Penguin* trait extends the *Bird* trait, so the type of the aPenguin variable is more specific than the type of the aBird variable. As a result, the connection of a penguin object's canFly signal to false has a higher priority than the connection of a bird object's canFly signal to true. In this way, penguin behavior **overrides** more generic bird behavior.

Besides being used to prioritize connections, type extension is also used in Super-Glue to refine inner object types. Generic typing is achieved in SuperGlue by refining inner object types when their containers are extended. As an example, the *List* trait, which is declared in Figure 12, describes list items through its T inner object type. The T inner object type can be refined whenever the *List* trait is extended, imported, or exported. As an example, consider the following code:

```
atom TableView {
  inner Row { ... }
  inner Rows imports List {
    refine T extends Row;
  }
  import rows : Rows;
}
```

In this code, the Rows inner object type is declared to extend the *List* trait through the **imports** keyword. As a result, the Rows inner object type has the *List* trait's

```
trait List extends Array {
  inner T;
  port size  : Int;
  port index : Int;
  port item  : T;
}
```

Fig. 12. The declaration of the **List** trait

T inner object type, which itself can be refined to extend the Row inner object type declared in the **TableView** component prototype. As a result, any element of the rows list will be an object that is or is connected from a row object. The refinement of a single inner object type in a trait is a common operation and is supported by SuperGlue with syntactic sugar so that the above SuperGlue code can be re-written as follows:

```
atom TableView {
  inner Row { ... }
  import rows : List[T : Row];
}
```

In this code, the colon operator is used twice as a short hand for extension: the colon expresses that the T inner object type from the *List* trait extends Row and that the type of the rows signal imports the *List* trait. Similar syntax was used to declare list signals in Figure 8, Figure 9, and Figure 10.

3.4 Array Signals and Streams

Multi-element data is expressed in SuperGlue with signals whose types extend the built-in *Array* trait, which we refer to as *array signals*. The *List* trait is declared in Figure 12 to extend *Array* so any signal that is declared with the *List* trait will be an array signal. Array signals are similar to SQL tables–an individual element of an array can only be accessed through an SQL-like query that selects the element according to the values of its sub-signals. As an example, the following SuperGlue code selects the first element of a table's list of rows:

```
table.rows(index = 0).item
```

This SuperGlue code is similar in behavior to the following pseudo-SQL query:

```
SELECT item FROM table.rows WHERE index = 0
```

Alternatively, SuperGlue provides syntactic sugar to access list elements; e.g., **table-**.rows[0] is equivalent to the above SuperGlue code. Array signal queries are also used to express arithmetic expressions. For example, the expression x + y is syntactic sugar for x.plus(operand = y).result. We use query syntax rather than argument binding for an important reason: the coercions that are described in Section 3.2 can be directly applied to query bindings, which would be problematic with parameter passing semantics.

So that entire interactive programs can be expressed in SuperGlue, SuperGlue supports *streams* that can be used to manipulate discrete events and imperative commands. There are two kinds of streams in SuperGlue: event streams, which intercept discrete events, and command streams, which perform imperative commands. As an example of how streams are used, consider the following SuperGlue code that implements delete email message behavior:

```
let delete_button = new Button;
on (delete_button.pushed)
  if (msg : Mailbox.Message = messageView.selected)
    do msg.delete;
```

The last three lines of this code use streams. The **on** statement intercepts events where the delete button is pushed. When the delete button is pushed, each email message selected in the message view table is deleted by executing its `delete` command stream in a **do** statement. Streams in SuperGlue are convenience abstractions that enable imperative programming without sacrificing the benefits of SuperGlue's signals. Unlike signals, we do not claim that there is a significant advantage to using SuperGlue to express components interactions through streams.

4   Evaluation

Our evaluation of SuperGlue focuses on our claim that SuperGlue can substantially reduce the amount of glue code needed to build an interactive program out of components. More importantly, we claim that this code reduction corresponds to a similar reduction in complexity. This section evaluates our claims using the case study of implementing a complete email client in SuperGlue, which has been used as our primary example in this paper. We then compare this SuperGlue implementation of an email client to a feature-equivalent implementation in Java. As part of this comparison, we have designed a strategy to compare complexity that accounts for differences between SuperGlue and Java syntax.

Our email client is composed of user-interface and email components. For this case study, we have implemented the necessary SuperGlue component libraries by wrapping the Swing [24] and JavaMail [23] class libraries, which are used directly in the Java email client. How a Java class library is wrapped into a SuperGlue component library is described in Section 5. By far, the most complicated wrapping involves Swing's **JTree** and **JTable** classes, which require 444 and 611 lines of Java code, respectively. This code is devoted to translating the Java-centric abstractions of the original classes into SuperGlue signal abstractions. Component wrappers involve a lot of code that is not counted in our case study because the resulting component libraries are reusable in multiple applications. On the other hand, the need for wrapper code represents a significant amount of complexity that must be amortized by reusing the components in many programs.

A screen shot of the SuperGlue email client is shown in Figure 13. Our comparison case study is organized according to the code that is needed to express the following email client features:

- **Navigation**, which allows a user to navigate mailboxes, folders, and messages. Navigation is divided into three views: a folder view tree, which views the folders of installed mailboxes, a message view table, which views rows of message headers, and a body view form, which views the contents of a message. In Figure 13, the folder view is in the upper left-hand corner, the message view is in the upper right-hand corner, and the content view is in the bottom portion of the screen shot.
- **Deletion**, which allows a user to delete email messages. Deleted messages are highlighted in the message view table, and the user can expunge deleted messages in a folder that is selected in the tree view.
- **Composition**, which allows a user to compose and send a new message, and reply to an existing message.

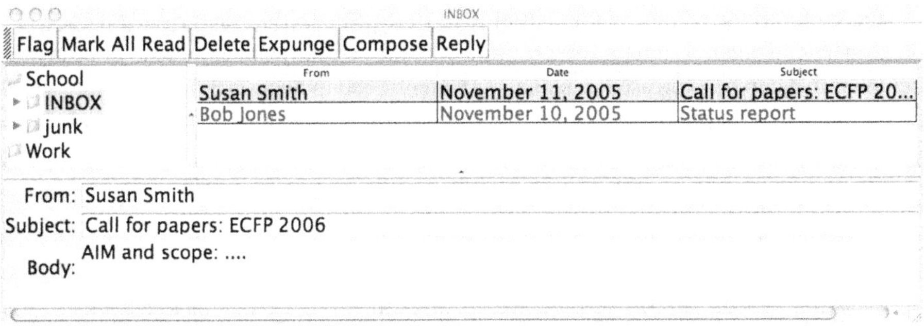

Fig. 13. A screen shot of an email client that is implemented in SuperGlue

The methodology used in our comparison case study involves measuring two metrics in each implementation: lines of code and number of operations. While line counts are accurate measures of verbosity, they are not necessarily accurate measures of complexity. Verbosity and complexity are only loosely related, and code that is more verbose can aid in readability and is not necessarily more complicated. For this reason, we also measure the number of operations needed to implement a feature. We count only operations that are defined by libraries and not built into the programming language. We do not count type declarations, local variable assignments, control flow constructs, and so on, which contribute to verbosity but do not make a library more difficult to use. For example, a method call in Java or a signal connection in SuperGlue are both counted as an operation each, while variable uses in both Java and SuperGlue are not counted as operations. Because the operations we count are related to using a library, they are a more accurate measure of complexity than line count.

The results of our comparison are shown in Figure 14. In these results, the line count and operation metrics are similar for each feature so, at least in this case study, operation density per line is similar between SuperGlue and Java. By far the largest reduction in program complexity is obtained in the SuperGlue implementation of the navigation feature. This reduction is large because the navigation feature uses trees, tables, and forms, which are components with a large amount of signal-based functionality. Besides the navigation feature, the deletion and composition features involve only a minor amount of continuous behavior, and so their implementations do not benefit very much from SuperGlue. Overall, SuperGlue's reduces the amount of code needed to implement an email client by almost half because the navigation feature requires much more Java code to implement than the other two features combined.

	Line Counts			Operations		
Features	*Java*	*SuperGlue*	$\frac{Java}{SuperGlue}$	*Java*	*SuperGlue*	$\frac{Java}{SuperGlue}$
Navigation	147	51	2.8	265	110	2.4
Deletion	24	23	1.0	45	35	1.3
Composition	54	43	1.3	96	76	1.3
Total	225	117	1.9	406	221	1.8

Fig. 14. A comparison of email client features as they are implemented in SuperGlue and Java

According to the results of this initial case study, SuperGlue can provide a code reduction benefit when an interactive program contains a significant amount of continuous behavior that can be expressed as signals. As mentioned in Section 3.4, SuperGlue's use is of little benefit in programs that involve a lot of non-continuous behavior; i.e., behavior that is discrete or imperative.

5   Syntax, Semantics, and Implementation

Our prototype of SuperGlue can execute many realistic programs, including the email client described in Section 4. Our prototype consists of an interpreter that evaluates the circuits of signals at run-time to drive component communication. This prototype can deal with components that are implemented either in SuperGlue (compounds) or Java (atoms). The discussion in this section describes informally the syntax, semantics, and implementation of SuperGlue. For space reasons, our discussion omits the following language features: **else** clauses, array signals, and streams. Our discussion also does not cover syntactic sugar that was described in Section 3.

5.1   Component and Trait Declarations

The syntax used to declare components and traits is expressed informally in Figure 15. **Notation:** the horizontal over-arrow indicates zero-to-many repetition, while the vertical bar indicates choice. A program consists of a collection of atoms, compounds, and traits. Atom s have Java implementations, which are described in Section 5.3. Compounds are implemented in SuperGlue code (*glue-code*) to glue other constituent components together. SuperGlue code is described in Section 5.2. SuperGlue code always exists in compound components, and a self-contained SuperGlue program is a compound that lacks imports and exports.

Atoms, compounds, traits, and inner object types all have declarations (*decls*) of their extended traits, signals, and inner object types. Sub-typing ($<_t$) is established by trait extension for components, traits, and inner object types, and by inner object type extension for inner object types. Inheritance behaves in the usual way; i.e., a type inherits all signals and inner object types of its super-types. An inner object type is a subtype of any inner object type it mirrors in its container's super-types: if $B <_t A$, then $B.anInner <_t A.anInner$ if $anInner$ is declared in A. Additionally, inner object types are extended virtually: if $A.anInnerY <_t A.anInnerX$ and $B <_t A$, then $B.anInnerY <_t B.anInnerX$. Because of this virtual extension behavior, as inner object types are refined via the **refine** keyword, all extending inner object types with the same container type automatically inherit the refinements.

When declaring a signal or extending a trait within the declaration of an atom or compound, the import/export polarity of the declared signal or the extended trait's signals must be specified via the **import(s)** and **export(s)** keywords. When declaring a signal or extending a trait within a trait declaration, import/export polarity is not specified so the **port** or **extends** keywords are used instead. When a trait is imported or exported into a component or inner object type of a component, the trait's signals are inherited under the same import/export polarity, which also applies to the signals of the

```
program      ≡   atom | compound | trait
atom         ≡   atom AtomName decls
compound     ≡   compound CompoundName decls with { glue-code }
trait        ≡   trait TraitName decls
decls        ≡   implements { inner | signal }
inner        ≡   (inner | refine) InnerName extends AnInner decls
implements   ≡   (imports | exports | extends) ATrait
signal       ≡
    (import | export | port) signalName : (ATrait | AnInner)
```

Fig. 15. Informal syntax for SuperGlue programs as well as components and traits

trait's inner object types. Likewise, when a trait is used as a signal's type, the signal inherits the trait's signals with its own import/export polarity.

5.2 SuperGlue Code

SuperGlue code, which forms the body of a compound component, is a collection of let statements, variable declarations, and rules whose syntax are described in Figure 16. For brevity, we assume that each rule is expressed in its own single **if** statement, although **if** nesting is possible in the actual language. We also do not address **else** statements, which act to negate the conditions in a corresponding **if** clause.

Expressions (e) in SuperGlue are values that have run-time representations. Evaluation determines how an expression is connected to another expression. Evaluation can be applied successively to determine what value that an expression is terminally connected to. This value will either be a constant as a number, string, handle, or an exception, which indicates failure in the evaluation.

The evaluation of a signal expression (e_z.aSignal) involves evaluating the signal's circuit of prioritized rules if the signal connected with SuperGlue code. The rules in a signal's circuit are prioritized according to the type specificity of each rule's target expression (e_x). Given two rules with target expressions e_a and e_b, the first rule is of a higher priority than the second rule if e_a's type is a subtype of e_b's type. If the target expressions of two rules do not have a sub typing relationship, then the rules have the same priority and are ambiguous.

To evaluate a rule, the e_x.aSignal expression of the rule is connected if possible to the evaluated signal expression e_z.aSignal. This is represented and evaluated as the connection query $e_x = e_z$, which is the implied first antecedent of every rule. Given a specific evaluated signal expression (e_z.aSignal), a rule is instantiated into the following:

if ($e_z = e_x$ && $\overrightarrow{query}$) e_z.aSignal = e_y

The connection queries that are a rule's antecedents perform a uni-directional form of unification in logic programming languages: the query $e_v = e_w$ is true if e_v is connected to an expression that is equivalent to e_w, where variables referred to by e_w can be bound to expressions in e_v to meet the equivalence condition. A connection query successively evaluates e_v until an expression is yielded that is equivalent to e_w, or until an end-point expression is reached, in which case the connection query fails.

```
glue-code ≡   let | var | rule
rule      ≡   if (query) eₓ.aSignal = e_y;
let       ≡   let instanceName = new aComponent;
var       ≡   var varName : (aTrait | aComponent | e.anInner)
query     ≡   e_v = e_w
e ≡ anInstance | aVar | e.aSignal | aConstant | anException
```

Fig. 16. Informal syntax for the SuperGlue code that is inside a compound component

A variable can be bound to an expression in a connection query if it is not already bound and the expression is of a type that is compatible with the variable's declared type. The binding of a variable does not cause the variable to be replaced with its bound-to expression. Instead, the variable ($aVar$) becomes connected to the bound-to expression (e) so that $aVar$ evaluates to e.

A rule is active if all of its antecedents evaluate to true. If the highest-priority active rule of a circuit is unambiguous, then $e_z.aSignal$ evaluates to e_a where e_y evaluates to e_a in an environment of any variable bindings that are created when the rule's connection queries are evaluated. If no rule is active, then the expression is unconnected. If multiple highest-priority rules are active, then the expression is connected to an ambiguity exception. Any other kind of exception that occurs during evaluation, such as dividing by zero, will also be propagated as the result of the evaluation.

If the evaluated signal expression $e_z.aSignal$ lacks a circuit, which occurs when e_z is a variable, or its circuit evaluates to an unconnected exception, then e_z is evaluated into e_n. If e_n has a type that declares $aSignal$, then the expression $e_n.aSignal$ is used as $e_z.aSignal$'s evaluation. In this way, we uniformly deal with variables and expressions, as well as establish default connections between container expressions that extend common traits, as described in Section 3.2.

5.3   Component Implementations

Signals that are imported into atoms or compounds or are exported from compounds are implemented with SuperGlue code. Evaluating a compound's exported signals is similar to evaluating imported signals, although the evaluation environments between the outside and inside of a compound are different. Signals that are exported from atoms are implemented with Java code. Atoms implement their exported signals and use their imported signals according to a Java interface that is described in Figure 17. This interface declares an eval method that allows an atom's Java code to implement the circuits of its exported signals directly and also enables access to the SuperGlue-based circuits of an atom's imported signals.

The eval method of the *Signal* interface accepts an observer that is notified when the result of the eval method has changed. When implementing a signal, Java code can install this observer on the Java resource being wrapped by the atom. For example, when implementing the exported selected nodes signal of a user-interface tree, this observer can be translated into a selection observer that is installed on a wrapped **JTree** object. When a signal is being used, Java code can provide an observer to notify the Java resource that is being wrapped of some change. For example, when using the imported rows signal of

```
interface Signal {
  Value eval(Value target, Context context, Observer o);
  Signal signal(Value target, Port port);
} interface Observer {
  void notify(Context context);
}
```

Fig. 17. Java interfaces used to implement signals

a user-interface table, an observer is implemented that translates imported row changes into notifyRowsAdded and notifyRowsRemoved calls on a wrapped **JTable** object.

An atom's Java code can either return arbitrary values when implementing an eval method or pass arbitrary values as targets when using an eval method. As a result, an atom has a lot of flexibility when manipulating inner objects. For example, an atom can create new inner objects on the fly and pass them into the right signal eval methods. This occurs when wrapping a **JTree** object, where parameters of methods in the tree model object are used as targets when querying the imported signals of inner **Node** objects.

5.4 Continuous Evaluation

The observers that are implemented in and used by Java code form the underlying infrastructure for *continuous evaluation* in SuperGlue, where evaluation results are updated continuously as state changes in the program's atoms. When an imported signal is evaluated from within an evaluating atom, the atom can specify an observer that is installed on dependent evaluations. Eventually, when evaluation reaches the exported signals of other atoms, this observer is installed in those atoms. When state changes in any of these other atom implementations, the evaluating atom is notified through the observer it defined. The evaluating atom can then re-evaluate the changed imported signal to refresh its view of state in other components.

When the state of an atom's imported signal changes, the atom will uninstall its observer on the signal's old evaluation and install its observer on the signal's new evaluation. The atom may also compute changes in the state of its own exports, where observers that are defined in other atoms and are installed on the atom are notified of these changes. A naive implementation of continuous evaluation processes all state changes as soon as they occur. However, this strategy results in *glitches* that cause atoms to observe inconsistent old and new signal evaluations. In the case of a glitch, an observer is not uninstalled and installed in the correct evaluation contexts, and therefore atoms will begin to miss changes in state.

Avoiding glitches in SuperGlue involves a sophisticated interpreter that adheres to the following guidelines:

- During the processing of a change in the evaluation of an atom's exported signal, ensure that both the signal's old and new evaluations are computable. This allows clients to compute old evaluations for derived signals so that observers can be uninstalled as necessary.
- The evaluation of an atom's exported signal cannot exhibit a new value until the corresponding change is processed and observers are notified of this new value.

This is an issue when a signal changes rapidly so that the processing of its new evaluations could overlap.

- A change in the value of an atom's exported signal is processed in two phases. The first phase only discovers what exported signals in other atoms have changed as a result of the first exported signal's change. As a result of this discovery, the second phase updates observers for each changing signal together. The separation of these two phases allow multiple dependent signals to change together and avoid situations where they exhibit combinations of evaluations that are inconsistent; e.g., where both b and !b evaluate to true.

5.5   Cycles, Termination, and Performance

Cycles in the signal graph occur when the evaluation of a signal expression yields itself. In SuperGlue, cycles are detected at run-time and rejected with a cyclic connection exception. Although cycles created solely in SuperGlue code can be statically detected, a cycle can also occur because of dependencies between an atom's imported and exported signals. For example, a table view imports a list of rows and exports a list of these rows that are selected. Connecting the exported selected rows of a table view to its imported rows creates a cycle.

Even without cycles in the signal graph, non-termination can still occur in a Super-Glue program. Because SuperGlue lacks recursion that is strong enough to traverse data structures, SuperGlue code by itself will never be the sole cause of non-termination. However, atoms can be implemented with arbitrary Java code, and how the atom is connected by SuperGlue code can influence whether this Java code terminates. For example, a tree view atom will not terminate if it is configured to expand all tree nodes and is connected to a tree model of an unbounded size.

Our prototype implementation of SuperGlue is not tuned in any way for performance. According to microbenchmarks, SuperGlue code is between two and 144 times slower than equivalent Java code, depending on the connections and evaluations being compared. As a worst case, the continuous evaluation of a circuit whose highest-priority active rule is always changing is 144 times slower than Java code that implements the equivalent behavior. For the interactive programs that we have explored so far, most of the work is being performed in atoms that are implemented in Java, so SuperGlue's performance penalty is not very noticeable. On the other hand, if SuperGlue code is to be used in more computationally intensive ways, higher performance will be necessary. Given SuperGlue's lack of strong recursion, the direct effects of SuperGlue code on performance is linearly related to the number of rules in the program. However, as with cycles and termination, the presence of atoms implemented with arbitrary Java code make it difficult to reason about how overall program performance is affected by SuperGlue code.

6   Related Work

The signal abstraction originates from the functional-reactive programming (FRP) language Fran [10], which extends Haskell with signals. FRP is itself based on various synchronous data-flow languages such as Esterel [4], Lustre [6], and Signal [3].

More recent FRP languages include Fran's successor, Yampa [14], and FatherTime (Fr-Time) [8], which extends Scheme with signals. SuperGlue differs from Fran and Yampa and resembles FrTime in that it supports an asynchronous rather than synchronous concurrency model. By supporting an asynchronous concurrency model, SuperGlue code can easily integrate with imperative Java code, although we must deal with "glitches" that are described in Section 5. Unlike SuperGlue, both Fran and FrTime support signals with higher-order and recursively-defined functions. While the use of functions presents programmers with a well-understood functional programming model, function calls obscure the state-viewing relationships between components when compared to SuperGlue's connection-based programming model. Frappé [9] is an implementation of FRP for Java that is based on Fran. Because signals in Frappé are manipulated purely as Java objects, it suffers from the verbosity problems described in Section 2.

SuperGlue connections resemble simple constraints. Kaleidoscope [11, 12] supports general constraint variables whose values can be updated imperatively. Kaleidoscope constraints are more powerful than SuperGlue signals: its constraints are multi-way and it directly supports the expression of imperative code. However, these features also make Kaleidoscope more complicated than SuperGlue: the mixing of constraint and imperative constructs complicates the language, and the duration of its constraints must be explicitly programmed.

SuperGlue supports the expression of graph-like state with object-oriented abstractions. Inner objects with virtual refinement in SuperGlue resembles pattern nesting in BETA [17]. As described in Section 3.2, traits can be used to add new behavior to objects. As a result, SuperGlue's objects and traits are similar to the mixin [5], open classes [7], or views [21] that are used to add new methods to existing classes. Super-Glue's rules are similar to rules in logic programming languages such as Prolog [22], which query and prove logical relations. Although connections in SuperGlue are similar to simple relations, SuperGlue does not use first-order logic to manipulate connections. While logic programming focuses on expressing computations declaratively, SuperGlue focuses on the expression of glue code with as little expressiveness as possible. In this way, SuperGlue is more similar to SQL than Prolog.

Connections have long been used to describe dependencies between components–see various work on architecture description languages [16, 18, 20]. Visual tools in JavaBeans can be used to wire the bean properties of components together. ArchJava [1] is a language that uses the port-connection model to specify how components can interact in the implementation of a software architecture. ArchJava has a custom connector abstraction [2] that can be used to express a wide-variety of port types. In contrast, although SuperGlue only supports signals, it can support them with abstractions that cannot be easily expressed in ArchJava.

7   Conclusion

SuperGlue combines signal, object, and rule abstractions into a novel language for building interactive programs out of components. By focusing on glue code instead of component implementations, SuperGlue's abstractions sacrifice expressiveness so that glue code is easy to write. One consequence of this tradeoff is that SuperGlue does not have the control flow or recursion constructs found in general-purpose programming languages. The use of these constructs in glue code is often neither necessary nor desirable as they can often be replaced by rules that are more concise.

SuperGlue's design demonstrates how connections, an object system, and a declarative rule system can be effectively integrated together. The key to this integration is the use of object-oriented types to abstract over component connection graphs that are potentially unbounded in size. SuperGlue's support for connection prioritization via type extension and coercions via traits are all directly related to the use of types to abstract over connections.

7.1   Future Work

Although the features presented in this paper are complete, SuperGlue is still under development. We are currently refining our implementation of array signals, which were briefly described in Section 3.4. Additionally, we are improving component instantiation to be more dynamic. As presented in this paper, our language only supports a fixed number of components per program, which is too restrictive for many programs.

We have implemented SuperGlue with an initial prototype that is capable of running the case study described in Section 4. SuperGlue's implementation can be improved in two ways. First, compilation rather than interpretation can improve performance so SuperGlue can be used in computationally-intensive areas. Second, SuperGlue should be implemented in a way so that its programs can be developed interactively. This would allow the editing of a program's circuits while the program is running.

We plan to explore how SuperGlue can be used to build more kinds of interactive programs. We are currently investigating how a complete user-interface library in SuperGlue can enable user-interface programs that are more interactive. Beyond user interfaces, many programs can benefit from being more interactive than they currently are. For example, programming tools such as compilers are more useful when they are interactive. With the appropriate component libraries, SuperGlue would be a very good platform for developing these new kinds of interactive programs.

Acknowledgements

We thank Craig Chambers, Matthew Flatt, Gary Lindstrom, Gail Murphy, and the anonymous reviewers for comments on drafts of this paper and the preceeding research. Sean McDirmid and Wilson Hsieh were supported during this research in part by NSF CAREER award CCR–9876117. Wilson Hsieh is currently employed at Google.

References

1. J. Aldrich, C. Chambers, and D. Notkin. Architectural reasoning in ArchJava. In *Proceedings of ECOOP*, volume 2374 of *Lecture Notes in Computer Science*, pages 334–367. Springer, 2002.
2. J. Aldrich, V. Sazawal, C. Chambers, and D. Notkin. Language support for connector abstractions. In *Proceedings of ECOOP*, Lecture Notes in Computer Science. Springer, 2003.

3. A. Benveniste, P. L. Geurnic, and C. Jacquemot. Synchronous programming with events and relations: the Signal language and its semantics. In *Science of Computer Programming*, 1991.
4. G. Berry. *The Foundations of Esterel*. MIT Press, 1998.
5. G. Bracha and W. Cook. Mixin-based inheritance. In *Proceedings of of OOPSLA and ECOOP*, volume 25 (10) of *SIGPLAN Notices*, pages 303–311. ACM, 1990.
6. P. Caspi, D. Pilaud, N. Halbwachs, and J. A. Plaice. LUSTRE: a declarative language for programming synchronous systems. In *Proceedings of POPL*, 1987.
7. C. Clifton, G. T. Leavens, C. Chambers, and T. D. Millstein. Multijava: Modular open classes and symmetric multiple dispatch for Java. In *Proceedings of OOPSLA*, volume 35 (10) of *SIGPLAN Notices*, pages 130–145. ACM, 2000.
8. G. H. Cooper and S. Krishnamurthi. Embedding dynamic dataflow in a call-by-value language. To appear in ESOP, 2006.
9. A. Courtney. Frappé: Functional reactive programming in Java. In *Proceedings of PADL*, volume 1990 of *Lecture Notes in Computer Science*, pages 29–44. Springer, 2001.
10. C. Elliott and P. Hudak. Functional reactive animation. In *Proceedings of ICFP*, volume 32 (8) of *SIGPLAN Notices*, pages 263–273. ACM, 1997.
11. B. N. Freeman-Benson. Kaleidoscope: Mixing objects, constraints and imperative programming. In *Proceedings of of OOPSLA and ECOOP*, volume 25 (10) of *SIGPLAN Notices*, pages 77–88. ACM, 1990.
12. B. N. Freeman-Benson and A. Borning. Integrating constraints with an object-oriented language. In *Proceedings of ECOOP*, volume 615 of *Lecture Notes in Computer Science*, pages 268–286. Springer, 1992.
13. A. Goldberg and D. Robson. *SmallTalk-80: The Language and its Implementation*. Addison Wesley, Boston, MA, USA, 1983.
14. P. Hudak, A. Courtney, H. Nilsson, and J. Peterson. Arrows, robots, and functional reactive programming. In *Advanced Functional Programming*, volume 2638 of *Lecture Notes in Computer Science*, pages 159–187. Springer, 2002.
15. IBM. *The Eclipse Project*. http://www.eclipse.org/.
16. D. Luckham and J. Vera. An event-based architecture definition language. In *IEEE Transactions on Software Engineering*, volume 21, 1995.
17. O. L. Madsen and B. Moeller-Pedersen. Virtual classes - a powerful mechanism for object-oriented programming. In *Proceedings of OOPSLA*, pages 397–406, Oct. 1989.
18. J. Magee, N. Dulay, S. Eisenbach, and J. Kramer. Specifying distributed software architectures. In *Proceedings of ESEC*, 1995.
19. Y. Matsumoto. *Ruby: Programmers' Best Friend*. http://www.ruby-lang.org/en/.
20. N. Medvidovic, P. Oreizy, and R. N. Taylor. Reuse of off-the-shelf components in C2-style architectures. In *Proceedings of ICSE*, pages 692–700. IEEE Computer Society, 1997.
21. M. Odersky and et. al. The scala language specification. Technical report, EPFL, Lausanne, Switzerland, 2004. http://scala.epfl.ch.
22. L. Sterling and E. Shapiro. *The Art of Prolog: Advanced Programming Techniques*. MIT Press, Cambridge, MA, USA, 1986.
23. Sun Microsystems, Inc. *The JavaMail API*. http://java.sun.com/products/javamail/.
24. Sun Microsystems, Inc. *The Swing API*. http://java.sun.com/products/jfc/.
25. G. van Rossum and F. L. Drake. *The Python Language Reference Manual*, Sept. 2003. http://www.python.org/doc/current/ref/ref.html.

Ambient-Oriented Programming in AmbientTalk

Jessie Dedecker*, Tom Van Cutsem*, Stijn Mostinckx**,
Theo D'Hondt, and Wolfgang De Meuter

Programming Technology Laboratory
Vrije Universiteit Brussel, Belgium
{jededeck, tvcutsem, smostinc, tjdhondt, wdmeuter}@vub.ac.be

Abstract. A new field in distributed computing, called Ambient Intelligence, has emerged as a consequence of the increasing availability of wireless devices and the mobile networks they induce. Developing software for mobile networks is extremely hard in conventional programming languages because the network is dynamically demarcated. This leads us to postulate a suite of characteristics of future *Ambient-Oriented Programming* languages. A simple reflective programming language, called AmbientTalk, that meets the characteristics is presented. It is validated by implementing a collection of high level language features that are used in the implementation of an ambient messenger application.

1 Introduction

Software development for mobile devices is given a new impetus with the advent of *mobile networks*. Mobile networks surround a mobile device equipped with wireless technology and are demarcated dynamically as users move about. Mobile networks turn isolated applications into cooperative ones that interact with their environment. This vision of ubiquitous computing, originally described by Weiser [38], has recently been termed *Ambient Intelligence* (AmI for short) by the European Council's IST Advisory Group [12].

Mobile networks that surround a device have several properties that distinguish them from other types of networks. The most important ones are that connections are volatile (because the communication range of wireless technology is limited) and that the network is open (because devices can appear and disappear unheraldedly). This puts extra burden on software developers. Although system software and networking libraries providing uniform interfaces to the wireless technologies (such as JXTA and M2MI [21]) have matured, developing application software for mobile networks still remains difficult. The main reason for this is that contemporary programming languages lack abstractions to deal with the mobile hardware characteristics. For instance, in traditional programming languages failing remote communication is usually dealt with using a classic exception handling mechanism. This results in application code

---

* Research Assistant of the Fund for Scientific Research Flanders, Belgium (F.W.O.).
** Funded by a doctoral scholarship of the Institute for the Promotion of Innovation through Science and Technology in Flanders (IWT-Vlaanderen), Belgium.

D. Thomas (Ed.): ECOOP 2006, LNCS 4067, pp. 230–254, 2006.
© Springer-Verlag Berlin Heidelberg 2006

polluted with exception handling code because failures are the rule rather than the exception in mobile networks. Observations like this justify the need for a new *Ambient-Oriented Programming* paradigm (AmOP for short) that consists of programming languages that explicitly incorporate potential network failures in the very heart of their basic computational steps.

The goal of our research is threefold:

- First, we want to gain insight in the structure of AmOP applications.
- Second, we want to come up with AmOP language features that give programmers expressive abstractions that allow them to deal with the characteristics of the mobile networks.
- Third, we want to distill the fundamental semantic building blocks that are at the scientific heart of AmOP language features in the same way that current continuations are at the heart of control flow instructions and environments are the essence of scoping mechanisms.

As very little experience exists in writing AmOP applications, it is hard to come up with AmOP language features based on software engineering requirements. Therefore, our research is grounded in the hardware phenomena that fundamentally distinguish mobile from stationary networks. These phenomena are listed in section 2.1 and form the basis from which we distill a number of fundamental programming language characteristics that define the AmOP paradigm. These characteristics are the topic of section 3. A concrete scion of the AmOP paradigm — called AmbientTalk — is presented starting from section 4. AmbientTalk's design is directly based on our analysis of the hardware phenomena and features a number of fundamental semantic building blocks designed to deal with these hardware phenomena. Since AmbientTalk was conceived as a reflectively extensible language kernel, the semantic building blocks turn AmbientTalk into a language laboratory that allows us to investigate the language features that populate the AmOP paradigm. Section 5 validates this by realising three language features that facilitate high-level collaboration of objects running on devices connected by a mobile network. The language features are used in a concrete experiment we conducted, namely the implementation of an ambient peer-to-peer instant messaging application that was deployed on smart phones.

2   Motivation

The hardware properties of the devices constituting a mobile network engender a number of phenomena that have to be dealt with by distributed programming languages and/or middleware. We summarize these hardware phenomena below and describe how existing programming languages and middleware fail to deal with them. These shortcomings form the main motivation for our work.

2.1   Hardware Phenomena

With the current state of commercial technology, mobile devices are often characterised as having scarcer resources (such as lower CPU speed, less memory and limited battery life) than traditional hardware. However, in the last couple of years, mobile devices and full-fledged computers like laptops are blending more and more. That is why we do not consider such restrictions as fundamental as the following phenomena which are inherent to mobile networks:

Connection Volatility. Two devices that perform a meaningful task together cannot assume a stable connection. The limited communication range of the wireless technology combined with the fact that users can move out of range can result in broken connections at any point in time. However, upon re-establishing a broken connection, users typically expect the task to resume. In other words, they expect the task to be performed in the presence of a volatile connection.

Ambient Resources. If a user moves with his mobile device, remote resources become dynamically (un)available in the environment because the availability of a resource may depend on the location of the device. This is in contrast with stationary networks in which references to remote resources are obtained based on the explicit knowledge of the availability of the resource. In the context of mobile networks, the resources are said to be ambient.

Autonomy. Most distributed applications today are developed using the client-server approach. The server often plays the role of a "higher authority" which coordinates interactions between the clients. In mobile networks a connection to such a "higher authority" is not always available. Every device should be able to act as an autonomous computing unit.

Natural Concurrency. In theory, distribution and concurrency are two different phenomena. For instance in a client-server setup, a client device might explicitly wait for the results of a request to a serving device. But since waiting undermines the autonomy of a device, we conclude that concurrency is a natural phenomenon in software running on mobile networks.

2.2 Distributed Languages

To the best of our knowledge no distributed language has been designed that deals with all the characteristics of mobile hardware just described. Languages like Emerald [19] and Obliq [6] are based on synchronous communication which is irreconcilable with the autonomy and the connection volatility characteristics. Languages like ABCL/f [31] and Argus [23] that promote a scheme based on futures [14] partially solve this but their objects block when accessing unresolved futures. Other languages based on the actor model, such as Janus [20], Salsa [35] and E [27] use pure asynchronous communication. However, these languages offer no support to discover ambient resources or to coordinate interactions among autonomous computing units in the face of volatile connections.

2.3 Distributed Middleware

An alternative to distributed languages is middleware. Over the past few years a lot of research has been invested in middleware for mobile networks [25]. It can be categorised in several groups.

RPC-based Middleware like Alice [13] and DOLMEN [29] are attempts that focus mainly on making ORBs suitable for lightweight devices and on improving the resilience of the CORBA IIOP protocol against volatile connections. Others deal with such connections by supporting temporary queuing of RPCs [18] or by rebinding [30]. However, these approaches remain variations of synchronous communication and are thus irreconcilable with the autonomy and connection volatility phenomena.

Data Sharing-oriented Middleware tries to maximize the autonomy of temporarily disconnected mobile devices using weak replica management (cf. Bayou [32], Rover [18] and XMiddle [40]). However, since replicas are not always synchronisable upon reconnection, potential conflicts must be resolved at the application level. In spite of the fact that these approaches foster fruitful ideas to deal with the autonomy characteristic, to the best of our knowledge, they do not address the ambient resources phenomenon.

Publish-subscribe Middleware adapts the publish-subscribe paradigm [10] to cope with the characteristics of mobile computing [7, 5]. Such middleware allows asynchronous communication, but has the disadvantage of requiring manual callbacks to handle communication results, which severely clutters object-oriented code.

Tuple Space based Middleware [28, 24] for mobile computing has been proposed more recently. A tuple space [11] is a shared data structure in which processes can asynchronously publish and query tuples. Most research on tuple spaces for mobile computing attempts to distribute a tuple space over a set of devices. Tuple spaces are an interesting communication paradigm for mobile computing. Unfortunately, they do not integrate well with the object-oriented paradigm because communication is achieved by placing data in a tuple space as opposed to sending messages to objects.

2.4   Problem Statement

Neither existing distributed programming languages nor existing middleware solutions deal with *all* hardware phenomena listed above. Some middleware proposals offer partial solutions, but do not fit the object-oriented paradigm. However, the object-oriented paradigm has proven its merit w.r.t. dealing with distribution (and its induced concurrency) because it successfully aligns encapsulated objects with concurrently running distributed software entities [3]. We claim that these observations motivate the need for an Ambient-Oriented Programming paradigm which consists of concurrent distributed object-oriented programming languages offering well-integrated facilities to deal with all the hardware phenomena engendered by mobile networks.

3   Ambient-Oriented Programming

In the same way that referential transparency can be regarded as a defining property for pure functional programming, this section presents a collection of language design characteristics that discriminate the AmOP paradigm from classic concurrent distributed object-oriented programming. These characteristics have been described earlier [8] and are repeated in the following four sections.

3.1 Classless Object Models

As a consequence of argument passing in the context of remote messages, objects are copied back and forth between remote hosts. Since an object in a class-based programming language cannot exist without its class, this copying of objects implies that classes have to be copied as well. However, a class is – by definition – an entity that is conceptually shared by all its instances. From a conceptual point of view there is only one single version of the class on the network, containing the shared class variables and method implementations. Because objects residing on different machines can autonomously update a class variable of "their" copy of the class or because a device might upgrade to a new version of a class thereby "updating" its methods, a classic distributed state consistency problem among replicated classes arises. Independent updates on the replicated class – performed by autonomous devices – can cause two instances of the "same" class to unexpectedly exhibit different behaviour. Allowing programmers to manually deal with this phenomenon requires a *full* reification of classes and the instance-of relation. However, this is easier said than done. Even in the absence of wireless distribution, languages like Smalltalk and CLOS already illustrate that a serious reification of classes and their relation to objects results in extremely complex meta machinery.

A much simpler solution consists of favouring entirely self-sufficient objects over classes and the sharing relation they impose on objects. This is the paradigm defined by prototype-based languages like Self [34]. In these languages objects are *conceptually* entirely idiosyncratic such that the above problems do not arise. Sharing relations between different prototypes can still be established (such as e.g. traits [33]) but the point is that these have to be explicitly encoded by the programmer at all times[1]. For these reasons, we have selected prototype-based object models for AmOP. Notice that this confirms the design of existing distributed programming languages such as Emerald, Obliq, dSelf and E which are all classless.

3.2 Non-blocking Communication Primitives

Autonomous devices communicating over volatile connections necessitate non-blocking communication primitives since blocking communication would harm the autonomy of mobile devices. First, blocking communication is a known source of (distributed) deadlocks [36] which are extremely hard to resolve in mobile networks since not all parties are necessarily available for communication. Second, blocking communication primitives would cause a program or device to block

---

[1] Surely, a runtime environment can optimise things by sharing properties between different objects. But such a sharing is not part of the language definition and can never be detected by objects.

long-lastingly upon encountering volatile connections or temporary unavailability of the communication partner [25, 28]. As such, the availability of resources and the responsiveness of applications would be seriously diminished.

Non-blocking communication is often confused with asynchronous sending, but this neglects the (possibly implicit) corresponding 'receive' operation. Non-blocking reception gives rise to event-driven applications, responsive to the stream of events generated by spontaneously interacting autonomous devices. We conclude that an AmOP language needs a concurrency model without blocking communication primitives.

3.3 Reified Communication Traces

Non-blocking communication implies that devices are no longer implicitly synchronised while communicating. However, in the context of (autonomously) collaborating devices, synchronisation is necessary to prevent the communicating parties from ending up in an inconsistent state. Whenever such an inconsistency is detected, the parties must be able to restore their state to whatever previous consistent state they were in, such that they can synchronise anew based on that final consistent state. Examples of the latter could be to overrule one of the two states or deciding together on a new state which both parties can use to resume their computation. Therefore, a programming language in the AmOP paradigm has to provide programmers with an *explicit representation* (i.e. a reification) of the communication details that led to the inconsistent state. Having an explicit reified representation of whatever communication that happened, allows a device to properly recover from an inconsistency by reversing (part of) its computation.

Apart from supporting synchronisation in the context of non-blocking communication, reified communication traces are also needed to be able to implement different message delivery policies. A broad spectrum of such policies exists. For example, in the M2MI library [21], messages are asynchronously broadcasted without guarantees of being received by any listening party. In the actor model on the other hand, all asynchronous messages are expected to be eventually received by their destination actor [1]. This shows that there is no single "right" message delivery policy because the desired delivery guarantee depends on the semantics of the application. Reifying outgoing communication traces allow one to make a tradeoff between different delivery guarantees. Programming languages in the AmOP paradigm ought to make this possible.

3.4 Ambient Acquaintance Management

The combination of autonomous devices and ambient resources which are dynamically detected as devices are roaming implies that devices do not necessarily rely on a third party to interact with each other. This is in contrast to client-server communication models where clients interact through the mediation of a server (e.g. chat servers or white boards). The fact that communicating parties do not need an explicit reference to each other beforehand (whether directly or indirectly through a server) is known as distributed naming [11]. Distributed naming provides a mechanism to communicate without knowing the address of an ambient resource. For example, in tuple space based middleware this property is achieved, because a process can publish data in a tuple space, which can then be consulted by the other processes based on a pattern matching basis. Another example is M2MI [21], where messages can be broadcast to all objects implementing a certain interface.

We are not arguing that all AmOP applications must necessarily be based on distributed naming. It is perfectly possible to set up a server for the purposes of a particular application. However, an AmOP language should allow an object to spontaneously get acquainted with a previously unknown object based on an intensional description of that object rather than via a fixed URL. Incorporating such an acquaintance discovery mechanism, along with a mechanism to detect and deal with the loss of acquaintances, should therefore be part of an AmOP language. We will refer to the combination of these mechanisms as ambient acquaintance management.

3.5   Discussion

Having analysed the implications of the hardware phenomena on the design of programming languages, we have distilled the above four characteristics. We will henceforth refer to programming languages that adhere to them as *Ambient-oriented Programming Languages*. Surely, it is impossible to prove that these are strictly necessary characteristics for writing the applications we target. After all, AmOP does not transcend Turing equivalence. However, we do claim that an AmOP language will greatly enhance the construction of such applications because its distribution characteristics are designed with respect to the hardware phenomena presented in section 2.1. AmOP languages incorporate transient disconnections and evolving acquaintance relationships in the heart of their computational model.

4   The AmbientTalk Kernel

Having defined the AmOP paradigm, we now present AmbientTalk, a language that was explicitly designed to satisfy its characteristics. As explained in the introduction, AmbientTalk is a reflectively extensible kernel that can be used as a language laboratory to experiment with AmOP language features. First, the essential characteristics of its object model are explained.

4.1   A Double-Layered Object Model

AmbientTalk has a concurrent object model that is based on the model of ABCL/1 [39]. This model features active objects which consist of a perpetually running thread, updateable state, methods and a message queue. These concurrently running active objects communicate using asynchronous message passing. Upon reception, messages are scheduled in the active object's message queue and are processed one by one by the active object's thread. By excluding simultaneous message processing, race conditions on the updateable state are avoided. The merit of the model is that it unifies imperative object-oriented programming and concurrent programming without suffering from omnipresent race conditions. We will henceforth use the term 'active object' or 'actor' interchangeably for ABCL/1-like active objects.

To avoid having every single object to be equipped with heavyweight concurrency machinery and having every single message to be thought of as a concurrent one, an object model that distinguishes between active and passive (i.e. ordinary) objects is adopted. This allows programmers to deal with concurrency only when strictly necessary (i.e. when considering semantically concurrent and/or distributed tasks). Since passive objects are not equipped with an execution thread, the "current thread" flows from the sender into the receiver, thereby implementing synchronous message passing. However, it is important to ensure that a passive object is never shared by two different active ones because this easily leads to race conditions. AmbientTalk's object model avoids this by obeying the following rules:

- *Containment.* Every passive object is contained within exactly one active object. Therefore, a passive object is never shared by two active ones. The only thread that can enter the passive object is the thread of its active container.
- *Argument Passing Rules.* When an asynchronous message is sent to an active object, objects may be sent along as arguments. In order not to violate the containment principle, a passive object that is about to leave its active container this way, is passed by copy. This means that the passive object is deep-copied up to the level of references to active objects. Active objects process messages one by one and can therefore be safely shared by two different active objects. Hence, they are passed by reference.

This pragmatic marriage between the functional actor model, the imperative thread model and the prototype-based object model was chosen as the basis for AmbientTalk's distribution model. Active objects are defined to be AmbientTalk's unit of distribution and are the only ones allowed to be referred to across device boundaries. Therefore, AmbientTalk applications are conceived as suites of active objects deployed on autonomous devices. Several active objects can run on a device and every active object contains a graph of passive objects. Objects in this graph can refer to active objects that may reside on any device. In other words, AmbientTalk's remote object references are always references to active objects. The rationale of this design is that synchronous messages (as sent to passive objects) cannot be reconciled with the non-blocking communication characteristic presented in section 3.2.

AmbientTalk does not know the concept of proxies on the programming language level. An active object a_1 can 'simply' refer to another active object a_2 that resides on a different machine. If both machines move out of one another's communication range and the connection is (temporarily) lost, a_1 conceptually remains referring to a_2 and can keep on sending messages as if nothing went wrong. Such messages are accumulated in a_1 and will be transparently delivered after the connection has been re-established. Hence, AmbientTalk's default delivery policy strives for eventual delivery of messages. The mechanism that takes care of this transparency is explained in section 4.4. First we discuss both layers of AmbientTalk's object model in technical detail.

4.2 The Passive Object Layer

Following the prototype-based tradition, AmbientTalk passive objects are conceived as collections of slots mapping names to objects and/or methods. The code below shows an implementation for stacks in AmbientTalk:

```
makeStack(size)::object({        // makeStack continued
  els:makeVector(size);          pop()::{
  top:0;                           if(this.isEmpty(),
  isEmpty()::{ size=0 };            { error("Stack Underflow") },
  isFull()::{ size=top };           { val: els.get(top);
  push(item)::{                       top:=top-1;
    if(this.isFull(),                 val })
      { error("Stack Overflow") },  }
      { top:=top+1;              })
        els.set(top,item) })
};
```

Objects are created using the `object(...)` form[2]. It creates an object by executing its argument expression, typically a block of code (delimited by curly braces) containing a number of slot declarations. Slots can be mutable (declared with :) or immutable (declared with ::). Mutable slots are always private and immutable slots are always public (for the rationale of this design decision we refer to [9]). Both method invocation and public slot selection use the classic dot notation. Objects are lexically scoped such that names from the surrounding scope can be used in the `object(...)` form. As illustrated by `makeStack(size)`, the form can be used in the body of a function in order to generate objects. Such a function will be referred to as a constructor function and is AmbientTalk's idiom to replace the object instantiation role of classes. Objects can also be created by extending existing ones: the `extend(p,...)` form creates an object whose parent is `p` and whose additional slots are listed in a block of code, analogous to the `object(...)` form. Messages not understood by the newly created object are automatically delegated to the parent. Furthermore, a Java-like **super** keyword can be used to manually delegate messages to the parent object. Following the standard delegation semantics proposed by Lieberman [22] and Ungar [34], references to **this** in the parent object denote the newly created child object.

Apart from objects, AmbientTalk features built-in numbers, strings, a null value **void** and functions. However, these 'functions' are actually nothing but methods in AmbientTalk. For example, the **makeStack** constructor function is actually a method of the root object which is the global environment of the AmbientTalk interpreter. Methods can be selected from an object (e.g. `myPush:aStack.push`). Upon selection, a first-class closure object is created which encapsulates the receiver (`aStack`) and which can be called using canonical syntax, e.g., `myPush(element)`. Closure objects are actually passive objects

---

[2] A 'form' is a Scheme-like special form, i.e., a built-in 'function' whose parameters are treated in an ad hoc way. `if(test,exp1,exp2)` is another example of a form.

with a single `apply` method. Finally, a syntactic sugar coating allows anonymous closures to be created given a list of formal parameters and a body, e.g., `lambda(x,y) -> {x+y}`. When bound to a name (e.g., as the value of a slot `f` or when bound to a formal parameter `f`), a closure is called using canonical syntax, e.g., `f(1,2)`.

4.3   The Active Object Layer

As explained in section 4.1, AmbientTalk actors have their own message queues and computational thread which processes incoming messages one by one by executing their corresponding method. Therefore, an actor is entirely single-threaded such that state changes using the classic assignment operator `:=` cannot cause race conditions. Messages sent to the passive objects it contains (using the dot notation) are handled synchronously. Actors are created using the `actor(o)` form where o must be a passive object that specifies the behaviour of the actor. In order to respect the containment principle, a copy of o is made before it is used by the `actor` form because o would otherwise be shared by the creating and the created actor. A newly created actor is immediately sent the `init()` message and `thisActor` denotes the current actor. These concepts are exemplified by the following code excerpt which shows the implementation of a friend finder actor running on a cellular phone. When two friend finders discover one another (which is explained later on) they send each other the `match` message, passing along an `info` passive object that contains objects representing the age (with an `isInRangeOf` method) and hobbies (containing a method that checks whether two hobby lists have anything in common).

```
makeFriendFinder(age,hobbies)::actor(object({
  init()::{ display("Friend Finder initialized!") };
  beep()::{ display("Match Found - BEEP!") };
  match(info)::{
    if(and(age.isInRangeOf(info.age),
           hobbies.intersectsWith(info.hobbies)),
      { thisActor#beep() })
  }})))
```

Actors can be sent asynchronous messages using the `#` primitive which plays the same role for actors as the dot notation for passive objects. E.g., if `ff` is a friend finder (possibly residing on another cellular phone), then `ff#match(myInfo)` asynchronously sends the `match` message to `ff`. The return value of an asynchronous message is `void` and the sender never waits for an answer. Using the `#` operator without actual arguments (e.g., `ff#match`) yields a first-class message object that encapsulates the sending actor (`thisActor`), the destination actor (`ff`) and the name of the message. First-class messages are further explained in section 4.5 that describes AmbientTalk's meta-level facilities. Finally, using the dot notation for actors (resp. `#` for passive objects) is considered to be an error.

When passing along objects as arguments to message sends, caution is required in order not to breach the containment principle. In the case of synchronous messages of the form `po.m(arg`$_1$`, ... arg`$_n$`)` between two objects that are contained in the same actor, the arguments do not "leave" the actor and can therefore be safely passed by reference. In the case of asynchronous messages of the form ao#m($arg_1, \ldots arg_n$), the arguments "leave" the actor from which the message is sent. In order to respect the containment principle, this requires the arguments to be passed by copy as explained in section 4.1. In the friend finder example, the info object is thus passed by copy.

4.4   First-Class Mailboxes

AmbientTalk's concurrent object model presented above is classless and supports non-blocking communication. This already covers two of the four characteristics of AmOP as presented in section 3. However, with respect to the other two, the model presented so far still has some limitations which it directly inherits from the original actor model [15, 2]:

- The model does not support the ambient acquaintance management characteristic of the AmOP paradigm because traditionally, actors can only gain acquaintances through other actors. ActorSpace [4] is an extension of the actor model that explicitly addresses this problem. However, it is not clear how this extension behaves in mobile networks exhibiting the hardware phenomena listed in section 2.1.
- Actor formalisms do not support the reified communication traces we argued for in section 3.

To enable these two properties, AmbientTalk replaces the single message queue of the original actor model by a system of eight first-class mailboxes which is described below.

When scrutinising the communication of a typical actor, four types of messages are distinguished: messages that have been sent by the actor (but not yet received by the other party), outgoing messages that have been acknowledged to be received, incoming messages that have been received (but not yet processed) and messages that have been processed. The AmbientTalk interpreter stores each type in a dedicated mailbox associated with the actor. An actor has access to its mailboxes through the names outbox, sentbox, inbox and rcvbox. The combined behaviour of the inbox and outbox mailboxes was already implicitly present in the original actor model in the form of a single message queue. As we will show in the remainder of the paper, AmbientTalk's mailboxes are the fundamental semantic buidling blocks for implementing advanced language constructs on top of the non-blocking communication primitives. Indeed, conceptually, the mailboxes rcvbox and sentbox allow one to peek in the communication history of an actor. Likewise, the mailboxes inbox and outbox represent an actor's continuation, because they contain the messages the actor will process and deliver in the future. Together, the four explicit mailboxes cover the need for reified communication traces that have been prescribed by the AmOP paradigm.

In order to cover the ambient acquaintance management requirement of AmOP, AmbientTalk actors have four additional predefined mailboxes called joinedbox, disjoinedbox, requiredbox and providedbox. An actor that wants to make itself available for collaboration on the network can broadcast this fact by adding one or more descriptive tags (e.g. strings) in its `providedbox` mailbox (using the `add` operation described below). Conversely, an actor that needs other actors for collaboration can listen for actors broadcasting particular descriptive tags by adding these tags to its `requiredbox` mailbox. If two or more actors join by entering one another's communication range while having an identical descriptive tag in their mailboxes, the mailbox `joinedbox` of the actor that *required* the collaboration is updated with a *resolution object* containing the corresponding descriptive tag and a (remote) reference to the actor that *provided* that tag. Conversely, when two previously joined actors move out of communication range, the resolution is moved from the `joinedbox` mailbox to the `disjoinedbox` mailbox. This mechanism allows an actor not only to detect new acquaintances in its ambient, but also to detect when they have disappeared from the ambient. It is AmbientTalk's technical realisation of the ambient acquaintance management characteristic discussed in section 3.4.

Mailboxes are first-class passive objects contained in the actor. Due to the containment principle for passive objects, mailboxes can never be shared among multiple actors. However, mailboxes are necessarily shared between the actor and the AmbientTalk interpreter because this interpreter puts messages into the mailboxes (e.g. upon reception of a message or upon joining with another actor). To avoid race conditions on mailboxes, the interpreter is not given access to them while the actor is processing a message because it may then manipulate its own mailboxes. Mailboxes provide operators to add and delete elements (such as messages, descriptive tags and resolutions): if `b` is a mailbox, then `b.add(elt)` adds an element to `b`. Similarly, `b.delete(elt)` deletes an element from a mailbox. `b.iterate(f)` applies the closure `f` to all elements that reside in the mailbox `b`. Moreover, the changes in a mailbox can be monitored by registering observers with a mailbox: `b.uponAdditionDo(f)` (resp. `b.uponDeletionDo(f)`) installs a closure `f` as a listener that will be triggered whenever an element is added to (resp. deleted from) the mailbox `b`. The element is passed as an argument to `f`. The closure is invoked when the mailbox's actor is ready to accept the next incoming message as to avoid internal concurrency.

The following code excerpt exemplifies these concepts by extending the friend finder example of the previous section with ambient acquaintance management in order for two friend finders to discover each other. The initialisation code shows that the actor advertises itself as a friend finder and that it requires communication with another friend finder. When two friend finders meet, a resolution is added to their `joinedbox`, which will trigger the method `onFriendFinderFound` that was installed as an observer on that mailbox. This resolution contains a `tag` slot (in this case `"<FriendFinder>"`) and a `provider` slot corresponding to the providing actor. The latter is sent the `match` message (as described in the previous section).

```
makeFriendFinder(age,hobbies)::actor(object({
  ...as above...
  onFriendFinderFound(aResolution)::{
    aResolution.provider#match(makeInfo(age, hobbies))
  };
```

```
init()::{
  provided.add("<FriendFinder>");
  required.add("<FriendFinder>");
  joinedbox.uponAdditionDo(this.onFriendFinderFound)
}}))
```

4.5   AmbientTalk as a Reflective Kernel

This section explains how to reflectively extend AmbientTalk's kernel which consists of the double-layered object model along with the system of eight built-in mailboxes. The mailboxes and their observers (installed using `uponAdditionDo` and `uponDeletionDo` as described above) can already be regarded as part of AmbientTalk's metaobject protocol (MOP) since they partially reify the state of the interpreter. Indeed, they constantly reflect the past and future of the communication state between actors as well as the evolving state of the ambient. Additionally, the MOP allows a programmer to override the default message sending and reception mechanisms. Just like ABCL/R [37, 26], AmbientTalk has a MOP for a concurrent active object model (hence what follows is only applicable to active objects, there is no MOP for passive objects). The operations of the MOP presented in this section by default reside in any actor and can be redefined by overriding them in any idiosyncratic actor. This mechanism is at the heart of AmbientTalk's ability to act as a programming language laboratory for AmOP. The remainder of this section describes the different MOP operations.

In order to explain the MOP, it is crucial to understand how asynchronous messages are sent between two actors (that might reside on different machines). When an actor a_1 sends a message of the form a_2#m(...), the interpreter of a_1 creates a first-class message object and places it in the `outbox` of a_1. After having successfully transmitted that message between the interpreter of a_1 and the interpreter of a_2, the interpreter of a_2 stores it in the `inbox` of a_2. Upon receiving a notification of reception, the interpreter of a_1 moves the message from the `outbox` of a_1 to the `sentbox` of a_1. a_2 processes the messages in its `inbox` one by one and stores the processed messages in the `rcvbox` of a_2. Each stage in this interplay (namely message creation, sending, reception and processing) between the two interpreters is reified in the MOP.

Message creation is reified in the MOP using the constructor function `createMessage(sender, dest, name, args)` which generates first-class messages. A message is a passive object which has four slots: the sending actor `sender`, the destination actor `dest`, the name of the message `name` and a vector object `args` containing the actual arguments. Remember from section 4.3 that a first-class message is also created upon field selection with an expression of the form `anActor#msgName` which results in a first-class message with sender `thisActor`, destination `anActor`, name `msgName` and an empty argument vector.

Message sending is reified in the MOP by adding messages to the `outbox` which is accomplished by the MOP's message sending operation `send`. In other words, an expression of the form `anActor#msg(arg_1, ..., arg_n)` is base-level terminology for an equivalent call to the meta-level method `send`, passing along a newly created first-class message object. The default behaviour of `send` is:

send(msg)::{outbox.add(msg) }. It is possible to override this behaviour by
redefining the method **send**. The example below illustrates how **send** can be
overridden for logging purposes.

```
send(msg)::{
  display("sending..."+msg.getName());
  super.send(msg)
}
```

Every actor has a perpetually running thread that receives incoming messages
in the **inbox** and transfers them to the **rcvbox** after processing them. **Message
reception** is reified in the MOP by adding messages to an actor's **inbox** which
can be intercepted by adding an observer to that mailbox. **Message processing**
is reified in the MOP by invoking the parameterless **process** method on that
message (which will execute the recipient's method corresponding to the message
name) and by subsequently placing that message in the **rcvbox**. The latter event
can be trapped by installing an observer on that mailbox.

4.6 Summary: AmbientTalk and AmOP

In summary, AmbientTalk features a classless double-layered object model. Actors are visible in mobile networks and communicate with each other in a non-
blocking way. Internally, they contain a graph of passive objects. Actors have four
mailboxes which reify their communication traces and four mailboxes which are
causally connected to the outside world to reflect the evolution of acquaintances
in the ambient. These properties turn AmbientTalk into an AmOP language
as discussed in section 3. AmbientTalk's fundamental semantic building blocks
can be used along with the MOP's reflective facilities to experiment with new
AmOP language constructs and their interactions. This is extensively shown in
the following section.

5   AmbientTalk at Work: AmbientChat

In order to validate AmbientTalk's concepts, we have implemented an instant
messenger application that epitomises all the difficulties of mobile network applications in which multiple parties dynamically join and disjoin and collaborate
without presuming a centralised server. The instant messenger runs on a mobile device and spontaneously discovers chat buddies appearing in its proximity.
Conceived as an actor, the messenger's functionality suggests the following conceptual constructions which are non-existent in the AmbientTalk kernel. Their
reflective implementation is the topic of this section:

Ambient References can be thought of as active object references which "sniff
the ambient" given a textual description (e.g. a nickname). Ambient references discover actors matching that description and are resilient to the effects
of volatile connections: upon disconnection ambient references try to rebind
to a (potentially different) actor in the ambient matching the description.

Futures [14, 23] are a classic technique to reconcile return values of methods with asynchronous message sends without resorting to manual callback methods or continuation actors. A future is a placeholder that is immediatly returned from an asynchronous send and that is eventually *resolved* with the expected result. Computations that access an unresolved future block until it is resolved. However, this contradicts the *non-blocking communication* characteristic of AmOP. AmbientTalk's futures avoid this problem by adopting the technique that was recently proposed in E [27]. It allows for a transparent forwarding of messages sent to a future to its resolution and features a when(aFuture, closure) construct to register a closure that is to be applied upon resolving the future.

Due-blocks are similar to try-catch blocks. They consist of a block of code, a handler and a deadline that is imposed on the transmission of all asynchronous messages sent during the execution of the block. The handler is invoked should the deadline expire. This mechanism is used by the messenger to visualize undelivered messages by greying them out in the GUI.

These language constructs are implemented by using and overriding the MOP operations described in the previous section. We use a mixin-based technique to implement them in a modular way: an AmbientTalk construct and its supporting MOP operations are grouped in what we call a *language mixin*; a function that returns an extension of its argument with new meta-level behaviour (i.e. it overrides send, createmessage, process and/or installs observers on mailboxes). The idea is to apply such a language mixin to a passive object before that passive object is used to create an actor. This way, a newly created actor will exhibit the required behaviour.

Given these three language abstractions, the code for the instant messenger follows. An instant messenger in AmbientTalk is conceived as an actor created by the constructor function makeInstantMessenger given a nickname, a guiActor (representing the application's graphical user interface) and a maxTimeOut value that indicates how resilient the messenger will be w.r.t. volatile connections. The actor's MOP is extended with the three language constructs by applying the DueMixin, the FuturesMixin and the AmbientRefMixin to the passive object representing its behaviour. The usage of the language constructs is indicated in comments.

```
makeInstantMessenger(nickname, guiActor, maxTimeOut)::
  actor(AmbientRefMixin(FuturesMixin(DueMixin(object({
    buddies : makeHashmap();
    statusLine: "Available";
    getStatusLine() :: { statusLine };
    setStatusLine(newStatus) :: { statusLine := newStatus };
    buddyAppears(buddyNick) :: {
      when(buddies.get(buddyNick)#getStatusLine(),          // FUTURES
           lambda(status) -> { guiActor#onlineColor(buddyNick,status) })
    };
    buddyDisappears(buddyNick) :: {
      guiActor#offlineColor(buddyNick)
    };
    addBuddy(buddyNick) :: {
      bAmsg:thisActor#buddyAppears;
      bDmsg:thisActor#buddyDisappears;
```

```
    bAmsg.getArgs().set(1,buddyNick);
    bDmsg.getArgs().set(1,buddyNick);
    buddies.put(buddyNick, makeAmbientRef("<Messenger id="+buddyNick+">", bAmsg, bDmsg))
  };                                                // AMBIENT REFERENCES
receiveText(from, text) :: {
  guiActor#showText(from,text)
};
failedDelivery(msg) :: {
  text: msg.getArgs().get(2);
  guiActor#unableToSend(text)
};
talkTo(buddyNick,text) :: {
  due(maxTimeOut, lambda() -> {                     // DUE BLOCKS
      buddies.get(buddyNick)#receiveText(nickname,text)
  }, thisActor#failedDelivery)
};
init() :: {
  guiActor#register(thisActor);
  broadcast("<Messenger id="+nickname+">")
}})))));
```

An instant messenger actor has a slot `statusLine` and a slot `buddies` mapping nicknames to ambient references that represent instant messengers on other mobile devices. Upon creation, its `init` method registers the messenger with the GUI and broadcasts its presence in the ambient. The latter is accomplished by the `broadcast` function which is merely a thin veneer of abstraction to hide the fact that a descriptive tag is added to the `providedbox` of the actor (i.e. `broadcast(tag)::{providedbox.add(tag)}`). Instant messenger actors have three methods (`addBuddy`, `setStatusLine` and `talkTo`) that are called from the GUI when the user adds a buddy (given a nickname), changes his status line or sends a `text` message to one of his buddies. Two other methods (`getStatusLine` and `receiveText`) are invoked by other instant messengers to retrieve a buddy's status line and to send a message to a buddy.

Upon adding a buddy, `addBuddy` creates an ambient reference (which searches for a messenger) based on the nickname and a couple of first-class callback messages (`bAmsg` and `bDmsg`) which are to be invoked by the ambient reference whenever that buddy appears or disappears in the ambient. The first-class callback message `bAmsg` (resp. `bDmsg`) is created by the expression `thisActor#buddy-Appears` (resp. `thisActor#buddyDisappears`) and given the buddy's nickname as its first and only argument. Whenever an actor matching the ambient reference's tag appears (resp. disappears) `buddyAppears` (resp. `buddyDisappears`) will thus be invoked. `buddyAppears` subsequently asks for the status line of its communication partner. This yields a future, that will trigger the `when` language construct upon resolution. In the closure that is passed to the `when` construct, the resolved future can be accessed as a parameter (e.g. `status`). Finally, whenever the GUI invokes `talkTo` to communicate with a buddy, `receiveText` is sent to the ambient reference representing that buddy. It is the ambient reference's task to forward that message to the actual messenger it denotes. The send of `receiveText` occurs in a `due` block which tries to send it within the prescribed time period. Should the message expire, `failedDelivery` is invoked which in turn informs the GUI about this event.

This AmbientTalk application illustrates that it is relatively straightforward to build an AmOP application, given the futures, ambient references and due-block language extensions. The remainder of this section presents their implementation one by one.

5.1   Ambient References

As explained above, ambient references are active object references – "pointing into the ambient" – that constantly represent a remote actor matching some textual description. The following language mixin contains the `makeAmbientRef` constructor function to create an ambient reference actor given a textual description `tag` and two first-class messages `uponJoinMsg` and `uponDisjoinMsg` that need to be sent upon establishing or losing a connection with an actor matching the description.

```
AmbientRefMixin(actorBehaviour)::extend(actorBehaviour, {
  makeAmbientRef(tag, uponJoinMsg, uponDisjoinMsg)::actor(object({
    principal : void;

    forwardMsg(msg) :: {
      if(not(is_void(principal)), {
        outbox.add(msg.setDestination(principal));
        inbox.delete(msg)
      })
    };
    handleActorJoined(resolution) :: {
      if(is_void(principal), {
        principal := resolution.provider;
        send(uponJoinMsg);
        inbox.iterate(this.forwardMsg)
      })
    };
    handleActorDisjoined(resolution) :: {
      if(resolution.provider = principal, {
        principal := void;
        send(uponDisjoinMsg);
        outbox.iterate(lambda(msg) -> {
          outbox.delete(msg);
          inbox.addToFront(msg)
        })
      });
      disjoined.delete(resolution)
    };
    init() :: {
      requiredbox.add(tag);
      inbox.uponAdditionDo(this.forwardMsg);
      joinedbox.uponAdditionDo(this.handleActorJoined);
      disjoinedbox.uponAdditionDo(this.handleActorDisjoined)
    }})))})
```

The ambient reference is initialised by adding the `tag` to the `requiredbox` making it listen for actors broadcasting this tag, and by installing three mailbox observers to be triggered when messages arrive in the `inbox` and when resolutions appear in the `joinedbox` or `disjoinedbox`. An ambient reference has a private slot `principal`, the value of which is toggled between an actor broadcasting the tag, and `void` when no such actors are currently available in the ambient. This toggling is accomplished by the `joinedbox` observer `handleActorJoined` (called whenever an actor was discovered) and the `disjoinedbox` observer `handleActorDisjoined` (that voids the principal when it has moved out of communication range). When a message is sent to the ambient reference, the `inbox` observer `forwardMsg` is called since it is the ambient reference's task to forward messages to the actor it represents. This is implemented by changing the destination actor of the message from the ambient reference to the principal and by moving it from the `inbox` of the ambient reference to its `outbox`. The AmbientTalk interpreter will henceforth handle the delivery of the message as explained in section 4.5. Messages may be accumulated in the `inbox` of the ambient reference while its `principal` is `void`[3]. Therefore, `handleActorJoined` flushes all unsent messages in the `inbox` by forwarding them to the newly discovered actor. Similarly the `handleActorDisjoined` method will ensure that messages that were not delivered yet and were accumulated in the `outbox` are transferred to the `inbox` of the reference in order to make sure they will be resent upon rebinding to another principal.

5.2   Non-blocking Futures

As explained above, AmbientTalk's implementation of futures is based on E. The main difference with existing proposals for futures is the fact that futures are non-blocking. Futures are represented as AmbientTalk actors and messages sent to them are transparently forwarded to the future's value. The `when` construct is used to register a block of code that will be triggered upon resolution of the future. The first part of the language mixin implementing futures is shown below:

```
FuturesMixin(actorBehaviour)::extend(actorBehaviour, {
  makeFuture() :: actor(object({
    value: void;
    whenObservers: makeList();

    forward(msg) :: {
      if(not(has_slot(this, msg.getName())),
        if(is_actor(value),
          { inbox.delete(msg);
            outbox.add(msg.setDestination(value)) }))
    };
    register(aWhenObserver) :: {
      if(is_void(value),
        { whenObservers.add(aWhenObserver) },
        { aWhenObserver.notify(value) })
    };
    resolve(computedValue) :: {
      value:=computedValue;
      whenObservers.iterate(lambda(observer) -> { observer.notify(value) });
      inbox.iterate(this.forward)
    };
    init() :: { inbox.uponAdditionDo(this.forward) }
  }));              // CONTINUED
```

The language mixin introduces the `makeFuture` constructor function which generates new futures. Futures contain a method `forward` to forward messages to the actor it resolved to, except for messages for which the future actor itself has a method slot (such as `register` and `resolve`). Every usage of `when(aFuture, closure)` gives rise to the registration of a 'when-observer object' with the

---

[3] If an actor has no method to process an incoming message, the default behaviour is to leave it waiting in the `inbox`.

future using `register`. Upon resolution, the future notifies all its registered
when-observers and forwards all previously accumulated messages.

To introduce futures in the MOP of actors, `createMessage` is overridden
such that asynchronous messages are intercepted in order to be extended with a
`future` slot. Furthermore, the message's `process` method (which will be invoked
by the destination actor) is refined in order to resolve the message's future with
the computed value. The overridden `send` first performs a super-send to delegate
message sending to the default implementation. However, instead of returning
`void`, the new implementation returns the future contained in the extended
message.

```
                    // FuturesMixin, CONTINUED
createMessage(sender,dest,name,args)::{
  extend(super.createMessage(sender,dest,name,args), {
    future :: makeFuture();
    process()::{
      computedValue: super.process();
      future#resolve(computedValue);
      computedValue
    };
  })
};
send(message)::{
  super.send(message);
  message.future
};

whenBlocks: makeHashmap();
whenIdCtr : 1;

invokeWhen(whenBlockID, computedValue)::{
  whenBlocks.get(whenBlockID)(computedValue);    //curried call
  whenBlocks.delete(whenBlockID)
};
makeWhenObserver(callBackActor, whenBlockID): object({
  notify(computedValue):: {
    callBackActor#invokeWhen(whenBlockID, computedValue) }
});
when(aFuture, whenBlock)::{
  whenBlocks.put(whenIdCtr, whenBlock);
  aFuture#register(makeWhenObserver(thisActor, whenIdCtr));
  whenIdCtr := whenIdCtr + 1
}})
```

The `when(aFuture, closure)` language extension registers a closure that is
applied when the future gets resolved. Caution is required since a closure is a
passive object and passing it to the future actor would cause it to be copied
as a consequence of the containment principle. As this implies deep-copying the
entire closure, side effects in the lexical scope would go by unnoticed. Hence,
passing closures to another actor must be avoided. This is achieved by creating
an observer object (created with the `makeWhenObserver` constructor function)
which encapsulates an actor and an ID that identifies a local closure in the
`whenBlocks` vector of that actor. It is this observer that is registered with the
future. Whenever the future gets resolved, all observers are sent `notify` which in
turn ask their encapsulating actor (through `invokeWhen`) to invoke the closure
registered on the future by passing along the closure's ID and the result value.

5.3   Due: Handling Failures

As explained in section 4.1, AmbientTalk's default delivery policy guarantees eventual delivery of messages. Messages are stored indefinitely in the outbox of an actor until they can be delivered. The **due** language construct alters this policy by putting an expiration deadline on outgoing messages. A **due**-block consists of a timeout value (relative to the time at which a message is sent), a 'body' closure and a handler message to be sent upon expiration. When a message sent during the execution of the body expires, it is removed from the actor's outbox and the handler message is sent with the expired message as argument. The implementation of the **due** construct consists of two separate language mixins:

- The **DueMixin** defines the **due** construct which stamps all asynchronous messages sent while executing its body with an expiration deadline and a handler message to be sent upon expiration.
- The **ExpiryCheckMixin** observes an actor's mailbox for expirable messages. Upon encountering an expirable message, the actor will check when its expiration deadline has passed whether that message has been sent.

The reason for separating the **DueMixin** and the **ExpiryCheckMixin** is that messages often get forwarded through different actors before reaching their destination. A typical example thereof is when actors are referred to indirectly via an ambient reference as explained in section 5.1: a message may expire in the inbox or outbox of the intermediary actor rather than in the outbox of the actor which originally sent the message. Such intermediary actors must therefore be able to detect expired messages even though they do not use the **due** construct. Hence, the **ExpiryCheckMixin** has to be applied to both ambient references and futures. This was omitted in the previous sections for didactic purposes. The language mixin **DueMixin** is defined as follows:

```
DueMixin(actorBehaviour) :: extend(actorBehaviour, {
  dueTimeout: void;
  dueHandlerMsg: void;
  due(deadline, body, handlerMsg) :: {
    tmpTimeout: dueTimeout;
    tmpHandler: dueHandlerMsg;
    dueTimeout := deadline;
    dueHandlerMsg := handlerMsg;
    value: body();
    dueTimeout := tmpTimeout;
    dueHandlerMsg := tmpHandler;
    value
  };
  send(msg) :: {
    if(!is_void(dueTimeout),
      { expirableMsg : extend(msg, {
          deadline :: time() + dueTimeout;
          handlerMsg :: dueHandlerMsg.copy() });
        super.send(expirableMsg) },
      { super.send(msg) }) } })
```

The **DueMixin** installs the **due** construct in an actor and overrides the way its outgoing messages are sent in order to stamp those messages by extending them with a **deadline** slot and a 'complaint address' in the form of a **handlerMsg** which will determine how to react when the deadline expires. The overridden send method extends msg with these slots provided that it was invoked in the dynamic context of a due-block (i.e. if dueTimeout contains a meaningful value rather than void). The message is then sent by delegating to the overridden implementation. At any particular time on the execution path of an actor, at most one active due-block exists (cf. try-catch). Its timeout value and its handler are stored in the slots dueTimeout and dueHandlerMsg. To allow dynamic nesting of due-blocks, the current values of dueTimeout and dueHandlerMsg are saved in temporary variables and are restored upon returning from the due body closure.

The ExpiryCheckMixin is parameterized by an actor behaviour and a mailbox name. The mixin adds a mailbox observer to the mailbox corresponding to the mailbox name. Whenever a message stamped with a deadline is added to that mailbox, a closure is scheduled for execution when the message's deadline has passed (using AmbientTalk's after form). The closure checks whether the message is still present in either the inbox or the outbox and if so, removes it from that mailbox and sends its handler message to deal with the expiration.

```
ExpiryCheckMixin(actorBehaviour, mbxName) :: extend(actorBehaviour,{
  init() :: { super.init(); getMailbox(mbxName).uponAdditionDo(this.checkExpired) };
  checkExpired(msg) :: {
    if(has_slot(msg, "deadline"), {
      after(msg.deadline - time(), lambda() -> {
        this.retractMsgInMailbox(msg, outbox); this.retractMsgInMailbox(msg, inbox)
      })
    }) };
  retractMsgInMailbox(aMsg, aMailbox) :: {
    if(aMailbox.contains(aMsg), {
      aMailbox.delete(aMsg);
      aMsg.handlerMsg.setArgs(makeVector(1).set(1, aMsg));
      send(aMsg.handlerMsg)
  }) } })
```

The mailbox to be observed by the checkExpired method depends on the kind of actor. Actors using due should observe their outbox for outgoing expirable messages. Intermediary actors such as ambient references and futures should observe their inbox, as they may receive expirable messages from other actors which they must forward. An expirable message may be stored in either the inbox or outbox before it can be forwarded, which is why both mailboxes are checked when the deadline has passed.

5.4   Evaluation

This section has presented three tentative high-level AmOP language features: ambient references, due-blocks and non-blocking futures. We have adhered to the (functional programming) tradition of modular interpreters to formulate these features as modular semantic building blocks — called language mixins — that enhance AmbientTalk's kernel. AmbientTalk's basic semantic building blocks (consisting of the eight first-class mailboxes, its mailbox observers and its reflective facilities) have been shown to be sufficient to implement these abstractions. The abstractions have been validated in the context of the instant messenger application. Indeed, the essence of communication between two messengers consists of making the corresponding actors get acquainted and in handling the delivery, processing and result propagation of asynchronously sent messages between two autonomous actors that are separated by a volatile connection. To support these different aspects of communication,

Ambient References establish and maintain a meaningful connection between two actors on top of a volatile connection. The implementation of ambient references heavily relies on AmbientTalk's ambient acquaintance management facilities (in order to manage the appearance and disappearance of communication partners) as well as its reified communication traces (to flush messages accumulated during disconnection).

Non-blocking Futures in combination with the `when` construct allow one to link an asynchronous message send to the code that is to be executed upon result propagation. The `when` construct thus bridges the computational context in which the message was sent and the one in which its result is handled. Furthermore, AmbientTalk's non-blocking futures delay the delivery of received messages until the expected result is ready to receive them. As mentioned in section 3.3, this shows that reified communication traces are at the heart of realigning synchronisation with communication while strictly relying on non-blocking communication primitives as prescribed by the AmOP paradigm.

Due-blocks allow the sender to define, detect and deal with permanent disconnections. The `due` language construct shows that although AmbientTalk's default message delivery policy (discussed in section 4.1) implements a resumable communication model (where disconnections are not aligned with failures), one can still cope with permanent failures by reflecting upon an actor's communication traces: by having access to an actor's outgoing message queue which reifies its outgoing messages yet to be delivered, expired messages can be cancelled.

Surely, it is impossible to prove that AmbientTalk's building blocks are necessary and sufficient to cover all future AmOP features. Nevertheless, our analysis in section 3 strongly argues for their necessity and the expressiveness of our reflective extensions detailed in section 5 forms compelling evidence for their sufficiency. Thanks to the abstraction barriers offered by these reusable language constructs, our prototypical messenger application counts merely 35 lines of AmbientTalk code. A chat application with similar goals – called BlueChat [16] – implemented in Java using Bluetooth counts no less than 545 lines of code. BlueChat allows for ambient acquaintance discovery but has no provisions whatsoever to deal with volatile connections.

Currently, a prototype AmbientTalk interpreter was implemented in Java on top of J2ME. It is written in continuation passing style and relies on sockets for inter-device communication over WLAN. Efficiency was not our primary concern in conceiving the implementation. The messenger experiment has been conducted on QTek 9090 cellular phones.

6 Conclusion and Future Work

As explained in the introduction, the goal of our research is to a) obtain a better understanding of the structure of future AmOP applications, b) invent expressive programming language abstractions facilitating their construction and c) get insight in the semantic building blocks lying behind these abstractions in the same vein continuations are the foundations of control flow and environments are at the heart of scoping mechanisms.

Since the conception of AmOP applications is currently still in its infancy, it is hard to come up with good software engineering criteria for future AmOP language features. That is why our research methology has been based on an unraveling of the hardware characteristics that fundamentally discriminate mobile devices (connected by mobile networks) from classic desktop machines (connected by stationary networks). We have defined the AmOP paradigm as a set of characteristics for programming languages that directly deal with these hardware phenomena in the very heart of their basic computational abstractions.

Instead of proposing a number of haphazardly chosen language features, we have used our analysis of the hardware phenomena to conceive an extensible kernel that comprises a set of fundamental semantic building blocks to implement future AmOP language features. The essence of the semantic experimentarium consists of a double-layered object model, the active objects of which form the basis for concurrency and distribution. Active objects are further equipped with a MOP and a system of eight mailboxes that constantly reflect their computational history as well as the state of the hardware surrounding them. Although it is impossible to prove that these provisions are both necessary and sufficient, we feel that AmbientTalk provides a good basis for further experiments in language design and that the language features proposed here merely scratch the surface of an interesting new branch in distributed computing research. E.g., it remains an open question of how transaction management in classic distributed systems can be transposed to the AmOP setting in which devices holding a lock may leave and never return. Reified communication traces may once again prove useful here, as already exemplified by optimistic process collaboration approaches such as the Time Warp mechanism [17]. Additionally, more insight is required on how to map AmOP features on efficient implementation technology. E.g., new distributed memory management techniques are required because existing techniques are not intended for use in mobile networks.

References

1. G. Agha. *Actors: a Model of Concurrent Computation in Distributed Systems.* MIT Press, 1986.
2. G. Agha and C. Hewitt. Concurrent programming using actors. *Object-oriented concurrent programming*, pages 37–53, 1987.
3. J.-P. Briot, R. Guerraoui, and K.-P. Lohr. Concurrency and distribution in object-oriented programming. *ACM Computing Surveys*, 30(3):291–329, 1998.

4. C. J. Callsen and G. Agha. Open heterogeneous computing in ActorSpace. *Journal of Parallel and Distributed Computing*, 21(3):289–300, 1994.
5. M. Caporuscio, A. Carzaniga, and A. L. Wolf. Design and evaluation of a support service for mobile, wireless publish/subscribe applications. *IEEE Transactions on Software Engineering*, 29(12):1059–1071, December 2003.
6. L. Cardelli. A Language with Distributed Scope. In *Proceedings of the 22nd ACM SIGPLAN-SIGACT Symposium on Principles of Programming Languages*, pages 286–297. ACM Press, 1995.
7. G. Cugola and H.-A. Jacobsen. Using publish/subscribe middleware for mobile systems. *SIGMOBILE Mob. Comput. Commun. Rev.*, 6(4):25–33, 2002.
8. J. Dedecker, T. Van Cutsem, S. Mostinckx, T. D'Hondt, and W. De Meuter. Ambient-Oriented Programming. In *OOPSLA '05: Companion of the 20th annual ACM SIGPLAN conference on Object-oriented programming, systems, languages, and applications*. ACM Press, 2005.
9. T. D'Hondt and W. De Meuter. Of first-class methods and dynamic scope. *RSTI - L'objet no. 9/ 2003. LMO 2003*, pages 137–149, 2003.
10. P. Eugster, P. Felber, R. Guerraoui, and A.-M. Kermarrec. The many faces of publish/subscribe. *ACM Comput. Surv.*, 35(2):114–131, 2003.
11. D. Gelernter. Generative communication in Linda. *ACM Transactions on Programming Languages and Systems*, 7(1):80–112, Jan 1985.
12. IST Advisory Group. Ambient intelligence: from vision to reality, September 2003.
13. M. Haahr, R. Cunningham, and V. Cahill. Supporting corba applications in a mobile environment. In *MobiCom '99: Proceedings of the 5th annual ACM/IEEE international conference on Mobile computing and networking*, pages 36–47, New York, NY, USA, 1999. ACM Press.
14. R. Halstead, Jr. Multilisp: a language for concurrent symbolic computation. *ACM Trans. Program. Lang. Syst.*, 7(4):501–538, 1985.
15. C. Hewitt. Viewing control structures as patterns of passing messages. *Artificial Intelligence*, 8:323–364, 1977.
16. B. Hui. Go wild wirelessly with bluetooth and java. *Java Developer's Journal*, 9(2), February 2004.
17. D. R. Jefferson. Virtual time. *ACM TOPLAS*, 7(3):404–425, 1985.
18. A. D. Joseph, J. A. Tauber, and M. F. Kaashoek. Mobile computing with the rover toolkit. *IEEE Transactions on Computers*, 46(3):337–352, 1997.
19. E. Jul, H. Levy, N. Hutchinson, and A. Black. Fine-grained mobility in the Emerald system. *ACM Transactions on Computer Systems*, 6(1):109–133, February 1988.
20. K. Kahn and Vijay A. Saraswat. Actors as a special case of concurrent constraint (logic) programming. In *OOPSLA/ECOOP '90: Proceedings of the European conference on object-oriented programming on Object-oriented programming systems, languages, and applications*, pages 57–66, New York, NY, USA, 1990. ACM Press.
21. A. Kaminsky and H.-P. Bischof. Many-to-many invocation: a new object oriented paradigm for ad hoc collaborative systems. In *OOPSLA '02: Companion of the 17th annual ACM SIGPLAN conference on Object-oriented programming, systems, languages, and applications*, pages 72–73, New York, NY, USA, 2002. ACM Press.
22. H. Lieberman. Using prototypical objects to implement shared behavior in object-oriented systems. In *Conference proceedings on Object-oriented Programming Systems, Languages and Applications*, pages 214–223. ACM Press, 1986.
23. B. Liskov and L. Shrira. Promises: linguistic support for efficient asynchronous procedure calls in distributed systems. In *Proceedings of the ACM SIGPLAN 1988 conference on Programming Language design and Implementation*, pages 260–267. ACM Press, 1988.

24. M. Mamei and F. Zambonelli. Programming pervasive and mobile computing applications with the TOTA middleware. In *PERCOM '04: Proceedings of the Second IEEE International Conference on Pervasive Computing and Communications*, page 263, Washington, DC, USA, 2004. IEEE Computer Society.
25. C. Mascolo, L. Capra, and W. Emmerich. Mobile Computing Middleware. In *Advanced lectures on networking*, pages 20–58. Springer-Verlag, 2002.
26. H. Masuhara, S. Matsuoka, and A. Yonezawa. Implementing parallel language constructs using a reflective object-oriented language. In *Proceedings of Reflection Symposium '96*, pages 79–91, April 1996.
27. M. Miller, E. D. Tribble, and J. Shapiro. Concurrency among strangers: Programming in E as plan coordination. In *Symposium on Trustworthy Global Computing*, volume 3705 of *LNCS*, pages 195–229. Springer, 2005.
28. A. Murphy, G. Picco, and G.-C. Roman. Lime: A middleware for physical and logical mobility. In *Proceedings of the The 21st International Conference on Distributed Computing Systems*, pages 524–536. IEEE Computer Society, 2001.
29. P. Reynolds and R. Brangeon. DOLMEN - service machine development for an open long-term mobile and fixed network environment. 1996.
30. A. Schill, B. Bellmann, W. Bohmak, and S. Kummel. Infrastructure support for cooperative mobile environments. *Proceedings of the Fourth Workshop on Enabling Technologies: Infrastructure for Collaborative Enterprises.*, pages 171–178, 1995.
31. K. Taura, S. Matsuoka, and A. Yonezawa. Abcl/f: A future-based polymorphic typed concurrent object-oriented language - its design and implementation. In *Proceedings of the DIMACS workshop on Specification of Parallel Algorithms*, number 18 in Dimacs Series in Discrete Mathematics and Theoretical Computer Science, pages 275–292, 1994.
32. D. B. Terry, K. Petersen, M. J. Spreitzer, and M. M. Theimer. The case for non-transparent replication: Examples from Bayou. *IEEE Data Engineering Bulletin*, 21(4):12–20, december 1998.
33. D. Ungar, C. Chambers, B.-W. Chang, and U. Hölzle. Organizing programs without classes. *Lisp Symbolic Computing*, 4(3):223–242, 1991.
34. D. Ungar and R. Smith. Self: The power of simplicity. In *Conference proceedings on Object-oriented Programming Systems, Languages and Applications*, pages 227–242. ACM Press, 1987.
35. C. Varela and G. Agha. Programming dynamically reconfigurable open systems with salsa. *SIGPLAN Not.*, 36(12):20–34, 2001.
36. C. Varela and G. Agha. What after java? from objects to actors. In *WWW7: Proceedings of the seventh international conference on World Wide Web 7*, pages 573–577, Amsterdam, The Netherlands, The Netherlands, 1998. Elsevier Science Publishers B. V.
37. T. Watanabe and A. Yonezawa. Reflection in an object-oriented concurrent language. In *Conference proceedings on Object-oriented programming systems, languages and applications*, pages 306–315. ACM Press, 1988.
38. M. Weiser. The computer for the twenty-first century. *Scientific American*, pages 94–100, september 1991.
39. A. Yonezawa, J.-P. Briot, and E. Shibayama. Object-oriented concurrent programming in ABCL/1. In *Conference proceedings on Object-oriented programming systems, languages and applications*, pages 258–268. ACM Press, 1986.
40. S. Zachariadis, L. Capra, C. Mascolo, and W. Emmerich. Xmiddle: information sharing middleware for a mobile environment. In *ICSE '02: Proceedings of the 24th International Conference on Software Engineering*, pages 712–712, New York, NY, USA, 2002. ACM Press.

Responders: Language Support for Interactive Applications

Brian Chin and Todd Millstein

University of California, Los Angeles
{naerbnic, todd}@cs.ucla.edu

Abstract. A variety of application domains are *interactive* in nature: a primary task involves responding to external actions. In this paper, we introduce explicit programming language support for interactive programming, via the concept of a *responder*. Responders include a novel control construct that allows the interactive logic of an application to be naturally and modularly expressed. In contrast, the standard approaches to interactive programming, based on the event-driven style or the state design pattern, fragment this logic across multiple handlers or classes, with the control flow among fragments expressed only indirectly. We describe ResponderJ, an extension to Java supporting responders. A responder is simply a class with additional abilities, and these abilities interact naturally with the existing features of classes, including inheritance. We have implemented ResponderJ as an extension to the Polyglot compiler for Java. We illustrate ResponderJ's utility in practice through two case studies: the implementation of a GUI supporting drag-and-drop functionality, and a re-implementation of the control logic of JDOM, a Java library for parsing and manipulating XML files.

1 Introduction

Many applications are fundamentally *interactive*: an important part of their functionality consists in responding to external actions. For example, a graphical user interface (GUI) for an editor responds to mouse clicks, possibly causing a change to the internal state of the editor and to the display. As another example, an application that is configured by an external XML file is typically structured to respond to events arising from an XML parsing API like SAX [16].

Unfortunately, interactive programming in today's object-oriented (OO) languages is tedious and error prone. Typically, an interactive application is structured as a set of *event handlers*, each able to respond to one kind of external action (or *event*). Because control is transferred back to the external environment after each handler is run, the logical flow of control among the handlers is obscured, expressed only indirectly through modifications to state. Also because of the need to transfer control back to the environment, the application cannot use the call stack to manage state. Instead, all state must be shared across all handlers, making it difficult to understand how state is being used and to ensure that each handler only manipulates the state that is relevant for its task.

To make these problems concrete, the rest of this section describes a simple interactive application and considers two common implementation strategies. Suppose we wish to create a guessing game that works as follows. When the player presses the start

D. Thomas (Ed.): ECOOP 2006, LNCS 4067, pp. 255–278, 2006.
© Springer-Verlag Berlin Heidelberg 2006

```
class GuessingGame {
  static final int GAME_NOT_RUNNING = 0;
  static final int GAME_RUNNING = 1;
  private int currState = GAME_NOT_RUNNING;
  private Random rand = new Random();
  private int correctAnswer;
  GuessResult startGame() {
    switch(currState) {
      case GAME_NOT_RUNNING:
        currState = GAME_RUNNING;
        correctAnswer = rand.nextInt(50);
        return null;
      case GAME_RUNNING:
        return GuessResult.HAVENOTFINISHED;
    }
    return null;
  }
  GuessResult guess(int i) {
    switch(currState) {
      case GAME_NOT_RUNNING:
        return GuessResult.HAVENOTSTARTED;
      case GAME_RUNNING:
        //... compare i to correctAnswer
    }
    return null;
  }
}
```

Fig. 1. The guessing game in an event-driven style

button, the game chooses a random integer in some range and asks the player for a guess. If the player's guess is lower than the target number, the game responds with "too low!" and asks for another guess, and similarly if the player's guess is too high. If the player guesses correctly, the game is over and the player may press the start button to play again. Pressing the start button has no effect and emits a warning message if the player is in the middle of a game. Similarly, making a guess has no effect and emits a warning message if the game has not yet started.

1.1   An Event-Driven Implementation

A common implementation strategy for interactive applications is the event-driven style. In this style, there is one event handler (a method) per external event. An event loop waits for external events, dispatching each to the appropriate handler. Figure 1 shows a portion of a Java implementation of the guessing game in an event-driven style. The game has two events, leading to two event handlers, startGame and guess.

Even in this simple example, the problems with the event-driven style are apparent. The game has two logical internal states, corresponding to whether or not the game has started; a more interesting game would have several possible states. The GuessingGame class uses a currState field to record the current state, which is represented as an in-

```
class GuessingGame {
  public static interface GameState {
    GuessResult guess(int guess);
    GuessResult startGame();
  }
  private Random rand = new Random();
  private GameState currState = new GameStartState();
  public class GameStartState implements GameState {
    public GuessResult startGame() {
      currState = new GameRunningState();
      return null;
    }
    public GuessResult guess(int i) {
      return GuessResult.HAVENOTSTARTED;
    }
  }
  public class GameRunningState implements GameState {
    private int correctAnswer;
    public GameRunningState() {
      correctAnswer = rand.nextInt(50);
    }
    public GuessResult startGame() {
      return GuessResult.HAVENOTFINISHED;
    }
    public GuessResult guess(int i) {
      // ... compare i to correctAnswer
    }
  }
}
```

Fig. 2. A state-based implementation of the guessing game

teger, and each event handler switches on the value of currState to determine the
appropriate response. In this way, the implementation of each logical state is fragmented across the different handlers, making it difficult to understand the behavior
of each state. Further, state transitions occur only indirectly through modifications to
currState. Finally, the correctAnswer field is only well-defined when the game is
in the GAME_RUNNING state. However, this fact is difficult to ascertain from the code,
and there is nothing preventing an event handler from manipulating that field in the
GAME_NOT_RUNNING state.

1.2   A State-Based Implementation

The *state* design pattern [6] is an attempt to avoid several of these problems. The basic
idea is to reify each internal state as its own class, thereby modularizing the application logic by state rather than by event. An implementation of our guessing game using
the state pattern is shown in Figure 2. Each state class contains its own methods for
handling events, thereby avoiding the switch statements necessary in the event-driven
implementation. Each state class also has its own local fields, which is an improvement

on the event-driven style. However, state transitions are still expressed indirectly through updates to currState, and the logical flow of the game is now fragmented across the various state classes.

1.3 Our Contributions

In this paper, we describe explicit language support that resolves the problems for inter-active programming described above. We introduce the concept of a *responder*, which is a class containing a *responding block* to encapsulate the control logic of an inter-active application. A responding block employs a novel control-flow construct called an eventloop, which implements the logic of an internal state of the computation. An eventloop dispatches on a signaled event to handle it appropriately and uses ordinary control-flow constructs to move to another eventloop if desired, before returning con-trol back to the caller. The next time the responding block is invoked with an event to handle, execution resumes from the current eventloop. In this way, state transitions are explicit in the responding block's control flow, rather than implicit through updates to shared data. Further, responding blocks allow ordinary local variables to be used to hold state, allowing such state to be locally scoped and making it easier to modularly ensure that state is properly manipulated.

We have instantiated our notion of responders as a backward-compatible extension to Java [3, 7] that we call *ResponderJ*. In addition to the benefits described above, re-sponders interact naturally with OO inheritance in order to allow the logic of an inter-active application to be extended in subclasses. We have designed a modular compila-tion strategy for responders and implemented ResponderJ using the Polyglot extensible Java compiler framework [13]. Finally, we have evaluated ResponderJ through two case studies. First, we implemented a GUI containing drag-and-drop functionality in three styles: the event-driven style in Java, the state-based style in Java, and using responders in ResponderJ. A detailed study of these three implementations concretely illustrates the benefits of ResponderJ over existing approaches. Second, we have rewritten JDOM [8], a Java library for manipulating XML files from Java programs, to use ResponderJ. This case study illustrates that existing applications can naturally benefit from ResponderJ's features.

The remainder of this paper describes our contributions in detail. In Section 2, we describe the novel language constructs in ResponderJ through a number of examples, including our solution to the guessing game. Section 3 explains our compilation strategy for ResponderJ. In Section 4 we present our two case studies, and in Section 5 we discuss some limitations of the current language and compilation strategy and our ideas for future work. Section 6 compares ResponderJ against related work, and Section 7 concludes.

2 Responders

2.1 Responding Blocks, Events, and Event Loops

We explain the basic concepts of responders using a ResponderJ implementation of the guessing game, which is shown in Figure 3. A *responder* is an ordinary Java class that

```
class GuessingGame {
  public revent StartGame();
  public revent Guess(int num);
  responding yields GuessResult {               //A
    Random rand = new Random();
    eventloop {                                 //B
      case StartGame() {                        //C
        int correctAnswer = rand.nextInt(50);
        eventloop {                             //D
          case Guess(int guess) {               //E
            if(guess > correctAnswer) {
              emit GuessResult.LOWER;
            } else if(guess < correctAnswer) {
              emit GuessResult.HIGHER;
            } else {
              emit GuessResult.RIGHT;
              break;
            }
          }
          default {                             //F
            emit GuessResult.HAVENOTFINISHED;
          }
        }
      }
      default {
        emit GuessResult.HAVENOTSTARTED;
      }
    }
  }
}
```

Fig. 3. An implementation of the guessing game in ResponderJ

```
GuessingGame game = new GuessingGame();  //A → B
game.StartGame();        //C → D, emits {}, correctAnswer = 30
game.Guess(20);          //E → D, emits { GuessResult.HIGHER }
game.StartGame();        //F → D, emits { GuessResult.HAVENOTFINISHED }
game.Guess(30);          //E → B, emits { GuessResult.RIGHT }
```

Fig. 4. An example execution of the guessing game in ResponderJ

additionally contains a *responding block*, denoted by the keyword responding. The responding block encapsulates a responder's logic for handling external events. When a responder instance is created via new, the appropriate constructor is run as usual. The newly constructed object's responding block is then executed until an eventloop is reached, at which point control returns to the caller and program execution continues normally. In Figure 3, a new instance of GuessingGame initializes the random-number generator before passing control back to the caller.

An object's responding block resumes when a *responder event* is signaled on the object. GuessingGame in Figure 3 declares two responder events using the revent keyword, StartGame and Guess. From a client's perspective, these events are signaled as ordinary method calls. For example, to signal that the player has pressed the start button, a client of a GuessingGame instance game simply signals the event as follows: game.StartGame();. Signaling the Guess event is analogous, with the guessed value passed as an argument.

When an event is signaled on a responder, its responding block resumes execution from the eventloop where it last paused. An eventloop behaves like a while(true) loop. An eventloop's body performs a case analysis of the different possible events declared for the responder. When a responding block resumes at an eventloop, control is dispatched to the case clause that matches the signaled event, or to the default case if no other case matches. The appropriate case is then executed normally, with the responding block again suspending execution and returning control to the caller when the top of an eventloop is reached. Unlike the cases in a Java switch statement, a case inside an eventloop implicitly ends that iteration of the loop when its end is reached, instead of falling through to the next case.

For example, suppose the responding block of an instance of GuessingGame is paused at the outer eventloop, which represents the state where the game has not yet started. If the StartGame event is signaled, the game chooses a random number and pauses execution at the inner eventloop, thereby changing to the state where the game has started. On the other hand, if the Guess event is signaled, then the outer default case is executed, which emits an error message (the emit statement is discussed below) and pauses execution at the top of the outer eventloop once again.

As the example shows, eventloops, like ordinary loops, can be nested. An eventloop also has the same rules for variable scoping as any other Java loop structure. Finally, eventloops support the standard control constructs for loops, namely break and continue. For example, the inner eventloop in Figure 3 uses break to return to the outer eventloop when the player has won, thereby allowing a new game to begin.

An emit statement allows a responding block to communicate information back to clients without ending execution of the responding block, as a return statement would. For example, as mentioned above, the GuessingGame uses an emit statement to signal an error when a guess is made before the game is started; execution continues after the emit statement as usual. Once the responding block pauses execution, all values emitted since the responding block was last paused are provided in an array as the call's result. Using an array allows the responding block to emit any number of values, including zero, for use by the caller.

For the purposes of static typechecking, each responding block uses a yields clause to declare the type of values it emits; a responder that does not perform any emits can omit this clause. For example, the GuessingGame is declared to emit values of type GuessResult, so all responder events implicitly return a value of type GuessResult[]. We use a single type of emitted values across the entire responder instead of using a different type per event, since the presence of nested eventloops as well as the use of break and continue make it difficult to statically know to which event a particular emit statement corresponds.

Figure 4 recaps the semantics of ResponderJ through a small example execution trace. The comment after each statement indicates the starting and ending control locations of the responder as part of executing that statement, as well as the result array arising from the emit statements.

Responders solve the problems for interactive programming illustrated by the event-driven and state-based implementations of the guessing game. Unlike those approaches, which perform state transitions indirectly via modifications to shared fields like currState, ResponderJ uses simple and local control flow among eventloops, each of which represents a single internal state. In Figure 3, it is easy to understand the ways in which control can move from one eventloop to another, making it easier to debug and extend the interaction logic. Further, ResponderJ allows ordinary local variables to be used to hold data, unlike the usage of fields required to share data across event handlers in the other approaches. For example, in Figure 3 ordinary scoping rules ensure that correctAnswer is only accessible in the inner event loop. This makes it impossible for the variable to be accidentally manipulated in the wrong state, and it allows for modular inspection to ensure that the variable is manipulated properly.

Responders may have all the same kinds of members as ordinary classes, and these members are accessible inside of the responding block. For example, the responding block can manipulate the class's fields or invoke methods of the class. Similarly, a responding block can access the visible methods and fields of any objects in scope, for example passed as an argument to an event. Responding blocks can also instantiate classes, including other responders. Further, responder classes may be used as types, just as ordinary classes are. For example, a class (including a responder) can have a field whose type is a responder or a method that accepts a responder as an argument. Responders can inherit from non-responder classes as well as from other responders; this latter capability is discussed in more detail below.

2.2   Another Example

To motivate some other features of ResponderJ, we illustrate an example from the domain of user interfaces in Figure 5. The DragDropPanel responder defines a subclass of the JPanel class from Java's Swing library, in order to support simple drag-and-drop functionality. The responder defines three events, corresponding to clicking, releasing, and moving the mouse. The drag-and-drop control logic is natural expressed via control flow among eventloops. When the mouse is clicked initially, control moves from the outer eventloop to the first nested one. If the mouse is then moved a sufficient distance, we break out of that eventloop and move to the subsequent one, which represents dragging mode. In dragging mode, moving the mouse causes a new moveByOffset method (definition not shown) to be invoked, in order to move the panel as directed by the drag. Dragging mode continues until the mouse is released, at which time we return to the outer eventloop. This example also illustrates the usage of Java's labeled continue construct and labeled statements, which allow the state machine to transition to the initial state when the mouse is released without having moved a sufficient distance.

```
class DragDropPanel extends JPanel {
  public revent MouseDown(Point p);
  public revent MouseUp(Point p);
  public revent MouseMove(Point p);
  responding {
    outer: eventloop {
      case MouseDown(Point initialPoint) {
        eventloop {
          case MouseUp(Point dummy) { continue outer; }
          case MouseMove(Point movePoint) {
            if(initialPoint.distance(movePoint) > 3)
              break;
          }
          default {
          }
        }
        eventloop { //Dragging mode
          case MouseMove(Point dragPoint) {
            this.moveByOffset(initialPoint, dragPoint);
          }
          case MouseUp(Point dummy) { break; }
          default {
          }
        }
      }
      // ... handle the other events
    }
  }
}
```

Fig. 5. A GUI panel supporting drag-and-drop

2.3 Responding Methods

A *responding method* is a regular method annotated with the responding modifier.
Like a responding block, responding methods may contain eventloops and emit
statements, and they therefore serve as a form of procedural abstraction for responding blocks. For example, Figure 6 shows how the logic for the dragging mode in
DragDropPanel can be pulled out of the responding block and into a separate method.
We note the use of return, which behaves as usual, in this case ending the method and
returning control to the caller.

Like any standard method, responding methods can be called recursively. This ability
provides an elegant and powerful way to "remember" past states and return to them
after visiting conceptually nested states. We have relied on this technique heavily in
the JDOM case study described in Section 4, since JDOM's control logic has a natural
nesting structure. With the event-driven style or the state design pattern, the state history
would instead have to be explicitly maintained by the programmer and consulted to
decide how to update currState.

```
class DragDropPanel extends JPanel {
  protected responding void doDrag(Point initialPoint) {
    eventloop {
      case MouseMove(Point dragPoint) {
        this.moveByOffset(initialPoint, dragPoint);
      }
      case MouseUp(Point dummy) { return; }
      default {
      }
    }
  }
  responding {
    outer: eventloop {
      case MouseDown(Point initialPoint) {
        eventloop {
          //...
        }
        doDrag(initialPoint);
      }
      // ... handle the other events
    }
  }
}
```

Fig. 6. A responding method

One disadvantage of responding methods is that they are in a different static scope from the responding block and hence do not have access to the responding block's local variables. Therefore, any state needed by a responding method must be explicitly passed as an argument, as with the initialPoint argument to doDrag in Figure 6. Of course, the fact that a responding method has its own scope also provides the usual benefits of procedural abstraction. For example, a responding method that encapsulates some common control logic can be invoked from multiple places within a responder, with the method's arguments serving to customize this logic to the needs of each caller.

Because a responding method can contain eventloops and emits, it only makes sense to invoke such a method as part of the execution of an object's responding block. We statically enforce this condition through three requirements. First, a responding method must be declared private or protected, to ensure that it is inaccessible outside of its associated class and subclasses. Second, a responding method may only be invoked from a responding block or from another responding method. Finally, we require that every call to a responding method have either the (possibly implicit) receiver this or super. This requirement ensures that the responding method is executed on the same object whose responding block is currently executing.

2.4 Responder Inheritance

As shown with DragDropPanel in Figure 5, responders can inherit from non-responders. As usual, the responder inherits all fields and methods of the superclass and can override superclass methods. Responders may also inherit from other responders. In this case, the subclass additionally inherits and has the option to override both

```
class DragHoldPanel extends DragDropPanel {
  protected responding void doDrag(Point initialPoint) {
    eventloop {
      case MouseMove(Point dragPoint) {
        this.moveByOffset(initialPoint, dragPoint);
      }
      case MouseUp(Point dummy) { break; }
      default {
      }
    }
    eventloop {
      case MouseMove(Point dragPoint) {
        this.moveByOffset(initialPoint, dragPoint);
      }
      case MouseUp(Point dummy) { return; }
      default {
      }
    }
  }
}
```

Fig. 7. Overriding responding methods

the superclass's responding block as well as any responding methods. The subclass also inherits the superclass's `yields` type. We disallow narrowing the `yields` type in the subclass, as this would only be safe if the subclass overrode the superclass's responding block and all responding methods, to ensure that all `emit`s are of the appropriate type.

The ability to override responding methods allows an existing responder's behavior to be easily modified or extended by subresponders. For example, the `DragHoldPanel` responder in Figure 7 inherits the responding block of `DragDropPanel` but overrides the `doDrag` responding method from Figure 6. The overriding `doDrag` method uses two `eventloop`s in sequence to change the behavior of a drag. Under the new semantics, the user can release the mouse but continue to drag the panel. Drag mode only ends after a second `MouseUp` event occurs, which causes the `doDrag` method to return. It would be much more tedious and error prone to make this kind of change using an event-driven or state-based implementation of the drag-and-drop panel.

The example above shows how subresponders can easily add new states and state transitions to a responder. Subresponders also have the ability to add new responder events. For example, the `DragKeyPanel` responder in Figure 8 subclasses from `DragDropPanel` and adds a new event representing a key press. `DragKeyPanel` then overrides the `doDrag` responding method in order to allow a key press to change the color of the panel while it is in drag mode. Because of the possibility for subresponders to add new events, a responding block may be passed events at run time that were not known when the associated responder was compiled. To ensure that all events can nonetheless be handled, we require each `eventloop` to contain a `default` case.

Overriding in ResponderJ is expressed at the level of entire responding methods. It would be interesting to consider forms of overriding and extension for individual `eventloop`s. Without such features, subresponders sometimes have no choice but to

```
class DragKeyPanel extends DragDropPanel {
  public revent KeyDown(char key);
  protected void changeColor(char c) {
    // ...
  }
  protected responding void doDrag(Point initialDragPoint) {
    eventloop {
      case MouseMove(Point dragPoint) {
        this.moveByOffset(initialPoint, dragPoint);
      }
      case KeyDown(char c) {
        this.changeColor(c);
      }
      case MouseUp(Point dummy) { return; }
      default {
      }
    }
  }
}
```

Fig. 8. Adding new responder events in subresponders

duplicate code. For example, DragKeyPanel's doDrag method is identical to the original doDrag method from Figure 6 but additionally contains a case for the new KeyDown event.

2.5 Exceptional Situations

There are two exceptional situations that can arise through the use of responders that are not easily prevented statically. Therefore, we have chosen instead to detect these situations dynamically and throw a runtime exception. First, it is possible for a responder object to (possibly indirectly) signal an event on itself while in the middle of executing its responding block in response to another event. If this situation ever occurs, a RecursiveResponderException is thrown. Second, it is possible for a responding block to complete execution, either by an explicit return statement in the block or simply by reaching the block's end. If an event is ever signaled on a responder object whose responding block has completed, a ResponderTerminatedException is thrown.

3 Compilation

ResponderJ is implemented as an extension to the Polyglot extensible Java compiler framework [13], which translates Java 1.4 extensions to Java source code. Each responder class is augmented with a field base of type ResponderBase, which orchestrates the control flow between the responding block (and associated responding methods) and the rest of the program. To faithfully implement the semantics of eventloops, ResponderBase runs all responding code in its own Java thread, and ResponderBase includes methods that yield and resume this thread as appropriate. Although our current implementation uses threads, we use standard synchronization primitives to ensure that

```
protected static class GuessEvent extends Event {
  public int num;
}

public GuessResult[] Guess(int num) {
  GuessEvent e = new GuessEvent();
  e.num = num;
  return (GuessResult[])base.passInput(e, new GuessResult[0]);
}
```

Fig. 9. Translation of the Guess responder event from Figure 3

```
while(true) {
  Event temp = (Event)base.passOutput();
  if(temp instanceof GuessEvent) {
    int guess = ((GuessEvent)temp).num;
    {
      // Implementation
      if(guess > correctAnswer) {
        base.emitOutput(GuessResult.LOWER);
      } else if(guess < correctAnswer) {
        base.emitOutput(GuessResult.HIGHER);
      } else {
        base.emitOutput(GuessResult.RIGHT);
        break;
      }
    }
    continue;
  } else {
    // default handler
    base.emitOutput(GuessResult.HAVENOTFINISHED);
  }
}
```

Fig. 10. Translation of the inner eventloop from Figure 3

only one thread is active at a time, thereby preserving ResponderJ's purely sequential semantics and also avoiding concurrency issues like race conditions and deadlocks. As we discuss in Section 5, in future work we plan to do away with threads entirely in our compilation strategy.

First we describe the compilation of responder events. Each revent declaration in a responder is translated into both a method of the specified visibility and a simple class. This class contains a field for every formal parameter of the declared responder event. When the responder event's method is called, the method body creates an instance of the class, fills its fields with the given parameters, and passes this instance to the ResponderBase object. For example, Figure 9 shows the translation of the Guess responder event from the guessing game in Figure 3. The passInput method in ResponderBase passes our representation of the signaled event to the responding thread and resumes its execution from where it last yielded.

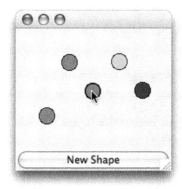

Fig. 11. A screenshot of the drag-and-drop application

Each eventloop is implemented as a simple while loop, as shown in Figure 10. The first statement of the loop body calls the ResponderBase instance's passOutput method, which yields the responding thread to the caller until an event is passed in via passInput, when the thread resumes. The rest of the loop body contains a sequence of if statements, one for each case clause of the original eventloop, in order to perform the event dispatch.

Responding methods are translated into ordinary methods of the responding class. The static typechecks described in Section 2 are sufficient to guarantee that these methods are only called from within the responding thread. Each emit statement is translated into a method call on the class's ResponderBase instance. For example, the statement emit GuessResult.RIGHT is translated as base.emitOutput(GuessResult.RIGHT). The emitOutput method appends the given argument to an internal array of output values. When the responding thread next yields at the top of an eventloop, control returns to the calling thread and that array is passed as the result.

Finally, each responder class includes a method startResponder(), which initializes the responding thread. Our translation strategy ensures that this method is invoked on an instance of a responder class immediately after the instance is constructed. The run method of the thread begins executing the (translation of the) responding block.

4   Case Studies

In order to demonstrate the practical applicability of ResponderJ, we performed two case studies. First, we expanded the drag-and-drop GUI example shown in Section 2 into a complete application that interfaces with Java's Swing library. We implemented and compared three versions of the application: using responders in ResponderJ, using the event-driven style in Java, and using the state design pattern in Java. Second, we rewrote an existing application to use ResponderJ. JDOM [8] is a library that makes it easy to access and manipulate XML files from Java programs. JDOM parses XML files via the SAX API [16], which signals events as an XML file is parsed (e.g., when a tag is read). We rewrote in ResponderJ the portion of JDOM that responds to SAX events in order to create a tree of Java objects that represents the parsed XML data.

```
responding {
  outer: eventloop {
    case Paint(Graphics g) {
      this.paintAll(g);
    }
    case MouseDown(Point initial) {
      //We eventually expect a mouseUp, so we do a nested eventloop
      Shape currentShape = null;
      //set currentShape to clicked-on shape
      if(currentShape == null)
        continue;
      this.repaint();
      //While the mouse is down and a shape is selected
      eventloop {
        case MouseUp(Point p2) {
          //Drag is over
          this.repaint();
          continue outer;
        }
        case Paint(Graphics g) {
          this.paintExcept(g, currentShape);
          currentShape.drawSelected(g);
        }
        case MouseMove(Point p2) {
          if(Math.abs(initial.getX() - p2.getX()) > 3 ||
               Math.abs(initial.getY() - p2.getY()) > 3)
            break;
        }
        default {
        }
      }
      this.doDrag(initial, currentShape);
    }
    default {
    }
  }
}
```

Fig. 12. Main responding block from DragDropPanel

4.1 Drag and Drop

Figure 11 shows a screenshot of the drag-and-drop application we built. The program provides a window with a button. When the button is pressed, a new circle appears on the panel above. The user can use the mouse to drag shapes around the screen.

ResponderJ Implementation. As in the example from Section 2, we created a DragDropPanel class that inherits from Swing's JPanel class. Swing has an event-driven structure; a JPanel must implement methods to handle the various kinds of events. For example, the processMouseMotionEvent is called when the user moves the mouse. To interface between Swing's events and the responder events of DragDropPanel, we simply implemented the Swing event handlers to invoke the corresponding revent methods. Since the revents are never meant to be accessed externally, we made them protected.

Figure 12 shows the implementation of the responding block in DragDropPanel. There are two main enhancements to the logic, as compared to the version described in Section 2. First, this version has to manage multiple draggable entities. Therefore, when the user clicks initially, the code determines which shape (if any) has been clicked and stores it in the local variable currentShape. If no shape was clicked, we do nothing and end this iteration of the outer eventloop. Otherwise, we continue to the first inner eventloop, employing currentShape as needed.

Second, we added a responder event Paint that takes a Graphics object, and this event is invoked from the panel's paintComponent method. The repaint method inherited from JPanel causes Swing to schedule a painting event to be executed at some point in the future; at that point, the paintComponent method will be invoked to handle the event. We call repaint in the code in Figure 12 whenever the screen needs to be redrawn because of some change. The repaint method only schedules an event for later execution, rather than actually signaling the event, so there is no danger of incurring a RecursiveResponderException. As shown in the figure, we handle the Paint event differently depending on the current state. If no shape has been clicked (the outer eventloop), all shapes are drawn as normal. If a shape has been selected (the inner eventloop), then it is drawn specially.

As we described in Section 2, we use the doDrag method to encapsulate the logic of drag-and-drop. This method is shown in Figure 13. The logic is analogous to what we described in Section 2, except for the addition of the painting event. The Paint handler is identical to the Paint handler from the inner loop in Figure 12. We could abstract this code into a separate method that is called from both places, passing along any local variables needed for the method body. However, there is no direct way to share handlers among eventloops.

Finally, we created a version of DragKeyPanel, as was shown in Figure 8, to incorporate a KeyDown event allowing a shape's color to change during a drag. DragKeyPanel inherits the responding block of DragDropPanel but overrides the doDrag method to handle the KeyDown event, as shown in the figure. As mentioned earlier, ResponderJ currently has no mechanism for inheriting portions of an overridden eventloop, so much of the code in the original doDrag method's code had to be duplicated in the overriding version. Conceptually, however, the change was quite straightforward to implement, requiring only a single additional case in the method's eventloop.

Event-Driven Implementation. In the event-driven approach, DragDropPanel has an integer field currState to represent the current state. Each event has an associated handler method in the class, which switches on the current state to decide what action to perform. For example, the Paint method in the class is shown in Figure 14.

The biggest problem of this approach as compared with the ResponderJ implementation is the fact that control flow is expressed only implicitly, through updates

```
protected responding void doDrag(Point start, Shape currShape) {
  int offsetx = (int)(currShape.getX() - start.getX());
  int offsety = (int)(currShape.getY() - start.getY());
  this.requestFocus();
  eventloop {
    case Paint(Graphics g) {
      this.paintExcept(g, currShape);
      currShape.drawSelected(g);
    }
    case MouseMove(Point p) {
      currShape.setCenter((int)(p.getX() + offsetx),
                          (int)(p.getY() + offsety));
      this.repaint();
    }
    case MouseUp(Point p) {
      //We're done!
      this.repaint();
      return;
    }
    default {
    }
  }
}
```

Fig. 13. doDrag() method from DragDropPanel

```
protected void Paint(Graphics g) {
  switch(currState) {
    case NORMAL_STATE:
      paintExcept(g, null);
      break;

    case MOUSEDOWN_STATE:
    case DRAG_STATE:
      paintExcept(g, currShape);
      currShape.draw(g, 2);
      break;
  }
}
```

Fig. 14. One handler method in the event-driven implementation of DragDropPanel

to currState. Another problem is the need to store all data as fields of the class. DragDropPanel has four fields used for this purpose, including the currShape field used in Figure 14. The four fields are used for different purposes and in different states in the control flow, but it is difficult to understand the intuition behind each field and whether it is being used properly across all handlers. A final problem with the event-driven approach is that there is no single place to execute code that should be run upon

```
private class DragState extends SelectedShapeState implements DragDropState {
  private int offsetx, offsety;
  public DragState(Shape currShape, Point initialPoint) {
    super(currShape);
    this.offsetx = (int)(currShape.getX() - initialPoint.getX());
    this.offsety = (int)(currShape.getY() - initialPoint.getY());
  }
  public void mouseMove(Point p) {
    currShape.setCenter((int)(p.getX() + offsetx),
                        (int)(p.getY() + offsety));
    repaint();
  }
  public void mouseUp(Point p) {
    repaint();
    currState = new NormalState();
  }
  //... Other event handlers
}
```

Fig. 15. A class to represent the dragging state

reaching a particular state. Instead, this code must be duplicated in each event handler that can cause a transition to that state.

The event-driven approach does have some advantages over the ResponderJ implementation. First, it is easy to share event-handling code across states. An example is shown in Figure 14, which handles the paint event identically for the mouse-down and drag states, without any code duplication.Second, it is straightforward to add a new event like KeyDown in a subclass — the subclass simply needs to add a KeyDown method and can inherit all the other event-handling methods. However, adding a new state in a subclass, for example to change the way a drag works as shown in Figure 7, would necessitate overriding every event-handling method to include a case for the new state, as well as modifying existing logic to transition appropriately to the new state.

State-Pattern Implementation. In this version, we define an interface DragDropState that has a method for each kind of event. Then each state is represented by an inner class of DragDropPanel that meets this interface, as demonstrated by the example state class in Figure 15. DragDropPanel has a field currState of type DragDropState; changing states involves creating an instance of the appropriate state class, passing the necessary arguments to the constructor, and storing the result in currState.

This version has some of the advantages of ResponderJ's version over the event-driven implementation. The logic is grouped by state, making it easier to understand and extend the behavior of each state. Further, each state class has its own fields, making it somewhat easier to ensure their proper usage. Finally, any code to be executed upon entering a state can written once and placed in the corresponding state class's constructor.

To address the duplication of the event-handling code for Paint across multiple states, we employed inheritance. We created an abstract state class Selected-ShapeState that implements the Paint method appropriately. The states that should employ that behavior for Paint simply subclass from SelectedShapeState, as shown in Figure 15. However, this technique does not work in general, for example if overlapping sets of states need to share code for different event handlers, because of Java's lack of multiple inheritance. Therefore, some code duplication is still required in some cases.

The most apparent disadvantage of the state pattern is its verbosity. Several classes must be defined, each with its own constructor and fields. Having multiple state classes can also cause problems for code evolution. For example, if a state needs to be augmented to use a new field, that field will likely need to be initialized through an extra argument to the state class's constructor, thereby requiring changes to all code that constructs instances of the class. By using ordinary local variables, ResponderJ avoids this problem. Further, while the behavior of a single state is easier to understand than in the event-driven approach, the control flow now jumps among several different state classes, which causes its own problems for code comprehension.

Finally, augmenting the drag-and-drop panel to support a new event like KeyDown requires all state classes to be overridden to add a new method and to meet an augmented interface that includes the new method. This approach necessitates type casts when manipulating the inherited currState field, since it is typed with the old interface. Using inheritance to add a new state is easier, requiring the addition of a new state class, but it also requires existing state classes to be overridden to appropriately use the new state.

4.2   JDOM 1.0

JDOM 1.0 is a Java class library that uses the SAX API to construct its own implementation of DOM [5], which is an object model for XML data. At the core of JDOM is the SAXHandler class, which implements several of the standard SAX interfaces. An instance of SAXHandler is given to the SAX parser, which in turn passes events to that object while parsing an XML file. The SAXHandler is supposed to respond to these events by constructing the corresponding DOM tree.

The original event-driven version of SAXHandler utilized 17 fields to store local state. Most of these fields were booleans that kept track of whether or not the handler was currently in a particular mode. Others were data members that stored information needed to implement the class's functionality. The remaining few fields were integers used to keep track of the nesting depth in the structure of the XML document as it is parsed. Altogether it was difficult to determine the exact purpose of each of the variables and to make sure each was used properly.

To parse into a DOM document, the JDOM SAXHandler maintains an explicit stack of nodes in the DOM tree whose subtrees have not yet been fully parsed. When a start tag is seen in the XML data, a new node is pushed on the stack. When the associated end tag is seen, the node is popped off the stack and linked as a subtree of the next node on the stack. Since there are different kinds of nodes (e.g., the root document node, element nodes), switching logic is used to decide what action to take at a given point, based on what kind of node is on the top of the stack.

```
protected void pushElement(Element element) {
  if (atRoot) {
    document.setRootElement(element);
    atRoot = false;
  }
  else {
    factory.addContent(currentElement, element);
  }
  currentElement = element;
}

public void processingInstruction(String target, String data)
    throws SAXException
{
  if (suppress) return;
  flushCharacters();
  if (atRoot) {
    factory.addContent(document,
                       factory.processingInstruction(target, data));
  } else {
    factory.addContent(getCurrentElement(),
                       factory.processingInstruction(target, data));
  }
}
```

Fig. 16. Some code from the original SAXHandler class

Figure 16 shows a representative subset of the original SAXHandler code. The field atRoot is used to keep track of whether or not the element on top of the stack is currently in an element node or a document node. This field is then explicitly checked (and set) throughout the code. In a similar vein, the processingInstruction method starts with a check of the member variable suppress: nothing is done if we are currently in suppress mode. This dependency on multiple fields that serve as flags for various conditions pervades the class's code, making the logical control flow extremely difficult to follow.

In contrast, the ResponderJ implementation relies on ordinary control flow among eventloops to implicitly keep track of the various modes of computation, with local variables storing the data needed in each mode. A representative responding method from the ResponderJ version of SAXHandler is shown in Figure 17. The buildElement method handles the logic for creating the DOM representation of an XML element, which is roughly the data between a given start- and end-tag pair of the same name. The method first creates the element instance, storing its associated tag name along with any associated XML attributes, before waiting at an eventloop. The logic of the eventloop makes use of the fact that SAX's start-tag and end-tag events are always properly nested. If a new start-tag is seen, we recursively use buildElement to parse the nested element. Since the call stack is saved when an eventloop yields to a caller, all of the pending enclosing elements are still available the next time the responder resumes. If an end-tag is seen, then we know that construction of the element has completed.

```
protected responding Element buildElement(String initname,
                                            Attributes initatts ) {
  Element element = factory.element(initname);
  //... Process Attributes
  eventloop {
    case onStartElement(String name, Attributes atts) {
      element.addElement(buildElement(name, atts));
    }
    case onEndElement() {
      return element;
    }
    case onProcessingInstruction(String target, String data) {
      factory.addContent(element,
                          factory.processingInstruction(target, data));
    }
    //... Handling other supported events
    default {
    }
  }
}
```

Fig. 17. A responding method from the ResponderJ version of SAXHandler

```
private revent onProcessingInstruction(String target, String data);
public void processingInstruction(String target, String data)
    throws SAXException
{
  handleOutput(this.onProcessingInstruction(target, data));
}
```

Fig. 18. Handling exceptions thrown in the responding block

Other types of events, like onProcessingInstruction, cause the new element to be augmented with new content as appropriate.

As in the drag-and-drop case study, we used the SAXHandler's event-handling methods to forward SAX events to the responding block by invoking the corresponding responder events. The original event-handling methods were declared to throw SAXException, which is thrown if an error occurs during XML parsing. To handle such exceptions, we wrapped the entire body of the responding block in a try/catch statement, which catches a SAXException, creates an object that wraps the thrown exception and meets the yields type of the responding block, and emits this new object. The event-handling methods must then unwrap any such objects and re-throw the exception. We encapsulate this behavior in a handleOutput method that is called from the event-handling methods, as shown in Figure 18.

Of the 17 original fields in SAXHandler, we were able to do away with 10 of them in the ResponderJ version. The code that was originally scattered across several methods, with boolean flags to determine the control flow, is now gathered into five well-structured responding methods in addition to the responding block. The responding block handles building the root document in the DOM tree, while each of the other five methods handles the building of an individual kind of XML construct (e.g., an element).

This refactoring of the code made it much easier to understand its behavior, leading to further simplifications of the logic. In the original class, the `startEntity` method was possibly the most complex, explicitly keeping track of the XML document's nesting depth by counting the number of `onStartEntity` and `onEndEntity` calls. The boolean logic in the method was rather confusing, reading and setting no fewer than four boolean fields. The ResponderJ version of this code aided understanding greatly, allowing us to find a much simpler way to express the logic. We created a method `ignoreEntities` that calls itself recursively on every `onStartEntity` event and returns at every `onEndEntity` event, similar to the style shown for `buildElement`'s logic in Figure 17. This method avoids the need to count explicitly and encapsulates the simpler logic in a separate method. Our refactoring also led us to discover several redundancies in the usage of boolean fields, whereby a field's value is tested even though its value is already known from an earlier test. These kinds of redundancies, as well as similar kinds of errors, are easy to make in the programming style required of the Java version of the code.

Finally, the need to explicitly forward calls from the SAX-level event-handling methods to the appropriate responder events, while verbose, provided an unexpected benefit in the ResponderJ version of `SAXHandler`. One of the original event-handling methods executed a particular statement before doing a `switch` on the current state. While the logic of the `switch` was moved to the responding block's `eventloops`, that first statement could remain in the event-handling method. In essence, the event-handling method now serves as a natural repository for any state-independent code to be executed when an event occurs. Without this method, such code would have to be duplicated in each `eventloop`'s case for that event.

5 Discussion

There are several potential directions for future work, many of which are inspired by issues encountered during the case studies described above. Since the responding block and associated responding methods store state in ordinary local variables, this state cannot easily be shared. We could of course use fields to share state, but that approach leads to the kinds of difficulties described earlier for the event-handling and state-pattern programming styles. One possibility is to define a notion of a *local method*, which could be nested within a responding block or responding method, thereby naturally obtaining access to the surrounding local variables while still allowing the usual benefits of procedural abstraction.

If a responder subclass wishes to modify an `eventloop` from the superclass, say to include a new `revent`, the entire `eventloop` must currently be duplicated in the subclass. We are pursuing approaches for allowing subclasses to easily customize superclass `eventloops` to their needs. The key question is how to convey information about the local variables in the superclass `eventloop` for use in the subclass `eventloop`, while maintaining modularity.

Responders encode state transitions implicitly by the control flow from `eventloop` to `eventloop`. This approach naturally represents sequential as well as nested state logic, but it cannot easily represent arbitrary control flow among states. To increase expressiveness, we are considering language support for directly jumping among named `eventloops`. The challenge is to provide the desired expressiveness while preserving traditional code structure and scoping.

In addition to events, it may be useful to allow callers to query the responder for some information without actually changing state. Such queries can currently be encoded via events, but specialized language support would make this idiom simpler and easier to understand. For example, separating queries from more general kinds of events would allow queries to return a single value in the usual way, instead of returning an unspecified number of results indirectly through `emits`.

Finally, as described earlier, our current implementation strategy relies on Java threads. Although we avoid concurrency concerns by appropriate use of synchronization primitives, there is still overhead simply by using threads. However, since ResponderJ's semantics is purely sequential, it is possible to implement the language without resorting to threads. Our idea is to instead break the responding block and responding methods into multiple methods, using the yield points as boundaries. When a responding event is signaled, the appropriate one of these methods would be dispatched to as directed by the semantics of the original responding code. Each method would explicitly save and restore its local state, and a liveness analysis of the original responding code's local variables could be used to minimize the amount of state that each method requires.

6 Related Work

The *coroutine* [9] is a general control structure that allows multiple functions to interact in order to complete a task. During execution, a function can explicitly yield control to another function. When control is eventually yielded back to the first function, it resumes execution from where it left off, with its original call stack and local variables restored.

The control-flow semantics of ResponderJ's `eventloop` construct can be viewed as a specialization of the coroutine idea to the domain of event-driven programming. This specialization entails several novel design choices and extensions. First, the `eventloop` bundles the coroutine-style control flow with an event dispatch loop in a natural way. Second, the interaction among coroutines is symmetric, with each explicitly yielding control to the others. In contrast, our approach is asymmetric: the responder yields to its caller, but callers are insulated from the coroutine-like control flow by the responder events, which appear as ordinary methods to clients. Third, we have shown how responding blocks can make use of procedural abstraction through the notion of responding methods. Finally, we have integrated responders with object orientation, allowing responders to be refined through inheritance.

CLU iterators [10] and their variants (e.g., Sather iterators [12] and Python generators [15]) are functions that are used to produce a sequence of values one-by-one for manipulation by clients. The body of an iterator function emits a value and yields control to the client. When the client asks for the next value, the iterator resumes from where it left off. *Interruptible iterators* [11] additionally allow clients to interrupt an iterator through an exception-like mechanism, for example to perform an update during iteration.

CLU-style iterators and `eventloops` specialize the coroutine for very different purposes. Iterators specialize the coroutine in order to interleave the generation of values with their manipulation by clients, while `eventloops` specialize the coroutine to naturally represent the internal state logic of an interactive application. However, it is possible to use an `eventloop` to implement an iterator, with the `emit` statement generating consecutive values appropriately. Further, a form of iterator interruptions can be supported, with responder events playing the role of interrupts and `eventloops` playing the role of the interrupt handlers. In fact, interrupt handlers support a very similar style of control flow as `eventloops`, employing a form of `break` and `continue` [11].

Cooperative multitasking (e.g., [17]) is an alternative to preemptive multitasking whereby a thread explicitly yields control so that another thread can be run, saving state like in any other context switch. There is a related body of work on the event-driven approach to I/O (e.g., [14]), in which fine-grained event handlers run cooperatively in response to asynchronous I/O events. Further, researchers have explored language and library support to make this application of event-driven programming easier and more reliable [2, 4, 1].

ResponderJ is targeted at a significantly different class of event-driven applications than these systems, namely those that must be *deterministic*. With both cooperative multitasking and event-driven I/O, a central scheduler decides which of the pending threads or event handlers should be executed upon a yield. In contrast, program execution in ResponderJ is dictated entirely by the order of responder events invoked by clients. Such determinism is critical for a large class of event-driven programs, for example computer games and GUIs, where events must be processed in a specific order. The deterministic semantics carries the additional benefits of being easier to test and analyze.

7   Conclusions

We have introduced the *responder*, a new language construct supporting interactive applications. Responders allow the control logic of an application to be expressed naturally and modularly and allow state to be locally managed. In contrast, existing approaches to interactive programming fragment the control logic across multiple handlers or classes, making it difficult to understand the overall control flow and to ensure proper state management. We instantiated the notion of responders in ResponderJ, an extension to Java, and described its design and implementation. We have employed our ResponderJ compiler in two case studies, which illustrate that responders can provide practical benefits for application domains ranging from GUIs to XML parsers.

Acknowledgments

This research was supported in part by NSF ITR award #0427202 and by a generous gift from Microsoft Research.

References

1. Ada 95 reference manual. http://www.adahome.com/Resources/refs/rm95.html.
2. A. Adya, J. Howell, M. Theimer, W. Bolosky, and J. Douceur. Cooperative task management without manual stack management. In *Proc. Usenix Tech. Conf.*, 2002.
3. K. Arnold, J. Gosling, and D. Holmes. *The Java Programming Language Third Edition*. Addison-Wesley, Reading, MA, third edition, 2000.
4. R. Cunningham and E. Kohler. Making events less slippery with EEL. In *HotOS X: Hot Topics in Operating Systems*, 2005.
5. Dom home page. http://www.w3.org/DOM.
6. E. Gamma, R. Helm, R. E. Johnson, and J. Vlissides. *Design Patterns: Elements of Reusable Object-Oriented Software*. Addison-Wesley, Massachusetts, 1995.
7. J. Gosling, B. Joy, G. Steele, and G. Bracha. *The Java Language Specification Second Edition*. The Java Series. Addison-Wesley, Boston, Mass., 2000.
8. Jdom home page. http://www.jdom.org.
9. D. Knuth. *Fundamental Algorithms, third edition*. Addison-Wesley, 1997.
10. B. Liskov. A history of CLU. *ACM SIGPLAN Notices*, 28(3):133–147, 1993.
11. J. Liu, A. Kimball, and A. C. Myers. Interruptible iterators. In *POPL '06: Conference record of the 33rd ACM SIGPLAN-SIGACT Symposium on Principles of Programming Languages*, pages 283–294, New York, NY, USA, 2006. ACM Press.
12. S. Murer, S. Omohundro, D. Stoutamire, and C. Szyperski. Iteration abstraction in Sather. *ACM Transactions on Programming Languages and Systems*, 18(1):1–15, January 1996.
13. N. Nystrom, M. R. Clarkson, and A. C. Myers. Polyglot: An extensible compiler framework for Java. In *Proceedings of CC 2003: 12'th International Conference on Compiler Construction*. Springer-Verlag, Apr. 2003.
14. J. K. Ousterhout. Why threads are a bad idea (for most purposes). Invited talk at the 1996 USENIX Technical Conference, Jan. 1996.
15. PEP 255: Simple generators. http://www.python.org/peps/pep-0255.html.
16. Sax home page. http://www.saxproject.org.
17. M. Tarpenning. Cooperative multitasking in C++. *Dr. Dobb's Journal*, 16(4):54, 56, 58–59, 96, 98–99, Apr. 1991.

Variance and Generalized Constraints for C♯ Generics

Burak Emir[1], Andrew Kennedy[2], Claudio Russo[2], and Dachuan Yu[3]

[1] EPFL, Lausanne, Switzerland
[2] Microsoft Research, Cambridge, U.K.
[3] DoCoMo Communications Laboratories USA, San Jose, California

Abstract. Generic types in C♯ behave invariantly with respect to subtyping. We propose a system of type-safe variance for C♯ that supports the declaration of covariant and contravariant type parameters on generic types. To support more widespread application of variance we also generalize the existing constraint mechanism with arbitrary subtype assertions on classes and methods. This extension is useful even in the absence of variance, and subsumes equational constraints proposed for Generalized Algebraic Data Types (GADTs). We formalize the subtype relation in both declarative and syntax-directed style, and describe and prove the correctness of algorithms for constraint closure and subtyping. Finally, we formalize and prove a type safety theorem for a featherweight language with variant classes and generalized constraints.

1 Introduction

The Generics feature of C♯ 2.0 introduced *parametric polymorphism* to the language, supporting type parameterization for types (classes, interfaces, structs, and delegates) and methods (static and instance). Being object-oriented, C♯ already offers *subtype polymorphism*, namely the ability for a value of type T to be used in a context that expects type U, if T is a subtype of U.

As it stands, though, subtype and parametric polymorphism interact only through subclassing. In particular, there is no subtyping relationship between distinct instantiations of the same generic type – type parameters are said to behave *invariantly* with respect to subtyping. This leads to a certain inflexibility: a method whose parameter has type IEnumerable<Control> cannot be passed an argument of type IEnumerable<Button>, even though this is safe: since Button is a subclass of Control, something that enumerates Buttons also enumerates Controls. Dually, a method expecting a parameter of type IComparer<Button> cannot be passed an argument of type IComparer<Control>, even though this is safe: something that can compare Controls can also compare Buttons.

1.1 Variance

We can increase the flexibility of generic types by declaring *variance* properties on type parameters. For example, IEnumerable is declared covariant (+) in its

D. Thomas (Ed.): ECOOP 2006, LNCS 4067, pp. 279–303, 2006.
© Springer-Verlag Berlin Heidelberg 2006

type parameter, and IComparer is declared contravariant (-), meaning that if $T <: U$ ("T is a subtype of U") then IEnumerable<T><:IEnumerable<U> and IComparer<U><:IComparer<T>. In our extension, these interfaces are declared as follows:

```
interface IEnumerable<+T> { IEnumerator<T> GetEnumerator(); }
interface IEnumerator<+T> { T Current { get; } }
interface IComparer<-T>   { int Compare(T x, T y); }
interface IComparable<-T> { int CompareTo(T other); }
```

To be safe, covariant type parameters can be used only in 'producer' positions in signatures (e.g. as result types, as in the GetEnumerator method and Current property above), and contravariant type parameters can be used only in 'consumer' positions (e.g. as argument types, as in the Compare and CompareTo methods above). These stringent requirements can make it hard to apply variance where it is desired. For example, a List<+T> type representing functional-style lists cannot even declare an append operation (T occurs in argument position):

```
class List<+T> {
  public List<T> Append(T other); // illegal
  public List<T> Append(List<T> other); // also illegal
```

Without such restrictions, there would be nothing to stop an *implementation* of the Append method updating the receiver list with its argument:

```
class List<+T> { private T head; private List<T> tail;
  public List(T head, List<T> tail){ this.head=head; this.tail=tail; }
  public T Hd(){ return head;} public List<T> Tl(){ return tail;}
  public List<T> Append(T other){ this.head=other; return this; }
  public List<T> Append(List<T> other){ this.tail=other; return this; }
}
```

This is unsafe: a List<Button> object could be updated with a VScrollBar value by first coercing it to List<Control>. As VScrollBar subtypes Control, but not Button, this violates safety:

```
List<Button> lb = new List<Button>(new Button(),null);
((List<Control>) lb).Append(new VScrollBar());
Button b = lb.Hd(); // we just read a scrollbar as a button
```

1.2   Generalized Constraints

We can overcome these restrictions through the use of *type constraints*:

```
class List<+T> { ...
  List<U> Append<U>(U other) where T : U { ... }
  List<U> Append<U>(List<U> other) where T : U { ... }
```

Here Append is parameterized on an additional type U, constrained to be a supertype of the element type T. So an implementation of Append cannot place its argument in the list, as U is not a subtype of T, but it can create a new list cell of type List<U> with tail of type List<T>, as List<T> is a subtype of List<U>. It is easy to check that these refined signatures for Append rule out the unsafe implementations above, while still allowing the intended, benign ones:

```
class List<+T> { ...
  public List<U> Append<U>(U other) where T : U
    { return new List<U>(head,new List<U>(other,null));}
  public List<U> Append<U>(List<U> other) where T : U
    { return new List<U>(head, tail==null? other: tail.Append(other));}
```

Notice how this is actually *less* constraining for the client code – it can always instantiate Append with T, but also with any supertype of T. For example, given a List<Button> it can append a Control to produce a result of type List<Control>. The designers of Scala [12] identified this useful pattern.

The type constraint above is not expressible in C♯ 2.0, which supports only 'upper bounds' on method type parameters. Here we have a lower bound on U. Alternatively, it can be seen as an additional upper bound of the type parameter T of the enclosing class, a feature that is useful in its own right, as the following example demonstrates:

```
interface ICollection<T> { ...
  void Sort() where T : IComparable<T>;
  bool Contains(T item) where T : IEquatable<T>; ...
```

Here, constraints on T are localized to the methods that take advantage of them.

We therefore propose a generalization of the existing constraint mechanism to support arbitrary subtype constraints at both class and method level. This neatly subsumes both the existing mechanism, which has an unnatural asymmetry, and the *equational* constraint mechanism proposed previously [10]: any equation T=U between types can be expressed as a pair of subtype constraints T:U and U:T.

1.3   Contribution and Related Work

Adding variance to parametric types has a long history [1], nicely summarized by [8]. More recently, others have proposed variance for Java. NextGen, one of the original designs for generics in Java, incorporated definition-site variance annotations, but details are sketchy [2]. Viroli and Igarashi described a system of *use-site* variance for Java [8], which is appealing in its flexibility. It was since adopted in Java 5.0 through its *wildcard* mechanism [16]. However, use-site variance places a great burden on the user of generic types: annotations can become complex, and the user must maintain them on every use of a generic type. We follow the designers of Scala [11] and place the burden on the library designer, who must annotate generic definitions, and if necessary, factor them into covariant and contravariant components.

Our type constraints generalize the 'F-bounded polymorphism' of Java [7] and C♯ and the bounded method type parameters of Scala [11], and also subsume previous work on equational constraints [10]. The treatment of constraint *closure* was inspired by previous work on constrained polymorphism for functional programming languages [14, 17] but has been adapted to handle Java-style inheritance.

We present the first formalization and proof of type safety for an object system featuring definition-site variance and inheritance in the style of Java or C♯. Independently, variance for generics in the .NET Common Language Runtime has recently been formalized and proved sound [5].

We present an algorithm to decide subtyping in the presence of contravariance and generic inheritance. Previous systems have been presented in a non-algorithmic fashion [8, 16]. This is sufficient for showing soundness, but as we demonstrate, a naïve reading even of syntax-directed subtyping rules as a procedure leads to non-termination.

2   Design Issues

In this section, we study variance and generalized constraints in more detail, considering issues of type safety and language expressivity informally in code fragments. Sections 3 and 4 provide a formal foundation, proving the correctness of a subtyping algorithm and the soundness of the type system.

2.1   Variant Interfaces

Use-site variance, as first proposed by Viroli and Igarashi [8] and recast as *wildcards* in Java 5.0 [16], requires no annotations on type parameters at type definitions. Instead, an annotation on the *use* of a generic type determines (a) its properties with respect to subtyping, and (b) the members of the type that are 'visible' for that variance annotation. For example, a mutable List<X> class can be used covariantly, permitting values of type List<+String> to be passed at type List<+Object> (in Java, List<? extends String> passed at type List<? extends Object>), and restricting invocation to 'reader' methods such as Get. Conversely, the class can be used contravariantly, permitting values of type List<-Object> to be passed at type List<-String> (in Java, List<? super Object> passed at type List<? super String>), and restricting invocation to 'writer' methods such as Add.

With definition-site variance, the library designer must prepare for such uses ahead of time. One natural way to achieve this is to expose covariant and contravariant behaviour through the implementation of covariant and contravariant *interfaces*. For example, a non-variant mutable list class could implement two interfaces, one containing 'reader' methods, and the other 'writer' methods.

```
interface IListReader<+X> {
  X Get(int index);
  void Sort(IComparer<X> comparer); ...
}
interface IListWriter<-Y> {
  void Add(Y item);
```

```
    void AddRange(IEnumerable<Y> items); ...
  }
  class List<Z> : IListReader<Z>, IListWriter<Z> {
    private Z[] arr; public List() { ... }
    public Z Get(int index) { ... } ...
  }
```

To be safe, covariant type parameters must not appear in argument positions, and contravariant parameters must not appear in result positions. To see why, consider the following counterexample:

```
interface IReader<+X> {
  public X Get();            // this is legal
  public void BadSet(X x)    // this is illegal
}
interface IWriter<-Y> {
  public void Set(Y y);      // this is legal
  public Y BadGet();         // this is illegal
}
class Bad<T> : IReader<T>, IWriter<T> {
  private T item; public Bad(T item) { this.item = item; }
  public void T Get() { return this.item ; }
  public void BadSet(T t) { this.item = t; }
  public void Set(T t) { this.item = t ; }
  public Z BadGet() { return this.item; }
}
  IReader<object> ro = new Bad<string>("abc");
  ro.BadSet(new Button()); // we just wrote a button as a string
  ...
  IWriter<string> ws = new Bad<object>(new Button());
  string s = ws.BadGet(); // we just read a button as a string
```

This might give the impression that type safety violations necessarily involve reading and writing of object fields. This is not so: the toy subset of C$^\sharp$ studied in Section 4 is purely functional, but nevertheless it is worthwhile proving soundness, as the following example illustrates:

```
interface IComparer<+T> { int Compare(T x, T y); } // this is illegal
class LengthComparer : IComparer<string> {
  int Compare(string x, string y)
    { return Int32.Compare(x.Length, y.Length); }
}
... IComparer<object> oc = new LengthComparer();
    int n = oc.Compare(3,new Button()); // takes Length of int & button
```

2.2   Variant Delegates

Variance on interfaces has a very simple design: interfaces represent a pure contract, with no code or data, so there are no interactions with mutability, access qualifiers, or implementation inheritance. C$^\sharp$'s *delegates* have a similar feel – they can be considered as degenerate interfaces with a single `Invoke` method. It is natural to support variance on generic delegates too. Here are some examples, taken from the .NET base class library:

```
delegate void Action<-T>(T obj);
delegate int Comparison<-T>(T x, T y);
delegate bool Predicate<-T>(T obj)
delegate TOutput Converter<-TInput,+TOutput>(TInput input);
```

Variance on interfaces and delegates is already supported by the .NET Common Language Runtime (and was recently proved sound [5]). Although no CLR languages currently expose variance in their type system, it is expected that Eiffel's (unsafe) covariant generic classes will be represented by covariant generic interfaces, making use of the CLR's support for exact runtime types to catch type errors at runtime.

2.3   Variant Classes

The Adaptor pattern provides another means of factoring variant behaviour. Here, rather than implement variant interfaces directly, *adaptor* methods in a non-variant class provide alternative views of data by returning an object that implements a variant interface – or, if supported, a variant abstract class:

```
abstract class ListReader<+X> {
  abstract X Get(int index);
  abstract void Sort(IComparer<X> comparer); ...
}
abstract class ListWriter<-Y> {
  abstract void Add(Y item);
  abstract void AddRange(IEnumerable<Y> items); ...
}
class List<Z> {
  public ListReader<Z> AsReader() { ... }
  public ListWriter<Z> AsWriter() { ... } ...
}
```

Concrete variant classes are also useful. For example, here is a covariant class Set that implements immutable sets:

```
class Set<+X> : IEnumerable<X> where X : IComparable<X> {
  private RedBlackTree<X> items;
  public Set() { ... }
  public Set(X item) { ... }
  public bool All(Predicate<X> p) { ... }
  public bool Exists(Predicate<X> p) { ... }
  public IEnumerator<X> GetEnumerator() { ... } ...
}
```

When are covariant and contravariant parameters on classes safe? First, note that no restrictions need be placed on the signatures of constructors or static members, as the class type parameters cannot vary. The second constructor above has X appearing in a contravariant position (the argument), but this is safe: once an object is created, the constructor cannot be invoked at a supertype. For the same reason, constraints declared on a class may make unrestricted use of variant type parameters, as in the example above.

In general, fields behave invariantly and so their types must not contain any covariant or contravariant parameters. Fields marked readonly, however, can be treated covariantly – as we do in our formalization in Section 4.

No restrictions need be placed on private members, which is handy in practice when re-factoring code into private helpers. It is also useful on fields, as above, where a field can be mutated from within the class – for example, to re-balance the RedBlackTree representing the Set above. However, we must take care: if private is interpreted as a simple lexical restriction – "accessible from code lexically in this class" – then a type hole is the result:

```
class Bad<+X> { private X item;
  public void BadAccess(Bad<string> bs) {
    Bad<object> bo = bs;
    bo.item = new Button(); } // we just wrote a button as a string
}
```

A suitable safe interpretation of private is "accessible only through type-of-this". Here, that means access only through objects of type Bad<X>; bo.item would be inaccessible as bo has type Bad<object>.

The base types of a generic type must, of course, behave covariantly, otherwise we could circumvent our restrictions through inheritance.

2.4   Generalized Constraints

As we saw in the introduction, restrictions on the appearance of variant type parameters in signatures can be very limiting. For example, we cannot define a set-union operation for the class above because its argument has type Set<X>. But using generalized constraints, we *can* define it, as follows:

```
class Set<+X> : IEnumerable<X> where X : IComparable<X> { ...
  public Set<Y> Union<Y>(Set<Y> that) where X : Y { ... }
}
```

Note that Java cannot express such a signature, because it does not support lower bounds on method type parameters; though the use of bounded wildcards can achieve the same effect for type parameters used for a single argument.

What restrictions, if any, should we apply to occurrences of class type parameters within method level constraints? The answer is that a constraint on a method behaves covariantly on the left of the constraint, and contravariantly on the right. To see why this must be the case, consider the following pair of interfaces, which attempt to avoid occurrences of covariant (contravariant) parameters in argument (result) positions, by introducing illegal bounds:

```
interface IReader<+X> {
  public X Get();                         // this is legal
  public void BadSet<Z>(Z z) where Z : X; // this is illegal
}
interface IWriter<-Y> {
  public void Set(Y y);                   // this is legal
  public Z BadGet<Z>() where Y : Z;       // this is illegal
}
class Bad<T> : IReader<T>, IWriter<T> {
  private T item; public Bad(T item) { this.item = item; }
  public void T Get() { return this.item ; }
  public void BadSet<Z>(Z z) where Z : T { this.item = z; }
  public void Set(T t) { this.item = t ; }
  public Z BadGet<Z>() where T : Z { return this.item; }
}
... IReader<object> ro = new Bad<string>("abc");
    ro.BadSet<Button>(new Button()); // we wrote a button as a string
... IWriter<string> ws = new Bad<object>(new Button());
    string s = ws.BadGet<string>(); // we read a button as a string
```

2.5   Deconstructing Constraints

In earlier work [10], we made the observation that the interesting class of Generalized (rather than Parametric) Algebraic Datatypes, currently a hot topic in Functional Programming, are already definable using Generics in C$^\sharp$. However, capturing the full range of programs over such GADTs requires the addition of both equational constraints on methods and some equational reasoning on types.

Perhaps the smallest example requiring equational constraints and reasoning is implementing strongly-typed equality over type-indexed expressions. The special case for tuple expressions highlights the issues (see [10] for the full example):

```
abstract class Exp<T> {
  public abstract T Eval();
  public abstract bool Eq(Exp<T> that);
  public abstract bool EqTuple<C,D>(Tuple<C,D> that)
    where Tuple<C,D> : Exp<T>;
}
class Tuple<A,B>: Exp<Pair<A,B>> { public Exp<A> e1; public Exp<B> e2;
  public Tuple(Exp<A> e1,Exp<B> e2) { this.e1 = e1; this.e2 = e2; }
  public override Pair<A,B> Eval(){
    return new Pair<A,B>(e1.Eval(),e2.Eval()); }
  public override bool Eq(Exp<Pair<A,B>> that) {
    return that.EqTuple<A,B>(this);} // NB: Tuple<A,B><:Exp<Pair<A,B>>
  public override bool EqTuple<C,D>(Tuple<C,D> that) {
    // where Tuple<C,D><:Exp<Pair<A,B>>
    return e1.Eq(that.e1) && e2.Eq(that.e2); }
}
```

In [10], we add the equational constraint where Pair<C,D> = T to the abstract EqTuple method to allow the override in the specialized Tuple subclass to typecheck. In the override, the constraint specializes to the assumption `Pair<A,B>=Pair<C,D>` which the type system can deconstruct (since all generic type constructors are both injective and invariant) to deduce the equations `A=C` and `B=D`. From this it follows that `Exp<C><:Exp<A>` and `Exp<D><:Exp<B>`, justifying, respectively, the calls to methods `e1.Eq(that.e1)` and `e2.Eq(that.e2)`.

With subtype constraints we can employ the more natural pre-condition `Tuple<C,D><:Exp<T>`, shown here, which directly relates the type of `that` to the type of `this` using a bound rather than an oblique equation on T. In the override, the inherited bound yields the assumption `Tuple<C,D><:Exp<Pair<A,B>>`. From the class hierarchy, it is evident that `Exp<Pair<C,D>><:Exp<Pair<A,B>>`, since the only way `Tuple<C,D>` can subtype `Exp<Pair<A,B>>` is if its declared superclass, `Exp<Pair<C,D>>`, does so too. Since `Exp<T>` is invariant, we can deconstruct this constraint to conclude that `Pair<C,D><:Pair<A,B>` and, symmetrically, `Pair<A,B><:Pair<C,D>`. Deconstructing yet again, assuming that `Pair` is covariant, we obtain `C<:A,D<:B` and `A<:C,B<:D`. Shuffling these inequalities we can derive `Exp<C><:Exp<A>` and `Exp<D><:Exp<B>` which, finally, justify the recursive calls to `e1.Eq(that.e1)` and `e2.Eq(that.e2)`. To accommodate this sort of reasoning in general, our subtype judgement must be able to both deconstruct the inheritance relation, to obtain lower bounds on superclass instantiations, and deconstruct subtype relationships betweens different instantiations of the same generic class, to deduce relationships between corresponding type arguments, oriented by the variance properties of the class.

3   Types and Subtyping

We begin our formal investigation of variance and constraints with a description of the subtype relation, presented in both declarative and syntax-directed styles. Types, ranged over by T, U and V, are of two forms:

- *type variables*, ranged over by X, Y and Z, and
- *constructed types*, ranged over by K, of the form $C<\overline{T}>$ where C is a class or interface name, and $\overline{T}$ is a sequence of zero or more type arguments.

(As is common, we write vectors such as $\overline{T}$ as shorthand for $T_1, \ldots, T_n$.)

The subtype relation $<:$ is determined by a class hierarchy (subclassing *is* subtyping in C♯), and by variance properties of generic types. We therefore assume a set of declarations which specify for each class C its formal type parameters $\overline{X}$, variance annotations on those parameters $\overline{v}$, and base class and interfaces $\overline{K}$. We write $C<\overline{v}\overline{X}>:\overline{K}$ for such a declaration. A variance annotation v is one of ○ (invariant), + (covariant), and - (contravariant). In our examples, omitted annotations are implicitly ○ (for backwards compatibility with C♯).

For type soundness it is necessary to impose restrictions on how variant type parameters appear in signatures. Formally, we define a judgment $\overline{v}\overline{X} \vdash T$ *mono* which states that a type T behaves 'monotonically' with respect to its type variables $\overline{X}$ whose variance annotations are $\overline{v}$. This predicate on types is presented in Figure 1, with extension to subtype assertions. It makes use of a negation operation on variance annotations, with the obvious definition.

$$\frac{v_i \in \{\circ, +\}}{\overline{vX} \vdash X_i \; mono} \; \text{V-VVAR} \qquad \frac{X \notin \overline{X}}{\overline{vX} \vdash X \; mono} \; \text{V-VAR}$$

$$\frac{C<\overline{w}\,\overline{Y}>:\overline{K} \qquad \begin{array}{l} \forall i \; w_i \in \{\circ, +\} \Rightarrow \overline{vX} \vdash T_i \; mono \\ \forall i \; w_i \in \{\circ, -\} \Rightarrow \neg\overline{vX} \vdash T_i \; mono \end{array}}{\overline{vX} \vdash C<\overline{T}> \; mono} \; \text{V-CON} \qquad \neg v = \begin{cases} \text{-, if } v = \text{+,} \\ \circ, \text{ if } v = \circ, \\ \text{+, if } v = \text{-} \end{cases}$$

$$\frac{\neg\overline{vX} \vdash T \; mono \quad \overline{vX} \vdash U \; mono}{\overline{vX} \vdash T<:U \; mono} \; \text{V-SUB}$$

Fig. 1. Variance validity of types and subtypes

$$\frac{\Delta \vdash T<:U \quad \Delta \vdash U<:V}{\Delta \vdash T<:V} \; \text{TRAN} \qquad \frac{}{\Delta \vdash X<:X} \; \text{VAR} \qquad \frac{T<:U \in \Delta}{\Delta \vdash T<:U} \; \text{HYP}$$

$$\frac{C<\overline{vX}>:\overline{K} \quad \forall i, v_i \in \{\circ, +\} \Rightarrow \Delta \vdash T_i<:U_i \text{ and } v_i \in \{\circ, -\} \Rightarrow \Delta \vdash U_i<:T_i}{\Delta \vdash C<\overline{T}><:C<\overline{U}>} \; \text{CON}$$

$$\frac{C<\overline{vX}>:\overline{K}}{\Delta \vdash C<\overline{T}><:[\overline{T}/\overline{X}]K_i} \; \text{BASE} \qquad \frac{C<\overline{T}> \triangleleft D<\overline{U}> \quad \Delta \vdash C<\overline{T}><:D<\overline{V}>}{\Delta \vdash D<\overline{U}><:D<\overline{V}>} \; \text{DEBASE}$$

$$\frac{C<\overline{vX}>:\overline{K} \quad \Delta \vdash C<\overline{T}><:C<\overline{U}> \quad v_i \in \{\circ, +\}}{\Delta \vdash T_i<:U_i} \; \text{DECON}^+$$

$$\frac{C<\overline{vX}>:\overline{K} \quad \Delta \vdash C<\overline{T}><:C<\overline{U}> \quad v_i \in \{\circ, -\}}{\Delta \vdash U_i<:T_i} \; \text{DECON}^-$$

Fig. 2. Subtyping rules

Before defining the subtyping relation proper, we introduce an auxiliary relation $\triangleleft$ over constructed types, denoting the reflexive transitive closure of the 'is an immediate base class of' relation. It is defined as follows.

$$\frac{}{K \triangleleft K} \qquad \frac{C<\overline{vX}>:\overline{K} \quad [\overline{T}/\overline{X}]K_i \triangleleft K}{C<\overline{T}> \triangleleft K}$$

We impose three restrictions on the class hierarchy. First, that it is *acyclic*: if $C<\overline{vX}>:\overline{K}$ and $K_i \triangleleft D<\overline{T}>$ then $C \neq D$. Second, that generic instantiations are *uniquely determined*: if $C<\overline{X}> \triangleleft D<\overline{T}>$ and $C<\overline{X}> \triangleleft D<\overline{U}>$ then $\overline{T} = \overline{U}$. Third, that it *respects variance*: if $C<\overline{vX}>:\overline{K}$ then $\overline{vX} \vdash \overline{K} \; mono$. It is easy to show that this extends transitively: under the same definition of C, if $C<\overline{X}> \triangleleft K$ then $\overline{vX} \vdash K \; mono$.

We are now ready to specify subtyping. Let Δ range over lists of subtype assumptions of the form $T<:U$. Our subtyping relation is defined by a judgment $\Delta \vdash T<:U$ which should be read "under assumptions Δ we can deduce that T is a subtype of U". A declarative presentation of this relation is given in Figure 2.

Ignoring Δ for the moment, ground subtyping requires just three rules: we assert that subtyping is transitive (TRAN), that instantiations of the same class vary according to the annotations on the type parameters (CON), and that subclassing induces subtyping (BASE). Observe that reflexivity is admissible (by repeated use of CON), and that the induced equivalence relation for ground types is just syntactic equality.

Now suppose that subtyping judgments are open and we make use of assumptions in Δ. We add reflexivity on type variables (VAR), and hypothesis (HYP). This lets us deduce, for example, for contravariant I that $X<:C \vdash I<C><:I<X>$.

These rules alone are insufficient to check code such as in Section 2.5. Suppose our subtype assumptions include $C<X><:C<Y>$. Take any ground instantiation of X and Y, say $[T/X, U/Y]$. If C is invariant or covariant then $\vdash C<T><:C<U>$ can hold only if $\vdash T<:U$. Dually, if C is invariant or contravariant then $\vdash C<T><:C<U>$ can hold only if $\vdash U<:T$. This justifies inverting rule CON to obtain rules DECON$^+$ and DECON$^-$ that 'deconstruct' a type according to its variance.

In a similar vein, suppose our subtype assumptions include $C<X><:D<Y>$, for class definitions $C<\circ Z>:D<Z>$ and $D<-Z>:\mathtt{object}$. Consider any ground instantiation of X and Y, say $[T/X, U/Y]$. Then a derivation of $\vdash C<T><:D<U>$ exists only if $\vdash D<T><:D<U>$ and thus $\vdash U<:T$. We are justified in 'inverting' rule BASE to obtain DEBASE that uses the class hierarchy to derive a subtype relationship between two instantiations of the same class.

It is straightforward to prove standard properties of subtype entailment.

Lemma 1 (Substitution). *If $\Delta \vdash T<:U$ then $S\Delta \vdash ST<:SU$ for any substitution $S = [\overline{T/X}]$.*

Proof. By induction on the derivation, using a similar property of $\lhd$. □

Lemma 2 (Weakening). *If $\Delta \vdash \Delta'$ and $\Delta' \vdash T<:U$ then $\Delta \vdash T<:U$.*

Proof. By induction on the subtyping derivation. □

We will also make use of the following lemma, which states that subtype assertions lift through type formers according to variance.

Lemma 3 (Subtype lifting). *Suppose that $\overline{v}\overline{X} \vdash V$ mono, and for all i, if $v_i \in \{\circ, +\}$ then $\Delta \vdash T_i<:U_i$, and if $v_i \in \{\circ, -\}$ then $\Delta \vdash U_i<:T_i$. Then $\Delta \vdash [\overline{T/X}]V<:[\overline{U/X}]V$.*

Proof. By induction on the variance validity derivation. □

3.1 Syntax-Directed Subtyping

The declarative presentation of subtyping is direct, and it is easy to prove properties such as Substitution and Weakening, but it is not easy to derive an algorithm from the rules: reading the rules backwards, we can always apply rule TRAN to introduce new subgoals. So we now consider an alternative set of *syntax-directed*

$$\frac{}{\Psi \succ X <: X} \text{ S-VAR} \qquad \frac{C<\overline{v}\overline{X}>:\overline{K} \qquad \Psi \succ [\overline{T}/\overline{X}]K_i <: D<\overline{U}> \qquad C \neq D}{\Psi \succ C<\overline{T}> <: D<\overline{U}>} \text{ S-BASE}$$

$$\frac{\Psi \succ T <: U \quad U <: X \in \Psi \quad T \neq X}{\Psi \succ T <: X} \text{ S-LOWER} \qquad \frac{X <: T \in \Psi \quad \Psi \succ T <: K}{\Psi \succ X <: K} \text{ S-UPPER}$$

$$\frac{C<\overline{v}\overline{X}>:\overline{K} \quad \forall i, v_i \in \{\circ, +\} \Rightarrow \Psi \succ T_i <: U_i \text{ and } v_i \in \{\circ, -\} \Rightarrow \Psi \succ U_i <: T_i}{\Psi \succ C<\overline{T}> <: C<\overline{U}>} \text{ S-CON}$$

Fig. 3. Syntax-directed subtyping rules

subtyping rules, where the structure of the types determines uniquely a rule (scheme) to apply. These are presented in Figure 3.

We write $\Psi \succ T <: U$ to mean that "under context Ψ we can deduce that T is a subtype of U". As is usual, we eliminate the transitivity rule TRAN, rolling it into rules S-BASE, S-UPPER, and S-LOWER. We also work with a different form of context: instead of an arbitrary set of subtype assertions, the context Ψ provides upper or lower bounds for type variables. In place of a hypothesis rule, we have rules S-UPPER and S-LOWER that replace a type variable by one of its bounds.

For transitivity to be admissible, we need to impose some restrictions on the context Ψ. For example, consider the context $\Psi = \{C<X> <: Z, Z <: C<Y>\}$ for covariant C. Clearly we have $\Psi \succ C<X> <: Z$ and $\Psi \succ Z <: C<Y>$, but not $\Psi \succ C<X> <: C<Y>$. We need to add $X <: Y$ to Ψ to achieve this. We define a notion of *consistency* for contexts (see Pottier [14] and Trifonov and Smith [17] for similar ideas).

Definition 1 (Consistency). *A context Ψ is consistent if for any pair of assertions $T <: X \in \Psi$ and $X <: U \in \Psi$ it is the case that $\Psi \succ T <: U$.*

We should now have enough to relate the syntax-directed and declarative rules: given a consistent context Ψ that is equivalent to a set of constraints Δ (in the sense that $\Psi \succ \Delta$ and $\Delta \vdash \Psi$), the relation $\Psi \succ - <: -$ should coincide with $\Delta \vdash - <: -$. The proof of this rests on the admissibility of transitivity: if $\Psi \succ T <: U$ and $\Psi \succ U <: V$ then $\Psi \succ T <: V$. Attempts at a direct proof of transitivity fail (for example, by induction on the total height of the derivations). There are two difficult cases. If the first derivation ends with rule S-CON and the second ends with S-BASE then we need to 'push' the premises of S-CON through the second derivation. We use an auxiliary result (Lemma 6) to achieve this. If the first derivation ends with rule S-LOWER (so we have a proof of $\Psi \succ T <: X$) and the second ends with S-UPPER (so we have a proof of $\Psi \succ X <: V$) then we need to make use of the consistency of Ψ in the side-conditions of these rules ($T' <: X \in \Psi$ and $X <: U' \in \Psi$) to obtain a derivation of $\Psi \succ T' <: U'$. But to apply the induction hypothesis on this derivation we need to bound its size.

Lemma 4. *For any consistent context Ψ there exists a context Ψ' such that $\Psi \succ \Psi'$ and $\Psi' \succ \Psi$ and satisfying the following property: if $T <: X <: U \in \Psi'$ then there is a derivation $\Psi' \succ T <: U$ in which all uses of rules S-LOWER and S-UPPER are trivial, namely, that the premise is of the form $\Psi' \succ V <: V$.*

$$\frac{}{\Psi \succ_{b,m} X <: X} \text{ R-VAR} \qquad \frac{C<\overline{v}\overline{X}>:\overline{K} \quad \Psi \succ_{b,m} [\overline{T}/\overline{X}]K_i <:D<\overline{U}> \quad C \neq D}{\Psi \succ_{b,m} C<\overline{T}> <:D<\overline{U}>} \text{ R-BASE}$$

$$\frac{\Psi \succ_{b,m} T <:U \quad U <:X \in \Psi \quad T \neq X}{\Psi \succ_{b+1,m} T <:X} \text{ R-LOWER} \qquad \frac{X <:T \in \Psi \quad \Psi \succ_{b,m} T <:K}{\Psi \succ_{b+1,m} X <:K} \text{ R-UPPER}$$

$$\frac{C<\overline{v}\overline{X}>:\overline{K} \quad \forall i, v_i \in \{\circ, +\} \Rightarrow \Psi \succ_{b,n} T_i <:U_i \text{ and } v_i \in \{\circ, -\} \Rightarrow \Psi \succ_{b,n} U_i <:T_i}{\Psi \succ_{b,n+1} C<\overline{T}> <:C<\overline{U}>} \text{ R-CON}$$

Fig. 4. Ranked syntax-directed subtyping rules

Proof. By consistency of Ψ, for any $T <:X <:U \in \Psi$ we have a derivation of $\Psi \succ T <:U$. For every sub-derivation that ends with the conclusion $\Psi \succ V <:X$, add $V <:X$ to the context, likewise for every sub-derivation that ends with $\Psi \succ X <:V$, add $X <:V$ to the context. If we repeat this process the resultant context $\Psi' \supseteq \Psi$ has the desired property. □

Figure 4 presents a 'ranked' variant of the syntax-directed rules, where the judgment $\Psi \succ_{b,m} T <:U$ is indexed by natural numbers b and m, where b is a bound on the height of the derivation with respect to rules R-LOWER and R-UPPER, and n is a bound on the height with respect to rule R-CON. Note that rule R-BASE does not count towards either measure: in our proofs we make use of the following lemma that lets us elide inheritance.

Lemma 5 (Variant inheritance). *If $\Psi \succ_{b,m} C<\overline{T}> <:D<\overline{U}>$ then $C<\overline{T}> \lhd D<\overline{V}>$ and $\Psi \succ_{b,m} D<\overline{V}> <:D<\overline{U}>$ for some $\overline{V}$.*

Proof. By induction on the subtyping derivation. □

Lemma 6. *Fix some $n, c, l, \overline{T}, \overline{U}$. Suppose that for any $m \leqslant n$, any $b \leqslant c$ and any W, if $\Psi \succ_{b,m} T_i <:W$ and $v_i \in \{\circ, +\}$, then there exists r such that $\Psi \succ_{b+l,r} U_i <:W$. Likewise suppose that for any $m \leqslant n$, any $b \leqslant c$ and any W, if $\Psi \succ_{b,m} W <:T_i$ and $v_i \in \{\circ, -\}$, then there exists r such that $\Psi \succ_{b+l,r} W <:U_i$.*

1. *For any T and V such that $\overline{v}\overline{X} \vdash T$ mono, if $\Psi \succ_{c,n} [\overline{T}/\overline{X}]T <:V$ then $\Psi \succ_{c+l,r} [\overline{U}/\overline{X}]T <:V$ for some r.*
2. *For any U and V such that $\neg\overline{v}\overline{X} \vdash U$ mono, if $\Psi \succ_{c,n} V <:[\overline{T}/\overline{X}]U$ then $\Psi \succ_{c+l,r} V <:[\overline{U}/\overline{X}]U$ for some r.*

Proof. By simultaneous induction on the subtyping derivations in (1) and (2).

Lemma 7 (Transitivity). *Let Ψ be a consistent context. If $\Psi \succ T <:U$ and $\Psi \succ U <:V$ then $\Psi \succ T <:V$.*

Proof. Using Lemma 4, assume that Ψ satisfies the stronger conditions described there. We now prove the following equivalent 'ranked' statement. If $\mathcal{D}_1$ and $\mathcal{D}_2$ are derivations of $\Psi \succ_{b,m} T <:U$ and $\Psi \succ_{c,n} U <:V$, then $\Psi \succ_{b+c,r} T <:U$ for some r. We proceed by induction on $(b+c, m+n)$, ordered lexicographically. We make use of Lemma 6 for R-BASE against R-CON. □

Theorem 1 (Equivalence of syntax-directed and declarative rules).
Provided Ψ is consistent, $\Psi \succ \Delta$ and $\Delta \vdash \Psi$, then $\Psi \succ T <: U$ iff $\Delta \vdash T <: U$.

Proof. By induction on the derivations, using Lemma 7 for rule TRAN.   □

3.2   Subtyping Algorithm

Our syntax-directed rules can be interpreted as a procedure for checking subtypes: if a subtype assertion holds, then the procedure terminates with result *true*. To show that the procedure will terminate with *false* if the relation does *not* hold, it suffices to find some measure on subtype judgments that strictly decreases from conclusion to premises of the syntax-directed rules. Unfortunately, there is no such measure for the rules of Figure 3. Consider the following classes:

$$N <\!\!-X> : \texttt{object} \qquad \text{and} \qquad C : N <\!N\!<\!C\!>\!>$$

Now consider checking the subtype assertion $C <: N<C>$. If we attempt to construct a derivation, we end up back where we started:

$$
\cfrac{
\cfrac{
\cfrac{
\begin{array}{c} \vdots \end{array}
}{\succ C <: N<C>}
}{\succ N<N<C>> <: N<C>}\ \text{S-CON}
}{\succ C <: N<C>}\ \text{S-BASE}
$$

A similar issue arises with constraints. Suppose that $\Psi = \{X <: N<N<X>>\}$, and consider checking the subtype assertion $X <: N<X>$. Even simple equations on type variables, expressed as bounds, such as $\{X <: Y, Y <: X\}$, can induce looping behaviour, for example testing $X <: \texttt{object}$.

These examples can be dealt with straightforwardly if the algorithm keeps a set of goals 'already seen', returning *false* when asked to prove an assertion from the set. Unfortunately this solution is not universal. Consider these definitions:

$$N <\!\!-X> : \texttt{object} \qquad \text{and} \qquad D<Y> : N<N<D<D<Y>>>>$$

Now consider checking $D^m<T> <: N<D^m<T>>$ where D^m has the obvious interpretation as m iterations of the type constructor D:

$$
\cfrac{
\cfrac{
\cfrac{
\cfrac{
\cfrac{
\begin{array}{c} \vdots \end{array}
}{\succ D^{m+1}<T> <: N<D^{m+1}<T>>}
}{\succ N<N<D^{m+1}<T>>> <: N<D^{m+1}<T>>}\ \text{S-CON}
}{\succ D^m<T> <: N<D^{m+1}<T>>}\ \text{S-BASE}
}{\succ N<N<D^{m+1}<T>>> <: N<D^m<T>>}\ \text{S-CON}
}{\succ D^m<T> <: N<D^m<T>>}\ \text{S-BASE}
$$

After four rules we end up at the subgoal $D^{m+1}<T> <: N<D^{m+1}<T>>$, demonstrating that there is no derivation.

We have not yet devised an algorithm that can check this assertion; nor have we proved that the problem is undecidable. Instead, we impose a natural restriction on class hierarchies that guarantees termination. We introduce the notion of *closure* of a set of types under decomposition and inheritance.

$\text{Sub}(\Xi, \Psi, T, U) =$
   if $(T, U) \in \Xi$ then *false*
   else let $\text{Sub}'(T', U') = \text{Sub}(\{(T, U)\} \cup \Xi, \Psi, T', U')$ in
   case T, U of
      $X, X \Rightarrow true$
      $T, X \Rightarrow \bigvee_{T_i <: X \in \Psi} \text{Sub}'(T, T_i)$
      $X, K \Rightarrow \bigvee_{X <: T_i \in \Psi} \text{Sub}'(T_i, K)$
      $C\texttt{<}\overline{T}\texttt{>}, D\texttt{<}\overline{U}\texttt{>} \Rightarrow \bigvee_{K \in \overline{K}} \text{Sub}'([\overline{T}/\overline{X}]K, D\texttt{<}\overline{U}\texttt{>})$, if $C \neq D$ and $C\texttt{<}\overline{v}\overline{X}\texttt{>}: \overline{K}$
      $C\texttt{<}\overline{T}\texttt{>}, C\texttt{<}\overline{U}\texttt{>} \Rightarrow \bigwedge_{i|v_i \in \{\circ, +\}} \text{Sub}'(T_i, U_i) \wedge \bigwedge_{i|v_i \in \{\circ, -\}} \text{Sub}'(U_i, T_i)$, if $C\texttt{<}\overline{v}\overline{X}\texttt{>}: \overline{K}$

Fig. 5. Subtyping algorithm

Definition 2 (Closure of types). *A set of types $\mathcal{S}$ is* closed *if whenever $C\texttt{<}\overline{T}\texttt{>} \in \mathcal{S}$ then $\overline{T} \subseteq \mathcal{S}$ (decomposition) and whenever $K \in \mathcal{S}$ and $K \lhd K'$ then $K' \in \mathcal{S}$ (inheritance). The* closure *of $\mathcal{S}$ is the least closed superset of $\mathcal{S}$.*

Now consider the closure of the set $\{D\texttt{<object>}\}$ with respect to the above class definitions. It is easy to see that it is infinite. We rule out such classes; in fact, the .NET Common Language Runtime already imposes the same restriction [4, Partition II, §9.2], which enables eager loading of superclasses.

Definition 3 (Finitary definitions). *A set of class definitions is* finitary *if for any set of types $\mathcal{S}$ making use of those classes, its closure is finite.*

Fortunately, there is an algorithm that can check whether or not a set of class definitions is finitary [18, §6].
   Figure 5 presents our subtyping algorithm in functional style. The additional parameter Ξ is a set of pairs of types representing subtype assertions already visited. The algorithm assumes that class definitions are finitary.

Definition 4 (Small derivations). *A derivation of $\Psi \vdash T <: U$ is* small *if each proper sub-derivation has a conclusion other than $\Psi \vdash T <: U$, and is itself small.*

It is easy to see that an arbitrary derivation can be transformed into a small derivation. We make use of this fact in the proof of completeness.

Theorem 2 (Soundness and completeness of subtyping algorithm). $\text{Sub}(\{\}, \Psi, T, U) = true$ iff $\Psi \vdash T <: U$.

Proof. Soundness ($\Rightarrow$). By induction on the call tree. *Completeness* ($\Leftarrow$). Let $\mathcal{P} = \{(T, U) \mid \Psi \vdash T <: U \text{ is a sub-derivation of } \mathcal{D}\}$. We show, by induction on $\mathcal{D}$, that if $\mathcal{D}$ is a small derivation of $\Psi \vdash T <: U$ and $\Xi \cap \mathcal{P} = \emptyset$ then $\text{Sub}(\Xi, \Psi, T, U) = true$. □

Theorem 3 (Termination). *For any Ξ, any consistent, finite Ψ and any T and U, the procedure $\text{Sub}(\Xi, \Psi, T, U)$ terminates with result* true *or* false*.*

Proof. Let $\mathcal{S} = \{T, U\} \cup \{T \mid T <: U \in \Psi\} \cup \{U \mid T <: U \in \Psi\}$. Call its closure $\mathcal{T}$, which is finite if we assume finitary class definitions. Then it is easy to see that at each recursive call to Sub, the cardinality of $(\mathcal{T} \times \mathcal{T}) \setminus \Xi$ decreases by one. Hence the algorithm terminates. □

3.3   Constraint Closure

There remains one piece of the subtyping jigsaw to put in place: given a set of constraints Δ, as declared or inherited by a method, determining an equivalent, consistent context Ψ, used as input to the subtyping algorithm when type-checking the body of the method.

Not all constraint sets are useful: in particular, constraints between types that are unrelated in the hierarchy can never be satisfied. That's not enough, though: a constraint set may *entail* unsatisfiable constraints. (For example, the set $\{C<:X, X<:D\}$ is unsatisfiable if C is unrelated to D in the class hierarchy.) So we define a notion of *closure* for constraint sets.

Definition 5 (Closure). *A constraint set Δ is* closed *if it is closed under transitivity, inheritance and decomposition:*

- *If $T<:U \in \Delta$ and $U<:V \in \Delta$ then $T<:V \in \Delta$.*
- *If $C<\overline{T}><:D<\overline{U}> \in \Delta$ and $C<\overline{T}> \triangleleft D<\overline{V}>$ with $D<\overline{v}\overline{X}>:\overline{K}$ then for each i, if $v_i \in \{\circ, +\}$ then $V_i<:U_i \in \Delta$ and if $v_i \in \{\circ, -\}$ then $U_i<:V_i \in \Delta$.*

The closure *of Δ, written $\mathrm{Cl}(\Delta)$, is the least closed superset of Δ.*

Definition 6 (Consistency of constraint sets). *A constraint set Δ is* consistent *if for any constraint $C<\overline{T}><:D<\overline{U}> \in \mathrm{Cl}(\Delta)$ there exists some $\overline{V}$ such that $C<\overline{T}> \triangleleft D<\overline{V}>$.*

To construct a context Ψ from a constraint set Δ we make use of a partial function Dec which takes an arbitrary constraint $T<:U$ and produces a set of constraints on type variables through a combination of inheritance and decomposition (Pottier defines a similar notion [14]).

$$\mathrm{Dec}(X<:T) = \{X<:T\}$$
$$\mathrm{Dec}(T<:X) = \{T<:X\}$$
$$\mathrm{Dec}(C<\overline{V}><:D<\overline{U}>) = \begin{cases} \bigcup_{i|v_i\in\{\circ,+\}} \mathrm{Dec}(T_i<:U_i) \cup \bigcup_{i|v_i\in\{\circ,-\}} \mathrm{Dec}(U_i<:T_i) \\ \quad \text{if } C<\overline{V}> \triangleleft D<\overline{T}> \text{ for some } \overline{T} \text{ where } D<\overline{v}\overline{X}>:\overline{K} \\ \text{undefined otherwise.} \end{cases}$$

We combine this with transitive closure in the following Lemma.

Lemma 8 (Context construction). *Let Δ be a set of constraints. Define*

$$\Psi_0 = \bigcup_{T<:U\in\Delta} \mathrm{Dec}(T<:U)$$
$$\Psi_{n+1} = \Psi_n \cup \sum_{T<:X<:U\in\Psi_n} \mathrm{Dec}(T<:U).$$

If the class definitions are finitary, and Δ is consistent, then Ψ_n is defined for each n and has a fix-point $\Psi = \Psi_\infty$. Then Ψ is consistent, $\Delta \vdash \Psi$ and $\Psi \succ \Delta$.

This provides a means of computing a consistent Ψ that models a set of constraints Δ, or rejecting the constraints as unsatisfiable if they are found to be inconsistent. In practice one might want to *simplify* constraints further, using techniques such as those described by Pottier [14], though constraint sets in $C^\sharp$ are unlikely to be large.

$$
\begin{array}{rll}
\text{(class def)} & cd & ::= \texttt{class } C\texttt{<}\,\overline{v}\,\overline{X}\texttt{>} : K \;\boxed{\texttt{where } \Delta}\; \{\,\boxed{\overline{P}}\;\overline{T}\,\overline{f};\; kd\;\overline{md}\} \\
\text{(constr def)} & kd & ::= \texttt{public } C(\overline{T}\,\overline{f}) : \texttt{base}(\overline{f})\,\{\texttt{this}.\overline{f} = \overline{f};\} \\
\text{(field qualifier)} & \boxed{P} & ::= \texttt{public readonly} \\
\text{(method qualifier)} & Q & ::= \texttt{public virtual} \mid \texttt{public override} \\
\text{(method def)} & md & ::= Q\;T\;m\texttt{<}\overline{X}\texttt{>}(\overline{T}\,\overline{x})\;\boxed{\texttt{where }\Delta}\;\{\texttt{return } e;\} \\
\text{(expression)} & e & ::= x \mid e.f \mid e.m\texttt{<}\overline{T}\texttt{>}(\overline{e}) \mid \texttt{new } K(\overline{e}) \mid (T)e \\
\text{(value)} & v, w & ::= \texttt{new } K(\overline{v}) \\
\text{(typing environment)} & \Gamma & ::= \overline{X}, \overline{x} : \overline{T}, \Delta \\
\text{(method signature)} & & ::= \texttt{<}\overline{X}\;\boxed{\texttt{where }\Delta}\texttt{>}\overline{T} \to T \quad (\overline{X} \text{ is bound in } \Delta, \overline{T}, T) \\
\text{(substitutions)} & & ::= [\overline{T}/\overline{X}], [\overline{e}/\overline{x}]
\end{array}
$$

Fig. 6. Syntax of C$^\sharp$ minor with variance and constraints

4   C$^\sharp$ Minor with Variance and Generalized Constraints

In this section we formalize variance and generalized constraints as extensions of a small, but representative fragment of C$^\sharp$. After presenting the type system and operational semantics, we prove the usual *Preservation* and *Progress* theorems (Theorems 4 and 5) that establish *Type Soundness* (Theorem 6). Preservation tells us that program evaluation preserves types. Progress tells us that well-typed programs are either already fully evaluated, may be evaluated further, or are stuck, but only at the evaluation of an illegal cast (but not, say, at an undefined runtime member lookup). The fact that we have to accommodate stuck programs has nothing to do with our extensions; it is just the usual symptom of supporting runtime-checked downcasts.

We formulate our extensions for 'C$^\sharp$ minor' [9], a small, purely-functional subset of C$^\sharp$ version 2.0 [15, 6]. Its (extended) syntax, typing rules and small-step reduction semantics are presented in Figures 6–8. To aid the reader, we emphasize the essential differences to basic C$^\sharp$ minor using shading. C$^\sharp$ minor itself is based on Featherweight GJ [7] and has similar aims: it is just enough for our purposes but does not "cheat" – valid (constraint-free) programs in C$^\sharp$ minor really are valid C$^\sharp$ programs. The differences from FGJ are as follows:

- Instead of bounds on type parameters, we allow *subtype constraints* on types, specified at class and virtual method definitions but implicitly inherited at method overrides. In this way, a virtual method may further constrain its outer class type parameters as well as its own method type parameters.
- We include a separate rule for subsumption instead of including subtyping judgments in multiple rules.
- We fix the reduction order to be call-by-value.

Like Featherweight GJ, this language does not include object identity and encapsulated state, which arguably are defining features of the object-oriented programming paradigm, nor does it model interfaces. It does include dynamic

Subtyping:

$$(\text{sub-incl}) \dfrac{\Delta \vdash T{<}:U}{\overline{X}, \overline{x}{:}\overline{T}, \Delta \vdash T <: U}$$

Well-formed types and constraints:

$$\dfrac{}{\Gamma \vdash \texttt{object } ok} \qquad \dfrac{X \in \Gamma}{\Gamma \vdash X \ ok} \qquad \dfrac{\mathcal{D}(C) = \texttt{class } C{<}\,\overline{v}\,\overline{X}{>} : K \ \texttt{where } \Delta \ \{\ldots\} \quad \Gamma \vdash \overline{T} \ ok \quad \Gamma \vdash [\overline{T}/\overline{X}]\Delta}{\Gamma \vdash C{<}\overline{T}{>} \ ok}$$

$$\dfrac{\Delta \equiv \overline{T}{<}:\overline{U} \quad \Gamma \vdash \overline{T}, \overline{U} \ ok}{\Gamma \vdash \Delta \ ok}$$

Typing:

$$(\text{ty-var}) \dfrac{}{\Gamma, x{:}T \vdash x : T} \qquad (\text{ty-fld}) \dfrac{\Gamma \vdash e : K \ fields(K) = \overline{P} \ \overline{T} \ \overline{f}}{\Gamma \vdash e.f_i : T_i}$$

$$(\text{ty-cast}) \dfrac{\Gamma \vdash U \ ok \quad \Gamma \vdash e : T}{\Gamma \vdash (U)e : U} \qquad (\text{ty-sub}) \dfrac{\Gamma \vdash e : T \quad \Gamma \vdash U \ ok \quad \Gamma \vdash T <: U}{\Gamma \vdash e : U}$$

$$(\text{ty-new}) \dfrac{\Gamma \vdash K \ ok \quad fields(K) = \overline{P} \ \overline{T} \ \overline{f} \quad \Gamma \vdash \overline{e} : \overline{T}}{\Gamma \vdash \texttt{new } K(\overline{e}) : K}$$

$$(\text{ty-meth}) \dfrac{\Gamma \vdash e : K \quad mtype(K.m) = {<}\overline{X} \ \texttt{where } \Delta {>}\overline{U} \to U \quad \Gamma \vdash \overline{T} \ ok \quad \Gamma \vdash [\overline{T}/\overline{X}]\Delta \quad \Gamma \vdash \overline{e} : [\overline{T}/\overline{X}]\overline{U}}{\Gamma \vdash e.m{<}\overline{T}{>}(\overline{e}) : [\overline{T}/\overline{X}]U}$$

Method and Class Typing:

$$(\text{ok-virtual}) \dfrac{\begin{array}{c}\mathcal{D}(C) = \texttt{class } C{<}\,\overline{v}\,\overline{X}{>} : K \ \texttt{where } \Delta_1 \ \{\ldots\} \ mtype(K.m) \text{ not defined} \\ \neg\overline{v}\overline{X} \vdash \Delta_2, \overline{T} \ mono \quad \overline{v}\overline{X} \vdash T \ mono \quad \Delta_1, \Delta_2 \ consistent \\ \overline{X}, \overline{Y}, \Delta_1, \Delta_2 \vdash T, \overline{T}, \Delta_2 \ ok \quad \overline{X}, \overline{Y}, \Delta_1, \Delta_2, \overline{x}{:}\overline{T}, \texttt{this}{:}C{<}\overline{X}{>} \vdash e : T\end{array}}{\vdash \texttt{public virtual } T \ m{<}\overline{Y}{>}(\overline{T} \ \overline{x}) \ \texttt{where } \Delta_2 \ \{\texttt{return } e;\} \ ok \ in \ C{<}\overline{X}{>}}$$

$$(\text{ok-override}) \dfrac{\begin{array}{c}\mathcal{D}(C) = \texttt{class } C{<}\,\overline{v}\,\overline{X}{>} : K \ \texttt{where } \Delta_1 \ \{\ldots\} \\ mtype(K.m) = {<}\overline{Y} \ \texttt{where } \Delta_2 {>}\overline{T} \to T \\ \Delta_1, \Delta_2 \ consistent \quad \overline{X}, \overline{Y}, \Delta_1, \Delta_2, \overline{x}{:}\overline{T}, \texttt{this}{:}C{<}\overline{X}{>} \vdash e : T\end{array}}{\vdash \texttt{public override } T \ m{<}\overline{Y}{>}(\overline{T} \ \overline{x}) \ \{\texttt{return } e;\} \ ok \ in \ C{<}\overline{X}{>}}$$

$$(\text{ok-class}) \dfrac{\begin{array}{c}\overline{v}\overline{X} \vdash K, \overline{T} \ mono \quad \Delta \ consistent \quad \overline{X}, \Delta \vdash K, \Delta, \overline{T} \ ok \\ fields(K) = \overline{P} \ \overline{U} \ \overline{g} \quad \overline{f} \text{ and } \overline{g} \text{ disjoint} \\ \vdash \overline{md} \ ok \ in \ C{<}\overline{X}{>} \quad kd = \texttt{public } C(\overline{U} \ \overline{g}, \overline{T} \ \overline{f}) \ \texttt{base}(\overline{g}) \ \{\texttt{this}.\overline{f}{=}\overline{f}; \}\end{array}}{\vdash \texttt{class } C{<}\,\overline{v}\,\overline{X}{>} : K \ \texttt{where } \Delta \ \{\overline{P} \ \overline{T} \ \overline{f}; \ kd \ \overline{md}\} \ ok}$$

Fig. 7. Typing rules for $C^\sharp$ minor with variance and constraints

Operational Semantics:
(reduction rules)

$$(\text{r-fld}) \frac{\mathit{fields}(K) = \overline{P}\ \overline{T}\ \overline{f}}{\texttt{new }K(\overline{v}).f_i \to v_i} \qquad (\text{r-meth}) \frac{\mathit{mbody}(K.m\texttt{<}\overline{T}\texttt{>}) = \langle \overline{x}, e' \rangle}{\texttt{new }K(\overline{v}).m\texttt{<}\overline{T}\texttt{>}(\overline{w}) \to [\overline{w}/\overline{x}, \texttt{new }K(\overline{v})/\texttt{this}]e'}$$

$$(\text{r-cast}) \frac{\vdash K <: T}{(T)\texttt{new }K(\overline{v}) \to \texttt{new }K(\overline{v})}$$

(evaluation rules)

$$(\text{c-new}) \frac{e \to e'}{\texttt{new }K(\overline{v}, e, \overline{e}) \to \texttt{new }K(\overline{v}, e', \overline{e})} \qquad (\text{c-fld}) \frac{e \to e'}{e.f \to e'.f}$$

$$(\text{c-cast}) \frac{e \to e'}{(T)e \to (T)e'} \qquad (\text{c-meth-rcv}) \frac{e \to e'}{e.m\texttt{<}\overline{T}\texttt{>}(\overline{e}) \to e'.m\texttt{<}\overline{T}\texttt{>}(\overline{e})}$$

$$(\text{c-meth-arg}) \frac{e \to e'}{v.m\texttt{<}\overline{T}\texttt{>}(\overline{v}, e, \overline{e}) \to v.m\texttt{<}\overline{T}\texttt{>}(\overline{v}, e', \overline{e})}$$

Field lookup:

$$\frac{}{\mathit{fields}(\texttt{object}) = \{\}} \qquad \frac{\mathcal{D}(C) = \texttt{class }C\texttt{<}\ \overline{v}\ \overline{X}\texttt{>} : K \ \boxed{\texttt{where }\Delta} \ \{\ \overline{P_1}\ \overline{U_1}\ \overline{f_1};\ kd\ \overline{md}\} \quad \mathit{fields}([\overline{T/X}]K) = \overline{P_2}\ \overline{U_2}\ \overline{f_2}}{\mathit{fields}(C\texttt{<}\overline{T}\texttt{>}) = \overline{P_2}\ \overline{U_2}\ \overline{f_2}, \overline{P_1}\ [\overline{T/X}]\overline{U_1}\ \overline{f_1}}$$

Method lookup:

$$\frac{\mathcal{D}(C) = \texttt{class }C\texttt{<}\ \overline{v}\ \overline{X_1}\texttt{>} : K \ \boxed{\texttt{where }\Delta} \ \{\dots\ \overline{md}\} \quad m \text{ not defined public virtual in } \overline{md}}{\mathit{mtype}(C\texttt{<}\overline{T_1}\texttt{>}.m) = \mathit{mtype}([\overline{T_1/X_1}]K.m)}$$

$$\frac{\mathcal{D}(C) = \texttt{class }C\texttt{<}\overline{X_1}\texttt{>} : K \ \boxed{\texttt{where }\Delta_1} \ \{\dots\ \overline{md}\} \quad \texttt{public virtual } U\ m\texttt{<}\overline{X_2}\texttt{>}(\overline{U}\ \overline{x}) \ \boxed{\texttt{where }\Delta_2} \ \{\texttt{return }e;\} \in \overline{md}}{\mathit{mtype}(C\texttt{<}\overline{T_1}\texttt{>}.m) = [\overline{T_1/X_1}](\texttt{<}\overline{X_2}\ \boxed{\texttt{where }\Delta_2}\texttt{>}\overline{U} \to U)}$$

Method dispatch:

$$\frac{\mathcal{D}(C) = \texttt{class }C\texttt{<}\ \overline{v}\ \overline{X_1}\texttt{>} : K \ \boxed{\texttt{where }\Delta} \ \{\dots\ \overline{md}\} \quad m \text{ not defined in } \overline{md}}{\mathit{mbody}(C\texttt{<}\overline{T_1}\texttt{>}.m\texttt{<}\overline{T_2}\texttt{>}) = \mathit{mbody}([\overline{T_1/X_1}]K.m\texttt{<}\overline{T_2}\texttt{>})}$$

$$\frac{\mathcal{D}(C) = \texttt{class }C\texttt{<}\ \overline{v}\ \overline{X_1}\texttt{>} : K \ \boxed{\texttt{where }\Delta_1} \ \{\dots\ \overline{md}\} \quad Q\ U\ m\texttt{<}\overline{X_2}\texttt{>}(\overline{U}\ \overline{x}) \ \boxed{\texttt{where }\Delta_2} \ \{\texttt{return }e;\} \in \overline{md}}{\mathit{mbody}(C\texttt{<}\overline{T_1}\texttt{>}.m\texttt{<}\overline{T_2}\texttt{>}) = \langle \overline{x}, [\overline{T_1/X_1}, \overline{T_2/X_2}]e \rangle}$$

Fig. 8. Evaluation rules and helper definitions for C♯ minor with variance and constraints

dispatch, generic methods and classes, and runtime casts. Despite the lack of mutation, unrestricted use of variant type parameters leads to unsoundness:

```
class C<-X> { public readonly X x; public C(X x) { this.x = x; } }
// Interpret a Button as a string!
((C<string>) (new C<object>(new Button()))).x
```

For readers unfamiliar Featherweight GJ we summarize the language here.

Type variables X, types T, classes C, constructed types K, constraints $T <: U$, constraint lists Δ and indeed the declarative subtyping relation $\Delta \vdash T <: U$ are as in Section 3 and not re-defined here; object abbreviates object<>.

A **class definition** cd consists of a class name C with formal, variance-annotated type parameters $\overline{v}\,\overline{X}$, single base class (superclass) K, constraints Δ, constructor definition kd, typed instance fields $\overline{P}\ \overline{T}\ \overline{f}$ and methods $\overline{md}$. Method names in $\overline{md}$ must be distinct *i.e.* there is no support for overloading.

A **field qualifier** P is always public readonly, denoting a publicly accessible field that can be read, but not written, outside the constructor. Readonly fields behave covariantly.

A **method qualifier** Q is either public virtual, denoting a publicly-accessible method that can be inherited or overridden in subclasses, or public override, denoting a method that overrides a method of the same name and type signature in some superclass.

A **method definition** md consists of a method qualifier Q, a return type T, name m, formal type parameters $\overline{X}$, formal argument names $\overline{x}$ and types $\overline{T}$, constraints Δ and a body consisting of a single statement return e;. The constraint-free sugar $Q\ T\ m<\overline{X}>(\overline{T}\ \overline{x})$ {return e;} abbreviates a declaration with an empty where clause ($|\Delta| = 0$). By design, the typing rules only allow constraints to be placed on a *virtual* method definition: constraints are inherited, modulo base-class instantiation, by any overrides of this virtual method. Implicitly inheriting constraints matches $C^{\sharp}$'s implicit inheritance of bounds on type parameters. Note that if Δ contains a bound on a class type parameter, then it may become a general constraint between types in any overrides of this method (by virtue of base class specialization). This is why we accommodate arbitrary constraints, not just bounds, in constraint sets Δ.

A **constructor** kd initializes the fields of the class and its superclass.

An **expression** e can be a method parameter x, a field access $e.f$, the invocation of a virtual method at some type instantiation $e.m<\overline{T}>(\overline{e})$ or the creation of an object with initial field values new $K(\overline{e})$. A **value** v is a fully-evaluated expression, and (always) has the form new $K(\overline{v})$.

A **class table** $\mathcal{D}$ maps class names to class definitions. The distinguished class object is not listed in the table and is dealt with specially.

A typing environment Γ has the form $\Gamma = \overline{X}, \overline{x}{:}\overline{T}, \Delta$ where free type variables in $\overline{T}$ and Δ are drawn from $\overline{X}$. We write $\cdot$ to denote the empty environment. Judgment forms are as follows. The subtype judgment $\Gamma \vdash T <: U$ extracts Δ from Γ and defers to subtype judgment of Figure 2. To do this we define the predicates $C<\overline{v}\overline{X}>{:}\overline{K}$ of Section 3 to mean $|\overline{K}| = 0$ and $C<\overline{v}\overline{X}> \equiv$ object<> or $|\overline{K}| = 1$ and $\mathcal{D}(C) =$ class $C<\overline{v}\overline{X}> : K_1 \ldots$. The formation judgment

$\Gamma \vdash T$ ok states "in typing environment Γ, the type T is well-formed with respect to the class table, type variables and constraints declared in Γ". The typing judgment $\Gamma \vdash e : T$ states that "in the context of a typing environment Γ, the expression e has type T" with type variables in e and T drawn from Γ. The method well-formedness judgment $\vdash md$ ok in $C{<}\overline{X}{>}$ states that "method definition md is valid in class $C{<}\overline{X}{>}$." The class well-formedness judgment $\vdash cd$ ok states that "class definition cd is valid". The judgment $e \to e$ states that "(closed) expression e reduces, in one step, to (closed) expression e'." As usual, the reduction relation is defined by both primitive *reduction* rules and contextual *evaluation* rules.

All of the judgment forms and helper definitions of Figures 7 and 8 assume a class table $\mathcal{D}$. When we wish to be more explicit, we annotate judgments and helpers with $\mathcal{D}$. We say that $\mathcal{D}$ is a *valid* class table if $\vdash^{\mathcal{D}} cd$ ok for each class definition cd in $\mathcal{D}$ and the class hierarchy is a tree rooted at `object` (which we could easily formalise but do not).

The operation $mtype(T.m)$, given a statically known class $T \equiv C{<}\overline{T}{>}$ and method name m, looks up the generic signature of method m, by traversing the class hierarchy from C to find its virtual definition. The operation also computes the inherited constraints of m so it cannot simply return the syntactic signature of an intervening override but must examine its virtual definition.

The operation $mbody(T.m{<}\overline{T}{>})$, given a runtime class $T \equiv C{<}\overline{U}{>}$, method name m and method instantiation $\overline{T}$, walks the class hierarchy from C to find the most specific override of the virtual method, returning its instantiated body.

Now some comments on the differences in our rules. Rule (ty-meth) imposes an additional premise: the actual, instantiated constraints of the method signature (if any) must be derivable from the constraints in the context. In turn, rules (ok-virtual) and (ok-override) add the class constraints and any declared or inherited formal method constraints to the environment, before checking the method body: the body may assume the constraints hold, thus allowing more code to type-check. Note that we may apply subsumption, including subtyping through variance, to the receiver of a method call or field lookup: for safety, the run-time type or signature of the field or method must always be a subtype of this static type. To this end, rule (ok-class) restricts field types to be monotonic in the variance of class type parameters. Because the base class must be monotonic too, this property is preserved by the types of any inherited fields (it is easy to show that monotonicity is preserved by monotonic substitution). Rule (ok-virtual) on the other hand, requires the method constraints and argument types to be anti-monotonic in the variance of the class type parameters, but the return type to be monotonic.

Our type checking rules are not algorithmic in their current form. In particular, the rules do not give a strategy for proving subtyping judgments and the type checking rules for expressions are not syntax-directed because of rule (ty-sub). As a concession to producing an algorithm, rules (ok-virtual) and (ok-override) require that the declared constraints in Δ are *consistent*. This ensures that an algorithm will only have to cope with the bodies of methods that have consistent constraints. This does not rule out any useful programs: methods with inconsistent constraints are effectively dead, since the pre-conditions for calling them can never be established. However, imposing consistency means that subtype relations can be decided by appealing to our subtyping algorithm.

Nevertheless, our proof of Type Soundness does *not* rely on the notion of *consistency*. Type soundness holds even if we omit the consistency premises.

We now outline the proof (eliding standard lemmas like *Well-formedness*, *Weakening* and *Inversion*). The class table implicit in all results is assumed to be valid.

We prove the usual type and term substitution properties that follow, but a key lemma for our system is Lemma 11, that lets us discharge proven hypothetical constraints from various judgment forms (a similar lemma appears in [10], but for equations).

Lemma 9 (Substitution Property for Lookup).

– If $\mathit{fields}(K) = \overline{P}\,\overline{T}\,\overline{f}$ then $\mathit{fields}([\overline{U}/\overline{Y}]K) = \overline{P}\,[\overline{U}/\overline{Y}]\overline{T}\,\overline{f}$.
– $\mathit{mtype}(K.m) = \texttt{<}\overline{X}$ where $\Delta\texttt{>}\overline{T} \to T$ *implies*
  $\mathit{mtype}(([\overline{U}/\overline{Y}]K).m) = [\overline{U}/\overline{Y}](\texttt{<}\overline{X}$ where $\Delta\texttt{>}\overline{T} \to T)$.
– $\mathit{mtype}(K.m)$ *is undefined then* $\mathit{mtype}(([\overline{U}/\overline{Y}]K).m)$ *is undefined.*

Lemma 10 (Substitution for types). *Let* $\mathcal{J}$ *range over the judgment forms of subtyping* $(T\texttt{<:}U)$, *type well-formedness* $(T\ ok)$ *and typing* $(e : T)$:
If $\overline{X}, \overline{Y}, \overline{x}{:}\overline{T}, \Delta \vdash \mathcal{J}$ *and* $\overline{Y} \vdash \overline{U}$ *ok then* $\overline{Y}, \overline{x}{:}[\overline{U}/\overline{X}]\overline{T}, [\overline{U}/\overline{X}]\Delta \vdash [\overline{U}/\overline{X}]\mathcal{J}$.

Proof. Straightforward induction on the derivation of $\mathcal{J}$, using Lemma 9.   □

Lemma 11 (Constraint Elimination). *Let* $\mathcal{J}$ *range over the judgment forms of subtyping* $(T\texttt{<:}U)$, *type well-formedness* $(T\ ok)$ *and typing* $(e : T)$:
If $\Gamma, \Delta \vdash \mathcal{J}$ *and* $\Gamma \vdash \Delta$ *then* $\Gamma \vdash \mathcal{J}$.

Proof. Induction on the derivation of $\mathcal{J}$.   □

Lemma 12 (Substitution for terms). *If* $\Gamma, \overline{x}{:}\overline{T} \vdash e : T$ *and* $\Gamma \vdash \overline{v} : \overline{T}$ *then* $\Gamma \vdash [\overline{v}/\overline{x}]e : T$.

Proof. By induction on the typing derivation.   □

To prove Preservation we also need the following properties of (ground) subtyping. The first two lemmas tell us that the types of members are preserved by subtyping, but only up to subtyping, since fields and method signatures behave covariantly (subtyping on method signatures may be defined in the usual contra-co fashion, treating constraints contra-variantly). The proofs of these lemmas rely on the monotonicity restrictions on base classes, fields and method signatures enforced by rules (ok-class) and (ok-virtual): these, in turn, justify appeals to Lemma 3 in the proofs.

Lemma 13 (Field Preservation). *If* $\cdot \vdash T, U$ *ok and* $\cdot \vdash T \texttt{<:} U$, *then* $\mathit{fields}(U) = \overline{P}\,\overline{U}\,\overline{g}$ *and* $\mathit{fields}(T) = \overline{P}\,\overline{T}\,\overline{f}$ *implies* $\cdot \vdash T_i \texttt{<:} U_i$ *and* $f_i = g_i$ *for all* $i \leq |\overline{g}|$.

Lemma 14 (Signature Preservation).
If $\cdot \vdash T, U$ ok and $\cdot \vdash T <: U$ then $mtype(U.m) = \texttt{<}\overline{X}$ where $\Delta_1\texttt{>}\overline{V}_1 \to V_1$ implies $mtype(T.m) = \texttt{<}\overline{X}$ where $\Delta_2\texttt{>}\overline{V}_2 \to V_2$ where $\Delta_1 \vdash \Delta_2$ and $\cdot \vdash \overline{V}_1 <: \overline{V}_2$ and $\cdot \vdash V_2 <: V_1$.

Lemma 15 (Soundness for Dispatch). *If $mbody(T.m\texttt{<}\overline{T}\texttt{>}) = \langle \overline{x}, e \rangle$ then, provided $\cdot \vdash T, \overline{T}$ ok and $mtype(T.m) = \texttt{<}\overline{X}$ where $\Delta\texttt{>}\overline{U} \to U$ and $\cdot \vdash [\overline{T}/\overline{X}]\Delta$, there must be some type V such that $\cdot \vdash V$ ok, $\cdot \vdash T <: V$ and $\overline{x}{:}[\overline{T}/\overline{X}]\overline{U}, \texttt{this}{:}V \vdash e : [\overline{T}/\overline{X}]U$.*

Proof. By induction on the relation $mbody(T.m\texttt{<}\overline{T}\texttt{>}) = \langle \overline{x}, e \rangle$ using Substitution Lemmas 10 and 9 and Lemma 11. □

Theorem 4 (Preservation). *If $\cdot \vdash e : T$ then $e \to e'$ implies $\cdot \vdash e' : T$.*

Proof. By induction on the reduction relation using Lemmas 12–15. □

The proof of Progress relies on Lemma 16. The lemma guarantees the presence of a dynamically resolved field or method body, given the existence of a member of the same name in a statically known superclass.

Lemma 16 (Runtime Lookup). *If $\cdot \vdash T, U$ ok and $\cdot \vdash T <: U$ then*

- *$fields(U) = \overline{P}\ \overline{U}\ \overline{g}$ implies $fields(T) = \overline{P}\ \overline{T}\ \overline{f}$, for some $\overline{T}, \overline{f}$, with $\cdot \vdash T_i <: U_i$ and $f_i = g_i$ for all $i \le |\overline{g}|$.*
- *$mtype(U.m) = \texttt{<}\overline{X}$ where $\Delta\texttt{>}\overline{V} \to V$ implies $mbody(T.m\texttt{<}\overline{T}\texttt{>}) = \langle \overline{x}, e \rangle$ for some $\overline{x}, e$ with $|\overline{x}| = |\overline{V}|$.*

To state the Progress Theorem in the presence of casts, as for FGJ, we first characterize the implicit *evaluation contexts*, $\mathcal{E}$, defined by the evaluation rules:

$$\mathcal{E} ::= [] \mid \texttt{new } K(\overline{v}, \mathcal{E}, \overline{e}) \mid \mathcal{E}.f \mid \mathcal{E}.m\texttt{<}\overline{T}\texttt{>}(\overline{e}) \mid v.m\texttt{<}\overline{T}\texttt{>}(\overline{v}, \mathcal{E}, \overline{e}) \mid (T)\mathcal{E}$$

We define $\mathcal{E}[e]$ to be the obvious expression obtained by replacing the unique hole $[]$ in $\mathcal{E}$ with e.

Theorem 5 (Progress). *If $\cdot \vdash e : T$ then:*

- *$e = v$ for some value v (e is fully evaluated), or*
- *$e \to e'$ for some e' (e can make progress), or*
- *$e = \mathcal{E}[(U)\texttt{new } K(\overline{v})]$, for some evaluation context $\mathcal{E}$, types U and K and values $\overline{v}$ where $\not\vdash K <: U$ (e is stuck, but only at the evaluation of a failed cast).*

Proof. By (strong) induction on the typing relation, applying Lemma 16. □

Theorem 6 (Type Soundness). *Define $e \to^\star e'$ to be the reflexive, transitive closure of $e \to e'$. If $\cdot \vdash e : T$, $e \to^\star e'$ with e' a normal form, then either e' is a value with $\cdot \vdash e' : T$, or a stuck expression of the form $\mathcal{E}[(U)\texttt{new } K(\overline{v})]$ where $\not\vdash K <: U$.*

Proof. An easy induction over $e \to^\star e'$ using Theorems 5 and 4. □

5   Conclusion

We have described and formalized a significant generalization of the $C^\sharp$ generics design. Generalized constraints, in particular, are useful in their own right, and easy to understand. In a sense, they are simply a lifting of a restriction imposed in both Java and $C^\sharp$: that the type on the left of a class constraint must be a class type parameter, and that the type on the left of a method constraint must be a method type parameter.

The practicality of definition-site variance is less clear, bearing in mind the refactoring of libraries that is necessary to make good use of the feature. The experience of Scala users will be valuable, as Scala adopts a very similar design for variant types.

For future work, we would like to develop an algorithm for – or prove undecidable – the extension of subtyping to infinitary inheritance. These results would transfer almost directly to variant subtyping in Viroli and Igarashi's system [8] and to wildcards in Java, which have similar inheritance and variance behaviour.

Our formalization could be extended to support interfaces, and perhaps also mutable fields in objects. Finally, we are studying the generalization of our previous work on type-preserving translations from variants of System F into $C^\sharp$, providing some handle on the expressivity of the extensions. It does not seem possible to translate Full $F_{<:}$, for which subtyping is undecidable [13]. Neither is it possible to translate Kernel $F_{<:}$. But a third variant, called $F_{<:}^\top$ [3], can be translated into $C^\sharp$ with variance and upper bounds.

The first author has completed a prototype implementation of variant interfaces, variant delegates, and generalized constraints. We hope to release this as a 'diff' to the shared source release of $C^\sharp$ 2.0.

References

1. P. America and F. van der Linden.   A parallel object-oriented language with inheritance and subtyping. In *Proceedings of the ACM SIGPLAN Conference on Object-Oriented Programming, Systems, Languages and Applications/European Conference on Object-Oriented Programming (OOPSLA/ECOOP'90)*, pages 161–168. ACM Press, 1990.
2. R. Cartwright and G. L. Steele. Compatible genericity with run-time types for the Java programming language. In *Object-Oriented Programming: Systems, Languages, Applications (OOPSLA)*, Vancouver, October 1998. ACM.
3. G. Castagna and B. Pierce. Decidable bounded quantification. In *Proceedings of the Twenty-First ACM SIGPLAN–SIGACT Symposium on Principles of Programming Languages (POPL), Portland, Oregon*. ACM, Jan. 1994.
4. ECMA International.   ECMA Standard 335: Common Language Infrastructure, 3rd edition, June 2005. Available at
   http://www.ecma-international.org/publications/standards/Ecma-335.htm.
5. N. G. Fruja. Type Safety of Generics for the .NET Common Language Runtime. In P. Sestoft, editor, *European Symposium on Programming*, pages 325–341. Springer-Verlag, Lecture Notes in Computer Science 3924, 2006.

6. A. Hejlsberg, S. Wiltamuth, and P. Golde. C# version 2.0 specification, 2005. See
http://msdn.microsoft.com/vcsharp/team/language/default.aspx.

7. A. Igarashi, B. C. Pierce, and P. Wadler. Featherweight Java: a minimal core
calculus for Java and GJ. *ACM Trans. Program. Lang. Syst.*, 23(3):396–450, 2001.

8. A. Igarashi and M. Viroli. Variant parametric types: A flexible subtyping scheme for
generics. *ACM Transactions on Programming Languages and Systems (TOPLAS)*,
2006. To appear.

9. A. Kennedy and D. Syme. Transposing F to C♯: Expressivity of parametric polymorphism in an object-oriented language. *Concurrency and Computation: Practice
and Experience*, 16:707–733, 2004.

10. A. J. Kennedy and C. V. Russo. Generalized algebraic data types and object-
oriented programming. In *Object-Oriented Programming: Systems, Languages, Applications (OOPSLA)*, San Diego, October 2005. ACM.

11. M. Odersky, P. Altherr, V. Cremet, B. Emir, S. Micheloud, N. Mihaylov, M. Schinz,
E. Stenman, and M. Zenger. The Scala language specification, 2005. Available from
http://scala.epfl.ch/.

12. M. Odersky and M. Zenger. Scalable component abstractions. In *Object-Oriented
Programming: Systems, Languages, Applications (OOPSLA)*. ACM, 2005.

13. B. C. Pierce. Bounded quantification is undecidable. *Information and Computation*, 112(1):131–165, July 1994.

14. F. Pottier. Simplifying subtyping constraints: a theory. *Information and Computation*, 170(2):153–183, Nov. 2001.

15. P. Sestoft and H. I. Hansen. *C# Precisely.* MIT Press, October 2004.

16. M. Torgersen, E. Ernst, and C. P. Hansen. Wild FJ. In *Workshop on Foundations
of Object-Oriented Languages (FOOL)*, January 2005.

17. V. Trifonov and S. Smith. Subtyping constrained types. In *Static Analysis Symposium (SAS)*, volume 1145 of *Lecture Notes in Computer Science*, pages 349–365.
Springer Verlag, Sept. 1996.

18. M. Viroli and A. Natali. Parametric polymorphism in Java through the homogeneous translation LM: Gathering type descriptors at load-time. Technical Report
DEIS-LIA-00-001, Università degli Studi di Bologna, April 2000.

A Semantic Analysis of C++ Templates[*]

Jeremy Siek and Walid Taha

Rice University,
Houston, TX 77005, USA
Jeremy.G.Siek@rice.edu, taha@rice.edu

Abstract. Templates are a powerful but poorly understood feature of
the C++ language. Their *syntax* resembles the parameterized classes of
other languages (e.g., of Java). But because C++ supports template specialization, their *semantics* is quite different from that of parameterized
classes. Template specialization provides a Turing-complete sub-language
within C++ that executes at compile-time. Programmers put this power
to many uses. For example, templates are a popular tool for writing
program generators.

The C++ Standard defines the semantics of templates using natural
language, so it is prone to misinterpretation. The meta-theoretic properties of C++ templates have not been studied, so the semantics of templates has not been systematically checked for errors. In this paper we
present the first formal account of C++ templates including some of the
more complex aspects, such as template partial specialization. We validate our semantics by proving type safety and verify the proof with the
Isabelle proof assistant. Our formalization reveals two interesting issues
in the C++ Standard: the first is a problem with member instantiation
and the second concerns the generation of unnecessary template specializations.

1 Introduction

We start with a review of C++ templates, demonstrating their use with some basic
examples. We then review more advanced uses of templates to perform compile-
time computations and to write program generators. We give an overview of the
technical contributions of this paper at the end of this section.

The following definition is an example of a *class template* that defines a container parameterized on the element type T and length n.

```
template<class T, int n>
class buffer {
  T data[n];
public:
  void set(int i, T v) { data[i] = v; }
  T get(int i) { return data[i]; }
};
```

---

[*] This work was supported by NSF ITR-0113569 Putting Multi-Stage Annotations
to Work, Texas ATP 003604-0032-2003 Advanced Languages Techniques for Device
Drivers, and NSF SOD-0439017 Synthesizing Device Drivers.

D. Thomas (Ed.): ECOOP 2006, LNCS 4067, pp. 304–327, 2006.
© Springer-Verlag Berlin Heidelberg 2006

A *template specialization* provides an alternate implementation of a template for concrete template arguments. For example, the above template is not space-efficient when T=**bool** because a **bool** may be larger than a single bit in C++. The following specialization for element type **bool** uses a compressed representation, dedicating a single bit for each element.

```
template<int n>
class buffer<bool, n> {
    int data[(n + BITS_PER_WORD − 1)/BITS_PER_WORD];
public:
    void set(int i, bool v) { /* complicated bit masking */ }
    T get(int i) { /* complicated bit masking */ }
};
```

The above definition is called a *partial template specialization* because there is still a template parameter left. We refer to <**bool**,n> as the *specialization pattern*. The following is an example of a *full specialization*:

```
template<>
class buffer<bool, 0> {
public:
    void set(int i, bool v) { throw out_of_range(); }
    T get(int i) { throw out_of_range(); }
};
```

When a template is used, C++ performs *pattern matching* between the template arguments and the specialization patterns to determine which specialization to use, or whether a specialization needs to be generated from a class template or a partial specialization. Consider the following program that defines three objects.

```
int main() {
    buffer<int,3> buf1;
    buffer<bool,3> buf2;
    buffer<bool,0> buf3;
}
```

The type buffer<**int**,3> matches neither of the specializations for buffer, so C++ will generate a specialization from the original buffer template by substituting **int** for T and 3 for n. This automatic generation is called *implicit instantiation*. The resulting template specialization is shown below.

```
template<>
class buffer<int,3> {
    int data[3];
public:
    void set(int i, int v);
    int get(int i);
};
```

Note that definitions (implementations) of the members set and get were not generated. Only the declarations of the members were generated. The definition of a member is generated only if a call to the member appears in the program. So, for example, the following code

```
buf1.get(2);
```

causes C++ to generate a member definition for buffer<int,3>::get.

```
template<>
int buffer<int,3>::get(int i) { return data[i]; }
```

The above is an example of a member defined separately from a class.

Going back to the second line of the main function, consider the use of type buffer<bool,3>. This matches the partial specialization buffer<bool,n> but not the full specialization buffer<bool,0>, so C++ will generate a specialization from the partial specialization buffer<bool,n>.

In the third line of main, the type buffer<bool,0> type matches the full specialization of buffer, so C++ does not need to generate a specialization.

1.1   Compile-Time Programming with Templates

The buffer<bool,n> specialization contains a small compile-time computation for the length of the data array:

```
int data[(n + BITS_PER_WORD − 1)/BITS_PER_WORD];
```

The ability to pass values as template parameters and to evaluate expressions at compile time provides considerable computational power. For example, the following power template computes the exponent x^n at compile-time.

```
template<int x, int n> struct power {
   static const int r = x ∗ power<x, n − 1>::r;
};
template<int x> struct power<x, 0> {
   static const int r = 1;
};
int array[power<3, 2>::r];
```

The static keyword means the member is associated with the class and not with each object. The const keyword means the member is immutable.

There are limitations, however, to what kinds of expressions C++ will evaluated at compile time: only arithmetic expressions on built-in integer-like types. There are similar restrictions on the kinds of values that may be passed as template parameters. For example, a list value can not be passed as a template parameter. Fortunately, it is possible to encode data structures as types, and types can be passed as template parameters. The following creates a type encoding for cons-lists.

```
template<class Head, class Tail> struct Cons { };
struct Nil { };
typedef Cons< int, Cons< float, Nil > > list_of_types;
```

In general, templates can be used to mimic algebraic datatypes [5], such as those found in SML [10] and Haskell [1]. Furthermore, templates are "open ended" so they can mimic the extensible variants of Objective Caml [9].

This paper omits value template parameters and compile-time expressions because they are technically redundant: we can encode computations on integer-like values as computations on types. For example, the following types encode natural numbers.

```
template<class T> struct succ { };
struct zero { };
typedef succ<zero> one;
typedef succ< succ<zero> > two;
```

The following is the power template reformulated for types. The definition of mult is left as an exercise for the reader.[1]

```
template<class x, class n> struct power { };

template<class x, class p> struct power<x, succ<p> > {
  typedef mult<x, power<x, p>::r>::r r;
};
template<class x> struct power<x, zero> {
  typedef one r;
};
```

1.2 Metaprogramming with Templates

The combination of templates and member functions enables compile-time program generation in C++, often referred to as *template metaprogramming* [3, 4, 19]. Member functions can be used to represent run-time program fragments while templates provide the ability to compose and select fragments. We revisit the power example, but this time as a staged metaprogram that takes n as a compile-time parameter and generates a program with a run-time parameter x.

```
template<class n> struct power { };

template<class p>
struct power< succ<p> > {
  static int f(int x){ return x * power<p>::f(x); }
};
template<> struct power<zero> {
  static int f(int x) { return 1; }
};
int main(int argc, char* argv[]) {
  return power<two>::f(atoi(argv[1])); // command-line input
}
```

---

[1] A C++ expert will notice missing **typename** keywords in our examples. We do this intentionally to avoid confusing readers unfamiliar with C++ and its syntactic clutter.

The bodies of functions, such as in main and f, contain run-time code. Type expressions, such as power<two> and power<p> represent escapes from the run-time code back into the compile-time level. The power metaprogram is recursive but the generated program is not. The generated program has a static call tree of height 3. An optimizing C++ compiler is likely to simplify the generated program to the following:

```
int main(int argc, char* argv[]) {
    int x = atoi(argv[1]);
    return x * x;
}
```

Such optimization is not required by the C++ Standard. However, if the compiler performs inlining, it must preserve the call-by-value semantics. We might label function f with the **inline** keyword, but this is only a suggestion to the compiler. The performance of the generated programs is therefore brittle and non-portable. Compilers rarely publicize the details of their inlining algorithm, and the algorithms are heuristic in nature and hard to predict. Furthermore, the inlining algorithm can vary dramatically from one compiler to the next. See [7] for an alternative approach based on macros that guarantees inlining.

The subset of C++ we study in the paper includes just enough features to exhibit both the compile time and run time computations needed to write template metaprograms.

1.3   Contributions

We present the first formal account of C++ templates. We identify a small subset of C++ called C++.T and give a semantics to C++.T by defining:

1. template lookup (Section 2.2)
2. type evaluation (Section 2.3),
3. expression evaluation and well-typed expressions (Section 3), and
4. template instantiation (Section 4).

C++.T includes the partial specialization feature of C++, so template lookup is nontrivial. To maintain a clear focus, C++.T does not include features of C++ that are orthogonal to templates, such as statements, imperative assignment, and object-oriented features such as inheritance.

A C++.T program is "valid" if and only if the template instantiation process terminates without error. This definition is unusual because some potentially non-terminating evaluation (type evaluation) is performed as part of determining whether a program is "valid". In particular, this means that determining validity is undecidable. We show that C++.T is type safe in the sense that if template instantiation succeeds, run-time execution of the program will not encounter type errors (Theorem 1, Section 4.3). We wrote the proof in the Isar proof language [11, 21] and mechanically verified the proof using the Isabelle proof assistant [12]. Due to space considerations, we do not present the Isar proof in this paper but refer the reader to the accompanying technical report [17].

Formalizing C++.T revealed two issues with the C++ Standard:

1. The Standard's rule for member instantiation requires the point of instantiation to come too soon, possibly before the definition of the member. In our semantics we delay member instantiation to the end of the program, which corresponds to the current practice of the GNU and Edison Design Group C++ compilers.
2. The template instantiation process converts a program into an expanded program with more template specializations. The Standard requires the generation of a template specialization whenever a member is accessed. However, if such a specialization is only needed temporarily, the compiler should be allowed to omit the specialization from the resulting program, analogously to the way procedure activation frames are discarded when a function returns, thereby improving the space-complexity for template programs.

1.4   Overview of the Formalization

C++.T contains syntactic categories for types, expressions (or terms), and definitions. A program is a sequence of definitions. The semantics of C++.T includes compile-time and run-time components. The main semantic definitions for the compile-time aspects of C++.T are:

Type evaluation. We define a big step evaluation function that reduces type expressions to simpler type expressions in §2.3.
Well-formed types. We define when a type expression is valid in §2.4.
Type evaluation in expressions. Types may occur within expressions, so we define how type evaluation is performed within expressions in §3.
Well-typed expressions. We define type checking for C++.T expressions in §3.
Program instantiation. The instantiation process expands a program by generating the necessary template specializations and member function specializations. Program instantiation is defined in §4. A **valid** C++.T program is one in which program instantiation completes successfully.

The run-time aspect of C++.T consists of one definition: expression evaluation, which we cover in §3. Fig. 1 shows the dependencies between the semantic definitions for C++.T.

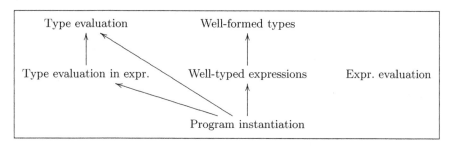

Fig. 1. Semantic definitions and their dependencies

The main technical result is that valid programs are type safe. That is, if a program successfully instantiates, then the run-time evaluation will result in a value of the appropriate type, provided that evaluation terminates. The type safety theorem is proved in Section 4. The lemmas and definitions in the following sections lead up to this result.

2   Types and Templates

The syntax of types and templates is defined by the following grammar. We use an abstract syntax for the sake of conciseness and readability for those unfamiliar with C++ template syntax.

Abstract syntax of types and templates $\tau \in \mathbb{T}$ $\qquad \mathcal{T}$

$$
\begin{array}{lll}
\text{Type variables} & \alpha \in \mathsf{TyVar} \\
\text{Template names} & t \in \mathsf{TmName} \\
\text{Member names} & m, f, a \in \mathsf{MemName} \\[2mm]
\text{Type expressions} & \tau \in \mathbb{T} ::= \alpha \mid \tau.a \mid t\langle \tau..\tau \rangle \mid \tau \to \tau \mid \mathtt{int} \\
\text{Member kind} & \kappa \in \mathcal{K} ::= \mathtt{fun} \mid \mathtt{type} \\
\text{Templates} & \mathcal{T} ::= t\langle \pi..\pi \rangle \{m : \kappa\ \tau\} \\[2mm]
\text{Type patterns} & \pi \in \Pi ::= \alpha \mid t\langle \pi..\pi \rangle \mid \pi \to \pi \mid \mathtt{int} \\
\text{Residual types} & r \in \mathbb{R} ::= t\langle r..r \rangle \mid r \to r \mid \mathtt{int}
\end{array}
$$

A type in C++.T can be a type variable α, member access $\tau.a$, template identifier $t\langle \tau_1..\tau_2 \rangle$, function type $\tau_1 \to \tau_2$, or $\mathtt{int}$. There are no variable binders in $\mathbb{T}$ so the set of free type variables (FTV) of a type is simply the type variables occurring in the type. A type is **closed** if it contains no type variables. We pick out two subsets of $\mathbb{T}$: type patterns Π and residual types $\mathbb{R}$. Type patterns do not include member access types. Residual types are restricted to template identifiers, functions, and $\mathtt{int}$. When applied to closed types, type evaluation produces residual types.

Member access $\tau.a$ refers to a type definition for a within the template specialization identified by τ. In the concrete syntax of C++, type member access is written $\tau::a$. A template identifier $t\langle \tau_1..\tau_n \rangle$ refers to the specialization of template t for the type arguments $\tau_1..\tau_n$. A function type $\tau_1 \to \tau_2$ corresponds to the C++ syntax $\tau_2(*)(\tau_1)$.

The abstract syntax $t\langle \pi_1..\pi_n \rangle \{m : \kappa\ \tau\}$ is used for both class templates and class template specializations, where t is the name of the template and $\langle \pi_1..\pi_n \rangle$ is the specialization pattern. The body contains the declaration of a single member $m : \kappa\ \tau$, where m is the name, κ is the kind, and τ is its type. When all of the patterns $\pi_1..\pi_n$ are variables, the declaration is a class template, such as $t\langle \alpha_1..\alpha_n \rangle \{m : \kappa\ \tau\}$. When the patterns contain no type variables, then the declaration is a full specialization of a class template, such as $t\langle\tau_1..\tau_n\rangle\{m:\kappa\ \tau\}$ where $FTV(t\langle\tau_1..\tau_n\rangle) = \emptyset$. Everything in between corresponds to partial specializations of class templates. When referring to things of the general form $t\langle\tau_1..\tau_n\rangle\{m:\kappa\ \tau\}$ we will use the term "template" even though we ought to say "template or specialization".

We restrict templates to contain just a single member to reduce clutter in the semantics. Expressiveness is not lost because a template with multiple members can always be expressed using multiple templates. In the following example, we split template A into two templates A1 and A2 and change the use of x to A1<T>::x.

```
template<class T>
struct A {
  typedef T x;
  typedef foo<x> y;
};
```

$\Longrightarrow$

```
template<class T>
struct A1 {
  typedef T x;
};
template<class T>
struct A2 {
  typedef foo<A1<T>::x> y;
};
```

A type member is written m : type τ and is equivalent to the C++ syntax typedef τ m;. A member function declaration is written f : fun $\tau_1 \rightarrow \tau_2$ and is equivalent to the C++ syntax static τ_2 $f(\tau_1)$;. The implementation of a member function is written separately and the syntax for that is introduced in Section 3.

2.1   Type Substitution

A *substitution* S is a function mapping type variables to types that acts like the identity function on most of its domain except for a finite number of elements. A *renaming* is an injective substitution whose codomain is restricted to type variables. We use renaming to define α-equivalence for types and the injective property is needed to disallow mapping distinct variables to the same variable. We extend substitution to types with the following definition.

Simultaneous substitution on types. $S(\tau) \in \mathbb{T}$

$$S(\alpha) = S\ \alpha$$
$$S(\tau_1 \rightarrow \tau_2) = S(\tau_1) \rightarrow S(\tau_2)$$
$$S(t\langle\tau_1..\tau_n\rangle) = t\langle S(\tau_1)..S(\tau_n)\rangle$$
$$S(\tau.a) = S(\tau).a$$
$$S(\texttt{int}) = \texttt{int}$$

The case $S(\alpha) = S\ \alpha$ in the definition of substitution on types is not a circular definition. We are given a function S on type variables and we are building a function, also called S, on type expressions.

Proposition 1. $FTV(S(\tau)) = \bigcup_{\alpha \in FTV(\tau)} FTV(S(\alpha))$

Proof. By induction on the structure of τ.

2.2 Template Lookup, Matching, and Ordering

As mentioned in Section 1, template lookup is non-trivial because C++ supports partial specialization. The use of a template resolves to the most specialized template that matches the given template arguments, according to Section [14.5.4.1 p1] of the C++ Standard. So our goal is to define "most specific" and "matches".

Template arguments are matched against the specialization pattern of candidate templates. In the C++ Standard, the matching is called *template argument deduction* (see Section [14.8.2.4 p1] of the Standard). The following defines matching.

Definition 1. *A type τ_1 **matches** a type τ_2 iff there exists a substitution S such that $S(\tau_2) = \tau_1$.*

To define "most specialized" we first need to define the "at least as specialized" relation on types. This relation is defined in terms of matching. (See Sections [14.5.4.2 p1] and [14.5.5.2 p2-5] of the C++ Standard.)

Definition 2. *If τ_1 matches τ_2, then we write $\tau_2 \leq \tau_1$ and say that τ_1 is **at least as specialized as** τ_2.*

The $\leq$ relation is a quasi-order, i.e., it is reflexive and transitive. If we identify type patterns up to renaming type variables then we have antisymmetry and the $\leq$ relation is a partial order.

Proposition 2. *If $\tau_1 \leq \tau_2$ and $\tau_2 \leq \tau_1$ then there exists a renaming S such that $S(\tau_2) = \tau_1$.*

We use the notation $\doteq$ for type pattern equivalence and use it to define a notion of duplicate template definitions. The symbol $\triangleq$ means "is defined to be".

Definition 3.

- $\pi_1 \doteq \pi_2 \triangleq \pi_1 \leq \pi_2$ *and* $\pi_2 \leq \pi_1$.
- *Template* $\pi_1\{m_1 : \kappa_1 \; \tau_1'\}$ *and template* $\pi_2\{m_2 : \kappa_2 \; \tau_2'\}$ *are **duplicates** if* $\pi_1 \doteq \pi_2$.
- *There **are no duplicates in** T if no two templates in T are duplicates of one another.*

We extend the relation $\leq$ to templates as follows:

Definition 4. $\pi_1\{m_1 : \kappa_1 \; \tau_1\} \leq \pi_2\{m_2 : \kappa_2 \; \tau_2\} \triangleq \pi_1 \leq \pi_2$

This extension is a partial order on the set of template definitions in a valid C++.T program because we do not allow duplicate templates (duplicates would cause antisymmetry to fail).

Definition 5. *Given a set of template definitions T and the ordering $\leq$, the* ***most specific template***, *if it exists, is the greatest element of T, written* $\max T$.

We define the following *lookup* function to capture the rule that the use of a template resolves to the most specific template that matches the given template arguments.

$$lookup : \mathsf{Set}\ \mathcal{T} \times \mathbb{T} \to \mathcal{T}_\perp$$

$$lookup(T, \tau) \triangleq \begin{cases} \lfloor \max\{\pi\{m : \kappa\ \tau\} \in T \mid \pi \leq \tau\} \rfloor & \text{if the max exists} \\ \perp & \text{otherwise} \end{cases}$$

The *inst* function maps a set of templates and a type to the template specialization obtained by instantiating the best matching template from a set of templates. The condition that $S(\pi) = \tau$ fully determines the action of S on free variables in π, and because the free variables in τ' are required to be a subset of those in π, the type $S(\tau')$ is unique.

$$inst : \mathsf{Set}\ \mathcal{T} \times \mathbb{T} \to \mathcal{T}_\perp$$

$$inst(T, \tau) \triangleq \begin{cases} \lfloor \tau\{m : \kappa\ S(\tau')\} \rfloor & \text{where } lookup(T, \tau) = \lfloor \pi\{m : \kappa\ \tau'\} \rfloor \\ & \text{and } S(\pi) = \tau \\ \perp & \text{otherwise} \end{cases}$$

The following *lookupmem* function maps a set of templates, a type, and a member name to a type.

$$lookupmem : \mathsf{Set}\ \mathcal{T} \times \mathbb{T} \times \mathsf{MemName} \to (\mathcal{K} \times \mathbb{T})_\perp$$

$$lookupmem(T, \tau, m) \triangleq \begin{cases} \lfloor (\kappa, \tau') \rfloor & inst(T, \tau) = \lfloor \tau\{m : \kappa\ \tau'\} \rfloor \\ \perp & \text{otherwise} \end{cases}$$

Next we show that member lookup produces closed types. For this lemma we need to define the free type variables of a set of template definitions.

Definition 6. $FTV(T) \triangleq \{\alpha \mid \pi\{m : \kappa\ \tau\} \in T \wedge \alpha \in FTV(\tau) - FTV(\pi)\}$

Lemma 1. *(Member lookup produces closed types.) If* $lookupmem(T, \tau, m) = \lfloor (\kappa, \tau') \rfloor$ *and* $FTV(\tau) = \emptyset$ *and* $FTV(T) = \emptyset$ *then* $FTV(\tau') = \emptyset$

Proof. A straightforward use of Proposition 1.

2.3 Type Evaluation

The rules for type evaluation are complicated by the need to evaluate types underneath type variable binders. In the following example, the type `A<A<int>::u>` is underneath the binder for `T` but it must be evaluated to `A<float>`.

```
template<class T>                        template<class T>
struct A {                               struct A {
  typedef float u;                         typedef float u;
};                                       };
template<class T>           ⟹            template<class T>
struct B {                               struct B {
  static int foo(A<A<int>::u> x)           static int foo(A<float> x)
    { return x; }                            { return x; }
};                                       };
```

The need for evaluation under variable binders is driven by the rules for determining the point of instantiation for a template. Section [14.6.4.1 p3] of the C++ Standard [8] says that the point of instantiation for a specialization precedes the first declaration that contains a use of the specialization in an instantiation context, unless the enclosing declaration is a template and the use is dependent on the template parameters. Otherwise the point of instantiation is immediately before the point of instantiation for the enclosing template. In the above example, the type A<A<int>::u> is in an instantiation context and does not depend on the template parameter T. So we need to instantiate A<A<int>::u>, but we must first reduce it to A<float> to check whether the type was already instantiated.

The type evaluation judgment has the form $T; P \vdash \tau \Downarrow \tau'$ where T is the set of in-scope template definitions and P is the set of in-scope type parameters. Type evaluation reduces type τ to τ'. The type evaluation rules do not include error handling cases because it is not important for us to distinguish between errors and non-termination of type evaluation. A C++.T program is invalid if the instantiation process does not terminate.

The evaluation rules for type expressions are defined in Fig. 2. The rule (C-VART) says a type variable α evaluates to itself provided α is in scope. The rule (C-MEMT1) that defines type member access $\tau.a$ is reminicent of a function call. First evaluate τ. If the result is of the form $t\langle \tau_1..\tau_n \rangle$ and has no free variables, lookup the type definition τ' for member a. The lookup function takes care of substituting the type arguments $\tau_1..\tau_n$ for template parameters. The member type is evaluated to τ'' and that is the result. An alternative design of the rules would be to perform the lookup and substitution whenever a template identifier such as $t\langle \tau_1..\tau_n \rangle$ is evaluated. We choose to delay the lookup and instantiation to the last possible moment to better reflect the on-demand nature of C++ instantiation.

Rule (C-MEMT2) handles the case when the τ in $\tau.a$ evaluates to a type τ' with free variables. In this case the result is just $\tau'.a$. The rest of the rules are straightforward; they simply evaluate the nested types and put the type back together.

Several of the type evaluation rules test if a type contains free variables, which is not a constant-time operation. However, an implementation of type evaluation could keep track of whether types contain any free variables by returning a boolean value in addition to the resulting type.

The *names* function returns the set of template names from a set of templates.

$$names(T) \triangleq \{t \mid t\langle \pi_1..\pi_n \rangle \{m : \kappa \; \tau\} \in T\}$$

$$T; P \vdash \tau \Downarrow \tau$$

(C-VART)
$$\frac{\alpha \in P}{T; P \vdash \alpha \Downarrow \alpha}$$

(C-MEMT1)
$$\frac{\begin{array}{cc} T; P \vdash \tau \Downarrow_n t\langle \tau_1..\tau_n \rangle & \bigcup_i \text{FTV}(\tau_i) = \emptyset \\ lookupmem(T, t\langle \tau_1..\tau_n \rangle, a) = \lfloor (\text{type}, \tau') \rfloor \\ T; P \vdash \tau' \Downarrow \tau'' \end{array}}{T; P \vdash \tau.a \Downarrow \tau''}$$

(C-MEMT2)
$$\frac{T; P \vdash \tau \Downarrow \tau' \quad \text{FTV}(\tau') \neq \emptyset}{T; P \vdash \tau.a \Downarrow \tau'.a}$$

(C-TMT)
$$\frac{t \in names(T) \quad \forall i \in 1..n.\ T; P \vdash \tau_i \Downarrow \tau_i'}{T; P \vdash t\langle \tau_1..\tau_n \rangle \Downarrow t\langle \tau_1'..\tau_n' \rangle}$$

(C-ARROWT)
$$\frac{T; P \vdash \tau_1 \Downarrow \tau_1' \quad T; P \vdash \tau_2 \Downarrow \tau_2'}{T; P \vdash \tau_1 \to \tau_2 \Downarrow \tau_1' \to \tau_2'}$$

(C-INTT)
$$\frac{}{T; P \vdash \text{int} \Downarrow \text{int}}$$

Fig. 2. Type evaluation

Proposition 3. *(Properties of type evaluation)*

1. *If $T; P \vdash \tau \Downarrow \tau'$ then $FTV(\tau') \subseteq P$.*
2. *If $T; \emptyset \vdash \tau \Downarrow \tau'$ then $\tau' \in \mathbb{R}$.*

It is worth mentioning that type evaluation may diverge for some types and therefore it is impossible to build a derivation for those types (the derivation would need to be infinite). For example, let $T = \{A\langle \alpha \rangle \{x : \text{type } A\langle A\langle \alpha \rangle \rangle.x\}\}$ and $P = \emptyset$. Then we can not build an derivation for $A\langle \text{int} \rangle.x$.

2.4 Well-Formed Types

Well-formed types are types that do not contain out-of-scope type parameters or use undefined template names. The definition of well-formed types is given in Fig. 3. The well-formed type judgment has the form $T; P \vdash \tau$ wf where T is the set of in-scope templates and P is the set of in-scope type parameters. In the case for member access, we do not check that the member name is indeed a member of the given type τ, as that would require us to evaluate τ. The purpose of the well-formed type judgment is not to ensure a safety property for type evaluation, it is merely to check for uses of undefined type variables or template names.

$$T; P \vdash \tau \text{ wf}$$

$$\frac{\alpha \in P}{T; P \vdash \alpha \text{ wf}} \qquad \frac{T; P \vdash \tau \text{ wf}}{T; P \vdash \tau.a \text{ wf}} \qquad \frac{t \in names(T) \quad \forall i \in 1..n. \; T; P \vdash \tau_i \text{ wf}}{T; P \vdash t\langle \tau_1..\tau_n \rangle \text{ wf}}$$

$$\frac{T; P \vdash \tau_1 \text{ wf} \quad T; P \vdash \tau_2 \text{ wf}}{T; P \vdash \tau_1 \to \tau_2 \text{ wf}} \qquad T; P \vdash \text{int wf}$$

Fig. 3. Well-formed types

Proposition 4. *(Properties of well-formed types)*

1. *If* $T; P \vdash \tau$ wf *then* $FTV(\tau) \subseteq P$.
2. *If* $T; P \vdash \tau$ wf *and* $T \subseteq T'$ *then* $T'; P \vdash \tau$ wf.

Lemma 2. *(Well-formed types in an empty type variable environment are closed.) If* $T; \emptyset \vdash \tau$ wf *then* $FTV(\tau) = \emptyset$.

Proof. By induction on the well-formed type judgment.

3   Expressions and Functions

The expressions of C++.T include variables x, integers n, object creation $\text{obj } \tau$, static member function access $\tau.f$, and function application $e_1 \, e_2$. (In C++ the syntax for object creation is $\tau()$, static member access is $\tau::f$, and function application is $e_1(e_2)$.)

Abstract syntax of expressions. $e \in \mathcal{E} \qquad \mathcal{F}$

Expressions	$e \in \mathcal{E} ::= x \mid n \mid \text{obj } \tau \mid \tau.f \mid e \, e$
Values	$v \in \mathcal{V} ::= n \mid \text{obj } \tau \mid \tau.f$
Member functions	$\mathcal{F} ::= t\langle \pi..\pi \rangle \text{ has } f(x{:}\tau) \to \tau\{e\}$
Errors	$\epsilon ::= \text{Error} \mid \text{Abort}$
Answers	$ans ::= v \mid \epsilon$

A static member function definition has the form $(\tau \text{ has } f(x : \tau_1) \to \tau_2\{e\})$. The type τ is the owner of the function and f is the name of the function. The function has a parameter x of type τ_1 and return type τ_2. The expression e is the body of the function.

When a member function is instantiated, all the types in the member function are evaluated, including those occurring in the body expression.

Definition 7. *(Type evaluation inside an expression)* $T; P \vdash e \Downarrow e'$ *iff every type τ occurring in expression e is replaced with τ' where $T; P \vdash \tau \Downarrow \tau'$ to produce expression e'.*

Substitution of expressions for expression variables is defined below. There are no variable binders inside expressions, so substitution is straightforward. We also extend type-substitution to expressions.

Substitution on expressions $\qquad\qquad e[y := e] \in \mathcal{E} \qquad S(e) \in \mathcal{E}$

$$
x[y := e] = \begin{cases} e & y = x \\ x & \text{otherwise} \end{cases}
$$
$$
(e_1\ e_2)[y := e] = e_1[y := e]\ e_2[y := e]
$$
$$
\tau.f[y := e] = \tau.f
$$
$$
\mathsf{obj}\ \tau[y := e] = \mathsf{obj}\ \tau
$$
$$
n[y := e] = n
$$

$$
S(x) = x
$$
$$
S(e_1\ e_2) = S(e_1)\ S(e_2)
$$
$$
S(\tau.f) = S(\tau).f
$$
$$
S(\mathsf{obj}\ \tau) = \mathsf{obj}\ S(\tau)
$$
$$
S(n) = n
$$

The following defines when a type is defined and when a type is complete, two notions that will be used in the evaluation semantics.

Definition 8.

- A type τ **is defined in** T iff $\exists \tau', m, \kappa, \tau''.\ \tau' \doteq \tau \wedge \tau'\{m{:}\kappa\ \tau''\} \in T$.
- A type τ **is complete** in T iff τ is defined in T and $\tau \in \mathbb{R}$.

We present a big-step semantics for the run-time evaluation of expressions with a judgment of the form $F; T \vdash e \hookrightarrow_n ans$, defined in Fig. 4. The F is a set of member function definitions and T is a set of template definitions. Evaluation produces an answer that is either a value, Error, or Abort. The n is used to limit the derivation depth by aborting when n reaches 0. This lets us distinguish between erroneous programs versus nonterminating programs and thereby strengthen the statement of type safety and ensure that all cases are handled by the evaluation rules [6].

The main computational rule is (R-App), which evaluates a function application expression. The expression e_1 evaluates to a member function expression $\tau.f$ and the operand e_2 evaluates to e_2'. The body of the member function $\tau.f$ is found in F. The argument e_2' is substituted for parameter x in the body e, which is then evaluated. The parameter and return types are required to be complete types because C++ has pass-by-value semantics: we need to know the layout of the types to perform the copy.

Similarly, in the (R-OBJ) rule, the type of the object must be complete so that we know how to construct the object. The semantics includes error propagation rules so that we can distinguish between non-termination and errors. The (R-APPE1) rule states that a function application results in an error if either e_1 or e_2 evaluates to an error. Strictly speaking, this would force an implementation of C++.T to interleave the evaluation of e_1 and e_2 so that non-termination of either would not prevent encountering the error. This is not the intended semantics, but a precise treatment is rather verbose. Our type safety result still holds for any sequential implementation because the behavior only differs on programs that are rejected by the type system.

$$F; T \vdash e \hookrightarrow_n ans$$

(R-INT)
$$\frac{0 < k}{F; T \vdash n \hookrightarrow_k n}$$

(R-OBJ)
$$\frac{\tau \text{ is complete in } T \quad 0 < n}{F; T \vdash \mathsf{obj}\ \tau \hookrightarrow_n \mathsf{obj}\ \tau}$$

(R-MEM)
$$\frac{0 < n}{F; T \vdash \tau.f \hookrightarrow_n \tau.f}$$

(R-APP)
$$\frac{F; T \vdash e_1 \hookrightarrow_n \tau.f \quad F; T \vdash e_2 \hookrightarrow_n v_2 \quad \tau \text{ has } f(x{:}\tau_1) \to \tau_2\{e\} \in F}{\tau_1 \text{ and } \tau_2 \text{ are complete in } T \quad F; T \vdash e[x := v_2] \hookrightarrow_n v}{F; T \vdash e_1\ e_2 \hookrightarrow_{n+1} v}$$

Error introduction rules

$$\frac{0 < n}{F; T \vdash x \hookrightarrow_n \mathsf{Error}} \qquad \frac{\tau \text{ is not complete in } T \quad 0 < n}{F; T \vdash \mathsf{obj}\ \tau \hookrightarrow_n \mathsf{Error}} \qquad \frac{}{F; T \vdash e \hookrightarrow_0 \mathsf{Abort}}$$

$$\frac{F; T \vdash e_1 \hookrightarrow_n \tau.f}{\neg \exists x, \tau_1, \tau_2, e.\ \tau \text{ has } f(x{:}\tau_1) \to \tau_2\{e\} \in F}{F; T \vdash e_1\ e_2 \hookrightarrow_{n+1} \mathsf{Error}} \qquad \frac{F; T \vdash e_1 \hookrightarrow_n \tau.f}{\tau \text{ has } f(x{:}\tau_1) \to \tau_2\{e\} \in F}{\exists i \in 1, 2.\ \tau_i \text{ is not complete in } T}{F; T \vdash e_1\ e_2 \hookrightarrow_{n+1} \mathsf{Error}}$$

Error propagation rules

(R-APPE1)
$$\frac{\exists i \in 1, 2.\ F; T \vdash e_i \hookrightarrow_n \epsilon}{F; T \vdash e_1\ e_2 \hookrightarrow_{n+1} \epsilon} \qquad \frac{F; T \vdash e_1 \hookrightarrow_n \tau.f \quad F; T \vdash e_2 \hookrightarrow_n v_2}{\tau \text{ has } f(x{:}\tau_1) \to \tau_2\{e\} \in F}{F; T \vdash e_1[x := v_2] \hookrightarrow_n \epsilon}{F; T \vdash e_1\ e_2 \hookrightarrow_{n+1} \epsilon}$$

Fig. 4. Run-time evaluation

Well-typed expressions are defined by a judgment of the form $T; P; \Gamma \vdash e : \tau_?$, shown in Fig. 5. This judgment is used to type check expressions in the body of member functions of templates and specializations. If an expression contains a type with a type variable, the type of the expression cannot be determined and the typing judgment returns ? (for unknown). Thus, type checking within template definitions is incomplete in the sense that it does not guarantee that instantiating a member function will result in a well-typed body. When the member function is instantiated, type variables are replaced by closed types and the body is type checked again (See Section 4).

Lemma 3. *(Substitution preserves well-typed expressions) If $T; \emptyset; x : \tau_1 \vdash e : \tau_2$ and $T; \emptyset; \emptyset \vdash e' : \tau_1$ then $T; \emptyset; \emptyset \vdash e[x := e'] : \tau_2$.*

Proof. By induction on the typing judgment.

Lemma 4. *(Environment weakening for well-typed expressions) If $T; P; \Gamma \vdash e : \tau_2$ and $T \subseteq T'$ then $T'; P; \Gamma \vdash e : \tau_2$.*

Proof. By induction on the typing judgment. The cases for (T-OBJ1) and (T-MEM1) use Proposition 4.

In what follows we give a formal definition of what it means for a member function to be used in an expression and to be used in a set of function definitions.

Definition 9.

- $\tau.f \in e \triangleq \tau.f$ *is a subexpression of e and $\tau \in \mathbb{R}$.*
- $funused(e) \triangleq \{\tau.f \mid \tau.f \in e\}$
- $\tau.f \in F \triangleq$ *there is a member function π **has** $f'(x : \tau_1) \rightarrow \tau_2\{e\} \in F$ such that $\tau.f \in e$.*
- $funused(F) \triangleq \{\tau.f \mid \tau.f \in F\}$
- *A function $\tau.f$ **is defined in** F iff $\exists \tau', x, \tau_1, \tau_2, e. \ \tau' \doteq \tau \wedge \tau'$ **has** $f(x : \tau_1) \rightarrow \tau_2\{e\} \in F$.*
- $fundef(F) \triangleq \{\tau.f \mid \tau.f$ *is defined in* $F\}$

Lemma 5. *If $F; T \vdash e \hookrightarrow_n e'$ then $funused(e')$ is a subset of $funused(e) \cup funused(F)$.*

Proof. By induction on the evaluation judgment. The case for application relies on the fact that the functions used in $e_1[x := e_2]$ are a subset of the functions used in e_1 and e_2.

Definition 10. *(Well typed function environment) We write $T \vdash F$ if, for all full member specializations r **has** $f(x : \tau_1) \rightarrow \tau_2\{e\} \in F$ we have*

1. $r\{f : \mathbf{fun} \ \tau_1 \rightarrow \tau_2\} \in T$
2. $T; \emptyset; x : \tau_1 \vdash e : \tau_2$
3. τ_1 *and* τ_2 *are complete in* T

$$T; P; \Gamma \vdash e : \tau?$$

(T-VAR1)	$\dfrac{x : \tau \in \Gamma \quad \mathrm{FTV}(\tau) = \emptyset}{T; P; \Gamma \vdash x : \lfloor \tau \rfloor}$
(T-VAR2)	$\dfrac{x : \tau \in \Gamma \quad \mathrm{FTV}(\tau) \neq \emptyset}{T; P; \Gamma \vdash x : ?}$
(T-INT)	$\dfrac{}{T; P; \Gamma \vdash n : \lfloor \mathtt{int} \rfloor}$
(T-OBJ1)	$\dfrac{t\langle \tau_1 .. \tau_n \rangle \text{ is complete in } T}{T; P; \Gamma \vdash \mathtt{obj}\ t\langle \tau_1 .. \tau_n \rangle : \lfloor t\langle \tau_1 .. \tau_n \rangle \rfloor}$
(T-OBJ2)	$\dfrac{\mathrm{FTV}(\tau) \neq \emptyset}{T; P; \Gamma \vdash \mathtt{obj}\ \tau : ?}$
(T-MEM1)	$\dfrac{T; P \vdash \tau \text{ wf} \quad \mathrm{FTV}(\tau) = \emptyset \quad \tau\{f : \mathtt{fun}\ \tau'\} \in T}{T; P; \Gamma \vdash \tau.f : \lfloor \tau' \rfloor}$
(T-MEM2)	$\dfrac{\mathrm{FTV}(\tau) \neq \emptyset}{T; P; \Gamma \vdash \tau.f : ?}$
(T-APP1)	$\dfrac{T; P; \Gamma \vdash e_1 : \tau \to \tau' \quad T; P; \Gamma \vdash e_2 : \tau}{T; P; \Gamma \vdash e_1\ e_2 : \lfloor \tau' \rfloor}$
(T-APP2)	$\dfrac{T; P; \Gamma \vdash e_1 : a_1 \quad T; P; \Gamma \vdash e_2 : a_2 \qquad a_1 =? \vee a_2 =?}{T; P; \Gamma \vdash e_1\ e_2 : ?}$

Fig. 5. Well-typed expressions

The next lemma is type safety for expression evaluation. The appearance of $F; T \vdash e \hookrightarrow_n ans$ in the conclusion of this lemma, and not as a premise, would normally be a naive mistake because not all programs terminate. However, by using n-depth evaluation, we can construct a judgment regardless of whether the program is non-terminating. Further, by placing $F; T \vdash e \hookrightarrow_n ans$ in the conclusion, this lemma proves that our evaluation rules are complete, analogous to a progress lemma for small-step semantics. We learned of this technique from Ernst et al. [6].

Lemma 6. *(Type safety of expression evaluation) If*

1. $T; \emptyset; \emptyset \vdash e : \lfloor \tau \rfloor$ *and*
2. *every function used in e and F is defined in F and*
3. $T \vdash F$ *and*
4. *there are no duplicates in T*

then for all n, $F; T \vdash e \hookrightarrow_n ans$ and either $ans = $ Abort or there exists v such that $ans = v$ and $T; \emptyset; \emptyset \vdash v : \lfloor \tau \rfloor$.

Proof. By strong induction on n, followed by case analysis on the final derivation step in the typing judgment for e. The cases for application (including the cases for error propagation) rely on the assumptions that $T \vdash F$, every function used in e and F is defined in F, and that there are no duplicates in T. Also, the application cases use Proposition 2 (Well-formed types in an empty type variable environment are closed), Lemma 3 (Substitution preserves well-typed expressions), and Lemma 5. The cases for object construction rely on the requirement for a complete type in the typing rule (T-Obj1). The other cases are straightforward.

4   Programs and the Instantiation Process

A program is a sequence of template and function definitions. To review, templates $\mathcal{T}$ were defined in Section 2 and functions $\mathcal{F}$ were defined in Section 3.

Abstract syntax of programs	$p \in \mathcal{P}$

$$\text{Definitions } d \in \mathcal{D} ::= \mathcal{T} \mid \mathcal{F}$$
$$\text{Programs } \quad p \in \mathcal{P} ::= d^*$$

The program instantiation judgment has the form $T; F \vdash p \Downarrow T'; F'$, where T is a set of templates, F a set of member function definitions, and p is the program. The result of instantiation is an updated set T' of templates and of member functions F'. The program instantiation judgment performs type evaluation, template instantiation, and type checking on each definition. The following auxiliary definitions are used in the definition of program instantiation.

Definition 11.

– *We write $\tau \in e$ iff $\mathbf{obj}\,\tau$ is a subexpression of e and $\tau \in \mathbb{R}$.*
– *The notation X, z stands for $\{z\} \cup X$ where $z \notin X$.*

4.1   Member Function Processing

During program instantiation there are two places where member function definitions are processed: when a user-defined function definition is encountered and when a member function is instantiated. We abstract the member function processing into a judgment of the form $T; F \vdash \pi$ has $f(x : \tau) \rightarrow \tau'\{e\} \Downarrow T'; F'$ with a single rule (MEMFUN). This rule evaluates the type expressions that occur in the member function then records all of the types that need to be instantiated in the set N'. The results of template lookup for each type in N' is placed in set T_2, which is then instantiated to the set T_3 (The listof function converts a set into a list). We type check the body of the function in an environment extended with T_3. If there are free type variables in the template pattern π, then type checking may result in ?. Otherwise the type of the body must be identical to the return type.

Process member function $\qquad T; F \vdash \pi$ has $f(x : \tau) \rightarrow \tau\{e\} \Downarrow T; F$

(MEMFUN)

$$
\begin{array}{c}
T_1; \mathrm{FTV}(\pi) \vdash \tau_1 \Downarrow \tau_1' \quad T_1; \mathrm{FTV}(\pi) \vdash \tau_2 \Downarrow \tau_2' \quad T_1; \mathrm{FTV}(\pi) \vdash e \Downarrow e' \\
N = \{\tau \mid \tau \in e'\} \cup \{\pi, \tau_1', \tau_2'\} \\
N' = \{\tau \in N \mid \tau \text{ is not defined in } T_1\} \quad \forall \tau \in N'. \ inst(T_1, \tau) \neq \bot \\
T_2 = \{\tau\{m : \kappa \, \tau'\} \mid \tau \in N' \land inst(T_1, \tau) = \lfloor \tau\{m : \kappa \, \tau'\} \rfloor\} \\
T_1; F_1 \vdash \mathsf{listof}(T_2) \Downarrow T_3; F_1 \\
T_3; \mathrm{FTV}(\pi); x : \tau_1' \vdash e' : a \quad (\mathrm{FTV}(\pi) \neq \emptyset \land a = ?) \lor a = \lfloor \tau_2' \rfloor \\
F_2 = \{\pi \text{ has } f(x : \tau_1') \rightarrow \tau_2'\{e'\}\} \\
\hline
T_1; F_1 \vdash \pi \text{ has } f(x : \tau_1) \rightarrow \tau_2\{e\} \Downarrow T_3; F_1 \cup F_2
\end{array}
$$

4.2   Program Instantiation

The definition of the program instantiation judgment is in Fig. 6 and the following describes each rule.

(C-NIL): Program instantiation is finished when there are definitions for all of the functions used in the program. The symbol [] is used for the empty list.

(C-INSTFUN): Once the entire program has been processed we instantiate member functions that are used but not yet defined. and instantiates the function. We find the best matching template and the corresponding member function definition. The matching substitution S is applied to the type parameters and the body of the function. We then process the instantiated member function with rule (MEMFUN).

(C-TM): For template definition, we check that the template is not already defined and then evaluate the template's member. We then insert the evaluated template into T and process the rest of the program.

(C-FUN): For member function definitions, we check that there is a template defined with a member declaration for this function. Then we check that there is not already a definition for this function. We apply the (MEMFUN) rule to the member function and then process the rest of the program.

$$T; F \vdash p \Downarrow T; F$$

(C-NIL)
$$\dfrac{\textit{funused}(F) \subseteq F}{T; F \vdash [\,] \Downarrow T; F}$$

(C-INSTFUN)
$$\dfrac{\begin{array}{c} \tau.f \in \textit{funused}(F_1) - F_1 \qquad \textit{lookup}(T_1, \tau) = \lfloor \pi \{ f : \mathtt{fun}\ \tau_1 \to \tau_2 \} \rfloor \\ \pi\ \mathtt{has}\ f(x{:}\tau_1) \to \tau_2 \{e\} \in F_1 \qquad S(\pi) = \tau \\ T_1; F_1 \vdash \tau\ \mathtt{has}\ f(x{:}S(\tau_1)) \to S(\tau_2)\{S(e)\} \Downarrow T_2; F_2 \qquad T_2; F_2 \vdash [\,] \Downarrow T'; F' \end{array}}{T_1; F_1 \vdash [\,] \Downarrow T'; F'}$$

(C-TM)
$$\dfrac{\begin{array}{c} \pi\ \text{is not defined in}\ T \qquad T; \mathrm{FTV}(\pi) \vdash \tau \Downarrow \lfloor \tau' \rfloor \\ \{\pi\{m{:}\kappa\ \tau'\}\} \cup T; F \vdash p_1 \Downarrow T'; F' \end{array}}{T; F \vdash \pi\{m{:}\kappa\ \tau\} :: p_1 \Downarrow T'; F'}$$

(C-FUN)
$$\dfrac{\begin{array}{c} \pi.f\ \text{is not defined in}\ F_1 \qquad \textit{lookupmem}(T_1, \pi, f) = \lfloor (\mathtt{fun}, \tau_1 \to \tau_2) \rfloor \\ T_1; F_1 \vdash \pi\ \mathtt{has}\ f(x{:}\tau_1) \to \tau_2 \{e\} \Downarrow T_2; F_2 \qquad T_2; F_2 \vdash p_1 \Downarrow T'; F' \end{array}}{T_1; F_1 \vdash \pi\ \mathtt{has}\ f(x{:}\tau_1) \to \tau_2 \{e\} :: p_1 \Downarrow T'; F'}$$

Fig. 6. Program instantiation

4.3   Type Safety

For the purposes of proving type safety, we need to show that the semantics of program instantiation establish the appropriate properties needed by Lemma 6 (Type soundness for evaluation). The following lemma captures the invariants that are maintained during program instantiation to achieve this goal.

Lemma 7. *(Instantiation produces a well-typed program) If $T; F \vdash p \Downarrow T'; F'$, and*

1. *$T \vdash F$, and*
2. *there are no duplicates in T, and*
3. *$FTV(T) = \emptyset$*

then

1. *$\textit{funused}(F') \subseteq F'$, and*
2. *$T' \vdash F'$, and*
3. *there are no duplicates in T', and*
4. *$FTV(T') = \emptyset$*

Proof. By induction on the instantiation of p. The case for template definitions uses Proposition 3 (Properties of type evaluation) and and Lemma 4 (Environment weakening for well-typed expressions). The cases for member function definitions and member function instantiation also use Proposition 3 and Lemma 4. In addition they use Lemma 1 (Member lookup produces closed types).

The proof of the type-safety theorem is a straightforward use of Lemma 7 (Instantiation produces a well-typed program) and Lemma 6 (Type safety of expression evaluation).

Theorem 1. *(Type Safety) If*

1. $\emptyset; \emptyset; \emptyset \vdash p \Downarrow T; F$, *and*
2. $Main\langle\rangle\{main : int \to int\} \in T$, *and*
3. $Main\langle\rangle$ *has* $main(x : int) \to int\{e\} \in F$, *and*

then for all n, $F; T \vdash Main\langle\rangle.main(n) \hookrightarrow_n ans$ *and either* $ans = Abort$ *or there exists* v *such that* $ans = v$ *and* $T; \emptyset; \emptyset \vdash v : int$.

Proof. From $Main\langle\rangle\{main : int \to int\} \in T$ we have $T; \emptyset; \emptyset \vdash Main\langle\rangle.main(n) : int$. By Lemma 7 we know that all the functions used in F are defined, $T \vdash F$, there are no duplicates in T, and there are no free type variables in T. From $Main\langle\rangle$ has $main(x:int) \to int\{e\} \in F$ we know that the function used in $Main\langle\rangle.main(n)$ is defined, so we apply Lemma 6 to obtain the conclusion.

5 Discussion

The semantics defined in this paper instantiates fewer templates than what is mandated by the C++ standard. In particular, the C++ standard says that member access, such as `A<int>::u`, causes the instantiation of `A<int>`. In our semantics, the member access will obtain the definition of member u but it will not generate a template specialization for `A<int>`. We only generate template specializations for types that appear in residual program contexts that require complete types: object construction and function parameters and return types. Our type-safety result shows that even though we produce fewer template specializations, we produce enough to ensure the proper run-time execution of the program. The benefit of this semantics is that the compiler is allowed to be more space efficient.

The semantics of member function instantiation is a point of some controversy. Section [14.6.4.1 p1] of the Standard says that the point of instantiation for a member function immediately follows the enclosing declaration that triggered the instantiation (with a caveat for dependent uses within templates). The problem with this rule is that uses of a member function may legally precede its definition and the definition is needed to generate the instantiation. (A use of a member function must only come after the *declaration* of the member function, which is in the template specialization.) In general, the C++ Standard is formulated to allow for compilation in a single pass, whereas the current rules for member instantiation would require two passes. Also, there is a disconnect between the Standard and the current implementations. The Edison Design Group and GNU compilers both delay the instantiation of member functions to the end of the program (or translation unit). We discussed this issue on C++ committee[2] and

---

[2] A post to the C++ committee email reflector on September 19, 2005, with a response from John Spicer.

the opinion was that this is a defect in the C++ Standard and that instantiation of member functions should be allowed to occur at the end of the program. Therefore, C++.T places instantiations for member functions at the end of the program.

6 Related Work

Recently, Stroustrup and Dos Reis proposed a formal account of the type system for C++ [13, 14]. However, they do not define the semantics of evaluation and they do not study template specialization. The focus of the work by Stroustrup and Dos Reis is to enable the type checking of template definitions separately from their uses. Siek et al. [16] also describe an extension to improve the type checking of template definitions and uses.

Wallace studied the dynamic evaluation of C++, but not the static aspects such as template instantiation [20].

C++ templates are widely used for program generation. There has been considerable research on language support for program generation, resulting in languages such as MetaOCaml [2] and Template Haskell [15]. These languages provide first-class support for program generation by including a hygienic quasi-quotation mechanism. The advanced type system used in MetaOCaml guarantees that the generated code is typable. There are no such guarantees in C++. The formal semantics defined in this paper will facilitate comparing C++ with languages such as MetaOCaml and will help in finding ways to improve C++. The C++ Standards Committee has begun to investigate improved support for metaprogramming [18].

7 Conclusion

This paper presents a formal account of C++ templates. We identify a small subset, named C++.T, that includes templates, specialization, and member functions. We define the compile-time and run-time semantics of C++.T, including type evaluation, template instantiation, and a type system. The main technical result is the proof of type safety, which states that if a program is valid (template instantiation succeeds), then run-time execution of the program will not encounter type errors. In the process of formalizing C++.T, we encountered two interesting issues: the C++ Standard instantiates member functions too soon and generates unnecessary template specializations.

From the point of view of language semantics and program generation research, it was interesting to see that C++.T involves a form of evaluation under variable binders at the level of types but not at the level of terms. However, evaluation of open terms is not allowed. We plan to investigate how this affects the expressivity of C++ templates as a mechanism for writing program generators.

Acknowledgments

We thank the anonymous reviewers for their careful reading of this paper. We thank Emir Pasalic and Ronald Garcia for reading drafts and suggesting improvements and we thank Jaakko Järvi, Doug Gregor, Todd Veldhuizen, and Jeremiah Willcock for helpful discussions. We especially thank John Spicer and Daveed Vandevoorde of Edison Design Group for help with interpreting the C++ Standard.

Bibliography

[1] *Haskell 98 Language and Libraries: The Revised Report*, December 2002. http://www.haskell.org/onlinereport/index.html.

[2] MetaOCaml: A compiled, type-safe multi-stage programming language. Available online from http://www.metaocaml.org/, 2004.

[3] David Abrahams and Aleksey Gurtovoy. *C++ Template Metaprogramming: Concepts, Tools, and Techniques from Boost and Beyond*. Addison-Wesley Longman Publishing Co., Inc., Boston, MA, USA, 2004.

[4] Andrei Alexandrescu. *Modern C++ design: generic programming and design patterns applied*. Addison-Wesley Longman Publishing Co., Inc., Boston, MA, USA, 2001.

[5] Krzysztof Czarnecki and Ulrich W. Eisenecker. *Generative programming: methods, tools, and applications*. ACM Press/Addison-Wesley Publishing Co., New York, NY, USA, 2000.

[6] Erik Ernst, Klaus Ostermann, and William R. Cook. A virtual class calculus. In *POPL'06: Conference record of the 33rd ACM SIGPLAN-SIGACT symposium on Principles of programming languages*, pages 270–282, New York, NY, USA, 2006. ACM Press.

[7] Steven E. Ganz, Amr Sabry, and Walid Taha. Macros as multi-stage computations: type-safe, generative, binding macros in MacroML. In *ICFP '01: Proceedings of the sixth ACM SIGPLAN international conference on Functional programming*, pages 74–85, New York, NY, USA, 2001. ACM Press.

[8] International Organization for Standardization. *ISO/IEC 14882:2003: Programming languages — C++*. Geneva, Switzerland, October 2003.

[9] Xavier Leroy. The Objective Caml system: Documentation and user's manual, 2000. With Damien Doligez, Jacques Garrigue, Didier Rémy, and Jérôme Vouillon.

[10] Robin Milner, Mads Tofte, and Robert Harper. *The Definition of Standard ML*. MIT Press, 1990.

[11] Tobias Nipkow. Structured proofs in Isar/HOL. In *Types for Proofs and Programs (TYPES 2002)*, number 2646 in LNCS, 2002.

[12] Tobias Nipkow, Lawrence C. Paulson, and Markus Wenzel. *Isabelle/HOL — A Proof Assistant for Higher-Order Logic*, volume 2283 of *LNCS*. Springer, 2002.

[13] Gabriel Dos Reis and Bjarne Stroustrup. A formalism for C++. Technical Report N1885=05-0145, ISO/IEC JTC1/SC22/WG21, 2005.

[14] Gabriel Dos Reis and Bjarne Stroustrup. Specifying c++ concepts. In *POPL '06: Conference record of the 33rd ACM SIGPLAN-SIGACT symposium on Principles of programming languages*, pages 295–308, New York, NY, USA, 2006. ACM Press.

[15] Tim Sheard and Simon Peyton Jones. Template meta-programming for haskell. In *Haskell '02: Proceedings of the 2002 ACM SIGPLAN workshop on Haskell*, pages 1–16, New York, NY, USA, 2002. ACM Press.

[16] Jeremy Siek, Douglas Gregor, Ronald Garcia, Jeremiah Willcock, Jaakko Järvi, and Andrew Lumsdaine. Concepts for C++0x. Technical Report N1758=05-0018, ISO/IEC JTC 1, Information Technology, Subcommittee SC 22, Programming Language C++, January 2005.

[17] Jeremy Siek and Walid Taha. C++.T formalization in Isar. Technical Report TR05-458, Rice University, Houston, TX, December 2005.

[18] Daveed Vandevoorde. Reflective metaprogramming in C++. Technical Report N1471/03-0054, ISO/IEC JTC 1, Information Technology, Subcommittee SC 22, Programming Language C++, April 2003.

[19] Todd Veldhuizen. Using C++ template metaprograms. *C++ Report*, 7(4):36–43, May 1995. Reprinted in C++ Gems, ed. Stanley Lippman.

[20] Charles Wallace. *Specification and validation methods*, chapter The semantics of the C++ programming language, pages 131–164. Oxford University Press, Inc., New York, NY, USA, 1995.

[21] Markus Wenzel. *The Isabelle/Isar Reference Manual*. TU München, April 2004.

Session Types for Object-Oriented Languages*

Mariangiola Dezani-Ciancaglini[1], Dimitris Mostrous[2],
Nobuko Yoshida[2], and Sophia Drossopoulou[2]

[1] Dipartimento di Informatica, Università di Torino
[2] Department of Computing, Imperial College London

Abstract. A session takes place between two parties; after establishing a connection, each party interleaves local computations with communications (sending or receiving) with the other. Session types characterise such sessions in terms of the types of values communicated and the shape of protocols, and have been developed for the π-calculus, CORBA interfaces, and functional languages. We study the incorporation of session types into object-oriented languages through MOOSE, a multi-threaded language with session types, thread spawning, iterative and higher-order sessions. Our design aims to consistently integrate the object-oriented programming style and sessions, and to be able to treat various case studies from the literature. We describe the design of MOOSE, its syntax, operational semantics and type system, and develop a type inference system. After proving subject reduction, we establish the progress property: once a communication has been established, well-typed programs will never starve at communication points.

1 Introduction

Object-based communication oriented software is commonly implemented using either sockets or remote method invocation, such as Java RMI and C# remoting. Sockets provide generally untyped stream abstractions, while remote method invocation offers the benefits of standard method invocation in a distributed setting. However, both have shortcomings: socket-based code requires a significant amount of dynamic checks and type-casts on the values exchanged, in order to ensure type safety; remote method invocation does ensure that methods are used as mandated by their type signatures, but does not allow programmers to express design patterns frequently arising in distributed applications, where *sequences* of messages of different types are exchanged through a single connection following fixed protocols. A natural question is the seamless integration of tractable descriptions of type-safe communication patterns with object-oriented programming idioms.

A *session* is such a sequence of interactions between two parties. It starts after a connection has been established. During the session, each party may execute its own local

* This work was funded in part by the Information Society Technologies programme of the European Commission, Future and Emerging Technologies under the IST-2005-015905 MOBIUS project, and FP6-2004-510996 Coordination Action TYPES, and by MIUR Cofin'04 project McTafi, and by EPSRC GR/T03208, GR/S55538, GR/T04724 and GR/S68071. This paper reflects only the authors' views and the Community is not liable for any use that may be made of the information contained therein.

D. Thomas (Ed.): ECOOP 2006, LNCS 4067, pp. 328–352, 2006.
© Springer-Verlag Berlin Heidelberg 2006

computation, interleaved with several communications with the other party. Communications take the form of sending and receiving values over a channel, and additionally, throughout interaction between the two parties, there should be a perfect matching of sending actions in one with receiving actions in the other, and vice versa. This form of structured interaction is found in many application scenarios.

Session types have been proposed in [18], aiming to characterise such sessions, in terms of the types of messages received or sent by a party. For example, the session type `begin.!int.!int.?bool.end` expresses that two `int`-values will be sent, then a `bool`-value will be expected to be received, and then the protocol will be complete. Thus, session types specify the communication behaviour of a piece of software, and can be used to verify the safety, in terms of communication, of the composition of several pieces of software executing in parallel. Session types have been studied for several different settings, *i.e.*, for π-calculus-based formalisms [6, 7, 13, 18, 20, 26], for CORBA [27], for functional languages [15, 29], and recently, for CDL, a W3C standard description language for web services [3, 8, 30].

In this paper we study the incorporation of session types into object-oriented languages. To our knowledge, except for our earlier work [10], such an integration has not been attempted so far. We propose the language MOOSE, a multi-threaded object-oriented core language augmented with session types, which supports thread spawning, iterative sessions, and higher-order sessions.

The design of MOOSE was guided by the wish for the following properties:

object oriented style. We wanted MOOSE programming to be as natural as possible to people used to mainstream object oriented languages. In order to achieve an object oriented style, MOOSE allows sessions to be handled modularly using methods.

expressivity. We wanted to be able to express common case studies from the literature on session types and concurrent programming idioms [24], as well as those from the WC3 standard documents [8, 30]. In order to achieve expressivity, we introduced the ability to spawn new threads, to send and receive sessions (*i.e.*, higher-order sessions), conditional, and iterative sessions.

type preservation. The guarantee that execution preserves types, *i.e.*, the subject reduction property, proved to be an intricate task. In fact, several session type systems in the literature fail to preserve typability after reduction of certain subtle configurations, which we identified through a detailed analysis of how types of communication channels evolve during reduction. Type preservation requires linear usage of channels; in order to guarantee this we had to prevent aliasing of channels, manifested by the fact that channel types cannot be assigned to fields.

progress. We wanted to be able to guarantee that once a session has started, *i.e.*, a connection has been established, threads neither starve nor deadlock at the points of communication during the session, a highly desirable property in communication-based programs. Establishing this property was an intricate task as well, and, to the best of our knowledge, no other session type system in the literature can ensure it. The combination of higher-order sessions, spawn and the requirement to prevent deadlock during sessions posed the major challenge for our type system.

The paper is organised as follows: §2 illustrates the basic ideas through an example. §3 defines the syntax of the language. §4 presents the operational semantics. §5 describes design decisions. §6 illustrates the typing system. §7 states basic theorems on type safety and communication safety. §8 discusses the related work, and §9 concludes.

A full version of this paper, [1], includes complete definitions and proofs. Also, more detailed explanations and examples can be found in [24].

2   Example: Business Protocol

We describe a typical collaboration pattern that appears in many web service business protocols [8, 30] using MOOSE. This simple protocol contains essential features by which we can demonstrate the expressivity of MOOSE: it requires a combination of session establishing, higher-order session passing, spawn, conditional and deadlock-freedom during the session.

In Fig. 1 we show the sequence diagram for the protocol which models the purchasing of items as follows: first, the Seller and Buyer participants initiate interaction over channel c1; then, the Buyer sends a product id to the Seller, and receives a price quote in return; finally, the Buyer may either accept or reject this price. If the price received is acceptable then the Seller connects with the Shipper over channel c2. First the Seller sends to the Shipper the details of the purchased item. Then the Seller delegates its part of the remaining activity with the Buyer to the Shipper, that is realised by sending c1 over c2. Now the Shipper will await the Buyer's address, before responding with the delivery date. If the price is not acceptable, then the interaction terminates.

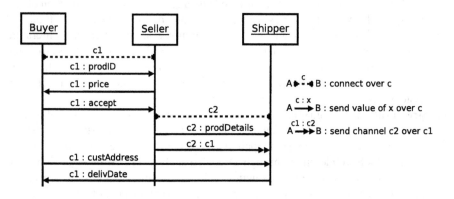

Fig. 1. Sequence diagram for item purchasing protocol

In Fig. 2 we declare the necessary session types, and in Fig. 3 we encode the given scenario in MOOSE, using one class per protocol participant. The session types Buy-Product and RequestDelivery describe the communication patterns between Buyer and Seller, and Seller and Shipper, respectively. The session type BuyProduct models the sending of a String, then the reception of a double, and finally a conditional behaviour, in which a bool is (implicitly) sent before a branch is followed: the first branch requires that an Address is sent, then a DeliveryDetails received, and finally that the session is closed; the second branch models an empty communication sequence and the closing of the session. We write $\overline{\texttt{BuyProduct}}$ for the *dual* type, which is constructed by taking `BuyProduct` and changing occurrences of ! to ? and vice versa; hence, these types represent the two complementary behaviours associated with a session, in which the sending of a value in one end corresponds to its reception at the other. In other words, $\overline{\texttt{BuyProduct}}$ is the same as `begin.?String.!double.?<?Address.!DeliveryDetails.end,end>`. Note that in the case of the conditional, the thread with ! in its type decides which branch is to be followed and communicates the boolean value, while the other thread passively awaits the former thread's decision. The session type `RequestDelivery` describes sending a `ProductDetails` instance, followed by sending a 'live' session channel of type `?Address.!DeliveryDetails.end`.

```
1  session BuyProduct =
2     begin.!String.?double.!<!Address.?DeliveryDetails.end,end>
3  session RequestDelivery =
4     begin.!ProductDetails.!(?Address.!DeliveryDetails.end).end
```

Fig. 2. Session types for the buyer-seller-shipper example

Sessions can start when two compatible `connect ...` statements are active. In Fig. 3, the first component of `connect` is the shared channel that is used to start communication, the second is the session type, and the third is the *session body*, which implements the session type. The method `buy` of class `Buyer` contains a `connect` statement that implements the session type `BuyProduct`, while the method `sell` of class `Seller` contains a `connect` statement over the same channel and the dual session type. When a `Buyer` and a `Seller` are executing concurrently their respective methods, they can engage in a session, which will result in a fresh channel being replaced for occurrences of the shared channel `c1` within both session bodies; freshness guarantees that the new channel only occurs in these two session bodies, therefore the objects can proceed to perform their interactions without the possibility of external interference.

Once the session has started in the body of method `buy`, the product identifier, `prodID`, is sent using `c1.send(prodID)` and the price quote is received using `c1.receive`. If the price is acceptable, *i.e.*, `c1.receive <= maxPrice`, then `true` is sent and the first branch of the conditional is taken, starting on line 9. In this case, the customer's address, `addr`, is sent and an instance of `DeliveryDetails` is received. If the price is not acceptable, then `false` is sent and the second branch of the conditional starting on line 11 is taken, and the connection closes.

The body of method `sell` implements behaviour dual to the above. Note that in `c1.receiveIf{...}{...}` the branch to be selected depends on the boolean value received from the other end, which will execute the complementary expression `c1.sendIf(..){...}{...}`. The first branch of the former conditional contains a nested `connect` in line 25, via which the product details are sent to the `Shipper`, followed by the actual runtime channel that was substituted for `c1` when the outer `connect` took place; the latter is sent through the construct `c2.sendS(c1)`, which realises *higher-order session communication*. Notice that the code in lines 25-26 is within a `spawn`, which reduces to a new thread with the enclosed expression as its body.

```
1    class Buyer {
2
3      Address addr;
4
5      void buy( String prodID, double maxPrice ) {
6        connect c1 BuyProduct {
7          c1.send( prodID );
8          c1.sendIf( c1.receive <= maxPrice ) {
9             c1.send( addr );
10            DeliveryDetails delivDetails := c1.receive;
11         }{ null; /* buyer rejects price, end of protocol */ }
12       } /* End connect */
13     } /* End method buy */
14   }
15
16   class Seller {
17     void sell() {
18       connect c1 BuyProduct {
19         String prodID := c1.receive;
20         double price := getPrice( prodID ); // implem. omitted
21         c1.send( price );
22         c1.receiveIf { // buyer accepts price
23           ProductDetails prodDetails := new ProductDetails();
24           // ... init prodDetails with prodID, size, etc
25           spawn { connect c2 RequestDelivery {
26                    c2.send( prodDetails ); c2.sendS( c1 );} }
27         }{ null; /* receiveIf : buyer rejects */ }
28       } /* End connect */
29     } /* End method sell */
30   }
31
32   class Shipper {
33     void delivery() {
34       connect c2 RequestDelivery {
35         ProductDetails prodDetails := c2.receive;
36         c2.receiveS( x ) {
37         Address custAddress := x.receive;
38         DeliveryDetails delivDetails := new DeliveryDetails();
39         //... set state of delivDetails
40         x.send( delivDetails ); }
41       } /* End connect */
42     } /* End method delivery */
43   }
```

Fig. 3. Code for the buyer, seller and shipper

Method delivery of class Shipper should be clear, with the exception of c2.receiveS (x){..} which is dual to c2.sendS(c1). In the former expression, the received channel is bound to variable x.

The above example shows how MOOSE achieves deadlock-freedom during a session: because sessions take place between threads with complementary communication

(type)	$t ::= C \mid$ bool $\mid s \mid (s, \bar{s})$
(class)	$class ::=$ class C extends $C \{ \tilde{f}\tilde{t} \ \tilde{meth} \}$
(method)	$meth ::=$ t m $(\tilde{t}\,\tilde{x}) \ \{e\} \mid$ t m $(\tilde{t}\,\tilde{x}, \eta x) \ \{e\}$
(expression)	$e ::=$ x $\mid$ v $\mid$ this $\mid$ e ; e $\mid$ e.f $:=$ e $\mid$ e.f $\mid$ e.m $(\,\tilde{e}\,) \mid$ new $C \mid$ new $(s, \bar{s})$
	$\mid$ NullExc $\mid$ spawn $\{ e \} \mid$ connect u s $\{e\}$
	$\mid$ u.receive $\mid$ u.send (e) $\mid$ u.receiveS (x) $\{e\} \mid$ u.sendS (u)
	$\mid$ u.receiveIf $\{e\}\{e\} \mid$ u.sendIf (e) $\{e\}\{e\}$
	$\mid$ u.receiveWhile $\{e\} \mid$ u.sendWhile (e) $\{e\}$
(identifier)	$u ::=$ c $\mid$ x
(value)	$v ::=$ c $\mid$ null $\mid$ true $\mid$ false $\mid$ o
(thread)	$P ::=$ e $\mid P \mid P$
(heap)	$h ::= \emptyset \mid h \cdot [o \mapsto (C, \tilde{f} : \tilde{v})] \mid h \cdot c$

Fig. 4. Syntax, where syntax occurring only at runtime appears shaded

patterns, whenever we have c.send(v) eventually an expression of the shape c.receive will appear in the other thread, unless the thread diverges or an exception occurs or there is a connect instruction waiting for the dual connect instruction. Likewise for the other communication expressions. Therefore, no session will remain incomplete, because for every action we can guarantee that the co-action will eventually appear and the communication will take place, again, unless one of the above mentioned cases occurs.

3 A Concurrent Object Oriented Language with Sessions

In Fig. 4 we describe the syntax of MOOSE. We distinguish *user syntax, i.e.,* source level code, and *runtime syntax,* which includes null pointer exceptions, threads and heaps. The syntax is based on FJ [21] with the addition of imperative and communication primitives similar to those from [4, 6, 10, 18, 20, 29]. We designed MOOSE as a multi-threaded concurrent language for simplicity of presentation although it can be extended to model distribution; see § 8.

Channels. We distinguish *shared channels* and *live channels.* Shared channels have not yet been connected; they are used to decide if two threads can communicate, in which case they are replaced by fresh live channels. After a connection has been created the channel is live; data may be transmitted through such active channels only. The types of MOOSE enforce the condition that there are exactly two threads which contain occurrences of the same live channel: we call it *bilinearity condition.*

User syntax. The metavariable t ranges over types for expressions, C ranges over class names and s ranges over session types. Each session type s has one corresponding *dual,* denoted $\bar{s}$, which is obtained by replacing each ! (output) by ? (input) and vice versa. We use η to denote the type of a live channel. We introduce the full syntax of types in § 6. Class and method declarations are as expected, except for the restriction that at most one parameter can be a live channel. This condition is explained in Example 5.4.

The syntax of user expressions e, e' is standard but for the channel constructor new $(s, \bar{s})$, and the *communication expressions, i.e.*, connect $u\, s\{e\}$ and all the expressions in the last three lines.

The first line gives parameter, value, the receiver this, sequence of expressions, assignment to fields, field access, method call, object and channel creation, and new $(s, \bar{s})$, which builds a fresh shared channel used to establish a private session. The values are channels, null, and the literals true and false. Thread creation is declared using spawn $\{\, e\, \}$, in which the expression e is called the *thread body*.

The expression connect $u\, s\{e\}$ starts a session: the channel u appears within the term $\{e\}$ in session communications that agree with session type s. The remaining eight expressions, which realise the exchanges of data, are called *session expressions*, and start with "u._"; we call u the *subject* of such expressions. In the below explanation session expressions are pairwise coupled: we say that expressions in the same pair and with the same subject are *dual* to each other.

The first pair is for exchange of values (which can be shared channels): u.receive receives a value via u, while u.send(e) evaluates e and sends the result over u. The second pair expresses live channel exchange: in u.receiveS$(x)\{e\}$ the received channel will be bound to x within e, in which x is used for communications. The expression u.sendS(u') sends the channel u' over u. The third pair is for *conditional* communication: u.receiveIf$\{e\}\{e'\}$ receives a boolean value via channel u, and if it is true continues with e, otherwise with e'; the expression u.sendIf$(e)\{e'\}\{e''\}$ first evaluates the boolean expression e, then sends the result via channel u and if the result was true continues with e', otherwise with e''. The fourth is for *iterative* communication: the expression u.receiveWhile$\{e\}$ receives a boolean value via channel u, and if it is true continues with e and iterates, otherwise ends; the expression u.sendWhile$(e)\{e'\}$ first evaluates the boolean expression e, then sends its result via channel u and if the result was true continues with e' and iterates, otherwise ends.

Runtime syntax. The runtime syntax (shown shaded in Fig. 4) extends the user syntax: it introduces threads running in parallel; adds NullExc to expressions, denoting the null pointer error; finally, extends values to allow for object identifiers o, which denote references to instances of classes. Single and multiple *threads* are ranged over by P, P'. The expression $P\,|\,P'$ says that P and P' are running in parallel.

Heaps, ranged over h, are built inductively using the heap composition operator '$\cdot$', and contain mappings of object identifiers to instances of classes, and channels. In particular, a heap will contain the set of objects and *fresh* channels, both shared and live, that have been created since the beginning of execution. The heap produced by composing $h \cdot [o \mapsto (C, \tilde{f} : \tilde{v})]$ will map o to the object $(C, \tilde{f} : \tilde{v})$, where C is the class name and $\tilde{f} : \tilde{v}$ is a representation for the vector of distinct mappings from field names to their values for this instance. The heap produced by composing $h \cdot c$ will contain the fresh channel c. Heap membership for object identifiers and channels is checked using standard set notation, we therefore write it as $o \in h$ and $c \in h$, respectively. Heap update for objects is written $h[o \mapsto (C, \tilde{f} : \tilde{v})]$, and field update is written $(C, \tilde{f} : \tilde{v})[f \mapsto v]$.

4   Operational Semantics

This section presents the operational semantics of MOOSE, which is inspired by the standard small step call-by-value reduction of [4, 5, 25] and mainly of [10]. We only discuss the more interesting rules. First we list the evaluation contexts.

$$E ::= \quad [\,]\mid E.\mathsf{f}\mid E;\mathsf{e}\mid E.\mathsf{f}:=\mathsf{e}\mid\mathsf{o}.\mathsf{f}:=E\mid E.\mathsf{m}\,(\tilde{\mathsf{e}})\mid\mathsf{o}.\mathsf{m}\,(\tilde{\mathsf{v}},E,\tilde{\mathsf{e}})$$
$$\mid\ \mathsf{c}.\mathsf{send}\,(E)\mid\mathsf{u}.\mathsf{sendIf}\,(E)\{\mathsf{e}\,\}\{\mathsf{e}'\}$$

Notice that connect u s$\{E\}$, u.receiveS $(\mathsf{x})\{E\}$, u.sendIf $(\mathsf{e})\{E\}\{\mathsf{e}\}$, u.sendIf $(\mathsf{e})\{\mathsf{e}\}\{E\}$, u.receiveIf $\{E\}\{\mathsf{e}\}$, u.receiveIf $\{\mathsf{e}\}\{E\}$, u.receiveWhile $\{E\}$, and u.sendWhile $(\mathsf{e})\{E\}$ are not evaluation contexts: the first would allow session bodies to run before the start of the session; the second would allow execution of an expression waiting for a live channel before actually receiving it; the remaining would allow parts of a conditional or iterative session to run before determining which branch should be selected, or whether the iteration should continue.

Fld
$$\frac{h(\mathsf{o}) = (C,\tilde{\mathsf{f}}:\tilde{\mathsf{v}})}{\mathsf{o}.\mathsf{f}_i\,,h\longrightarrow\mathsf{v}_i,h}$$

Seq
$$\frac{\mathsf{e}_1,h\longrightarrow\mathsf{v},h'}{\mathsf{e}_1;\mathsf{e}_2,h\longrightarrow\mathsf{e}_2,h'}$$

FldAss
$$\frac{h' = h[\mathsf{o}\mapsto h(\mathsf{o})[\mathsf{f}\mapsto\mathsf{v}]]}{\mathsf{o}.\mathsf{f}:=\mathsf{v},h\longrightarrow\mathsf{v},h'}$$

NewC
$$\frac{\mathsf{fields}(C) = \tilde{\mathsf{f}}\tilde{\mathsf{t}}\quad\mathsf{o}\notin h}{\mathsf{new}\ C,h\longrightarrow\mathsf{o},h\cdot[\mathsf{o}\mapsto(C,\tilde{\mathsf{f}}:\mathsf{init}(\mathsf{t}))]}$$

NewS
$$\frac{\mathsf{c}\notin h}{\mathsf{new}\ (\mathsf{s},\bar{\mathsf{s}}),h\longrightarrow\mathsf{c},h\cdot\mathsf{c}}$$

Cong
$$\frac{\mathsf{e},h\longrightarrow\mathsf{e}',h'}{E[\mathsf{e}],h\longrightarrow E[\mathsf{e}'],h'}$$

Meth
$$\frac{h(\mathsf{o}) = (C,\dots)\quad\mathsf{mbody}(\mathsf{m},C) = (\tilde{\mathsf{x}},\mathsf{e})}{\mathsf{o}.\mathsf{m}\,(\tilde{\mathsf{v}}),h\longrightarrow\mathsf{e}[\mathsf{o}/\mathtt{this}][\tilde{\mathsf{v}}/\tilde{\mathsf{x}}],h}$$

NullProp
$$E[\mathsf{NullExc}],h\longrightarrow\mathsf{NullExc},h$$

NullFldAss
$$\mathsf{null}.\mathsf{f}:=\mathsf{v},h\longrightarrow\mathsf{NullExc},h$$

NullFld
$$\mathsf{null}.\mathsf{f}\,,h\longrightarrow\mathsf{NullExc},h$$

NullMeth
$$\mathsf{null}.\mathsf{m}\,(\tilde{\mathsf{v}}),h\longrightarrow\mathsf{NullExc},h$$

In **NewC**, init(bool) = false otherwise init(t) = null.

Fig. 5. Expression Reduction

Expressions. Fig. 5 shows the rules for execution of expressions which correspond to the sequential part of the language. These are standard [5, 11, 21], but for the addition of a fresh shared channel to the heap (rule **NewS**). In rule **NewC** the auxiliary function fields(C) examines the class table and returns the field declarations for C. The method invocation rule is **Meth**; the auxiliary function mbody(m,C) looks up m in the class C, and returns a pair consisting of the formal parameter names and the method's code. The result is the method body where the keyword this is replaced by the receiver's object identifier o, and the formal parameters $\tilde{\mathsf{x}}$ are replaced by the actual parameters $\tilde{\mathsf{v}}$. Note that the replacement of this by o cannot lead to unwanted behaviours since the receiver cannot change during the execution of the method body.

Struct $P | \text{null} \equiv P$ $P | P_0 \equiv P_0 | P$ $P | (P_0 | P_1) \equiv (P | P_0) | P_1$

Spawn   **Par**   **Str**

$E[\text{spawn}\{ \ e \ \}], h \longrightarrow E[\text{null}] | e, h$ $\dfrac{P, h \longrightarrow P', h'}{P | P_0, h \longrightarrow P' | P_0, h'}$ $\dfrac{P_1, h \longrightarrow P_2, h' \quad P_i \equiv P'_i \ i \in \{1, 2\}}{P'_1, h \longrightarrow P'_2, h'}$

Connect

$E_1[\text{connect c s}\{e_1\}] | E_2[\text{connect c } \bar{s}\{e_2\}], h \ \longrightarrow \ E_1[e_1[^{c'}\!/\!c]] | E_2[e_2[^{c'}\!/\!c]], h \cdot c' \quad c' \notin h$

ComS

$E_1[\text{c.send}\,(\mathsf{v})] | E_2[\text{c.receive}], h \ \longrightarrow \ E_1[\text{null}] | E_2[\mathsf{v}], h$

ComSS

$E_1[\text{c.receiveS}\,(\mathsf{x})\{e\}] \ | \ E_2[\text{c.sendS}\,(c')], h \ \longrightarrow \ E_1[\text{null}] \ | \ e\,[^{c'}\!/\!\mathsf{x}] \ | \ E_2[\text{null}], h$

ComSIf-true

$E_1[\text{c.sendIf}\,(\text{true})\{e_1\}\{e_2\}] | E_2[\text{c.receiveIf}\,\{e_3\}\{e_4\}], h \ \longrightarrow \ E_1[e_1] | E_2[e_3], h$

CommSIf-false

$E_1[\text{c.sendIf}\,(\text{false})\{e_1\}\{e_2\}] | E_2[\text{c.receiveIf}\,\{e_3\}\{e_4\}], h \ \longrightarrow \ E_1[e_2] | E_2[e_4], h$

ComSWhile

$E_1[\text{c.sendWhile}\,(e)\{e_1\}] | E_2[\text{c.receiveWhile}\,\{e_2\}], h \ \longrightarrow$
$E_1[\text{c.sendIf}\,(e)\{e_1; \text{c.sendWhile}\,(e)\{e_1\}\}\{\text{null}\}]$
$\qquad\qquad\qquad\qquad\qquad | \ E_2[\text{c.receiveIf}\,\{e_2; \text{c.receiveWhile}\,\{e_2\}\}\{\text{null}\}], h$

Fig. 6. Thread Reduction

Threads. The reduction rules for threads, shown in Fig. 6, are given modulo the standard structural equivalence rules of the π-calculus [23], written $\equiv$. We define *multi-step* reduction as: $\longrightarrow\!\!\!\!\longrightarrow \ \overset{\text{def}}{=} \ (\longrightarrow \cup \equiv)^*$.

When spawn$\{ \ e \ \}$ is the active redex within an arbitrary evaluation context, the *thread body* e becomes a new thread, and the original spawn expression is replaced by null in the context.

Rule **Connect** describes the opening of sessions: if two threads require a session on the same channel name c with dual session types, then a new fresh channel c' is created and added to the heap. The freshness of c' guarantees privacy and bilinearity of the session communication between the two threads. Finally, the two connect expressions are replaced by their respective session bodies where the shared channel c has been substituted by the live channel c'.

Rule **ComS** gives simple session communication: value v is sent by one thread and received by another. Rule **ComSS** formalises the act of delegating a session. One thread awaits to receive a live channel, which will be bound to the variable x within the expression e, and another thread is ready to send such a channel. Notice that when the channel is exchanged, the receiver spawns a new thread to handle the consumption of the delegated session. This strategy is necessary in order to avoid deadlocks in the presence of circular paths of session delegation; see Example 4.1.

In rules **ComSIf-true** and **ComSIf-false**, depending on the value of the boolean, execution proceeds with either the first or the second branch. Rule **CommSWhile** simply expresses the iteration by means of the conditional. This operation allows to repeat a sequence of actions within a single session, which is convenient when describing practical communication protocols (see [8, 10]).

The following example justifies some aspects of our operational semantics.

Example 4.1. demonstrates the reason for the definition of rule **ComSS** which creates a new thread out of the expression in which the sent channel replaces the channel variable. A more natural and simpler formulation of this rule would avoid spawning a new thread:

$$E_1[c.\mathsf{receiveS}\,(x)\{e\}] \mid E_2[c.\mathsf{sendS}\,(c')], h \longrightarrow E_1[e[c'/x]] \mid E_2[\mathsf{null}], h$$

However, using the above version of the rule the threads P_1 and P_2 in the table below reduce to

$$c_1'.\mathsf{send}\,(5); c_1'.\mathsf{receive} \mid \mathsf{null}, \quad h \cdot c\,1'$$

where c_1' is the fresh live channel that replaced c_1 when the connection was established. Notice that both ends of the session are in one thread, so the last configuration is stuck.

```
1   connect c1 begin.?int.end {
2     connect c2 begin.?(!int.end).end {
3       c2.receiveS(x) { x.send(5)} };
4     c1.receive
5   }
```

$$P_1$$

```
1   connect c1 begin.!int.end{
2     connect c2 begin.!(!int.end).end {
3       c2.sendS(c1)
4     }
5   }
```

$$P_2$$

5   Motivating the Design of the Type System

This section discusses the key ideas behind the type system introduced in § 6 with some examples, focusing on type preservation and progress.

Type preservation. In order to achieve subject reduction, we need to ensure that at any time during execution, no more than two threads have access to the same live channel, and also, that no thread has aliases (*i.e.*, more than one reference) to a live channel.

Example 5.1. demonstrates that bilinearity is required for type preservation, and that in order to guarantee bilinearity we need to restrict aliases on live channels. Assume in the following, that in the threads P_1, P_2 and P_3 the variables x, y and z, all point to the same live channel c in heap h.

$$\underbrace{x.\mathsf{send}\,(3); x.\mathsf{send}\,(true)}_{P_1} \mid \underbrace{y.\mathsf{send}\,(4); y.\mathsf{send}\,(false)}_{P_2} \mid \underbrace{z.\mathsf{receive}; z.\mathsf{receive}}_{P_3}, \quad h$$

It is clear that P_3 expects to receive first an integer and then a boolean via channel c; but P_3 could communicate first with P_1 and then with P_2 (or vice versa) receiving two integers. Therefore we need to distinguish a *shared* channel (one where a connection has not been established yet) from a *live* channel (one where a connection has been established). In order to make this distinction, shared channel types start with begin. To avoid the creation of aliases on live channels, we do not allow live channel types to be used as the types of fields, nor do we allow more than one live channel parameter in methods.

Example 5.2. demonstrates that guaranteeing bilinearity requires restrictions on sending/receiving live channels. In the following, assuming that the three threads, P_1, P_2 and P_3 could be typed, for some s_1 and s_2,

```
1   connect c1 s1 {
2       connect c2 s2 {
3           c2.sendS(c1) };
4       c1.receive }
```
$$P_1$$

```
1   connect c1 s̄1 {
2       c1.receive;
3       c1.send(3)
4   }
```
$$P_2$$

```
1   connect c2 s̄2 {
2       c2.receiveS(x){ x.send(4) }
3   }
```
$$P_3$$

then, starting with a heap h, the above three threads in parallel reduce to:

$$c_1'.\text{receive} \mid c_1'.\text{receive} ; c_1'.\text{send}(3) \mid c_1'.\text{send}(4), \quad h \cdot c_1' \cdot c_2'$$

where c_1' and c_2' are the fresh live channels that replaced respectively c_1 and c_2 when the sessions began. Clearly, this configuration violates the bilinearity condition.

We therefore need a notion of whether a live channel has been *consumed*, *i.e.*, whether it can still be used for the communication of values. There is no explicit user syntax for consuming channels. Instead, channels are implicitly consumed 1) at the end of a connection, 2) when they are sent over a channel, and 3) when they are used within spawn. However, types distinguish consumed channels using the end suffix. Hence, when a live channel is passed as parameter in a method call it can potentially become consumed. In § 6.1 we show that P_1 is type incorrect for any s_1 and s_2.

Progress in MOOSE means that indefinite waiting may only happen at the point where a connection is required, and in particular when the dual of a connect is missing. In other words, there will never be a deadlock at the communication points. This can only be guaranteed if the communications are always processed in a given order, *i.e.*, if there is no interleaving of sessions.

Example 5.3. demonstrates how session interleaving may cause deadlocks.

```
1   connect c1 begin.!int.end {
2       connect c2 begin.?int.end {
3           c1.send(3); c2.receive}
4   }
```
$$P_1$$

```
1   connect c1 begin.?int.end {
2       connect c2 begin.!int.end {
3           c2.send(5); c1.receive}
4   }
```
$$P_2$$

In the above example we have indefinite waiting after establishing the connection, because P_1 cannot progress unless P_2 reaches the statement c_1.receive, and P_2 cannot progress unless P_1 reaches the statement c_2.receive, and so we have a deadlock at a communication point. Note that *nesting* of sessions does not affect progress. Let us consider the following processes:

$P_1' = $ connect c_1 begin.?int.end$\{c_1$.receive;connect c_2 begin.!int.end$\{c_2$.send$(5)\}\}$

$P_2' = $ connect c_1 begin.!int.end$\{c_1$.send(3);connect c_2 begin.?int.end$\{c_2$.receive$\}\}$

$P_3' = $ connect c_1 begin.!int.end$\{$connect c_2 begin.?int.end$\{c_2$.receive$\}$;c_1.send$(3)\}$

Parallel execution of P_1' and P_2' does not cause deadlock, while parallel execution of P_1' with P_3' does, but it does so at the connection point for c_2. However, such deadlock is acceptable, since it would disappear if we placed a suitable connect in parallel.

In order to avoid interleaving at live channels, we require that within each "scope" no more than one live channel can be used for communication; we call this the "hot set." The formal definition can be found in § 6. In § 6.1, we show that P_1 and P_2 are type incorrect.

Example 5.4. demonstrates that allowing methods with multiple live channel parameters may cause interleaving. Consider a method m of class C with two parameters x and y both of type ?int and body x.receive;y.receive. In this case the two threads P_1 and P_2 below produce a deadlock due to the interleaving of sessions.

```
1   connect c1 begin.!int.end {
2     connect c2 begin.!int.end {
3       c1.send(3); c2.send(3)}
4   }
```
P_1

```
1   connect c1 begin.?int.end {
2     connect c2 begin.?int.end {
3       new C.m(c2,c1)}
4   }
```
P_2

In order to avoid problems like the above, we restrict the number of live channel parameters to at most one.

We argue that the above conditions on live channels are not that restrictive. First, we can represent most of the communication protocols in the session types literature, as well as traditional synchronisation [24, § 3], while at the same time ensuring progress. Secondly, since these conditions are only essential for progress, if we remove hot sets from typing judgements, we will obtain a more relaxed type system which allows deadlock on live channels, but still preserves type safety.

6   Type System

Types. The full syntax of the types is given below.

$$t ::= C \mid \mathsf{bool} \mid s \mid (s,\bar{s}) \qquad \dagger ::= ! \mid ?$$
$$s ::= \mathsf{begin}.\rho \qquad \rho ::= \pi.\mathsf{end} \mid \pi.\dagger\langle\rho,\rho\rangle \qquad \eta ::= \pi \mid \rho$$
$$\pi ::= \varepsilon \mid \dagger t \mid \dagger(\rho) \mid \dagger\langle\pi,\pi\rangle \mid \dagger\langle\pi\rangle^* \mid \pi.\pi$$

Each session type s starts with the keyword begin and has one or more endpoints, denoted by end. Between the start and each ending point, a sequence of session parts describe the communication protocol.

Session parts, ranged over π, represent communications and their sequencing; $\dagger$ is a convenient abbreviation that ranges over $\{!,?\}$. The types !t and ?t express respectively the sending and reception of a value of type t, while $!(\rho)$ and $?(\rho)$ represent the exchange of a live channel, and therefore of an active session, with remaining communications determined by type ρ.

The *conditional* session part has the shape $\dagger\langle\pi_1,\pi_2\rangle$: when $\dagger$ is ! this type describes sessions which send a boolean value and proceed with π_1 if the value is true, or π_2 if the value is false; when $\dagger$ is ? the behaviour is the same, except that the boolean that determines the branch is to be received instead. The *iterative* session part $\dagger\langle\pi\rangle^*$ describes sessions that respectively send or receive a boolean value, and if that value is true continue with π, *iterating*, while if the value is false, continue to following session parts, if any. Session parts can be composed into sequences using '.', hence forming longer session parts inductively; note that we use ε for the empty sequence. A *complete session part* is a session part concatenated either with end or with a conditional whose branches in turn are both complete session parts. We use ρ to range over complete session parts and η to range over both complete and incomplete session parts. Each session type s has a corresponding dual, denoted $\bar{s}$, which is obtained as follows:

- $\bar{?} =!$ $\bar{!} =?$
- $\overline{\text{begin}.\rho} = \text{begin}.\bar{\rho}$
- $\overline{\pi.\text{end}} = \bar{\pi}.\text{end}$ $\overline{\pi.\dagger\langle\rho_1,\rho_2\rangle} = \bar{\pi}.\bar{\dagger}\langle\bar{\rho_1},\bar{\rho_2}\rangle$
- $\overline{\dagger t} = \bar{\dagger}t$ $\overline{\dagger(\rho)} = \bar{\dagger}(\rho)$ $\overline{\dagger\langle\pi_1,\pi_2\rangle} = \bar{\dagger}\langle\bar{\pi_1},\bar{\pi_2}\rangle$ $\overline{\dagger\langle\pi\rangle^*} = \bar{\dagger}\langle\bar{\pi}\rangle^*$ $\overline{\pi_1.\pi_2} = \bar{\pi_1}.\bar{\pi_2}$

Type System. We type expressions and threads with respect to a fixed class table, so only the classes declared in this table are types. We could easily extend the syntax to allow dynamic class creation, but this is orthogonal to session typing. We use the same table to judge subtyping $<:$ on class names: we assume the subtyping between classes causes no cycle as in [21]. In addition, we have $(s,\bar{s}) <: s$ and $(s,\bar{s}) <: \bar{s}$, as in standard π-calculus channel subtyping rules [19]: a channel on which both communication directions are allowed may also transmit data following only one of the two directions.

The typing judgements for threads have two environments, *i.e.*, they have the shape:

$$\Gamma;\Sigma \vdash P:\text{thread}$$

where the *standard environment* Γ associates types to this, parameters and objects, while the *session environment* Σ contains only judgements for live channels. These environments are defined as follows, under the condition that no subject occurs twice.

$$\Gamma ::= \emptyset \mid \Gamma,x:t \mid \Gamma,\text{this}:C \mid \Gamma,o:C \qquad \Sigma ::= \emptyset \mid \Sigma,u:\eta \mid \Sigma,u:\updownarrow$$

When typing expressions we need also to take into account which is the unique (if any) channel identifier currently used to communicate data. This is necessary in order to avoid session interleaving. Therefore we record a third set, the *hot set* S, which can be either empty or can contain a single channel identifier belonging to the session environment. Thus the typing judgements for expressions have the shape:

$$\Gamma; \Sigma; S \vdash e : t$$

where S is either $\emptyset$ or $\{u\}$ with $u \in \text{dom}(\Sigma)$.

We adopt the convention that typing rules are applicable only when the session environments in the conclusions are defined.

Spawn

$$\dfrac{\Gamma; \Sigma; S \vdash e : t \quad closed(\Sigma)}{\Gamma; \Sigma; S \vdash \text{spawn} \{ e \} : Object}$$

Weak

$$\dfrac{\Gamma; \Sigma; \emptyset \vdash e : t \quad u \in \text{dom}(\Sigma)}{\Gamma; \Sigma; \{u\} \vdash e : t}$$

Seq

$$\dfrac{\Gamma; \Sigma; S \vdash e : t \quad \Gamma; \Sigma'; S \vdash e' : t'}{\Gamma; \Sigma.\Sigma'; S \vdash e; e' : t'}$$

Meth

$$\dfrac{\Gamma; \Sigma_0; S \vdash e : C \quad \Gamma; \Sigma_i; S \vdash e_i : t_i \quad i \in \{1 \ldots n\}}{\Gamma; \Sigma_0.\Sigma_1 \ldots \Sigma_n; S \vdash e.m(e_1 \ldots e_n) : t} \qquad mtype(m, C) = t_1 \ldots t_n \rightarrow t$$

MethLin

$$\dfrac{\Gamma; \Sigma_0; \{u\} \vdash e : C \quad \Gamma; \Sigma_i; \{u\} \vdash e_i : t_i \quad i \in \{1 \ldots n\}}{\Gamma; \Sigma_0.\Sigma_1 \ldots \Sigma_n.\{u : \eta\}; \{u\} \vdash e.m(e_1 \ldots e_n, u) : t} \qquad mtype(m, C) = t_1 \ldots t_n, \eta \rightarrow t$$

Fig. 7. Some Typing Rules for Standard Expressions

Expressions. We highlight the interesting typing rules for expressions in Fig. 7 and Fig. 8. Looking at these rules two observations on hot sets are immediate:

- in all rules except **Conn**, **ReceiveS** and **Weak** the hot sets of all the premises and of the conclusion coincide;
- in all rules whose conclusion is a session expression the hot set of the conclusion is the subject of the session expression.

These two conditions ensure that all communications use the same live channel, *i.e.*, that sessions are not interleaved. In rule **Conn** the live channel becomes shared, and therefore in the conclusion the hot set is empty. Since $u.\text{receiveS}(x)\{e\}$ in rule **ReceiveS** receives along the live channel u a channel that will be replaced to x, the hot set of the premise is $\{x\}$ while that of the conclusion is $\{u\}$. Lastly, rule **Weak** allows to replace an empty hot set by a set containing an arbitrary element of the domain of the session environment.

The session environments of the conclusions are obtained from those of the premises and possibly other session environments using the *concatenation* defined below.

- $\eta.\eta' = \eta.\eta'$ if $\eta = \pi$ or $\eta' = \varepsilon$ otherwise $\eta.\eta' = \bot$.
- $\Sigma.\Sigma' = \Sigma \setminus \text{dom}(\Sigma') \cup \Sigma' \setminus \text{dom}(\Sigma) \cup \{u : \Sigma(u).\Sigma'(u) \mid u \in \text{dom}(\Sigma) \cap \text{dom}(\Sigma')\}$

The concatenation of two live channel types η and η' is the unique live channel type (if it exists) which prescribes all the communications of η followed by all those of η'. The

Conn
$$\frac{\Gamma;\emptyset;\emptyset \vdash u:\text{begin}.\rho \quad \Gamma\backslash u\,;\Sigma,u:\rho;\{u\} \vdash e:t}{\Gamma;\Sigma;\emptyset \vdash \text{connect } u \text{ begin}.\rho\,\{e\}:t}$$

Send
$$\frac{\Gamma;\Sigma;\{u\} \vdash e:t}{\Gamma;\Sigma.\{u:!t\};\{u\} \vdash u.\text{send}(\,e\,):Object}$$

Receive
$$\frac{\Gamma \vdash \text{ok} \quad \vdash t:tp}{\Gamma;\{u:?t\};\{u\} \vdash u.\text{receive}:t}$$

ReceiveS
$$\frac{\Gamma\backslash x\,;\Sigma,x:\rho;\{x\} \vdash e:t \quad closed(\Sigma)}{\Gamma;\{u:?(\rho)\}.\Sigma;\{u\} \vdash u.\text{receiveS}(x)\{e\}:Object}$$

SendS
$$\frac{\Gamma \vdash \text{ok} \quad \vdash \rho:tp}{\Gamma;\{u':\rho,u:!(\rho)\};\{u\} \vdash u.\text{sendS}(u'):Object}$$

ReceiveIf
$$\frac{\Gamma;\Sigma,u:\eta_i;\{u\} \vdash e_i:t \quad i\in\{1,2\}}{\eta'=?\langle\eta_1,\eta_2\rangle}$$
$$\frac{}{\Gamma;\Sigma,u:\eta';\{u\} \vdash u.\text{receiveIf}\{e_1\}\{e_2\}:t}$$

SendIf
$$\frac{\Gamma;\Sigma_1;\{u\} \vdash e:bool \quad \eta'=!\langle\eta_1,\eta_2\rangle}{\Gamma;\Sigma_2,u:\eta_i;\{u\} \vdash e_i:t \quad i\in\{1,2\}}$$
$$\frac{}{\Gamma;\Sigma_1.\{\Sigma_2,u:\eta'\};\{u\} \vdash u.\text{sendIf}(e)\{e_1\}\{e_2\}:t}$$

ReceiveWhile
$$\frac{\Gamma;\{u:\pi\};\{u\} \vdash e:t}{\Gamma;\{u:?\langle\pi\rangle^*\};\{u\} \vdash u.\text{receiveWhile}\{e\}:t}$$

SendWhile
$$\frac{\Gamma;\{u:\pi\};\{u\} \vdash e:bool \quad \Gamma;\{u:\pi'\};\{u\} \vdash e':t}{\Gamma;\{u:\pi.!\langle\pi'.\pi\rangle^*\};\{u\} \vdash u.\text{sendWhile}(e)\{e'\}:t}$$

Fig. 8. Typing Rules for Communication Expressions

extension to session environments is straightforward. The typing rules concatenate the session environments to take into account the order of execution of expressions.

In the following we discuss the three most interesting typing rules for expressions.

Rule **Spawn** requires that all sessions used by the spawned thread are finally consumed, *i.e.*, they are all complete live channel types. This is necessary in order to avoid configurations that break the bilinearity condition, such as spawn{ c.send(1) }; c.send(true). To guarantee the consumption we define:

$$closed(\Sigma) = \forall u:\eta \in \Sigma \,\exists\rho.\,\eta = \rho$$

Rule **MethLin** retrieves the type of the method m from the class table using the auxiliary function mtype(m, C). This rule expects the last actual parameter u to be a channel identifier that will be used within the method body directly as if it was part of an open session. Therefore the hot sets of all the premises and of the conclusion must be {u}. The session environments of the premises are also concatenated with {u:η} which represents the communication protocol of the live channel u during the execution of the method body.

Rule **Conn** ensures that a session body properly uses its unique channel according to the required session type. The first premise says that the channel identifier used for the session (u) can be typed with the appropriate shared session type (begin.ρ). The second premise ensures that the session body can be typed in the restricted environment Γ\u with a session environment containing u:ρ and with hot set {u}.

Methods. The following rules define well-formed methods.

M-ok	**MLin-ok**
$\mathtt{this}:C,\tilde{x}:\tilde{t}\,;\,\emptyset\,;\,\emptyset\vdash e:t$	$\mathtt{this}:C,\tilde{x}:\tilde{t}\,;\,x:\eta\,;\,\{x\}\vdash e:t$
$\mathtt{t\,m}\,(\tilde{t}\,\tilde{x})\;\{e\}:\mathtt{ok\,in}\,C$	$\mathtt{t\,m}\,(\tilde{t}\,\tilde{x},\eta x)\;\{e\}:\mathtt{ok\,in}\,C$

Rule **M-ok** checks that a method that does not have live channel parameters is well-formed, by type-checking its body and succeeding with both an empty session environment and an empty hot set, *i.e.*, it ensures that no channel can be used outside the scope of a session within the method body. Rule **MLin-ok** performs the same check, but requires that the last parameter is a live channel which is the element of the hot set in the typing of the method body.

Thread. In the typing rules for threads, we need to take into account that the same channel can occur with dual types in the session environments of two premises. For this reason we compose the session environments of premises using the *parallel composition* defined below.

- $\eta\|\eta'=\updownarrow$ if $\eta=\overline{\eta'}$ otherwise $\eta\|\eta'=\bot$; and $\updownarrow\|\eta=\eta\|\updownarrow=\updownarrow\|\updownarrow=\bot$.
- $\Sigma\|\Sigma'=\Sigma\setminus\mathrm{dom}(\Sigma')\cup\Sigma'\setminus\mathrm{dom}(\Sigma)\cup\{u:\Sigma(u)\|\Sigma'(u)\mid u\in\mathrm{dom}(\Sigma)\cap\mathrm{dom}(\Sigma')\}$

Using the above operator, the typing rules for processes are straightforward. Rule **Start** promotes an expression to the thread level; and rule **Par** types a composition of threads if the composition of their session environments is defined.

Start	**Par**
$\Gamma;\Sigma;\mathcal{S}\vdash e:t$	$\Gamma;\Sigma\vdash P:\mathtt{thread}\quad\Gamma;\Sigma'\vdash P':\mathtt{thread}$
$\Gamma;\Sigma\vdash e:\mathtt{thread}$	$\Gamma;\Sigma\|\Sigma'\vdash P\,|\,P':\mathtt{thread}$

6.1 Justifying Examples

In this subsection we discuss the typing of the threads shown in § 5.

Example 5.1. The thread $P_1\,|\,P_2$ is not typable since the parallel composition of the corresponding session environments is undefined.

Example 5.2. The thread P_1 cannot be typed since:

- the expression in line 3 can only be typed by rule **SendS** which requires for the sent channel c_1 a live channel type terminating by end in the session environment;
- the expression in line 4 can only be typed by rule **Receive** which requires also a live channel type different from ε for the channel c_1 in the session environment;
- to type the composition of these two expressions, **Seq** requires the concatenation of the corresponding session environments to be defined, but this is false since a type terminating by end cannot be concatenated to a live channel type different from ε.

Examples 5.3. Neither thread can be typed. For example, to type the expressions in line 3 in P_1 using rule **Send**, $\{c_1\}$ and $\{c_2\}$ should be the hot sets, respectively. Thus rule **Seq** cannot type the composition of these two expressions, since this rule requires the premises to share the same hot set.

Example 5.4. It is clear from the rules **Meth** and **MethLin** that a method can have at most one live parameter, so the method is not typable.

ConnI

$$\frac{\Gamma \vdash e : t \parallel \Sigma; \mathcal{S} \quad \Sigma(\!(u)\!) = \eta \quad s = begin.\sigma(\eta \downarrow) \quad u \notin dom(\Gamma) \quad \Gamma' = \Gamma \text{ if } u \text{ name else } \Gamma, u : s}{\Gamma' \vdash connect\ u\ s\ \{e\} : \sigma(t) \parallel \sigma(\Sigma) \setminus u; \emptyset}$$

ReceiveI

$$\frac{\Gamma \vdash ok}{\Gamma \vdash u.receive : \phi \parallel \{u : ?\phi\}; \{u\}}$$

ReceiveSI

$$\frac{\Gamma \vdash e : t \parallel \Sigma; \mathcal{S} \quad x \notin \Gamma \quad \mathcal{S} \subseteq \{x\} \quad \Sigma(\!(x)\!) = \eta}{\Gamma \vdash u.receiveS\,(x)\{e\} : Object \parallel \{u : ?(\eta \downarrow)\}.\Sigma \downarrow; \{u\}}$$

SendSI

$$\frac{\Gamma \vdash ok}{\Gamma \vdash u.sendS\,(u') : Object \parallel \{u' : \psi.end, u : !(\psi.end)\}; \{u\}}$$

Fig. 9. Some Inference Rules

6.2 Inference of Session Environments, Hot Sets, and Session Types for connect

Although the type system is flexible enough to express interesting protocols, typing as described so far is somewhat inconvenient, in that it requires a) the hot sets, and the session environments to be assumed (or "guessed"), and b) the session types to be stated explicitly for connect expressions.

To address (a), in this section, we develop *inference rules* for expressions and threads which have the shape

$$\Gamma \vdash e : t \parallel \Sigma; \mathcal{S} \qquad \text{and} \qquad \Gamma \vdash P : thread \parallel \Sigma$$

and which express that session environments and hot sets are derived rather than assumed. Based on these rules, at the end of the section, we address (b) and show how session types can be inferred for connect expressions.

Fig. 9 gives some of the inference rules. The rules are applicable only if all sets in the conclusion are defined. We extend the syntax of types with *type variables*, ranged over by ϕ, which stand for types, and *part of session type variables*, ranged over by ψ, which stand for part of session types. Rule **ReceiveI** introduces ϕ, since we do not know the type of the data that will be received. Rule **SendSI** introduces ψ, since we do not know the type of the channel that will be sent.

As usual, the inference rules are structural, *i.e.*, depend on the structure of the expression being typed; typically, the inference system does not have rules like **Weak**. Therefore, the inference rules must play also the role of the non-structural type rules.

Because in rule **ConnI** we do not know if the session environment inferred for e contains a premise for u, we define:

$$\Sigma(\!(u)\!) = \text{ if } u \in dom(\Sigma) \text{ then } \Sigma(u) \text{ else } \varepsilon.$$

Furthemore, the operator $\downarrow$ appends end to η if η is a session part, propagates inside the final branches of η if η is of the shape $\pi.\dagger\langle\eta_1,\eta_2\rangle$, and does nothing otherwise.

An *inference substitution*, σ, maps type variables to types, and part of session type variables to part of session types. We use inference substitution only in rule **ConnI** in order to unify the session type s with begin.η where $\eta\downarrow$ being inferred may contain variables. That is, we require s $=$ begin.$\sigma(\eta\downarrow)$.

The following proposition states that inference computes the least session environments and hot sets.

Proposition 6.1. *1. If* $\Gamma;\Sigma;S \vdash e:t$ *then* $\Gamma \vdash e:t' \parallel \Sigma';S'$ *where* $\sigma(t') = t$ *and* $\sigma(\Sigma') \subseteq \Sigma$ *for some inference substitution* σ *and* $S' \subseteq S$.

2. If $\Gamma \vdash e:t \parallel \Sigma;S$ *then for all inference substitutions* σ *we get:* $\Gamma;\sigma(\Sigma);S \vdash e:\sigma(t)$.

3. If $\Gamma;\Sigma \vdash P:$thread *then* $\Gamma \vdash P:$thread $\parallel \Sigma'$ *where* $\sigma(\Sigma') \subseteq \Sigma$ *for some inference substitution* σ.

4. If $\Gamma \vdash P:$thread $\parallel \Sigma$ *then for all inference substitutions* σ *we get:* $\Gamma;\sigma(\Sigma) \vdash P:$thread.

Note that the inference of Σ does not rely on S so that we can obtain the same result for the system without S.

$$\dfrac{\dfrac{\dfrac{0 \vdash 5:\text{int} \parallel 0;0}{0 \vdash x.\text{send}\,(5):Object \parallel \{x:!\text{int}\};\{x\}}}{0 \vdash c_2.\text{receiveS}\,(x)\{x.\text{send}\,(5)\}:Object \parallel \{c_2:?(!\text{int}.\text{end})\};\{c_2\}} \quad \dfrac{0 \vdash e:Object \parallel 0;0 \qquad 0 \vdash e':\phi \parallel \{c_1:?\phi\};\{c_1\}}{\dfrac{0 \vdash e;e':\phi \parallel \{c_1:?\phi\};\{c_1\}}{0 \vdash \text{connect}\,c_1\,\text{begin}.?\text{int}.\text{end}\{e;e'\}:\text{int} \parallel 0;0}}}{}$$

where e $=$ connect c_2 begin.?($!$int.end).end$\{c_2$.receiveS $(x)\{x$.send $(5)\}\}$, e$' = c_1$.receive.

Fig. 10. An Example of Inference

As an example we show the inference for the thread P_1 of Example 4.1 in Fig. 10.

We can now address (b), *i.e.*, the inference of session types in connect expressions. This requires to modify the syntax by dropping the session types in the connect expressions. It is enough to modify the inference rule for connect avoiding to use the inference substitution for obtaining the required session types. Thus, the new inference rule is:

ConnI$'$
$$\dfrac{\Gamma \vdash e:t \parallel \Sigma;S \quad \Sigma(\!(u)\!) = \eta \quad u \notin \text{dom}(\Gamma) \quad \Gamma' = \Gamma \text{ if } u \text{ is a name else } \Gamma,u:s}{\Gamma' \vdash \text{connect}\,u\,\{e\}:t \parallel \Sigma\setminus u;0}$$

With this rule, users would not need to declare session types explicitly in connect; for example, they could write connect c $\{c$.send (true);c.send (false)$\}$ instead of writing connect c begin.!bool.!bool.end $\{c$.send (true);c.send (false)$\}$.

Since explicit declarations are useful for program documentation, the inclusion of type inference for connect should be up to the individual language designer.

7 Type Safety and Communication Safety

7.1 Subject Reduction

We will consider only reductions of well-typed expressions and threads. We define agreement between environments and heaps in the standard way and we denote it by $\Gamma \vdash h : \text{ok}$. A convenient notation is $\Gamma;\Sigma;S \vdash e;h$, which is short for $\Gamma;\Sigma;S \vdash e : t$ for some t and $\Gamma \vdash h : \text{ok}$. Similarly $\Gamma;\Sigma \vdash P;h$ means $\Gamma;\Sigma \vdash P : \text{thread}$ and $\Gamma \vdash h : \text{ok}$. We first show that the type system of §6 satisfies the subject reduction property.

Theorem 7.1 (Subject Reduction).

- $\Gamma;\Sigma;S \vdash e : t$, and $\Gamma;\Sigma;S \vdash e;h$ and $e,h \longrightarrow e',h'$ imply $\Gamma';\Sigma';S \vdash e';h'$ and $\Gamma';\Sigma';S \vdash e' : t$ with $\Gamma \subseteq \Gamma'$ and $\Sigma \subseteq \Sigma'$.
- $\Gamma;\Sigma \vdash P;h$ and $P,h \longrightarrow P',h'$ imply $\Gamma';\Sigma' \vdash P';h'$ with $\Gamma \subseteq \Gamma'$ and $\Sigma \subseteq \Sigma'$.

The proof uses generation lemmas and substitution lemmas in a standard way. The novelty of this proof relies on a detailed analysis of the relations between session environments for typing expressions inside evaluation contexts and the filled contexts. More precisely we introduce a partial order on session environments in Definition 7.2. When proving type preservation for the case $E[e],h \longrightarrow E[e'],h'$, we apply Lemma 7.3 to extrapolate properties of the session environment used for typing e out of that used for typing $E[e]$. Similarly for the case when two threads communicate by the communication rules in Fig. 6.

Definition 7.2 (Prefix Order on Session Environments).

1. $\eta \preceq \eta'$ is the smallest partial order such that $\pi \preceq \pi.\eta$;
2. $\Sigma \preceq \Sigma'$ if $u : \eta \in \Sigma$ implies $u : \eta' \in \Sigma'$ and $\eta \preceq \eta'$.

Notice that $\Sigma \preceq \Sigma'$ iff $\Sigma' = \Sigma.\Sigma''$ for some Σ''.

Lemma 7.3 (Subderivations).

If a derivation $\mathcal{D}$ proves $\Gamma;\Sigma;S \vdash E[e] : t$ then $\mathcal{D}$ contains a subderivation whose conclusion is the typing of the showed occurrence of e: $\Gamma;\Sigma';S' \vdash e : t'$ and $\Sigma' \preceq \Sigma$.

The proof is by induction on evaluation contexts.

7.2 Communication Safety

Even more interesting than subject reduction, are the following properties:

P1 (communication error freedom) no communication error can occur, *i.e.*, there cannot be two sends or two receives on the same channel in parallel in two different threads;

P2 (progress) typable threads can always progress unless one of the following situations occurs:
- a null pointer exception is thrown;
- there is a connect instruction waiting for the dual connect instruction.

P3 (communication-order preserving) after a session has begun the required communications are always executed in the expected order.

These properties hold for a thread obtained by reducing a well-typed closed thread in which all expressions are user expressions. We write $\prod_{0 \leq i < n} e_i$ for $e_0 \mid e_1 \mid \ldots \mid e_{n-1}$. We say a thread P is *initial* if $0; 0 \vdash P$: thread is derivable and $P \equiv \prod_{0 \leq i < n} e_i$ where e_i is a user expression. Notice that this implies $0; 0 \vdash P; 0$. For stating **P1**, we add a new constant CommErr *(communication error)* to the syntax and the following rule:

$$E_1[e] \mid E_2[e'] \longrightarrow \text{CommErr}$$

if e and e' are session expressions with the same subject and they are not dual of each other. We can now prove that we never reach a state containing such incompatible expressions.

Corollary 7.4 (CommErr **Freedom**). *Assume P_0 is initial and $P_0, 0 \longrightarrow\!\!\!\rightarrow P, h$. Then P does not contain* CommErr, *i.e., there does not exist P' such that $P \equiv P' \mid$ CommErr.*

The proof of the above theorem is straightforward from the subject reduction theorem. Next we show that the progress property **P2** holds in our typing system.

Theorem 7.5 (**Progress**). *Assume P_0 is initial and $P_0, 0 \longrightarrow\!\!\!\rightarrow P, h$. Then one of the following holds.*

- *In P, all expressions are values, i.e., $P \equiv \prod_{0 \leq i < n} v_i$;*
- *$P, h \longrightarrow P', h'$;*
- *P throws a null pointer exception, i.e., $P \equiv$ NullExc $\mid Q$; or*
- *P stops with a connect waiting for its dual instruction, i.e., $P \equiv E[\text{connect } c \, s \, \{e\}] \mid Q$.*

The key in showing progress is the natural correspondence between irreducible session expressions and parts of session types formalised in the following definition.

Definition 7.6. *Define $\propto$ between irreducible session expressions and parts of session types as follows:*

$$\text{c.receive} \propto ?t \quad \text{c.send}(v) \propto !t \quad \text{c.receiveS}(x)\{e\} \propto ?(\rho) \quad \text{c.sendS}(c') \propto !(\rho)$$
$$\text{c.receiveIf}\{e_1\}\{e_2\} \propto ?\langle \eta_1, \eta_2 \rangle \quad \text{c.sendIf}(v)\{e_1\}\{e_2\} \propto !\langle \eta_1, \eta_2 \rangle$$
$$\text{c.receiveWhile}\{e\} \propto ?\langle \pi \rangle^* \quad \text{c.sendWhile}(v)\{e\} \propto !\langle \pi \rangle^*$$

Notice, that the relation $e \propto \pi$ reflects the "shape" of the session, rather than the precise types involved. For example, $e \propto ?t$ implies $e \propto ?t'$ for any type t'.

Using the generation lemmas and Lemma 7.3 we can show the correspondence between an irreducible session expression inside an evaluation context and the type of the live channel which is the subject of the expression.

Lemma 7.7. *Let e be an irreducible session expression with subject c and $\Gamma; \Sigma \vdash E[e]$: thread. Then $\Sigma(c) = \pi.\eta$ with $e \propto \pi$.*

The proof of Theorem 7.5 argues that if the configuration does not contain waiting connects or null pointer errors, but contains an irreducible session expression e_1, then by subject reduction and well-formedness of the session environment, the rest of the thread independently moves or it contains the dual of that irreducible expression, e_2. Then by Lemma 7.7, we get $e_1 \propto \pi$ and $e_2 \propto \bar{\pi}$. Therefore e_1 and e_2 are dual of each other and can communicate.

Note that Theorem 7.5 shows that *threads can always communicate at live channels.* From the above theorem, immediately we get:

Corollary 7.8 (Completion of Sessions). *Assume P_0 is initial and $P_0, \emptyset \longrightarrow\!\!\!\rightarrow P, h$. Suppose $P \equiv \prod_{0 \leq i < n} e_i$ and irreducible. Then either all e_i are values $(0 \leq i < n)$ or there is some j $(0 \leq j < n)$ such that $e_j \in \{\text{NullExc}, E[\text{connect } c \, s \, \{e\}]\}$.*

Finally we state the main property (**P3**) of our typing system. For this purpose, we define the partial order $\sqsubseteq$ on live channel types as the smallest partial order such that: $\eta \sqsubseteq \pi.\eta$; $\pi_i.\eta \sqsubseteq \dagger\langle\pi_1, \pi_2\rangle.\eta$ $(i \in \{1,2\})$; $\rho_i \sqsubseteq \dagger\langle\rho_1, \rho_2\rangle$ $(i \in \{1,2\})$; and $\dagger\langle\pi.\langle\pi\rangle^*, \varepsilon\rangle.\eta \sqsubseteq \langle\pi\rangle^*.\eta$.

This partial order takes into account reduction as formalised in the following theorem: any configuration $E[e_0] \, | \, Q, h$ reachable from the initial configuration and containing the irreducible session expression e_0, if it proceeds, then either (1) it does so in the sub-thread Q, or (2) Q contains the dual expression e_0', which (a) interacts with e_0, and (b) has a dual type at c (and therefore, through application of Lemma 7.7 the two expressions conform to the "shape" of their type, *i.e.*, $\eta = \pi.\eta_0$ with $e_0 \propto \pi$ and $e_0' \propto \bar{\pi}$), and (c) then the type of channel c "correctly shrinks" as $\eta' \sqsubseteq \eta$.

Theorem 7.9 (Communication-Order Preservation). *Let P_0 be initial. Assume that $P_0, \emptyset \longrightarrow\!\!\!\rightarrow E[e_0] \, | \, Q, h \longrightarrow P', h'$ where e_0 is an irreducible session expression with subject c. Then:*

1. *$P' \equiv E[e_0] \, | \, Q'$, or*
2. *$Q \equiv E'[e_0'] \, | \, R$ with e_0' dual of e_0 and*
   (a) *$E[e_0] \, | \, E'[e_0'] \, | \, R, h \longrightarrow e \, | \, e' \, | \, R', h'$;*
   (b) *$\Gamma; \Sigma, c : \eta \vdash E[e_0] :$ thread and $\Gamma; \Sigma', c : \bar{\eta} \vdash E'[e_0'] :$ thread; and*
   (c) *$\Gamma; \hat{\Sigma}, c : \eta' \vdash e :$ thread and $\Gamma; \hat{\Sigma}', c : \bar{\eta}' \vdash e' :$ thread with $\eta' \sqsubseteq \eta$.*

8   Related Work

Linear typing systems. Session types for the π-calculus originate from linear typing systems [19, 22], whose main aim is to guarantee that a channel is used exactly or at most once within a term.

In the context of programming languages, [12] proposes a type system for checking protocols and resource usage in order to enforce linearity of variables in the presence of aliasing. They implemented the typing system in Vault [9], a low level C-like language. The main issue that they had to address is that a shared component should not refer to linear components, since aliasing of the shared component can result in non-linear usage of any linear elements to which it provides access. To relax this condition, they proposed operations for safe sharing, and for controlled linear usage. In our system non-interference is ensured by operational semantics in which substitution of shared fresh channels takes place when reducing `connect`, and therefore we do not need explicit constructs for this purpose. Finally, note that the system of [12] is not readily applicable in a concurrent setting, and hence in channel-based communication.

Programming languages and sessions. In [29] the authors extend previous work [15], and define a concurrent functional language with session primitives. Their language supports sending of channels and higher-order values, and incorporates branching and selection, along with recursive sessions and channel sharing. Moreover, it incorporates the multi-threading primitive fork, whose operational semantics is similar to that of spawn. Finally, their system allows live channels as parameters to functions, and tracks aliasing of channels; as a result, their system is polymorphic.

In [27], the authors formalise an extension to CORBA interfaces based on session types, which are used to determine the order in which available operations can be invoked. The authors define *protocols* consisting of *sessions*, and use labelled branches and selection to model method invocation within each session. Labelled branches are also used to denote exceptions, and their system incorporates recursive session types. However, run-time checks are considered in order to check protocol conformance, and there is no formalisation in terms of operational semantics and type system.

We developed our formalism building upon previous experience with $\mathcal{L}_{doos}$ [10], a distributed object-oriented language with basic session capabilities. In the present work we have chosen to simplify the substrate to that of a concurrent calculus, and focus on the integration of advanced session types. In [10], shared channels could only be associated with a single session type each, and therefore runtime checks were not required for connections; however, this assumption is not necessary, and we preferred to compromise such superficial type-checking — the essence of our system is in typing a session body against the session type.

In our new formulation we chose not to model RMI, and in fact, an interesting question is whether we can encode RMI as a form of degenerate session in the spirit of [27]. Also, we have now introduced more powerful primitives for thread and (shared) channel creation, along with the ability to delegate live sessions via method invocation and higher-order sessions. None of these features are considered in [10]. We discovered a flaw in the progress theorem in $\mathcal{L}_{doos}$ [10], and developed the new type system with hot sets in order to guard against the offending configurations.

Subject Reduction and Progress. In all previously mentioned papers on session types, typability guarantees absence of run-time communication errors. However, not all of them have the subject reduction property: the problem emerges when sending a live channel to a thread which already uses this channel to communicate, as in Example 4.1. This example can be translated into the calculi studied in [6, 14, 20, 29], and this issue has been discussed with some of their authors [2].

MOOSE has been inspired by the previously mentioned papers, however, we believe that it is the only calculus which guarantees absence of starvation on live channels. For example, we can encode the counterpart of Example 5.3 in the calculi of [6, 14, 20, 29]. More details on these two issues can be found in [1].

Note that we can flexibly obtain a version of the typing system which preserves the type safety and type inference results, but allows deadlock on live channels like the above mentioned literature, by simply dropping the hot set. In this sense, our system is not only theoretically sound, but also modular.

9   Conclusion and Future Work

This paper proposes the language MOOSE, a simple multi-threaded object-oriented language augmented with session communication primitives and types. MOOSE provides a clean object-oriented programming style for structural interaction protocols by prescribing channel usages as session types. We develop a typing system for MOOSE and prove type safety with respect to the operational semantics. We also show that in a well-typed MOOSE program, there will never be a communication error, starvation on live channels, nor an incorrect completion between two party interactions. These results demonstrate that a consistent integration of object-oriented language features and session types is possible where well-typedness can guarantee the consistent composition of communication protocols. To our best knowledge, MOOSE is the first application of session types to a concurrent object-oriented class-based programming language. Furthermore, type inference on session environments (Proposition 6.1), and the progress property on live channels (Theorem 7.5) have never been proved in any work on session types including those in the π-calculus.

Advanced session types. An issue that arises with the use of sessions is how to group and distinguish different behaviours within a program or protocol. In [20] and subsequently in [29] the authors utilise labelled *branching* and *selection*; the first enables a process to offer alternative session paths indexed by labels, and the second is used dually to choose a path by selecting one of the available labels. In [13, 17, 20, 28], branching and selection are considered as an effective way to simulate methods of objects. Several advancements have been made, ranging from simple session subtyping [13] to more complex bounded session polymorphism [17], which corresponds to parametric polymorphism within session types. Our conditional constructs are a simplification of branching and selection, therefore the same behaviour realised by branching types can also be expressed using our types.

As another study on the enrichment of basic session types, in [6] the authors integrate the *correspondence assertions* of [16] with standard session types to reason about multi-party protocols comprising of standard interleaved sessions.

In this work, our purpose was to produce a reliable and extensible object-oriented core, and not to include everything in the first attempt; however, such richer type structures are attractive in an object-oriented framework. MOOSE can be used as a core extensible language incorporating other typing systems.

We plan to study transformations from methods with more than one live channel parameters to methods with only one live channel parameter; and from interleaved sessions to non-interleaved ones for investigating expressiveness of our type system.

Exceptions, timeout and implementation. Another feature not considered in our system, although important in practice, is exceptions; in particular, we did not provide any way for a session type to declare that it may throw a *checked* exception, so that when this occurs both communicating processes can execute predefined error-handling code. One obvious way to encode an exception would be to use a branch as in [27]. In addition, when a thread becomes blocked waiting for a session to commence, in our operational semantics, it will never escape the waiting state unless a connection occurs. In practice, this is unrealistic, but it could have been ameliorated by introducing a 'timeout' version of our basic connection primitive such as `connect(timeout)u s {e}`. However, controlling exceptions during session communication and realising timeout would be non-trivial if we wish to preserve the progress property on live channels.

Finally, we are considering a prototype implementation using source to source translation from MOOSE to Java code. Firstly, the current notation for session types is convenient for our calculus, but sessions can be long and complex in large programs, making the types difficult to understand. We are developing an equivalent but more scalable way to describe sessions, using an alternative notation in which sessions are declared as nominal interface-like types. Other interesting issues are the choice of a suitable runtime representation for both shared and linear channels, the ability to detect and control implicit multi-threading, and the efficient implementation of higher-order sessions.

Acknowledgments. Eduardo Bonelli, Adriana Compagnoni, Kohei Honda, Simon Gay, Pablo Garralda, Elsa Gunter, Antonio Ravara and Vasco Vasconcelos, discussed with us subject reduction and progress for systems with sessions types. Vasco Vasconcelos and the ECOOP reviewers gave useful suggestions. Discussions with Marco Carbone, Kohei Honda, Robin Milner and the members of W3C Web Services Choreography Working Group for their collaboration on [8, 30] motivated the example in Section 2.

References

1. A full version of this paper. http://www.doc.ic.ac.uk/~dm04.
2. Personal communication by e-mails between the authors of [6, 7, 13, 15, 18, 20, 26, 27, 29].
3. Conversation with Steve Ross-Talbot. *ACM Queue*, 4(2), 2006.
4. A. Ahern and N. Yoshida. Formalising Java RMI with Explicit Code Mobility. In *OOPSLA '05*, pages 403–422. ACM Press, 2005.
5. G. Bierman, M. Parkinson, and A. Pitts. MJ: An Imperative Core Calculus for Java and Java with Effects. Technical Report 563, Univ. of Cambridge Computer Laboratory, 2003.
6. E. Bonelli, A. Compagnoni, and E. Gunter. Correspondence Assertions for Process Synchronization in Concurrent Communications. *J. of Funct. Progr.*, 15(2):219–248, 2005.
7. E. Bonelli, A. Compagnoni, and E. Gunter. Typechecking Safe Process Synchronization. In *FGUC 2004*, volume 138 of *ENTCS*, pages 3–22. Elsevier, 2005.
8. M. Carbone, K. Honda, and N. Yoshida. A Theoretical Basis of Communication-centered Concurrent Programming. Web Services Choreography Working Group mailing list, to appear as a WS-CDL working report.
9. R. DeLine and M. Fahndrich. Enforcing High-Level Protocols in Low-Level Software. In *PLDI '01*, volume 36(5) of *SIGPLAN Notices*, pages 59–69. ACM Press, 2001.
10. M. Dezani-Ciancaglini, N. Yoshida, A. Ahern, and S. Drossopoulou. A Distributed Object Oriented Language with Session Types. In *TGC'05*, volume 3705 of *LNCS*, pages 299–318. Springer-Verlag, 2005.
11. S. Drossopoulou. Advanced issues in object oriented languages course notes. http://www.doc.ic.ac.uk/~scd/Teaching/AdvOO.html.

12. M. Fahndrich and R. DeLine. Adoption and focus: practical linear types for imperative programming. In *PLDI '02*, pages 13–24. ACM Press, 2002.
13. S. Gay and M. Hole. Types and Subtypes for Client-Server Interactions. In *ESOP'99*, volume 1576 of *LNCS*, pages 74–90. Springer-Verlag, 1999.
14. S. Gay and M. Hole. Subtyping for Session Types in the Pi-Calculus. *Acta Informatica*, 42(2/3):191–225, 2005.
15. S. Gay, V. T. Vasconcelos, and A. Ravara. Session Types for Inter-Process Communication. TR 2003–133, Department of Computing, University of Glasgow, 2003.
16. A. D. Gordon and A. Jeffrey. Typing Correspondence Assertions for Communication Protocols. In *MFPS'01*, volume 45 of *ENTCS*, pages 379–409. Elsevier, 2001.
17. M. Hole and S. J. Gay. Bounded Polymorphism in Session Types. Technical Report TR-2003-132, Department of Computing Science, University of Glasgow, 2003.
18. K. Honda. Types for Dyadic Interaction. In *CONCUR'93*, volume 715 of *LNCS*, pages 509–523. Springer-Verlag, 1993.
19. K. Honda. Composing Processes. In *POPL'96*, pages 344–357. ACM Press, 1996.
20. K. Honda, V. T. Vasconcelos, and M. Kubo. Language Primitives and Type Disciplines for Structured Communication-based Programming. In *ESOP'98*, volume 1381 of *LNCS*, pages 22–138. Springer-Verlag, 1998.
21. A. Igarashi, B. C. Pierce, and P. Wadler. Featherweight Java: a Minimal Core Calculus for Java and GJ. *ACM TOPLAS*, 23(3):396–450, 2001.
22. N. Kobayashi, B. C. Pierce, and D. N. Turner. Linearity and the Pi-Calculus. *ACM TOPLAS*, 21(5):914–947, Sept. 1999.
23. R. Milner, J. Parrow, and D. Walker. A Calculus of Mobile Processes, Parts I and II. *Information and Computation*, 100(1), 1992.
24. D. Mostrous. Moose: a Minimal Object Oriented Language with Session Types. Master's thesis, Imperial College London, 2005.
25. B. C. Pierce. *Types and Programming Languages*. MIT Press, 2002.
26. K. Takeuchi, K. Honda, and M. Kubo. An Interaction-based Language and its Typing System. In *PARLE'94*, volume 817 of *LNCS*, pages 398–413. Springer-Verlag, 1994.
27. A. Vallecillo, V. T. Vasconcelos, and A. Ravara. Typing the Behavior of Objects and Components using Session Types. In *FOCLASA'02*, volume 68(3) of *ENTCS*. Elsevier, 2002.
28. V. Vasconcelos. Typed Concurrent Objects. In *ECOOP'94*, volume 821 of *LNCS*, pages 100–117. Springer-Verlag, 1994.
29. V. T. Vasconcelos, A. Ravara, and S. Gay. Session Types for Functional Multithreading. In *CONCUR'04*, volume 3170 of *LNCS*, pages 497–511. Springer-Verlag, 2004.
30. Web Services Choreography Working Group. Web Services Choreography Description Language. http://www.w3.org/2002/ws/chor/.

Parameterized Modules for Classes and Extensible Functions

Keunwoo Lee and Craig Chambers

University of Washington
Department of Computer Science and Engineering
Box 352350, Seattle WA 98195-2350, USA
{klee, chambers}@cs.washington.edu

Abstract. We present F(EML), a language that combines classes, extensible functions, symmetric multiple dispatching, and a practical system for *parameterized modules*. Parameterized modules permit subclasses and function extensions to be defined and typechecked once, and then reused to extend multiple argument modules. F(EML)'s predecessor, EML, supported classes and extensible functions with multiple dispatch, but its support for parameterized modules was weak. F(EML)'s key novel features are *alias declarations*, *generalized type relations* in module signatures, and a nontrivial definition of *signature subsumption*.

1 Introduction

Programmers should be able to write code so it can later be extended—with new cases of existing data types, and new cases of existing functions. Programmers should also be able to write these extensions so they can be reused to extend a wide range of base modules. Finally, these extensions should support modular reasoning, including modular typechecking. Unfortunately, it is hard to support all of these desiderata at once.

Consider the core of an interpreter in a language like Java:

```
package Lang;
abstract class Expr {
  Expr() {}
  abstract Int eval(); }
```

In the classic "expression problem" [35, 41], one wishes to add both new types of `Expr` and new functions over `Expr` types. In object-oriented languages, one can straightforwardly do the former without changing the original code:

```
package ConstPackage;
class Const extends Expr {
  Int value;
  Const(Int v_in) {value=v_in;}
  Int eval() {return value;} }
```

D. Thomas (Ed.): ECOOP 2006, LNCS 4067, pp. 353–378, 2006.
© Springer-Verlag Berlin Heidelberg 2006

However, to add a new dispatching function for Expr — say, print — we must invasively alter the original code:

```
abstract class Expr {          ... // as before
  abstract String print(); }
class Const extends Expr {    ... // as before
  String print() { return value.toString(); } }
```

Traditional functional languages have the converse problem: adding new functions is easy, but adding new cases to data types requires invasive changes, either to the original source code, or to existing clients.

Previous work on EML [28] and related languages [27, 10] integrates both object-oriented and functional extensibility in a single unified framework. These languages include extensible class hierarchies and method overriding (as in traditional object-oriented languages), while also allowing functions to be added externally to classes, and to dynamically dispatch on any subset of their arguments (as in traditional functional languages). In EML, we would write:

```
module Lang = { abstract class Expr() of {}
                abstract fun eval:Expr -> Int }
```

It is straightforward to add new data types:

```
module ConstMod uses Lang = {
  class Const(v_in:Int) extends Lang.Expr() of {value:Int = v_in}
  extend fun Lang.eval(Const {value=v}) = v }
```

Note that extends adds a new subclass to an existing class, and extend fun adds a new (pattern-matching) case to an existing function.

It is also straightforward to add new functions:

```
module PrintMod uses Lang, ConstMod = {
  fun print:Lang.Expr -> String
  extend fun print(Lang.Expr) = ""
  extend fun print(ConstMod.Const {value=v})= Std.intToString(v) }
```

EML therefore supports both data type and function extensibility (with some restrictions, which is why print has a default case for Expr — see Section 3.2).

Now, we would like it to support code reuse as well. Suppose the interpreter code base had many *features* — i.e., expression types, and functions over those types — and we wished to combine various subsets to produce a *product line* [24] of interpreters. In this case, we would like to define a feature once, typecheck it once, and reuse it to extend several interpreter instances.

Like ML [23, 30, 19, 11], EML supports *functors*, or parameterized modules:

```
signature LangSig = sig { abstract class Expr() of {}
                          abstract fun eval:Expr -> Int }
```

```
module MakePlus = (L:LangSig) -> {
  class Plus(l_in:Int, r_in:Int) extends L.Expr()
      of {left:Int = l_in, right:Int = r_in}
  extend fun L.eval(Plus {left=l, right=r}) = L.eval(l)+L.eval(r)}
```

```
module PlusMod = MakePlus(Lang)
```

MakePlus defines a function over modules; it can be applied to any module that implements LangSig, to produce a module containing a (freshly minted) class Plus and its eval implementation.

Note that Plus inherits from L.Expr, a class provided by the module parameter. In principle, such parameterization supports and subsumes many useful idioms, including mixins [5, 17] (Plus is a mixin), mixin layers [37] (which apply mixins to multiple classes at once), and certain aspect-oriented extensions [21] that extend members of multiple base modules.

However, limitations in EML prevent it from realizing this potential:

- EML functors are sensitive to the names of classes and functions in their arguments. In our example, MakePlus could only be applied to modules with a class named Expr. However, a truly reusable functor should be insensitive to inessential details like class names — other mixin systems, for example, do not constrain the names of classes with which a mixin may be composed.
- EML's signature language could only specify *direct* subclassing relations in functor arguments. Therefore, for example, it would be impossible to write an EML functor that extended a transitive subclass of Expr.
- EML included no useful form of *signature subsumption*. Therefore, for example, a module that provided all the features of Lang, plus some extra declarations, would be incompatible with LangSig.

In combination, these limitations meant that EML functors were not truly reusable. The contributions of the present work are as follows:

- We have designed F(EML), a language that combines EML's data type and function extensibility with practical, reusable parameterized modules. F(EML) enriches EML with three key features that lift the above limitations: (1) constructs for renaming declarations, and controlling the aliasing that results; (2) generalized type relations, including freshness information; and (3) useful signature subsumption.
- We have formalized the essence of F(EML) in a core language, Mini-F(EML). Section 3 summarizes the semantics and soundness properties; details will appear in a companion report [22].
- We have implemented a prototype F(EML) interpreter, and verified that it can typecheck interesting idioms. Our interpreter also supports some extensions (such as information hiding via *signature ascription*) which we do not discuss in this paper.

Finally, Sections 4 and 5 discuss related work and conclude.

2   Motivation and Design Overview

Fig. 1 gives the grammar of a F(EML) subset which we call F(EML)⁻; except
for shallow syntactic differences, this sublanguage corresponds roughly to EML.
In the remainder of this section, we informally explain the semantics of this
language using examples (Sections 2.1 and Section 2.2), show its limitations
(Section 2.3), and then present our solution (Section 2.4). We conclude by high-
lighting and motivating a few of F(EML)'s *unusual* technical features informally
(Section 2.5) prior to the more formal treatment in Section 3.

Module declarations, expressions, bodies

$Md ::=$ module M uses $\overline{M}$ = Me

$Me ::=$ $\{\ \overline{Mb}\ \}\ |\ (M : Se)$ -> $Me\ |\ M(M')$

$Mb ::=$ [abstract] class $c(\overline{x:\tau})$ [extends $C(\overline{e})$] of $\{\overline{l : \tau' = e'}\}$

      | fun $f : \tau^{\#}$ -> τ'

      | extend fun $F\ P$ = e

      | val x = e

Core expressions, patterns, types

$e ::= (\overline{e})\ |\ C\ (\overline{e})\ |\ F\ |\ e\ e'\ |\ x\ |\ \hat{M}.x$

$P ::= (\overline{P})\ |\ C\ \{\overline{L = P}\}\ |\ x\ [\text{as}\ P]\ |\ \_$

$\tau ::= (\overline{\tau})\ |\ C\ \{\overline{L : \tau}\}\ |\ \tau$ -> $\tau'\ |$ bottom

$\tau^{\#} ::= (\overline{\tau}, \tau_i^{\#}, \overline{\tau'})\ |\ \#C\ \{\overline{L : \tau}\}\ |\ C\ \{\overline{L : \tau}, L : \tau^{\#}, \overline{L' : \tau'}\}$

Signatures

$Sd ::=$ signature S uses $\overline{M}$ = Se

$Se ::=$ sig $\{\ \overline{Sb}\ \}\ |\ (M : Se)$ -> $Se'\ |\ S$

$Sb ::=$ [abstract] class $c(\overline{\tau})$ [extends C] of $\{\overline{L : \tau'}\}$

      | fun $f : \tau^{\#}$ -> τ'

      | extend fun $F\ \tau$

      | val $x : \tau$

Qualified names, identifiers

$\hat{M} ::= M\ |$ ThisMod $C ::= \hat{M}.c$ $F ::= \hat{M}.f$ $L ::= \hat{M}.l$

          $S, M, f, c, l, x ::= identifier$

Fig. 1. Syntax of F(EML)⁻

2.1   Ground Modules and Declarations

We have already seen examples of ground (non-functor) modules; here, we give
a more systematic description of each construct in Fig. 1. Returning to `Lang`:

```
module Lang = { abstract class Expr() of {}
                abstract fun eval:Expr -> Int }
```

This module declaration (Md) declares a new ground module (or *structure*)
named `Lang`, having two members (Mb). The first member is a *fresh class* declaration for an abstract class named `Expr`, which has the trivial constructor argument () and the trivial representation {}. Since `Expr` specifies no superclass,
it is assumed to inherit from the distinguished root class `Object`.

The second member is a *fresh function* declaration, having the type
`Expr -> Int`. Note that in Fig. 1, a function's argument type must be a *marked
type* $\tau^\#$, wherein exactly one class type is prefixed by a hash mark `#`. If no
mark is present, we mark the topmost, leftmost class by default — in this case,
`Expr`. We explain marked types further Section 3, but intuitively, they statically
constrain future extensions so that they will not be ambiguous with each other.

Next, consider our `ConstMod` example, slightly extended:

```
module ConstMod uses Lang = {
    class Const(v_in:Int) extends Lang.Expr() of {value:Int = v_in}
    extend fun Lang.eval(Const {value=v}) = v
    val zero = Const(0) }
```

This module declares another fresh class `Const`, a *fresh method* that extends
`eval`, and a *value binding* named `zero`. `Const` has a non-trivial constructor
specification with one argument `v_in` of type `Int`.

`Const` extends `Lang.Expr`; the name reference must be qualified with the
module path `Lang` because it is not a local class.[1] All module paths used in a
module body must appear in the `uses` clause of the enclosing module declaration, or one of the (transitive) `uses` clauses of used modules. `Const` also invokes
`Lang.Expr`'s constructor, passing an argument tuple of appropriate type (in this
case, the empty tuple, but in general any tuple of expressions may appear here).
Finally, `Const` defines a representation containing one *field* (in addition to any
inherited fields, although here the superclass has no fields), having *label* `value`.[2]
and type `Int`. This field is initialized to the value of `v_in`, which is bound in the
constructor argument. As with superclass constructor arguments, field initializers may be arbitrary expressions.

The fresh method `extend fun Lang.eval` adds a case to the function `eval`
in `Lang`.[3] Methods define an argument pattern P, similar in spirit to pattern
matching constructs in functional languages. This method's pattern is `Const`
`{value=v}`, which specifies that this method overrides `eval` on arguments of class
`Const` (or any subclass), matching on the `value` field, and assigning that field's
value to the variable `v`, which is bound in the method body expression (patterns
may also be tuples $(\overline{P})$, binders x [as P], or wildcards _). This method's body
is `v`, so it returns the `v` bound during pattern matching.

Finally, a *value binding* evaluates a core language expression and binds it to a
name. In the case of the `zero` binding, the expression is `Const(0)`, which applies
the `Const` constructor to the single-element argument tuple `(0)`.

The syntax of core language expressions e, from left to right in Fig. 1, is
as follows: tuples $(\overline{e})$, which construct tuple values; object constructors C $(\overline{e})$,

---

[1] Technically, references to local declarations and standard classes like `Object` are
automatically qualified with the paths `ThisMod` and `Std` respectively.

[2] Internally, field labels are qualified by a module name; this is a technical point which,
for presentation purposes, we will ignore in the rest of this paper.

[3] Note that EML, unlike many other object-oriented languages, distinguishes explicitly
between *introduction* of functions (`fun` declarations) and *overriding* of a function by
a method (`extend fun` declarations).

which construct a fresh value of class C by invoking its constructor with the argument tuple $(\bar{e})$; named function references F; message sends $e\ e'$, which apply e to e'; local pattern-bound variables x; or val-bound variables $M.x$.

At runtime, a message send dispatches to the *globally most-specific case* among all method cases that have been defined for the invoked function. The specificity relation between method cases is defined by the subtyping relation between the patterns in their arguments (Section 3.1 gives a formal description of the dispatch semantics). The dynamic semantics of dispatch give no priority to any particular position in (the abstract syntax tree of) a method's argument pattern — i.e., dispatching is *symmetric*.

2.2   Basic Signatures and Functors

Following ML, we call a module interface a *signature*. A module definition implicitly defines a *principal signature* (which is generated automatically from the module by the type system), but F(EmL) also supports explicit interfaces.

Signature body declarations Sb have four cases, paralleling the four basic kinds of declarations that can appear in a module. Recall our LangSig example:

```
signature LangSig = sig {
  abstract class Expr() of {}
  abstract fun eval:Expr -> Int }
```

This signature has a *class signature* and a *function signature*. Class signatures indicate whether the class is abstract, give the class name and constructor argument types, the class's superclass, and a list of field names and types. Function signatures simply give the function name and type.

The following signature is equivalent to the principal signature generated for the ConstMod from the previous section:

```
sig { class Const(Int) extends Lang.Expr of {value:Int}
      extend fun Lang.eval(Const {value:Int})
      val zero:Const }
```

Const's class signature shows that it is a concrete class with a constructor of type Int and a representation with a single field. A *method signature* extend fun $F\ \tau$ names the extended function F (here, Lang.eval) and the argument type τ at which the method overrides the function (here, Const {value:Int}). A *value signature* val $x : \tau$ gives the name and type of the bound name.

For this paper's purposes, the most important use of explicit signatures is to describe the arguments of parameterized modules. Recall our MakePlus example:

```
module MakePlus = (L:LangSig) -> {
  class Plus(l_in:Int, r_in:Int) extends L.Expr()
      of {left:Int = l_in, right:Int = r_in}
  extend fun L.eval(Plus {left=l, right=r}) = L.eval(l)+L.eval(r)}
```

A parameterized module expression begins with a parameter definition (M : Se), where M is the formal parameter name and Se is a signature expression.

In `MakePlus`, the parameter definition is `(L:LangSig)`; L is the formal parameter name, and `LangSig` is the formal parameter's signature. The parameter declaration is followed by an arrow `->` and a module expression. As one might expect, in the module body, declarations specified by the argument signature are available as names qualified by the formal parameter name.

A functor application $M(M')$ applies the module named by M to the argument M'. For presentation, we follow Leroy [23] and Harper et al. [18], and limit functor application expressions to named modules; a practical implementation would perform "lambda lifting" to allow applications of arbitrary functors to arbitrary argument modules. Informally, the application $M(M')$ copies the body of M to a new module expression Me' and substitutes M' for the formal name in Me'. For example, `MakePlus(Lang)` generates the following module expression:

```
{ class Plus(l_in:Int, r_in:Int) extends Lang.Expr()
      of {left:Int = l_in, right:Int = r_in}
  extend fun Lang.eval(Plus {left=l, right=r})
      = Lang.eval(l) + Lang.eval(r) }
```

2.3 Problem: Limited Reuse

To explore the limitations of this language, we now examine a more complex example. Consider Fig. 2. The signature `Algebra` defines an abstract class `Expr` with two concrete direct subclasses, `Plus` and `Times`. The `MakeDist` functor provides `dist`, which distributes occurrences of `Times` over `Plus`. Notice that this operation defines four cases. The first case is a default, which leaves other `Expr` forms unchanged. One case each is defined for a root expression of `Times` with `Plus` on the left subtree, the right subtree, and both subtrees.

```
signature Algebra = sig {
  abstract class Expr() of {}
  class Plus(Expr, Expr) extends Expr of {left:Expr, right:Expr}
  class Times(Expr, Expr) extends Expr of {left:Expr, right:Expr} }

module MakeDist = (A:Algebra) -> {
  fun dist:A.Expr -> A.Expr
  extend fun dist(e as A.Expr) = e
  extend fun dist(A.Times { left=(A.Plus {left=l,right=r}), right=r_outer }) =
      A.Plus(A.Times(l, r_outer), A.Times(r, r_outer))
  extend fun dist(A.Times { left=l_outer, right=(A.Plus {left=l,right=r}) }) =
      A.Plus(A.Times(l, l_outer), A.Times(r, l_outer))
  extend fun dist(A.Times { left=(A.Plus {left=l,right=r}),
                            right=(r_outer as A.Plus {left=_, right=_}) }) =
      A.Plus(dist(A.Times(l, r_outer)), dist(A.Times(r, r_outer))) }
```

Fig. 2. The `Algebra` signature and `MakeDist` functor

Now, recall that we would like to reuse this extension in many contexts. However, consider the following reasonable definition of an "algebra". First, use `Lang` and `PlusMod` as defined in Section 1; finally, define a third module:

```
module TimesMod uses Lang = {
  abstract class DistOp extends Lang.Expr() of {}
  class OpTimes(l_in:Lang.Expr, r_in:Lang.Expr)
    extends DistOp() of {left:Lang.Expr=l_in, right:Lang.Expr=r_in}
  extend fun eval(OpTimes {...}) = ... }
```

Considered together, `Lang`, `PlusMod`, and `TimesMod` contain all the pieces needed for an "algebra", yet they do not constitute an `Algebra`, for several reasons:

- First, and most obviously, this functor assumes a particular prior modularization strategy. `Algebra` is the signature of a single module, but in this case the client chose to factor the declarations into separate modules.
- Second, `Algebra` requires a declaration named `Times`, not `OpTimes`.
- Third, `Algebra` requires classes that *directly* extend `Expr`. `OpTimes` *transitively* extends `Expr`, so again it would be incompatible with `Algebra`. More generally, one might wish to specify direct subclassing, strict subclassing, inequality, and other relations; for example, inequality constraints might help prove the non-ambiguity of two methods. However, the language presented so far cannot express these constraints.

Finally, we note briefly one further problem that is not obvious from the examples' syntax, but arises in typechecking. EML did not permit *signature subsumption*; an EML module could be incompatible with a signature having fewer declarations, or less-precise information. Hence, even if we bundled all the declarations in one module and allowed `Algebra` to accept a transitive subclass of `Expr` for `Times`, the presence of the `DistOp` class or the `eval` function would render the module incompatible with `Algebra`. Clearly, this greatly reduces the utility of `MakeDist`. This was not merely an oversight in the EML design; as we shall see in Section 3, signature subsumption turns out to be rather tricky.

2.4   Solution: An Enriched Language

The limitations described in the previous section share a common theme: the argument signature makes the functor depend on *inessential details* of the extended code. Our solution is to enrich the language so as to remove these dependencies — either by generalizing the signature language, or by letting the programmer "adapt" a potential argument to the required signature.

The enriched grammar is shown in Fig. 3. Note that we extend the syntax of module bodies, but replace the syntax of signatures; the signatures in Fig. 1 are legal, but F(EML) rewrites them internally into the form shown.

There are three general kinds of changes. First, we add *alias declarations*; second, we add *relation constraints* to signatures; third, we enable *selective sealing* of class and function declarations. In the rest of this subsection, we discuss these changes in turn, and then revisit our `MakeDist` example.

Alias Declarations. Alias declarations define a new module declaration that aliases an existing declaration rather than creating a new one. An *alias class* `alias class c = C` defines a module member named `c` that refers to the existing

Module expressions and bodies

$$Mb ::= \ldots$$
$$| \ \texttt{alias class } c = C$$
$$| \ \texttt{alias fun } f = F$$
$$| \ \texttt{alias extend fun } F \ \tau \ \texttt{in } \hat{M}$$

Signatures

$$Se ::= \texttt{sig } \{ \ \overline{Sb} \ \texttt{fresh } \phi \ \texttt{where } \rho \ \} \ | \ (M : Se) \ \texttt{-> } Se' \ | \ S$$
$$Sb ::= [\texttt{closed}] \ \texttt{class } c \ [(\overline{\tau})] \ \texttt{of } \{\overline{L : \tau}\} \ [\texttt{abstract on } \overline{F}]$$
$$| \ \texttt{fun } f : \tau^{\#} \ \texttt{-> } \tau' \ \texttt{open below } \tau''$$
$$| \ \texttt{extend fun } F \ \tau$$
$$| \ \texttt{val } x : \tau$$
$$\phi ::= \overline{y} \qquad\qquad \rho ::= \overline{r} \qquad y ::= c \ | \ f \ | \ q$$
$$q ::= F.\tau \qquad\quad Q ::= \hat{M}.q$$
$$r ::= C \ \mathcal{R}_C \ C' \ | \ F \ \mathcal{R}_F \ F' \ | \ Q \ \mathcal{R}_Q \ Q'$$

Class, function, method, and type relations

$$\mathcal{R}_C ::= \top \ | \ \bot \ | \ \leq \ | \ \neq \ | \ \varnothing \ | \ < \ | \ <^0 \ | \ <^1 \ | \ <^2 \ | \ \ldots$$
$$\mathcal{R}_F ::= = \ | \ \neq \qquad \mathcal{R}_Q ::= = \ | \ \neq$$
$$\mathcal{R}_\tau ::= \top \ | \ \bot \ | \ \leq \ | \ \neq \ | \ \varnothing \ | \ < \ | \ =$$

Fig. 3. Syntax of F(EML) (diff from Fig. 1)

class C. An *alias function* alias fun $f = F$ defines a member named f that refers to F. An *alias method* alias extend fun $F \ \tau$ in $\hat{M}$ defines an alias for the method found in module $\hat{M}$ that extends the function F on type τ. The need for function and class aliases is relatively straightforward, as we shall see shortly in Section 2.4; however, the need for method aliases is somewhat technical, and we postpone further discussion of them to Section 3.

Relation Constraints. There are two kinds of relation information: *binary relations* ρ, and *freshness* information ϕ.

Binary relations describe the relationships between two declarations. Classes have the richest language of relations, including general subclassing $\leq$, inequality $\neq$, disjointness $\varnothing$ (sharing no common subclasses; in ASCII we write disjoint), strict subclassing $<$, and k-level subclassing $<^k$ (for $k \in \{0, 1, 2, \ldots\}$). $<^0$ is reflexive subclassing, i.e. equality, and can be written $=$; $<^1$ is direct subclassing, and can be written extends. $\top$ and $\bot$ denote "unknown" and "impossible" relations respectively; these are a technical convenience permitting certain rules to be stated more concisely, and we will not discuss them further in this paper.

Class relations serve two purposes. First, they enrich the language of constraints that a programmer can describe in a signature. Second, they permit the programmer to track the aliasing that results from the use of alias classes. It turns out that typechecking often requires knowledge that two classes, for example, are *not* aliases for each other. This second rationale also applies to functions and methods, so we require relations for these as well; function and method relations include only aliasing ($=$) or non-aliasing ($\neq$).

It is impossible for a signature to anticipate all the must-not-alias relation-ships that future clients might need. Therefore, F(EML) also tracks freshness information: when a name appears in the **fresh** ϕ portion of a signature, it indi-cates that the name (which must be bound by the enclosing signature) describes a fresh declaration and not an alias declaration. When a name appears in a **fresh** clause, its referent therefore is known not to alias any other **fresh** name, without requiring an explicit $\neq$ relation between the two names.

Selective Sealing. Class and function signatures in F(EML) have additional clauses, which restrict how they may be used. These restrictions play a key role in signature subsumption; for the moment we explain only their informal meaning, postponing the details of *how* they make subsumption safe to Section 3.

Class signatures change in several ways. First, they may be marked **closed**, indicating that clients may not extend them *through this signature* (although other aliases of the underlying class may not be marked **closed**, so **closed** is not equivalent to Java's **final**). Second, class constructors are optional in signatures; when the constructor argument type is absent, the constructor is hidden, and the class may not be instantiated. Third, class signatures may have an **abstract on** clause, naming a list of functions that need an implementing case for this class. Note that functions no longer carry an optional **abstract** flag; **abstract on** replaces **abstract** on the functions.

Function signatures gain one piece: an **open below** clause, which names the *extension type* of that function. If a function has the signature **fun** $f : \tau^{\#}$ -> τ' **open below** τ'', then methods outside of f's module can only extend f on τ if τ is a strict subtype of τ'' (again, other aliases of f may have a more permissive extension type).

A revised Algebra. Fig. 4 gives an alternative definition of the **Algebra** sig-nature, and a module that remodularizes the declarations we defined previously to fit this signature.

```
signature Algebra = sig {
  closed class Expr of {}
  closed class Plus(Expr, Expr) of {left:Expr, right:Expr}
  closed class Times(Expr, Expr) of {left:Expr, right:Expr}
  fresh .
  where Plus < Expr, Times < Expr, Plus != Times }

module LangAlgebra uses Lang = {
  alias class Expr = Lang.Expr
  alias class Plus = PlusMod.Plus
  alias class Times = TimesMod.OpTimes }
```

Fig. 4. Revision of **Algebra** from Fig. 2, and a module satisfying this signature

If we use this revised **Algebra**, then both the functor definition **MakeDist** and the functor application **MakeDist(LangAlgebra)** will typecheck. Our fix uses all

three of the extensions described previously. First, we use alias declarations to
"repackage" existing declarations so they can be extended by the functor. Second, we use generalized class relations to specify exactly the relations needed for
MakeDist to conclude that no two cases of dist are ambiguous with each other.
Third, we seal all the classes in the signature, marking them closed, which constitutes a "promise" that MakeDist's body will not subclass any of these classes.
This promise is necessary to make Algebra compatible with LangAlgebra, for
a somewhat subtle reason. Consider the signature of LangAlgebra.Expr:

    class Expr() of {} abstract on Lang.eval   // (1)

because its source class (Lang.Expr) is abstract on eval. But (1) is not compatible with (not a valid subsignature of)

    class Expr() of {}   // (2)

A hypothetical concrete subclass of (2) would not need to implement a case
for eval, whereas any valid concrete subclass of (1) *must* implement a case for
eval. Hence, valid clients of (2) are not necessarily valid clients of (1).

   However, a closed class with a hidden constructor cannot be subclassed or
instantiated, so its signature may freely "forget" about its abstract functions.
Therefore, the signature (1) *is* a valid subsignature of the following signature
(the absence of the tuple of constructor argument types signifies that the constructor cannot be called):

    closed class Expr of {}   // (3)

because no client can use (3) inconsistently with legal uses of (1).

2.5   Discussion: Unusual Features, and Their Motivation

Before diving into our semantics, we highlight a few forces, arising from certain
design choices, which motivate specific unusual supporting technical features.

   First, as previously noted, combining extensibility and symmetric multiple dispatch raises the problem of ambiguous function implementation. As a result, our
type relations include *inequality*, *disjointness*, and *strict subtyping*, which can be
used to deduce non-ambiguity of methods. For example, methods that override
a function on disjoint argument types can never apply to the same argument,
and hence cannot be ambiguous. This is unusual because most type systems either do not care about distinctness (ML signatures, for example, transmit type
equalities, but not inequalities) or treat inequality only implicitly.

   Second, because F(EML) aims to support modular programming, we cannot
require programmers to list all useful inequality constraints for every class —
for any class C, it may be useful to know that C is distinct from classes that are
not visible or not yet defined at the point of C's declaration. Therefore, F(EML)
explicitly tracks the *freshness* of classes and other declarations, and deduces, for
example, that two fresh class declarations always name distinct classes. This is
unusual because, again, most type systems treat freshness only implicitly.

   Third, because F(EML) permits class and function extension from outside the
original declaration, F(EML) requires fine-grained *selective sealing* to restrict the

extensibility of declarations. As we've shown in the previous section, sealing is crucial to signature subsumption. This is unusual because most languages either lack extensibility, or conflate a construct's visibility with permission to extend it, or permit coarse-grained limits on extensibility to express programmer intent (e.g., Java's `final`) but never require it for soundness.

3   Semantics and Typechecking

We have formalized the essence of F(EML) in a reduced language called Mini-F(EML). Actually, the language presented thus far *is* Mini-F(EML), except for the differences in Fig. 5. This grammar also specifies which subsets of module and core expressions are module language and core language values.

Module values, bodies

$Mv ::= \{ \ \overline{Mb} \ \} \mid (M : Sv) \ \text{->} \ Me$

$Mb ::= \ldots ((\text{alias}) \ \text{classes and (alias) functions as before})$
$\quad \mid \text{extend fun } F \text{ with } q \ P = e$
$\quad \mid \text{alias extend fun } F \text{ with } q = Q$
$\quad \mid \ \text{\sout{val } x = e}$

Signature values, bodies

$Sv ::= \text{sig } \{ \ \overline{Sb} \ \text{fresh } \phi \text{ where } \rho \ \} \mid (M : Sv) \ \text{->} \ Sv'$

$Sb ::= [\text{closed}] \ \text{class } c \ [(\overline{\tau})] \ \text{of } \{\overline{L : \tau}\} \ [\text{abstract on } \overline{F}]$
$\quad \mid \text{fun } f : \tau^{\#} \ \text{->} \ \tau \ \text{open below } \tau^{P}$
$\quad \mid \text{extend fun } F \text{ with } q \ \tau^{P}$

Core patterns, types, expressions, values

$P ::= (\overline{P}) \mid C \ \{\overline{L = P}\} \mid x \text{ as } P \mid \_$

$\tau ::= (\overline{\tau}) \mid C \ \{\} \mid \tau \ \text{->} \ \tau'$

$\tau^{P} ::= (\overline{\tau^{P}}) \mid C \ \{\overline{L : \tau^{P}}\} \mid \tau \ \text{->} \ \tau' \mid \text{bottom}$

$\tau^{\#} ::= (\overline{\tau}, \tau^{\#}, \overline{\tau'}) \mid \#C \ \{\}$

$e ::= (\overline{e}) \mid C \ \{\overline{L = e}\} \mid C \ (\overline{e}) \mid F \mid e \ e' \mid x$

$v ::= (\overline{v}) \mid C \ \{\overline{L = v}\} \mid F$

Method names (bare and qualified); qualified names; fresh names

$q ::= identifier \quad Q ::= \hat{M}.q \quad Y ::= C \mid F \mid Q \quad \phi ::= \overline{Y}$

Fig. 5. Syntax of Mini-F(EML) (diff from Fig. 3)

We summarize the changes (made for technical convenience) as follows. First, in F(EML), methods do not have names, and are referenced by profile only; in Mini-F(EML), for convenience, each method is named by an identifier q. Second, we omit `val` bindings, as these can be simulated by functions with a dummy argument and exactly one case. Third, we eliminate named signature expressions, and require signatures to be expanded inline. Fourth, the `as` P clause in binding patterns is mandatory. Fifth, we separate types into two syntactic kinds: we restrict first-class types τ to tuples, functions, and class types, with tracking of field types, whereas τ^P (the type of a pattern) may include more precise information about fields. Restricting the type syntax in this manner simplifies our proof strategy, while still requiring us to deal with the essence of the ambiguity and incompleteness problems arising from extensibility and multiple dispatch. Sixth, lists of fresh names ϕ are fully qualified, and may include method names. Lastly, we include instances $C \{\overline{L = e}\}$ in the grammar of expressions; these are not available at source level, but arise when defining small-step reduction.

The challenge in designing a type system that is both useful and sound arises from the combination of F(EML)'s uniform, symmetric dispatching model and its powerful extensibility constructs. In Section 3.1, we elaborate on the dynamic semantics of dispatching, focusing on how evaluation can go wrong. In Section 3.2, we describe typechecking. Section 3.3 states the soundness theorems. The full formalization of F(EML) will appear in our companion report [22].

3.1   Linkage and Evaluation

A Mini-F(EML) program consists of a list of module declarations $\overline{Md}$, followed by a "main expression" e. Execution has two phases: first, $\overline{Md}$ is linked to produce a *dynamic context* Δ, and then e is evaluated in the context of Δ.

Δ is a finite map $\overline{M \mapsto Me}$ from module names to ("compiled") module expressions. Fig. 6 shows a subset of the linkage rules. $[\overline{x \mapsto v}]e$ denotes the substitution of each v_i for its respective x_i in an expression e.

$$\frac{}{\Delta \vdash \epsilon \Downarrow^* \Delta} \text{(Link-Empty)} \qquad \boxed{\Delta \vdash \overline{Md} \Downarrow^* \Delta'}$$

$$\frac{\Delta \vdash \overline{Md} \Downarrow^* \Delta' \qquad \Delta' \vdash M = Me \Downarrow Mv}{\Delta' \vdash \overline{Md}; (\texttt{module } M \texttt{ uses } \overline{M} \texttt{ = } Me) \Downarrow^* \Delta', M \mapsto Mv} \text{(Link-Mod)}$$

$$\boxed{\Delta \vdash M = Me \Downarrow Mv}$$

$$\frac{}{\Delta \vdash M = (M' : Sv) \texttt{ -> } Me \Downarrow (M' : Sv) \texttt{ -> } Me} \text{(L-Funct)}$$

$$\frac{\Delta, \texttt{ThisMod} \mapsto \{ \overline{Mb} \} \vdash \text{dealias}(\{ \overline{Mb} \}) = \{ \overline{Mb'} \}}{\Delta \vdash M = \{ \overline{Mb} \} \Downarrow [\texttt{ThisMod} \mapsto M]\{ \overline{Mb'} \}} \text{(L-Struct)}$$

$$\frac{\Delta(M) = (M_1 : Sv) \texttt{ -> } Me_1 \qquad Me' = [M_1 \mapsto M']Me_1 \qquad \Delta \vdash M_0 = Me' \Downarrow Mv'}{\Delta \vdash M_0 = M(M') \Downarrow Mv'}$$
$$\text{(L-App)}$$

Fig. 6. Selected linkage rules

Linkage performs three operations. First, it expands functor applications into module values (L-App); since we restrict applications to named module expressions, we simply substitute the actual argument name for the formal argument name in the body, and then link the body if necessary. Second, for ground modules, linkage eliminates references to alias declarations; we omit the definition of the $\Delta \vdash$ dealias(Me) judgment, but informally, for every name that refers to an alias, it (transitively) "chases aliases" until it finds a fresh declaration, and replaces the reference to the alias with a reference to that fresh declaration source. Third, for structures, linkage rewrites self-references via ThisMod to refer to the module's linked name.

Fig. 7 gives the (small-step, operational) semantics of core expression evaluation and auxiliary judgments. Execution uses the dynamic context Δ, but otherwise these rules are exactly analogous to those for EML [28]. We include fairly complete rules here for reference, but we will only discuss those parts absolutely necessary to explain the typechecking problems that follow.

Note that some syntactic sequences with an overbar have a superscripted range, e.g. $\overline{v}^{1..n}$; this is shorthand for $v_1, \ldots, v_n$. We use the set membership operator $\in$ on syntactic sequences, e.g. $Mb \in \overline{Mb}$ indicates that the Mb is an element of the sequence $\overline{Mb}$. We write $Mb \in \Delta(M)$ as shorthand for $(\Delta(M) = \{ \overline{Mb} \}) \wedge (Mb \in \overline{Mb})$. We use a long double arrow $\Longrightarrow$ for logical implication, to distinguish it from $\rightarrow$ (for small-step evaluation) and $\Rightarrow$ (for signature generation, which we will see in in Section 3.2). Superscripted brackets $[\ ]^k$ around a part of the rule indicate that those parts are optional, but either all bracketed portions superscripted with the same k must be present, or all must be absent.

Evaluation uses the dynamic subpattern and subclass relations, which are given in Fig. 7. Note that these judgments are entirely distinct from the *static* relation deduction that we describe later.

Evaluation can get stuck in two cases. First, the program could attempt to construct a class marked abstract; call this an *abstract instantiation* error. Second, the program could send a message for which $\Delta \vdash \text{lookup}(F, v) = \langle q, B, e \rangle$ is not derivable, which can occur in two ways. Informally, the premises of LOOKUP specify that there must exist some (fresh) method in Δ such that (1) its pattern P matches the argument value, and (2) P is strictly more specific than the patterns of all other matching methods in Δ. Therefore, this rule can fail either if there are *zero* applicable methods, or if there are *multiple* applicable methods, none of which is strictly more specific than all the others. The former case is a *message not understood* error; the latter case is an *ambiguous message* error.

3.2 Typechecking

In this section, we first describe the general structure of typechecking; then, in later subsections, we describe in more detail those portions of the semantics most directly relevant to supporting parameterized modules. Fig. 8 summarizes the major static judgment forms.

A signature context Γ is a finite map from module names $\hat{M}$ to signature values Sv; the dependency context $\mathcal{D}$ is a finite map from module names M to depended-upon module names $\overline{M}$. The relation context $\mathcal{K}$ is a pair $\langle \phi, \rho \rangle$ where ϕ is a set of fresh names and ρ is a set of binary relations. Auxiliary rules used by these judgments will also use the contexts β (mapping pattern-bound variables x to types τ) and R (mapping class names C to representations $\{\overline{L : \tau}\}$).

The top-level typing judgments (the first two lines in Fig. 8) essentially typecheck each module declaration in $\overline{Md}$ from left to right (i.e., they construct Γ

$$\frac{\Delta \vdash e_1 \to e_2}{\Delta \vdash e_1 \; e' \to e_2 \; e'} \text{(E-App-L)} \qquad \frac{\Delta \vdash e_1 \to e_2}{\Delta \vdash v \; e_1 \to v \; e_2} \text{(E-App-R)} \qquad \boxed{\Delta \vdash e \to e'}$$

$$\frac{\begin{array}{c}\Delta \vdash \text{concrete}(C) \\ \Delta \vdash \text{rep}(C \; (\overline{v})) = \{\overline{L = e'}\}\end{array}}{\Delta \vdash C \; (\overline{v}) \to C \; \{\overline{L = e'}\}} \text{(E-New)} \qquad \frac{\Delta \vdash e_1 \to e_2}{\begin{array}{c}\Delta \vdash C \; \{\overline{L = v}, L = e_1, \overline{L' = e'}\} \\ \to C \; \{\overline{L = v}, L = e_2, \overline{L' = e'}\}\end{array}} \text{(E-Rep)}$$

$$\frac{\Delta \vdash e_1 \to e_2}{\Delta \vdash (\overline{v}, e_1, \overline{e'}) \to (\overline{v}, e_2, \overline{e'})} \qquad \frac{\Delta \vdash \text{lookup}(F, v) = \langle q, B, e \rangle}{\Delta \vdash F \; v \to [B]e} \text{(E-App-Red)}$$
$$\text{(E-Tuple)}$$

$$\boxed{\Delta \vdash \text{concrete}(C)}$$

$$\frac{(\textbf{class} \; c \; \_ \; [\textbf{extends} \; \_ \; \_] \; \textbf{of} \; \{\_\}) \in \Delta(M)}{\Delta \vdash \text{concrete}(M.c)} \text{(Concrete)}$$

$$\frac{\begin{array}{c}([\textbf{abstract}] \; \textbf{class} \; c \; (\overline{x : \tau}^{1..n}) \; [\textbf{extends} \; C(\overline{e''})]^1 \qquad \boxed{\Delta \vdash \text{rep}(C \; (\overline{v})) = \{\overline{L = e}\}} \\ \textbf{of} \; \{\overline{L' : \tau' = e'}\}) \in \Delta(M) \\ [\Delta \vdash \text{rep}(C \; ([\overline{x \mapsto v}^{1..n}]\overline{e''})) = \{\overline{L = e'''}\}]^1\end{array}}{\Delta \vdash \text{rep}(M.c \; (\overline{v}^{1..n})) = \{[\overline{L = e'''}]^1, \overline{M.l' = [\overline{x \mapsto v}^{1..n}]e'}\}} \text{(Rep)}$$

$$\frac{\begin{array}{c}\Delta \vdash \text{match}(P, v) = B \\ (\textbf{extend fun} \; F \; \textbf{with} \; q \; P \; \textbf{=} \; e) \in \Delta(M) \\ (\forall M' \in \text{dom}(\Delta).\forall(\textbf{extend fun} \; F \; \textbf{with} \; q' \; P' \; \textbf{=} \; e') \in \Delta(M'). \\ ((\Delta \vdash \text{match}(P', v) = B') \wedge (M.q \neq M'.q')) \Longrightarrow ((\Delta \vdash P \leq P') \wedge \neg(\Delta \vdash P' \leq P)))\end{array}}{\Delta \vdash \text{lookup}(F, v) = \langle q, B, e \rangle} \qquad \boxed{\Delta \vdash \text{lookup}(F, v) = \langle q, B, e \rangle}$$
$$\text{(Lookup)}$$

$$\boxed{\Delta \vdash \text{match}(P, v) = B}$$

$$\frac{\Delta \vdash \text{match}(P, v) = B}{\Delta \vdash \text{match}(x \; \textbf{as} \; P, v) = x \mapsto v, B} \text{(Match-Bind)} \qquad \frac{}{\Delta \vdash \text{match}(\_, v) = \epsilon} \text{(Match-Wild)}$$

$$\frac{\Delta \vdash C' \leq C \qquad \forall_{i=1}^n.(\Delta \vdash \text{match}(P_i, v_i) = B_i)}{\Delta \vdash \text{match}(C \; \{\overline{L = P}^{1..n}\}, C' \; \{\overline{L = v}^{1..n}, \overline{L' = v'}\}) = \cup_1^n B} \text{(Match-Class)}$$

$$\frac{\forall_{i=1}^n.(\Delta \vdash \text{match}(P_i, v_i) = B_i)}{\Delta \vdash \text{match}((\overline{P}^{1..n}), (\overline{v}^{1..n})) = \cup_1^n B} \text{(Match-Tuple)}$$
$$\boxed{\Delta \vdash P \leq P'}$$

$$\frac{\Delta \vdash P \leq P'}{\Delta \vdash (x \; \textbf{as} \; P) \leq P'} \qquad \frac{\Delta \vdash P \leq P'}{\Delta \vdash P \leq (x \; \textbf{as} \; P')} \qquad \frac{}{\Delta \vdash P \leq \_}$$
$$\text{(PSub-Bind-L)} \qquad\qquad \text{(PSub-Bind-R)} \qquad\qquad \text{(PSub-Wild)}$$

$$\frac{\forall_{i=1}^n.\Delta \vdash P_i \leq P_i'}{\Delta \vdash (\overline{P}^{1..n}) \leq (\overline{P'}^{1..n})} \qquad \frac{\Delta \vdash C \leq C' \qquad \forall_1^n i.\Delta \vdash P_i \leq P_i''}{\Delta \vdash C \; \{\overline{L = P}^{1..n}, \overline{L' = P'}\} \leq C' \; \{\overline{L = P''}^{1..n}\}}$$
$$\text{(PSub-Tuple)} \qquad\qquad \text{(PSub-Class)}$$

$$\frac{([\textbf{abstract}] \; \textbf{class} \; c \; \_ \; \textbf{extends} \; C \; \_ \; \textbf{of} \; \{\_\}) \in \Delta(M)}{\Delta \vdash M.c \leq C} \text{(CSub-Ext)} \qquad \boxed{\Delta \vdash C \leq C'}$$

Fig. 7. Dynamic semantics: Evaluation and auxiliary rules

$$\Gamma, \mathcal{D} \vdash \overline{Md} \Rightarrow^* \Gamma', \mathcal{D}' \qquad \text{Program typechecking}$$
$$\Gamma, \mathcal{D} \vdash Md \Rightarrow M : \langle Sv, \overline{M'} \rangle \qquad \text{Module declaration typechecking}$$
$$\Gamma; \overline{M} \vdash Me : Sv \qquad \text{Module principal signatures}$$
$$\Gamma, \overline{M} \vdash Sv \text{ OK arg} \qquad \text{OK functor argument signature}$$
$$\text{declRels}(\overline{Mb}) = \mathcal{K} \qquad \text{Relation context formation}$$
$$\langle \Gamma, \mathcal{K}, \overline{Mb} \rangle \vdash Mb : Sb \qquad \text{Signature of a module body decl}$$
$$\langle \Gamma, \mathcal{K}, \overline{Mb} \rangle \vdash Y : \langle \hat{M}, Sb \rangle \qquad \text{Lookup or compute sig for a name}$$
$$\Gamma, \overline{M} \vdash Mb \text{ OK in } \overline{Sb} \qquad \text{Module body decl well-formedness}$$
$$\Gamma \vdash Sv \leq Sv' \qquad \text{Signature subsumption}$$
$$\Gamma, \mathcal{K}, \overline{Sb} \vdash Sb \leq Sb' \qquad \text{Sig body decl subsumption}$$
$$\Gamma, \mathcal{K}, \overline{Sb} \vdash Sb \text{ droppable} \qquad \text{Sig body width subsumption}$$
$$\mathcal{K} \vdash C_1 \mathcal{R}_C C_2 \qquad \text{Class relation deduction}$$
$$\mathcal{K} \vdash F_1 \mathcal{R}_F F_2 \qquad \text{Function relation deduction}$$
$$\mathcal{K} \vdash Q_1 \mathcal{R}_Q Q_2 \qquad \text{Method relation deduction}$$
$$\mathcal{K} \vdash \tau_1 \mathcal{R}_\tau \tau_2 \qquad \text{Type relation deduction}$$
$$\Gamma, \mathcal{K}, \beta \vdash e : \tau \qquad \text{Expression typing}$$
$$\mathcal{K}, R \vdash \text{ptype}(P, \tau) = \langle \tau^P, \beta \rangle \qquad \text{Type and bindings of a pattern}$$
$$\langle \Gamma, \overline{Mb} \rangle \vdash \text{rep}(C) = \{\overline{L : \tau}\} \qquad \text{Class representation lookup}$$

Fig. 8. Static semantics: Selected judgment forms

and $\mathcal{D}$ with a left-to-right fold on the module declaration list), so we skip directly to the "meat" of module expression typechecking, shown in Fig. 9. $DN(\overline{Mb})$ is an auxiliary function that extracts the set of class, function, and method names introduced in $\overline{Mb}$. There are three cases for module expression typechecking: structures, functors, and functor applications.

For structures, informally, the premises of MOD-STRUCT specify that: (line 1) the module's declared names must be unique; (line 2) we extract a "relation context" $\mathcal{K} = \langle \phi, \rho \rangle$ from the members $\overline{Mb}$, and a principal signature can be generated for $\overline{Mb}$; (lines 3-4) in the context enriched by the relation and declaration signatures, each Mb is well-formed.

For functors, we typecheck the body in the context extended with the formal argument's signature. Informally, the Sv OK arg judgment checks that the **fresh** ϕ clause in Sv is empty, since declarations in functor arguments are never fresh (declarations in a functor formal argument are always potentially aliases).

For functor applications, we check that an alias of the actual argument's signature would be subsumed by the formal argument signature. (Informally, the aliasOf function, whose definition we omit, erases freshness information and adds equality relations between declarations in the actual and formal parameters.) We then substitute the actual argument name for the formal name in the signature body. Notice that we do not need to typecheck the functor body again.

Recall the major technical innovations that F(EML) adds relative to EML: generalized relations, alias declarations, and a non-trivial definition of signature subsumption. Before describing the mechanics of these features, we must first show how signatures are constructed, and summarize certain implementation restrictions inherited from EML; we do this in the next two subsections. Then,

$$\forall_1^n i.\mathrm{DN}(Mb_i) \cap \mathrm{DN}(\overline{Mb}^{1..(i-1)}; \overline{Mb}^{(i+1)..n}) = \emptyset$$

$$\boxed{\Gamma; \overline{M} \vdash Me : Sv}$$

$$\mathrm{declRels}(\overline{Mb}^{1..n}) = \langle \phi, \rho \rangle \qquad \forall_1^n i.\langle \Gamma, \langle \phi, \rho \rangle, \overline{Mb} \rangle \vdash Mb_i : Sb_i$$

$$\Gamma' = \Gamma, \mathtt{ThisMod} \mapsto (\mathtt{sig} \; \{ \; \overline{Sb}^{1..n} \; \mathtt{fresh} \; \phi \; \mathtt{where} \; \rho \; \})$$

$$\frac{\forall Mb_i \in \overline{Mb}^{1..n}.\Gamma' \vdash Mb_i \; \mathrm{OK} \; \mathrm{in} \; \overline{Sb}^{1..n}}{\Gamma; \overline{M} \vdash \{ \; \overline{Mb}^{1..n} \; \} : \mathtt{sig} \; \{ \; \overline{Sb}^{1..n} \; \mathtt{fresh} \; \phi \; \mathtt{where} \; \rho \; \}} \text{(MOD-STRUCT)}$$

$$\Gamma; \overline{M} \vdash Sv \; \mathrm{OK} \; \mathrm{arg}$$

$$\frac{(\Gamma, M \mapsto [\mathtt{ThisMod} \mapsto M]Sv); (\overline{M}, M) \vdash Me : Sv'}{\Gamma; \overline{M} \vdash ((M : Sv) \; \mathtt{->} \; Me) : ((M : Sv) \; \mathtt{->} \; Sv')} \text{(MOD-FUNCT)}$$

$$\frac{\Gamma(M_1) = (M : Sv_1) \; \mathtt{->} \; Sv_1' \qquad \Gamma(M_2) = Sv_2 \qquad \Gamma \vdash \mathrm{aliasOf}(Sv_2, M_2) \le Sv_1}{\Gamma; \overline{M} \vdash M_1(M_2) : [M \mapsto M_2]Sv_1'} \text{(MOD-APP)}$$

Fig. 9. Static semantics: Module typechecking

we describe how typechecking must be adjusted to accommodate aliases and generalized relations. Finally, we summarize our rules for signature subsumption.

Building Signatures. Fig. 10 shows selected rules for generating the signatures of module body declarations, and the extraction of initial relation information: fresh declarations generate an element of ϕ; alias declarations generate equality relations; and a subclass generates a direct subclassing ($<^1$) relation.

Function signatures (S-FUN) are trivial; the auxiliary function unmark($\tau^\#$), whose definition we omit, simply erases the hash mark from a marked type.

To generate a method signature (S-METHOD), we first compute a finite map R from all visible class names C to representation types $\{\overline{L : \tau}\}$ (informally, the reps function iterates over all classes in Γ and $\overline{Mb}$, and builds the mapping by accumulating field lists). Then, we compute the type of the argument pattern. Lastly, we sanity-check that the function to be extended exists. Note that this last check uses the judgment for signature lookup *or* computation from Fig. 8; this looks either in the global context Γ for the signature, or computes the signature from $\overline{Mb}$ if it refers to a locally defined name.

Signatures for fresh class declarations are more involved. The premises of S-CLASS and S-ABS-CLASS compute the class's representation and abstract functions. Representation computation involves looking up the superclass representation (if a superclass is declared) and "copying it down" into the current class's signature. Abstract function computation involves looking up all functions "owned" by this class and checking whether there is a default implementing case; if no such default exists, then the function is abstract for this class, and must appear in the class's **abstract on** clause. We revisit owners in Section 3.2.

We omit the rules that generate signatures for alias declarations, as they are verbose but straightforward. Informally, these lookup or compute the signature of their right-hand side, and then substitute the alias declaration's name for the referred-to declaration's name. For example, for **alias class C1 = M.C2**, we would look up the signature of M.C2 in the environment, and C1's signature

$$\boxed{\langle \Gamma, \mathcal{K}, \overline{Mb}\rangle \vdash Mb : Sb}$$

$$\frac{\text{unmark}(\tau^{\#}) = \tau}{\langle \Gamma, \mathcal{K}, \overline{Mb}\rangle \vdash (\text{fun } f : \tau^{\#} \text{ -> } \tau') : (\text{fun } f : \tau^{\#} \text{ -> } \tau' \text{ open below } \tau)} \text{ (S-Fun)}$$

$$\frac{R = \text{reps}(\Gamma, \overline{Mb}) \qquad \text{unmark}(\tau^{\#}) = \tau_f \qquad \mathcal{K}, R \vdash \text{ptype}(P, \tau_f) = \langle \tau^P, \beta\rangle}{\langle \Gamma, \mathcal{K}, \overline{Mb}\rangle \vdash \hat{M}.f : \langle \hat{M}, \text{fun } f : \tau^{\#} \text{ -> } \_ \text{ open below } \_\rangle}$$
$$\overline{\langle \Gamma, \mathcal{K}, \overline{Mb}\rangle \vdash (\text{extend fun } \hat{M}.f \text{ with } q \ P = e) : (\text{extend fun } \hat{M}.f \text{ with } q \ \tau^P)} \text{ (S-Method)}$$

$$\frac{[\langle \Gamma, \overline{Mb}\rangle \vdash \text{rep}(C) = \{\overline{L''' : \tau'''}^{1..k}\}]^1 \qquad \langle \Gamma, \mathcal{K}, \overline{Mb}\rangle \vdash \text{abstractFuns}(c[, C]^1) = \emptyset}{\langle \Gamma, \mathcal{K}, \overline{Mb}\rangle \vdash \text{class } c \ (\overline{x : \tau}^{1..m}) \ [\text{extends } C \ (\overline{e})]^1 \text{of } \{\overline{l : \tau'' = e''}^{1..n}\}}$$
$$: \text{class } c \ (\overline{\tau}^{1..m}) \text{ of } \{\overline{\text{ThisMod}.l : \tau''}^{1..n}[, \overline{L''' : \tau'''}^{1..k}]^1\} \text{ (S-Class)}$$

$$\frac{[\langle \Gamma, \overline{Mb}\rangle \vdash \text{rep}(C) = \{\overline{L''' : \tau'''}^{1..k}\}]^1 \qquad \langle \Gamma, \mathcal{K}, \overline{Mb}\rangle \vdash \text{abstractFuns}(c[, C]^1) = \overline{F}}{\langle \Gamma, \mathcal{K}, \overline{Mb}\rangle \vdash \text{abstract class } c \ (\overline{x : \tau}^{1..m}) \ [\text{extends } C \ e]^1 \text{ of } \{\overline{l : \tau'' = e''}^{1..n}\}}$$
$$: \text{class } c \ (\overline{\tau}^{1..m}) \text{ of } \{\overline{\text{ThisMod}.l : \tau''}^{1..n}[, \overline{L''' : \tau'''}^{1..k}]^1\} \text{ abstract on } \overline{F} \text{ (S-Abs-Class)}$$

$$\boxed{\text{declRels}(\overline{Mb}) = \mathcal{K}}$$

$$\frac{\forall_{i=1}^{n}.\text{fresh}(Mb_i) = \phi_i \qquad \forall_{i=1}^{n}.\text{rel}(Mb_i) = \rho_i \qquad \langle \phi, \rho\rangle = \langle \cup_{i=1}^{n}\phi_i, \cup_{i=1}^{n}\rho_i\rangle}{\text{declRels}(Mb_1, \ldots, Mb_n) = \langle \phi, \rho\rangle} \text{ (Decl-Rels)}$$

Mb	$\text{fresh}(Mb)$	$\text{rel}(Mb)$
[abstract] class $c(\_)$ of $\{\_\}$	ThisMod.c	—
[abstract] class $c(\_)$ extends $C(\_)$ of $\{\_\}$	ThisMod.c	ThisMod.$c <^1 C$
alias class $c = C$	—	ThisMod.$c <^0 C$
fun $f : \_ \text{ -> } \_$	ThisMod.f	—
alias fun $f = F$	—	ThisMod.$f = F$
extend fun F with $q \ P \text{ -> } e$	ThisMod.q	—
alias extend fun F with $q = Q$	—	ThisMod.$q = Q$

Fig. 10. Static semantics: Principal signatures (selected rules)

would have the same representation, constructor (if present), and **abstract on** clause (if present), but with C1 substituted for C2.

Well-Formedness of Module Declarations. After a module's principal signature is generated, each of its declarations is checked for well-formed implementation ($\Gamma \vdash Mb$ OK in $\overline{Sb}$). The well-formedness rules contain much that is standard — for example, part of the well-formedness rule for methods typechecks the method body in the environment formed by the bindings in the method's argument. In this section, we focus only on the (relatively) non-standard requirements imposed by the unusual mechanisms of F(EML) (note that some of these requirements are adapted with only minor changes from EML).

Recall, from Section 3.1, the three kinds of dynamic errors: abstract instantiations, messages not understood, and ambiguous messages. Abstract instantiations can be prevented relatively easily: when typechecking a constructor invocation, verify that the constructor is visible and that class's signature does not have an **abstract on** clause.

However, preventing message-not-understood and ambiguous message errors is harder, because modular typechecking context does not, in general, contain all the concrete classes and methods in the program. New subclasses and new methods can be added by modules that are not visible in any given scope. Hence, a function may appear to be implemented on all concrete subtypes of its argument, but other concrete subtypes may still exist; similarly, all the visible cases of a function may appear to be unambiguous with each other, but other ambiguous methods may still exist. Therefore, F(EML) adapts from EML several restrictions that, taken together, prevent these errors.

Recall that function argument types must be *marked types* $\tau^\#$. Define the *owner position* of $\tau^\#$ as the position in its abstract syntax tree that is marked with a hash #; define a function's *owner* as the class at the owner position in its argument type (note that, unlike a *receiver* class, the owner is a purely static notion; dynamic dispatch remains symmetric); and define a method's *owner* as the class at the owner position of the method's argument pattern's type. Then, the following well-formedness conditions must hold for methods, functions, and classes respectively. First, each method must be defined in either the same module as its owner, or the same module as the function it extends. Second, for any function F declared in a different module from its owner, a *global default* case (which covers F's declared argument type) must be defined in the same module as F. Third, any concrete subclass C of an abstract class C' must define a *local default* case for each function F that appears in the **abstract on** clause of C''s signature; the local default case for each F must cover the argument type $\tau^\#$ of F, but with C substituted at the owner position of $\tau^\#$.

Previous work [28] has shown how the above restrictions intuitively support (more than) the union of object-oriented and functional styles of extensibility — they are crafted to permit extension with both (a) new subclasses of existing classes, and (b) new functions on existing types.

The restrictions above rule out incompleteness errors. To completely rule out ambiguity errors, we must add one further condition to method well-formedness: we must check that each method is *pairwise unambiguous* with all other visible methods. Informally, two methods are pairwise unambiguous if either: (1) they extend different functions, (2) they have *disjoint* argument types, (3) one has an argument type that *strictly subtypes* the other's argument type, (4) their argument types share a common subtype, for which a *disambiguating* case exists that is more specific than both, or (5) they are aliases of the same method.

Finally, F(EML) imposes one further requirement on function aliases. If a module M aliases a function F from module M', then that M must also contain aliases of all F's methods from M'. The reason for this is subtle; there are cases (as we shall see in Section 3.2) when subsumption may not safely hide a method. Our rules check for these conditions before allowing a method to be hidden; however, if it were possible to alias functions freely without aliasing their methods, then those methods would be hidden from clients of the alias function, bypassing these subsumption conditions and rendering typechecking unsound.

Deducing Relations. We have seen that typechecking requires several kinds of knowledge about the relationships between classes, types, functions, and methods. In most object-oriented languages with nominal subtyping — e.g., in Java — subtyping is the only type relation relevant to typechecking, and the typechecker computes subtyping by inspecting the actual inheritance graph of classes. In F(EML), we can make use of richer information about types — e.g., the fact that classes are disjoint can be used to prove two methods unambiguous — and we must also deduce function and method relations. F(EML) performs all such deductions with a set of judgments that depend only on a relation context $\mathcal{K} = \langle \phi, \rho \rangle$. To form this context, we gather the union of all ϕ and ρ from all structure signatures $\texttt{sig} \{ \_ \texttt{fresh } \phi \texttt{ where } \rho \}$ in the range of the context Γ (during principal signature generation, we also add the initial declRels($\overline{Mb}$), as computed in Fig. 10), and run the deduction rules in this context.

Fig. 11 gives a sampling of rules for deducing class and type relations. The class deduction rules should be fairly intuitive upon inspection. Notice that CREL-NEQ implements the rule, mentioned in Section 2.4, that all fresh classes are known to be distinct from each other. The type deduction rules simply then "lift" the various class relations to the level of structured types.

$$\frac{\mathcal{K} \vdash C_1 <^i C_2 \quad \mathcal{K} \vdash C_2 <^j C_3}{\mathcal{K} \vdash C_1 <^{i+j} C_3}$$
(CREL-TRANS-COUNT)

$$\frac{C_1 \; \mathcal{R}_C \; C_2 \in \rho}{\langle \phi, \rho \rangle \vdash C_1 \; \mathcal{R}_C \; C_2} \qquad \boxed{\mathcal{K} \vdash C_1 \; \mathcal{R}_C \; C_2}$$
(CREL-LOOKUP)

$$\frac{\{\hat{M}.c, \hat{M}'.c'\} \subseteq \phi}{(\hat{M} \neq \hat{M}') \vee (c \neq c')}$$ (CREL-NEQ)
$$\frac{}{\langle \phi, \rho \rangle \vdash \hat{M}.c \neq \hat{M}'.c'}$$

$$\frac{\mathcal{K} \vdash C_1 \neq C_2 \qquad \mathcal{K} \vdash C_1 <^k C \quad \mathcal{K} \vdash C_2 <^k C}{\mathcal{K} \vdash C_1 \not\!\!\mathrel{/} C_2}$$ (CREL-DIS)

$$\frac{\forall_{i=1}^n.(\mathcal{K} \vdash \tau_i \; \leq \; \tau_i')}{\mathcal{K} \vdash (\overline{\tau}^{1..n}) \; \leq \; (\overline{\tau'}^{1..n})}$$ (R-TUPLE-SUB) $$\boxed{\mathcal{K} \vdash \tau_1 \; \mathcal{R}_\tau \; \tau_2}$$

$$\frac{\mathcal{K} \vdash C \leq C' \qquad \forall_1^n i.\mathcal{K} \vdash \tau_i \leq \tau_i'}{\mathcal{K} \vdash C \; \{\overline{L : \tau}^{1..n}, \overline{L : \tau}^{(n+1)..m}\} \; \leq \; C' \; \{\overline{L : \tau'}^{1..n}\}}$$ (R-CLASS-SUB)

Fig. 11. Static relation deduction (selected rules)

We do not show function and method relation deduction rules, but these are straightforwardly parallel to a subset of the class relation rules. For example, FREL-LOOKUP looks up a function relation $F_1 \; \mathcal{R}_F \; F_2$ in ρ, and FREL-NEQ deduces that all function names in ϕ refer to (pairwise) distinct functions.

Signature Subsumption and Selective Sealing. To be reusable, a functor should accept actual arguments whose signatures have "more information than" its formal argument signature. However, defining signature subtyping is not as simple as it would seem at first. Intuitively, subsumption hides information from a client, and unrestricted information hiding would sometimes grant a client permission to perform actions that would be prohibited by the more informative signature. In particular, hiding a function F on which a class is abstract could permit a client to create a concrete subclass of that class without providing an implementing case for F; and hiding a method Q could permit a client to define a method that is ambiguous with Q without providing a disambiguating case.

F(EML)'s signature language therefore contains features that *selectively revoke* the privileges to perform potentially harmful actions — in particular, to subclass a class, and to extend a function — and permits hiding only when the client does not possess dangerous privileges. Fig. 12 and gives the subsumption rules that bear directly these problems. Note that relsInContext(Γ) simply extracts all the relations ϕ and ρ from each structure signature in Γ. We now describe how these rules manage the two kinds of potentially unsafe subsumption we have just mentioned — hiding functions, and hiding method cases.

First, a client can conflict with a hidden function by defining a new subclass of an abstract class C, while failing to implement the corresponding cases for a hidden abstract function. Therefore, we cannot *both* permit a client to subclass an abstract class, *and* hide a function on which that class is abstract. Notice that SB-CLOSED-ABS only permits abstract functions to be forgotten if the class is closed, so that clients cannot subclass it (this rule also permits the abstract on clause to be forgotten entirely, provided the client forgoes the privilege of invoking the constructor as well). Then, DROP-FUN requires that any dropped function not be referenced anywhere in the signature (including the abstract on clause of a class). Taken together, these rules encode the constraint we require — a client cannot forget about a function *and* create a concrete subclass of a class abstract on that function.

Second, a client can conflict with a hidden method by defining a new method that is ambiguous with the hidden method. Therefore, we cannot *both* permit a client to extend a function on some type, *and* hide a case that may be ambiguous with that type. Now, recall that a class may not extend a function F from outside F's enclosing module, except on a *strict subtype* of F's extension type. The DROP-METHOD rule requires that a method can be hidden only if it extends a local function on a *supertype* of its extension type, guaranteeing that future methods will not be ambiguous with the hidden method. By itself, this rule would be overly restrictive, since functions use their argument type as the default extension type (see S-FUN in Fig. 10). However, SB-SEAL permits us to seal a function to a subtype of that function's original extension type; one can apply SB-SEAL to make a method droppable, and then DROP-METHOD to hide it.

3.3 Soundness

Previous work [28] established the soundness of Mini-EML (the formal core of EML, analogous to Mini-F(EML)) via the following standard theorems:

Theorem 1 (Mini-Eml Subject Reduction). *Given: (1)* $\forall Bn \in dom(BT)$. $BT(Bn)$ *OK, (2)* $\vdash E : T$ *in the context of* BT, *and (3)* $E \longrightarrow E'$ *in the context of* BT, *then* $\vdash E' : T'$ *for some* T' *such that* $T' \leq T$.

Theorem 2 (Mini-Eml Progress). *Given: (1)* $\forall Bn \in dom(BT)$. $BT(Bn)$ *OK, (2)* $\vdash E : T$ *in the context of* BT, *and (3)* E *is not a value, then* $\exists E'.E \longrightarrow E'$.

$$\boxed{\Gamma \vdash Sv \leq Sv'}$$

$$\frac{\Gamma, \mathcal{K}, (\overline{Sb}; \overline{Sb'}) \vdash Sb \text{ droppable}}{\text{relsInContext}(\Gamma) = \langle \phi', \rho' \rangle \qquad \mathcal{K} = \langle (\phi, \phi'), (\rho, \rho') \rangle}{\Gamma \vdash \text{sig } \{\ \overline{Sb}; Sb; \overline{Sb'} \text{ fresh } \phi \text{ where } \rho\ \} \leq \text{sig } \{\ \overline{Sb}; \overline{Sb'} \text{ fresh } \phi \text{ where } \rho\ \}} \text{ (SUB-WIDTH)}$$

$$\frac{\Gamma, \mathcal{K}, (\overline{Sb}; \overline{Sb'}) \vdash Sb \leq Sb'}{\text{relsInContext}(\Gamma) = \langle \phi', \rho' \rangle \qquad \mathcal{K} = \langle (\phi, \phi'), (\rho, \rho') \rangle}{\Gamma \vdash \text{sig } \{\ \overline{Sb}; Sb; \overline{Sb'} \text{ fresh } \phi \text{ where } \rho\ \} \leq \text{sig } \{\ \overline{Sb}; Sb'; \overline{Sb'} \text{ fresh } \phi \text{ where } \rho\ \}} \text{ (SUB-DEPTH)}$$

$$\boxed{\Gamma, \mathcal{K}, \overline{Sb} \vdash Sb \leq Sb'}$$

$$\frac{}{\Gamma, \mathcal{K}, \overline{Sb} \vdash \text{class } c\ (\overline{\tau}) \text{ of } \{\overline{L:\tau}\} \text{ [abstract on } \overline{F}]^1 \atop \leq \text{closed class } c\ (\overline{\tau}) \text{ of } \{\overline{L:\tau}\} \text{ [abstract on } \overline{F}]^1} \text{ (SB-CLOSE)}$$

$$\frac{[\overline{F'} \subseteq \overline{F}]^1}{\Gamma, \mathcal{K}, \overline{Sb} \vdash \text{closed class } c\ (\overline{\tau}) \text{ of } \{\overline{L:\tau}\} \text{ abstract on } \overline{F} \atop \leq \text{closed class } c\ [(\overline{\tau})]^1 \text{ of } \{\overline{L:\tau}\} \text{ [abstract on } \overline{F'}]^1} \text{ (SB-CLOSED-ABS)}$$

$$\frac{\mathcal{K} \vdash \tau' \leq \tau}{\Gamma, \mathcal{K}, \overline{Sb} \vdash \text{fun } f : \tau^{\#} \text{ -> } \tau_r \text{ open below } \tau \leq \text{fun } f : \tau^{\#} \text{ -> } \tau_r \text{ open below } \tau'} \text{ (SB-SEAL)}$$

$$\frac{(\text{fun } f : \_ \text{ -> } \_ \text{ open below } \tau_f^P) \in \overline{Sb} \qquad \boxed{\Gamma, \mathcal{K}, \overline{Sb} \vdash Sb \text{ droppable}}}{\text{ThisMod.}q \notin \text{freeNames}(\overline{Sb}) \qquad \mathcal{K} \vdash \tau_f^P \leq \tau^P}{\Gamma, \mathcal{K}, \overline{Sb} \vdash (\text{extend fun ThisMod.}f \text{ with } q\ \tau^P) \text{ droppable}} \text{ (DROP-METHOD)}$$

$$\frac{\text{ThisMod.}c \notin \text{freeNames}(\overline{Sb})}{\Gamma, \mathcal{K}, \overline{Sb} \vdash (\ [\text{abstract}] \text{ class } c \ldots) \text{ droppable}} \text{ (DROP-CLASS)}$$

$$\frac{\text{ThisMod.}f \notin \text{freeNames}(\overline{Sb})}{\Gamma, \mathcal{K}, \overline{Sb} \vdash (\text{fun } f : \_ \text{ -> } \_ \text{ open below } \_) \text{ droppable}} \text{ (DROP-FUN)}$$

Fig. 12. Static semantics: Signature subsumption (selected rules)

Here, the "block table" BT is a finite map from block names Bn to *blocks* (module values), E is a Mini-EML core expression, and T is a Mini-EML type. $BT(Bn)$ OK denotes the Mini-EML judgment that the block $BT(Bn)$ is well-formed. $\vdash E : T$ denotes that E has the Mini-EML type T. $E \longrightarrow E'$ is the Mini-EML small-step evaluation relation. Now, we define a function $\lfloor\ \rfloor$ which translates Mini-F(EML) syntax into Mini-EML: $\lfloor \mathcal{D}; \Delta; e \rfloor$ denotes the translation of a compiled Mini-F(EML) program into a Mini-EML program $BT; E$, assuming the module dependency relation $\mathcal{D}$. We then require two extra properties:

Theorem 3 (Well-Formed Translation). *If (1)* $\emptyset, \emptyset \vdash \overline{Md} \Rightarrow^* \Gamma, \mathcal{D}$, *(2)* $\emptyset \vdash \overline{Md} \Downarrow^* \Delta$, *and (3)* $\lfloor \mathcal{D}, \Delta \rfloor = BT$, *then (G1)* $\forall Bn \in dom(BT).BT(Bn)$ *OK.*

Theorem 4 (Type Preservation). *If (1)* $\emptyset, \emptyset \vdash \overline{Md} \Rightarrow^* \Gamma, \mathcal{D}$, *(2)* $\emptyset \vdash \overline{Md} \Downarrow^*$ Δ, *(3)* $\lfloor \mathcal{D}, \Delta; e \rfloor = BT; E$, *and (4)* $\Gamma, \emptyset, \emptyset \vdash e : \tau$, *then (G1)* $\vdash E : \lfloor \tau \rfloor$ *in* BT.

Provided the above properties hold, it follows that if a Mini-F(EML) program typechecks, then its Mini-EML translation typechecks, and the translated program does not go wrong. We working towards completion of the proofs, which will appear in a companion technical report [22].

4   Related Work

As previously mentioned, the direct predecessor to F(EML) is EML [28]. A sibling of EML is MultiJava [10, 29], which explores many of the same issues and could be extended with parameterized modules in closely analogous ways. Nice [3] resembles EML (though it is built on a different formalism) in providing multiple dispatch and a form of modular typechecking, without parameterized modules.

A *mixin* [5, 17] is a class that inherits from a parameter to be provided later. Bracha and Cook first proposed mixins [5] for a single-dispatch object-oriented language. Statically typed mixin languages prior to our work generally have not supported multiple dispatch, or permitted addition of dispatching functions from outside the receiver class. *Traits* [36, 38, 32] are a mixin-like multiple inheritance mechanism wherein classes can inherit *one* ordinary superclass and *multiple* traits, where traits may not define constructors or state. Traits languages would still gain additional flexibility if combined with functors: a class defining constructors and state could (by functorization of the containing module) be parameterized by a superclass that also defined constructors and state.

Many languages allow general multiple inheritance, which can support mixin-like idioms. Multiple inheritance comes with a number of known problems, e.g., the "diamond inheritance" problem. Like traditional mixin languages, F(EML) sidesteps these problems (with some loss of expressiveness) by offering single inheritance, plus the alternative composition mechanism of parameterization.

Virtual types (or *virtual classes* [25]) extend class-level inheritance with *overridable type members* nested inside classes. Virtual types can statically typecheck many idioms like those supported by parameterized classes and modules [7, 40, 14]. In languages like **gbeta** [13], Scala [32], Jx [31], and CAESARJ [2], virtual types also support *family polymorphism* [13], an idiom for writing code that is generic over multiple instantiations of related groups of types. Virtual and parametric types share deep connections, and we suspect that any given language feature raises closely analogous issues in either style of system. For example, if one added multiple dispatch to virtual type systems, then determining whether a type member could be safely overridden in a subclass might raise issues like those that F(EML) encounters in defining subsumption for classes in functor argument signatures. Conversely, adding family polymorphism support to F(EML) might require dependent type mechanisms akin to those in virtual type systems.

F(EML)'s functors are inspired by ML's parameterized module system [19]. Many extensions to ML parameterized modules have been proposed [23, 18, 11], but none have incorporated extensible data types, extensible functions, *and* symmetric multiple dispatch. OML [34], OCaml [33], and Moby [15] combine ML-style modules orthogonally with object-oriented classes, but these classes are traditional receiver-oriented constructs: dispatching methods can only be declared with their receiver class, and cannot be externally added without modifying the original declaration. ML$_\leq$ [4] generalizes ML datatypes with subtyping and symmetric dispatch, but does not support addition of new cases to existing functions from outside of the extended declaration's original module. Several proposals extend ML with *mixin modules* [12, 20]; these systems do not currently support subtyping among datatype cases, ruling out object-oriented idioms.

Jiazzi [26] (based on Units [16]) and JavaMod [1] extend Java with parameterized modules that support many idioms, including mixins. These languages only support single dispatch, so in this sense they are more restrictive than F(EML); however, conversely, they support recursive module linkage, which our work does not (although we believe recursive linkage could be added to F(EML)). Jiazzi also supports the addition of dispatching functions externally to a class, through an *open class* design pattern, though this requires more advance planning than in F(EML), where external functions can be added directly.

Classes in C++ templates [39] can inherit from a template parameter, but templates do not support separate typechecking of template bodies. Parameterized classes in GJ [6] support separate typechecking, but disallow inheritance from the type parameter, ruling out idioms like mixins.

5   Conclusions and Future Work

We have described a parameterized module system with several novel features in the module and signature language. The module language includes aliasing declarations, which permit potential arguments to be adapted to the naming and modularization requirements of a parameterized module. The signature language allows a parameterized module to specify two important kinds of requirements of its argument: how its declarations are *related* to each other, and how *extensible* the classes and functions must be. These constraints enable the body of the parameterized module to be typechecked separately from instantiations, even in the face of extensible classes, extensible functions, and methods with symmetric multiple dispatching. At the same time, these constraints remain weak enough to allow the parameterized module to be applied to a wide range of arguments.

In the future, we would like to study relaxing F(EML)'s modular typechecking restrictions, along the lines of Relaxed MultiJava [29], to give the programmer more control over the trade-off between modular typechecking and programming flexibility. We also think it would be interesting to explore the ideas in this paper in the context of a virtual type-based system. Finally, we plan to adapt and implement these ideas in Diesel, a language which adds a module system to an underlying core language based on Cecil [8, 9].

Acknowledgments. This work has been supported in part by NSF grants CCR-0204047 and ACI-0203908. We wish to thank Erik Ernst, Todd Millstein, the University of Washington WASP group, and anonymous reviewers of this work (and its earlier incarnations) for their invaluable feedback and discussions.

References

1. D. Ancona, E. Zucca. True Modules for Java-like Languages. *15th ECOOP*, 2001.
2. I. Aracic, V. Gasiunas, M. Mezini, K. Ostermann. An Overview of CaesarJ. *Trans. on Aspect-Oriented Development I*, LNCS 3880 pp. 135-173, Feb. 2006.

3. D. Bonniot. Type-checking multi-methods in ML (A modular approach). *FOOL 9*, 2002.
4. F. Bourdoncle, S. Merz. Type checking higher-order polymorphic multi-methods. *24th POPL*, 1997.
5. G. Bracha, W. Cook. Mixin-based Inheritance. In *OOPSLA*, 1990.
6. G. Bracha, M. Odersky, D. Stoutamire, P. Wadler. Making the Future Safe for the Past: Adding Genericity to the Java Programming Language. *OOPSLA*, 1998.
7. K. B. Bruce, M. Odersky, P. Wadler. A Statically safe alternative to virtual types. *12th ECOOP*, 1998.
8. C. Chambers. Object-Oriented Multi-Methods in Cecil. *6th ECOOP*, 1992.
9. C. Chambers, Cecil Group. The Cecil Language: Specification and Rationale. Univ. of Washington Technical Report UW-CSE-93-03-05, 1993-2004.
10. C. Clifton, G. T. Leavens, C. Chambers, T. Millstein. MultiJava: Modular Open Classes and Symmetric Multiple Dispatch for Java. *OOPSLA*, 2000.
11. D. Dreyer, K. Crary, R. Harper. A Type System for Higher-Order Modules. *30th POPL*, 2003.
12. D. Duggan, C. Sourelis. Mixin modules. In *First ICFP*, Philadelphia PA, 1996.
13. E. Ernst. Family Polymorphism. *15th ECOOP*, June 2001.
14. E. Ernst, K. Ostermann, W. R. Cook. A Virtual Class Calculus. *POPL*, 2006.
15. K. Fisher, J. Reppy. The design of a class mechanism for Moby. *PLDI*, June 1999.
16. M. Flatt, M. Felleisen. Units: Cool modules for HOT languages. *PLDI*, 1998.
17. M. Flatt, S. Krishnamurthi, M. Felleisen. Classes and Mixins. *25th POPL*, 1998.
18. R. Harper, M. Lillibridge. A Type-theoretic approach to higher-order modules with sharing. *POPL*, 1994.
19. R. Harper, C. Stone. A Type-theoretic interpretation of Standard ML. Carnegie Mellon Dept. of CS Technical Report CMU-CS-97-147, 1997.
20. T. Hirschowitz, X. Leroy. Mixin modules in a call-by-value setting. *European Symp. on Programming*, LNCS 2305, D. Le Metayer, ed., 2002.
21. G. Kiczales, J. Lamping, A. Menhdhekar, C. Maeda, C. Lopes, J.-M. Loingtier, J. Irwin. Aspect-Oriented Programming. *11th ECOOP*, 1997.
22. K. Lee, C. Chambers. Parameterized modules for extensible classes and functions. Univ. of Washington Technical Report UW-CSE-2005-07-01, 2006 (forthcoming).
23. X. Leroy. Manifest types, modules, and separate compilation. *21st POPL*, 1994.
24. R. E. Lopez-Herrejon, D. Batory, W. Cook. Evaluating Support for Features in Advanced Modularization Technologies. *19th ECOOP*, 2005.
25. O. L. Madsen, B. Møller-Pedersen. Virtual classes: a powerful mechanism in object-oriented programming. In *Conf. OOPSLA*, 1989.
26. S. McDirmid, M. Flatt, W. C. Hsieh. Jiazzi: New age modules for old-fashioned Java. *16th OOPSLA*, pp. 211-222, Tampa Bay FL, 2001.
27. T. Millstein, C. Chambers. Modular Statically Typed Multimethods. *13th ECOOP*, 1999.
28. T. Millstein, C. Bleckner, C. Chambers. Modular Typechecking for Hierarchically Extensible Datatypes and Functions. *ACM TOPLAS* 26(5):836-889, 2004.
29. T. Millstein, M. Reay, C. Chambers. Relaxed MultiJava: Balancing Extensibility and Modular Typechecking. In *OOPSLA*, Oct. 2003.
30. R. Milner, M. Tofte, R. Harper, D. MacQueen. *Def. of Standard ML (Revised)*. MIT Press, 1997.
31. N. Nystrom, S. S. Chong, A. C. Myers. Scalable Extensibility via Nested Inheritance. *OOPSLA*, 2004.

32. M. Odersky, P. Altherr, V. Cremet, B. Emir, S. Maneth, S. Micheloud, N. Mihaylov, M. Schinz, E. Stenman, M. Zenger. An Overview of the Scala Programming Language. EPFL Technical Report IC/2004/64. EPFL Lausanne, 2004.

33. D. Rémy, J. Vouillon. Objective ML: a simple object-oriented extension of ML. *24th POPL*, 1997.

34. J. Reppy, J. Riecke. Simple objects for Standard ML. *1996 PLDI*, 1996.

35. J. C. Reynolds. User defined types and procedural data structures as complementary approaches to data abstraction. In *Programming Methodology, A Collection of Articles by IFIP WG2.3*, D. Gries, ed., Springer-Verlag, 1978.

36. N. Schärli, S. Ducasse, O. Nierstrasz, A. Black. Traits: Composable Units of Behavior. *18th ECOOP*, LNCS 2743, July 2003.

37. Y. Smaragdakis, D. Batory. Mixin Layers: An Object-Oriented Implementation Technique for Refinements and Collaboration Designs. *ACM TSEM* 11(2):215-255, April 2002.

38. C. Smith, S. Drossopoulou. Chai: Traits for Java-like Languages. *ECOOP*, 2005.

39. B. Stroustrup. *The C++ Programming Language, 3rd Ed.* Addison-Wesley, 2000.

40. K. K. Thorup, M. Torgersen. Unifying genericity – combining the benefits of virtual types and parameterized classes. *13th ECOOP*, 1999.

41. Philip Wadler. The Expression Problem. Java-genericity email list, Nov. 1998.

The Closing of the Frontier

Ralph E. Johnson

Dept of Computer Science, 201 N Goodwin Ave, Urbana IL 61820, USA
University of Illinois at Urbana-Champaign
johnson@cs.uiuc.edu

Abstract. Software design is usually discussed as if the system is being created "de novo", but most programmers are working on systems that have already been released. This is a sign of success, since software is now good enough to keep and is worth improving. But the way we talk about design and the way we teach it is stuck in the twentieth century. The software frontier is closing.

Although there are still new projects, it is more accurate to say "there are no new software projects" than it is to say "all software projects are new". What would the world be like if there were no new software projects?

If a software project has been going for fifty years then a programmer who has been on the project for twenty years will be more valuable than someone who is new to the project. Old programmers will be more valuable than young programmers.

If a software project is going to last another fifty years and will be actively developed during that time then it is worthwhile to keep it in good shape. It is worth fixing pesky bugs that only appear once every year. It is worth spending some time improving the documentation. It is worth rewriting parts of the system that are complex and buggy.

If a software project is on version 129 then it is clear that software development is program transformation. Each iteration transforms version N into version N+1. Although user requirements are important, version N+1 depends more on version N than it does on the latest requests from the users.

Fortunes can be made both on the frontier and in cities. The frontier and cities are different, however, and some of the rules of success of the frontier must change for the cities.

D. Thomas (Ed.): ECOOP 2006, LNCS 4067, p. 379, 2006.
© Springer-Verlag Berlin Heidelberg 2006

Augmenting Automatically Generated Unit-Test Suites with Regression Oracle Checking

Tao Xie

Department of Computer Science
North Carolina State University
Raleigh, NC 27695
xie@csc.ncsu.edu

Abstract. A test case consists of two parts: a test input to exercise the program under test and a test oracle to check the correctness of the test execution. A test oracle is often in the form of executable assertions such as in the JUnit testing framework. Manually generated test cases are valuable in exposing program faults in the current program version or regression faults in future program versions. However, manually generated test cases are often insufficient for assuring high software quality. We can then use an existing test-generation tool to generate new test inputs to augment the existing test suite. However, without specifications these automatically generated test inputs often do not have test oracles for exposing faults. In this paper, we have developed an automatic approach and its supporting tool, called Orstra, for augmenting an automatically generated unit-test suite with regression oracle checking. The augmented test suite has an improved capability of guarding against regression faults. In our new approach, Orstra first executes the test suite and collects the class under test's object states exercised by the test suite. On collected object states, Orstra creates assertions for asserting behavior of the object states. On executed observer methods (public methods with non-void returns), Orstra also creates assertions for asserting their return values. Then later when the class is changed, the augmented test suite is executed to check whether assertion violations are reported. We have evaluated Orstra on augmenting automatically generated tests for eleven subjects taken from a variety of sources. The experimental results show that an automatically generated test suite's fault-detection capability can be effectively improved after being augmented by Orstra.

1   Introduction

To expose faults in a program, developers create a test suite, which includes a set of test cases to exercise the program. A test case consists of two parts: a test input to exercise the program under test and a test oracle to check the correctness of the test execution. A test oracle is often in the form of runtime assertions [2, 36] such as in the JUnit testing framework [19]. In Extreme Programming [7] practice, writing unit tests has become an important part of software development. Unit tests help expose not only faults in the current program version but also regression faults introduced during program changes: these written unit tests allow developers to change their code in a continuous and controlled way. However, some special test inputs are often overlooked by developers and

D. Thomas (Ed.): ECOOP 2006, LNCS 4067, pp. 380–403, 2006.
© Springer-Verlag Berlin Heidelberg 2006

typical manually created unit test suites are often insufficient for assuring high software quality. Then developers can use one of the existing automatic test-generation tools [31, 8, 42, 11, 12, 43, 44] to generate a large number of test inputs to complement the manually created tests. However, without specifications, these automatically generated test inputs do not have test oracles, which can be used to check whether test executions are correct. In this paper, we have developed a new automatic approach that adds assertions into an automatically generated test suite so that the augmented test suite has an improved capability of guarding against regression faults.

Our approach focuses on object-oriented unit tests, such as the ones written in the JUnit testing framework [19]. An object-oriented unit test consists of sequences of method invocations. Our approach proposes a framework for asserting the behavior of a method invocation in an object-oriented unit-test suite. Behavior of an invocation depends on the state of the receiver object and method arguments at the beginning of the invocation. Behavior of an invocation can be asserted by checking at the end of the invocation the return value of the invocation (when the invocation's return is not void), the state of the receiver object, and the states of argument objects (when the invocation can modify the states of the argument objects). Automatic test-generation tools often do not create assertions but rely on uncaught exceptions or program crashes to detect problems in a program [11, 12].

To address insufficient test oracles of an automatically generated test suite, we have developed an automatic tool, called Orstra, to augment the test suite for guarding against regression faults. Orstra executes tests in the test suite and collects the class under test's object states exercised by the test suite; an object's state is characterized by the values of the object's transitively reachable fields [43]. On collected object states, Orstra invokes observers (public methods with non-void returns) of the class under test, collects their actual return values, and creates assertions for checking the returns of observers against their actual collected values. In addition, for each collected object state S, Orstra determines whether there is another collected object state S' that is *equivalent* to S (state equivalence is defined by graph isomorphism [8, 43]); if so, Orstra reconstructs S' with method sequences and creates an assertion for checking the state equivalence of S and S'.

This paper makes the following main contributions:

- We propose a framework for asserting the behavior of a method invocation in an object-oriented unit-test suite.
- We develop an automatic test-oracle-augmentation tool that systematically adds assertions into an automatically generated test suite in order to improve its capability of guarding against regression faults.
- We evaluate our approach on augmenting automatically generated tests for eleven Java classes taken from a variety of sources. The experimental results show that our test-oracle augmentation can effectively improve the fault-detection capability of a test suite.

The rest of this paper is organized as follows. Section 2 presents an illustrating example. Section 3 presents our framework for asserting behavior of a method invocation in a test suite. Section 4 presents our Orstra tool for automatically augmenting a test suite.

Section 5 presents an experiment to assess our approach. Section 6 discusses issues of the approach. Section 7 reviews related work, and Section 8 concludes.

2 Example

We next illustrate how Orstra augments an automatically generated test suite's regression oracle checking. As an illustrating example, we use a Java implementation of a bounded stack that stores unique elements. Stotts et al. [40] used this Java implementation to experiment with their algebraic-specification-based approach for systematically creating unit tests. In the abbreviated implementation shown in Figure 1, the class MyInput is the comparable type of elements stored in the stack. In the class implementation of the bounded stack, the array elems contains the elements of the stack, and numberOfElements is the number of the elements and the index of the first free location in the stack. The max is the capacity of the stack. The public methods in the class interface include two standard stack operations: push and pop, as well as five observer methods, whose returns are not void.

Given a Java class, existing automatic test-generation tools [31, 11, 12, 43, 44] can generate a test suite automatically for the class. For example, Jtest [31] allows users to set the length of calling sequences between one and three, and then generates random calling sequences whose lengths are not greater than the user-specified one. JCrasher [11] automatically constructs method sequences to generate non-primitive arguments and uses default data values for primitive arguments. JCrasher generates tests as calling sequences with the length of one.

For example, given the UBStack class, existing automatic test-generation tools [31, 11, 12, 43, 44] can generate test suites such as the example *test suite* UBStackTest with two tests (exported in the JUnit testing framework [19]) shown in Figure 2. Each *test* has several method sequences on the objects of the class. For example, test1 creates a stack s1 and invokes push, top, pop, and isMember on it in a row.

Note that there are no assertions generated in the UBStackTest test suite. Therefore, when the test suite is run, tools such as JCrasher [11] and CnC [12] detect problems by observing whether uncaught exceptions are thrown; tools such as Korat [8] detect problems by observing whether the execution of the test suite violates design-by-contract annotations [28, 23, 9] (equipped with the program under test), which are translated into run-time assertions [2, 36].

Given a test suite such as UBStackTest, Orstra systematically augments the test suite to produce an augmented test suite such as UBStackAugTest shown in Figure 3. For illustration, we annotate UBStackAugTest with line numbers and mark in bold font those lines of statements that correspond to the statements in UBStackTest. The augmented test suite UBStackAugTest is equipped with comprehensive assertions, which reflect the behavior of the current program version under test. These new assertions can guard against regression faults introduced in future program versions.

We next illustrate how Orstra automatically creates assertions for UBStackTest to produce UBStackAugTest. By running UBStackTest, Orstra dynamically monitors the method sequences executed by UBStackTest and collects the exercised state of a UBStack-receiver object by collecting the values of the re-

```
public class MyInput implements Comparable {
    private int o;
    public MyInput(int i) { o = i; }
    public boolean equals(Object that) {
        if (!(that instanceof MyInput)) return false;
        return (o == ((MyInput)that).o);
    }
}

public class UBStack {
    private Comparable[] elems;
    private int numberOfElements;
    private int max;
    public UBStack() { ... }
    //standard stack operations
    public void push(Comparable i) { ... }
    public void pop() { ... }
    //stack observer methods
    public int getNumberOfElements() { ... }
    public boolean isFull() { ... }
    public boolean isEmpty() { ... }
    public boolean isMember(Comparable i) {... }
    public MyInput top() { ... }
}
```

Fig. 1. A bounded stack implementation (UBStack) in Java

```
public class UBStackTest extends TestCase {
    public void test1() {
        UBStack s1 = new UBStack();
        MyInput i1 = new MyInput(3);
        s1.push(i1);
        s1.top();
        s1.pop();
        s2.isMember(i1);
    }

    public void test2() {
        UBStack s2 = new UBStack();
        s2.isEmpty();
        s2.isFull();
        s2.getNumberOfElements();
    }
}
```

Fig. 2. An automatically generated test suite UBStackTest for UBStack

ceiver object's transitively reachable fields. Based on the collected method invocations, Orstra identifies UBStack's observer methods that are invoked by UBStackTest: top(), isMember(new MyInput(3)), isEmtpy(), isFull(), and getNumberOfElements().

Then on each UBStack-receiver-object state exercised by UBStackTest, Orstra invokes the collected observer methods. For example, after the constructor invocation (shown in Line 2 of Figure 3), Orstra invokes the five observer methods on the UBStack object s1. After invoking these observer methods, Orstra collects their return values and then makes an assertion for each observer method by adding a JUnit assertion method (assertEquals), whose first argument is the observer method's return and second argument is the collected return value. The five inserted assertions are shown in Lines 4-9. Similarly, Orstra inserts assertions after the push invocation (shown in Line 12) for asserting the state of the receiver s1. Because in test1 of UBStackTest, there is

```
0  public class UBStackAugTest extends TestCase {
1   public void testAug1() {
2    UBStack s1 = new UBStack();
3    //start inserting new assertions for observers
4    assertEquals(s1.isEmpty(), true);
5    assertEquals(s1.isFull(), false);
6    assertEquals(s1.getNumberOfElements(), 0);
7    MyInput temp_i1 = new MyInput(3);
8    assertEquals(s1.isMember(temp_i1), false);
9    assertEquals(s1.top(), null);
10   //finish inserting new assertions for observers
11   MyInput i1 = new MyInput(3);
12   s1.push(i1);
13   //start inserting new assertions for observers
14   assertEquals(s1.isEmpty(), false);
15   assertEquals(s1.isFull(), false);
16   assertEquals(s1.getNumberOfElements(), 1);
17   assertEquals(s1.isMember(temp_i1), true);
18   //finish inserting new assertions for observers
19   assertEquals(Runtime.genStateStr(s1.top()), "o:3;");
20   //insert no new assertions for top
21   s1.pop();
22   //start inserting new assertions for state equivalence
23   UBStack temp_s1 = new UBStack();
24   EqualsBuilder.reflectionEquals(s1, temp_s1);
25   //finish inserting new assertions for state equivalence
26   assertEquals(s2.isMember(i1), false);
27   //insert no new assertions for isMember
28  }
29
30  public void testAug2() {
31   UBStack s2 = new UBStack();
32   //insert no new assertions because the equivalent state
33   //has been asserted in test1
34   assertEquals(s2.isEmpty(), true);
35   assertEquals(s2.isFull(), false);
36   assertEquals(s2.getNumberOfElements(), 0);
37  }
39 }
```

Fig. 3. An Orstra-augmented test suite for UBStackTest

an observer method top invoked immediately after the push invocation, in the inserted assertions for s1 after the push invocation, Orstra does not include another duplicate top observer invocation. Then Orstra still adds an assertion for the original top invocation (shown in Line 19). When Orstra collects the return value of top, it determines that the value is not of a primitive type but of the MyInput type. It then invokes its own runtime helper method (**Runtime**.genStateStr) to collect the state-representation string of the MyInput-type return value. The string consists of the values of all transitively reachable fields of the MyInput-type object, represented as "o:3;", where o is the field name and 3 is the field value.

After the top invocation (shown in Line 19), Orstra inserts no new assertion for asserting the state of s1 immediately after the top invocation, because Orstra dynamically determines top to be a state-preserving or side-effect-free method: all its invocations in the test suite do not modify the state of the receiver object.

After the pop invocation (shown in Line 21), Orstra detects that s1's state is equivalent to another collected object state that is produced by a shorter method sequence: an object state produced after the constructor invocation; Orstra determines state equivalence of two objects by comparing their state-representation strings. Therefore, instead of invoking observer methods on s1, Orstra constructs an assertion for asserting that the state of s1 is equivalent to the state of temp_s1, which is produced after the constructor is invoked. Orstra creates the assertion by using an equals-assertion-builder method (**EqualsBuilder**.reflectionEquals) from the Apache Jakarta Commons subproject [4]. This method uses Java reflection mechanisms [5] to determine if two objects are equal based on field-by-field comparison. If an equals method is defined as a public method of the class under test, Orstra can also alternatively use the equals method for building the assertion.

After the isMember invocation (shown in Line 26), Orstra inserts no new assertion for asserting the state of s1 immediately after the isMember invocation, because Orstra dynamically determines isMember to be a state-preserving method.

When augmenting test2, Orstra does not insert assertions for the state of s2 immediately after the constructor invocation, because the object state that is produced by the same method sequence has been asserted in testAug1. In testAug2, Orstra adds assertions only for those observer-method invocations that are originally in test2 (shown in Lines 34-36).

3 Framework

This section formalizes some notions introduced informally in the previous section. We first describe approaches for representing states of non-primitive-type objects and then compare these approaches. We finally describe how these state representations can be used to build assertions for the receiver object and return value of a method invocation.

3.1 State Representation

When a variable (such as the return of a method invocation) is of a primitive type or a primitive-object type such as String and Integer, Orstra asserts its value by comparing it with an expected value. When a variable (such as the return or receiver of a method invocation) is a non-primitive-type object, Orstra constructs assertions by using several types of state representations: method-sequence representation [43], concrete-state representation [43], and observer-abstraction representation [46].

Method-Sequence Representation.   The method-sequence-representation technique [43] represents the state of an object by using sequences of method invocations that produce the object (following Henkel and Diwan [22] who use the representation in mapping Java classes to algebras). Then Orstra can reconstruct or clone an object state by re-executing the method invocations in the method-sequence representation; the capability of reconstructing an object state is crucial when Orstra wants to assert that the state of the object under consideration is equivalent to that of another object constructed elsewhere.

The state representation uses symbolic expressions with the grammar shown below:

$$\begin{aligned}
&\text{exp} ::= \text{prim} \mid \text{invoc ".state"} \mid \text{invoc ".retval"}\\
&\text{args} ::= \epsilon \mid \text{exp} \mid \text{args "," exp}\\
&\text{invoc} ::= \text{method "(" args ")"}\\
&\text{prim} ::= \text{"null"} \mid \text{"true"} \mid \text{"false"} \mid \text{"0"} \mid \text{"1"} \mid \text{"-1"} \mid \ldots
\end{aligned}$$

Each object or value is represented with an expression. Arguments for a method invocation are represented as sequences of zero or more expressions (separated by commas); the receiver of a non-static, non-constructor method invocation is treated as the first method argument. A static method invocation or constructor invocation does not have a receiver. The `.state` and `.retval` expressions denote the state of the receiver after the invocation and the return of the invocation, respectively. For brevity, the grammar shown above does not specify types for the expressions. A method is represented uniquely by its defining class, name, and the entire signature. (For brevity, we do not show a method's defining class or signature in the state-representation examples of this paper.) For example, in `test1`, the state of the object `s1` after the `push` invocation is represented by

```
push(UBStack<init>().state, MyInput<init>(3).state).state.
```

where `UBStack<init>` and `MyInput<init>` represent constructor invocations.

Note that the state representation based on method sequences allows tests to contain loops, arithmetic, aliasing, and polymorphism. Consider the following two tests `test3` and `test4`:

```
public void test3() {
  UBStack t = new UBStack();
  UBStack s3 = t;
  for (int i = 0; i <= 1; i++)
    s3.push(new MyInput(i));
}

public void test4() {
  UBStack s4 = new UBStack();
  int i = 0;
  s4.push(new MyInput(i));
  s4.push(new MyInput(i + 1));
}
```

Orstra dynamically monitors the invocations of the methods on the actual objects created at runtime and collects the actual argument values for these invocations. For example, it represents the states of both `s3` and `s4` at the end of `test3` and `test4` as `push(push(UBStack<init>().state, MyInput<init>(0)).state, MyInput<init>(1)).state`.

The above-shown grammar does not capture a method execution's side effect on an argument: a method can modify the state of a non-primitive-type argument and this argument can be used for another later method invocation. Following Henkel and Diwan's suggested extension [22], we can enhance the first grammar rule to address this issue:

$$\text{exp} ::= \text{prim} \mid \text{invoc ``.state''} \mid \text{invoc ``.retval''} \mid \text{invoc ``.}arg_i\text{''}$$

where the added expression (invoc "$.arg_i$") denotes the state of the modified ith argument after the method invocation.

If test code modifies directly some public fields of an object without invoking any of its methods, these side effects on the object are not captured by method sequences in the method-sequence representation. To address this issue, Orstra can be extended to create a public field-writing method for each public field of the object, and then monitor object-field accesses in the test code. If Orstra detects at runtime the execution of the object's field-write instruction in the test code, it can insert a corresponding field-writing method invocation in the method-sequence representation.

```
Map ids; // maps nodes into their unique ids
String linearize(Node root, Heap <O,E>) {
  ids = new Map();
  return lin("root", root, <O,E>);
}

String lin(String fieldName, Node root, Heap <O,E>) {
  if (ids.containsKey(root))
    return fieldName+":"+String.valueOf(ids.get(root))+";";
  int id = ids.size() + 1;
  ids.put(root, id);
  StringBuffer rep = new StringBuffer();
  rep.append(fieldName+":"+String.valueOf(id)+";");
  Edge[] fields = sortByField({ <root, f, o> in E });
  foreach (<root, f, o> in fields) {
    if (isPrimitive(o))
      rep.append(f+":"+String.valueOf(o)+";");
    else
      rep.append(lin(f, o, <O,E>));
  }
  return rep.toString();
}
```

Fig. 4. Pseudo-code of the linearization algorithm

Concrete-State Representation. A program is executed upon the program state that includes a program heap. The concrete-state representation of an object [43] considers only parts of the heap that are reachable from the object. We also call each part a "heap" and view it as a graph: nodes represent objects and edges represent fields. Let P be the set consisting of all primitive values, including $null$, integers, etc. Let O be a set of objects whose fields form a set F. (Each object has a field that represents its class, and array elements are considered index-labelled object fields.)

Definition 1. A heap *is an edge-labelled graph* $\langle O, E \rangle$, *where* $E = \{\langle o, f, o' \rangle | o \in O, f \in F, o' \in O \cup P\}$.

Heap isomorphism is defined as graph isomorphism based on node bijection [8].

Definition 2. *Two heaps* $\langle O_1, E_1 \rangle$ *and* $\langle O_2, E_2 \rangle$ *are* isomorphic *iff there is a bijection* $\rho : O_1 \to O_2$ *such that:*

$$E_2 = \{\langle \rho(o), f, \rho(o') \rangle | \langle o, f, o' \rangle \in E_1, o' \in O_1\} \cup$$
$$\{\langle \rho(o), f, o' \rangle | \langle o, f, o' \rangle \in E_1, o' \in P\}.$$

The definition allows only object identities to vary: two isomorphic heaps have the same fields for all objects and the same values for all primitive fields.

The state of an object is represented with a *rooted* heap, instead of the whole program heap.

Definition 3. *A* rooted heap *is a pair* $\langle r, h \rangle$ *of a root object* r *and a heap* h *whose all nodes are reachable from* r.

Orstra linearizes rooted heaps into strings such that checking heap isomorphism corresponds to checking string equality. Figure 4 shows the pseudo-code of the linearization algorithm. The linearization algorithm traverses the entire rooted heap in the depth-first order, starting from the root. When the algorithm visits a node for the first time, it assigns a unique identifier to the node, and keeps this mapping in ids so that already assigned identifiers can be reused by nodes that appear in cycles. We can show that the linearization normalizes rooted heaps into strings. The states of two objects are *equivalent* if their strings resulted from linearization are the same.

Observer-Abstraction Representation. The observer abstraction technique [46] represents the state of an object by using abstraction functions that are constructed based on observers. We first define an observer following Henkel and Diwan's work [22] on specifying algebraic specifications for a class:

Definition 4. *An* observer *of a class c is a method ob in c's interface such that the return type of ob is not void.*

An observer invocation is a method invocation whose method is an observer. Given an object o of class c and a set of observer calls $OB = \{ob_1, ob_2, ..., ob_n\}^1$ of c, the observer abstraction technique represents the state of o with n values $OBR = \{obr_1, obr_2, ..., obr_n\}$, where each value obr_i represents the return value of observer call ob_i invoked on o.

When behavior of an object is to be asserted, Orstra can assert the observer-abstraction representation of the object: asserting the return values of observer invocations on the object.

Among different user-defined observers for a class, toString() [41] deserves special attention. This observer returns a string representation of the object, often being concise and human-readable. java.lang.Object [41] defines a default toString, which returns the name of the object's class followed by the unsigned hexadecimal representation of the hash code of the object. The Java API documentation [41] recommends developers to override this toString method in their own classes.

Comparison. In this section, we compare different state representations in terms of their relationships and the extent of revealing implementation details, as well as their effects on asserting method invocation behavior.

We first define subsumption relationships among state representations as follows. State representation S_1 *subsumes* state representation S_2 if and only if any two objects that have the same S_1 representations also have the same S_2 representations. State representation S_1 *strictly subsumes* state representation S_2 if S_1 subsumes S_2 and for some objects o and o', the S_1 representations differ but the S_2 representations do not. State representations S_1 and S_2 are *incomparable* if neither S_1 subsumes S_2 nor S_2 subsumes S_1. State representations S_1 and S_2 are *equivalent* if S_1 subsumes S_2 and S_2 subsumes S_1.

If state representation S_1 subsumes state representation S_2, and S_1 has been asserted (by checking whether the actual state representation is the same as the expected one), it is not necessary to assert S_2: asserting S_2 is *redundant* after we have asserted S_1.

The method-sequence representation strictly subsumes the concrete-state representation. The concrete-state representation strictly subsumes the observer-abstraction

---

[1] Orstra does not use an observer defined in java.lang.Object [41].

representation. Among different observers, the representation resulting from the toString() observer often subsumes the representation resulting from other observers and is often equivalent to the concrete-state representation.

Different state representations expose different levels of implementation details. If a state representation exposes more implementation details of a program, it is often more difficult for developers to determine whether the program behaves as expected once an assertion for the state representation is violated. In addition, If a state representation exposes more implementation details, developers can be overwhelmed by assertion violations that are not symptoms of regression faults but due to expected implementation changes (such as during program refactoring [18]). Although these assertion violations can be useful during software impact analysis [6], we prefer to put assertions on state representations that reveals fewer implementation details.

Among the three representations, the concrete-state representation exposes more implementation details than the other two representations: the concrete-state representation of an object is sensitive to changes on the object's field structure or the semantic of its fields, even if these changes do not cause any behavioral difference in the object's interface. To address this issue of the concrete-state representation, when Orstra creates an assertion for an object's concrete-state representation, instead of directly asserting the concrete-state representation string, Orstra asserts that the object is equivalent to another object produced with a different method sequence if such an object can be found (note that state equivalence is still determined based on the comparison of representation strings). This strategy is inspired by state-equivalence checking in algebraic-specifications-based testing [16, 22]. One such example is in Line 24 of Figure 3.

3.2 Method-Execution-Behavior Assertions

The execution of a test case produces a sequence of method executions.

Definition 5. *A method execution is a sextuple* $e = (m, S_{args}, S_{entry}, S_{exit}, S_{args'}, r)$ *where* m, S_{args}, S_{entry}, S_{exit}, $S_{args'}$, *and* r *are the method name (including the signature), the argument-object states at the method entry, the receiver-object state at the method entry, the receiver-object state at the method exit, the argument-object states at the method exit, and the method return value, respectively.*

Note that when m's return is *void*, r is *void*; when m is a static method, S_{entry} and S_{exit} are empty; when m is a constructor method, S_{entry} is empty.

When a method execution e is a public method of the class under test C and none of e's indirect or direct callers is a method of C, we call that e is invoked on the interface of C. For each such method execution e invoked on the interface of C, if S_{exit} is not empty, S_{exit} can be asserted by using the following ways:

- If another method sequence can be found to produce an object state S' that is expected to be equivalent to S_{exit}, an assertion is created to compare the state representations of S' and S_{exit}.
- If an observer method ob is defined by the class under test, an assertion is created to compare the return of an ob invocation on S_{exit} with the expected value (the ways of comparing return values are described below).

As is discussed in Section 3.1, we do not create an assertion that directly compares the concrete-state representation string of the receiver object with the expected string, because such an assertion is too sensitive to some internal implementation changes that may not affect the interface behavior.

If a method invocation is a state-preserving method, then asserting S_{exit} is not necessary; instead, the existing purity analysis techniques [37, 39] can be exploited to statically check its purity if its purity is to be asserted.

Similarly, we can assert $S_{args'}$ in the same way as asserting S_{exit}. If a method invocation does not modify argument objects' states, then asserting $S_{args'}$ is not necessary.

For each method execution e that is invoked on the interface of the class under test, if r is not *void*, its return value r can be asserted by using the following ways:

- If r is of a primitive type (including primitive-type objects such as String and Integer), an assertion is created to compare r with the expected primitive value.
- If r is of the class-under-test type (which is a non-primitive type), an assertion is created by using the above ways of asserting a receiver-object state S_{exit}.
- If r is of a non-primitive type R but not the class-under-test type,
  — if the observer method toString is defined by R, an assertion is created to compare the return of the toString invocation on r with the expected string value;
  — otherwise, an assertion is created to compare r's concrete-state representation string with the expected representation string value[2].

When a method execution throws an uncaught exception, we can add an assertion for asserting that the exception is to be thrown and it is not necessary to add other assertions for S_{exit}, $S_{args'}$, or r.

4   Automatic Test-Oracle Augmentation

The preceding section presents a framework for asserting the behavior exhibited by a method execution in a test suite. Although developers can manually write assertions based on the framework, it is tedious to write comprehensive assertions as specified by the framework. Some automatic test-generation tools such as JCrasher [11] do not generate any assertions and some tools such as Jtest [31] generate a limited number of assertions. In practice, the assertions in an automatically generated test suite are often insufficient to provide strong oracle checking. This section presents our Orstra tool that automatically adds new assertions into an automatically generated test suite based on the proposed framework. The automatic augmentation consists of two phases: state-capturing phase and assertion-building phase. In the state-capturing phase, Orstra dynamically collects object states exercised by the test suite and the method sequences that are needed to reproduce these object states. In the assertion-building phase, Orstra builds assertions that assert behavior of the collected object states and the returns of observer methods.

---

[2] Note that we do not intend to create another method sequence that produces an object state that is expected to be equivalent to r but directly assert r's concrete-state representation string, because r is not of the class-under-test type and its implementation details often remain relatively stable.

4.1   State-Capturing Phase

In the state-capturing phase, Orstra runs a given test suite T (in the form of a JUnit test class [19]) for the class under test C and dynamically rewrites the bytecodes of each class at class loading time (based on the Byte Code Engineering Library (BCEL) [13]).

Orstra rewrites the T class bytecodes to collect receiver object references, method names, method signatures, arguments, and returns at call sites of those method sequences that lead to C-object states or argument-object states for C's methods. Then Orstra can use the collected method call information to reconstruct the method sequence that leads to a particular C-object state or argument-object state. The reconstructed method sequence can be used in constructing assertions for C-object states in the assertion-building phase.

Orstra also rewrites the C class bytecodes in order to collect a C-object's concrete-state representations at the entry and exit of each method call invoked through the C-object's interface. Orstra uses Java reflection mechanisms [5] to recursively collect all the fields that are reachable from a C-object and uses the linearization algorithm (shown in Figure 4) to produce the object's state-representation string.

Additionally Orstra collects the set OM of observer-method invocations exercised by T. These observer-method invocations are used to inspect and assert behavior of an C-object state in the assertion-building phase.

4.2   Assertion-Building Phase

In the assertion-building phase, Orstra iterates through each C-object state o exercised by the initial test suite T. If o is equivalent to a nonempty set O of some other object states exercised by T, Orstra picks the object state o' in O that is produced by the shortest method sequence m'. Then Orstra creates an assertion for asserting state equivalence by using the techniques described in Section 3.2.

In particular, if an `equals` method is defined in C's interface, Orstra creates the following JUnit assertion method (`assertTrue`) [19] to check state equivalence after invoking the method sequence m' to produce o':

```
C o' = m';
assertTrue(o.equals(o'))
```

Note that m' needs to be replaced with the actual method sequence in the exported assertion code.

If no `equals` method is defined in C's interface, Orstra creates an assertion by using an equals-assertion-builder method (`EqualsBuilder.reflectionEquals`), which is from the Apache Jakarta Commons subproject [4]. This method uses Java reflection mechanisms [5] to determine if two objects are equal by comparing their transitively reachable fields. We can show that if two objects o and o' have the same state representation strings, the return value of `EqualsBuilder.reflectionEquals(o, o')` is `true`. Orstra creates the following assertion to check state equivalence after invoking the method sequence m' to produce o':

```
C o' = m';
EqualsBuilder.reflectionEquals(o, o')
```

If o is not equivalent to any other object state exercised by T, Orstra invokes on o each observer method om in OM collected in the state-capturing phase. Orstra collects the return value r of the om invocation and makes an assertion by using the techniques described in Section 3.2.

In particular, if r is of a primitive type, Orstra creates the following assertion to check the return of om:

```
assertEquals(o.om, r_str);
```

where r_str is the string representation of r's value.

If r is of the C type, Orstra uses the above-described technique for constructing an assertion for a C object if there exist any other object states that are equivalent to r.

If r is of a non-primitive type R but not the C type, Orstra creates the following assertion if a toString method is defined in R's interface:

```
assertEquals((o.om).toString(), t_str);
```

where t_str is the return value of the toString method invocation. If no toString method is defined in R's interface, Orstra creates the following assertion:

```
assertEquals(Runtime.genStateStr(o.om), s_str);
```

where Runtime.genStateStr is Orstra's own runtime helper method for returning the concrete-representation string of an object state, and s_str is the concrete-state representation string of r.

The preceding assertion building techniques are generally exhaustive, enumerating possible mechanisms that developers may use to write assertions manually for these different cases.

In the end of the assertion-building phase, Orstra produces an augmented test suite, which is an exported JUnit test suite, including generated assertions together with the original tests in T.

Note that an automatically generated test suite can include a high percentage of redundant tests [43], which generally do not add value to the test suite. It is not necessary to run these redundant tests or add assertions for these redundant tests. To produce a compact test suite with necessary assertions, the implementation of Orstra actually first collects all nonequivalent method executions and creates assertions only for these method executions; therefore, the tests in the actually exported JUnit test suite may not correspond one-on-one to the tests in the original JUnit test suite.

5   Experiment

This section presents our experiment conducted to address the following research question:

- RQ: Can our Orstra test-oracle-augmentation tool improve the fault-detection capability (which approximates the regression-fault-detection capability) of an automatically generated test suite?

Table 1. Experimental subjects

class	meths	public meths	ncnb loc	Jtest tests	JCrasher tests	faults
IntStack	5	5	44	94	6	83
UBStack	11	11	106	1423	14	305
ShoppingCart	9	8	70	470	31	120
BankAccount	7	7	34	519	135	42
BinSearchTree	13	8	246	277	56	309
BinomialHeap	22	17	535	6205	438	310
DisjSet	10	7	166	779	64	307
FibonacciHeap	24	14	468	3743	150	311
HashMap	27	19	597	5186	47	305
LinkedList	38	32	398	3028	86	298
TreeMap	61	25	949	931	1000	311

5.1 Experimental Subjects

Table 1 lists eleven Java classes that we use in the experiment. These classes were previously used in evaluating our previous work [43] on detecting redundant tests. UBStack is the illustrating example taken from the experimental subjects used by Stotts et al. [40]. IntStack was used by Henkel and Diwan [22] in illustrating their approach of discovering algebraic specifications. ShoppingCart is an example for JUnit [10]. BankAccount is an example distributed with Jtest [31]. The remaining seven classes are data structures previously used to evaluate Korat [8]. The first four columns show the class name, the number of methods, the number of public methods, and the number of non-comment, non-blank lines of code for each subject.

To address the research question, our experiment requires automatically generated test suites for these subjects so that Orstra can augment these test suites. We then use two third-party test-generation tools, Jtest [31] and JCrasher [11], to automatically generate test inputs for these eleven Java classes. Jtest allows users to set the length of calling sequences between one and three; we set it to three, and Jtest first generates all calling sequences of length one, then those of length two, and finally those of length three. JCrasher automatically constructs method sequences to generate non-primitive arguments and uses default data values for primitive arguments. JCrasher generates tests as calling sequences with the length of one. The fifth and sixth columns of Table 1 show the number of tests generated by Jtest and JCrasher.

Although our ultimate research question is to investigate how much better an augmented test suite guards against regression faults, we cannot collect sufficient real regression faults for the experimental subjects. Instead, in the experiment, we use general fault-detection capability of a test suite to approximate regression-fault-detection capability. In particular, we measure the fault-detection capability of a test suite before and after Orstra's augmentation. Then our experiment requires faults for these eleven Java classes. These Java classes were not equipped with such faults; therefore, we used Ferastrau [24], a Java mutation testing tool, to seed faults in these classes. Ferastrau modifies a single line of code in an original version in order to produce a faulty version.

We configured Ferastrau to produce around 300 faulty versions for each class. For three relatively small classes, Ferastrau generates a much smaller number of faulty versions than 300. The last column of Table 1 shows the number of faulty versions generated by Ferastrau.

5.2 Measures

To measure the fault-detection capability of a test suite, we use a metric, *fault-exposure ratio* (FE): the number of faults detected by the test suite divided by the number of total faults. A higher fault-exposure ratio indicates a better fault-detection capability. The JUnit testing framework [19] reports that a test fails when an assertion in the test is violated or an uncaught exception is thrown from the test. An initial test suite generated by JCrasher or Jtest may include some failing tests when being run on the original versions of some Java classes shown in Table 1, because some automatically generated tests may be illegal, violating (undocumented) preconditions of some Java classes. Therefore, we determine that a test suite exposes the seeded fault in a faulty version if the number of failing tests reported on the faulty version is larger than the number of failing tests on the original version. We measure the fault-exposure ratio FE_{orig} of an initial test suite and the fault-exposure ratio FE_{aug} of its augmented test suite. We then measure the *improvement factor*, given by the equation: $\frac{FE_{aug}-FE_{orig}}{FE_{orig}}$. A higher improvement factor indicates a more substantial improvement of the fault-detection capability.

5.3 Experimental Results

Table 2 shows the experimental results. The results for JCrasher-generated test suites are shown in Columns 2-4 and the results for Jtest-generated test suites are shown in

Table 2. Fault-exposure ratios of Jtest-generated, JCrasher-generated, and augmented test suites, and improvement factors of test augmentation

class	JCrasher-gen tests			Jtest-gen tests		
	orig	aug	improve	orig	aug	improve
IntStack	9%	40%	3.36	47%	47%	0.00
UBStack	39%	53%	0.36	60%	60%	0.00
ShoppingCart	0%	48%	∞	56%	56%	0.00
BankAccount	0%	98%	∞	98%	98%	0.00
BinSearchTree	8%	20%	1.58	20%	27%	0.34
BinomialHeap	18%	95%	4.19	85%	95%	0.12
DisjSet	23%	31%	0.36	26%	43%	0.65
FibonacciHeap	9%	96%	9.28	55%	96%	0.74
HashMap	14%	76%	4.30	22%	76%	2.43
LinkedList	7%	35%	3.73	45%	45%	0.01
TreeMap	2%	89%	54.40	12%	89%	6.29
Average	12%	62%	9.06	48%	67%	0.96
Median	9%	53%	3.55	47%	60%	0.12

Columns 5-7. Columns 2 and 5 show the fault-exposure ratios of the original test suites (before test-oracle augmentation). Columns 3 and 6 show the fault-exposure ratios of the test suites augmented by Orstra. Columns 4 and 7 show the improvement factors of the augmented test suites over the original test suites. The last two rows show the average and median data for Columns 2-7.

Without containing any assertion, a JCrasher-generated test exposes a fault if an uncaught exception is thrown during the execution of the test. We observed that JCrasher-generated tests has 0% fault-exposure ratios for two classes (ShoppingCart and BankAccount), because no seeded faults for these two classes cause uncaught exceptions. Jtest equips its generated tests with some assertions: these assertions typically assert those method invocations whose return values are of primitive types. (Section 7 discusses main differences between Orstra and Jtest's assertion creation.) Generally, Jtest-generated test suites have higher fault-exposure ratios than JCrasher-generated test suites. The phenomenon is due to two factors: Jtest generates more test inputs (with longer method sequences) than JCrasher, and Jtest has stronger oracle checking (with additional assertions) than JCrasher.

After Orstra augments the JCrasher-generated test suites with additional assertions, we observed that the augmented test suites achieve substantial improvements of fault-exposure ratios. After augmenting the JCrasher-generated test suite for TreeMap, Orstra achieves an improvement factor of even beyond 50. The augmented Jtest-generated test suites also gain improvements of fault-exposure ratios (although not substantially as JCrasher-generated test suites), except for the first four classes. These four classes are relatively simple and seeded faults for these classes can be exposed with a less comprehensive set of assertions; Jtest-generated assertions are already sufficient to expose those exposable seeded faults.

5.4   Threats to Validity

The threats to external validity primarily include the degree to which the subject programs and their existing test suites are representative of true practice. Our subjects are from various sources and the Korat data structures have nontrivial size for unit testing. Our experiment had used initial test suites automatically generated by two third-party tools, one of which (Jtest) is popular and used in industry. These threats could be further reduced by experiments on more subjects and third-party tools. The main threats to internal validity include instrumentation effects that can bias our results. Faults in our tool implementation, Jtest, or JCrasher might cause such effects. To reduce these threats, we have manually inspected the source code of augmented tests and execution traces for several program subjects. The main threats to construct validity include the uses of those measurements in our experiment to assess our tool. To assess the effectiveness of our test-oracle-augmentation tool, we measure the exposure ratios of faults seeded by a mutation testing tool to approximate the exposure ratios of real regression faults introduced as an effect of changes made in the maintenance process. Although empirical studies showed that faults seeded by mutation testing tools yield trustworthy results [3], these threats can be reduced by conducting more experiments on real regression faults.

6   Discussion

6.1   Analysis Cost

In general, the number of assertions generated for an initial test suite can be approximately characterized as

$$|assertions| = O(|nonEqvStates| \times |observers| + \\ |statesEqvToAnother|)$$

where $|nonEqvStates| \times |observers|$ is the number of nonequivalent object states exercised by the initial test suite being multiplied by the number of observer calls exercised by the initial test suite; recall that Orstra generates an assertion for the return of an observer invoked on a nonequivalent object state. $|statesEqvToAnother|$ is the number of object states (produced by nonequivalent method executions in the initial test suite) that can be found to be equivalent to another object state produced by a different method sequence; recall that Orstra generates an assertion for asserting that an object state produced by a method sequence is equivalent to another object state produced by a different method sequence if any.

Using Orstra in regression testing activities incurs two types of extra cost. The first type is the cost of augmenting the initial test suite. In our experiment, the elapsed real time of running our test augmentation is reasonable, being up to several seconds, determined primarily by the class complexity, the number of tests in the test suite, the number of generated assertions. Note that Orstra needs to be run once when the initial test suite is augmented for the first time, and later to be run when reported assertion violations are determined not to be caused by regression faults. In future work, following the idea of repairing GUI regression tests [27], we plan to improve Orstra so that it can fix those violated assertions in the augmented test suite without re-augmenting the whole initial test suite.

The second type of cost is the cost of running additional assertion checking in the augmented test suite, determined primarily by the number of generated assertions. Although this cost is incurred every time the augmented test suite is run (after the program is changed), running the initial unit-test suite is often fast and running these additional assertion checking slows down the execution of the test suite within several factors. Indeed, if an initial test suite exercises many non-equivalent object states and the program under test has many observer methods, the cost of both augmenting the test suite and running the augmented test suite could be high. Under these situations, developers can configure Orstra to trade weaker oracle checking for efficiency by invoking a subset of observer methods during assertion generation. In addition, regression test prioritization [15] or test selection [20] for Java programs can be used to order or select tests in the Orstra-augmented test suite for execution when the execution time is too long.

6.2   Fault-Free Behavioral Changes

Orstra observes behavior of the program under test when being exercised by a test suite and then automatically adds assertions to the test suite to assert the program behavior is preserved after future program changes. Indeed, sometimes violations of inserted assertions do not necessarily indicate real regression faults. For example, consider that the program under test contains a fault, which is not exposed by the initial test suite. Orstra runs the test suite on the current (faulty) version and create assertions, some of which assert wrong behavior. Later developers find the fault and fix the program. When running the Orstra-augmented test suite on the new program version, assertion violations are reported but there are no regression faults. In addition, although Orstra has been carefully designed to assert as few implementation details in object-state representation as possible, some program changes may violate inserted assertions but still preserve program behavior that developers care about. To help developers to determine whether an assertion violation in an augmented test suite indicates real regression faults, we can use change impact analysis tools such as Chianti [33] to identify a set of affecting changes that were responsible for the assertion violation.

Some types of programs (such as multi-threaded programs or programs whose behaviors are related to time) may exhibit nondeterministic or different behaviors across multiple runs: running the same test suite twice may produce different observer returns or receiver-object states. For example, a getTime method returns the current time and a getRandomNumber method returns a random number. After we add assertions for these types of method returns in a test suite, running the augmented test suite on the current or new program version can report assertion violations, which do not indicate real faults or regression faults. To address this issue, we can run a test suite multiple times on the current program version and remove those assertions that are not consistently satisfied across multiple runs.

6.3 Availability of Observers

Orstra creates assertions for the returns of observers of the class under test. These observer calls may already exist in the initial test suite or may be invoked by Orstra to assert object-state behavior. Although observers are common in a class interface, there are situations where a class interface includes few or no observers. Even when a class interface includes no observer, we can still apply Orstra to augment a test suite generated for the class by asserting that a receiver-object state produced by a method sequence is equivalent to another receiver-object state produced by a different method sequence.

6.4 Iterations of Augmentation

Orstra runs an automatically generated test suite and then adds assertions to the test suite to produce an augmented test suite. When some observer methods are state-modifying methods, running them for preparing assertion checking in the augmented test suite can produce new receiver-object states that are not exercised by the initial test suite. Therefore, if we apply Orstra on the augmented test suite again, the second iteration of augmentation can produce a test suite with more assertion checking and thus often stronger oracle checking. However, if the augmented test suite after the first iteration does not produce any new receiver-object state, the second or later iteration of augmentation adds no new assertions to the test suite.

6.5   Quality of Automatically Generated Unit-Test Suites

The tests generated by JCrasher and Jtest (the two third-party test-generation tools used in the experiment) include a relatively high number of redundant tests [43], which do not contribute to achieving new structural coverage or better fault-detection capability. Rostra and Symstra (two test-generation tools developed in our previous work [43, 44]) can generate a test suite of higher quality (e.g., higher structural coverage) than a test suite generated by JCrasher or Jtest. Augmenting a test suite generated by Rostra or Symstra can achieve a higher improvement factor than augmenting a test suite generated by JCrasher or Jtest. In general, the higher quality a test suite is of, the higher improvement factor Orstra can achieve when augmenting the test suite.

6.6   Augmentation of Other Types of Test Suites

Although Orstra focuses on augmenting a unit-test suite, it is straightforward to extend Orstra to augment an integration-test suite, which intends to test the interactions of multiple classes. When we assert the return values of a method execution in an integration-test suite, we can directly apply Orstra without any modification. When we assert the receiver-object state at a method exit, we can adapt Orstra to invoke on the receiver object the observer methods of the receiver-object class rather than the observer methods of all the classes under test because there are multiple classes under test for an integration-test suite.

So far Orstra has been evaluated on augmenting an automatically generated test suite. Generally Orstra can also be used to augment a manually generated test suite, because the input to Orstra is simply a JUnit test class no matter whether it is generated automatically or manually. Because it is tedious to manually write comprehensive assertions for a test suite, a manually written test suite often does not have comprehensive assertions. We hypothesize that applying Orstra to augment a manually generated test suite can also improve the test suite's fault-detection capability. We plan to validate this hypothesis in our future experiments.

6.7   Incorporation of Oracle Augmentation in Test Generation

Orstra has been developed as an independent component that can augment any test suite in the form of a JUnit test class. Orstra can also be incorporated into the test-generation process of an existing test-generation tool as a two-step process. In the first step, the tool generates test inputs and runs these generated test inputs to collect method returns and object states. This step combines the existing test-generation process and Orstra's state capturing phase. The second step includes Orstra's assertion-building phase. Some existing test-generation tools such as JCrasher do not run generated test inputs during their test-generation process. Then these tools can loosely incorporate Orstra by adopting this two-step process. Some existing tools such as Jtest, Rostra [43], and Symstra [44] actually run generated test inputs during their test-generation process. Then these tools can tightly incorporate Orstra by including Orstra's state-capturing and assertion-building phases when these tools run the generated test inputs during the test-generation process. In fact, Orstra has been incorporated into Rostra and Symstra as an optional component for adding assertions to their generated tests.

7   Related Work

Richardson [34] developed the TAOS (Testing with Analysis and Oracle Support) toolkit, which provides different levels of test oracle support. For example, in lower levels, developers can write down expected outputs for a test input, specify ranges for variable values, or manually inspect actual outputs. The oracle support provided by our Orstra tool is in TAOS' lower levels: generating expected outputs for test inputs. In higher levels, developers can use specification languages (such as Graphical Interval Logic Langauge and Real-Time Interval Logic Language) to specify temporal properties. There exist a number of proposed approaches for providing oracle supports based on different types of specifications [35, 32, 14, 26, 9]. In particular, for testing Java programs, Cheon and Leavens [9] developed a runtime verification tool for Java Modelling Language (JML) [23] and then provided oracle supports for automatically generated tests. This oracle checking approach was also adopted by automatic specification-based test generation tools such as Korat [8]. Different from these specification-based oracle supports, Orstra does not require specifications but Orstra can enhance oracle checking only for exposing regression faults.

When specifications do not exist, automatic test-generation tools such as JCrasher [11] and CnC [12] use program crashes or uncaught exceptions as symptoms of the current program version's faulty behavior. Like Orstra, Jtest [31] can also create some assertions for its generated tests. Orstra differs from Jtest in several ways. Jtest creates assertions for its own generated tests only, whereas Orstra can augment any third-party test suite. Jtest creates assertions for method invocations whose return values are of primitive types, whereas Orstra creates more types of assertions, such as asserting returns with non-primitive types and asserting behavior of receiver-object states. Unlike Orstra, Jtest does not systematically or exhaustively create assertions to assert exercised program behavior. Our experimental results (shown in Section 5.3) indicate that Orstra can still effectively augment a Jtest-generated test suite, which has been equipped with Jtest-generated assertions.

Saff and Ernst [38] as well as Orso and Kennedy [29] developed techniques for capturing and replaying interactions between a selected subsystem (such as a class) and the rest of the application. Their techniques focus on creating fast, focused unit tests from slow system-wide tests, whereas our Orstra tool focuses on adding more assertions to an existing unit-test suite. In addition, Orstra's techniques go beyond capturing and replaying, because Orstra creates new helper-method invocations for assertion checking and these new method invocations might not be exercised in the original test suite.

Memon et al. [25] model a GUI state in terms of the widgets that the GUI contains, their properties, and the values of the properties. Their experimental results show that comparing more-detailed GUI states (e.g., GUI states associated with all or visible windows) from two versions can detect faults more effectively than comparing less-detailed GUI states (e.g., GUI states associated with the active window or widget). Our experiment shows a similar result: checking more-detailed behavior (with augmented test suites) can more effectively expose regression faults.

Both Harrold et al's spectra comparison approach [21] and our previous value-spectra comparison approach [47] also focus on exposing regression faults. Program spectra usually capture internal program execution information and these approaches compare program spectra from two program versions in order to expose regression faults. Our new Orstra tool compares interface-visible behavior of two versions without comparing internal execution information. On one hand, Orstra may not report behavioral differences that are reported by spectra comparison approaches, if these internal behavioral differences cannot cause behavioral differences in the interface. On the other hand, Orstra may report behavioral differences that are not reported by spectra comparison approaches, if these behavioral differences are exhibited only by new Orstra-invoked observers (spectra comparison approaches do not create any new method invocation).

When there are no oracles for a large number of automatically generated tests, developers cannot afford to inspect the results of such a large number of tests. Our previous operational violation approach [45] selects a small subset of automatically generated tests for inspection; these selected tests violates the operational abstractions [17] inferred from the existing test suite. Pacheco and Ernst [30] extended the approach by additionally using heuristics to filter out illegal test inputs. Agitar Agitator [1] automatically generates initial tests, infers operational-abstraction-like observations, lets developers confirm these observations to assertions, and generates more tests to violate these inferred and confirmed observations. The operational violation approach primarily intends to expose faulty behavior exhibited by new generated tests on the current program version, whereas Orstra intends to enhance the oracle checking of an existing test suite so that it has an improved capability of exposing faulty behavior exhibited by the same test suite on future program versions.

Orstra has been implemented based on our two previous approaches. Our previous Rostra approach [43] provides state representation and comparison techniques, but Rostra compares states in order to detect redundant tests out of automatically generated tests. Our previous Obstra approach [46] also invokes observers on object states exercised by an existing test suite. Obstra uses the return values of observers to abstract concrete states and constructs abstract-object-state machines for inspection. Obstra allows developers to inspect the behavior of the current program version, whereas Orstra uses the return values of observers as well as receiver object states to assert that behavior of future program versions is the same as behavior of the current program version. In contrast to Rostra and Obstra, Orstra makes new contributions in developing an approach for enhancing the regression oracle checking of an automatically generated test suite.

8   Conclusion

An automatic test-generation tool can be used to generate a large number of test inputs for the class under test, complementing manually generated tests. However, without specifications these automatically generated test inputs do not have test oracles to guard against faults in the current program version or regression faults in future program versions. We have developed a new automated approach for augmenting an automatically generated test suite in guarding against regression faults. In particular, we have proposed a framework for asserting behavior of a method invocation in an object-oriented unit-test suite. Based on the framework, we have developed an automatic test-oracle-augmentation tool, called Orstra, that systematically adds assertions into an automatically generated test suite in order to improve its capability of guarding against regression faults. We have conducted an experiment to assess the effectiveness of augmenting tests generated by two third-party test-generation tools. The results show that Orstra can effectively increase the fault-detection capability of automatically generated tests by augmenting their regression oracle checking.

Acknowledgments

We would like to thank Alex Orso and Andreas Zeller for discussions that lead to the work described in this paper. We thank Darko Marinov for providing the Ferastrau mutation testing tool and Korat subjects used in the experiment.

References

1. Agitar Agitatior 2.0, Novermber 2004. http://www.agitar.com/.
2. D. M. Andrews. Using executable assertions for testing and fault tolerance. In *Proc. the 9th International Symposium on Fault-Tolerant Computing*, pages 102–105, 1979.
3. J. H. Andrews, L. C. Briand, and Y. Labiche. Is mutation an appropriate tool for testing experiments? In *Proc. 27th International Conference on Software Engineering*, pages 402–411, 2005.
4. The Jakarta Commons Subproject, 2005.
   http://jakarta.apache.org/commons/lang/apidocs/org/apache/commons/lang/builder/EqualsBuilder.html.
5. K. Arnold, J. Gosling, and D. Holmes. *The Java Programming Language*. Addison-Wesley Longman Publishing Co., Inc., 2000.
6. R. S. Arnold. *Software Change Impact Analysis*. IEEE Computer Society Press, 1996.
7. K. Beck. *Extreme programming explained*. Addison-Wesley, 2000.
8. C. Boyapati, S. Khurshid, and D. Marinov. Korat: automated testing based on Java predicates. In *Proc. International Symposium on Software Testing and Analysis*, pages 123–133, 2002.
9. Y. Cheon and G. T. Leavens. A simple and practical approach to unit testing: The JML and JUnit way. In *Proc. 16th European Conference Object-Oriented Programming*, pages 231–255, June 2002.
10. M. Clark. Junit primer. Draft manuscript, October 2000.
11. C. Csallner and Y. Smaragdakis. JCrasher: an automatic robustness tester for Java. *Software: Practice and Experience*, 34:1025–1050, 2004.
12. C. Csallner and Y. Smaragdakis. Check 'n' Crash: Combining static checking and testing. In *Proc. 27th International Conference on Software Engineering*, pages 422–431, May 2005.
13. M. Dahm and J. van Zyl. Byte Code Engineering Library, April 2003. http://jakarta.apache.org/bcel/.
14. L. K. Dillon and Y. S. Ramakrishna. Generating oracles from your favorite temporal logic specifications. In *Proc. 4th ACM SIGSOFT Symposium on Foundations of Software Engineering*, pages 106–117, 1996.
15. H. Do, G. Rothermel, and A. Kinneer. Empirical studies of test case prioritization in a JUnit testing environment. In *Proc. 15th International Symposium on Software Reliability Engineering*, pages 113–124, 2004.
16. R.-K. Doong and P. G. Frankl. The ASTOOT approach to testing object-oriented programs. *ACM Trans. Softw. Eng. Methodol.*, 3(2):101–130, 1994.
17. M. D. Ernst, J. Cockrell, W. G. Griswold, and D. Notkin. Dynamically discovering likely program invariants to support program evolution. *IEEE Trans. Softw. Eng.*, 27(2):99–123, 2001.

18. M. Fowler. *Refactoring: Improving the Design of Existing Code*. Addison Wesley, 1999.
19. E. Gamma and K. Beck. JUnit, 2003. http://www.junit.org.
20. M. J. Harrold, J. A. Jones, T. Li, D. Liang, and A. Gujarathi. Regression test selection for Java software. In *Proc. 16th ACM SIGPLAN Conference on Object-Oriented Programming, Systems, Languages, and Applications*, pages 312–326, 2001.
21. M. J. Harrold, G. Rothermel, K. Sayre, R. Wu, and L. Yi. An empirical investigation of the relationship between spectra differences and regression faults. *Journal of Software Testing, Verification and Reliability*, 10(3):171–194, 2000.
22. J. Henkel and A. Diwan. Discovering algebraic specifications from Java classes. In *Proc. 17th European Conference on Object-Oriented Programming*, pages 431–456, 2003.
23. G. T. Leavens, A. L. Baker, and C. Ruby. Preliminary design of JML: A behavioral interface specification language for Java. Technical Report TR 98-06i, Department of Computer Science, Iowa State University, June 1998.
24. D. Marinov, A. Andoni, D. Daniliuc, S. Khurshid, and M. Rinard. An evaluation of exhaustive testing for data structures. Technical Report MIT-LCS-TR-921, MIT CSAIL, Cambridge, MA, September 2003.
25. A. M. Memon, I. Banerjee, and A. Nagarajan. What test oracle should I use for effective GUI testing? In *Proc. 18th IEEE International Conference on Automated Software Engineering*, pages 164–173, 2003.
26. A. M. Memon, M. E. Pollack, and M. L. Soffa. Automated test oracles for GUIs. In *Proc. 8th ACM SIGSOFT International Symposium on Foundations of Software Engineering*, pages 30–39, 2000.
27. A. M. Memon and M. L. Soffa. Regression testing of GUIs. In *Proc. 9th European Software Engineering Conference held jointly with 11th ACM SIGSOFT International Symposium on Foundations of Software Engineering*, pages 118–127, 2003.
28. B. Meyer. *Eiffel: The Language*. Prentice Hall, 1992.
29. A. Orso and B. Kennedy. Selective capture and replay of program executions. In *Proc. 3rd International ICSE Workshop on Dynamic Analysis*, pages 29–35, St. Louis, MO, May 2005.
30. C. Pacheco and M. D. Ernst. Eclat: Automatic generation and classification of test inputs. In *Proc. 19th European Conference on Object-Oriented Programming*, pages 504–527, Glasgow, Scotland, July 2005.
31. Parasoft Jtest manuals version 4.5. Online manual, April 2003. http://www.parasoft.com/.
32. D. Peters and D. L. Parnas. Generating a test oracle from program documentation. In *Proc. 1994 Internation Symposium on Software Testing and Analysis*, pages 58–65, 1994.
33. X. Ren, F. Shah, F. Tip, B. G. Ryder, and O. Chesley. Chianti: a tool for change impact analysis of Java programs. In *Proc. 19th Annual ACM SIGPLAN Conference on Object-Oriented Programming, Systems, Languages, and Applications*, pages 432–448, 2004.
34. D. J. Richardson. TAOS: Testing with analysis and oracle support. In *Proc. 1994 ACM SIGSOFT International Symposium on Software Testing and Analysis*, pages 138–153, 1994.
35. D. J. Richardson, S. L. Aha, and T. O. O'Malley. Specification-based test oracles for reactive systems. In *Proc. 14th International Conference on Software Engineering*, pages 105–118, 1992.
36. D. S. Rosenblum. Towards a method of programming with assertions. In *Proc. 14th International Conference on Software Engineering*, pages 92–104, 1992.
37. A. Rountev. Precise identification of side-effect-free methods in Java. In *Proc. 20th IEEE International Conference on Software Maintenance*, pages 82–91, Sept. 2004.
38. D. Saff, S. Artzi, J. H. Perkins, and M. D. Ernst. Automatic test factoring for Java. In *Proc. 21st IEEE International Conference on Automated Software Engineering*, pages 114–123, Long Beach, CA, November 2005.

39. A. Salcianu and M. Rinard. Purity and side effect analysis for Java programs. In *Proc. 6th International Conference on Verification, Model Checking and Abstract Interpretation*, pages 199–215, Paris, France, January 2005.

40. D. Stotts, M. Lindsey, and A. Antley. An informal formal method for systematic JUnit test case generation. In *Proc. 2002 XP/Agile Universe*, pages 131–143, 2002.

41. Sun Microsystems. Java 2 Platform, Standard Edition, v 1.4.2, API Specification. Online documentation, Nov. 2003. http://java.sun.com/j2se/1.4.2/docs/api/.

42. W. Visser, C. S. Pasareanu, and S. Khurshid. Test input generation with Java PathFinder. In *Proc. 2004 ACM SIGSOFT International Symposium on Software Testing and Analysis*, pages 97–107, 2004.

43. T. Xie, D. Marinov, and D. Notkin. Rostra: A framework for detecting redundant object-oriented unit tests. In *Proc. 19th IEEE International Conference on Automated Software Engineering*, pages 196–205, Sept. 2004.

44. T. Xie, D. Marinov, W. Schulte, and D. Notkin. Symstra: A framework for generating object-oriented unit tests using symbolic execution. In *Proc. 11th International Conference on Tools and Algorithms for the Construction and Analysis of Systems*, pages 365–381, April 2005.

45. T. Xie and D. Notkin. Tool-assisted unit test selection based on operational violations. In *Proc. 18th IEEE International Conference on Automated Software Engineering*, pages 40–48, 2003.

46. T. Xie and D. Notkin. Automatic extraction of object-oriented observer abstractions from unit-test executions. In *Proc. 6th International Conference on Formal Engineering Methods*, pages 290–305, Nov. 2004.

47. T. Xie and D. Notkin. Checking inside the black box: Regression testing by comparing value spectra. *IEEE Transactions on Software Engineering*, 31(10):869–883, October 2005.

Automated Detection of Refactorings in Evolving Components

Danny Dig, Can Comertoglu, Darko Marinov, and Ralph Johnson

Department of Computer Science
University of Illinois at Urbana-Champaign
201 N. Goodwin Ave.
Urbana, IL 61801, USA
{dig, comertog, marinov, johnson}@cs.uiuc.edu

Abstract. One of the costs of reusing software components is updating applications to use the new version of the components. Updating an application can be error-prone, tedious, and disruptive of the development process. Our previous study showed that more than 80% of the disruptive changes in five different components were caused by refactorings. If the refactorings that happened between two versions of a component could be automatically detected, a refactoring tool could replay them on applications. We present an algorithm that detects refactorings performed during component evolution. Our algorithm uses a combination of a fast syntactic analysis to detect refactoring candidates and a more expensive semantic analysis to refine the results. The experiments on components ranging from 17 KLOC to 352 KLOC show that our algorithm detects refactorings in real-world components with accuracy over 85%.

1 Introduction

Part of maintaining a software system is updating it to use the latest version of its components. Developers like to reuse software components to quickly build a system, but reuse makes the system dependent on the components. Ideally, the interface of a component never changes. In practice, however, new versions of components often change their interfaces and require the developers to change the system to use the new versions of the components.

An important kind of change in object-oriented software is a refactoring. Refactorings [FBB+99] are program transformations that change the structure of a program but not its behavior. Example refactorings include changing the names of classes and methods, moving methods and fields from one class to another, and splitting methods or classes. An automated tool, called *refactoring engine*, can apply the refactorings to change the source code of a component. However, a refactoring engine can change only the source code that it has access to. Component developers often do not have access to the source code of all the applications that reuse the components. Therefore, refactorings that component developers perform preserve the behavior of the component but not of the applications that use the component; in other words, although the change is a refactoring from the component developers' point of view, it is not a refactoring from the application developers' point of view.

D. Thomas (Ed.): ECOOP 2006, LNCS 4067, pp. 404–428, 2006.
© Springer-Verlag Berlin Heidelberg 2006

One approach to automate the update of applications when their components change is to extend the refactoring engine to record refactorings on the component and then to replay them on the applications. Record-and-replay of refactorings was demonstrated in CatchUp [HD05] and JBuilder2005 [Bor] and recently incorporated in Eclipse 3.2 Milestone 4 [Ecl]. As component developers refactor their code, the refactoring engine creates a log of refactorings. The developers ship this log along with the new version of the component. An application developer can then upgrade the application to the new version by using the refactoring engine to play back the log of refactorings.

While replay of refactorings shows great promise, it relies on the existence of refactoring logs. However, logs are not available for the legacy versions of components. Also, logs will not be available for all future versions; some developers will not use refactoring engines with recording, and some developers will perform refactorings manually. To exploit the full potential of replay, it is therefore important to be able to automatically detect the refactorings used to create a new version of a component.

We propose a novel algorithm that detects a likely sequence of refactorings between two versions of a component. Previous algorithms [APM04, DDN00, GW05, GZ05, RD03] assumed closed-world development, where codebases are used only in-house and changes happen abruptly (e.g., one entity dies in a version and a new refactored entity starts from the next version). However, in the open-world development, components are reused outside the organization, therefore changes do not happen overnight but follow a long deprecate-replace-remove lifecycle. Obsolete entities will coexist with their newer counterparts until they are no longer supported. Also, multiple refactorings can happen to the same entity or related entities. This lifecycle makes it hard to accurately detect refactorings. Our algorithm works fine for both closed- and open-world paradigms.

We aim for our algorithm to help the developer infer a log of refactorings for replay. To be practical, the algorithm needs to detect refactorings with a high accuracy. On one hand, if the algorithm adds to a log a change that is not actually a refactoring (false positive), the developer needs to remove it from the log or the replay could potentially introduce bugs. On the other hand, if the algorithm does not add to a log an actual refactoring (false negative), the developer needs to manually find it and add it to the log. Previous algorithms [APM04, DDN00, GW05, GZ05, RD03] aimed at detection of refactorings for the purpose of program comprehension. Therefore, they can tolerate lower accuracy as long as they focus the developer's attention on the relevant parts of the software.

Our algorithm combines a fast syntactic analysis to detect refactoring candidates and a more expensive semantic analysis to refine the results. Our syntactic analysis is based on Shingles encoding [Bro97], a technique from Information Retrieval. Shingles are a fast technique to find similar fragments in text files; our algorithm applies shingles to source files. Most refactorings involve repartitioning of the source files, which results in similar fragments of source text between different versions of a component. Our semantic analysis is based on the *reference graphs* that represent references among source-level entities, e.g., calls among methods[1]. This analysis considers the semantic relationship between candidate entities to determine whether they represent a refactoring.

---

[1] These *references* do not refer to pointers between objects but to references among the source-code entities in each version of the component.

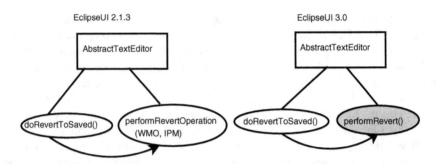

Fig. 1. An excerpt from Eclipse versions 2.1 and 3.0 showing two refactorings, rename method and changed method signature, applied to the same method. The squares represent classes, the ellipses methods, and arrows are method calls. The method that changes signature also changes name from performRevertOperation to performRevert.

We have implemented our algorithm as an Eclipse plugin, called RefactoringCrawler, that detects refactorings in Java components. The ideas in the algorithm can be applied to other programming languages. RefactoringCrawler currently detects seven types of refactorings, focusing on rename and move refactorings that we found to be the most commonly applied in several components [DJ05]. We have evaluated RefactoringCrawler on three components ranging in size from 17 KLOC to 352 KLOC. The results show that RefactoringCrawler scales to real-world components, and its accuracy in detecting refactorings is over 85%.

RefactoringCrawler and our evaluation results are available on the website [Ref].

2   Example

We next illustrate some refactorings that our algorithm detects between two versions of a component. We use an example from the EclipseUI component of the Eclipse development platform. We consider two versions of EclipseUI, from Eclipse versions 2.1.3 and 3.0. Each of these versions of EclipseUI has over 1,000 classes and 10,000 methods in the public API (of non-internal packages). Our algorithm first uses a fast syntactic analysis to find similar methods, classes, and packages between the two versions of the component. (Section 4 presents the details of our syntactic analysis.) For EclipseUI, our algorithm finds 231,453 pairs of methods with similar bodies, 487 pairs of similar classes, and 22 pairs of similar packages. (Section 8 presents more details of this case study.) These similar entities are candidates for refactorings. Our example focuses on two pairs of similar methods.

Figure 1 shows two pairs of similar methods from the two versions of the class `AbtstractTextEditor` from Eclipse 2.1 and 3.0. The syntactic analysis finds that the method `doRevertToSaved` in version 2.1 is similar to (although not identical with) the method `doRevertToSaved` in version 3.0, and the method `performRevertOperation` is similar to the method `performRevert`. Our algorithm then uses a semantic analysis to detect the refactorings that were performed on these pairs. As the result, our algorithm detects that the method `performRevertOperation` was renamed to `performOperation`, and its signature changed from having two arguments in the version 2.1 to no argument in the version 3.0. Our previous manual inspection [DJ05] of the Eclipse documentation and code indeed found that these two refactorings, renamed method and changed method signature, were performed.

Our semantic analysis applies a series of detection strategies that find whether candidate pairs of similar entities are indeed results of refactorings. The key information that the strategies consider is the *references* between the entities in each version. For methods, the references correspond to call edges. For our example methods, both `performRevertOperation` and `performRevert` have only one call in the entire EclipseUI: they are both called exactly once from `doRevertToSaved`. Our analysis represents this information with an edge, labeled with the number of calls, between these methods. We present how the two strategies for renamed methods and changed method signature proceed in our running example.

The strategy that detects renamed methods discards the pair of `doRevertToSaved` methods since they have the same name. This strategy, however, investigates further whether `performRevert` is a renaming of `performRevertOperation`. The strategy (lazily) finds the calls to these two methods and realizes that they are called (the same number of times) from the corresponding `doRevertToSaved` methods in both versions. Therefore, methods `performRevertOperation` and `performRevert` (i) are both in class `AbtstractTextEditor`, (ii) have similar method bodies, (iii) have similar incoming call edges, but (iv) differ in the name. The strategy thus concludes that `performRevert` is a renaming of `performRevertOperation`.

The strategy that detects changed method signatures also considers all pairs of similar methods. This strategy discards the pair of `doRevertToSaved` methods since they have the same signature. This strategy, however, investigates further `performRevertOperation` and `performRevert` methods, because they represent the same method but renamed. It is important to point out here that strategies *share detected refactorings*: although `performRevertOperation` and `performRevert` seemingly have different names, the RenameMethod strategy has already found that these two methods correspond. The ChangedMethodSignature strategy then finds that `performRevertOperation` and `performOperation` (i) have similar method bodies, (ii) "same" name, (iii) similar call edges, but (iv) different signatures. The strategy thus correctly concludes that a changed method signature refactoring was applied to `performOperation`.

3   Algorithm Overview

This section presents a high-level overview of our algorithm for detection of refactorings. Figure 2 shows the pseudo-code of the algorithm. The input are two versions of a component, and the output is a log of refactorings applied on `c1` to produce `c2`. The algorithm consists of two analyses: a fast *syntactic analysis* that finds candidates for refactorings and a precise *semantic analysis* that finds the actual refactorings.

Our syntactic analysis starts by parsing the source files of the two versions of the component into the *lightweight* ASTs, where the parsing stops at the declaration of the methods and fields in classes. For each component, the parsing produces a graph (more

```
Refactorings detectRefactorings(Component c1, c2) {
  // syntactic analysis
  Graph g1 = parseLightweight(c1);
  Graph g2 = parseLightweight(c2);
  Shingles s1 = annotateGraphNodesWithShingles(g1);
  Shingles s2 = annotateGraphNodesWithShingles(g2);
  Pairs pairs = findSimilarEntities(s1, s2);
  // semantic analysis
  Refactorings rlog = emptyRefactorings();
  foreach (DetectionStrategy strategy) {
    do {
      Refactorings rlog' = rlog.copy();
      foreach (Pair<e1, e2> from pairs relevant to strategy)
        if (strategy.isLikelyRefactoring(e1, e2, rlog))
          rlog.add(<e1, e2>, strategy);
    } while (!rlog'.equals(rlog)); // fixed point
  }
  return rlog;
}
```

Fig. 2. Pseudo-code of the conceptual algorithm for detection of refactorings

precisely, a tree to which analysis later adds more edges). Each node of the graphs represents a source-level entity, namely a package, a class, a method, or a field. Each node stores a fully qualified name for the entity, and each method node also stores the fully qualified names of method arguments to distinguish overloaded methods. Nodes are arranged hierarchically in the tree, based on their fully qualified names: the node $p.n$ is a child of the node p.

The heart of our syntactic analysis is the use of the *Shingles encoding* to find similar pairs of entities (methods, classes, and packages) in the two versions of the component. Shingles are "fingerprints" for strings with the following property: if a string changes slightly, then its shingles also change slightly. Therefore, shingles enable detection of strings with similar fragments much more robustly than the traditional string matching techniques that are not immune to small perturbations like renamings or small edits. Section 4 presents the computation of shingles in detail.

The result of our syntactic analysis is a set of pairs of entities that have similar shingles encodings in the two versions of the component. Each pair consists of an entity from the first version and an entity of the same kind from the second version; there are separate pairs for methods, classes, and packages. These pairs of similar entities are candidates for refactorings.

Our semantic analysis detects from the candidate pairs those where the second entity is a likely refactoring of the first entity. The analysis applies seven strategies for detecting specific refactorings, such as RenameMethod or ChangeMethodSignature discussed in section 2. Section 5 presents the strategies in detail. The analysis applies each strategy until it finds all possible refactorings of its type. Each strategy considers all pairs of entities $\langle e_1, e_2 \rangle$ of the appropriate type, e.g., RenameMethod considers only pairs of methods. For each pair, the strategy computes how likely is that e_1 was refactored into e_2; if the likelihood is above a user-specified threshold, the strategy adds the pair to the log of refactorings that the subsequent strategies can use during further analysis. Note that each strategy takes into account already detected refactorings; sharing detected refactorings among strategies is a key for accurate detection of refactorings when multiple types of refactorings applied to the same entity (e.g., a method was renamed and has a different signature) or related entities (e.g., a method was renamed and also its class was renamed). Our analysis cannot recover the list of refactorings in the order they were performed, but it finds *one path* that leads to the same result.

4 Syntactic Analysis

To identify possible candidates for refactorings, our algorithm first determines pairs of *similar* methods, classes, and packages. Our algorithm uses the Shingles encoding [Bro97] to compute a fingerprint for each method and determines two methods to be similar if and only if they have similar fingerprints. Unlike the traditional hashing functions that map even the smallest change in the input to a completely different hash value, the Shingles algorithm maps small changes in the input to small changes in the fingerprint encoding.

4.1 Computing Shingles for Methods

The Shingles algorithm takes as input a sequence of tokens and computes a multiset of integers called shingles. The tokens represent the method body or the Javadoc comments for the method (as interface methods and abstract methods have no body). The tokens do not include method name and signature because refactorings affect these parts. The algorithm takes two parameters, the length of the sliding window, W, and the maximum size of the resulting multiset, S. Given a sequence of tokens, the algorithm uses the sliding window to find all subsequences of length W, computes the shingle for each subsequence, and selects the S minimum shingles for the resulting multiset. Instead of selecting S shingles which have minimum values, the algorithm could use any other heuristic that deterministically selects S values from a larger set. Our implementation uses the Rabin's hash function [Rab81] to compute the shingles.

If the method is short and has fewer than S shingles, then the multiset contains all shingles. This is the case with many setters and getters and some constructors and other initializers. The parameter S acts as the upper bound for the space needed to represent shingles: a larger value of S makes calculations more expensive, and a smaller value makes it harder to distinguish strings. Our implementation sets the number of shingles proportional to the length of the method body/comments.

Figure 3 shows the result of calculating the shingles for two method bodies with $W = 2$ and $S = 10$. The differences in the bodies and the shingle values are in grey boxes. Notice that the small changes in the tokens produce only small changes in the shingle representation, enabling the algorithm to find the similarities between methods.

4.2 Computing Shingles for Classes and Packages

The shingles for methods are used to compute shingles for classes and packages. The shingles for a class are the minimum S_{class} values of the union of the shingles of

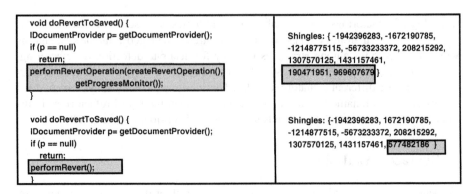

Fig. 3. Shingles encoding for two versions of `AbstractTextEditor.doRevertToSaved` between Eclipse 2.1 and 3.0. Notice that small changes (gray boxes) in the input strings produce small changes in the Shingles encoding.

the methods in that class. Analogously, the shingles for a package are the minimum $S_{package}$ values of the union of the shingles of the classes in that package. This way, the algorithm efficiently computes shingles values and avoids recalculations.

4.3 Finding Candidates

Our analysis uses the shingles to find candidates for refactorings. Each candidate is a pair of similar entities from the two versions of the component. This analysis is an effective way of eliminating a large number of pairs of entities, so that the expensive operation of computing the reference graphs is only done for a small subset of all possible pairs. More specifically, let M_1 and M_2 be the multisets of shingles for two methods, classes, or packages. Our analysis computes similarity between these two multisets. Let $|M_1 \cap M_2|$ be the cardinality of the intersection of M_1 and M_2. To compare similarity for different pairs, the algorithm *normalizes* the similarity to be between 0 and 1. More precisely, the algorithm computes the similarity as the *average* of similarity from M_1 to M_2 and similarity from M_2 to M_1 to address the cases when M_1 is similar to M_2 but M_2 is not similar to M_1 :

$$\frac{\frac{|M_1 \cap M_2|}{|M_1|} + \frac{|M_2 \cap M_1|}{|M_2|}}{2}.$$

If this similarity value is above the user-specified threshold, the pair is deemed similar and passed to the semantic analysis.

5   Semantic Analysis

We present the semantic analysis that our algorithm uses to detect refactorings. Recall from Figure 2 that the algorithm applies each detection strategy until it reaches a fixed point and that all strategies share the same log of detected refactorings, `rlog`. This sharing is crucial for successful detection of refactorings when multiple types of refactorings happened to the same entity (e.g., a method was renamed and has a different signature) or related entities (e.g., a method was renamed and also its class was renamed). We first describe how the strategies use the shared log of refactorings. We then describe *references* that several strategies use to compute the likelihood of refactoring. We also define the multiplicity of references and the similarity that our algorithm computes between references. We finally presents details of each strategy. Due to the sharing of the log, our algorithm imposes an order on the types of refactorings it detects first. Specifically, the algorithm applies the strategies in the following order:

1. RenamePackage (RP)
2. RenameClass (RC)
3. RenameMethod (RM)
4. PullUpMethod (PUM)
5. PushDownMethod (PDM)
6. MoveMethod (MM)
7. ChangeMethodSignature (CMS)

5.1   Shared Log

The strategies compare whether an entity in one graph corresponds to an entity in another graph *with respect to the already detected refactorings*, in particular with renaming refactorings. Suppose that the refactorings log `rlog` already contains several renamings that map fully qualified names from version `c1` to version `c2`. These renamings map package names to package names, class names to class names, or method names to method names. We define a renaming function ρ that maps a fully qualified name `fqn` from `c1` with respect to the renamings in `rlog`:

$$\rho(\texttt{fqn}, \texttt{rlog}) = \text{if } (\text{defined } \texttt{rlog}(\texttt{fqn})) \text{ then } \texttt{rlog}(\texttt{fqn})$$
$$\text{else } \rho(\text{pre}(\texttt{fqn}), \texttt{rlog}) + \texttt{"."} + \text{suf}(\texttt{fqn})$$
$$\rho(\texttt{""}, \texttt{rlog}) = \texttt{""},$$

where suf and pre are functions that take a fully qualified name and return its simple name (*suffix*) and the entire name but the simple name (*prefix*), respectively. The function ρ recursively checks whether a renaming of some part of the fully qualified name is already in `rlog`.

5.2   References

The strategies compute the likelihood of refactoring based on *references* among the source-code entities in each of the two versions of the component. In each graph that represents a version of the component, our algorithm (lazily) adds an edge from a node n' to a node n if the source entity represented by n' has a reference to a source entity represented by n. (The graph also contains the edges from the parse tree.) We define references for each kind of nodes/entities in the following way:

- There is a reference from a node/method m' to a node/method m iff m' calls m. Effectively, references between methods correspond to the edges in call graphs.

- There is a reference from a node n' to a node/class C iff:
  - n' is a method that has (i) an argument or return of type C, or (ii) an instantiation of class C, or (iii) a local variable of class C.
  - n' is a class that (i) has a field whose type is C or (ii) is a subclass of C.
- There is a reference from a node n' to a node/package p iff n' is a class that imports some class from the package p.

There can be several references from one entity to another. For example, one method can have several calls to another method or one class can have several fields whose type is another class. Our algorithm assigns to each edge a *multiplicity* that is the number of references. For example, if a method m' has two calls to a method m, then the edge from the node n' that represents m' to the node n that represents m has multiplicity two. Conceptually, we consider that there is an edge between any two nodes, potentially with multiplicity zero. We write $\mu(n', n)$ for the multiplicity from the node n' to the node n.

5.3 Similarity of References

Our algorithm uses a metric to determine the similarity of references to entities in the two versions of the component, with respect to a given log of refactorings. We write $n \in g$ for a node n that belongs to a graph g. Consider two nodes $n_1 \in g1$ and $n_2 \in g2$. We define the similarity of their incoming edges as follows. We first define the *directed similarity* between two nodes with respect to the refactorings. We then take the overall similarity between n_1 and n_2 as the average of directed similarities between n_1 and n_2 and between n_2 and n_1. The average of directed similarities helps to compute a fair grade when n_1 is similar to n_2 but n_2 is not similar to n_1.

We define the directed similarity between two nodes n and n' as the overlap of multiplicities of their *corresponding* incoming edges. More precisely, for each incoming edge from a node n_i to n, the directed similarity finds a node $n'_i = \rho(n_i, \texttt{rlog})$ that corresponds to n_i (with respect to refactorings) and then computes the overlap of multiplicities between the edges from n_i to n and from n'_i to n'. The number of overlapping incoming edges is divided by the total number of incoming edges. The formula for directed similarity is:

$$\delta(n, n', \texttt{rlog}) = \frac{\sum_{n_i} \min(\mu(n_i, n), \mu(\rho(n_i, \texttt{rlog}), n'))}{\sum_{n_i} \mu(n_i, n)}$$

The overall similarity is the average of directed similarities:

$$\sigma(n_1, n_2, \texttt{rlog}) = \frac{\delta(n_1, n_2, \texttt{rlog}) + \delta(n_2, n_1, \texttt{rlog}^{-1})}{2}$$

When computing the directed similarity between n_2 and n_1, the algorithm needs to take into account the inverse of renaming log, denoted by $\texttt{rlog}^{-1}$. Namely, starting from a node n_i in g_2, the analysis searches for a node $n_{i'}$ in g_1 such that the renaming of $n_{i'}$ (with respect to $\texttt{rlog}$) is n_i, or equivalently, $\rho(n_i, \texttt{rlog}^{-1}) = n_{i'}$.

We describe informally an equivalent definition of directed similarity based on the view of graphs with multiplicities as multigraphs that can have several edges between two same nodes. The set of edges between two nodes can be viewed as a multiset, and

Refactoring	Syntactic Checks	Semantic Checks
$RP(p_1, p_2)$	$p_2 \notin g1$ $\rho(\text{pre}(p_1), \texttt{rlog}) = \text{pre}(p_2)$ $\text{suf}(p_1) \neq \text{suf}(p_2)$	$\sigma(p_1, p_2, \texttt{rlog}) \geq T$
$RC(C_1, C_2)$	$C_2 \notin g1$ $\rho(\text{pre}(C_1), \texttt{rlog}) = \text{pre}(C_2)$ $\text{suf}(C_1) \neq \text{suf}(C_2)$	$\sigma(C_1, C_2, \texttt{rlog}) \geq T$
$RM(m_1, m_2)$	$m_2 \notin g1$ $\rho(\text{pre}(m_1), \texttt{rlog}) = \text{pre}(m_2)$ $\text{suf}(m_1) \neq \text{suf}(m_2)$	$\sigma(m_1, m_2, \texttt{rlog}) \geq T$
$PUM(m_1, m_2)$	$m_2 \notin g1$ $\rho(\text{pre}(m_1), \texttt{rlog}) \neq \text{pre}(m_2)$ $\text{suf}(m_1) = \text{suf}(m_2)$	$\sigma(m_1, m_2, \texttt{rlog}) \geq T$ $\rho(\text{pre}(m_1), \texttt{rlog})$ descendant-of $\text{pre}(m_2)$
$PDM(m_1, m_2)$	$m_2 \notin g1$ $\rho(\text{pre}(m_1), \texttt{rlog}) \neq \text{pre}(m_2)$ $\text{suf}(m_1) = \text{suf}(m_2)$	$\sigma(m_1, m_2, \texttt{rlog}) \geq T$ $\rho(\text{pre}(m_1), \texttt{rlog})$ ancestor-of $\text{pre}(m_2)$
$MM(m_1, m_2)$	$m_2 \notin g1$ $\rho(\text{pre}(m_1), \texttt{rlog}) \neq \text{pre}(m_2)$ $\text{suf}(m_1) = \text{suf}(m_2)$	$\sigma(m_1, m_2, \texttt{rlog}) \geq T$ $\neg\rho(\text{pre}(m_1), \texttt{rlog})$ anc.-or-desc. $\text{pre}(m_2)$ references-properly-updated
$CMS(m_1, m_2)$	$\rho(\text{fqn}(m_1), \texttt{rlog}) = \text{fqn}(m_2)$ $\text{signature}(m_1) \neq \text{signature}(m_2)$	$\sigma(m_1, m_2, \texttt{rlog}) \geq T$

Fig. 4. Syntactic and semantic checks performed by different detection strategies for refactorings: RP=RenamePackage, RC=RenameClass, RM=RenameMethod, PUM=PullUpMethod, PDM=PushDownMethod, MM=MoveMethod, and CMS=ChangeMethodSignature

finding the overlap corresponds to finding the intersection of one multiset of edges with the other multiset of edges (for nodes corresponding with respect to the refactorings). In this view, similarity between edges in the graph is conceptually analogous to the similarity of multisets of shingles.

5.4 Detection Strategies

We next precisely describe all detection strategies for refactorings. Each strategy checks appropriate pairs of entities and has access to the graphs g1 and g2 and the rlog of refactorings. (See the call to isLikelyRefactoring in Figure 2.) Figure 4 shows the seven strategies currently implemented in RefactoringCrawler. For each pair, the strategy first performs a fast syntactic check that determines whether the pair is relevant for the refactoring and then performs a semantic check that determines the likelihood of the refactoring. The semantic checks compare the similarity of references to the user-specified threshold value T.

RenamePackage (RP), RenameClass (RC), and RenameMethod (RM) strategies are similar. The first syntactic check requires the entity from g2 not to be in g1; otherwise, the entity is not new. The second check requires the two entities to have the same name prefix, modulo the renamings in rlog; otherwise, the refactoring is a potential move but not a rename. The third check requires the two entities to have different simple names.

PullUpMethod (PUM) and PushDownMethod (PDM) are the opposite of each other. Figure 5 illustrates a PUM that pulls up the declaration of a method from a subclass

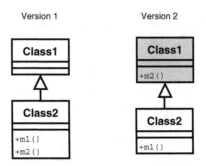

Fig. 5. PullUpMethod: method m2 is pulled up from the subclass C2 into the superclass C1

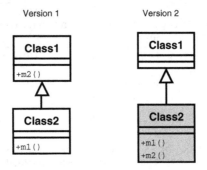

Fig. 6. PushDown: method m2 is pushed down from the superclass C1 into the subclass C2

into the superclass such that the method can be reused by other subclasses. Figure 6 illustrates a PDM that pushes down the declaration of a method from a superclass into a subclass that uses the method because the method is no longer reused by other subclasses. In general, the PUM and PDM can be between several classes related by inheritance, not just between the immediate subclass and superclass; therefore, PUM and PDM check that the original class is a *descendant* and an *ancestor*, respectively, of the target class. These inheritance checks are done on the graph g2.

MoveMethod (MM) has the second syntactic check that requires the parent classes of the two methods to be different. Without this check, MM would incorrectly classify all methods of a renamed class as moved methods. The second semantic check requires that the declaration classes of the methods not be related by inheritance; otherwise, the refactorings would be incorrectly classified as MM as opposed to a PUM/PDM. The third check requires that all references to the target class be removed in the second version and that all calls to methods from the initial class be replaced with sending a message to an instance of the initial class. We illustrate this check on the sample code in Figure 7. In the first version, method C1.m1 calls a method C1.xyz of the same class C1 and also calls a method C2.m2. After m1 is moved to the class C2, m1 can call any method in C2 directly (e.g., m2), but any calls to methods residing in C1 need to be executed through an instance of C1.

```
Version 1                              Version 2

Class C1 {                             Class C1 {
    public void m1(C2 c2) {                public void xyz() { ..... }
                                       }
        .......
        xyz();                         Class C2 {
        c2.m2();                           public void m1(C1 c1) {
        .........
                                           ..........
    }                                      c1.xyz();
                                           m2();
    public void xyz() { ..... }            ..............
}                                          }

Class C2 {
    public void m2() { .....}              public void m2() {....}
}                                      }
```

Fig. 7. Method m1 moves from class C1 in one version to class C2 in the next version. The method body changes to reflect that the local methods (e.g., m2) are called directly, while methods from the previous class (e.g., xyz) are called indirectly through an instance of C1.

ChangeMethodSignature (CMS) looks for methods that have the same fully qualified name (modulo renamings) but different signatures. The signature of the method can change by gaining/loosing arguments, by changing the type of the arguments, by changing the order of the arguments, or by changing the return type.

6   Discussion of the Algorithm

The example from Section 2 illustrates some of the challenges in automatic detection of refactorings that happened in reusable components. We next explicitly discuss three main challenges and present how our algorithm addresses them.

The first challenge is the size of the code to be analyzed. An expensive semantic analysis—for example finding similar subgraphs in call graphs (more generally, in the entire reference graphs)—might detect refactorings but does not scale up to the size of real-world components with tens of thousands of entities, including methods, classes, and packages. A cheap syntactic analysis, in contrast, might find many similar entities but is fallible to renamings. Also, an analysis that would not take into account the semantics of entity relationships would produce a large number of false positives. Our algorithm uses a hybrid of syntactic and semantic analyses: a fast syntactic analysis creates pairs of candidate entities that are suspected of refactoring, and a more precise semantic analysis on these candidates detects whether they are indeed refactorings.

The second challenge is the noise introduced by preserving backward compatibility in the components. Consider for example the following change in the Struts framework from version 1.1 to version 1.2.4: the method perform in the class Controller was renamed to execute, but perform still exists in the later version. However, perform is deprecated, all the internal references to it were replaced with references to execute, and the users are warned to use execute instead of perform. Since it is not feasible to perform an expensive analysis on all possible pairs of entities across two versions of

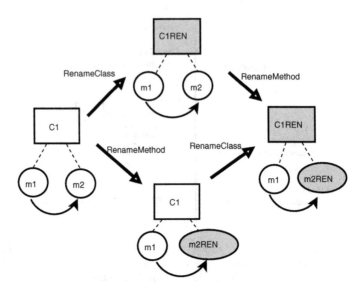

Fig. 8. Refactorings affect related entities class C1 and method m2. The class rename happens before the method rename in the upper path, the reverse happens in the bottom path. Both paths end up with the same result.

a component, any detection algorithm has to consider only a subset of pairs. Some previous algorithms [APM04, DDN00, GZ05] consider only the outdated entities that die in one version and then search for refactored counterparts that are created in the next version. The assumption that entities change in this fashion indeed holds in the closed-world development (where the only users of components are the component developers) but does not hold in the open-world development where outdated entities coexist with their refactored counterparts. For example, the previous algorithms cannot detect that perform was renamed to execute since perform still exists in the subsequent version. Our algorithm detects that perform in the first version and execute in the second version have the same shingles and their call sites are the same, and therefore our algorithm correctly classifies the change as a method rename.

The third challenge is multiple refactorings happening to the same entity or related entities. The example from Section 2, for instance, shows two refactorings, rename method and change method signature, applied to the same method. An example of refactorings happening to related entities is renaming a method along with renaming the method's class. Figure 8 illustrates this scenario. Across the two versions of a component, class C1 was renamed to C1REN, and one of its methods, m2, was renamed to m2REN. During component evolution, regardless of whether the class or method rename was executed first, the end result is the same. In Figure 8, the upper part shows the case when the class rename was executed first, and the lower part shows the case when the method rename was executed first.

Our algorithm addresses the third challenge by imposing an order on the detection strategies and sharing the information about detected refactorings among the detection strategies. Any algorithm that detects refactorings conceptually reconstructs the log of refactorings and thus not only the start and the end state of a component but also the intermediate states. Our algorithm detects the two refactorings in Figure 8 by following the upper path. When detecting a class rename, the algorithm takes into account only the shingles for class methods and not the method names. Therefore, our algorithm detects class C1REN as a rename of class C1 although one of its methods was renamed. This information is fed back into the loop; it conceptually reconstructs the state 2a, and the analysis continues. The subsequent analysis for the rename method checks whether the new-name method belongs to the same class as the old-name method; since the previous detection discovered that C1 is equivalent modulo rename with C1REN, m2REN can be detected as a rename of m2.

The order in which an algorithm detects the two refactorings matters. We described how our algorithm detects a class rename followed by a method rename. Consider, in contrast, what would happen to an algorithm that attempts to follow the bottom path. When analyzing what happened between the methods m2 and m2REN, the algorithm would need the intermediate state 2b (where m2REN belongs to C1) to detect that m2 was renamed to m2REN. However, that state is not given, and in the end state m2REN belongs to C1REN, so the algorithm would mistakenly conclude that m2REN was moved to another class (C1REN). The subsequent analysis of what happened between classes C1 and C1REN would presumably find that they are a rename and would then need to backtrack to correct the previously misqualified move method as a rename method. For this reason, our algorithm imposes an order on the detection strategies and runs detection of renamings top-down, from packages to classes to methods.

To achieve a high level of accuracy, our algorithm uses a fixed-point computation in addition to the ordering of detection strategies. The algorithm runs each strategy repeatedly until it finds no new refactorings. This loop is necessary because entities are intertwined with other entities, and a strategy cannot detect a refactoring in one entity until it detects a refactoring in the dependent entities. For instance, consider this example change that happened in the Struts framework between the versions 1.1 and 1.2.4: in the class ActionController, the method perform was renamed to execute. The implementation of perform in ActionController is a utility class that merely delegates to different subclasses of Action by sending them a perform message. For 11 of these Action classes, their callers consist mostly of the ActionController.perform. Therefore, unless a tool detects first that perform was renamed to execute, it cannot detect correctly the similarity of the incoming call edges for the other 11 methods. After the first run of the RenameMethod detection, our RefactoringCrawler tool misses the 11 other method renames. However, the feedback loop adds the information about the rename of perform, and the second run of the RenameMethod detection correctly finds another 11 renamed methods.

Even though we only analyze seven types of refactorings, conceptually similar combination of syntactic and semantic analysis can detect many other types of refactorings. A lot of the refactorings published by Fowler et al. [FBB+99] can be detected in this way, including extract/inline method, extract/inline package, extract/inline class or interface, move class to different package, collapse class hierarchy into a single class, replace record with data class, replace anonymous with nested class, replace type conditional code with polymorphism, as well as some higher-level refactorings to design patterns [GHJV95] including create Factory methods, form Template Method, replace type code with State/Strategy.

The largest extension to the current algorithm is required by 'replace type conditional code with polymorphism'. This refactoring replaces a switch statement whose branches type-check the exact type of an object (e.g., using *instanceof* in Java) with a call to a polymorphic method that is dynamically dispatched at run time to the right class. All the code in each branch statement is moved to the class whose type was checked in that branch. To detect this refactoring, the syntactic analysis should not only detect similar methods, but also similar statements and expressions within method bodies. This requires that shingles are computed for individual statements and expressions, which is overhead to the current implementation, but offers a finer level of granularity. Upon detection of similar statements in a switch branch and in a class method, the semantic analysis needs to check whether the class has the same type as the one checked in the branch and whether the switch is replaced in the second version with a call to the polymorphic method.

7   Implementation

We have implemented our algorithm for detecting refactorings in RefactoringCrawler, a plugin for the Eclipse development environment. The user loads the two versions of the component to be compared as projects inside the Eclipse workspace and selects the two projects for which RefactoringCrawler detects refactorings. To experiment with the accuracy and performance of the analysis, the user can set the values for different parameters, such as the size of the sliding window for the Shingles encoding (Section 4); the number of shingles to represent the digital fingerprint of methods, classes and package; and the thresholds used in computing the similarity of shingles encoding or the reference graphs. RefactoringCrawler provides a set of default parameter values that should work fine for most Java components.

RefactoringCrawler provides an efficient implementation of the algorithm shown in Figure 2. The syntactic analysis starts by parsing the source files of the two versions of the component and creates a graph representation mirroring the *lightweight* ASTs. We call it lightweight because the parsing stops at the declaration of the methods and fields in classes. RefactoringCrawler then annotates each method and field node with shingles values corresponding to the source code behind each node (e.g. method body or field initializers). From the leaves' shingles values, RefactoringCrawler annotates (bottom-up) with shingles values all the nodes corresponding to classes and packages. Since each node contains the fully qualified name of the source code entity, it is easy to navigate back and forth between the actual source code and the graph representation.

During the semantic analysis, RefactoringCrawler uses Eclipse's search engine to find the references among source code entities. The search engine operates on the source code, not on the graph. The search engine does a type analysis to identify the class of a reference when two methods in unrelated classes have the same name. Finding the references is an expensive computation, so RefactoringCrawler lazily runs this and caches the intermediate results by adding edges between the graph nodes that refer each other.

RefactoringCrawler performs the analysis and returns back the results inside an Eclipse view. RefactoringCrawler presents only the refactorings that happened to the public API level of the component since only these can affect the component users. RefactoringCrawler groups the results in categories corresponding to each refactoring strategy. Double clicking on any leaf Java element opens an editor having selected the declaration of that particular Java element. RefactoringCrawler also allows the user to export the results into an XML format compatible with the format that CatchUp [HD05] uses to load a log of refactorings. A similar XML format is used for the Eclipse 3.2 Milestone 4. Additionally, the XML format allows the developer to further analyze and edit the log, removing false positives or adding missed refactorings.

The reader can see screenshots and is encouraged to download the tool from the website [Ref].

8   Evaluation

We evaluate RefactoringCrawler on three real-world components. To measure the accuracy of RefactoringCrawler, we need to know the refactorings that were applied in the components. Therefore, we chose the components from our previous study [DJ05] that analyzed the API changes in software evolution and found refactorings to be responsible for more than 80% of the changes. The previous study considered components with good release notes describing the API changes. Starting from the release notes, we manually discovered the refactorings applied in these components. These manually discovered refactorings helped us to measure the accuracy of the refactoring logs that RefactoringCrawler reports. In general, it is easier to detect the false positives (refactorings that RefactoringCrawler erroneously reports) by comparing the reported refactorings against the source code than it is to detect the false negatives (refactorings that RefactoringCrawler misses). To determine false negatives, we compare the manually found refactorings against the refactorings reported by RefactoringCrawler. Additionally, RefactoringCrawler found a few refactorings that were not documented in the release notes. Our previous study and the evaluation of RefactoringCrawler allowed us to build a repository of refactorings that happened between the two versions of the three components. The case study along with the tool and the detected refactorings can be found online [Ref].

For each component, we need to choose two versions. The previous study [DJ05] chose two major releases that span large architectural changes because such releases are likely to have lots of changes and to have the changes documented. We use the same versions to evaluate RefactoringCrawler. Note, however, that these versions can present hard cases for RefactoringCrawler because they are far apart and can have large changes. RefactoringCrawler still achieves practical accuracy for these versions. We believe that RefactoringCrawler could achieve even higher accuracy on closer versions with less changes.

8.1   Case Study Components

Table 1 shows the size of the case study components. ReleaseNotes give the size (in pages) of the documents that the component developers provided to describe the API changes. We next describe the components and the versions that we analyze [DJ05].

Table 1. Size of the studied components

	Size KLOC	Packages	Classes	Methods	ReleaseNotes [Pages]
Eclipse.UI 2.1.3	222	105	1151	10285	-
Eclipse.UI 3.0	352	192	1735	15894	8
Struts 1.1	114	88	460	5916	-
Struts 1.2.4	97	78	469	6044	16
JHotDraw 5.2	17	19	160	1458	-
JHotDraw 5.3	27	19	195	2038	3

Eclipse Platform. [eclipse.org] provides many APIs and many different smaller frameworks. The key framework in Eclipse is a plug-in based framework that can be used to develop and integrate software tools. This framework is often used to develop Integrated Development Environments (IDEs). We focus on the UI subcomponent (Eclipse.UI) that contains 13 plug-ins.

We chose two major releases of Eclipse, 2.1 (March 2003) and 3.0 (June 2004). Eclipse 3.0 came with some major themes that affected the APIs. The *responsiveness* theme ensured that more operations run in the background without blocking the user. New APIs allow long-running operations like builds and searches to be performed in the background while the user continues to work. Another major theme in 3.0 is *rich-client platforms*. Eclipse was designed as a universal IDE. However many components of Eclipse are not particularly specific to IDEs and can be reused in other rich-client applications (e.g., plug-ins, help system, update manager, window-based GUIs). This architectural theme involved factoring out IDE-specific elements. APIs heavily affected by this change are those that made use of the filesystem resources. For instance IWorkbenchPage is an interface used to open an editor for a file input. All methods that were resource specific (those that dealt with opening editors over files) were removed from the interface. A client who opens an editor for a file should convert it first to a generic editor input. Now the interface can be used by both non-IDE clients (e.g., an electronic mail client that edits the message body) as well as IDE clients.

Struts. [struts.apache.org] is an open source framework for building Java web applications. The framework is a variation of the Model-View-Controller (MVC) design paradigm. Struts provides its own Controller component and integrates with other technologies to provide the Model and the View. For the Model, Struts can interact with standard data access technologies, like JDBC and EJB, and many third-party packages. For the View, Struts works with many presentation systems.

We chose two major releases of Struts, 1.1 (June 2003) and 1.2.4 (September 2004). All the API changes reveal consolidation work that was done in between the two releases. The developers eliminated duplicated code and removed unmaintained or buggy code.

JHotDraw. [jhotdraw.org] is a two-dimensional graphics framework for structured drawing editors. In contrast to the Swing graphics library, JHotDraw defines a basic skeleton for a GUI-based editor with tools in a tool palette, different views, user-defined

Table 2. Triples of (GoodResults, FalsePositives, FalseNegatives) for RenameMethod(RM), RenameClass(RC), RenamePackage(RP), MoveMethod(MM), PullUpMethod(PUM), PushDownMethod(PDM), ChangeMethodSignature(CMS)

	RM	RC	RP	MM	PUM	PDM	CMS	Precision	Recall
EclipseUI 2.1.3 - 3.0	2,1,0	0,0,0	0,0,0	8,2,4	11,0,0	0,0,0	6,0,0	90%	86%
Struts 1.2.1 - 1.2.4	20,0,1	1,0,1	0,0,0	20,0,7	1,0,0	0,0,0	24,0,1	100%	86%
JHotDraw 5.2 - 5.3	5,0,0	0,0,0	0,0,0	0,0,0	0,0,0	0,0,0	19,0,0	100%	100%

graphical figures, and support for saving, loading, and printing drawings. The framework has been used to create many different editors.

We chose two major releases of JHotDraw, 5.2 (February 2001) and 5.3 (January 2002). The purpose of 5.3 release was to clean up the APIs and fix bugs.

8.2   Measuring the Recall and Precision

To measure the accuracy of RefactoringCrawler, we use precision and recall, two standard metrics from the Information Retrieval field. *Precision* is the ratio of the number of relevant refactorings found by the tool to the total number of irrelevant and relevant refactorings found by the tool. It is expressed as the percentage:

$$PRECISION = GoodResults/(GoodResults + FalsePositives)$$

Recall is the ratio of the number of relevant refactorings found by the tool (good results) to the total number of actual refactorings in the component. It is expressed as the percentage:

$$RECALL = GoodResults/(GoodResults + FalseNegatives)$$

Ideally, precision and recall should be 100%. If that was the case, the reported refactorings could be fed directly into a tool that replays them to automatically upgrade component-based applications. However, due to the challenges mentioned in Section 6, it is hard to have 100% precision and recall.

Table 2 shows how many instances of each refactoring were found for the three components. These results use the default values for the parameters in RefactoringCrawler [Ref]. For each refactoring type, we show in a triple how many good results RefactoringCrawler found, how many false positives RefactoringCrawler found, and how many false negatives (according to the release notes [DJ05]) RefactoringCrawler found. For each component, we compute precision and recall that take into account the refactorings of all kinds.

We further analyzed why RefactoringCrawler missed a few refactorings. In Struts, for instance, method `RequestUtils.computeParameters` is moved to `TagUtils.computeParameters`, and method `RequestUtils.pageURL` is moved to `TagUtils.pageURL`. There are numerous calls to these methods from a test class. However, it appears that the test code was not refactored, and therefore it still calls the old method (that is deprecated), which results in quite different call sites for the old and the refactored method.

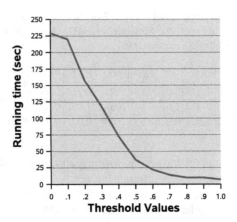

Fig. 9. Running time for JHotDraw decreases exponentially with higher threshold values used in the syntactic analysis

8.3   Performance

The results in Table 2 were obtained when RefactoringCrawler ran on a Fujitsu laptop with a 1.73GHz Pentium 4M CPU and 1.25GB of RAM. It took 16 min 38 sec for detecting the refactorings in EclipseUI, 4 min and 55 sec for Struts, and 37 sec for JHotDraw. Figure 9 shows how the running time for JHotDraw varies with the change of the method similarity threshold values used in the syntactic analysis. For low threshold values, the number of candidate pairs passed to the semantic analysis is large, resulting in longer analysis time. For high threshold values, fewer candidate pairs pass into the semantic analysis, resulting in lower running times. For JHotDraw, a .1 method similarity threshold passes 1842 method candidates to the RenameMethod's semantic analysis, a .5 threshold value passes 88 candidates, while a .9 threshold passes only 4 candidates.

The more important question, however, is how precision and recall vary with the change of the similarity threshold values. Very low threshold values produce a larger number of candidates to be analyzed, which results in a larger number of false positives, but increases the chance that all the relevant refactorings are found among the results. Very high threshold values imply that only those candidates that have almost perfect body resemblance are taken into account, which reduces the number of false positives but can miss some refactorings. We have found that threshold values between 0.5 and 0.7 result in practical precision and recall.

8.4   Strengths and Limitations

We next discuss the strengths and the limitations of our approach to detecting refactorings. We also propose new extensions to overcome the limitations.

Strengths

– **High precision and recall.** Our evaluation on the three components shows that both precision and recall of RefactoringCrawler are over 85%. Since RefactoringCrawler combines both syntactic and semantic analysis, it can process a realistic size of software with practical accuracy. Compared to other approaches [APM04, DDN00, GW05, GZ05, RD03] that use only syntactic analysis and produce large number of false positives, our tool requires little human intervention to validate the refactorings. RefactoringCrawler can significantly reduce the burden necessary to find refactoring logs that a replay tool uses to automatically upgrade component-based applications.

– **Robust.** Our tool is able to detect refactorings in the presence of noise introduced because of maintaining backwards compatibility, the noise of multiple refactorings, and the noise of renamings. Renamings create huge problems for other approaches but do not impede our tool. Since our tool identifies code entities (methods, classes, packages) based on their body resemblance and not on their names, our tool can successfully track the same entity across different versions, even when its name changes. For previous approaches, a rename is equivalent with an entity disappearing and a brand new entity appearing in the subsequent version. Another problem for previous approaches is the application of multiple refactorings to the same entity. Our tool takes this into account by sharing the log of refactorings between the detection strategies and repeating each strategy until it reaches a fixed point. Lastly, our tool detects refactorings in an open-world development where, due to backwards compatibility, obsolete entities coexist with their refactored counterparts until the former are removed. We can detect refactorings in such an environment because most of refactorings involve repartitioning the source code. This results in parts of the code from a release being spread in different places in the next release. Our algorithm starts by detecting the similarities between two versions.

– **Scalable.** Running expensive semantic analysis (like identifying similar subgraphs in the entire reference graph) on large codebases comprising of tens of thousands of nodes (methods, classes, packages) is very expensive. To avoid this, we run first an inexpensive syntactic analysis that reduces the whole input domain to a relatively small number of candidates to be analyzed semantically. It took RefactoringCrawler 16 min 38 sec to analyze for the org.eclipse.ui subcomponent (352 KLOC) of the Eclipse Platform.

Limitations

– **Poor support for interfaces and fields.** Since our approach tracks the identity of methods, classes, and packages based on their textual bodies and not on their names, it does not fit for those entities that lack a body. Both class fields and interface methods do not contain any body other than their declaration name. After the syntactic analysis, only entities that have a body resemblance are passed to the semantic analysis. Therefore, refactorings that happened to fields or interface methods cannot be detected. This was the case in org.eclipse.ui where between versions 2.1.3 and 3.0 many static fields were moved to other classes and many interface methods were moved to abstract classes. To counteract the lack of textual bodies for fields or interface methods, we treated their associated javadoc comments as their text bodies. This seems to work for some cases, but not all.

– **Requires experimentation.** As with any approach based on heuristics, coming up with the right values for the detection algorithms might take a few trials. Selecting threshold values too high reduces the false positives toward zero but can miss some refactorings as only those candidates that have perfect resemblance are selected. Selecting too low threshold values produces a large number of false positives but increases the chances that all relevant refactorings are found among the results. The default threshold values for RefactoringCrawler are between 0.5 and 0.7 (for various similarity parameters) [Ref]. When default values do not produce adequate results, users could start from high threshold values and reduce them until the number of false positive becomes too large.

9   Related Work

We provide an overview of related work on refactoring, automated detection of refactorings, and the use of Shingles encoding.

9.1   Refactoring

Programmers have been cleaning up their code for decades, but the term *refactoring* was coined much later [OJ90]. Opdyke [Opd92] wrote the first catalog of refactorings, while Roberts and Brant [RBJ97, Rob99] were the first to implement a refactoring engine. The refactoring field gained much popularity with the catalog of refactorings written by Fowler et al. [FBB+99]. Soon after this, IDEs began to incorporate refactoring engines. Tokuda and Batory [TB01] describe how large architectural changes in two frameworks can be achieved as a sequence of small refactorings. They estimate that automated refactorings are 10 times quicker to perform than manual ones.

More recent research on refactoring focuses on the analyses for automating powerful refactorings. Tip et al. [TKB03] use type constraints to support an analysis for refactorings that introduce type generalization. Donovan et al. [DKTE04] use a pointer analysis and a set-constraint-based analysis to support refactorings that replace the instantiation of raw classes with generic classes. Dincklage and Diwan [vDD04] use various heuristics to convert from non-generic classes to generic classes. Balaban et al. [BTF05] propose refactorings that automatically replace obsolete library classes with their newer counterparts. Component developers have to provide mappings between legacy classes and their replacements, and an analysis based on type constraints determines where the replacement can be done. Thomas [Tho05] points out that refactorings in the components result into integration problems and advocates the need for languages that would allow developers to specify refactorings to create customizable refactorings.

9.2   Detection of Refactorings

Researchers have already developed some tool support for detecting and classifying structural evolution, mostly spawned from the reengineering community. Detection of class splitting and merging was the main target of the current tools. Demeyer et al. [DDN00] use a set of object-oriented change metrics and heuristics to detect refactorings that will serve as markers for the reverse engineer. Antonio et al. [APM04] use a technique inspired from the Information Retrieval to detect discontinuities in classes (e.g., a class was replaced with another one, a class was split into two, or two classes merge into one). Based on Vector Space cosine similarity, they compare the class identifiers found in two subsequent releases. Therefore, if a class, say `Resolver`, was present in version n but disappears in version $n + 1$ and a new class `SimpleResolver` appears in version $n + 1$, they conclude that a class replacement happened. Godfrey and Zou [GZ05] are the closest to the way how we envision detecting structural changes. They implemented a tool that can detect some refactorings like renaming, move method, split, and merge for procedural code. Whereas we start from shingles analysis, they employ origin analysis along with a more expensive analysis on call graphs to detect and classify these changes. Rysselberghe and Demeyer [RD03] use a clone finding tool (Duploc) to detect methods that were moved across the classes. Gorg and Weisgerber [GW05] analyze subsequent versions of a component in configuration management repositories to detect refactorings.

Existing work on automatic detection of refactorings addresses some of the needs of reverse engineers who must understand at a high level how and why components evolved. For this reason, most of the current work focuses on detecting merging and splitting of classes. However, in order to automatically migrate component-based applications we need to know the changes to the API. Our work complements existing work because we must look also for lower level refactorings that affect the signatures of methods. We also address the limitations of existing work with respect to renamings and noise introduced by multiple refactorings on the same entity or the noise introduced by the deprecate-replace-remove cycle in the open-world components.

9.3 Shingles Encoding

Clone detection based on Shingles encoding is a research interest in other fields like internet content management and file storage. Ramaswamy et al. [RILD04] worked on automatic detection of duplicated fragments in dynamically generated web pages. Dynamic web pages cannot be cached, but performance can be improved by caching fragments of web pages. They used Shingles encoding to detect fragments of web pages that did not change. Manber [Man93] and Kulkarni et al. [KDLT04] employ shingles-based algorithms to detect redundancy in the file system. They propose more efficient storage after eliminating redundancy. Li et al. [LLMZ04] use shingles to detect clones of text in the source code of operating systems. They further analyze the clones to detect bugs due to negligent copy and paste.

10   Conclusions

Syntactic analyses are too unreliable, and semantic analyses are too slow. Combining syntactic and semantic analyses can give good results. By combining Shingles encoding with traditional semantic analyses, and by iterating the analyses until a fixed point was discovered, we could detect over 85% of the refactorings while producing less than 10% false positives.

The algorithm would work on any two versions of a system. It does not assume that the later version was produced by any particular tool. If a new version is produced by a refactoring tool that records the refactorings that are made, then the log of refactorings will be 100% accurate. Nevertheless, there may not be the discipline or the opportunity to use a refactoring tool, and it is good to know that refactorings can be detected nearly as accurately without it.

There are several applications of automated detection of refactorings. First, a log of refactorings helps in the automated migration of component-based applications. As our previous study [DJ05] shows, more than 80% of the API changes that break compatibility with existing applications are refactorings. A tool like Eclipse can replay the log of refactorings. The replay is done at the application site where both the component and the application reside in the same workspace. In this case, the refactoring engine finds and correctly updates all the references to the refactored entities, thus migrating the application to the new API of the component.

Second, a log of refactorings can improve how current configuration management systems deal with renaming. A tool like CVS looses all the change history for a source file whose main class gets renamed, since this appears as if the old source file was removed and a source file with a new name was added. A log of refactorings can help the configuration management system to correlate the old files/folders with the new files/folders when the main class or package was renamed.

Third, a log of refactoring can help a developer understand how an object-oriented system has evolved from one version to another. For example, an explicit list of renamings tells how the semantics of the refactored entity changed, while a list of moved methods tells how the class responsibilities shifted.

The tool and the evaluation results are available online [Ref].

Acknowledgments

We would like to thank Zheng Shao and Jiawei Han who suggested the use of shingles for detecting similar methods. Adam Kiezun, Russ Ruffer, Filip Van Rysselberghe, Danny Soroker, anonymous reviewers, and members of the SAG group at UIUC provided valuable feedback on the drafts of this paper. This work is partially funded through an Eclipse Innovation Grant for which we are very grateful to IBM.

References

[APM04]   Giuliano Antoniol, Massimiliano Di Penta, and Ettore Merlo. An automatic approach to identify class evolution discontinuities. In *IWPSE'04: Proceedings of International Workshop on Principles of Software Evolution*, pages 31–40, 2004.

[Bor]   What's new in Borland Jbuilder 2005. http://www.borland.com/resources/en/pdf/white_papers/jb2005_whats_new.pdf.

[Bro97]   Andrei Broder. On the resemblance and containment of documents. In *SEQUENCES '97: Proceedings of Compression and Complexity of Sequences*, pages 21–29, 1997.

[BTF05]   Ittai Balaban, Frank Tip, and Robert Fuhrer. Refactoring support for class library migration. In *OOPSLA '05: Proceedings of Object-oriented programming, systems, languages, and applications*, pages 265–279, New York, NY, USA, 2005. ACM Press.

[DDN00]   Serge Demeyer, Stéphane Ducasse, and Oscar Nierstrasz. Finding refactorings via change metrics. In *OOPSLA'00: Proceedings of Object oriented programming, systems, languages, and applications*, pages 166–177, 2000.

[DJ05]   Danny Dig and Ralph Johnson. The role of refactorings in api evolution. In *ICSM'05: Proceedings of International Conference on Software Maintenance*, pages 389–398, Washington, DC, USA, 2005. IEEE Computer Society.

[DKTE04]   Alan Donovan, Adam Kiezun, Matthew S. Tschantz, and Michael D. Ernst. Converting Java programs to use generic libraries. In *OOPSLA '04: Proceedings of Object-oriented programming, systems, languages, and applications*, volume 39, pages 15–34, New York, NY, USA, October 2004. ACM Press.

[Ecl]   Eclipse Foundation. http://eclipse.org.

[FBB+99]   Martin Fowler, Kent Beck, John Brant, William Opdyke, and Don Roberts. *Refactoring: Improving the Design of Existing Code*. Adison-Wesley, 1999.

[GHJV95]   Erich Gamma, Richard Helm, Ralph Johnson, and John Vlissides. *Design Patterns: Elements of Reusable Object-Oriented Software*. Addison-Wesley, 1995.

[GW05]   Carsten Gorg and Peter Weisgerber. Detecting and visualizing refactorings from software archives. In *IWPC'05: Proceedings of the 13th International Workshop on Program Comprehension*, pages 205–214, Washington, DC, USA, 2005. IEEE Computer Society.

[GZ05]   Michael W. Godfrey and Lijie Zou. Using origin analysis to detect merging and splitting of source code entities. *IEEE Transactions on Software Engineering*, 31(2):166–181, 2005.

[HD05]   Johannes Henkel and Amer Diwan. CatchUp!: Capturing and replaying refactorings to support API evolution. In *ICSE'05: Proceedings of International Conference on Software Engineering*, pages 274–283, 2005.

[KDLT04]   Purushottam Kulkarni, Fred Douglis, Jason D. LaVoie, and John M. Tracey. Redundancy elimination within large collections of files. In *USENIX Annual Technical Conference, General Track*, pages 59–72, 2004.

[LLMZ04]   Zhenmin Li, Shan Lu, Suvda Myagmar, and Yuanyuan Zhou. CP-Miner: A tool for finding copy-paste and related bugs in operating system code. In *OSDI'04: Proceedings of the Sixth Symposium on Operating System Design and Implementation*, pages 289–302, 2004.

[Man93]   Udi Manber. Finding similar files in a large file system. Technical Report 93-33, University of Arizona, 1993.

[OJ90]   Bill Opdyke and Ralph Johnson. Refactoring: An aid in designing application frameworks and evolving object-oriented systems. In *SOOPPA'90: Proceedings of Symposium on Object-Oriented Programming Emphasizing Practical Applications*, 1990.

[Opd92]   Bill Opdyke. *Refactoring Object-Oriented Frameworks*. PhD thesis, University of Illinois at Urbana-Champaign, 1992.

[Rab81]   Michael O. Rabin. Fingerprinting by random polynomials. Technical Report 15-81, Harvard University, 1981.

[RBJ97]   Don Roberts, John Brant, and Ralph E. Johnson. A refactoring tool for Smalltalk. *TAPOS*, 3(4):253–263, 1997.

[RD03]   Filip Van Rysselberghe and Serge Demeyer. Reconstruction of successful software evolution using clone detection. In *IWPSE'03: Proceedings of 6th International Workshop on Principles of Software Evolution*, pages 126–130, 2003.

[Ref]   RefactoringCrawler's web page:. https://netfiles.uiuc.edu/dig/RefactoringCrawler .

[RILD04]   Lakshmish Ramaswamy, Arun Iyengar, Ling Liu, and Fred Douglis. Automatic detection of fragments in dynamically generated web pages. In *WWW '04: Proceedings of the 13th international conference on World Wide Web*, pages 443–454, New York, NY, USA, 2004. ACM Press.

[Rob99]   Don Roberts. *Practical Analysis for Refactoring*. PhD thesis, University of Illinois at Urbana-Champaign, 1999.

[TB01]   Lance Tokuda and Don Batory. Evolving object-oriented designs with refactorings. *Automated Software Engineering*, 8(1):89–120, January 2001.

[Tho05]   Dave Thomas. Refactoring as meta programming? *Journal of Object Technology*, 4(1):7–11, January-February 2005.

[TKB03]   Frank Tip, Adam Kiezun, and Dirk Bauemer. Refactoring for generalization using type constraints. In *OOPSLA '03: Proceedings of Object-oriented programing, systems, languages, and applications*, volume 38, pages 13–26, New York, NY, USA, November 2003. ACM Press.

[vDD04]   Daniel von Dincklage and Amer Diwan. Converting Java classes to use generics. In *OOPSLA '04: Proceedings of Object-oriented programming, systems, languages, and applications*, pages 1–14. ACM Press, 2004.

Modeling Runtime Behavior in Framework-Based Applications

Nick Mitchell[1], Gary Sevitsky[1], and Harini Srinivasan[2]

[1] IBM TJ Watson Research Center 19 Skyline Drive, Hawthorne NY USA
[2] IBM Software Group Route 100, Somers NY USA
nickm@us.ibm.com, sevitsky@us.ibm.com, harini@us.ibm.com

Abstract. Our research group has analyzed many industrial, framework-based applications. In these applications, simple functionality often requires excessive runtime activity. It is increasingly difficult to assess if and how inefficiencies can be fixed. Much of this activity involves the transformation of information, due to framework couplings. We present an approach to modeling and quantifying behavior in terms of what transformations accomplish.

We structure activity into dataflow diagrams that capture the flow between transformations. Across disparate implementations, we observe commonalities in how transformations use and change their inputs. We introduce vocabulary of common phenomena of use and change, and four ways to classify data and transformations using this vocabulary. The structuring and classification enable evaluation and comparison in terms abstracted from implementation specifics. We introduce metrics of complexity and cost, including behavior signatures that attribute measures to phenomena. We demonstrate the approach on a benchmark, a library, and two industrial applications.

1 Introduction

Large-scale applications are being built from increasingly many reusable frameworks, such as web application servers (that use SOAP [5], EJB, JSP), portal servers, client platforms (Eclipse), and industry-specific frameworks. Over the past several years, our research group has analyzed the performance of dozens of industrial framework-based applications. In every application we looked at, an enormous amount of activity was executed to accomplish simple tasks. This was the case, even after some tuning effort has been applied. For example, a stock brokerage benchmark [13] executes 268 method calls and creates 70 new objects just to move a single date field from SOAP to Java. Beyond identifying bottlenecks, this paper presents an approach to understanding the general causes of runtime complexity and inefficiency in these applications.

In our experience, inefficiencies are not typically manifested in a few hot methods. They are mostly due to a constellation of transformations. Each transformation takes data produced in one framework and makes it suitable for another. Problems are less likely to be caused by poor algorithm choices, than by the combined design and implementation choices made in disparate frameworks. In

D. Thomas (Ed.): ECOOP 2006, LNCS 4067, pp. 429–451, 2006.
© Springer-Verlag Berlin Heidelberg 2006

a web-based server application, for example, the data arrives in one format, is transformed into a Java business object, and is sent to a browser or another system – e.g. from SOAP, to an EJB, and finally to XML. Surprisingly, inside each transformation are often many smaller transformations; inside these are often yet more transformations, each the result of lower-level framework coupling. In addition, many steps are often required to *facilitate* these transformations. For example, a chain of lookups may be needed to find the proper SOAP deserializer. In our benchmark example, moving that date from SOAP to Java took a total of 58 transformations.

How do we know if 58 transformations is excessive for this operation? And if so, what could possibly require so many? Traditional performance tools model runtime behavior in terms of implementation artifacts, such as methods, packages, and call paths [1, 2, 3, 8, 10, 20, 23]. Transformations, however, are implemented as sequences of method calls, spanning multiple frameworks. In this paper, we present an approach for understanding and quantifying behavior in terms of transformations and what they accomplish. We demonstrate how this model enables:

- Evaluation of an implementation to understand the nature of its complexity and costs, and assess whether they are excessive for what was accomplished. We show many examples of this throughout the paper.
- Comparison of implementations that accomplish similar functionality, but use different frameworks or physical data models. Section 5 gives two examples of this.

We model the behavior of a run by structuring it as the flow of data through transformations, and by classifying the data and transformations in multiple ways to give insight into what they accomplish. Both the structuring and classification are in terms that are abstracted from the specifics of any framework. This modeling approach enables powerful ways of evaluation and comparison, based on complexity and cost metrics we introduce. Generating a model and computing metrics are currently manual processes; parts are amenable to automation in the future. We now describe the approach in more detail.

Structuring Behavior: There often are multiple *physical representations* of the same *logical content*. For example, the same date may be represented as bytes within a SOAP message, and later as a Java Date object. Our approach structures runtime activity as data flow of logical content, as illustrated in Figure 1. We show the data flow as a hierarchy of data flow diagrams [7, 12]. Each edge represents the flow of a physical representation of some logical content. Each node represents a *transformation* — a change in logical content or physical representation of its inputs. Many types of processing can be viewed as transformations. For example, a transformation may be a physical change only, like converting information from bytes to characters or copying it from one location to another; it may be a lookup of associated information, such as finding a quote for a stock holding; or it may be implementing business logic, such as adding a commission to a stock sale record.

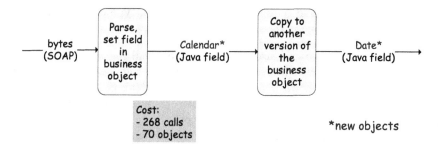

Fig. 1. A dataflow diagram of how the Trade benchmark transforms a date, from a SOAP message to a Java object

It is infeasible to have a dataflow diagram show an entire run. We introduce the concept of an *analysis scenario* that filters the analysis to show just the production of some specified information. We show how to group the activity and data of an analysis scenario into a hierarchy of dataflow diagrams.

Classifying Behavior: We classify transformations and the data flowing between them to gain insight into why they are necessary. Over years of analyzing industrial applications, we have seen many commonalities in how transformations use their inputs, and in how they change their inputs. To capture this, we introduce a number of orthogonal ways to classify by these common *phenomena* of use and change. We introduce a vocabulary of these phenomena.

For example, a transformation that converts a stock holding from SOAP to a Java object takes as input both the SOAP message and a parser. One of our classifications distinguishes these two inputs as serving different purposes in the transformation: the message is a *carrier* of the data being processed, and the parser is a *facilitator* of the conversion. We also classify the transformation by how it changes the physical representation of the carrier input data: it effects a *conversion*. Another classification is of the change in logical content: in this case we label the transformation as *information preserving*.

Phenomena such as these capture properties that are abstracted from the specifics of any one framework or application. Structuring and classifying in *framework-independent* terms enables evaluation and comparison across disparate implementations. To this end, we also introduce framework-independent metrics of runtime complexity and cost.

Quantifying Complexity: We use the number of transformations as an indicator of the magnitude of complexity. We aggregate this measure in two ways. First, we introduce metrics that aggregate based solely on the topology of the diagrams. For example, 58 transformations to convert one field seems excessive; knowing that 36 of these occurred while converting subfields indicates that the problem lies deep inside the standard Java libraries. Second, to surface the specific kinds of complexity in an implementation, we introduce *behavior signatures*. A behavior signature counts transformations by phenomenon. For example, the processing of each subfield requires five copies and six type changes, indicating poor framework coupling at the subfield level.

Quantifying Cost: We can also aggregate traditional resource costs, such as number of instructions executed, or objects created by topology and phenomena. Aggregating in these new ways, as opposed to by method, package, or call path, gives more powerful metrics of cost for framework-based applications. We give examples showing the benefits of reporting costs by transformation or analysis scenario. We also show the benefits of cost behavior signatures, that break down costs by phenomena. We give an example of a behavior signature that shows that, of the 70 objects created in the processing of a purchase date field, 59 were due to transformations that did not change the logical content of the field.

In summary, this paper contributes an approach to modeling and quantifying runtime behavior in framework-independent terms:

- A way to structure runtime behavior as the data flow of logical content through transformations. [Section 2]
- An in-depth example that illustrates the kinds of complexity in real-world framework-based applications. [Section 2]
- Three orthogonal dimensions to classify what transformations and data accomplish. [Section 3]
    - A vocabulary of common phenomena for each dimension.
    - A way to induce the purpose of transformations from the purpose of the data they help produce.
- New ways to measure complexity, and to aggregate complexity and resource cost measures. [Section 4]

Finally, in Section 5, we demonstrate the power of the metrics using two real-world examples.

2   Structuring Behavior

We model runtime behavior using data flow. Using the raw data flow information would give too much, and too low a level of information to make sense of. In this section we present our approach to filtering and grouping activity into a hierarchy of data flow diagrams.

Figure 1 shows a dataflow diagram from a configuration of the Trade 6 benchmark [13] that acts as a SOAP client.[1] The figure follows the flow of one small piece of information, a field representing the purchase date of a stock holding, from a web service response into a field of the Java object that will later be used for producing HTML. We follow this field because, of all the fields of a holding, it is the most expensive to process.

Each edge shows the flow of the physical form of some logical content. In the figure, the same purchase date is shown on three edges: first as some subset of the

---

[1] We omit the standard data flow notation for sources and sinks, and instead represent them as unterminated edges.

bytes in a SOAP response, then as a Java Calendar (and its subsidiary objects), and finally as a Java Date. Each node denotes a transformation of that data, and it groups together invocations of many methods or method fragments, drawn from multiple frameworks. In Sections 3.3 and 3.4 we discuss transformations and logical content in more depth.

Structuring in this way relates the cost of disparate activity to the data it produced. Figure 1 shows that the cost of the first transformation was 268 method calls and 70 new objects, mostly temporaries.[2] All this, just to produce an intermediate (Java object) form of the purchase date.

2.1 Filtering by Analysis Scenario

The extent of a diagram is defined by an *analysis scenario* that consists of the following elements:

- The output – the logical content whose production we follow
- The physical target of that logical content
- The physical sources of input data
- Optional filtering criteria that limit activity to a specified thread, or an interval of time.

For example, Figure 1 reflects an analysis scenario that follows the production of a purchase date field; its physical target is the Java object that will be used for generating HTML; its physical source is the SOAP message; filtering criteria limit the diagram to just one response to a servlet request, and to the worker thread that processes that request. Note how the filtering criteria allow us to construct a diagram that omits any advance work not specific to a servlet response, such as initializing the application server.

2.2 Grouping into Hierarchical Diagrams

Within an analysis scenario, the activity and data could be grouped into data flow diagrams in various ways. In this section we show how we group activity into transformations, to form an initial hierarchy of data flow diagrams. We then apply an additional rule that identifies groups of transformations to split out into additional levels of diagram.

Applications often have logical notions of *granularity* that cut across multiple type systems. For example, a stock holding record, whether represented as substrings of a SOAP message or as a Java object, may still be thought of as a record.

We follow the activity and intermediate data leading to the production of the scenario's output. The top-level diagram shows this at a single level of granularity, that of the output. Each transformation groups together all activity required to change either the logical content or physical representation of its input data.

---

[2] We used a publicly available application server and JVM. Once in a steady state, we used ArcFlow [1] and Jinsight [8] to gather raw information about the run, after JIT optimizations.

Section 3 gives more precise definitions of logical and physical change. Note that some of the inputs to a transformation will be facilitators, such as schemas or converters. In the diagram for that transformation, we also include the sequence of transformations needed to produce these facilitators. Section 3.1 discusses facilitators in more depth.

While one diagram shows data flow at a single level of granularity, it will also show those transformations that transition between that granularity and the next lower one. For example, the transformation that extracts a field from a record will be included in the diagram of the record.

We form additional levels of diagram to distinguish the parties responsible for a given cost. We define an *architectural unit* to be a set of classes. Given a set of architectural units, a hierarchical dataflow diagram splits the behavior so that the activity at one level of diagram is that caused by at most one architectural unit. The choice of architectural units allows flexibility in assigning responsibility for the existence of transformations. In our experience, architectural units do not necessarily align with package structure. The diagram of Figure 1 shows the field-level activity that the application initiates. Other field-level activity that SOAP is responsible for is grouped under the first node. To analyze the behavior that SOAP causes, we can zoom in, to explore a subdiagram.

2.3   The Diary of a Date

We now explore the structure of the first step of the diagram shown in Figure 1. This example illustrates how to apply the structuring approach, and also shows the kinds of complexity that we have seen in real-world framework-based applications. We chose a benchmark that has been well-tuned at the application level to demonstrate the challenges of achieving good performance in framework-based applications.

We present an additional three levels of diagram. Two are the result of splitting according to architectural units (SOAP and the standard Java library), and one according to granularity.

Diagram level 1. Figure 2 shows the field-granularity activity that SOAP is responsible for, within the first transformation of Figure 1. The purchase date field flows along the middle row of nodes. Just at this level, the input bytes undergo seven transformations before exiting as a Calendar field in the Java business object.

The first transformation extracts the bytes representing the purchase date from the XML text of a SOAP message, and converts it to a String. The String is passed to a deserializer for parsing. The SOAP framework allows registration of deserializers for datatypes that can appear in messages. In the lower left corner is a sequence of transformations that look up the appropriate deserializer given the field name.

We highlight as a group the five transformations related to parsing, to make it easier to see this functional relationship. The first step takes the String, extracts and parses the time zone and milliseconds, and copies the remaining characters into a new String. The reformatted date String is then passed to the SimpleDate-

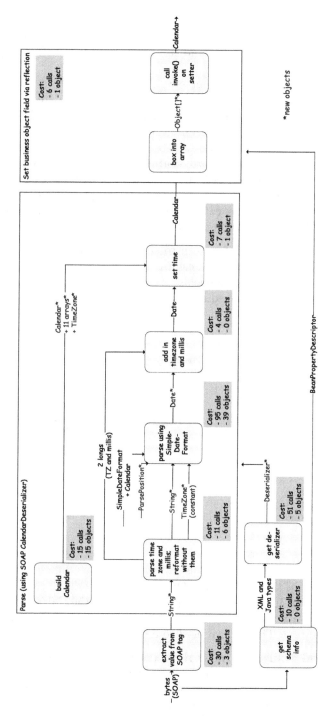

Fig. 2. Zooming in on the first step of Figure 1 shows how the SOAP framework transforms the purchase date field

Format library class for parsing. This is an expensive step, creating 39 objects (38 of them temporaries). Below, we explore that diagram to find out why.[3] It then returns a new Date object, and joins that object with the original time zone and milliseconds.

The Java library has two date classes. A Date object stores the number of milliseconds since a fixed point in time. A Calendar stores a date in two different forms, and can convert between them. One form is the same as in Date; the other is seventeen integer fields that are useful for operating on dates, such as year, month, day, hour, or day of the week.

In the top row is an expensive transformation that builds a new default Calendar from the current time. Our Date object is then used to set the value of this Calendar again. Finally, that Calendar becomes the purchase date field of our business object, via a reflective call to a setter method. Java's reflection interface requires the Calendar to first be packaged into an object array.

Diagram level 2. Figure 3 zooms in to show the Java library's responsibility for the SimpleDateFormat parse transformation. The String containing the date is input, and each of its six subfields – year, month, day, hour, minute, and second – is extracted and parsed individually.

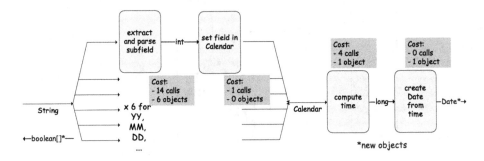

Fig. 3. Further zooming in on the parse using SimpleDateFormat step of Figure 2 shows how the standard Java library's date-handling code transforms the purchase date field

The SimpleDateFormat maintains its own Calendar, different from the one discussed earlier at the SOAP level. Once a subfield of date has been extracted and parsed into an integer, the corresponding field of the Calendar is set. After all six subfields are set, the Calendar converts this field representation into a time representation. This is then used to create a new Date object.

Diagram level 3. Figure 4 shows the detail of extracting and parsing a single date subfield, in this case, a year. Even at this microscopic level, the standard Java library requires six transformations to convert a few characters in the String (in "YYYY" representation) into the integer form of the year.

---

[3] It often seems that things named "Simple" are expensive.

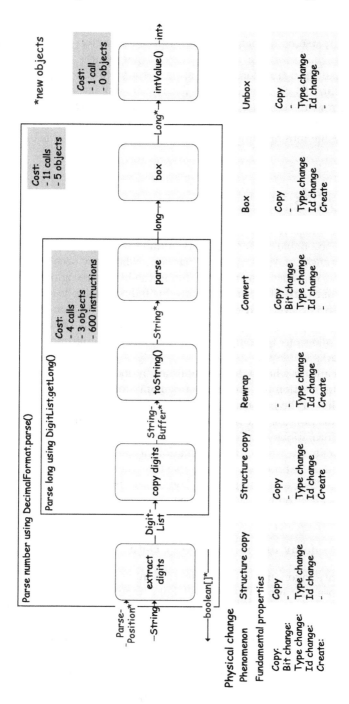

Fig. 4. Zooming into the first step of Figure 3 shows how the standard Java library's number-handling code transforms a subfield of a purchase date (such as a year, month, or day)

The first five transformations come from the general purpose DecimalFormat class. It can parse or format any kind of decimal number. SimpleDateFormat, however, uses it for a special case, to parse integer months, days, and years. The first, fifth, and sixth transformations are necessary only because of this overgenerality. The first transformation looks for a decimal point, an E for scientific notation, and rewraps the characters.[4] Furthermore, since DecimalFormat.parse() returns either a double or long value, the fifth transformation is needed to box the return value into an Object, and the sixth transformation is only necessary to unbox it.

3   Classifying Behavior

Section 2 describes how we structure an analysis scenario in terms of transformations. To enable a deeper understanding, we have identified four ways of classifying transformations and data based on what they accomplish.

All of these classifications revolve around the idea of recognizable phenomena drawn from our years of experience analyzing industrial applications. These same phenomena occur over and over again, from one application or framework to the next. Classifying transformations and data in terms of these recognizable phenomena allows us to compare what they are accomplishing independent of the frameworks employed.

We first capture what data accomplishes by looking at how transformations use that data. Section 3.1 presents a taxonomy for classifying the data at each edge according to the purpose it serves in the transformation into which it flows. We show in Section 3.2 how this can also be used to give insight into the purpose of the transformations that led to the production of that data.

We next capture what a transformation accomplishes by looking at how it changes the data it processes. We observe that there is an important distinction between the effect a transformation has on the physical representation of the data, and its effect on the logical content. Sections 3.3 and 3.4 present these two ways of classifying transformations.

3.1   A Taxonomy of the Purpose of Data

We introduce a taxonomy that classifies each input to a transformation according to the purpose that input data serves.[5] Some inputs provide the values that the transformation acts upon. We classify these as *carriers*. Other inputs provide ancillary data that facilitate the transformation. We classify these as *facilitators*. Framework-based applications expend a significant effort finding and creating facilitators, such as schemas, serializers, parsers, or connection handles. Table 1 shows common phenomena we have identified, arranged as a taxonomy.

---

[4] It checks fitsIntoLong() on a number representing a month!

[5] The outputs of the top-level diagram aren't classified; since they are the output of the analysis scenario, we don't know their eventual use. Outputs of subdiagrams are classified by the consuming transformation in the next higher diagram.

Table 1. We classify data flowing along an edge according to this taxonomy of how the subsequent transformation uses it

Phenomena			Example
carrier			the Java form of an Employee object
facilitator	metadata	schema	Java class info; record layout
		format	user preferences for web page layout
	converter		byte to char converter, SOAP deserializer
	protocol enabler	connection	database connection or file descriptor
		cursor	iterator or buffer position
		status	condition or error codes

Figure 5 shows the SOAP level of parsing of a Date, with the input of each transformation classified according to purpose. Note the carriers along the middle row. Also note facilitators such as *converters*: the Calendar in the top row, the SimpleDateFormat in the middle row, and the Deserializer in the bottom row. All three serve the same broad purpose, though their implementations and the kinds of conversions they facilitate are different. One input to the "parse using SimpleDateFormat" transformation is a ParsePosition, a Java library class that maintains a position in a String; it acts as a *cursor*.

Note that the same data may be used as input to more than one transformation. In this case, it may serve multiple purposes. The Calendar in the top row of Figure 5 first serves as a converter when it facilitates the "set time" transformation, and then as a carrier of the purchase date into the "box into array" transformation.

Classifying by purpose helps to assess the appropriateness of costs. For example, one would not expect the initialization of a converter to depend on the data being converted, but only on the type of data. It would seem strange, then, to see many converters for the parsing of fields. The scenario of Figure 5 requires three converters to process a field.

3.2   A Flow-Induced Classification of the Purpose of a Transformation

The classification of Section 3.1 tells us what input data are used for. Often, finding or creating that input data itself requires many transformations. The following algorithm takes a classification of data purpose and induces a classification on the transformations that contributed to the production of that data.

1. We denote the entire dataflow diagram as D. The *carrier subgraph* is that set $C \subseteq D$ consisting of the nodes and edges encountered on traversals from initial inputs to final outputs that are entirely composed of edges classified as carrier. The *facilitating subgraph* is $F = D - C$.
2. For each node $n \in D$, we compute a set L_n of induced labels as follows. If $n \in C$, then $L_n = \{carrier\}$. Otherwise, for each edge from F to C with label l, perform a backwards traversal within F and add l to L_i for each node i encountered in the traversal.

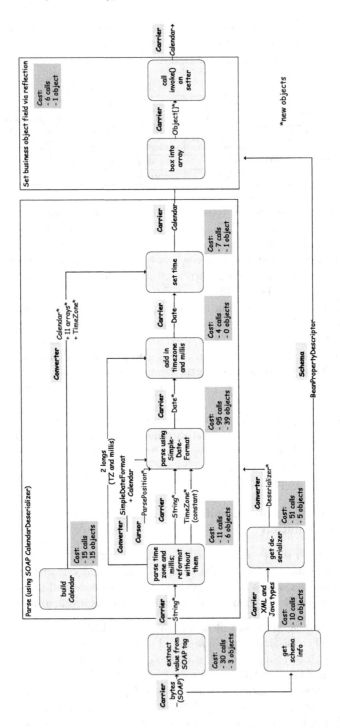

Fig. 5. Showing the same dataflow diagram as Figure 2, with the edges classified by data purpose

For example, the Deserializer in Figure 5 has been classified as a converter; the BeanPropertyDescriptor has been classified as a schema. The algorithm computes L for the "get schema info" transformation to be {*converter*, *schema*}, and for "get deserializer" transformation to be {*converter*}. In other words, the time spent getting schema information can be charged to a purpose.

3.3 How a Transformation Changes the Physical Representation of Its Input Data

We also classify each transformation by how it changes the physical representation of the data it processes. There are some common kinds of change to the physical form, despite the many implementations that accomplish that change. For example, the phenomena of *converting* data from one format to another occurs in many applications, implemented in a variety of ways. Note that this classification is based only on how the transformation changes carrier inputs, not facilitator inputs.

Table 2 shows four phenomena that commonly occur in framework-based applications. In Figure 4, the first row of labels below the diagram shows how we classify each transformation according to these phenomena.

Underlying these phenomena, we have identified five more fundamental properties of how a transformation changes the physical representation of its carrier inputs. The lower row of boxes in Figure 4 shows this classification.

- **Copy:** a transformation that copies the internal representation of the data to another location. The first transformation in Figure 4 copies characters from a String to a DigitList, a Java library object that maintains its own character array.
- **Bit change:** a transformation that modifies the internal representation of the data. Converting a number from characters to a binary form, for example, changes the bits. The "parse" step in the figure is an example of this.
- **Type change:** a transformation that changes the public interface to the data. The step labeled toString() takes a StringBuffer and produces a String containing the same characters. A type change reflects a change in the behavior available against the data.
- **Identity change:** a transformation that changes the owning reference to the data, without changing the actual data. The toString() transformation is an example of this. Note that identity change does not imply a copy. The Java library optimizes StringBuffer.toString() so as to share the character array between the new String and the StringBuffer, until it is modified.
- **Create:** a transformation that creates new storage for the output, rather than reusing existing storage. The first step, "extract digits", is not marked as create since it copies its data into an existing DigitList that it reuses.[6]

---

[6] A boolean classification is not always fine enough; e.g., we classify toString as a create, since it reuses part of its input. This has so far been sufficient, as long as there are some new objects.

Table 2. Common phenomena of change to physical representation. Each phenomenon either always ($\checkmark$), never ($\times$), or optionally (*) exhibits one of five fundamental properties of change.

Phenomena	Example	What changed?	
structure copy	String to StringBuffer	copy	$\checkmark$
		bit change	$\times$
		type change	*
		id change	$\checkmark$
		new object	*
rewrap	StringBuffer to String that reuses the underlying character array	copy	$\times$
		bit change	$\times$
		type change	*
		id change	$\checkmark$
		new object	$\checkmark$
conversion	bytes to characters	copy	$\checkmark$
		bit change	$\checkmark$
		type change	*
		id change	*
		new object	*
box or unbox	primitive int to Integer object	copy	$\times$
		bit change	$\times$
		type change	*
		id change	$\checkmark$
		new object	*

We can now express the phenomena in terms of these fundamental properties. For example, as shown in Table 2, what makes a transformation a conversion is that the data is copied, and the resulting bits are different from the input form. This finer classification lets us distinguish between the *essential* properties of a conversion and the variable ones (e.g. a conversion may or may not result in a new object). Furthermore, it exposes commonalities among distinct phenomena. For example, a conversion and a boxing may both result in a change in type, even though they are accomplishing completely different ends.

3.4   How a Transformation Changes the Logical Content of Its Input Data

Finally, we classify each transformation according to how it changes the logical content of the data it processes. This classification is orthogonal to how physical representation changes. For example, a transformation that converts a stock holding from a database record into a Java object changes the physical form, but the output represents the same stock holding as the input. We classify this transformation as *information preserving*, while we would classify it as a conversion at the physical level.

Similar to our classification of change in physical representation, we identify commonly occurring phenomena of logical content change, and introduce a finer

Table 3. Common phenomena of changes to logical content, expressed in terms of three fundamental properties

Phenomena	Example	What changed?	
information preserving	convert stock holding from a database record to a Java object	instance value granularity	× × ×
information exchange	get schema information given a type name	instance value granularity	✓ ✓ *
value added	add tax to a purchase total	instance value granularity	× ✓ ×
extract or combine	get or set the purchase date field of a Java stock holding object	instance value granularity	× × ✓
join or project	join stock holding and stock quote objects into a new object containing some fields of each	instance value granularity	✓ × ×

classification of fundamental properties. As in the previous section, we only consider how the transformation changes its carrier inputs, not facilitator inputs.

In Table 3 we identify common phenomena of change in logical content. For a given application, there are consistent notions of instance, value, and granularity of information that are independent of any physical representation of that information. We introduce a finer classification of logical content change based on change in these three fundamental properties.

- **Instance.** Consider the process of making a Java object to represent the database record of a stock holding. This transformation does not change the instance represented at a logical level; it is still the same stock holding, only its physical representation has changed. In contrast, a transformation that finds the current quote for a stock holding is an exchange between two essentially different pieces of information.
- **Value.** The stock holding transformation also results in no semantic change to the value of any of its constituents. It has the same stock name and a purchase date before and after, even if the two physical representations of the record are different. However, a transformation that adds shares would be a meaningful change in value, though not always in the actual bits.
- **Granularity.** Converting a stock holding from a database record to a Java data structure preserves its granularity as a record. Extracting the purchase date field from that record results in a change in granularity, from record to field.

As shown in Table 3, we can express common phenomena in terms of the above three properties. A transformation that preserves information content does not change the logical instance, value, or granularity. Other transformations may take one logical instance of information and return another (*information exchange)*, or alter just the value represented (*value add)*. Note that a given transformation may map to more than one phenomenon. For example, a transformation that formats stock holdings and quotes into HTML is both a *join* of the two sets of records, and is adding value by formatting them.

Figure 4 shows the six transformations to process a subfield of date in our Trade example. The first of the six transformations extracts the digits of the subfield (e.g. year, month, day) from a String representing the entire date. The last five of the six transformations preserve the information content. Looking at the analysis scenario in this way – as one extraction and five information preserving transformations – makes it clear what was (not) accomplished.

4   Quantifying Behavior

This section presents two classes of metrics for quantifying complexity and resource usage of framework-based applications. Both quantify behavior in terms independent of any one framework, enabling meaningful evaluation and comparison across applications.

4.1   Dataflow Topology-Based Metrics

The size and shape of the dataflow diagram for an analysis scenario are good indications of the complexity of an implementation. For example, we saw in Section 2.3 how long sequences of transformations, spread across many layers of diagram, indicate over-general implementations, impedance mismatches between frameworks, or misused APIs. We measure complexity by counting transformations, in three ways.

The *base size* metric counts transformations at a single level of diagram; *cumulative size* measures the entire hierarchy of diagrams. For example, the first top-level step of converting a date to a business object field in Figure 1 is implemented by a total of ten transformations at the next level down, and 58 transformations in total - a sign this is not a simple operation. Note that this assessment required a normalization relating the measured complexity to what was accomplished, in this case processing one field. We have found granularity of the output produced to be a useful, framework-independent unit of normalization for all of our metrics.

A *size histogram* breaks down cumulative size by level of diagram. In this example there are 8 transformations at the first level of depth, 14 at the second, and 36 at the third. This shows us that much of the activity is delegated to a distant layer.

The topology also lets us aggregate resource costs, such as number of calls or objects created, in ways that shed better light on framework-based applications than traditional ways of aggregating. A *cumulative cost* metric accumulates a resource cost for a transformation. For example, the transformation from Figure 2 that has a cumulative size of 58 transformations cost 268 calls and 70 new objects. A traditional profiling tool would aggregate costs by method, package, or path. For framework-based applications, showing costs by transformation or analysis scenario maps more closely to functions we are interested in analyzing, and allows us to make comparisons across disparate implementations.

4.2 Behavior Signatures

Topological metrics tell us how complex or costly an implementation is. To understand the nature of that complexity, we introduce a class of metrics based on behavior classification. A *behavior signature* is a complexity or cost measure, broken down according to one of our classifications. It captures how the complexity or costs of an implementation are attributed to various categories of behavior.

Table 4. A behavior signature of the analysis scenario of Figure 4, with transformations broken down by change in physical content

change in physical representation	*# transformations*
copies	5
bit changes	1
type changes	6

Table 4 summarizes the complexity of the analysis scenario of Figure 4 with a behavior signature aggregated by change in physical representation. Seeing so many type changes will lead the developer to ask whether she is using the wrong API calls, or calling a framework that was overly general for this task. Similarly, the existence of so many copies is a sign that either the developer or compiler is missing opportunities to optimize.

Table 5 shows a breakdown in terms of change in logical content, for the analysis scenario of Figure 3. It shows two behavior signatures. The second column measures complexity, by the number of transformations, and the third column measures cost, by the cumulative number of objects created (note that Figure 3 is not labeled by logical content change).

Table 5. Two behavior signatures of Figure 5, with transformations and object creations broken down by change in logical content

change in logical content	*# transformations*	*# objects created*
information preserving	6	59
information exchange	2	5
extract/combine	2	6

Note that for the latter behavior signature, while we measure objects created by all sub-transformations, in this case we chose to assign those costs based on the category label of just the top-level transformations. This allows the developer of the code at that level, who controls only how the top-level transformations affect logical content, to consider the cumulative costs incurred by his or her choices.

A *flow-induced behavior signature* is a behavior signature that aggregates according to the flow-induced transformation classification from Section 3.2. Table 6 illustrates two such signatures for Figure 5. It shows the costs incurred in the production of objects used for various purposes. They measure the number of calls and number temporary objects created aggregated by flow-induced label. The second row of the table pulls together all activity that leads to the production of converters. This includes the "build Calendar" and "get deserializer" transformations, which produced converters as their immediate output, as well as the "get schema info" transformation, which produced a carrier that was required for the production of the deserializer.

Table 6. Two flow-induced behavior signatures for Figure 5 that break down cost by the purpose of data produced

kind of flow	# method calls	# temps
flows that produce schema	10	0
flows that produce converters	76	18
carrier flows	192	52

In addition to evaluating one implementation, behavior signatures can also be used to compare two or more applications. Section 5.2 shows how this is useful for validating benchmarks. In future work, we will explore their use for identifying a baseline for evaluating a single application, and for characterizing classes of applications.

5   Further Examples

This section presents two examples that demonstrate the power of the metrics presented in Section 4.

5.1   Even Small Things Are Complex

We analyze the runtime complexity of the standard Java StringBuffer append methods. Over the years, the implementation has gone through three forms. It appears that appending a primitive value to a StringBuffer, a seemingly simple operation, is quite difficult to implement well. We use behavior signatures to understand the mistakes made in the first two implementations, and to see whether the third needs further tuning.

Table 7 presents the three implementations, for the case of appending a primitive integer. The first implementation, used up until Java 1.4.2, delegates responsibility for turning the integer to characters to the String.valueOf(int) method. It copies and converts the integer, creating a new String carrier object. The StringBuffer then delegates to its own append(String) method the job of copying the String to its private character array. The second, Java 1.4.2, implementation uses a single character array per thread to carry the characters. This eliminates the

Table 7. Behavior signatures help to compare three implementations of the standard Java library method `StringBuffer.append(int x)`. Even low-level operations such as this, which involve relatively few and insulated interactions, are difficult to get right.

	implementation *(fragments from various classes)*	*bit* *change*	*copy*	*exchange*	*carrier*
pre 1.4.2	`append(String.valueOf(x))`	1	2	0	1

1.4.2	`char[] A = threadLocal.get();`
	`Integer.getChars(x,A);`
	`append(A);`
		1	2	1	0

1.5.0	`ensureCapacity(stringSizeOfInt(x));`
	`char[] A = this.value;`
	`Integer.getChars(x,A);`
		1	1	0	0

construction of a new carrier object, but adds a lookup transformation instead (to fetch that array from thread-local storage). In the most recent, Java 1.5, implementation, StringBuffer simply asks Integer to fill in its own character array directly.

Each row of Table 7 is a behavior signature that captures the runtime complexity of an implementation. It is natural that appending should, at a minimum, require a copy. We'd also expect, since integers and characters have different representations, to see one bit-changing transformation. The behavior signature of the third implementation shows these and nothing more.

5.2   Validating a Benchmark

A benchmark should exhibit the same kinds of runtime complexity as the applications it is intended to represent. Behavior signatures can be used to validate benchmarks. We compare three web-based stock trading applications: a benchmark and two industrial applications deployed by large corporations.

Our analysis scenario follows a field from an external data source into the Java object that will be used for producing the output. Our scenario is restricted to transformations at the application level, which allows us to isolate the decisions that are under the control of the application developer from possibly inefficient implementations underneath.

Each column in Table 8 is a behavior signature that measures complexity according to phenomena of physical change. We study two types of fields, Dates and BigDecimals. Since app1 does not use BigDecimals we have omitted that column.

We quickly see that the benchmark's complexity is strikingly different from that of the real applications. For example, the Date field in app2 goes through eight transformations at the application level: conversion from a legacy COBOL data source into a String; structure copy into a StringBuffer; rewrap back to a String; conversion to a primitive integer; conversion back to a String; structure copy to a StringBuffer; rewrap back to a String; finally, conversion to a Date. For the benchmark, the Date field starts out as bytes in a SOAP response, is converted to a field in a Java object representing the server's data model, and is rewrapped into a slightly different Java object, in the client's model.

Table 8. Behavior signatures help to validate a benchmark against two applications of the kind it is intended to mimic. Each signature (a column) aggregates transformations by phenomena of physical change.

phenomena	Date field			BigDecimal field	
	app1	app2	benchmark	app2	benchmark
box/unbox	3	0	0	4	0
structure copy	0	2	0	1	0
rewrap	0	2	1	1	1
convert	1	4	1	5	1

Note that this analysis also highlights a difference between the two applications. Upon closer inspection, we found that the two applications used very different physical models for their business objects. This points out one of the challenges in designing good benchmarks for framework-based applications: to capture the great variety of reasons things can go wrong.

6   Related Work

The design patterns work provides a vocabulary of common architectural and implementation idioms [11]. Allowing developers to relate specific implementations to widely known patterns has been of immense value to how they conceptualize, communicate, and evaluate designs. While design patterns abstract the structure of an implementation, our phenomena abstract what a run accomplishes in the transformation of data. Other work introduces classification in abstract terms for component interconnections [18]. and for characterizing configuration complexity [6].

Recent work on mining jungloids [15] addresses a similar problem to ours, but at development time. They observe that, in framework-based applications, the coding process is difficult, due to the need to navigate long chains of framework calls.

There are many measures of code complexity and ways to normalize them, such as function points analysis [16], cyclomatic complexity [17], and the maintainability index [24]. Our measures are geared toward evaluating runtime behavior, especially as it relates to surfacing obstacles to good performance.

Performance understanding tools assign measurements to the artifacts of a specific application or framework [1, 2, 3, 8, 10, 14, 20, 23]. Some have identified that static classes do not capture the dynamic behavior of objects [3, 14]. Characterization approaches [9, 21], on the other hand, allow comparisons across applications, but usually in terms of low-level, highly aggregated physical measures, leaving little room for understanding what is occurring and why. By combining measurement with a framework-independent vocabulary of phenomena, we are able to provide a descriptive characterization. The work on characterizing configuration complexity [6] has similar benefits in its domain.

There is much work on using data flow diagrams, at design time, to capture the flow of information through processes at a conceptual level [7, 12]. In contrast, compilers and some tools analyze the data flow of program variables in source code [22]. In our work we use the data flow of logical content to structure runtime artifacts. This also sets us apart from existing performance tools, which typically organize activity based on control flow.

Finally, there is much work on recovering the design of complex applications [4, 19].

7 Ongoing and Future Work

We are currently exploring automating both the formation and classification of diagrams. Escape analysis and other analyses that combine static and dynamic information can aid in constructing the hierarchy of diagrams. The discovery of certain of the fundamental properties from Sections 3.3 and 3.4 can be automated. Other classifications will require annotation of frameworks by developers. Automation will enable further validation of our approach on more applications.

Our long-term goal in this work has been to develop a way to discuss and evaluate the complexities of designing framework-based applications. Toward this goal, we feel there are three main areas of exciting work.

First, we are developing additional classifications that relate runtime complexity more closely to design-time issues. One is in terms of design causes, such as late binding, eager evaluation, and generality of implementation. Another captures the complex issues of physical data modeling. We have found that some designs use the Java type system directly. Others implement entire type systems on top of Java. We are developing a classification that explains these varieties in more fundamental terms.

Second, in addition to evaluation and comparison of implementations, our approach is useful for characterizing whole classes of applications. For example, server and client applications both make heavy use of frameworks, but may be complex for different reasons. The former's excesses may lie largely in information-preserving transformations; the latter may spend more time on lookups and other information exchanges. Behavior signatures could capture this distinction. They can also capture the essential complexities in real applications, for use in designing good benchmarks, in establishing a baseline for evaluating a single implementation, or in establishing best practices. For example, the prevalence of certain phenomena indicate a need for better compiler design; others are a sign of poor API design; copying and boxing are in the realm of compilers, whereas information exchanges point to design issues, such as over-general implementations.

Third, we will investigate additional framework-independent metrics that can be derived from our model. Having a number of orthogonal classifications enables multidimensional analysis of complexity and costs. We are also exploring metrics that take into account additional context from the dataflow topology. For example, we would like to measure time spent facilitating the creation of facilitators (not an uncommon occurrence, in our experience).

8   Conclusions

That developers make such reuse of frameworks has been a boon for the development of large-scale applications. The flip side seems to be complex and poorly-performing programs. Developers can not make informed design decisions because costs are hidden from them. Moreover, framework designers can not predict the usage of their components. They must either design overly general frameworks, or ones specialized for use cases about which they can only guess. Our intent in this paper has been to introduce a way to frame discussions and analysis of this kind of complexity.

Acknowledgments

We wish to thank Tim Klinger, Harold Ossher, Barbara Ryder, Edith Schonberg, and Kavitha Srinivas for their contributions.

References

1. Alexander, W.P., Berry, R.F., Levine, F.E., Urquhart, R.J.: A unifying approach to performance analysis in the java environment. IBM Systems Journal 39(1) (2000)
2. Ammons, G., Choi, J., Gupta, M., Swamy, N.: Finding and removing performance bottlenecks in large systems. In: The European Conference on Object-Oriented Programming. (2004)
3. Arisholm, E.: Dynamic coupling measures for object-oriented software. In: Symposium on Software Metrics. (2002)
4. Bellay, B., Gall, H.: An evaluation of reverse engineering tool capabilities. Journal of Software Maintenance: Research and Practice 10 (1998)
5. Box, D., Ehnebuske, D., Kakivaya, G., Layman, A., Mendelsohn, N., Nielsen, H.F., Thatte, S., Winer, D.: Simple object access protocol (SOAP) 1.1. Technical Report 08, W3C World Wide Web Consortium (2000)
6. Brown, A.B., Keller, A., Hellerstein, J.L.: A model of configuration complexity and its application to a change management system. In: Integrated Management. (2005)
7. Coad, P., Yourdon, E.: Object-Oriented Analysis. 2 edn. Prentice-Hall, Englewood Cliffs, NJ (1991)
8. De Pauw, W., Mitchell, N., Robillard, M., Sevitsky, G., Srinivasan, H.: Drive-by analysis of running programs. In: Workshop on Software Visualization. (2001)
9. Dieckmann, S., Hlze, U.: A study of the allocation behavior of the SPECjvm98 Java benchmark. In: The European Conference on Object-Oriented Programming. (1999) 92–115
10. Dufour, B., Driesen, K., Verbrugge, L.J.H.C.: Dynamic metrics for java. In: Object-oriented Programming, Systems, Languages, and Applications. (2003) 149–168
11. Gamma, E., Helm, R., Johnson, R., Vlissides, J.: Design Patterns: Elements of Reusable Object-Oriented Software. Addison-Wesley (1994)
12. Gane, C., Sarson, T.: Structured Systems Analysis. Prentice-Hall, Englewood Cliffs, NJ (1979)
13. IBM: Trade web application benchmark.
    (http://www.ibm.com/software/webservers/appserv/wpbs_download.html)

14. Kuncak, V., Lam, P., , Rinard, M.: Role analysis. In: Symposium on Principles of Programming Languages. (2002)
15. Mandelin, D., Xiu, L., Bodik, R., Kimmelman, D.: Mining jungloids: Helping to navigate the api jungle. In: Programming Language Design and Implementation. (2005)
16. Marciniak, J.J., ed.: Encyclopedia of Software Engineering. John Wiley & Sons (2004)
17. McCabe, T.J., Watson, A.H.: Software complexity. Crosstalk, Journal of Defense Software Engineering **7**(12) (1994) 5–9
18. Mehta, N.R., Medvidovic, N., Phadke, S.: Towards a taxonomy of software connectors. In: International Conference on Software Engineering. (2000)
19. Richner, T., Ducasse, S.: Using dynamic information for the iterative recovery of collaborations and roles. In: International Conference on Software Maintenance. (2002)
20. Sevitsky, G., De Pauw, W., Konuru, R.: An information exploration tool for performance analysis of java programs. In: TOOLS Europe 2001, Zurich, Switzerland (2001)
21. Sherwood, T., Perelman, E., Hamerly, G., , Calder, B.: Automatically characterizing large scale program behavior. In: Architectural Support for Programming Languages and Operating Systems. (2002)
22. Tip, F.: A survey of program slicing techniques. Journal of Programming Languages (1995)
23. Walker, R.J., Murphy, G.C., Steinbok, J., Robillard, M.P.: Efficient mapping of software system traces to architectural views. In: CASCON. (2000) 31–40
24. Welker, K.D., Oman, P.W.: Software maintainability metrics models in practice. Crosstalk, Journal of Defense Software Engineering **8**(11) (1995) 19–23

Modular Software Upgrades for Distributed Systems

Sameer Ajmani[1], Barbara Liskov[2], and Liuba Shrira[3]

[1] Google, Inc.
[2] MIT Computer Science and Artificial Intelligence Laboratory
[3] Brandeis University Computer Science Department

Abstract. Upgrading the software of long-lived, highly-available distributed systems is difficult. It is not possible to upgrade all the nodes in a system at once, since some nodes may be unavailable and halting the system for an upgrade is unacceptable. Instead, upgrades must happen gradually, and there may be long periods of time when different nodes run different software versions and need to communicate using incompatible protocols. We present a methodology and infrastructure that make it possible to upgrade distributed systems automatically while limiting service disruption. We introduce new ways to reason about correctness in a multi-version system. We also describe a prototype implementation that supports automatic upgrades with modest overhead.

1 Introduction

Internet services face challenging and ever-changing requirements: huge quantities of data must be managed and made continuously available to rapidly growing client populations. Examples include online email services, search engines, persistent online games, scientific and financial data processing systems, content distribution networks, and file sharing networks.

The distributed systems that provide these services are large and long-lived and therefore will need changes (upgrades) to fix bugs, add features, and improve performance. Yet while a system is upgrading, it must continue to provide service to users. This paper presents a flexible and modular *upgrade system* that enables distributed systems to provide service during upgrades. We present a new methodology that makes it possible to upgrade distributed systems while minimizing disruption and without requiring all upgrades to be compatible.

Our system is designed to satisfy a number of requirements. To begin with, upgrades must be easy to define. In particular, we want *modularity*: to define an upgrade, the upgrader must understand only a few versions of the system software, e.g., the current and new versions.

In addition, we require *generality*: an upgrade should be able to change the software in arbitrary ways. This implies that the new version can be *incompatible* with the old one: it can stop supporting legacy behavior and can change communication protocols. Generality is important because otherwise a system must continue to support legacy behavior, which complicates software and makes it less robust. Our approach allows legacy behavior to be supported as needed, but in a way that avoids complicating the current version and that makes it easy to retire the legacy behavior when the time comes.

D. Thomas (Ed.): ECOOP 2006, LNCS 4067, pp. 452–476, 2006.
© Springer-Verlag Berlin Heidelberg 2006

A third point is that upgrades must be able to retain yet *transform* persistent state. Persistent state may need to be transformed in some application-dependent way, e.g., to move to a new file format; and transformations can be costly, e.g., if the local file state is large. We do not attempt to preserve volatile state (e.g., open connections) because upgrades can be scheduled (see below) to minimize inconvenience to users of losing volatile state.

A fourth requirement is *automatic deployment*. The systems of interest are too large to upgrade manually (e.g., via remote login). Instead, upgrades must be deployed automatically: the upgrader defines an upgrade at a central location, and the upgrade system propagates and installs it on each node.

A fifth requirement is *controlled deployment*. The upgrader must be able to control when nodes upgrade. Reasons for controlled deployment include: allowing a system to provide service while an upgrade is happening, e.g., by upgrading replicas in a replicated system one-at-a-time (especially when the upgrade involves a time-consuming persistent state transform); testing an upgrade on a few nodes before installing it everywhere; and scheduling an upgrade to happen at times when the load on nodes being upgraded is light.

A sixth requirement is *continuous service*. Controlled deployment implies there can be long periods of time when the system is running in *mixed mode*, i.e., when some nodes have upgraded and others have not. Nonetheless, the system must provide service, even when the upgrade is incompatible. This implies the upgrade system must provide a way for nodes running different versions to interoperate, without restricting the kinds of changes an upgrade can make.

Our system provides an upgrade infrastructure that supports these requirements. We make two main contributions. Ours is the first approach to provide a complete solution for automatic and controlled upgrades in distributed systems. It allows upgraders to define *scheduling functions* that control upgrade deployment, *transform functions* that control transforming persistent state, and *simulation objects* that enable the system to run in mixed mode. Our techniques are either entirely new, or are major extensions of what has been done before. We support all schedules used in real systems, and our support for mixed mode improves on what is done in practice and is more powerful than earlier approaches based on wrappers [12, 29, 24], which support only a very restricted set of upgrades.

Second, our approach provides a way to understand and specify mixed mode. In particular, we address the question: what should happen when a node runs several versions at once, and different clients interact with the different versions? We address this question by defining requirements for upgrades and providing a way to specify upgrades that enables reasoning about whether the requirements are satisfied. The specification captures the meaning of executions in which different clients interact with different versions of an object and identifies when calls must fail due to irreconcilable incompatibilities. The upgrade requirements and specification technique are entirely new.

We have implemented a prototype, called Upstart, that automatically deploys upgrades on distributed systems. We present results of experiments that show that our infrastructure introduces only modest overhead, and therefore our approach is practical.

We also discuss the usability of our approach in the context of several upgrades we have implemented and run.

The remainder of the paper is organized as follows. Section 2 presents an overview of our approach. Section 3 describes how to specify upgrades. Sections 4–6 discuss the three core components of our approach; Section 7 presents an example upgrade. Section 8 evaluates the overhead of our prototype, Section 9 discusses related work, and Section 10 concludes. A more detailed discussion of the approach can be found in a technical report [1].

2   Overview

This section presents an overview of our methodology and infrastructure.

We model a distributed system as a collection of objects. An object has an identity, a type that defines its behavior, and a state; it is an instance of a class that defines how it implements its type. Objects communicate by calling one another's methods (e.g., via RPC [27]); extending the model to general message-passing is future work. A portion of an object's state may be persistent. A node may fail at any point; when it node recovers, the object reinitializes itself from the persistent portion of its state.

To simplify the presentation, we assume each node runs a single top-level object that responds to remote calls. Thus, each node runs a top-level class—the class of the top-level object. Upgrades are limited to replacing top-level classes: we upgrade entire nodes at once. The top-level object may of course make use of other objects on its node to respond to requests, and an upgrade will also contain new code for these lower-level objects. We could extend this model to allow multiple top-level objects per node, in which case each could be upgraded independently.

An upgrade moves a system from one version to the next by specifying a set of *class upgrades*, one for each (top-level) class that is being replaced. The initial version

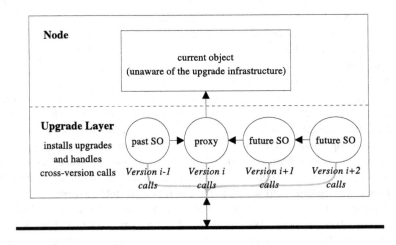

Fig. 1. The structure of a node

has version number one (1) and each subsequent version has the succeeding version number.

A class upgrade has six components: ⟨*oldClass, newClass, TF, SF, pastSO, futureSO*⟩. *OldClass* identifies the class that is now obsolete; *newClass* identifies the class that is to replace it. *TF* identifies a *transform function* that generates an initial persistent state for the new object from the persistent state of the old one. *SF* identifies a *scheduling function* that tells a node when it should upgrade. *PastSO* and *futureSO* identify classes for *simulation objects* that enable nodes to interoperate across versions. A *futureSO* object allows a node to support the new class's behavior before it upgrades; a *pastSO* object allows a node to support the old class's behavior after it upgrades. These components can be omitted when not needed.

The effect of an upgrade is (ultimately) to cause every node running an object of an old class to instead run an object of the new one. We could add *filters* to the model that would determine some subset of nodes that need to upgrade. Adding filters is enough to allow restructuring a system in arbitrary ways. Of course it is also possible (without using upgrades) to add new nodes to a system and to initialize them to run either existing classes or entirely new ones.

2.1   How an Upgrade Happens

Our system consists of an upgrade server, an upgrade database, and upgrades layers at the nodes. The *upgrade server* provides a central repository of information about upgrades, and the *upgrade database (UDB)* provides a central store for information about the upgrade status of nodes. Each node runs an *upgrade layer (UL)* that installs upgrades and handles cross-version calls; the UL also maintains a local database in which it stores information about the upgrade status of nodes with which this node has communicated recently.

The structure of a node is shown in Figure 1. The node's *current version* identifies the most recently installed upgrade (or the initial version); the node's *current object* is an instance of its *current class*, which is the new class of this upgrade. The node may also be running a number of simulation objects: *future SOs* to simulate versions not yet installed at the node, and *past SOs* to simulate versions that are older than the current version.

Past and future SOs are typically implemented using *delegation*: they call methods of the object for the next or previous version, which may be the current object or another SO. These calls all move toward the current object, as shown in Figure 1.

A node's UL labels outgoing calls with the version number of the caller: calls made by the current object are labeled with the node's current version number, and calls made by an SO are labeled with the SO's version number. The UL dispatches incoming calls by looking at their version number and sending them to the local object that handles that version number.

Nodes learn about upgrades because they receive a call from a node running a later version, through periodic communication with the upgrade server, or via gossip: nodes gossip with one another periodically about the newest version and their own status, e.g., their current version number and class.

When the UL learns of a newer version, it communicates with the upgrade server to download a small upgrade description. Then it checks whether the upgrade affects it, i.e., whether the upgrade contains an old class that is running at the node. (A node might be several versions behind, but it can process the upgrades one-by-one.) If the node is affected, the UL fetches the class upgrade components that concern it; drains any currently-executing RPCs; then starts a future SO if necessary, e.g., if the new type is a subtype of the old one, or if the upgrade is incompatible.

Next, the upgrade layer invokes the class upgrade's scheduling function, which runs in parallel with the node's other processing. The scheduling function notifies the UL when it is time to upgrade.

To upgrade, the UL restarts the node and runs the transform function to convert the node's persistent state to the representation required by the new class. After this, the UL does "normal" node recovery, during which it creates the current object and the SOs. Because SOs delegate toward the current object, the UL must create them in an order that allows this. First, it creates the current object, which recovers from the newly-transformed persistent state. Then it creates any past and future SOs as needed, in order of their distance from the current object.

Finally, the upgrade layer notifies the upgrade database that its node is running the new version.

When all nodes have moved to a new version, the previous version can be retired (or this could happen on command). Information about retirement arrives in messages from the upgrade server. In response, a UL discards past SOs for retired versions. This can be done lazily, since keeping past SOs around does not affect the behavior or performance of later versions.

3   Specifying Simulation

A key contribution of our approach is that we allow simulation so that nodes running different versions can nevertheless interact. But for simulation to make sense, we need to explain what it means.

Simulation enables a node to support multiple types. It implements its *current type* using its current object; it simulates old types (of classes that it upgraded from in the past) using past SOs and new types (of classes that it will upgrade to in the future) using future SOs. Some clients interact with the node via the current type, while others interact via an older or newer type. Yet all the objects implementing these types share a single identity and thus each call needs to affect and be affected by the others. It's straightforward to define these interactions when the old and new class implement the same type, or one is a subtype of the other [19], because in these cases the types already have a relationship that defines the meaning of the upgrade. Things get interesting, however, when there is an *incompatible upgrade*: when the two types are unrelated by subtyping.

This section explains what it means to simulate correctly. We capture the effects of simulation for a particular class upgrade by defining a specification for the upgrade; the specification guides the design of the simulation objects and transform function.

Correct simulation must support reasoning about client programs, not only when they call nodes that are running their own version, but also when they call nodes that are running newer or older versions, when they interact with other clients that are using the same node via a different version, and when the client itself upgrades and then continues using a node it was using before it upgraded. Furthermore upgrades of servers should be *transparent* to clients: clients should not notice when a node upgrades and changes its current type (except that more or fewer calls may fail as discussed below). Essentially, we want nodes to provide service that makes sense to clients, and we want this service to make sense across upgrades of nodes and clients.

We begin by defining some requirements that an upgrade must satisfy. Clearly, we require:

Type Requirement. The class for each version must implement its type.

In particular, the class implementing a future SO must implement the new type, and a class implementing the past SO must implement the old one. This requirement ensures that a client's call behaves as expected by that client.

However, we also need to define the effects of *interleaving*. Interleaving occurs when different clients running different versions interact with the same node, e.g.,

$O_1.m(args)$; $O_1.m(args)$; [version 2 introduced at server];
$O_1.m(args)$; $O_2.p(args)$; [server upgrades from 1 to 2];
$O_1.m(args)$; $O_2.p(args)$; [version 1 retired];
$O_2.p(args)$; $O_2.p(args)$;

where O_N is the object with which version N clients interact. Between the introduction of version 2 and the retirement of version 1, there can be an arbitrary sequence of calls to O_1 and O_2. If the server is supporting more than two types, calls to objects of all supported types can be interleaved. Although these calls can be running concurrently, we assume they occur one-at-a-time in some serial order; we discuss concurrency in Section 4.1.

To define what happens with interleaving we require:

Sequence Requirement. Each event in the computation at a node must reflect the effects of all earlier events in the computation in the order they occurred.

An event is a call, an upgrade, or the introduction of a version.

This requirement means method calls to a current object or SO must reflect the effects of calls made to the others. If the method is an observer, its return value must reflect all earlier modifications made via other objects; if it is a mutator, its effects must reflect all earlier modifications made via other objects, and must be visible to later calls made via other objects.

When the node upgrades and its current type changes, observations made via any of the objects after the upgrade must reflect the effects of all modifications made via any object before the upgrade. For example, if a node is running several versions of a file system, modifications to a file using one of the versions must be visible to clients using the others and must continue to be visible after the node upgrades.

Together, the type and sequence requirements can be overconstraining: it may not be possible to satisfy both of them for all possible computations. When this happens, we resolve the problem by *disallowing* calls. The system causes disallowed calls to fail (i.e., to throw a failure exception). In essence, we meet the requirements above by ruling out calls that would otherwise cause problems. However, we require:

Disallow Constraint. Calls to the current object must not be disallowed.

In other words, we can only disallow calls to past and future SOs. The rationale is that the current object provides the "real behavior" of the node, so it should not be affected by the node's support for other versions. Another point is that the code that implements the current object need not be concerned with whether there are simulation objects also running at its node, and therefore we simplify the implementation that really matters.

Disallowing takes advantage of the fact that any RPC can fail, e.g., because of network problems, so that clients won't be surprised by such a failure.

3.1 Specifying Upgrades

Now we describe how to specify an upgrade involving two types that are unrelated by subtyping, T_{new} and T_{old}. An upgrade specification has three parts, an invariant, a mapping function, and shadow methods.

The *invariant*, $I(O_{old}, O_{new})$, relates the old and new objects throughout the computation: assuming $I(O_{old}, O_{new})$ holds when a method call on one of the objects starts, $I(O_{old}, O_{new})$ also holds when the method returns. The invariant must be *total*: for each legal state O_{new} of T_{new}, there exists some legal state O_{old} of T_{old} such that $I(O_{old}, O_{new})$ holds, and vice versa.

The invariant is likely to be obvious to the upgrader. For example, if O_{old} and O_{new} are file systems, an obvious invariant is that the new and old file systems contain the same files (although some file properties may differ). However, weaker invariants can lead to fewer disallowed methods (as discussed in Section 3.2).

The *mapping function (MF)* defines an initial state for O_{new} given the state of O_{old} when T_{new} is introduced at the node. For example, the MF from the old file system to the new one would state that the new file system contains all the old files; it would also define initial values for any new file properties. The MF must be total and must *establish the invariant*: $I(O_{old}, MF(O_{old}))$ must hold.

I tells us something about what we expect from method calls. In particular, it constrains the behavior of mutators. For example, it wouldn't be correct to add a file to O_{new} but not to O_{old}. But *I* doesn't tell us exactly what effect a mutator on O_{new} should have on O_{old}, or vice versa. This information is given by *shadow methods*.

For each mutator $T_{old}.m$, we specify a related method, $T_{new}.\$m$. The specification of $T_{new}.\$m$ explains the effect on O_{new} of running $T_{old}.m$. Similarly, for each mutator $T_{new}.p$, we specify a related method, $T_{old}.\$p$, that explains the effect on O_{old} of running $T_{new}.p$.

A shadow method must be able to run whenever the corresponding real method can run. This means the precondition for a shadow method must hold whenever the precondition for the corresponding real method holds:

$$pre_m(O_{old}) \wedge I(O_{old}, O_{new}) \Rightarrow pre_{\$m}(O_{new})$$
$$pre_p(O_{new}) \wedge I(O_{old}, O_{new}) \Rightarrow pre_{\$p}(O_{old})$$

Also, shadow methods must *preserve the invariant*:

$$I(O_{old}, O_{new}) \Rightarrow I(O_{old}.m(args), O_{new}.\$m(args))$$
$$I(O_{old}, O_{new}) \Rightarrow I(O_{old}.\$p(args), O_{new}.p(args))$$

Given these constraints, we can prove that the invariant holds throughout the computation of a node that implements the old and new types simultaneously. The proof is by induction: the mapping function establishes the base case (when the new type is introduced), and shadow methods give us the inductive step (on each mutation).

As an example, consider a upgrade that replaces a set of colored integers with a set of flavored integers. This example is analogous to an upgrade that changes a property of files in a file system.

We begin by choosing an invariant I that we want to hold for each ColorSet (O_{old}) and FlavorSet (O_{new}). We could require that the two sets contain the same integers:

$$\{ x \mid \langle x, c \rangle \in O_{old} \} = \{ x \mid \langle x, f \rangle \in O_{new} \} \tag{1}$$

A stronger invariant maps colors to flavors:

$$\langle x, \text{blue} \rangle \in O_{old} \Leftrightarrow \langle x, \text{grape} \rangle \in O_{new},$$
$$\langle x, \text{red} \rangle \in O_{old} \Leftrightarrow \langle x, \text{cherry} \rangle \in O_{new},$$
$$\ldots \tag{2}$$

Whereas (1) treats colors and flavors as independent properties, (2) says these properties are related. A weaker invariant allows O_{new} to contain more elements than O_{old}:

$$\{ x \mid \langle x, c \rangle \in O_{old} \} \subseteq \{ x \mid \langle x, f \rangle \in O_{new} \} \tag{3}$$

The next step is to define a mapping function. For invariant (1), we might have:

$$O_{new} = MF(O_{old}) = \{ \langle x, \text{grape} \rangle \mid x \in O_{old} \} \tag{4}$$

As required, this MF establishes I.

Here are possible definitions of the shadow methods, assuming that both types have an insert method that adds an element with a specified color or flavor, and a delete method.

void ColorSet.$insertFlavor(x, f)
  effects: $\neg \exists \langle x, c \rangle \in this_{pre} \Rightarrow this_{post} = this_{pre} \cup \{\langle x, \text{blue}\rangle\}$
void ColorSet.$delete(x)
  effects: $this_{post} = this_{pre} - \{\langle x, c \rangle\}$

void FlavorSet.$insertColor(x, c)
  effects: $\neg \exists \langle x, f \rangle \in this_{pre} \Rightarrow this_{post} = this_{pre} \cup \{\langle x, \text{grape}\rangle\}$
void FlavorSet.$delete(x)
  effects: $this_{post} = this_{pre} - \{\langle x, f \rangle\}$

These definitions satisfy invariant (1). They do not work for invariant (2) since in that case the shadows must preserve the color-flavor mapping. Our original mapping function and shadow methods would work for invariant (3), but we could use weaker definitions, e.g., define FlavorSet.$delete to have no effect.

3.2 Disallowed Calls

There was no need to disallow any methods in the example above. But sometimes disallowing is needed.

When we specify an upgrade we implicitly define a "compound type," $T_{old\&new}$. This type has the methods of both T_{old} and T_{new}. Its objects contain the old state and the new state and they satisfy the invariant I.

The specification of a mutator is a combination of its original specification and its shadow specification provided in the upgrade; the former defines its effect on its own type, and the latter defines its effect on the other type in the upgrade. E.g., the specification of insertFlavor states its effect on the FlavorSet (its original specification) and on the ColorSet (as defined by the specification of ColorSet.$insertFlavor).

If $T_{old\&new}$ is a subtype of both the old and new types, the simulation is working properly, since users will always see the behavior they expect. In the case of the upgrade from FlavorSet to ColorSet, this subtype property holds. But sometimes it doesn't, and in this case we solve the problem by disallowing. We might disallow all calls to a method, or only some calls, based on the parameters of the call or the current state of the object.

For example, consider an upgrade that replaces GrowSet with IntSet; a GrowSet is like an IntSet except that it never shrinks because it has no delete method. The shadow of delete on a GrowSet object must remove the deleted object, assuming the invariant that the two objects have the same elements. Since GrowSet objects never shrink, we must disallow the delete method in the future SO for IntSet. However, once the node upgrades, we can no longer disallow this method since the current object is now an IntSet. Therefore the state of the past SO for GrowSet can shrink. Since this does not match the specification of GrowSet, we must disallow any GrowSet methods that would expose the problem. Thus we would need to disallow GrowSet.isIn.

Thus disallowing is done differently for the future SO and the past SO: for the future SO we only disallow methods of the new type, while in the past SO, we only disallow old type methods. These restrictions on disallowing follow from our disallow constraint: they ensure that all methods of the current object are allowed.

To disallow for the future SO, we proceed as follows. First we disallow all mutators of the new type whose shadow definitions for the old type would cause violations of the specification of the old type; this disallowing will ensure that $T_{old\&new}$ is a subtype of the old type. In addition, if the new shadows of any old type methods violate the specification of the new type, we disallow new methods that expose these violations; this ensures that users of the future SO won't notice that something strange is going on.

The situation for the old type is similar. We disallow any old methods whose shadows would cause violations of the specification of the new type; this way we will obtain a subtype of the new type. Also, if any shadows of the new type methods violate the specification of the old type, we disallow old methods that expose these violations to ensure that users won't see the odd behavior.

This notion of "exposing violations" has a different meaning for past and future SOs, because a future SO will eventually become the current object and at that point all its methods will be allowed. These calls represent another way of noticing a violation, and must be taken into account when disallowing. For example, consider the reverse upgrade (from IntSet to GrowSet). The future SO in this case must disallow both isIn and insert. It must disallow insert because once the GrowSet becomes the current object, calls of isIn will be allowed, and at that point the absence of an object that had previously been inserted into the GrowSet object would be noticed!

Weakening the invariant can reduce the need to disallow. For example, if we allowed the GrowSet object to contain a superset of the elements of the IntSet object, we would not need to disallow any methods in either the past or future SO.

In general, the upgrader should choose the weakest invariant that makes sense for the two types in the upgrade, in order to disallow as little as possible. Disallowing is unlikely to be what users want; therefore the upgrader may choose to avoid it by using an accelerated schedule for the upgrade (see Section 6).

3.3   Multiple Upgrades

The previous sections have discussed what is needed to specify and upgrade in isolation, assuming that no other upgrade is "active." In other words we considered a system that was everywhere running a particular version, and defined an upgrade to move it to the next version. Now we consider a more general case, in which more than one upgrade may be in progress.

If some upgrades are in progress when a new one is defined, and if some of those earlier upgrades are incompatible, we are in a situation where the previous upgrade is actually defining not T_{new} but in fact $T_{old\&new}$. Therefore, we need to extend our specification approach so that we define the intended behavior of these extra methods— the ones in $T_{old\&new}$ of the previous upgrade that aren't also in T_{new} of the previous upgrade. The extra methods are precisely the shadows of the mutators of the old type. (We do not need to consider the shadow definitions for the mutators of the new type because those details are handled by the previous implementation.)

Thus we need to provide shadows for these shadows. In addition, we need to use $T_{old\&new}$ from the previous upgrade when deciding what methods to disallow for the past and future SOs of the current upgrade.

As an example, suppose we define a second upgrade to follow the upgrade from ColorSet to FlavorSet. This second upgrade defines a CommentSet in which each element of the set has both a flavor and an associated comment. This upgrade is compatible since CommentSet is a subtype of FlavorSet.

However to define the upgrade we need to provide an explanation of the effect of a call on ColorSet.insertColor on the CommentSet. This is done by considering FlavorSet.$insertColor; the specification of this shadow explains the effect of running the insertColor on the FlavorSet. We provide a shadow for this method, CommentSet.$$insertColor, which explains the additional effect on the CommentSet. In this example, it isn't necessary to disallow any new methods because we have the subtype property.

One point about writing these specifications is that a kind of "transitive" disallowing is possible. Suppose the specification for the old upgrade disallows a method of the new type. Then when we shadow this method, there are two cases: either it is disallowed (because its upgrade hasn't yet been installed) or not. However, when the old method is disallowed, this necessarily implies that the new one is too. Therefore we require that the shadow specification only explain what happens when the method being shadowed is allowed.

The key question about specifying upgrades when many upgrades are in progress is modularity: how much does an upgrader need to know to specify an upgrade? Clearly the upgrader must know the old and new types of the current upgrade *plus* the specification of the earlier upgrade. However, this earlier upgrade has both an old and new type, and it's possible that in order to understand its specification it is necessary to understand both of them. Fortunately, this appears to not be necessary most of the time because the shadows of T_{old} methods are usually specified in terms of the T_{new} state; in this case the definer of the next upgrade need not understand T_{old}. The CommentSet example is like this, and so are all the real examples we looked at; the only ones that aren't are pathological examples we invented.[1]

If a pathological example were to arise, it may be possible to avoid the problem by changing the invariant. Otherwise it may be necessary to go arbitrarily far back in the chain of "active" upgrades (ones whose old type has not yet been retired). To avoid this, the upgrader might decide to use an eager schedule for the upgrade to limit the time during which defining future upgrades requires understanding of the old type.

4   Implementing Simulation

This section presents ways to use simulation objects to implement multiple types. The approaches differ in how calls are dispatched to objects (i.e., which objects implement which types) and how simulation objects can interact with one another. The first "direct" approach is simple and is similar to what others have proposed [12, 29, 24]. However it lacks expressive power, and therefore we instead use a much more powerful "interceptor" approach.

4.1   Direct Approach

In the *direct approach*, calls for each version are dispatched *directly* to the object that implements the type for that version. Each SO implements just its own type and can delegate calls to the next object closer to the current object: the next older object for future SOs, the next newer object for past SOs. When an upgrade is installed, a past SO for the old type is created if necessary (i.e., if the new type isn't a subtype of the old type). Figure 2 depicts how SOs are managed in the direct approach.

---

[1] An example that causes problems is the following. The old upgrade replaces ColorSet with FlavorSet, but the invariant specifies some function f that maps colors to flavors, where several colors map to the same flavor. Furthermore the specification of ColorSet.setColor states that the color of an item in the set can be changed only when its current color is blue. To define the shadow FlavorSet.$setColor, we need to consult the state of the ColorSet object to determine the current color of the item, since only then will we know what its flavor will be:

void FlavorSet.$setColor(x, c)
effects: $\langle x, blue \rangle \in prev.this_{pre} \Rightarrow this_{post} = this_{pre} - \{\langle x, * \rangle\} \cup \{\langle x, f(c) \rangle\}$

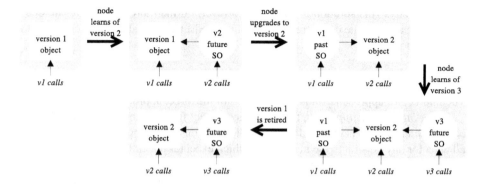

Fig. 2. The direct approach, presented as a sequence of states of a node. Large arrows are state transitions. In each state, the box is the current object, and the circles are SOs. Objects may delegate calls as indicated by the small arrows. Each object handles calls only for its own version.

The direct approach is simple but has limited expressive power. The most serious problem is that there is no way for an SO to be informed about calls that go directly to its delegate, and as a result it can do the wrong thing. For example, consider an SO that implements ColorSet by delegating to an object that implements IntSet. The delegate stores the state of the set (the integers in the set), and the SO stores the associated colors, which it updates when it runs its own methods. However, consider the following sequence of calls (here O refers to the SO's delegate): SO.insertColor(1, red); O.delete(1); O.insert(1); SO.getColor(1). The result of the final call will be "red," because the SO cannot know that 1 was ever removed; but because 1 was removed and re-inserted, its color should be the default color, e.g., "blue", as specified for the shadow of IntSet.insert(x).

Since we cannot prevent the SO state from being stale, our only recourse is to disallow SO methods (we cannot disallow O.delete because of the disallow constraint). It may seem that we must disallow SO.getColor, since it is the method that revealed the problem in our example, but in fact we must disallow SO.insertColor because otherwise we'll be able to observe the problem when the upgrade is installed (since at that point calls to the getColor will be allowed). And disallowing SO.insertColor is sufficient; we needn't disallow SO.getColor in addition (because every integer is blue).

A second problem is that the direct approach provides no way for the different versions to synchronize. Since calls go directly to the different versions, SOs have no way to control how calls are applied to their delegates. For example, suppose the current object implements a queue with methods enq and deq, and the future SO implements a queue with an additional method, deq2, that dequeues two consecutive items. With the direct model, how can the future SO ensure that two adjacent items are dequeued, since a client could call deq directly on the delegate while the SO is carrying out deq2?

It does not work for the upgrade layer to force methods to execute one-at-a-time, as this may cause the distributed system to deadlock. Instead, the delegate might provide some form of application-level concurrency control, such as a lockdeq method that locks the queue on behalf of the caller for any number of deq calls, but allows enq calls from other clients to proceed. The delegator can use lockdeq to implement deq2 correctly. This solution is complex, however. Furthermore, if the delegate does not provide appropriate concurrency control methods, the upgrader's only choice is to disallow deq2.

4.2   Interceptor Approach

The interceptor approach avoids the problems of the direct approach.

In the *interceptor approach*, the simulation object for the latest version handles all calls (it *intercepts* calls intended for the earlier versions). The upgrade layer dispatches all calls for any version to the newest SO, which executes the calls by delegating to the preceding object, which may be the current object or another SO.

If the current upgrade is compatible, then when the upgrade occurs, the node replaces its current object and the future SO with an instance of the new class, which becomes the current object of the node. The current object continues to handle all calls intended for its predecessor. There is no need for a past SO, because calls made by clients running at the old version are handled by the current object.

However, when the current upgrade is incompatible, the current object isn't sufficient since we want it to implement only the new behavior, and therefore it isn't prepared to handle calls for the old type of its upgrade. Therefore in this case, the upgrade replaces the future SO and current object with an instance of the new class *and* past SO. Furthermore all incoming calls are dispatched to the past SO, which simulates the old type's behavior and delegates to the current object. Figure 3 illustrates this approach.

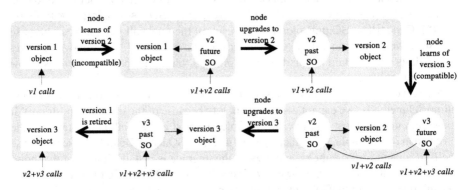

Fig. 3. The interceptor approach, presented as a sequence of states of a node. Large arrows are state transitions. In each state, the box is the current object, and the circles are SOs. Objects may delegate calls as indicated by the small arrows. One object in each state intercepts all calls.

If another upgrade is introduced, it receives a future SO, which must be prepared to handle the methods of the new type, the old type, *and* the old type of the previous upgrade. The future SO handles these methods by delegating to the past SO of the previous upgrade; because of this delegation, handling these extra calls isn't a burden.

This situation continues until the old type of the incompatible upgrade is retired. At this point the past SO can be removed and calls that used to be delegated to it will go directly to the current object. The calls won't be to methods of the old incompatible type, since that type is no longer in use.

The interceptor model works well as long as there is only one active incompatible upgrade. However, this model has only one past SO object in existence at any time, and this object must handle all the legacy behavior. It can do this by using the previous past SO as a subobject, which can delegate to the current object *if* the upgrade that just happened is compatible. Otherwise the new past SO will have to do more of the work of simulating past behavior.

Therefore a good upgrade strategy is to always retire an incompatible upgrade before introducing the next incompatible upgrade. We believe this is a reasonable approach since incompatible upgrades are introduced relatively infrequently.

4.3   Implementing SOs in the Interceptor Approach

Now we consider what is needed to implement SOs.

Obviously the implementation needs to satisfy the specification: the future SO needs to implement $T_{old\&new}$ of its upgrade with disallowing of T_{new} methods, while the past SO needs to implement $T_{old\&new}$ with disallowing of T_{old} methods.

These implementations must cause modifications of the state of the SO itself, but they must also do the right thing on other versions. For example, when the future SO handles a call on a mutator, it must also mutate its predecessor in the version chain. In our approach this is always done via delegation: an SO will call one or more methods on its predecessor (or successor if it is a past SO).

One interesting point is that the delegation may fail because that call is disallowed. When this happens, the call to the delegating object must also be disallowed. However, what happens due to disallowing can change during the lifetime of a future SO. Initially a call to the predecessor might be disallowed because it is a call to a method of the new type of the earlier upgrade, and upgrade hasn't happened yet. However, once that upgrade has happened, the call will be allowed, and therefore the call on the future SO should also be allowed. Thus the implementations in the future SO will typically be written to disallow if any disallowed calls are encountered, and to allow otherwise.

Each call that arrives from a client must be executed *atomically* at each object in the chain, and if some delegated call fails (whether because it is disallowed, or for some other reason), the states of all objects must be left unchanged (i.e., the call aborts). This can sometimes be tricky to ensure. For example, suppose that to carry out a call on method m of the future SO, two calls, to $p1$ and $p2$, are made to the predecessor object, where $p1$ is a mutator. The implementation in the future SO must be done in such a way that if the call to $p2$ is disallowed, the state of the predecessor doesn't change. This can be accomplished by checking in advance whether the call to $p2$ will succeed, assuming such a method exists. The method will exist if the old type of the upgrade is "complete" [16]; if not, it may sometimes be necessary to add extra observers to the predecessor to permit more access to its state. For example, if $p1$ is *insert(x)* and $p2$ is *remove(y)*, it may be necessary to check *isIn(y)* before calling $p1$ then $p2$.

A future SO comes into existence when the infrastructure at its node first learns about the upgrade. The node drains its currently-executing RPCs [26], and then creates the SO by running a default constructor. This code has no access to any arguments, nor can it access the object implementing the old version. Therefore it is unlikely to be able to fully implement the mapping function; instead it must leave the object in a partially-initialized state, and methods that are called after this point complete the initialization (e.g., by making calls on the delegate). This limitation on how an SO initializes is intentional so that SO installation can be a lightweight (and fast) operation.

5   Transform Functions

A transform function (TF) reorganizes a node's persistent state from the representation required by the old instance and future SO to that required by the new instance and past SO. It must implement the *identity mapping*: the post-TF abstract state of the past SO is the same as the pre-TF state of the old object, and the post-TF abstract state of the new object is the same as the pre-TF state of the future SO. Thus, clients do not notice that the node has upgraded, except that clients of the new type may see improved performance and fewer rejected calls, and clients of the old type may see decreased performance and more rejected calls.

A TF must be *restartable*, because the node might fail while the TF is running. If this happens, the upgrade infrastructure simply re-runs the TF, which must recover appropriately.

A TF may not call methods on other nodes, because we can make no guarantees about when one node upgrades relative to another, so other nodes may not be able to handle the calls a TF might make. This restriction does not limit expressive power; if a node needs to recover state from another node (e.g., in a replicated system), it can transfer this state *after* it has completed the upgrade. This restriction helps avoid deadlocks that may occur if nodes upgrading simultaneously attempt to obtain state from each other. It also makes TFs simpler to implement and reason about.

6   Scheduling Functions

Scheduling functions (SFs) allow an upgrader to control upgrade progress. SFs run on the nodes themselves, so they can consider the node's state in deciding when to upgrade. But often what's more important for SFs is the state of the system; in particular, the upgrade state of other nodes. Therefore we provide SFs with additional information: a central upgrade database (UDB) that records the upgrade status of every node and can contain user-defined tables (e.g., that authorize the upgrades of subsets of nodes), and per-node local databases (LDBs) that record information about the status of other nodes with which a node communicates regularly. Each class upgrade has its own scheduling function, which allows the upgrader to consider additional factors, such as the urgency of the class upgrade and how well the SOs for that class upgrade work.

When defining an SF, the first priority is to ensure that all nodes eventually upgrade. We guarantee this trivially by requiring that the upgrader specify a timeout for each SF.

The second priority is to minimize service disruption during the upgrade. How this is accomplished depends on how the system is designed. For example, Brewer [7] describes several upgrade schedules used in industry; each of these can be implemented easily as scheduling functions:

- A *rolling upgrade* causes a few nodes to upgrade at a time; this makes sense for replicated systems and can be implemented by an SF that queries its local database to decide when its node should upgrade, e.g., by waiting its turn in a sequence.
- A *big flip* causes half the nodes in a system to upgrade at once; this makes sense for systems that need to upgrade quickly and can be implemented by an SF that flips a coin to decide whether its node should be in the first or second upgrade group.
- A *fast reboot* causes all nodes to upgrade at once; this make sense when cross-version simulation is poor and can be implemented by an SF that causes its node to upgrade at a particular wall-clock time. Alternatively, this SF could wait for an explicit signal written to the UDB or sent via RPC.

The implementations of these SFs are each just a few lines of script.

A variety of other schedules are possible, e.g., "wait until the node's servers upgrade," "wait until all nodes of class C upgrade," "wait until the node is lightly loaded," and "avoid creating blind spots in the sensor network." Some of these schedules require centralized knowledge, which is provided via the UDB; others require local knowledge, which is provided via the node's state and LDB. Our goal is to provide sufficient flexibility so that upgraders can build a library of SFs according to the needs of their system; once this is done, an upgrader simply selects an SF for each class upgrade from the library.

Upgrade schedules can help the upgrader avoid implementing difficult SO features. For example, it may be impractical to simulate a certain method of a new server type. We can avoid the need to simulate this method by scheduling the upgrade such that servers upgrade to the new type before any clients upgrade; thus, the difficult-to-simulate method will not be called until the servers have upgraded.

An upgrader may want to test an upgrade on a few nodes and, if those upgrades fail, roll them back and abort the remaining upgrades. This policy is implementable with SFs (by recording upgrade failure in the UDB), though we do not discuss the details of how to rollback the failed upgrades here.

7   Example

In developing our methodology we looked at many examples, focusing on incompatible upgrades and real distributed systems including Thor [18], NFS [8], and DHash [9]. Some of the upgrades were ones that had actually happened, while others were invented. Our goal was to come up with challenging examples so that we could make sure our approach had sufficient expressive power, and so that we could understand the challenges in specifying upgrades and implementing SOs.

In this section we present a brief example of an incompatible upgrade to illustrate our approach. The example is a challenging one because the old and new types are quite different and there are several ways to resolve the differences. The upgrade replaces a file system that uses Unix-style permissions with one that uses per-file access control lists (ACLs) [15]. We assume the file system is distributed: the files are stored at many servers. The upgrade contains two class upgrades: one for clients (to switch to using ACLs) and one for servers (to switch to providing ACLs).

We assume there is no particular order in which nodes upgrade; thus clients might be ahead of servers and vice versa. A possible schedule might have a client SF that waits until the client is idle, while the server SF upgrades servers round-robin over some extended time period.

Each file in the old system has read, write, and execute bits for its owner, its group, and everyone else (the "world"). Thus, the old state (O_{old}) is a set of tuples:

⟨*filename, content, owner, or, ow, ox, group, gr, gw, gx, wr, ww, wx*⟩

Only the owner of a file can modify the file's permissions, group, or owner. The new state (O_{new}) is a set of

⟨*filename, content, acl*⟩

tuples, where *acl* is a sequence of zero or more ⟨*principal, r, w, x, a*⟩ tuples. Principals with the *a* permission are allowed to modify the ACL.

There are many invariants one could imagine for this example. Our invariant $I(O_{old},$ $O_{new})$ is very weak:

⟨*filename, content, owner, or, ow, ox, group, gr, gw, gx, wr, ww, wx*⟩ $\in O_{old}$
$\Leftrightarrow$ (⟨*filename, content, acl*⟩ $\in O_{new}$
    $\wedge$ (⟨*owner, or, ow, ox, "true"*⟩ $\in acl \vee$ (*owner* = "nobody" $\wedge \neg or \wedge \neg ow \wedge \neg ox$))
    $\wedge$ (⟨*group, gr, gw, gx, "false"*⟩ $\in acl \vee$ (*group* = "nobody" $\wedge \neg gr \wedge \neg gw \wedge \neg gx$))
    $\wedge$ (⟨*"system:world", wr, ww, wx, "false"*⟩ $\in acl \vee$ ($\neg wr \wedge \neg ww \wedge \neg wx$))

This invariant says that each file in O_{old} is in O_{new} with the same contents, and either the owner of the file in O_{old} appears in the ACL in O_{new} with the same permissions plus the ACL-modify permission, or the owner is the special user "nobody" and the owner permissions are all false, and similarly for the group and world permissions (except these have no ACL-modify permission). We need to include the "nobody" case so that I is total, i.e., so there is a defined state of O_{old} for each state of O_{new}, and vice versa (in particular, consider the case when the ACL is empty). Clearly other invariants are possible, e.g., to select a particular owner among several in the ACL to be the owner in the permissions.

The mapping function for this upgrade states that each file in O_{new} has the same contents as in O_{old} and an ACL containing the owner, group, and world permissions from O_{old}. The initial ACL grants ACL-modify permissions only to the owner.

The shadow methods must preserve I. When a client modifies a file in O_{old}, that file is also modified in O_{new}, and vice versa. Furthermore, the file system must only allow file operations that are consistent with the file's permissions (in the old system) or ACL (in the new system). But consistency is a problem, since ACLs are more expressive than permissions.

Let's consider the case of the future SO first. If the future SO allows modifications of ACLs, clients of the permissions system may see modifications made by clients of the new system that do not appear to have the correct permissions. For example, if an owner in the ACL system adds as a second owner a user of the permissions system, and later removes that user as an owner, a client using the permissions system and running as that user might notice odd behavior.

To prevent this, we might disallow such operations in the future SO. However, we cannot disallow modifications of ACLs once the server has upgraded, which means that we must figure out what to do for users of the permissions systems when such changes happen. A possible solution is to make it impossible for users of the permissions system to notice odd behavior by not allowing them to do anything at all. But this doesn't seem like a good idea: clearly we don't want to prevent users of the permissions system access to files. A second possibility is to disallow only cases where observation of odd behavior is possible. For example, we might disallow access only for files where there is more than one owner. This second solution is less draconian than the first but still seems undesirable.

In general when defining an upgrade it may not be possible to allow all behavior, and furthermore, almost always disallowing isn't desirable. In this particular example, however, we have an out because file systems don't guarantee that owners are in complete control, since the superuser can change anything: the specification of a file system does not rule out the kinds of odd behavior discussed above. Therefore we can in fact allow all methods in both the past and future SO.

Now let's consider how to implement the past and future SOs. Implementing the past SO is easy: it just needs to present the permissions corresponding to the ACLs in O_{new} and map any permissions modifications to the appropriate ACL modifications.

The implementation of the future SO is trickier. If it allows ACL mutations without restrictions it must keep track of all the entries in each ACL, not just the ones that map to permissions in O_{old} (O_{new} may be more permissive than O_{old} because of these extra ACL entries). Furthermore, it would need to run with superuser privileges in order to support the behavior in the ACL, which may be undesirable. Therefore the upgrader might choose to disallow the creation of ACLs via the future SO that have entries with no corresponding permissions in O_{old}.

The effort to implement the SOs is modest. SOs need to provide the extra behavior needed at that version, e.g., to store the extra information in the ACL for the future SO; the rest of the work is delegated. Furthermore, what is happening in the SO is similar to what will happen in the version it is simulating, once that becomes the current version, and therefore this code can be used in implementing the SO. For example, all the code for manipulating ACLs is available when the future SO for this upgrade is implemented.

The TF must produce the state of O_{new} (files and ACLs) from that of O_{old} (files and permissions) and the future SO (if it has state). Therefore, if we decide to allow unrestricted ACLs creation in the future SO, the TF would need to access to its state to create the current object.

The exact choice of what to allow is up to the definer of the upgrade, and as this example shows, there may be several possible choices. Furthermore, the decision might take into account implementation difficulties: the upgrader might choose to disallow some behavior because it would be difficult to implement.

8   Evaluation

This section evaluates Upstart, our prototype upgrade infrastructure. The purpose of this prototype is to demonstrate that our methodology can be realized efficiently, not to advocate any particular implementation. We describe Upstart, the results of microbenchmarks, and our experience running a distributed upgrade.

Upstart implements the upgrade server as an Apache web server. The upgrade server stores upgrade descriptions and code for upgrades. The upgrade descriptions are small; they identify the new code using URLs. To reduce load on the upgrade server, we use the Coral content distribution network [11] to cache and serve the code.

Upstart implements the upgrade database (UDB) as a PostGres database that resides on the upgrade server. Nodes append new records to the UDB periodically but do not write to the UDB directly, as this would cause too much contention in a large system. Instead, nodes send their header over UDP to a udb_logger process that in turn inserts records in the UDB. Under heavy load, some headers may be lost; but this is okay, as nodes will periodically resend updated headers.

The upgrade layer runs on each node, in a separate process from the application. This separation is important: if the application has a bug (e.g, that causes it to loop forever), the upgrade layer must be able to make progress so that it can download and install code that fixes the bug. The UL fetches upgrades from the upgrade server, runs the SF (in a separate process), runs SOs, installs upgrades, and writes status information to the UDB. Once a minute, the UL piggybacks headers on the messages it sends to other nodes it has communicated with lately to inform them of its status. Each UL maintains status information in a local PostGres database (LDB); scheduling functions can query the LDB to make scheduling decisions. To avoid writing to the LDB on the critical path, the UL passes headers to a local udb_logger process.

The UL is implemented as a TESLA handler [23]. TESLA is a dynamic interposition library that intercepts socket, read, and write calls made by an application and redirects them to *handler* objects. When the application creates a new socket, TESLA creates an instance of the UL handler. When the application writes data to the socket or when data arrives on that socket from the network, TESLA notifies the UL via method calls. Since TESLA is transparent to the application, the application can listen on its usual port and communicate normally, which is important for applications that exchange their network address with other nodes, such as peer-to-peer systems.

We implemented the UL and SOs in event-driven C++. To reduce the implementation burden on the upgrader, we provide code-generation tools that simplify the process of implementing SOs for systems that use Sun RPC [27]. Providing support for other kinds of systems is straightforward and requires no changes to the upgrade infrastructure.

8.1   Microbenchmarks

The most important performance issue is the overhead imposed by the upgrade layer when no upgrades are happening, as this is the common case. This section presents experiments that measure these overheads and show them to be modest.

We ran the experiments with the client and server on the same machine (connected over the loopback interface) and on separate machines (connected by a crossover cable). Each machine is a Dell PowerEdge 650 with four 3.06 GHz Intel CPUs, 512 KB cache, 2 GB RAM, and an Intel PRO/1000 gigabit ethernet card. We also ran experiments on the Internet; we do not report the results here, as the latency and bandwidth constraints of the network dwarf the overhead of the upgrade infrastructure.

In each experiment we ran a benchmark and compared its baseline performance with the costs imposed by our system. In the graphs, *Baseline* measures the performance of the benchmark alone. *TESLA* measures the performance of the benchmark running with the TESLA "dummy" handler on all nodes; it adds the overhead for interposing between the benchmark and the socket layer, context switching between the benchmark and the TESLA process, and copying data between the benchmark to the TESLA process. *Upstart* measures the performance of the benchmark running with the upgrade layer on all nodes; it adds the overhead for adding/removing version numbers on messages and bookkeeping in the proxy object. In our experiments, we disabled upgrade server polling and periodic header exchanges. In our prototype, prepending a version number to a message requires copying the message to a new buffer; so each RPC incurs two extra copies. These copies could be avoided by extending TESLA to support scatter-gather I/O.

Table 1 summarizes the results.

Table 1. Microbenchmark results (N=100000 for Null RPC, N=100 for TCP). For each experiment, the 5th, 50th (median), and 95th percentile latencies are given.

	Null RPC (loopback)			Null RPC (crossover)			100MB TCP transfer		
	5%	50%	95%	5%	50%	95%	5%	50%	95%
Baseline	50μs	51μs	53μs	247μs	382μs	769μs	896ms	896ms	923ms
TESLA	128μs	139μs	154μs	371μs	382μs	782μs	896ms	898ms	919ms
Upstart	192μs	206μs	223μs	245μs	388μs	819μs	897ms	908ms	936ms

In the Null RPC benchmark, a client issues empty RPCs to a server one-at-a-time using UDP. By instrumenting the code with timers, we found that the time spent in the client and server ULs is approximately equal, which is as expected since each side sends and receives one message per RPC. Half the time in the UL is spent in the proxy objects, and the other half is spent adding and removing version numbers.

Over the loopback interface, the latencies are normally distributed; but over the crossover cable, we see significant variance. This is due to *interrupt coalescing* done by the gigabit ethernet card, in which the card and/or driver delay interrupts so that one interrupt can be used for multiple packets. A cumulative distribution function of this data (not shown) reveals that the latencies cluster at 125μs intervals; this accounts for the fact that TESLA's 5th percentile is close to the median value.

In the TCP benchmark, a client transfers 100 MB of data to a server using TCP (without RPCs) over a crossover cable. The upgrade layer sees the 100 MB transfer as 12,800 8 KB messages (8 KB is the block size in the benchmark). The UL overhead is due to copying these messages and adding/removing version numbers.

8.2   Experience

To evaluate Upstart "in the field," we defined and ran a simple upgrade on PlanetLab, a large research testbed [21]. Specifically, we deployed DHash [9], a peer-to-peer storage system, on 205 nodes and installed a null upgrade on it. We chose a null upgrade to isolate the effect of the upgrade infrastructure on system performance and behavior.

Defining the upgrade was straightforward: no TF or SOs were required. The SF upgrades nodes gradually: it flips a biased coin periodically and signals if the coin is heads; we used a heads probability of 0.1 and a period of 3 minutes between flips (this SF is implemented as a 6-line Perl script). We set the time limit for the scheduling function to 6000 seconds (100 minutes); by this time, we expect 97% of nodes to have upgraded. The upgrade ran as expected, and the DHash network remained functional throughout.

We also ran an experiment to evaluate the effect of an upgrade on DHash client performance. Here the system consists of four nodes, each running a DHash server; one node also ran the DHash client. Before the upgrade began, we stored 256 8KB data blocks in the system. The client fetches the blocks one-at-a-time in a continuous loop and logs the latency of each fetch. Figure 4 depicts the fetch latencies over the course of the experiment.

The three non-client nodes upgrade round-robin, two minutes apart. The TF causes an upgrading node to sleep for one minute. Figure 4 reveals a stutter in client performance when each node goes down, but the client fetches resume well before each node recovers. The fetch performance while one node is down is slightly less than when all nodes are up.

The precise effect of an upgrade on clients depends somewhat on the application. With better timeouts, for example, the DHash client may see less stutter when nodes fail. Furthermore, we expect the client to see very little stutter in a larger system, as clients are less likely to need to access a node that is upgrading.

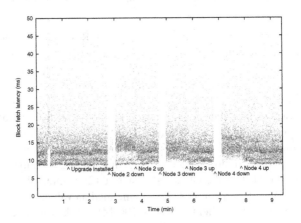

Fig. 4. DHash block fetch performance during an upgrade

9   Related Work

Distributed upgrades have been explored in systems with a wide variety of requirements, some similar, some different from ours. We compare our approach to the related work in research systems and to the current practice in real-world Internet systems.

9.1   Research on Upgrades

Reconfigurable distributed systems [5, 17, 14, 4, 22, 2] support the replacement of subsystems for specific distributed object systems, provided the new type implemented by a subsystem is compatible with the old one. These approaches do not support incompatible upgrades, and they stall when nodes in the subsystem fail.

A few systems support cross-version interaction using wrappers: PODUS [12] supports upgrades to individual procedures in a (possibly distributed) program, and the Eternal system [29] supports upgrades for replicated CORBA objects. But these systems do not consider the correctness issues of cross-version interoperation. Moreover, they use a weaker implementation model than Upstart since they do not allow chaining of wrappers and therefore do not meet our modularity requirement.

The closest approach to ours is Senivongse's "evolution transparency" approach [24], which uses chained *mapping operators* to support cross-version interoperation in a modular way. However, this work does not provide a correctness model: it does not define what system behavior clients can expect after they upgrade or when they communicate with clients running different versions.

Many of the correctness issues that arise in upgrading distributed systems also arise in schema evolution for object-oriented databases, where one object calls the methods of another, even though one of the objects has upgraded to a new schema, but the other has not. Some approaches transform the non-upgraded object just in time for the method call [6]; others [25, 20] use mixed mode: they allow objects of different versions to interact but do not consider general consistency issues. Encore [25] supports cross-version calls for a limited class of version changes via a version set interface that is a union of all the versions of that type. The work on views in O2 [3] provides a comprehensive study of how mutations made to one object type (a view type) are reflected on another (the base type) and so has much in common with our model for supporting multiple types on a single node. However, whereas a database can use schema information to detect correctness violations and reject mutations dynamically, the SO implementor must determine which calls to disallow statically.

Finally, we consider the state preservation requirement. The goal of *dynamic software updating* [10, 13, 28, 26] is to enable a node to upgrade its code and transform its volatile state without shutting down. These techniques require implementor to identify where in the program reconfiguration can take place and are typically language-specific. Furthermore, these points must guarantee that no future execution threads will reference the old types; this can be achieved either by draining the old threads [26] or by detecting such points statically [28]. Our approach guarantees this property by shutting down a node before changing its code. Dynamic updating is complementary to our approach and could be used to reduce downtime during upgrades.

9.2   Real-World Upgrades

Internet and web service providers must upgrade large-scale distributed systems regularly. How they do so depends on whether the upgrade is internal to the service or externally visible to clients and whether the upgrade is compatible or incompatible.

For web services, upgrades are either internal to the service or, if they are externally-visible, are usually compatible. Furthermore, it's acceptable for some clients of a service to see new behaviors while others see the old ones, which means its client-facing nodes may upgrade gradually.

Internally, Internet services are tiered: the topmost tier faces clients; middle tiers implement application logic; and the bottommost tiers manage persistent state. Internal upgrades change the code of one or more tiers and may change the protocols between them. Compatible upgrades are straightforward: the lowermost affected tier is restarted using a rolling upgrade [7], then the next-lowermost tier is upgraded, and so on up the stack. Since the upgrade is compatible, calls made by higher tiers can always be handled by the lower tiers.

Incompatible, internal upgrades are typically executed by upgrading datacenters round-robin: drain a datacenter of all traffic (and redirect its clients to other datacenters), upgrade all its nodes, warm up the datacenter, restore its traffic, then repeat for the next datacenter. Thus nodes in the same datacenter never encounter incompatibilities.

Incompatible, externally-visible upgrades are rare for web services that use HTTP but are more common in non-web services like persistent online games. In such systems, clients are forced to disconnect while the service upgrades and, when they reconnect, are forced to upgrade their client software to the latest version. This ensures that the service never needs to support old behaviors and that all clients see the same version of the service. Some systems support such upgrades by implementing multiple versions. For example, NFS servers implement both NFSv2 and NFSv3. The problem with this approach is that there is no barrier between these implementations, so one can corrupt the other; simulation objects prevent this by modularizing the implementation, and they furthermore make it easy to retire the old code.

Our methodology supports all these kinds of upgrades and enables systems to provide service during incompatible upgrades via simulation. Simulation eliminates the need to take down whole datacenters for incompatible upgrades and can allow clients to delay upgrading until convenient. Our methodology is especially important for peer-to-peer systems, since in those systems there are no tiers or clients; rather every node must upgrade, the upgrade must happen gradually, and even compatible upgrades require simulation so that upgraded nodes can call new methods on non-upgraded nodes.

10   Conclusions

We have presented a new automatic upgrade system. Our approach targets upgrades for large-scale, long-lived distributed systems that manage persistent state and need to provide continuous service. We support very general upgrades: the new version of the system may be incompatible with the old. Such incompatible upgrades, while infrequent, are important for controlling software complexity and bloat. We allow upgrades to be deployed automatically, but under control: upgraders can define flexible upgrade scheduling policies. Furthermore, our system supports mixed mode operation in which nodes running different versions can nevertheless interoperate.

In addition, we have defined a methodology for upgrades that takes mixed mode operation into account. Our methodology defines requirements for upgrades in systems running in mixed mode and provides a way to specify upgrades that enables reasoning about whether the requirements are satisfied. Our specification techniques are modular: only the old and new types of the upgrade must be considered, and possibly the specification of the previous upgrade.

We also presented a powerful implementation approach (running SOs as interceptors) that allows all behavior permitted by the upgrade specification to be implemented. Our approach allows the upgrader to define how long legacy behavior must be supported, by defining the deployment schedule for the incompatible upgrade.

We have implemented a prototype infrastructure called Upstart and shown that it imposes modest overhead. We have also evaluated the usability of our system by implementing a number of examples. The most challenging problem is defining SOs, but they can mostly be implemented by a combination of delegation and use of code that will be in the new version provided by the upgrade.

References

1. Sameer Ajmani. *Automatic Software Upgrades for Distributed Systems*. Ph.D., MIT, September 2004. Also available as technical report MIT-LCS-TR-1012.
2. Joao Paulo A. Almeida, Maarten Wegdam, Marten van Sinderen, and Lambert Nieuwenhuis. Transparent dynamic reconfiguration for CORBA, 2001.
3. S. Amer-Yahia, P. Breche, and C. Souza. Object views and updates. In *Journes Bases de Donnes Avances*, 1996.
4. C. Bidan, V. Issarny, T. Saridakis, and A. Zarras. A dynamic reconfiguration service for CORBA. In *Intl. Conf. on Configurable Dist. Systems*, pages 35–42, May 1998.
5. Toby Bloom. *Dynamic Module Replacement in a Distributed Programming System*. PhD thesis, MIT, 1983.
6. Chandrasekhar Boyapati, Barbara Liskov, Liuba Shrira, Chuang-Hue Moh, and Steven Richman. Lazy modular upgrades in persistent object stores. In *OOPSLA*, 2003.
7. Eric A. Brewer. Lessons from giant-scale services. *IEEE Internet Computing*, July 2001.
8. B. Callaghan, B. Pawlowski, and P. Staubach. NFS version 3 protocol specification. RFC 1813, Network Working Group, June 1995.
9. Frank Dabek, M. Frans Kaashoek, David Karger, Robert Morris, and Ion Stoica. Wide-area cooperative storage with CFS. In *SOSP*, October 2001.
10. R. S. Fabry. How to design systems in which modules can be changed on the fly. In *Intl. Conf. on Software Engineering*, 1976.
11. Michael J. Freedman, Eric Freudenthal, and David Mazières. Democratizing content publication with Coral. In *NSDI*, San Francisco, CA, March 2004.
12. Ophir Frieder and Mark E. Segal. On dynamically updating a computer program: From concept to prototype. *Journal of Systems and Software*, pages 111–128, 1991.
13. Michael W. Hicks, Jonathan T. Moore, and Scott Nettles. Dynamic software updating. In *Programming Language Design and Implementation*, pages 13–23, 2001.
14. Christine R. Hofmeister and James M. Purtilo. A framework for dynamic reconfiguration of distributed programs. Technical Report CS-TR-3119, University of Maryland, College Park, 1993.
15. Michael Kaminsky, George Savvides, David Mazières, and M. Frans Kaashoek. Decentralized user authentication in a global file system. In *SOSP*, pages 60–73, October 2003.
16. Deepak Kapur. Towards a theory for abstract data types. Technical Report MIT-LCS-TR-237, MIT, June 1980.
17. J. Kramer and J. Magee. The Evolving Philosophers Problem: Dynamic change management. *IEEE Transactions on Software Engineering*, 16(11):1293–1306, 1990.

18. Barbara Liskov, Miguel Castro, Liuba Shrira, and Atul Adya. Providing persistent objects in distributed systems. In *European Conf. on Object-Oriented Programming*, June 1999.
19. Barbara Liskov and Jeannette Wing. A behavioral notion of subtyping. *ACM Transactions on Programming Languages and Systems*, 16(6):1811–1841, November 1994.
20. Simon Monk and Ian Sommerville. A model for versioning of classes in object-oriented databases. In *British National Conf. on Databases*, pages 42–58, Aberdeen, 1992.
21. L. Peterson, D. Culler, T. Anderson, and T. Roscoe. A blueprint for introducing disruptive technology into the Internet. In *HotNets I*, October 2002.
22. Tobias Ritzau and Jesper Andersson. Dynamic deployment of Java applications. In *Java for Embedded Systems Workshop*, London, May 2000.
23. Jon Salz, Alex C. Snoeren, and Hari Balakrishnan. TESLA: A transparent, extensible session-layer architecture for end-to-end network services. In *USITS*, 2003.
24. Twittie Senivongse. Enabling flexible cross-version interoperability for distributed services. In *Distributed Objects and Applications*, 1999.
25. Andrea H. Skarra and Staney B. Zdonik. The management of changing types in an object-oriented database. In *OOPSLA*, pages 483–495, 1986.
26. Craig A. N. Soules, Jonathan Appavoo, Kevin Hui, Robert W. Wisniewski, Dilma Da Silva, Gregory R. Ganger, Orran Krieger, Michael Stumm, Marc Auslander, Michal Ostrowski, Bryan Rosenburg, and Jimi Xenidis. System support for online reconfiguration. In *USENIX Annual Technical Conf.*, 2003.
27. R. Srinivasan. RPC: Remote procedure call specification version 2. RFC 1831, Network Working Group, 1995.
28. G. Stoyle, M. Hicks, G. Bierman, P. Sewell, and I. Neamtiu. Mutatis mutandis: Safe and flexible dynamic software updating. In *Principles of Programming Languages*, 2005.
29. L. A. Tewksbury, L. E. Moser, and P. M. Melliar-Smith. Live upgrades of CORBA applications using object replication. In *ICSM*, pages 488–497, November 2001.

Demeter Interfaces: Adaptive Programming Without Surprises

Therapon Skotiniotis, Jeffrey Palm, and Karl Lieberherr

College of Computer & Information Science
Northeastern University, 360 Huntington Avenue
Boston, Massachusetts 02115 USA
{skotthe, jpalm, lieber}@ccs.neu.edu

Abstract. Adaptive Programming (AP) provides advanced modularization mechanisms for traversal related concerns over data structures in object-oriented programs. Computation along a traversal is defined through specialized visitors while the traversal itself is separately defined against a graph-based model of the underlying data structure with the ability to abstract over graph node names and edges. Modifying, under *certain* restrictions, the program's data structure does not alter the program's overall behavior. Even though AP is geared towards more easily evolvable systems, certain limitations of current AP tools hamper code reuse and system evolvability. Reasoning about adaptive code becomes difficult since there is no guarantee that a modification to a data structure will not alter the meaning of the program. Furthermore, adaptive programs are defined directly against a program's complete underlying data structure exposing unrelated information and introducing hardcoded dependencies decreasing reusability, modularity and hampering evolution. In this paper we present *Demeter Interfaces* through which a more thorough design method of adaptive programs allows for more resilient software. Traversal specifications and Visitors are defined against an interface class graph augmented with additional constraints that capture structural properties that *must* hold in order for the adaptive code to function correctly. A program implements a Demeter interface by providing a mapping between the program's concrete data structure and the interface class graph. We show how Demeter interfaces allow for higher levels of reusability and modularity of adaptive code while the static verification of constraints guards against behavior altering modifications. We also discuss the applicability of Demeter Interfaces to XML technologies.

1 Introduction

An adaptive program is written in terms of loosely coupled contexts, *i.e.*, data structure and behavior (computations) with a third definition succinctly binding the two contexts together. In DAJ [1], the most recent AP tool, a textual representation of the class hierarchy, called a *class dictionary*, defines the program's data structures. Specialized visitor classes define computation that takes place during the traversal of the program's data structures. The traversal specification, called a *strategy*, defines paths on the program's data structure to which visitor instances can be attached bridging together structure and behavior. Strategies are defined using a domain specific language that operates on a graph-based model of the program's data structure. Strategies can abstract over graph

D. Thomas (Ed.): ECOOP 2006, LNCS 4067, pp. 477–500, 2006.
© Springer-Verlag Berlin Heidelberg 2006

node names, edges and subpaths thus allowing certain modifications to the underlying data structure that do not alter the program's overall behavior.

This adaptive nature of AP programs better lends itself towards iterative software development [2, 3]. Programs are built in small iterations where each iteration adds a new small piece of program behavior. Typically modifications to the underlying data structure are necessary and often lead to code modifications of older iterations. The adaptive nature of AP systems assists in limiting, but not completely removing, such situations.

Consider a simple example of an application that collects information from a data structure that represents a bus route. The data structure consists of a list of BusRoute objects each one with a list of Bus objects as its data member. In turn, each bus maintains a list of Person objects as its member where each Person object holds the ticket price payed by each passenger. Calculating the total amount of ticket money collected from current bus passengers riding on a bus route requires a traversal to all Person objects, *i.e.*, using the strategy *"from BusRoute to Person"*, collecting the ticket price from each object along the way and adding the values together.

It is clear that the strategy depends on the names BusRoute and Person limiting its reusability but also the renaming of these classes in the program's data structure. The strategy makes the implicit assumption that all Person objects reached through a BusRoute object are all bus passengers. Extending the data structure so that a BusRoute also holds a list of BuStops which themselves contain a list of waiting passengers does not invalidate the strategy, but calculates the wrong amount of ticket money collected. DAJ (as well as the other AP tools DemeterJ and DJ) offers no way to define and check for such assumptions. Programmers resort to extensive testing as the only mechanism for identifying this kinds of violations.

The problems due to modifications that alter the meaning of the program make iterative and parallel development difficult. As dependencies between computations and traversals arise it becomes harder to properly test and detect bugs in adaptive programs. With larger AP software program comprehension decreases since strategies are defined directly on the complete data structure rather than just the important –from the adaptive code's viewpoint– information.

In this paper we propose Demeter Interfaces (DIs) as a mechanism within DAJ that allows the definition of an *Interface Class Graph* (ICG) [4, 5], which provides an interface for the concrete data structure. A DI further specifies its relevant traversal files which consist of traversal declarations, strategy declarations and *constraints*. Constraints define properties that both the ICG and the underlying data structure must satisfy. Computation is specified either as inter-type declarations (ala AspectJ) that introduce extra methods to classes, or as Visitors that are attached to traversals via adaptive methods. Visitors define methods that get to execute during the traversal of the data structure, *i.e.*, before and after specific nodes are reached. We further extend the concrete data structure definition with an implements clause used to specify which DI(s) are implemented along with a mapping between its concrete data members and the DI(s) data members. Finally we extend DAJ to statically verify the mapping provided and validate all constraints from the related Demeter Interfaces.

Demeter Interfaces hit a sweat spot between flexibility and safety. They restrict what AP can do but without going back to the old way of writing the Structural Recursion template manually [6]. They are safer because the adaptive program's intent is defined and used to check any future data type against it. As a result adaptive programs become better documented, more understandable and more reusable.

The remainder of this paper is structured as follows, section 2 introduces Demeter Interfaces by presenting an example application implemented in plain DAJ and then with Demeter Interfaces. Section 3 discusses some of the implementation details and section 4 describes the design benefits enjoyed by adaptive programs that deploy DIs. Section 5 discusses the connection between DIs and XML technologies, section 6 presents related work. Section 7 presents future work and section 8 concludes.

2   Demeter Interfaces

In this section we illustrate the usage of DIs and their advantages through an example of an equation system and the implementation of a semantic checker. We first provide a solution in DAJ [1, 7] which we also use to describe the DAJ system itself. We then iteratively extend the equation system, exposing the issues with the current DAJ implementation. We then show a solution for the same example using DIs and analyze the advantages over our initial implementation.

2.1   A Simple Equation System in DAJ

Our example is about systems of equations in which we want to check that all used variables are defined (we call this a *semantic checker*). We define a simple equation system where each equation introduces a new variable binding and bindings have global scope, *e.g.*, $x = 5; y = 9; z = x + y;$.

Adaptive programs in DAJ are defined through a Class Dictionary (*cd*), a set of Traversal Files (*trv*) and a mixture of Java and AspectJ code. Listing 1.1 shows the class dictionary for the simple equation system and Listing 1.3 shows the traversal, visitor and main class that implements the semantic checker. A cd file is a textual representation of the object oriented structure of the program which specifies classes and their members. Figure 1 provides the UML representation of the class dictionary in Listing 1.1. Each line of the class dictionary defines a class and its direct members. An equal sign ("=") defines a concrete class with the class name on the left hand side of the equals and the members of the class in the right hand side of the equals. Replacing the equal sign with a colon (":") defines an abstract class with its subclasses on the right of the colon. Names enclosed in "< >" define class member variable names, classes with no members are specified using an equal sign followed by a dot (A = .). The class dictionary further defines a graph-based model of the program's structure, referred to as a *class graph* with each class (concrete or abstract) represented as a node and each member variable represented as an edge (Figure 1). Inheritance is also represented as an edge, as in UML class diagrams, but with the direction of the arrow reversed to point to subclasses instead of the super class.

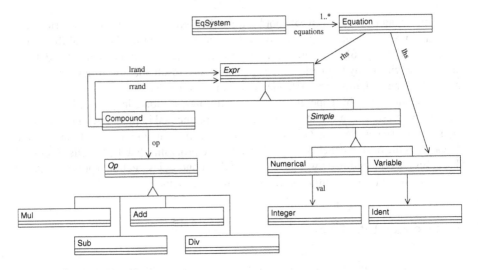

Fig. 1. The UML equivalent of Simple Equations Class Graph

Listing 1.1. Class Dictionary for Simple Equations

EqSystem = <equations> BList(Equation).
Equation = <lhs> Variable "=" <rhs> Expr.
Expr : Simple | Compound .
Simple : Variable | Numerical.
Variable = Ident.
Numerical = <val> Integer.
Compound = "(" <lrand> Expr <op> Op <rrand> Expr")".
Op : Add | Sub | Mul | Div.
Add = "+".
Sub = "−".
Mul = "∗".
Div = "/".
BList(S) ~ "(" S {";" S} ")".

The system uses a class dictionary as a grammar definition, providing a language that can parse in sentences and create the appropriate object instances. Tokens in the class dictionary surrounded in quotes define the generated language's syntax tokens (Listing 1.2). Parameterized classes are defined using a tilde ("~") operator, *e.g.*, BList(S) defines a list enclosed in parentheses of one (or more) elements of type S each element separated by a semicolon.

Listing 1.2. An instance of a simple equations system given as input to DAJ

(x = 5;
  y = (x − 2);
  z = ((y−x) + (y+9)))

Traversal files are an extension to AspectJ's aspect definition which allow inter-type declarations based on AspectJ's built-in extension capability: the declare statement. DAJ extends AspectJ's `declare` statement to define strategies and traversals. Strategy declarations provide a name for the strategy (*e.g.*, `defined` in Listing 1.3) followed by the strategy expression as a string. Strategies can refer to class nodes by name and to class edges using the syntax `-> Source,Label,Target.` (*e.g.*, class A with member c of type B can be expressed as `->A,c,B`). In place of a class name or edge name the `*` pattern is used to match any name. In our simple equation system the strategy `defined` visits all `Variable` objects starting form an `EqSystem` object and bypassing any edge with the name `rhs` along the way.

Listing 1.3. Additional traversal file (`SemanticChecker`), visitor class (`CollectDef`) and main driver class (`Main`) for the system of simple equations

```
// SemanticChecker.trv
aspect SemanticChecker {
  declare strategy : defined: "from EqSystem bypassing -> *,rhs,* to Variable";
  declare traversal: void printDefined(): defined(CollectDef);

  declare strategy : used :"from EqSystem bypassing -> *,lhs,* to Variable";
  declare traversal: void printUsed(): used(CollectDef);
}

// CollectDef.java Visitor
class CollectDef{
  void before (Variable v) { System.out.println("Found Ident :" + v.ident.toString()); }
}

// Main Class
import java.io.*;
class Main{
  public static void main(String args[]) {
    try {
      EqSystem eqSystem = EqSystem.parse(new File(args[0]));
      System.out.println("Defined are : ");
      eqSystem.printDefined();
      System.out.println("Used are : ");
      eqSystem.printUsed();
    }catch (Exception e){ e.printStackTrace(); }
  }
}
```

Traversal declarations require a method signature and a strategy with a visitor name as an argument. The method signature provided to a traversal declaration gets introduced as a new public method to the source class of the traversal's strategy. We call these methods *adaptive methods*. DAJ automatically generates the method body that performs the necessary calls for traversing the object's structure according to the given strategy. At each such call the attached visitor implementation is consulted and any applicable method is executed. Visitors in DAJ are Java classes where the one argument method names before, after and return hold a special meaning. During a traversal, if an object's type matches the argument type of a before method then that method is called before traversing the object. After methods behave in a similar way with the method being called after traversing the object. Return provides the final value of a traversal and is executed upon traversal termination. The return type of the return method must match the return type of the adaptive method that the visitor is attached to. In the simple equation system, before a Variable object is traversed the CollectDef visitor prints out the variable's name.

With the completed AP implementation of the semantic checker in place we can now evaluate our solution and verify the claims made, both in favor and against, AP. The principle behind AP [8] states

"A program should be designed so that the interface of objects can be changed within certain constraints without affecting the program *at all*."

For the simple equation system example, modifying the system so that equations are now in prefix notation does not affect the program's behavior. Doing so requires a single modification to the class dictionary,

```
Compound = ``(´´ <op> Op <lrand> Expr <rrand> Expr ``)´´.
```

No other changes are needed to the traversal file or the visitor. The modification simply changed the order between the Op data member and the first Expr data member of the Compound class. This is not surprising since even in plain Java, switching the order of member definitions does not change a program's behavior. Lets consider a more drastic extension, lets add exponent operations to our system but also impose precedence between operators. Listing 1.4 shows the complete class dictionary file, the definitions have been factored to accommodate for operator precedence. Again, no other changes are need to either the traversal file or the visitor. The semantic checker still functions correctly.

Why is the semantic checker unaffected by these changes? In both cases the modifications to the cd file did not falsify the strategy (*i.e.*, there is still a path from source to the target) and it did not affect the way by which variables are defined and used in the equation system (*i.e.*, there is no other way of binding a variable to equations other than ``=´´ and variables still have global scope). Any modification to the class dictionary that does not falsify the strategy and does not alter the assumptions about variable definition and usage within the equation system will not affect the semantic checker's code.

However any alteration that either

- modifies class and/or class member variable names that are explicitly referenced by traversals and/or visitors,
- or, breaks an assumption about the system on which adaptive code depends on (*e.g.*, adding a new variable binding construct to the equation system like let for local bindings or functions with arguments).

will alter the program's behavior.

For example, altering the equation system to allow for function definitions with arguments causes no compile time error, but results in erroneous program behavior. This modification breaks two assumptions:

1. There is only one new `Variable` defined at each equation.
2. All variables have global scope and thus can be used anywhere.

Listing 1.4. Extended class graph accommodating exponents and operator precedence

```
EqSystem = <equations> BList(Equation).
Equation = <lhs> Variable "=" <rhs> Expr.
Expr = <left> SimpleExp [ SimpleExpRest ].
SimpleExpRest = LowPrec <right> SimpleExp .
LowPrec : Add | Sub.
SimpleExp = <left> MultExp [ MultExpRest].
MultExpRest = MedPrec <right> MultExp.
MedPrec : Mul | Div.
MultExp = <left> PowerExp [PowerExpRest].
PowerExpRest = Raised <right> PowerExp.
Raised = "**".
PowerExp : Simple | BExpr .
BExpr = "(" Expr ")".
Simple : Variable | Numerical.
Variable = Ident.
Numerical = <val> Integer.
Add = "+".
Sub = "−".
Mul = "*".
Div = "/".
BList(S) ~ S {";" S}.
```

Adaptive methods, as well as the visitor, depend on these assumptions. However these assumptions are not explicitly captured in AP programs. There is no tool support to stop such modifications. In fact naively extending the equation system to accommodate for functions parameters, as in Listing 1.5, will generate a valid AP program that will provide the wrong results for the semantic checker.

With larger AP programs, it becomes nearly impossible to find all these implicit assumptions and even harder to predict which modifications will cause erroneous behavior. Programmers have to rely on exhaustive testing in order to increase their confidence that the program still behaves according to its specification. This in turn limits the effectiveness of AP and its application in iterative development since modifications to the data structure due to an iteration can introduce bugs in parts of the code developed in previous iterations.

These dependencies impede parallel development and decrease productivity. Addressing these issues requires

- The ability to define the assumptions made by adaptive code about the underlying data structure,
- Tool support to allow for the verification of these assumptions,
- Decrease the dependency on class and class member variable names,
- The modularization of only the relevant data structure information for each adaptive behavior instead of the whole class dictionary.

Listing 1.5. Class Graph for equation systems with functions of one argument

---

EqSystem = <equations> BList(Equation).
Equation = <lhs> VarOrFunc "=" <rhs> Expr.
VarOrFunc : Variable | Function.
Function = "*fun*" <fname> Variable "(" <args> Variable")".
Expr : FunCall | Simple | Compound .
Simple : Variable | Numerical.
Variable = Ident.
FunCall = <fname> Variable "(" <fargs> Simple ")".
Numerical = <val> Integer.
Compound = "(" <lrand> Expr <op> Op <rrand> Expr")".
Op : Add | Sub | Mul | Div.
Add = "+".
Sub = "−".
Mul = "*".
Div = "/".
BList(S) ˜ "(" S {";" S} ")".

2.2 A Simple Equation System with Demeter Interfaces

A Demeter Interface resides between a class graph and the *implementation* of adaptive behavior, *i.e.*, adaptive methods and visitor implementations. A DI defines the interface class graph as well as a list of traversal file names each defining strategies, traversals and constraints for this DI. A traversal file also defines a list of visitor class names that are used in its traversal declarations.

Figure 2 shows the Demeter Interface for the simple equation system along with its traversal file and visitor implementation. A diagrammatical representation (in UML) of the DI's interface class graph is given on the right.

The ICG [4, 5] serves as an abstraction of any class graph implementation of the ExprICG DI in order for the strategies defined in ExprICG to be applicable. The interface class graph captures only the necessary structural information. For the purpose of a semantic checker the interface class graph needs to capture the notions of variable definition and variable usage. Any other information, *e.g.*, operator precedence etc., is irrelevant for the semantic checker. Any definition in the equation system is viewed by the semantic checker as either defining a new variable or using some variables in the definition body. This is depicted in Listing 2 which defines an ESystem as a set of definitions, each definition having a def defining an entity (DThing) and a body part that uses (possibly many) entities (UThing).

The header for the DI defines, using a with statement, the traversal file name that uses this DI, in this case SemanticChecker. The SemanticChecker traversal file defines in its header, using a with statement, the visitor required by the traversals defined in its body. The three strategies defined are: the first for collecting all defined entities in an ESystem (gdefinedIdents), the second for collecting all used entities in an ESystem (gusedIdents) and the last strategy collects all defined entities from a Definition object (definedIdent).

Following the strategy definitions, two adaptive methods are introduced into the ESystem class, printDefined() uses the gdefinedIdents strategy along with

// *ExprICG.di*
di ExprICG **with** SemanticChecker{
   ESystem = List(Definition).
   Definition =
      <def> DThing "=" <body> Body.
   Body = List(UThing).
   UThing = Thing.
   DThing = Thing.
   Thing = .
   List(S) ~ "(" S ")".
}

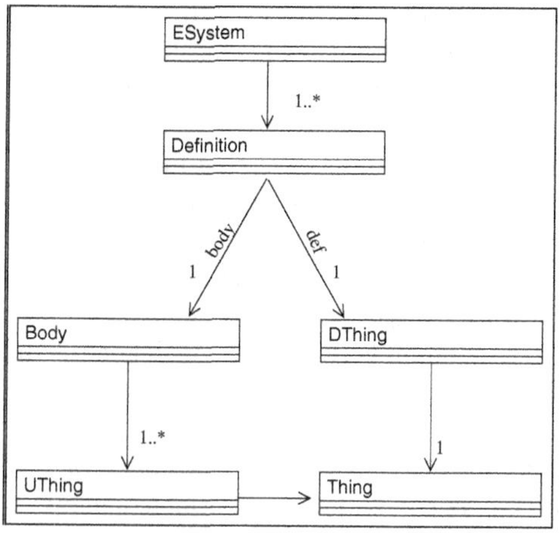

// *SemanticChecker.trv File*
aspect SemanticChecker **with** DVisitor{
   declare strategy: gdefinedIdents: *"from ESystem via DThing to Thing"*.
   declare strategy: gusedIdents: *"from ESystem via UThing to Thing"*.
   declare strategy definedIdent: *"from Definition via DThing to Thing"*.

   declare traversal: **void** printDefined(): gdefinedIdents(DVisitor);
   declare traversal: **void** printUsed(): gusedIdents(DVisitor);

   declare constraints:
      unique(definedIdent), **nonempty**(gusedIdents), **nonempty**(gdefinedIdents).
}

// *DVisitor.java File*
class DVisitor {
   public void before(Thing t){ System.out.println(t.toString()); }
}

Fig. 2. The Demeter Interface for the simple equations system defines an interface class graph, the SemanticChecker traversal file defines strategies traversals and constraints. The UML diagram is equivalent to the interface class graph defined in `ExprICG`.

the `DVisitor` to collect all defined entities. In a similar manner `printUsed()` uses the `gusedIdents` strategy along with `DVisitor` to collect all used (referenced) entities. Finally the three constraints state the assumptions that must hold for the ICG and later for any class dictionary that is mapped to this ICG. Specifically, that each `Definition` has a unique path to a defined entity, *i.e.*, a `Definition` defines one and only one new variable. The remaining two constraints specify that both `gusedIdents` and `gdefinedIdents` should have at least one path satisfying their strategy. These constraints can be checked statically.

A visitor implementation is a typical Java class containing one argument methods with the method name being either `before` or `after`. Execution of an adaptive method traverses the data structure according to the strategy provided with the adaptive method. Before traversing over an object, the visitor attached to this adaptive method is advised. If the type of the object to be traversed matches the argument type of a method, then the method is executed. As the method names imply, `before` methods are executed before traversing the object, `after` methods are executed after the object is traversed. Figure 3 gives an example implementation of the `ExprICG` Demeter Interface (on the right) along with a visitor implementation and a driver class (on the left). DAJ's class dictionaries are extended in two ways; a header is introduced allowing for an `implements` statement that specifies which DIs are being implemented and a mapping between the concrete class dictionary classes to the ICG's classes. The concrete class dictionary `InfixEQSystem` (Figure 3) provides a definition of its equation system and a mapping M between the classes in its class graph and all the classes in `ExprICG`'s interface class graph. The mapping definition can map class(es) to class(es), class member variable name(s) to class member variable name(s), a class to the target(s) of a strategy and a class member variable name to a strategy.

```java
import java.io.*;

class Main {
  public static void main(String[] args){
    try {
      InfixEQSystem ieqs =
        InfixEQSystem.parse(new File(args[0]));
      System.out.println("IDs in def:");
      ieqs.printDefined();
      System.out.println("IDs in use:");
      ieqs.printUsed();
    }catch(Exception e){
      e.printStackTrace();
    }
  }
}
```

```
cd InfixEQSystem implements ExprICG {
  EquationSystem = <eqs> List(Equation).
  List(S) ˜ "(" {S} ")".
  Equation = <lhs> Variable "="
    <rhs> Expr.
  Expr : Simple | Compound.
  Simple : Variable | Numerical.
  Variable = Ident.
  Numerical = <v> Integer.
  Compound = <lrand>List(Expr)
    <op> Op <rrand>List(Expr).
  Op : Add | Sub | Mul | Div.
  Add = "+".
  Sub = "−".
  Mul = "*".
  Div = "/".

  for ExprICG (
    use EquationSystem as ESystem,
    use Equation as Definition,
    use Expr as Body,
    use (−>*,lhs,Variable) as DThing,
    use (−>*,rhs,* to Variable) as UThing,
    use Variable as Thing
  )
}
```

Fig. 3. `InfixEQSystem` defines a class graph and a mapping of the entities in the class graph to the interface class graph of `ExprICG`. The driver class `Main` uses the adaptive methods introduced by `ExprICG`.

With the simple equation system implemented using Demeter Interfaces we now extend the system and verify that DIs assist the prevention of modifications that alter the program's behavior. We perform the same extensions as in Section 2.1 and show that in the situations where modifications did not affect the systems behavior are not affected by the incorporation of DIs. Modifications that did result in erroneous program behavior before, result in compile time errors in the presence of DIs.

As a first evolution step we want to change from infix notation to prefix notation. This is a modification that does not alter the program's behavior even in the original DAJ solution. Moving to a prefix notation requires to change the definition of `Compound` in `InfixEQSystem` to

```
Compound = <op> Op <lrand> List(Expr) <rrand> List(Expr).
```

This change does not affect the Demeter Interface at all. We update the equation system class graph while keeping the original mapping M. All constraints of the DI are still satisfied after they are mapped into the actual interface class graph and the adaptive methods function correctly.

It is important to note that during this evolution step, only the DI and the concrete implementation of the interface class graph was needed. Under the assumption that the DI's constraints capture the semantic checker's intend, the static assurances provided by the tool because of the DI, suffice to show that the strategies pick the correct paths and that the semantic checker still operates as expected. The Demeter Interface allows in this case for separate development and ease of evolution. The concrete class graph and its mapping can be a maintained separately while adaptive code can be developed based on the publicly available DI. Alterations made to the concrete class graph do not need to be visible to adaptive code maintainers unless it affects the mapping to an implemented DI. This form of data hiding through the Demeter Interface also provides for easier maintainability and higher system modularity.

As our next evolution step we extend the set of operators to include exponents and add operator precedence. Keeping the headers and mapping definition the same as in `InfixEQSystem` and replacing the data structure definition by that of Listing 1.4 gives us a working AP system. The modifications made to the data structure to accommodate for exponents and operator precedence do not invalidate any of the DI's constraints and the resulting AP program behaves as expected.

In the next evolution step we want to add functions with one argument to the equation system. This evolution step affects information that is relevant to the semantic checker. The semantic checker has to deal with parameter names on each function definition but also usages of function definitions that may appear on the right-hand side of equations. Unlike definitions so far function parameters do not have global scope, their scope is local to the function definition. A naive approach would be to alter the class dictionary as in Listing 1.6.[1] Altering the data structure and only the mapping to `DThing` results in a compile time error. The reason for this error is the predicate `unique(definedIdent)` from `ExprICG`, it no longer holds. The modification to allow functions with one parameter breaks one of the assumptions of the interface, in

---

[1] To keep the example simple we do not allow the usage of function calls as arguments to other functions, *i.e.*, $f(f(3))$.

```
// ParamExprICG.di File
di ParamExprICG
      with SemanticChecker{
   ESystem = List(Definition).
   Definition = <def> DThing
               <fnc> DFThing
               <body> Body.
   DThing = Thing.
   DFThing = <fname> DThing
             <fparam> DThing.
   Body = <fc> List(UFThing)
          List(UThing).
   UFThing = <name> UThing
             <aparam> UThing.
   UThing = Thing.
   Thing =.
   List(S) ~ "(" S ")".
}
```

```
// SemanticChecker.trv File
import java.util.*;
aspect SemanticChecker with PVisitor{
   declare strategy: definedIdents : "from ESystem to DThing".
   declare strategy: usedIdents : "from ESystem to UThing".
   declare strategy: dName : "from DFThing via −> *,fparam,* to Thing".
   declare strategy: uName : "from UFThing via −> *,aparam,* to Thing".
   declare strategy: dFName : "from DFThing via −> *,fname,* to Thing".
   declare strategy: uFName : "from UFThing via −> *,name,* to Thing".

   declare traversal: LinkedList getDefined(): definedIdents(PVisitor);
   declare traversal: LinkedList getUsed(): usedIdents(PVisitor);
   declare traversal: LinkedList getDefName(): dName(PVisitor);
   declare traversal: LinkedList getUsedName(): uName(PVisitor);
   declare traversal: LinkedList getDefArg(): dName(PVisitor);
   declare traversal: LinkedList getUsedArg(): uName(PVisitor);

   declare constraints:
      nonempty(definedIdents), nonempty(usedIdents), unique(dName),
      unique(uName), unique(dFName), unique(uFName).

   //Inter-type definition
   public boolean ESystem.checkBindings(LinkedList l1, LinkedList l2){
      // checks appropriate variable usage
   }}
```

Fig. 4. The evolved Demeter Interface and the UML representation of the extended Demeter Interface class graph

particular the fact that we can reach more than one variable through the left hand side of the equal sign. With one argument functions the meaning of what is defined and what is its scope has changed and these changes have to be reflected in the Demeter Interface.

Listing 1.6. Extending the class dictionary to accommodate function definitions using the ExprICG DI

```
cd ParamEquations implements ExprICG{
    EqSystem = <equations> BList(Equation).
    Equation = <lhs> VarOrFunc "=" <rhs> Expr.
    VarOrFunc : Variable | Function.
    Function = "fun" <fname> Variable "(" <args> Variable")".
    Expr : FunCall | Simple | Compound .
    Simple : Variable | Numerical.
    Variable = Ident.
    FunCall = <fname> Variable "(" <fargs> Simple ")".
    Numerical = <val> Integer.
    Compound = "(" <lrand> Expr <op> Op <rrand> Expr")".
    Op : Add | Sub | Mul | Div.
    Add = "+".
    Sub = "−".
    Mul = "*".
    Div = "/".
    BList(S) ~ "(" S {";" S} ")".

    for ExprICG (
        use EquationSystem as ESystem,
        use Equation as Definition,
        use Expr as Body,
        use (−>*,lhs,* to Variable) as DThing,
        use (−>*,rhs,* to Variable) as UThing,
        use Variable as Thing
    )
}
```

It is important to note that for this evolution step that the interface has to change (Figure 4). With a new interface class graph `ParamExprICG` we can abstractly reason about semantically checking systems with one argument functions. The two strategies `definedIdent` and `usedIdents` are used to navigate to definitions and references of variable names, both function names as well as simple variables. The strategies `dName` and `uName` are then used to collect arguments (at function definition) and actual arguments (at function invocation) respectively. Similarly `dFName` and `uFName` collect function names at function definitions and function usage respectively. The traversal declarations use the strategies to collect `Thing` objects. The implementation of the method `checkBindings` is introduced into `ESystem` and it is used to check the correct usage of variable and function definitions. The inputs to this function are two lists where the first represents variable and function definition names at different scopes and the second represents names of variables and functions references at their corresponding scope.

Listing 1.7. Modifications to the concrete class dictionary to accommodate single argument functions

```
cd ParamEquations implements ParamExprICG{
EqSystem = <equations> BList(Equation).
Equation = <lhs> VarOrFunc "=" <rhs> Expr.
VarOrFunc : Variable | Function.
Function = "fun" <fname> Variable "(" <args> Variable")".
Expr : FunCall | Simple | Compound .
Simple : Variable | Numerical.
Variable = Ident.
FunCall = <fname> Variable "(" <fargs> Simple ")".
Numerical = <val> Integer.
Compound = "(" <lrand> Expr <op> Op <rrand> Expr")".
Op : Add | Sub | Mul | Div.
Add = "+".
Sub = "−".
Mul = "∗".
Div = "/".
BList(S) ~ "(" S {";" S} ")".

for ParamExprICG(
    use EqSystem as ESystem,
    use Equation as Definition,
    use (−>,Equation,lhs,∗) bypassing Function to Variable as (−>,Definition,def,DThing)
    use (−>,Equation,lhs,∗) to Function as DFThing
    use (−>,Function,fname,Variable) as (−>,DFThing,fname,DThing)
    use (−>,Function,args,Variable) as (−>,DFThing,fparam,DThing)
    use (−>,Equation,rhs,∗) bypassing FunCall to Variable as UThing
    use Expr to FunCall as (−>,Body,fc,UFThing)
    use (−>,FunCall,fname,Variable) as (−>,UFThing,name,UThing)
    use (−>,FunCall,fargs,Variable) as (−>,UFThing,aparam,UThing)
    use Ident as Thing
    )
}
```

Listing 1.7 shows the class graph that implements `ParamExprICG`. The class dictionary maps the edge `args` to the edge `fparam` and its source and target nodes accordingly. Also the `fargs` edge is mapped to the edge `aparam` and `fname` is mapped to `name` with their source and target nodes mapped accordingly. `Function` is mapped to `DFThing` and `FunCall` to `UFThing`. All reachable `Variable` objects via the `lhs` edge of `Equation` that bypass `Function` are mapped to `DThing`. In a similar way all `Variable` objects that can be reached from the `rhs` edge of `Equation` by bypassing `FunCall` are mapped to `UThing`. Figure 5 shows the visitor implementation and the driver class. The visitor interface defines the method `return` which is called by DAJ at the end of a traversal. The return value of the `return` method is also the return value of the traversal.

In this evolution step, the Demeter Interface helped by disallowing a naive extension that would violate the intended behavior of the original Demeter Interface. The nature

```
import java.util.LinkedList;

class PVisitor {
  LinkedList env;

  PVisitor(){
    this.env = new LinkedList(); }
  public void before(Thing t) {
    env.add(t); }
  public void before(UFThing ud) {
    LinkedList rib = getUsedName();
    rib.addAll(getUsedArg());
    env.add(rib); }
  public void before(DFThing ud) {
    LinkedList rib = getDefName();
    ribaddAll(getDefArg());
    env.add(rib); }
  public LinkedList return(){
    return env; }
}
```

```
import java.io.*;

class Main {
  public static void main(String[] args){
    boolean codeOk ;

    PVisitor defV = new PVisitor();
    PVisitor useV = new PVisitor();
    ParamEquations pe = ParamEquations.
      parse(new File(args[0]));
    codeOk = pe.checkBindings(
      pe.getDefined(defV),
      pe.getUsed(useV));
    if (!codeOk)
      System.out.println(" Variables used
        before they where defined");
  }
}
```

Fig. 5. Changes to the interface affect `Main`. The definition of `PVisitor` is used to check for the local parameter names in parametric equations.

of the evolution required an extension of the interface and that resulted to changes in the driver class and a new concrete class dictionary. It is important to note how the Demeter Interface exposed the erroneous usage of the `ExprICG` interface for this evolution step and assisted in updating all the dependent components due to the definition of `ParamExprICG`.

Although Demeter Interfaces are a big improvement over traditional AP, their usage does not completely remove the need for testing adaptive code after modifications are made to the class graph. The mechanisms behind Demeter Interfaces rely on the appropriate constraints and mapping between the ICG and the class dictionary. Constraints in the interface could be too permissive allowing modifications to a class dictionary that lead to unintended behavior. Through testing we can verify the program's behavior and strengthen the program's constraints accordingly. The abstraction provided by the ICG assist programmers in this task allowing them to focus on the relevant subset of their application.

3   Compiling Demeter Interfaces

The previous sections have covered most of the features of Demeter Interfaces. In this section we provide a more detailed, informal, explanation of the current tool support for Demeter Interfaces in DAJ. We plan to introduce Demeter Interfaces to all Demeter Tools (DemeterJ and DJ) in the near future.

The incorporation of Demeter Interfaces into DAJ has resulted into two new compilation steps for AP software. A Demeter interface along with its supporting code (traversal files and visitor implementations) is compiled through a separate phase. This phase typechecks traversal files and visitor implementations, *i.e.*, names in strategy definitions and in visitor methods are defined in the DI's ICG. Also, the return type for traversal declarations matches the return type of the visitor's special `return` method. Finally, for this phase, the constraints defined inside traversal files are verified. Successful completion of the first phase produces an archive of the necessary files.

The second compilation phase takes as input a concrete class dictionary and an archive generated as output from a compilation of all required DIs for this concrete class dictionary. Using the mapping in the concrete class dictionary, DI code is expanded for the specific concrete class graph. After expansion the DI constraints are verified and finally the complete AP application is generated as compiled Java class files.

3.1 Mapping Concrete Class Dictionary to the Interface Class Graph

A mapping can be thought of as a relation between **all** classes and edges in an ICG and classes and edges in the concrete class dictionary. Informally, mapping directives allow mappings between:

- a concrete class to an ICG class
- a strategy in the concrete class graph to an ICG edge.
- the target(s) of a strategy in the concrete class graph to an ICG class

To make the mapping semantics in DAJ clear we use the definitions of class graphs and the notion of paths and path sets from previous work [9]. Formally a class graph is a labelled graph where nodes are class names and edges are field names or reverse inheritance edges, *i.e.*, the inheritance arrow points to the subclass instead of the super class. Fix a finite set C of *class names* where each class name is either *abstract* or *concrete*. We also fix a finite set $\mathcal{L}$ of *field names* or sometimes referred to as *labels*. We assume the existence of two distinguished symbols: this $\in \mathcal{L}$ and reverse inheritance edge $\diamond \notin \mathcal{L}$. A class graph model is a graph $G = (V, E, L)$ such that

- $V \subseteq C$, i.e., the nodes are class names.
- $L \subseteq \mathcal{L} \cup \{\diamond\}$, i.e., edges are labeled by field names or "$\diamond$".
- For each $v \in V$, the field names of all edges going out from v are distinct (but there may be many edges labeled by $\diamond$ going out from v).
- For each $v \in V$ such that v is concrete, $v \overset{\text{this}}{\rightarrow} v \in E$.
- The set of reverse inheritance edges is acyclic.

We use the (reflexive) notion of a *superclass*: given a class graph $G = (V, E, L)$, we say that $v \in V$ is a superclass of $u \in V$ if there is a (possibly empty) path of reverse inheritance edges from v to u. The collection of all super-classes of a class v is called the *ancestry* of v. We further define a *path* as a sequence $\langle v_0 l_1 v_1 l_2 \ldots l_n v_n \rangle$ where $v_{i-1} \overset{l_i}{\rightarrow} v_i \in E$ for all $0 < i \leq n$. For any path p we define $\mathsf{Source}(p) = v_0$ and $\mathsf{Target}(p) = v_n$. Any given strategy s with source node v_s and target node v_t can be defined as a set of paths from v_s to v_t and a set of predicates over each edge in a path. The set of predicates denote the strategy directives in s, *i.e.*, a directive such as `bypassing` A generates a predicate that fails on edges with A as their targets. Our representation of strategies in this setting correspond to the *embedded strategies* in [10]. Embedded strategies use directly names from the underlying class graph, *i.e.*, the ICG or the class dictionary.

Finally for a given class graph G and a strategy s we define $\mathsf{PathSet}_G(s)$ as the set containing all paths in G that satisfy s. A path p in G *satisfies* s if p is an expansion of a path from the source node of s to the target node of s and the predicate for each strategy edge is valid in p. We overload the definitions of Source and Target to accept path sets and return the set of source node and target nodes for each path p in the input.

Class dictionaries and ICGs are class graphs. The mapping between class dictionaries and ICGs reduces to a name map between nodes and edges of their corresponding class graphs. Given two class graphs $G_C = (V_C, E_C, L_C)$ for the class dictionary and $G_I = (V_I, E_I, L_I)$ for the ICG where labels and nodes between class graphs are distinct, we define a mapping M from V_I to V_C and from L_I to L_C.

The definition of a mapping M is given in the class dictionary for each of the DIs that it implements. The mapping of an ICG class to a concrete class, is straight forward. Mapping an ICG edge to a concrete edge maps the corresponding source and target classes but also the edge label. Mapping an ICG class to a strategy s in the concrete class graph G causes the target(s) of $\mathsf{Target}(\mathsf{PathSet}_G(s))$ to be mapped. Finally mapping a an ICG edge $v_1 \xrightarrow{l} v_2 \in E_I$ to a strategy s in the concrete class graph G maps the $\mathsf{Source}(\mathsf{PathSet}_G(s))$ to v_1, $\mathsf{Target}(\mathsf{PathSet}_G(s))$ to v_2 and each $p \in \mathsf{PathSet}_G(s)$ to l.

Since a concrete class graph can implement more than one DI, different DIs may map the same concrete class to different ICG classes. DAJ internally uses the name of the DI and the name of the ICG class for the mapping to resolve name clashes and name ambiguities. These issues come into play at strategy expansion. It is easy to see that classes can be mapped with different names and these can affect the path sets computed from strategies. Constraints on strategies can be used to define restrictions that the strategy, and by implication it's path set, must satisfy.

3.2 Constraints

Constraints may be placed on the ICG of a DI that further restrict the implementing class graphs. These are specified declaratively in the DI in a separate section as shown in Figure 2. Constraints take strategies as arguments and are evaluated on *Traversal Graphs* not the whole class graph. Traversal graphs are a specific view of a strategy under a specific class graph. That is, irrelevant nodes and edges that cannot help in satisfying the strategy s under a class graph G are removed. The AP Library represents traversal graphs as objects parameterized by a strategy and a class graph.

Currently the following primitive constraints for strategies s and t over a traversal graph G are provided in DAJ:

- **unique**(s): The size of $\mathsf{PathSet}_G(s)$ must be equal to one and the path itself must have no loops.
- **nonempty**(s): The size of $\mathsf{PathSet}_G(s)$ is greater than zero.

- **subset**(s,t): The path set of s is a subset of the path set of t, $\mathsf{PathSet}_G(s) \subseteq \mathsf{PathSet}_G(t)$
- **multiple**(s): The size of $\mathsf{PathSet}_G(s)$ is greater than one.

All primitives can be combined using common logical operators such as and (&&), or (| |), and negation !. With this ability one could, for example, define equivalence of two strategies s and t as:

$$\textbf{equiv}(s,t) = \textbf{subset}(s,t) \text{ \&\& } \textbf{subset}(t,s).$$

The equivalence predicate can be used to define the same set of paths using different strategies. In this way we can express variants of a strategy where each variant imposes different restrictions on the interface class graph and its mapped class dictionary.

The tool implements these primitives through functionality of the current AP Library [11]. **nonempty** can be implemented in the current release, while **subset** and **unique** are implemented through calls to the new interface `AlgorithmsI`[2]:

```
interface AlgorithmsI {
  Descriptive.Boolean isSubset(TraversalGraph t1,
                               TraversalGraph t2);
  Descriptive.Boolean isUnique(TraversalGraph t);
}
```

3.3 Strategy Expansion

At strategy expansion DAJ uses the mapping provided with the concrete class graph and all the related files (the archive generated by the DI's compilation) and regenerates the files based on the name mapping.

DAJ goes through the DI's traversal files and visitor implementations and systematically replaces strategy definitions and visitor method argument types according to the mapping provided by the concrete class dictionary. The translation is straight forward for when a class maps to a class. In the case where an edge is mapped to a class or a strategy is mapped to a class then this class cannot be an argument to a visitor method. Currently in DAJ visitor methods cannot deal with edges and so any mapping that takes an ICG class to an edge or strategy causes a compile time error. Finally, strategies that are part of a mapping directive may have to be altered before they are replaced inside the DI's strategy definitions. The last "to" directive of the strategy given in the mapping is replaced by a "via" directive if it is replacing any other segment of a strategy other than the target. If the strategy from a mapping definition is replacing the target class of a DI's strategy then the "from" directive of the DI's strategy is replaces by a "via" directive. In this way, the rewrite ensures that the resulting strategy is syntactically valid.

---

[2] `Descriptive.Boolean` is a utility class that contains a `boolean` value and descriptive reason *why* that value was returned.

4   Modularity and Demeter Interfaces

The introduction of Demeter Interfaces to AP development assists in designing, maintaining and understanding adaptive programs. The ideas behind DIs and their usage has revealed several design benefits.

During the design process of adaptive programs developers would first design a minimal class dictionary. Then iteratively both adaptive code and the class dictionary itself are developed with repeated testing to verify the behavior of adaptive code. Modifications to both the class dictionary as well as the adaptive code (the strategy and/or the visitor attached to traversal declarations) were necessary. As programs become larger in size distinguishing which parts of the class dictionary are involved in the different adaptive methods becomes difficult. Furthermore, modifications to class names in the class dictionary cause changes to traversal strategies and/or visitor methods due to the lack of abstraction over class names. For example, in the development of CONA [12, 13] a Design by Contract (DbC) extension to Java and AspectJ, the class dictionary is the whole Java and AspectJ language syntax. Understanding the dependencies between adaptive code and the class dictionary becomes a laborious and error prone process.

DIs provide solutions to both of these problems. The ICG provides an abstraction of the concrete class graph while the adaptive methods, traversal strategies and visitor interfaces localize all the information necessary for understanding the dependencies between adaptive code and the rest of the program. The mapping mechanism removes the tight dependence on naming conventions by providing an automatic renaming mechanism. The usage of DIs provides for higher modularity in AP systems.

To support our claim of modularity for DIs we borrow the definition for modular implementations as proposed by Kiczales and Mezini [14]

- it is textually local,
- there is a well-defined interface that describes how it interacts with the rest of the system,
- the interface is an abstraction of the implementation, in that it is possible to make material changes to the implementation without violating the interface.
- an automatic mechanism enforces that every module satisfies its own interface and respects the interface of all other modules, and
- the module can be automatically composed – by a compiler, loader, linker etc. – via various configurations with other modules to produce a complete system.

DIs are textually local with traversal strategies and visitors specifying exactly how adaptive methods interact with the rest of the system. DIs are an abstraction of the implementation of the class dictionary. The extensions made to the DAJ system provide automatic mechanisms that both check that modules satisfy their own interfaces as well as the interfaces of other modules. Composition of a DI with a concrete application is automatically managed by DAJ and configuration of this composition can be controlled via the implements keyword and the mapping specification.

5   Demeter Interfaces and XPath

Ideas in AP can be found in other technologies where the separation between navigation code and computation is necessary. According to the abstractions that strategies allow, the problems of surprise behavior are present in these systems as well. XML and XPath queries are technologies widely used today that share similar issues with AP. Specifically one can think of a DTD as a class dictionary and XPath expression as strategies [15]. The problems of surprise behavior are prominent in these technologies as well since modifications to the XML document might break assumptions that the XPath query depends upon. Consider the following DTD

```
<?xml version="1.0"?>
<!ELEMENT busRoute (bus*)>
<!ELEMENT bus (person*)>
<!ELEMENT person EMPTY>
<!ATTLIST bus number CDATA #REQUIRED>
<!ATTLIST person
        name CDATA #REQUIRED
        ticketprice CDATA #IMPLIED>
```

that defines busRoute containing a list of buses. Each bus contains a list of person which in turn contains a name for the person and a ticketprice for the bus fare. Consider the following XPath query

```
var nodes=xmlDoc.selectNodes(".//person")
```

that collects all person elements from a busRoute. We can think of a simple Java script that will iterate through nodes and calculate the total amount of money received by the current passengers riding the bus.

Making a correspondence between a DTD to class dictionary and an XPath query to a strategy it is straightforward to create a corresponding DAJ program. In fact, the two systems are so alike in this respect that they also share the same problems when it comes to modifications of their underlying data structure.

Leaving the JavaScript code and the XPath query the same we can extend the DTD (Listing 1.8) to accommodate for villages with bus stops along the bus route. The resulting amount this time is not the total of all passengers riding the bus, but instead the total amount for all passengers, both riding and waiting at bus stops. Similar problems are found in other XML technologies that use XPath like mechanisms, such as XLinq and XQuery, to select elements from a graph like structure.

Ideas from Demeter Interfaces can help to stop this kind of situations. Just like any XML document can define the DTD to which it confronts to, DTDs can define the XPath interfaces that they support and a mapping between the DTD's elements and the elements of the XPath interfaces that they implement. For instance, if the current total of all passengers riding the bus is to be supported by the DTD representing bus routes then it should make available an interface with XPath queries and constraints on these queries. The constraints are the guarantees provided to programmers by DTDs. At the same time, the mapping between the interface and the DTD itself allows for changes to the DTD to both names of entities as well as structure within the bounds of the constraints without imposing modifications to client code.

Listing 1.8. Extended DTD with BusStops

```
<?xml version="1.0"?>
<!ELEMENT busRoute (bus*,village*)>
<!ELEMENT bus (person*)>
<!ELEMENT village (busStop*)>
<!ELEMENT busStop (person*)>
<!ELEMENT person EMPTY>
<!ATTLIST bus number CDATA #REQUIRED>
<!ATTLIST person
     name CDATA #REQUIRED
     ticketprice CDATA #IMPLIED>
```

The usage of Demeter Interfaces also provides a clear distinct separation of responsibilities. In the case where an modification to the DTD breaks one of the XPath constraints then the blame lies with the DTD maintainer for breaking an interface that the DTD claims to implement.

6   Related Work

The idea of abstracting over a class graph in adaptive programs using an interface class graph was first introduced with adaptive plug-and-play-components (APPC) [4]. The mapping of interface class graphs allows for the mapping of a class name to a class name and for an edge to an edge or strategy. APPC have no provision for further constraints on interface class graphs or on concrete class dictionaries. A further development of APPC [5] allows for the mapping of methods resulting in a more general Aspect-Oriented system.

Ovlinger and Wand [6] propose a domain specific language as a means to specify recursive traversals of object structures used with the visitor pattern [16]. The domain specific language further allows for intermediate results from subtraversals supporting functional style visitor definitions. The explicit full definition of the recursive data structure provides an interface between visitors and the underlying data structure. This approach enforces that each object in a traversal is explicitly defined allowing no room for adaptiveness.

Modularity issues in AOSD [14, 17, 18] have received great attention recently. Kiczales and Mezini [14] advocate that in the presence of aspects, a module's interface has to further include pointcuts from aspects that apply to the module in question. These augmented interface definitions, named *aspect-aware interfaces*, can only be determined after the complete configuration of the system's components is known. Aspect-aware interfaces do not provide any extra information hiding capabilities to the base program's modules.

Open Modules [17] extend the traditional notion of a software module to include in its interface pointcut specifications. In this way a module can export, and as such make publicly available, pointcuts within its implementation. This approach gives a balanced control between module and aspect developers in terms of information hiding thus allowing for separate (parallel) evolution of aspects and modules on the agreed upon interface. The interface of a crosscutting concern can affect multiple modules at different join points on each one. Thus an aspect's interface is sprinkled along module interfaces and not localized making it harder (if not impossible at times) for aspect developers to develop their aspects.

Sullivan et. al. [18] advocate XPIs (crosscutting program interface) as a means to achieve separate development and define explicit dependencies between implementations of crosscutting concerns and base code. DIs can be viewed as a specialization of XPIs for AP. A more recent paper [19] by the same authors, demonstrated (partially) mechanized checking of XPIs through the usage of complementary aspects used to check for the appropriate interface constraints.

Kiczales and Mezini in [20] discuss the benefits of using different programming language mechanisms (procedures, annotations, advice and pointcuts) to provide separation of concerns at the code level. The resulting guidelines from their analysis sketch the situations where each mechanism will be most effective. The inherent modularity issues associated with each technology are not addressed.

In parallel to our work, Kellens et. al. [21] address the issue of the *fragile pointcut problem* [22, 23] in a general purpose AOP language. Pointcut definitions in AOP languages allow for the identification of points in the program's structure and/or execution where new functionality can be added. These pointcut definitions directly depend on the underlying program's structure causing aspects and the base system to be tightly coupled. As a result of this high coupling local modifications in the base program break pointcut semantics and hamper software evolution. This issue has been dubbed as *the fragile pointcut problem*. As a solution to this problem Kellens et. al. define a conceptual model of the base program against which pointcut definitions are declared and evaluated. The conceptual model further provides the means to define and verify structural and semantic constraints through their IntesiveVE [24] tool. Demeter Interfaces take a similar approach to the manifestation of the fragile pointcut problem in Adaptive Programming.

7   Future Work

Work is currently under way for allowing visitor methods to advise edges removing the limitation that classes mapped to edges cannot be advised by visitors.[3] The mapping definition can become long and difficult at times. A GUI tool that will help visualize ICG and class dictionaries as graphs will assist developers. Also a naive inferencing engine that can match mappings by structure, *i.e.*, mapping a class will automatically map its edges by position (as they appear in the class dictionary and the ICG) is already under development.

Another extension would be the provision of contracts on adaptive methods. Collaborations of adaptive methods exchange data and certain assumptions are being made that are not explicitly captured by the current system. The addition of pre- and postconditions would assist in both defining and validating these assumptions. The composition of Demeter Interfaces to provide new Demeter Interfaces is also an interesting

---

[3] For the latest release of DAJ with support for Demeter Interfaces visit DAJ's Beta Release web page [25].

future research direction. Also the interactions between DIs in an AP program still remains an open issue.

8 Conclusions

We introduce Demeter Interfaces as an extension to Adaptive Programming. Demeter interfaces encapsulate all the information and dependencies between the adaptive code and the underlying data structure. Through the definition of an interface class graph and a set of graph constraints Demeter Interfaces impose restrictions on any concrete data structure to which adaptive code will be attached. These restrictions are enforced at compile time disallowing modifications to the underlying data structure that would otherwise provide incorrect program results. With Demeter interfaces in place we have shown how modularity as well as understandability of adaptive programs increases dramatically leading to better program design and promoting parallel development.

Additional material related to this paper is available from `http://www.ccs.neu.edu/research/demeter/biblio/demeter-interf.html`.

References

1. The Demeter Group: The DAJ website. http://www.ccs.neu.edu/research/demeter/DAJ (2005)
2. Lieberherr, K.J., Orleans, D.: Preventive program maintenance in Demeter/Java (research demonstration). In: International Conference on Software Engineering, Boston, MA, ACM Press (1997) 604–605
3. Lieberherr, K.J., Riel, A.J.: Demeter: A CASE study of software growth through parameterized classes. Journal of Object-Oriented Programming **1**(3) (1988) 8–22 A shorter version of this paper was presented at the *10th International Conference on Software Engineering, Singapore, April 1988, IEEE Press*, pages 254-264.
4. Mezini, M., Lieberherr, K.J.: Adaptive plug-and-play components for evolutionary software development. In Chambers, C., ed.: Object-Oriented Programming Systems, Languages and Applications Conference, *in* Special Issue of SIGPLAN Notices, Vancouver, ACM (1998) 97–116
5. Lieberherr, K.J., Lorenz, D., Mezini, M.: Programming with Aspectual Components. Technical Report NU-CCS-99-01, College of Computer Science, Northeastern University, Boston, MA (1999)
6. Ovlinger, J., Wand, M.: A language for specifying recursive traversals of object structures. In: OOPSLA '99: Proceedings of the 14th ACM SIGPLAN conference on Object-oriented programming, systems, languages, and applications, New York, NY, USA, ACM Press (1999) 70–81
7. Sung, J.: Aspectual Concepts. Technical Report NU-CCS-02-06, Northeastern University (2002) Master's Thesis, http://www.ccs.neu.edu/home/lieber/theses-index.html.
8. Lieberherr, K.J.: Adaptive Object-Oriented Software: The Demeter Method with Propagation Patterns. PWS Publishing Company, Boston (1996) 616 pages, ISBN 0-534-94602-X.
9. Lieberherr, K., Patt-Shamir, B., Orleans, D.: Traversals of object structures: Specification and efficient implementation. ACM Trans. Program. Lang. Syst. **26**(2) (2004) 370–412
10. Lieberherr, K.J., Patt-Shamir, B.: The refinement relation of graph-based generic programs. In Jazayeri, M., Loos, R., Musser, D., eds.: 1998 Schloss Dagstuhl Workshop on Generic Programming, Springer (2000) 40–52 LNCS 1766.

11. Doug Orleans and Karl J. Lieberherr: AP Library: The Core Algorithms of AP: Home page. http://www.ccs.neu.edu/research/demeter/AP-Library/ (1999)
12. Skotiniotis, T., Lorenz, D.: Conaj: Generating contracts as aspects. Technical Report NU-CCIS-04-03, College of Computer and Information Science, Northeastern University (2004)
13. Skotiniotis, T., Lorenz, D.H.: Cona: aspects for contracts and contracts for aspects. In: OOPSLA '04: Companion to the 19th annual ACM SIGPLAN conference on Object-oriented programming systems, languages, and applications, New York, NY, USA, ACM Press (2004) 196–197
14. Kiczales, G., Mezini, M.: Aspect-oriented programming and modular reasoning. In: ICSE '05: Proceedings of the 27th International Conference on Software Engineering, New York, NY, USA, ACM Press (2005) 49–58
15. Lieberherr, K.J., Palm, J., Sundaram, R.: Expressiveness and complexity of crosscut languages. In: Proceedings of the 4th workshop on Foundations of Aspect-Oriented Languages (FOAL 2005). (2005)
16. Gamma, E., Helm, R., Johnson, R., Vlissides, J.: Design Patterns: Elements of Reusable Object-Oriented Software. Addison-Wesley (1995)
17. Aldrich, J.: Open Modules:modular reasoning about advice. In: European Conference on Object-Oriented Programming. (2005)
18. Sullivan, K., Griswold, W.G., Song, Y., Cai, Y., Shonle, M., Tewan, N., Rajan, H.: On the criteria to be used in decomposing systems into aspects. In: European Software Engineering Conference and International Symposium on the Foundations of Software Engineering. (2005)
19. Sullivan, K., Griswold, W.G., Song, Y., Shonle, M., Tewari, N., Cai, Y., Rajan, H.: Modular software design and crosscutting interfaces. In: IEEE Software, Special Issue on Aspect Oriented Programming. (2006)
20. Kiczales, G., Mezini, M.: Separation of concerns with procedures, annotations, advice and pointcuts. In: European Conference on Object-Oriented Programming. (2005)
21. Kellens, A., Mens, K., Brichau, J., Gybels, K.: Managing the evolutions of aspect-oriented software with model-based pointcuts. In: European Conference on Object Oriented Programming. (2006)
22. Koppen, C., Störzer, M.: PCDiff: Attacking the fragile pointcut problem. In: European Interactive Workshop on Aspects in Software (EIWAS). (2004)
23. Störzer, M., Graf, J.: Using pointcut delta analysis to support evolution of aspect-oriented software. In: 21st IEEE International Conference on Software Maintenance. (2005)
24. Mens, K., Kellens, A., Pluquet, F., Wuyts, R.: ¡co-evolving code and design with intensional views - a case study. Computer Languages, Systems and Structures (2006)
25. The Demeter Group: The DAJ beta website. http://www.ccs.neu.edu/home/skotthe/daj (2005)

Managing the Evolution of Aspect-Oriented Software with Model-Based Pointcuts

Andy Kellens[1,*], Kim Mens[2], Johan Brichau[1,3], and Kris Gybels[1]

[1] Programming Technology Lab
Vrije Universiteit Brussel, Belgium
{akellens, jbrichau, kris.gybels}@vub.ac.be
[2] Département d'Ingénierie Informatique
Université catholique de Louvain, Belgium
kim.mens@uclouvain.be
[3] Laboratoire d'Informatique Fondamentale de Lille
Université des Sciences et Technologies de Lille, France

Abstract. In spite of the more advanced modularisation mechanisms, aspect-oriented programs still suffer from evolution problems. Due to the *fragile pointcut problem*, seemingly safe modifications to the base code of an aspect-oriented program can have an unexpected impact on the semantics of the pointcuts defined in that program. This can lead to broken aspect functionality due to accidental join point misses and unintended join point captures. We tackle this problem by declaring pointcuts in terms of a conceptual model of the base program, rather than defining them directly in terms of how the base program is structured. As such, we achieve an effective decoupling of the pointcuts from the base program's structure. In addition, the conceptual model provides a means to verify where and why potential fragile pointcut conflicts occur, by imposing structural and semantic constraints on the conceptual model, that can be verified when the base program evolves. To validate our approach we implemented a *model-based pointcut* mechanism, which we used to define some aspects on SmallWiki, a medium-sized application, and subsequently detected and resolved occurrences of the fragile pointcut problem when this application evolved.

1 Introduction

Ever since its inception almost ten years ago, aspect-oriented software development (AOSD) has been promoted as a powerful development technique that extends the modularisation capabilities of existing programming paradigms such as object orientation [1]. To this extent, aspect-oriented programming languages provide a new kind of modules, called *aspects*, that allow one to modularise the implementation of crosscutting concerns which would otherwise be spread across various modules. The resulting improved modularity and separation of concerns intends not only to aid initial development, but also to allow developers to better

---

* Ph.D. scholarship funded by the "Institute for the Promotion of Innovation through Science and Technology in Flanders" (IWT Vlaanderen).

D. Thomas (Ed.): ECOOP 2006, LNCS 4067, pp. 501–525, 2006.
© Springer-Verlag Berlin Heidelberg 2006

manage software complexity, evolution and reuse [2]. Given the fact that maintenance and evolution of software applications account for the largest part of the software development process [3], the introduction and use of AOSD techniques looks promising.

Paradoxically, the essential techniques that AOSD proposes to improve software modularity seem to restrict the evolvability of that software. AOSD puts forward that aspects are not *explicitly* invoked but instead, are *implicitly* invoked [4]. This has also been referred to as the 'obliviousness' property of aspect orientation [5]. It means that the developer of the *base program* (i.e., the program without the aspects) does not need to explicitly invoke the aspects because the aspects themselves specify when and where they need to be invoked, by means of a *pointcut definition*. As a consequence, these pointcut definitions typically rely heavily on the structure of the base program.

This tight coupling of the pointcut definitions to the base program's structure and behaviour can hamper the evolvability of the software [6]: it implies that all pointcuts of each aspect need to be checked and possibly revised whenever the base program evolves. Indeed, due to changes to the base program, the pointcuts may unanticipatedly capture join points that were not supposed to be captured, or may no longer capture join points that should have been affected by the aspect. This problem has been coined *the fragile pointcut problem* [7,8].

We address the fragile pointcut problem by replacing the intimate dependency of pointcut definitions on the base program by a more stable dependency on a conceptual model of the program. These *model-based pointcut* definitions are less likely to break upon evolution, because they are no longer defined in terms of how the program happens to be structured at a certain point in time.

Because model-based pointcut definitions are decoupled from the actual structure of the base program, the fragile pointcut problem is thus transferred to a more conceptual level. Whereas traditional pointcut definitions may cause unanticipated captures and accidental misses of program entities upon evolution of the base program, model-based pointcut entities may lead to mismatches between the conceptual model of the program and the program entities to which the model is mapped. Hence, the fragile pointcut problem is transformed into the problem of keeping a conceptual model of the program synchronised with that program, when the program evolves.

To solve this derived problem, we rely on previous research that enables documenting the program structure and behaviour at a more conceptual level, where appropriate support is provided for keeping the 'conceptual model documentation' consistent with the source code when the program evolves. More specifically, we implement our particular solution to the fragile pointcut problem through an extension of the CARMA aspect language [9] combined with the formalism of *intensional views* [10]. The resulting approach tightly integrates the intensional views development tool with an aspect-oriented language. In essence, the pointcuts defined in the aspect language rely on the model that is built using the development tool. We validate our solution on SmallWiki, a medium-sized

Smalltalk application, where we illustrate how fragile pointcuts are detected and resolved more easily using model-based pointcuts, as opposed to using more traditional pointcuts.

2 The Fragile Pointcut Problem

In this section, we define the *fragile pointcut problem*, provide an analysis of possible causes of fragility of pointcut definitions, and illustrate each of them through a running example. We then study the fundamental causes underlying the problem, which will lead to our solution of *model-based pointcuts*.

2.1 Definitions

According to Stoerzer et al. [7,8], pointcuts are *fragile* because their semantics may change 'silently' when changes are made to the base program, even though the pointcut definition itself remains unaltered. The semantics of a pointcut change if the set of join points that is captured by that pointcut changes. Several other authors have observed symptoms of the fragile pointcut problem [6,11]. Before elaborating on these observations, we define the fragile pointcut problem:

> The **fragile pointcut problem** occurs in aspect-oriented systems when pointcuts unintentionally capture or miss particular join points as a consequence of their fragility with respect to seemingly safe modifications to the base program.

Therefore, in an aspect-oriented program, one cannot tell whether a change to the base code is safe simply by examining the base program in isolation. All pointcuts referring to the base program need to be examined as well.

Intuitively, because pointcuts capture a set of join points based on some structural or behavioural property shared by those join points, any change to the structure or behaviour of the base program can impact the set of join points that is captured by the pointcut definitions. If, upon evolution of the base program, source-code entities are altered which *accidentally* leads to the capture of a join point related to these source-code entities, we say that we have an **unintended join point capture**. Conversely, when the base program is changed in such a way that one of the join points that was originally captured by the pointcut is no longer captured, even though it was still supposed to be captured, we say we have an **accidental join point miss**. We define the **join point mismatches** (w.r.t. a given pointcut) as the union of the unintended join point captures and the accidental join point misses.

In literature, we find some interesting observations that confirm the existence of the fragile pointcut problem. Kiczales and Mezini [11] identified that aspects 'cut new interfaces' through the modules of a system and state that, in the presence of aspects, the complete interface of such a module can only be determined once the complete configuration of all modules in the system is known.

Sullivan et al. [6] observed that the criterion of *obliviousness* in AOSD comes at a considerable cost to aspect designers. They describe how aspect designers are confronted with complex pointcut definitions and extreme sensitivity of the validity of pointcuts to changes in the base program.

The fragile pointcut problem can be considered as the aspect-oriented equivalent of the *fragile base class problem* [12] found in object-oriented software development. In the fragile base class problem, one cannot tell whether a change to a base class is safe simply by examining the base class' methods in isolation; instead, one should examine all subclasses of that base class as well [13]. Analogously, in the fragile pointcut problem, one cannot tell whether a change to any part of the base program is safe without examining all pointcut definitions and determining the impact of that local change on each pointcut definition.

2.2   Examples

To understand the fundamental causes underlying the fragile pointcut problem, we study its various instantiations, and analyse how different kinds of pointcut definitions are fragile with respect to evolution of the base program. We observe that fragility of a pointcut depends on three fundamental properties of a pointcut definition:

1. The technique used to define the pointcut (e.g., enumeration of join points, pattern-based matching, . . .);
2. The expressiveness of the pointcut language (i.e., the structural and behavioural properties available to capture join points);
3. The join point model, more particularly, the kinds of join points that can be captured by a pointcut (method executions, method calls, variable assignments, . . .)

We illustrate the impact of these properties on the fragility of pointcuts, using a simple example: the Java implementation of a buffer object with a synchronisation aspect:

```
class Buffer {
        private Object content[];
        private int index = 0;
        ...
        public Object get() {
                ... return content[index] ... };
        public void set(Object el) {
                ... content[index] := el ... };
        ...
}
```

The implementation of a synchronisation aspect for this buffer contains a pointcut that captures all calls to the get() and set() accessor methods. Depending on the technique used to define it, the pointcut is fragile w.r.t. different modifications of the base program.

Enumeration pointcut. The simplest definition for this 'accessors' pointcut merely enumerates all join points that need to captured, by their exact signature:

```
pointcut accessors()
    call(void Buffer.set(Object)) || call(Object Buffer.get());
```

This pointcut definition is particularly fragile to accidental join point misses. Any change to the signature of the accessor methods requires a revision of the pointcut definition. Furthermore, consider an evolution of the buffer implementation where additional accessors are defined: e.g., the addition of `setAll` and `getAll` methods that get or set multiple objects at once in the buffer. Such an evolution requires revising the pointcut definition to explicitly add all new accessor methods to it. Otherwise, the pointcut would exhibit accidental misses of the call join points to these new accessor methods, and the synchronisation aspect would fail.

Pattern-based pointcut. In a pattern-based pointcut, we capture the desired join points by specifying a pattern, for example using wildcards over the signature. The following pattern captures all calls to methods of which the name starts with **set** or **get**:

```
pointcut accessors()
    call(* set*(..) ) || call(* get*(..) );
```

This pointcut is also fragile w.r.t. evolution of the base program. New methods can be added and existing ones can be removed such that they are captured by the pointcut definition, as long as they follow the naming convention encoded in the pattern. In addition, consider an evolution of the base code where a method named **setting** is added. A call to this method is unintendedly captured by the pointcut because its name happens to start with **set**.

Structural property-based pointcuts. In more advanced pointcut languages that allow to extract fine-grained structural properties of program elements to describe the join points, we can declare accessor methods as those methods that either assign to or return an instance variable directly. The following pointcut uses an AspectJ-like syntax[1] to illustrate a property-based pointcut that can, for example, be expressed in the CARMA pointcut language [9]. In CARMA, variables in pointcut definitions are prefixed with ?. The first pointcut expression captures all calls to methods that assign to an instance variable and the second pointcut expression captures all calls to 'getter' methods. The **assigns** and **returnsVariable** predicates reify the structural property of which variables that are assigned to or returned by the method[2]. The **instanceVariable** predicate reifies the instance variables defined in a class.

---

[1] We use this hypothetical AspectJ-like syntax to avoid having to explain the details of the CARMA syntax here.

[2] The predicates also consider indexing in arrays for variable accesses and assignments.

```
pointcut setters()
        call(?class.?method(..) ) &&
        assigns(?class.?method,?iv)  &&
        instanceVariable(?iv,?class);
pointcut getters()
        call(?class.?method(..) ) &&
        returnsVariable(?class.?method,?iv) &&
        instanceVariable(?iv,?class);
```

Although these pointcuts are no longer fragile w.r.t. changes in the name of the methods, they are still fragile because they capture only methods that respect the structural convention codified by the pointcut. Consider, for example, the following 'getter' method that does not directly return the instance variable in a return statement but returns another (temporary) variable:

```
Object get() {
   Object temp := content[index];
   ..
   return temp;
}
```

Although the variable `temp` contains the actual value of the instance variable, a call join point to this method would be missed by our previous pointcut definition. Hence, once again, the pointcut is fragile to changes in the base program's source code.

Behavioural property-based pointcuts. Behavioural properties that can be used in pointcut definitions mostly concern an application's execution history or runtime values during that history. A well-known behavioural property to qualify pointcuts is determined by the `cflow` predicate. Using `cflow`, we can specify join points that lie in the control flow of other join points. For example, the following pointcut captures only those join points that are 'getter' join points (as defined previously) but do not lie in the flow of control of other 'getter' join points. Using this `optimisedGetter` pointcut, we can prevent the execution of the synchronisation aspect if the running thread is already in the control flow of the synchronisation aspect (i.e., if the buffer is already synchronised).

```
pointcut optimisedGetter() :
        getters() &&
        !cflow(getters());
```

However, even behavioural property-based pointcuts are fragile to evolution of the source code, because they also need to refer to the source-code entities of which they want to characterise the behaviour. In this particular example, the pointcut is defined in terms of the `getters` pointcut. Because that latter pointcut is fragile, the `optimisedGetter` pointcut is equally fragile. Mind that this fragility also holds for many pointcuts that use dynamic values (of e.g. instance variables) because they often need to refer to the actual instance variables, of which they use the values, by name.

Uncapturable join points. While the previous examples illustrated the fragility of the pointcut due to the definition technique or the provided expressiveness of the pointcut language, another major reason for fragility lies in the fact that some intended join points simply cannot be captured because:

- The join point model is too restrictive and the code to be advised by the aspect is not confined to a join point. For example, most aspect languages today do not allow to advice pieces of method bodies. In our buffer example, this would mean that we must structure the possible critical sections in the buffer implementation as complete methods. Otherwise, they cannot be advised by the synchronisation aspect.
- The pointcut cannot be described because the join points do not share sufficient structural or behavioural properties to allow them to be qualified in a pointcut definition. As a consequence, developers are forced to use fragile enumeration-based pointcuts.

2.3 Problem Analysis

In all of the examples above, pointcuts are fragile because their definitions are tightly coupled to a particular structure or behaviour of the base program. Similar to how most programming paradigms rely on symbolic referencing (e.g. function calls by name), aspect-orientation relies on referencing more intricate structural and behavioural properties of the program as well. More precisely, pointcuts impose 'design rules' that developers of the base program must adhere to in order to prevent unintended join point captures or accidental join point misses (also see [6]). These rules originate from the fact that pointcuts try to define intended conceptual properties about the base program, based on structural and behavioural properties of the program. For example, the 'accessors' pointcut tries to define the conceptual property of an 'accessor method' by relying on coding conventions used to implement that method. Therefore, in general, base program developers need to adhere to such rules when implementing the base program, so that the pointcut definition can be expressed in terms of those rules. Because the rules themselves are not enforced by any mechanism, not only do the developers need to be aware of these rules, they also need to manually ensure not to break them when evolving the base program. This requires very disciplined developers that have a good understanding of the actual rules that the pointcut definitions depend on. Consequently, in practice these rules are likely to be violated upon evolution.

While the design rules imposed by enumeration-based pointcuts are very restrictive (i.e., only the explicitly enumerated join points can be advised), behavioural property-based pointcuts allow for more (structural) diversity in the base program but are also more complex to understand, write and verify. For example, we could define the 'accessors' pointcut by relying on the behavioural property that the method returns an instance variable value. However, this behavioural property cannot be statically verified upon program evolution in all cases. Moreover, although there are 'behavioural' design rules (that can be expressed using advanced pointcut languages [9,14,15]) that do not need to refer to structural properties in the program's source code, such structural properties are still required in many cases.

To the best of our knowledge, none of the proposed solutions that exist today (pointcut delta analysis [7], expressive pointcut languages [9,14,15], source-code annotations [16,17], design rules [6]) address *both* the too tight coupling of point-cuts to the structure of the program, and the brittleness of the imposed design rules upon program evolution. In the next section, we introduce a novel technique to define pointcuts, that achieves low coupling and provides a means to detect violations of the imposed rules. This technique is orthogonal to the techniques mentioned above, which are described in section 7.

3   Model-Based Pointcuts

We tackle the fragile pointcut problem with *model-based pointcuts*. This new pointcut definition mechanism achieves a low coupling of the pointcut definition with the source code, while at the same time providing a means of documenting and verifying the design rules on which the pointcut definitions rely.

Model-based pointcut definitions are defined in terms of a conceptual model of the base program, rather than referring directly to the implementation structure of that base program. Figure 1 illustrates this difference between *model-based* and traditional *source-code based* pointcuts. On the left-hand side, a traditional source-code based pointcut is defined directly in terms of the source code struc-ture. On the right-hand side, a model-based pointcut is defined in terms of a conceptual model of the base program. This conceptual model provides an ab-straction over the structure of the source code and classifies base program entities according to the concepts that they implement. As a result, model-based point-cuts capture join points based on conceptual properties instead of structural properties of the base program entities. In addition to decoupling the pointcut definitions from the base program's implementation structure, the classifications in the conceptual model are specifically conceived to provide support for detect-ing evolution conflicts between the conceptual model and the base program.

For example, assuming that the conceptual model contains a classification of all accessor methods in the buffer implementation, the model-based pointcut that captures all call join points to these accessor methods could be defined as:

```
pointcut accessors():
    classifiedAs(?methSignature,AccessorMethods) &&
    call(?methSignature);
```

where the expression `classifiedAs(?methSignature,AccessorMethods)` mat-ches all methods that are classified as accessor methods in the conceptual model of the buffer program and the variable `?methSignature` is bound to the method signature of such a method. This pointcut definition explicitly refers to the con-cept of an accessor method rather than trying to capture that concept by relying on implicit rules about the base program's implementation structure. Conse-quently, this pointcut does not need to be verified or changed upon evolution of

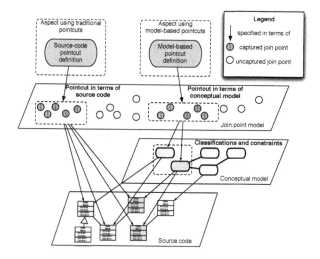

Fig. 1. Traditional pointcuts versus model-based pointcuts

the base program: if the conceptual model correctly classifies all accessor methods, this pointcut remains correct. In a certain sense, model-based pointcuts are similar to Kiczales and Mezini's *annotation-call* and *annotation-property* pointcuts [17]. Indeed, the classifications of source-code entities in the conceptual model could be constructed using annotations in the source code.

By defining pointcuts in terms of a conceptual model, the fragile pointcut problem has now been translated into the problem of keeping the classifications of the conceptual model consistent with the base program. To detect incorrectly classified source entities, the conceptual model goes beyond mere classification or annotation and defines extra constraints over the classifications that need to be respected by the source-code entities, for the model to be consistent. Formally, we distinguish two cases, defined below and illustrated by figure 2:

1. We define the set of possible *unintended captures* for a concept A as those entities that are classified as belonging to A but that do not satisfy some of the constraints defined on A:

$$UnintendedCaptures_A = \bigcup_{C \in \mathcal{C}_A} (A - ext(C))$$

where $\mathcal{C}_A$ is defined as the set of all constraints on A and $ext(C)$ denotes the set of all source-code entities satisfying constraint C. The intuition behind this definition is that if an entity belongs to A but does not satisfy the constraints defined on A then maybe the entity is misclassified.

2. We define the set of possible *accidental misses* as those entities that do not belong to A, but do satisfy at least one of the constraints C defined on A:

$$AccidentalMisses_A = \bigcup_{C \in \mathcal{C}_A} (ext(C) - A)$$

The intuition behind this definition is that if an entity does not belong to A but does satisfy some of the constraints defined on A, then maybe the entity should have been classified as belonging to A. To avoid having an overly restrictive definition (yet at the risk of having a too liberal one), we do not require the missed entity to satisfy *all* constraints defined on A. As soon as it satisfies one constraint, we flag it as a *potential* accidental miss.

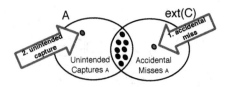

Fig. 2. Detecting potential unintended captures and accidental misses

The set of all *potential* unintended captures and accidental misses that can be detected is then defined as

$$Mismatches_A = \bigcup_{C \in \mathcal{C}_A} (A \; \Delta \; ext(C))$$

where Δ denotes symmetric difference. Whenever there is an unintended capture (resp. accidental miss) this can have one of 3 possible causes :

1. Either a source-code entity was misclassified and should be removed from (resp. added to) A;
2. Either a constraint C no longer applies and thus needs to be modified or removed;
3. Either a source-code entity accidentally satisfies (resp. invalidates) a constraint C and should be adapted.

In summary, model-based pointcuts provide support for detecting and resolving occurrences of the fragile pointcut problem because:

- Model-based pointcut definitions are decoupled from the source-code structure of the base program. They explicitly refer to a conceptual model of the program that classifies base program entities according to concepts that are of interest to define pointcuts.
- Although the conceptual model still classifies base program entities based on their implementation structure, the model does include constraints that allow verification of the consistency of the program's source code with respect to the classifications, when the source code evolves.

In practice, model-based pointcuts offer aspect developers a means to extract the structural dependencies from the pointcut definition and move these dependencies to the conceptual model specification, where they can be more easily enforced and checked. Upon evolution of the base program, the 'design rules' that govern these structural dependencies are automatically verified and the developer is notified of possible conflicts of the source code w.r.t. those rules.

4   View-Based Pointcuts

As a particular instantiation of model-based pointcuts, we introduce *view-based pointcuts*, which:

1. use the formalism of *intensional views* [10], and its associated tool suite IntensiVE[3], to express a conceptual model of a program and to keep it synchronised with the source code of that program;
2. specify pointcuts in terms of this conceptual model, using an extension to the aspect-oriented language *CARMA*.

We briefly present the formalism of intensional views and how it can be used to define a conceptual model of a program. Next, we introduce the CARMA aspect language and its extension to define aspects over intensional views. Throughout this section we use examples taken from the SmallWiki system. Section 5 explains this case in more detail.

4.1   Intensional Views

In earlier work [10], we presented the formalism of intensional views as a technique for describing a conceptual model of a program's structure and verifying consistency of that model with respect to the program. For the sake of completeness, we briefly repeat the formalism here, with a particular focus on those features that enable it to detect interesting evolution conflicts.

Intensional views describe concepts of interest to a programmer by grouping program entities (classes, methods, ...) that share some structural property. These sets of program entities are specified intensionally, using the logic metaprogramming language *Soul* [18]. (The *intension* — with an 's' — of a set is its description or defining properties, i.e., what is true about the members of the set. The extension of a set is its members or contents.)

For example, to model the concept of "all actions on Wiki pages" (save, login,...) in SmallWiki, we specify an intensional view named *Wiki Actions*, which groups all methods of which the name starts with execute, based on the observation that all action methods indeed respect that naming convention:

```
classInNamespace(?class,[SmallWiki]),
methodWithNameInClass(?entity,?name,?class),
['execute*' match: ?name asString]
```

Without explaining all details of the Soul syntax and semantics, upon evaluation the above query accumulates all solutions for the logic variable ?entity, such that ?entity is a method, implemented by a class in the SmallWiki namespace, whose name starts with execute. This query is the *intension* of the view.

Since the declared intension is sometimes too broad or too restrictive with respect to the actual program code, intensional views provide means to deal with *deviations* to a view, allowing to explicitly 'include' or 'exclude' specific program entities from a view. For example, if the SmallWiki implementation

---

[3] Available for download on http://www.intensional.be

would contain a method that starts with `execute` but does not perform an action, we would put that method in the *excludes set* of the *Wiki Actions* view.

Upon evolution of the program, a simple view such as the one defined above can capture or miss particular program entities accidentally, which is similar to the fragile pointcut problem. Therefore, a set of constraints on and between views (as defined in Section 3) is at the heart of the intensional views formalism. This set of constraints can be validated with respect to the program code and allows keeping an intensional view model synchronized with the program. We highlight two different types of constraints that can be defined on intensional views: *alternative intensions* and *intensional relations*.

Alternative Intensions. Often, the same set of program entities can be specified in different ways, e.g. when they share multiple naming or coding conventions. A first kind of constraints that can be declared on an intensional view is through the definition of multiple alternative intensions for that view. Each of these alternatives is required to be *extensionally consistent*, meaning that they need to describe exactly the same set of program entities. For example, all methods performing actions on Wiki pages do not only have a name that starts with `execute`, but are also implemented in a method protocol[4] called `action`. We can therefore define the *Wiki Actions* view in an alternative way, using a logic query that accumulates all SmallWiki methods implemented in that protocol. Since both alternatives are supposed to define the same concept (i.e. Wiki actions), we require both alternatives to capture the same set of methods.

Intensional Relations. Whereas alternative intensions declare an equality relation between the different alternatives of a view, a second means of specifying constraints is through *intensional relations*, which are binary relations between intensional views, of the canonical form:

$$Q_1 \; x \in View_1 : Q_2 \; y \in View_2 : x \; R \; y$$

where Q_i are logic quantifiers ($\forall$, $\exists$, $\exists!$ or $\nexists$), $View_i$ are intensional views, and R is a verifiable binary relation over the source-code entities (denoted by x and y) contained in those views. An example of such a constraint in SmallWiki is that all *Wiki Actions* should be implemented by *Action Handlers*. Assuming we have defined an *Action Handlers* view (a set of classes implementing actions), we express this dependency as:

$$\forall \; x \in WikiActions : \exists \; y \in ActionHandlers : x \; \texttt{isImplementedBy} \; y$$

where `isImplementedBy` is a binary predicate which verifies that a given method x is implemented by a given class y. Like for intensional views, explicit *deviations* can be declared on intensional relations.

As for checking extensional consistency, the IntensiVE tool suite can be used to verify the validity of the constraints imposed by intensional relations with

---

[4] In Smalltalk, the methods of a class are organised in logical groups called protocols.

respect to the program code. As explained in Section 3, invalidations of these constraints either indicate unintended captures or accidental misses, or maybe the constraint itself is simply no longer valid and should be modified or removed.

4.2 View-Based Pointcuts in CARMA

Having chosen the formalism in which to express the conceptual model of the base program, we still need a pointcut language that permits us to define pointcuts in terms of that model. Given that both the formalism of intensional views and the aspect-oriented programming language CARMA rely on the logic metaprogramming language Soul, to specify intensions and pointcuts respectively, we extended CARMA with the ability to define *view-based pointcuts*.

- reception(?joinpoint, ?message, ?arguments)
  Expresses that **?joinpoint** is a *message reception join point*, where the message with name **?message** is received with the arguments in the list **?arguments**.
- send(?joinpoint, ?message, ?arguments)
  The join point **?joinpoint** is a *message send join point* where the message with name **?message** is sent and passed the arguments in the list **?arguments**.
- within(?joinpoint, ?class, ?method)
  The join point **?joinpoint** is lexically associated to the method named **?method** in class **?class**. This means the join point was raised because of an expression in the body of that method or because of the execution of that method itself.
- withinClass(?joinpoint, ?class)
  The join point **?joinpoint** is lexically associated to the class **?class**. This means the join point was raised because of an execution of a method defined on that class or because of an expression in the body of a method of that class.

Fig. 3. Some basic predicates provided by CARMA for capturing join points

CARMA is very similar to the AspectJ language but features a logic pointcut language, and is an aspect-oriented extension to Smalltalk instead of Java. Pointcuts in CARMA are logic queries that can express structural as well as dynamic conditions over the join points that need to be captured by the pointcut. To this extent, a query can make use of a number of predefined predicates, stating conditions over join points, which form the heart of the CARMA language. Some basic CARMA predicates that are used in this paper are shown in Figure 3.

The expressive power of CARMA is a direct consequence of the logic language features of unification and recursive logic rules, together with a complete and open reification of the entire base program. CARMA has already proven useful to write more robust property-based and pattern-based pointcut definitions [9]. For this paper, we further enhanced CARMA with view-based pointcuts using an additional predicate classifiedAs(?entity,?view) that allows to define join points in terms of the intensional views defined over a program. For example, we can define a view-based pointcut that captures all calls to methods contained in the Wiki Actions view as:

```
pointcut wikiActionCalls():
    classifiedAs(?method,WikiActions),
    methodInClass(?method,?selector,?class),
    send(?joinpoint,?selector,?arguments)
```

The above pointcut definition is tightly coupled to the intensional view model of SmallWiki but it is decoupled from the actual program structure. In combination with the support for verifying consistency of the intensional views model with respect to the source code, we can thus alleviate part of the fragile pointcut problem, as is illustrated by the experiment in the following section.

5   Experiment: Aspects in SmallWiki

In this section, we demonstrate on a small but realistic program, on which two aspects were defined, how view-based pointcuts can detect occurrences of the fragile pointcut problem when the program evolves.

Case selection. The case study we selected is SmallWiki [19], a fully object-oriented and extensible Wiki framework, written by Lukas Renggli, that was developed entirely in VisualWorks Smalltalk. A Wiki is a collaborative web application that allows users to add content, but also allows anyone to edit the content. The original version of SmallWiki we studied was version 1.54, the first internal release of SmallWiki (14-12-2002), offering an operational Wiki server with rather limited functionality: only the rendering and editing of fairly simple Wiki pages was supported. This version contained 63 classes and 424 methods.

Set-up of the experiment. To illustrate our approach we conducted the following experiment:

1. We identified two aspects to be defined on the SmallWiki case.
2. Using an AOP approach with *traditional* pointcuts, we extended version 1.54 of SmallWiki with the extra functionality described by the aspects.
3. We applied the same aspects to version 1.304 of SmallWiki, an *evolved* version of the application dating one year after the release of version 1.54. We analyzed the impact of the changes in that evolution on the aspects. In particular, we assessed which changes gave rise to the *fragile pointcut problem*.
4. We made a *conceptual model* of Smallwiki's program structure. In practice, we merely reused a conceptual model which we conceived for an earlier experiment using intensional views and relations. (By selecting a set of intensional views that were already defined on the application, even before the aspects were identified, we show that our approach does not necessarily require the views to be defined in function of the aspects.)
5. We implemented the two aspects by means of *view-based pointcuts*, defined in terms of that *conceptual model*.
6. We reapplied these aspects to the evolved version of SmallWiki and observed how the evolved program gave rise to conflicts between the conceptual model

and the program. We compared the conflicting program entities with those that caused the fragile pointcut problem before. By using the feedback of the IntensiVE tool suite, we brought the program in sync with the conceptual model, and analysed the implication of these changes in the light of the fragile pointcut problem.

In the next subsections we elaborate on each of the steps of our experiment.

5.1 Two Aspects in SmallWiki

We extended our initial version 1.54 of SmallWiki with two simple aspects:

1. *logging of actions*: this aspect outputs information concerning which actions (like saving, opening a page, ...) are executed in SmallWiki.
2. *output in italics*: this aspect changes the output of SmallWiki by rendering all text in italics instead of a regular font.

5.2 A Traditional AOP Implementation

We implemented these two aspects in the (non-extended version of the) *CARMA* aspect language. Below, we highlight how we defined the pointcuts in terms of which those aspects were defined.

Implementing the 'logging' aspect. As mentioned earlier, all actions in the Wiki system are implemented by means of a method which starts with the string execute. Using this information we write down the following pointcut for the *logging of actions* aspect:

```
1    classInNamespace(?class,[SmallWiki]),
2    methodWithNameInClass(?method,?selector,?class),
3    ['execute*' match: ?selector],
4    reception(?joinpoint,?selector,?arguments)
```

Line 1 of this pointcut selects all classes in the SmallWiki namespace; line 2 and 3 select all methods within those classes whose name start with the string execute; finally, line 4 selects all message reception join points of those methods.

Implementing the 'output in italics' aspect. The output of Wiki pages is rendered by visitor objects which, for each different page component, generate some kind of output (HTML, Latex, save to disk). We wish to weave on all calls to these visitors originating from a Wiki page element. We declare this by means of the following pointcut:

```
1    classInNamespace(?class,[SmallWiki]),
2    or( classInHierarchyOf(?class,[PageComponent]),
3        classInHierarchyOf(?class,[Structure])),
4    classInHierarchyOf(?outputclass,[OutputVisitor]),
5    methodWithNameInClass(?method,?name,?outputclass),
6    within(?joinpoint,?class,?m),
7    send(?joinpoint,?name,?args)
```

Lines 1–3 collect all page element classes (i.e., all classes in SmallWiki which are either located in the hierarchy of `PageComponent` or in the hierarchy of `Structure`); lines 4–5 select all methods that render output (i.e., methods implemented on classes in the `OutputVisitor` hierarchy); finally, lines 6 and 7 select all join points from within Wiki page elements which perform a message send to a method that renders output.

5.3   Applying the Aspects to the Evolved Application

The evolved version of SmallWiki we selected was version 1.304, an internal release of almost a full year (16-11-2003) after the 1.54 release (14-12-2002). With 108 classes and 1219 methods, this evolved version was significantly larger than version 1.54.

When assessing the impact of this evolution on the pointcut of the *logging* aspect, we observed that all but two actions were correctly captured by the pointcut. The `save` and `authenticate` actions, which were added in version 1.304, were *not* captured by the pointcut, because their method names do not start with the string `execute`. The addition of these two methods thus caused two accidental join point misses in the evolved version of SmallWiki.

We mentioned earlier that the 'Wiki actions' are not only characterized by the fact that they all start with the string `execute`, but that they are also all categorized in a method protocol named `action`. We could have expressed the pointcut in terms of this alternative coding convention. This however would also have resulted in a join point mismatch when applying the pointcut to the evolved version of SmallWiki. Two other execute methods, namely `executeSearch` and `executePermission`, would have been missed by the pointcut because they have been misclassified in the `private` protocol instead of the `action` protocol.

The evolution step also had an impact on the pointcut for the *italic output* aspect. In the evolved version, a significant number of new Wiki page element components were added. For a number of these (i.e., `LinkInternal` and `LinkMailTo`) there did not exist a directly corresponding visit method (i.e., `visitLinkInternal` and `visitLinkMailTo`) in the `OutputVisitor` hierarchy, as was implicitly assumed by the pointcut declaration. Instead, for reasons of implementation reuse, they had their visit method implemented on the abstract `Visitor` class. From within this more abstract visit method, other visit methods, which *were* part of the `OutputVisitor` hierarchy, were then called. This subtle change in the implementation had a major impact on the correctness of the pointcut, causing the output generation methods of some of the newly added classes to be accidentally missed by the pointcut.

5.4   Intensional Views on SmallWiki

In a previous experiment we documented the conceptual structure of SmallWiki with 17 intensional views and 16 intensional relations [10]. For the current experiment, we reused that conceptual model, modulo the renaming of some intensional views to better reflect what SmallWiki concepts they represent. We do not show all views here[5], but limit ourselves to those interesting for the remainder of this paper, as summarized by Figure 4, and explained below.

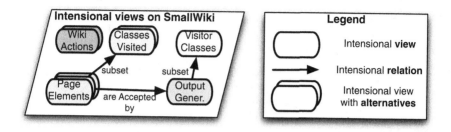

Fig. 4. Part of the conceptual model of SmallWiki version 1.54

- The *Wiki Actions* view groups all methods implementing an action on a Wiki page. Two alternative intensions for this view were explained in subsection 4.1.
- The *Page Elements* view groups all classes representing components out of which Wiki pages can be constructed (e.g., text, links, tables, lists). This view is defined by the following *alternative* intensions:
  1. All subclasses of either the `PageComponent` or `Structure` class;
  2. All classes in the Wiki system implementing a method named `accept`;
  3. All classes in the Wiki system containing a protocol named `visiting`.
  Alternatives 2 and 3 codify the knowledge that, in order to implement operations on Page Elements, SmallWiki relies heavily on the Visitor pattern.
- The *Output Generation* view groups all classes that generate output (e.g., HTML, Latex) for (the components of) a Wiki Page, and has as intension all subclasses of `OutputVisitor`.
- The *Visitor Classes* view groups all subclasses of `Visitor`.
- The *Classes Visited* view describes another aspect of the Visitor pattern and groups all classes that are visited by some `Visitor` in the SmallWiki system.

In addition to the constraint of extensional consistency between the different alternatives of each of these views, Figure 4 also shows 3 intensional relations that impose additional constraints on the views:

- The relation that the *Page Elements* view is a subset of the *Classes Visited* view codifies the knowledge that all page elements can be visited by a vistor.
- The `are Accepted by` relation captures the important fact that all page elements can be rendered by an *Output Generation* visitor.
- The third intensional relation states that the classes that render output are a particular kind of *Visitor Classes*.

---

[5] For a more exhaustive list of views that were defined on SmallWiki, and how they were defined, see [10].

5.5   Implementation with View-Based Pointcuts

In this subsection we show how we defined the pointcuts of the two aspects introduced earlier as *view-based pointcuts* in terms of the views discussed in subsection 5.4.

To implement the *logging of actions* aspect using a view-based pointcut, we use the following pointcut definition:

```
1   classifiedAs(?method,WikiActions),
2   methodWithName(?method,?message),
3   reception(?joinpoint,?message,?args),
4   withinClass(?joinpoint,?class)
```

This pointcut selects all reception join points of a message which is implemented by a method in the *Wiki Actions* view. Line 4 is added to the pointcut in order to propagate context information, concerning the class in which the join point is present, to the advice.

Analogously, we declare a view-based pointcut for the *italic output* aspect. We define this pointcut in terms of the *Page Elements* and *Output Generation* views discussed in subsection 5.4:

```
1   classifiedAs(?class,PageElements),
2   send(?joinpoint,?message,?args),
3   withinClass(?joinpoint,?class),
4   classifiedAs(?outputclass,OutputGeneration),
5   methodWithNameInClass(?method,?message,?outputclass)
```

Lines 1 and 2 select all message sends that occur in Wiki page elements. Lines 4 and 5 further restrict these sends to those invoking a method that generates output for the Wiki elements.

Note that both our traditional source-code based pointcut definitions and our view-based pointcut definitions provided a fine-grained description of the actual join points in the program execution that we wish to capture. Our model-based pointcut definitions, however, do not refer to the syntactical or structural organisation of the program on which they act.

5.6   Applying the Aspects to the Evolved Application

To assess the fragility of our view-based pointcuts, we reapply them to the evolved version 1.304 of SmallWiki. However, since view-based pointcuts are defined in terms of intensional views, before reapplying them, we first need to verify the impact of the evolution on the intensional view model and to try and resolve possible evolution conflicts at that level.

When checking extensional consistency of the *Wiki Actions* view, on which our *logging* pointcut is based, our IntensiVE tool suite warned us that the view had become inconsistent. The feedback provided by the tool informed us that the new actions save and authenticate did satisfy the second alternative, i.e. they belonged to the action method protocol, but they did not adhere to the first alternative, namely their name did not start with `execute`. Also, the tool reported that the `executeSearch` and `executePermission` were not captured by the second alternative, though they did satisfy the first alternative. Note that these inconsistencies match exactly the cases that caused the join point mismatches on our traditional implementation of the *logging* pointcut.

We resolved these mismatches between the model and the source code by performing the following two actions. First, we explicitly declared the `save` and `authenticate` methods as deviating cases to be included in the first alternative of the view. Second, we modified the classification of the `executeSearch` and `executePermission` so that they were correctly classified in the `action` protocol.

It is important to realise that, to detect and resolve these inconsistencies, we did not have to reason about the view-based pointcut itself, but only about the view(s) in terms of which it was defined. Furthermore, after having synchronised the conceptual model with the program again, the pointcut correctly captured the intended join points and we could safely apply the aspect to the code.

The *italic output* aspect depends on two intensional views: *Wiki Page Elements* and *Output Generation*. As for the *logging* aspect, before applying the aspect to the evolved code, we first verified validity of these views with respect to the source code. While the views themselves remained consistent during the considered evolution, our tool suite warned us that the relation *Wiki Page Elements are Accepted By Output Generation* was invalidated. More specifically, it informed us that the relation failed because of the classes `LinkInternal` and `LinkMailTo`. These are exactly the same classes that caused join point mismatches on our traditional implementation of the *italic output* pointcut.

Before applying the *italic output* aspect to the evolved code, we first resolved the conflict. The problem was that the conflicting classes did not have a corresponding visit method in the `OutputVisitor` hierarchy and thus were not directly visited by an output visitor. By adapting the *Output Generation* view so that these classes are explicitly defined as deviating cases to the view, we reconciled the intensional relation with the program. When applying the *italic output* aspect to the code now, it worked as desired.

6   Discussion

Our experiment showed that, when view-based pointcuts are used to implement the *logging of actions* and *italic output* aspects on SmallWiki, the formalism and tool suite of intensional views allowed us to discover exactly those evolution conflicts that caused join point mismatches in a more traditional implementation of the aspects. To do so, our tool did not reason about the pointcut definitions themselves, but only about the conceptual model in terms of which they were defined. Indeed, because the evolution we applied concerned changes to structure of the base program, only the structural dependencies contained in the conceptual model were affected. After resolving all detected inconsistencies, by synchronising the conceptual model with the evolved program, we could straightforwardly apply the aspects to that program, without having to alter the original view-based pointcut definition.

The core of our contribution lies in the observation that the fragile pointcut problem can be transferred to a problem space where the fundamental cause of the problem (i.e., the structural dependency of pointcuts on code) is isolated and easier to resolve. Rather than addressing the problem at the level of program code, we transfer it to the level of a conceptual model, where extra conceptual information is available that allows us to detect certain join point mismatches. The only requirement is the existence of a conceptual model which allows to express design-level constraints that can be verified against the code, and an aspect language that features model-based pointcuts which can refer to concepts in the conceptual model. Although view-based pointcuts provide a powerful instantiation of model-based pointcuts, one can easily imagine using other models and aspect languages, as we will describe in section 7.

We do not claim that our technique detects and resolves all occurrences of the fragile pointcut problem. Everything depends on the constraints imposed by the conceptual model. Since, in our particular example, we started from a case study which had already been well-documented with intensional views and relations before [10], we were able to detect and avoid all occurrences of the fragile pointcut problem as compared to a traditional AOP approach. In general, the more constraints defined by the conceptual model, the lesser the chance that certain inconsistencies go unnoticed. Further research is required on methodological guidelines to design the conceptual model such that it provides sufficient coverage to detect violations of the design rules.

Adoption of our model-based pointcut approach requires developers to describe a conceptual model of their program and its mapping to the program code. This should not be seen as a burden, because it provides an explicit and verifiable design documentation of the implementation. Such documentation is not only valuable for evolution of aspect-oriented programs but for the evolution of software in general. Providing a means of explicitly codifying and verifying the coding conventions and design rules employed by developers allows them to better respect these conventions and rules. The short term cost of having to design the conceptual model thus pays off on longer-term because it allows keeping the design consistent with the implementation and, consequently, allows detecting potential conflicts when the program evolves.

7   Related and Future Work

In subsection 2.3 we already mentioned some other solutions that have been proposed in the context of the fragile pointcut problem. We now take a closer look at these solutions and describe their differences to our proposed solution. We also describe other closely related work.

Expressive pointcut languages. To render pointcut definitions less fragile to base program evolution, more expressive pointcut languages are currently under investigation. The CARMA language, for example, offers a complete logic programming language for the definition of pointcuts. The language features of unification and recursion offer expressiveness to render pointcut definitions more robust [9]. The Alpha aspect language also uses a logic programming language for the specification of pointcuts and enhances the expressiveness by providing diverse automatically-derived models of the program and associated predicates that can, for example, reason over the entire state and execution history [15]. EAOP [14] and JAsCo [20] offer event-based or stateful pointcuts that allow to express the activation of an aspect based on a sequence of events during the program's execution.

Although such expressive pointcut languages permit to render pointcut definitions much less brittle, they do not make the problem disappear altogether. A pointcut definition still needs to refer to specific base program structure or behaviour to specify its join points. This dependency on the base program remains an important source of fragility. To deal with the fragility based on structural dependencies, the user-defined conceptual model, presented in this paper, would even complement the behavioural models used in Alpha and provide additional expressiveness for pointcuts that need to refer to structural properties. Furthermore, one could even argue that, in the occurrence of complex behavioural property-based pointcuts, the rules that the base program needs to respect become very complex to understand. Hence, although more expressive pointcut languages reduce the fragility of pointcut definitions, they may render the actual detection of broken pointcuts more difficult.

Annotations. An alternative solution that has been proposed is to define pointcuts in terms of explicit annotations in the code [16,17]. Similar to intensional views, annotations classify source-code entities and thereby make explicit additional semantics that would otherwise be expressed through implicit programming conventions. This solution, however, addresses the fundamental cause of the problem only partially. While the pointcut definitions are now defined in terms of semantic properties that would otherwise have remained implicit, the problem is displaced to the annotations themselves. Instead of requiring base developers to adhere to implicit programming rules, we now require them to annotate the base program explicitly. As a consequence, pointcuts are as brittle as the annotations to which they refer. When the base code has not been correctly annotated, or when annotations are not correctly updated when the base code evolves, the 'fragile pointcut problem' resurfaces. Havinga et al. [16] try to solve this problem by inserting the annotations in the code automatically by means of a pointcut that introduces them. However, this again translates the problem to the correctness of that pointcut expression, how well it captures the intention of the aspect developer, and how robust it is towards future changes. Nevertheless, we can easily imagine implementing model-based pointcuts using AspectJ's annotation-property pointcuts, extended with a conceptual model that imposes additional relations and constraints on the annotations that are used.

Pointcut-delta Analysis. Pointcut delta analysis [7] tackles the fragile pointcut problem by analysing the difference in captured join points, for each pointcut definition, before and after an evolution. The analysis considers statically determinable pointcut deltas and provides a static approximation of the join points which are newly captured or which are no longer captured. A developer can inspect these deltas and verify potential join point mismatches. He is aided in the process because the analysis also states which changes led to the delta.

While this approach can help to assess a number of interesting join point mismatches, accidental misses which result from the addition or modification of source-code entities that *should* be captured by a pointcut, but which are not, are impossible to detect using pointcut-delta analysis. For instance, if we look back at the *logging of actions* pointcut from Section 5, we see that the addition of the save method, which is accidentally missed by the pointcut, would not be detected by analyzing the sets of captured join points.

Nevertheless, the ideas proposed in pointcut-delta analysis can be used to create an interesting extension to the model of intensional views. Instead of comparing the sets of the different join points which are captured by the aspects before and after an evolution, we could do a delta analysis on the sets of source-code entities which belong to an intensional view. This way, a developer would be informed of elements which, for instance, change classification or which no longer belong to any classification. Using this feedback, the developer can then (re)classify the source-code entities if needed.

Open Modules, Design Rules and XPI. Yet another alternative approach is to explicitly include the pointcut descriptions in the design and implementation of the software and to require developers to adhere to this design. Sullivan et al. [6] propose such an approach by interfacing base code and aspect code through *design rules*. These rules are documented in interface specifications that base code designers are constrained to 'implement', and that aspect designers are licensed to depend upon. Once the interfaces are defined (and respected), aspect and base code become symmetrically oblivious to each others' design decisions. The bare design rules approach does not provide an explicit means to verify if developers adhere to these rules, as opposed to the intensional views model presented in this paper. More recently, the interfaces that are defined by the design rules can be implemented as *Explicit Pointcut Interfaces* (XPI's) using AspectJ [21]. Using XPIs, pointcuts are declared globally and some constraints can be verified on these pointcuts using other pointcuts. Our approach is different in the fact that we keep the pointcut description in the aspect, leaving more flexibility to the aspect developer. While XPIs fix all pointcut interfaces beforehand, our conceptual model only fixes a classification of the structural source code entities. Another approach is presented by Aldrich in his work on Open Modules [22]. In this approach, modules must advertise which join points can be captured by the aspects that are external to the module. The difference in applicability and expressiveness of these and our approaches remains to be investigated.

Demeter Interfaces. Independently of our work, Skotiniotis et al. [23] address a variant of the fragile pointcut problem, but in the context of adaptive programming, in a way that is very similar to our solution. Adaptive programming is a programming paradigm, akin to aspect-oriented programming, that allows for the separate definition of data structures and traversals over those data structures, with computations attached to the traversal. Current adaptive programming systems provide no mechanisms to warn or guard against modifications that will affect the meaning of a program. To allow for software that is more resilient towards such changes, they introduce *Demeter Interfaces*, which are very similar in spirit to our model-based pointcuts. Demeter Interfaces *decouple* the definition of an Interface Class Graph from the concrete data structure being traversed, thus leaving more flexibility for changes to this data structure. Demeter Interfaces also define structural *constraints* that both the Interface Class Graph and the underlying data structure must satisfy. Finally, the DAJ tool provides support to statically *verify* the mapping of the concrete data structure to the Interface Class Graph as well as the constraints imposed by the Demeter Interfaces.

Conceptual Models. Model-based pointcuts alleviate the fragile pointcut problem by specifying pointcuts in terms of a conceptual model. Although in our experiment we opted for the formalism of intensional views to define a conceptual model, we repeat that our approach is independent of the actual formalism chosen. Any formalism which allows the definition of a high-level model of the different concepts in a program, and provides means to keep this model consistent with the program code, can be used as a basis upon which to define model-based pointcuts. A number of such formalisms are the Concern Manipulation Environment (CME) [24], Cosmos [25], Reflexion Models [26], Conceptual Modules [27], ... With minimal effort, that is, given an extended pointcut language that allows to express pointcuts in terms of the concepts in those formalisms, these formalisms could be adopted to provide different flavours of model-based pointcuts, in the like of our 'view-based pointcuts'.

8   Conclusion

The fragile pointcut problem is a serious inhibitor to evolution of aspect-oriented programs. At the core of this problem is the too tight coupling of pointcut definitions with the base program's structure. To solve the problem we propose the novel technique of *model-based pointcuts*, which translates the problem to a more conceptual level where it is easier to solve. This is done, on the one hand, by decoupling the pointcut definitions from the actual structure of the base program, and defining them in terms of a conceptual model of the software instead. On the other hand, the conceptual model classifies program entities and imposes high-level conceptual constraints over those entities, which renders the conceptual model more robust towards evolutions of the base program. Potential evolution conflicts can now be detected at that level, and solving these conflicts requires changing either the conceptual model or its mapping to the program code, but leaves the model-based pointcut definitions themselves intact.

As a particularly powerful instantiation of model-based pointcuts, we implemented a formalism of *view-based pointcuts*, which extends the CARMA aspect language and combines it with the conceptual model of intensional views. We illustrated the formalism by defining two simple aspects on SmallWiki, an evolving Smalltalk application. When defining the aspects in terms of view-based pointcuts, we managed to discover automatically some instances of the fragile pointcut problem, that went unnoticed when using a more traditional aspect implementation.

Acknowledgements

The authors appreciate the feedback received on previous drafts of this paper. In particular, they wish to thank Yann-Gaël Guéhéneuc, Pascal Costanza, Kevin Sullivan, Sebastián González, Tom Tourwé, Mira Mezini and all anonymous reviewers.

References

1. Kiczales, G., Lamping, J., Mendhekar, A., Maeda, C., Lopes, C., Loingtoir, J., Irwin, J.: Aspect-oriented programming. In: European Conference on Object-Oriented Programming (ECOOP). LNCS, Springer Verlag (1997) 220–242
2. Parnas, D.L.: On the criteria to be used in decomposing systems into modules. Communications of the ACM **15**(12) (1972) 1053–1058
3. Sommerville, I.: Software Engineering, 6th edition. Pearson Education Ltd (2001)
4. Xu, J., Rajan, H., Sullivan, K.: Understanding aspects via implicit invocation. In: Automated Software Engineering (ASE), IEEE Computer Society Press (2004)
5. Filman, R., Friedman, D.: Aspect-oriented programming is quantification and obliviousness (2000) Workshop on Advanced Separation of Concerns (OOPSLA).
6. Sullivan, K., Griswold, W., Song, Y., Chai, Y., Shonle, M., Tewari, N., Rajan, H.: On the criteria to be used in decomposing systems into aspects. In: Symposium on the Foundations of Software Engineering joint with the European Software Engineering Conference (ESEC/FSE 2005), ACM Press (2005)
7. Stoerzer, M., Graf, J.: Using pointcut delta analysis to support evolution of aspect-oriented software. In: International Conference on Software Maintenance (ICSM), IEEE Computer Society Press (2005) 653–656
8. Koppen, C., Stoerzer, M.: Pcdiff: Attacking the fragile pointcut problem. In: First European Interactive Workshop on Aspects in Software (EIWAS). (2004)
9. Gybels, K., Brichau, J.: Arranging language features for more robust pattern-based crosscuts. In: Aspect-Oriented Software Development (AOSD). (2003)
10. Mens, K., Kellens, A., Pluquet, F., Wuyts, R.: Co-evolving code and design with intensional views - a case study. Computer Languages, Systems and Structures **32**(2-3) (2006) 140–156
11. Kiczales, G., Mezini, M.: Aspect-oriented programming and modular reasoning. In: International Conference on Software Engineering (ICSE), ACM Press (2005)
12. Mikhajlov, L., Sekerinski, E.: A study of the fragile base class problem. In: European Conference on Object-Oriented Programming (ECOOP). LNCS (1998)
13. Steyaert, P., Lucas, C., Mens, K., D'Hondt, T.: Reuse contracts: Managing the evolution of reusable assets. In: Object-Oriented Programming, Systems, Languages and Applications (OOPSLA'96), ACM Press (1996) 268–285

14. Douence, R., Fritz, T., Loriant, N., Menaud, J.M., Ségura, M., Südholt, M.: An expressive aspect language for system applications with arachne. In: Aspect-Oriented Software Development (AOSD). (2005)
15. Ostermann, K., Mezini, M. Bockisch, C.: Expressive pointcuts for increased modularity. In: European Conference on Object-Oriented Programming (ECOOP). (2005)
16. Havinga, W., Nagy, I., Bergmans, L.: Introduction and derivation of annotations in AOP: Applying expressive pointcut languages to introductions. In: First European Interactive Workshop on Aspects in Software. (2005)
17. Kiczales, G., Mezini, M.: Separation of concerns with procedures, annotations, advice and pointcuts. In: European Conference on Object-Oriented Programming (ECOOP). LNCS, Springer Verlag (2005)
18. Mens, K., Michiels, I., Wuyts, R.: Supporting software development through declaratively codified programming patterns. Special issue of Elsevier Journal on Expert Systems with Applications (2001)
19. Renggli, L.: Collaborative web : Under the cover. Master's thesis, University of Berne (2005)
20. Vanderperren, W., Suvee, D., Cibran, M.A., De Fraine, B.: Stateful aspects in JAsCo. In: Software Composition (SC). LNCS (2005)
21. Griswold, W., Sullivan, K., Song, Y., Shonle, M., Teware, N., Cai, Y., Rajan.H.: Modular software design with crosscutting interfaces. IEEE Software, Special Issue on Aspect-Oriented Programming (2006)
22. Aldrich, J.: Open modules: Modular reasoning about advice. In: Proceedings of the European Conference on Object-Oriented Programming. Volume 3586 of LNCS., Springer (2005) 144–168
23. Skotiniotis, T., Palm, J., Lieberherr, K.: Demeter interfaces: Adaptive programming without surprises. In: European Conference on Object-Oriented Programming (ECOOP). LNCS (2006)
24. Harrison, W., Ossher, H., Jr., S.M.S., Tarr, P.: Concern modeling in the concern manipulation environment. IBM Research Report RC23344, IBM Thomas J. Watson Research Center, Yorktown Heights, NY (2004)
25. Sutton, S., Rouvellou, I.: Modeling of software concerns in cosmos. In: Aspect-Oriented Software Development (AOSD), ACM (2002) 127–133
26. Murphy, G., Notkin, D., Sullivan, K.: Software reflexion models: Bridging the gap between source and high-level models. In: Symposium on the Foundations of Software Engineering (SIGSOFT), ACM Press (1995) 18–28
27. Baniassad, A.L.A., Murphy, G.C.: Conceptual module querying for software reengineering. In: International Conference on Software Engineering (ICSE), IEEE Computer Society (1998) 64–73

Author Index

Lecture Notes in Computer Science

For information about Vols. 1–3965

please contact your bookseller or Springer

Vol. 4010: S. Dunne, B. Stoddart (Eds.), Unifying Theories of Programming. VIII, 257 pages. 2006.

Vol. 4009: M. Lewenstein, G. Valiente (Eds.), Combinatorial Pattern Matching. XII, 414 pages. 2006.

Vol. 4007: C. Àlvarez, M. Serna (Eds.), Experimental Algorithms. XI, 329 pages. 2006.

Vol. 4006: L.M. Pinho, M. González Harbour (Eds.), Reliable Software Technologies – Ada-Europe 2006. XII, 241 pages. 2006.

Vol. 4005: G. Lugosi, H.U. Simon (Eds.), Learning Theory. XI, 656 pages. 2006. (Sublibrary LNAI).

Vol. 4004: S. Vaudenay (Ed.), Advances in Cryptology - EUROCRYPT 2006. XIV, 613 pages. 2006.

Vol. 4003: Y. Koucheryavy, J. Harju, V.B. Iversen (Eds.), Next Generation Teletraffic and Wired/Wireless Advanced Networking. XVI, 582 pages. 2006.

Vol. 4001: E. Dubois, K. Pohl (Eds.), Advanced Information Systems Engineering. XVI, 560 pages. 2006.

Vol. 3999: C. Kop, G. Fliedl, H.C. Mayr, E. Métais (Eds.), Natural Language Processing and Information Systems. XIII, 227 pages. 2006.

Vol. 3998: T. Calamoneri, I. Finocchi, G.F. Italiano (Eds.), Algorithms and Complexity. XII, 394 pages. 2006.

Vol. 3997: W. Grieskamp, C. Weise (Eds.), Formal Approaches to Software Testing. XII, 219 pages. 2006.

Vol. 3996: A. Keller, J.-P. Martin-Flatin (Eds.), Self-Managed Networks, Systems, and Services. X, 185 pages. 2006.

Vol. 3995: G. Müller (Ed.), Emerging Trends in Information and Communication Security. XX, 524 pages. 2006.

Vol. 3994: V.N. Alexandrov, G.D. van Albada, P.M.A. Sloot, J. Dongarra (Eds.), Computational Science – ICCS 2006, Part IV. XXXV, 1096 pages. 2006.

Vol. 3993: V.N. Alexandrov, G.D. van Albada, P.M.A. Sloot, J. Dongarra (Eds.), Computational Science – ICCS 2006, Part III. XXXVI, 1136 pages. 2006.

Vol. 3992: V.N. Alexandrov, G.D. van Albada, P.M.A. Sloot, J. Dongarra (Eds.), Computational Science – ICCS 2006, Part II. XXXV, 1122 pages. 2006.

Vol. 3991: V.N. Alexandrov, G.D. van Albada, P.M.A. Sloot, J. Dongarra (Eds.), Computational Science – ICCS 2006, Part I. LXXXI, 1096 pages. 2006.

Vol. 3990: J. C. Beck, B.M. Smith (Eds.), Integration of AI and OR Techniques in Constraint Programming for Combinatorial Optimization Problems. X, 301 pages. 2006.

Vol. 3989: J. Zhou, M. Yung, F. Bao, Applied Cryptography and Network Security. XIV, 488 pages. 2006.

Vol. 3988: A. Beckmann, U. Berger, B. Löwe, J.V. Tucker (Eds.), Logical Apporaches to Computational Barriers. XV, 608 pages. 2006.

Vol. 3987: M. Hazas, J. Krumm, T. Strang (Eds.), Location- and Context-Awareness. X, 289 pages. 2006.

Vol. 3986: K. Stølen, W.H. Winsborough, F. Martinelli, F. Massacci (Eds.), Trust Management. XIV, 474 pages. 2006.

Vol. 3984: M. Gavrilova, O. Gervasi, V. Kumar, C.J. K. Tan, D. Taniar, A. Laganà, Y. Mun, H. Choo (Eds.), Computational Science and Its Applications - ICCSA 2006, Part V. XXV, 1045 pages. 2006.

Vol. 3983: M. Gavrilova, O. Gervasi, V. Kumar, C.J. K. Tan, D. Taniar, A. Laganà, Y. Mun, H. Choo (Eds.), Computational Science and Its Applications - ICCSA 2006, Part IV. XXVI, 1191 pages. 2006.

Vol. 3982: M. Gavrilova, O. Gervasi, V. Kumar, C.J. K. Tan, D. Taniar, A. Laganà, Y. Mun, H. Choo (Eds.), Computational Science and Its Applications - ICCSA 2006, Part III. XXV, 1243 pages. 2006.

Vol. 3981: M. Gavrilova, O. Gervasi, V. Kumar, C.J. K. Tan, D. Taniar, A. Laganà, Y. Mun, H. Choo (Eds.), Computational Science and Its Applications - ICCSA 2006, Part II. XXVI, 1255 pages. 2006.

Vol. 3980: M. Gavrilova, O. Gervasi, V. Kumar, C.J. K. Tan, D. Taniar, A. Laganà, Y. Mun, H. Choo (Eds.), Computational Science and Its Applications - ICCSA 2006, Part I. LXXV, 1199 pages. 2006.

Vol. 3979: T.S. Huang, N. Sebe, M.S. Lew, V. Pavlović, M. Kölsch, A. Galata, B. Kisačanin (Eds.), Computer Vision in Human-Computer Interaction. XII, 121 pages. 2006.

Vol. 3978: B. Hnich, M. Carlsson, F. Fages, F. Rossi (Eds.), Recent Advances in Constraints. VIII, 179 pages. 2006. (Sublibrary LNAI).

Vol. 3977: N. Fuhr, M. Lalmas, S. Malik, G. Kazai (Eds.), Advances in XML Information Retrieval and Evaluation. XII, 556 pages. 2006.

Vol. 3976: F. Boavida, T. Plagemann, B. Stiller, C. Westphal, E. Monteiro (Eds.), NETWORKING 2006. Networking Technologies, Services, and Protocols; Performance of Computer and Communication Networks; Mobile and Wireless Communications Systems. XXVI, 1276 pages. 2006.

Vol. 3975: S. Mehrotra, D.D. Zeng, H. Chen, B. Thuraisingham, F.-Y. Wang (Eds.), Intelligence and Security Informatics. XXII, 772 pages. 2006.

Vol. 3973: J. Wang, Z. Yi, J.M. Zurada, B.-L. Lu, H. Yin (Eds.), Advances in Neural Networks - ISNN 2006, Part III. XXIX, 1402 pages. 2006.

Vol. 3972: J. Wang, Z. Yi, J.M. Zurada, B.-L. Lu, H. Yin (Eds.), Advances in Neural Networks - ISNN 2006, Part II. XXVII, 1444 pages. 2006.

Vol. 3971: J. Wang, Z. Yi, J.M. Zurada, B.-L. Lu, H. Yin (Eds.), Advances in Neural Networks - ISNN 2006, Part I. LXVII, 1442 pages. 2006.

Vol. 3970: T. Braun, G. Carle, S. Fahmy, Y. Koucheryavy (Eds.), Wired/Wireless Internet Communications. XIV, 350 pages. 2006.

Vol. 3969: Ø. Ytrehus (Ed.), Coding and Cryptography. XI, 443 pages. 2006.

Vol. 3968: K.P. Fishkin, B. Schiele, P. Nixon, A. Quigley (Eds.), Pervasive Computing. XV, 402 pages. 2006.

Vol. 3967: D. Grigoriev, J. Harrison, E.A. Hirsch (Eds.), Computer Science – Theory and Applications. XVI, 684 pages. 2006.

Vol. 3966: Q. Wang, D. Pfahl, D.M. Raffo, P. Wernick (Eds.), Software Process Change. XIV, 356 pages. 2006.